The Spirit of Capitalism

LIAH GREENFELD

The Spirit of Capitalism

*Nationalism and
Economic Growth*

HARVARD UNIVERSITY PRESS

Cambridge, Massachusetts, and London, England

338·9

First Harvard University Press paperback edition, 2003

Second printing, 2003

Library of Congress Cataloging-in-Publication Data

Greenfeld, Liah.
　The spirit of capitalism : nationalism and economic growth / Liah Greenfeld.
　　p.　cm.
　Includes bibliographical references and index.
　ISBN 0-674-00614-3 (cloth)
　ISBN 0-674-01239-9 (paper)
　1. Economic development.　2. Nationalism—Economic aspects.　I. Title.
　HD82.G655 2001
　338.9—dc21　　2001024608

To Gil

Contents

Acknowledgments   *ix*

Introduction   *1*

I **Another Take on How It All Began**   *27*

   1 The Capitalist Spirit and the British Economic Miracle   *29*

   2 "The Great Seventeenth-Century Exception"   *59*

II **The Spread of the New Economic Consciousness
    on the European Continent**   *105*

   3 The First Convert: France   *107*

   4 The Power of Concerted Action: Putting
      the Spirit of Capitalism to Work in Germany   *154*

III **The Asian Challenge: The Way of Japan**   *225*

   5 Japanese Nationalism   *227*

   6 Racing and Fighting   *299*

IV **The Economic Civilization:
    The Spirit of Capitalism in the New World**   *363*

   7 Searching for the American System   *369*

   8 The Thrust   *428*

Epilogue: Looking Backward from Year 2000   *473*

Notes   *487*

Index   *533*

Acknowledgments

An anonymous reviewer of the manuscript for this book wondered about the disciplinary affiliation of the author. Some parts of the manuscript suggested she was an economist, others seemed to reflect the hand of a historian, still others made the reviewer think of political science. The whole made for a difficult decision. I regard this as one of the most flattering compliments ever paid to my work (thus deserving the place at the head of this list of acknowledgments), all the more so since my "true" disciplinary identity—I was trained as a sociologist/social anthropologist—apparently remained hidden; I have mixed my accents well.

My reviewer's difficulty is a confirmation of the feasibility of the unified approach to the study of social reality whose validity for me admits no doubt. Spheres of social experience are intricately interrelated and interdependent, and to attempt to study any one of them in isolation is akin to creating independent subspecialties with an exclusive focus on legs or stomach in biology. All of this experience, whether economic, political, or familial, and however public and material, is culturally—that is, symbolically—defined, because culture is what distinguishes humanity from other species. To attempt to understand social reality while leaving culture out of the account is similar to addressing questions of modern biology while denying the relevance of genetics. Finally, social experience by definition takes place in history, the collective name for the multitude of social processes; to study it out of historical context is to limit one's knowledge of social reality to an unconnected snapshot of a multiplane, ever-changing, live moving picture.

The obvious validity of the unified cultural and historical approach to the study of social reality does not, however, make it any less unorthodox and its obviously unreasonable—topological, mechanistic, and ahistorical—alternative any less dominant. No one can safely challenge the reigning orthodoxy alone. It is, therefore, only thanks to the backing and encouragement of certain institutions and individuals that I could offend against the current notions of academic propriety, climbing over disciplinary fences and disregarding the clear "no trespassing" signs posted all along them, with (relative) impunity. It is literally true that the present book could not have been written without the support of the University Professors, a unique interdisciplinary college at Boston University, which provided me with a congenial and tolerant academic home; I am in particular grateful to John Silber and Claudio Véliz for bringing me there. This book also would not have been published without the help of David Landes, the great economic historian and an even greater man. I have no words to express my gratitude to him and only want him to know that I know how much I am in his debt.

Many colleagues, near and far, anthropologists, economists, historians, political scientists, sociologists, and even some biologists (!), both generalists and specialists in American, British, Dutch, French, German, and Japanese history and culture (including, obviously, economic history and culture) gave generously of their time, reading and commenting on chapters and sharing their expertise. I am grateful to them all and apologize for limiting myself to the shortest possible list, which must include Daniel Bell, Kevin Doak, Nathan Glazer, Richard John, Suzanne Keller, Hans Kornberg, John Lampe, Walter Laqueur, Charles Lindholm, Glenn Loury, Jeffrey Miron, Chandler Rosenberger, Chikako Takeishi, Michael Thurman, Claudio Véliz, and Ezra Vogel.

The Earhart Foundation funded a summer of research in the Bibliothèque Nationale in Paris in 1997, and the Woodrow Wilson International Center for Scholars a semester free of teaching, spent in the proximity of the Library of Congress, during which I was able to complete the chapters on Germany and Japan, in 1998. In Boston, thanks to Brendan Dooley, I could use yet another great library, the Widener (all the while thinking about the merits of nationalization of certain kinds of private property).

I am grateful to the former editor-in-chief of Harvard University Press, Aida Donald, for taking the book on and to my editor there, Michael Aronson, for his suggestions and capable handling of the process. Thanks are also due to anonymous reviewers for contributing the time a manuscript of this length required and for bearing with its author's controversial argument, as well as to copyeditor Amanda Heller for meticulous work on my (too numerous, in her view) commas and (insufficient) definite and indefinite articles, which after almost twenty years of life in English still remain for me "a hidden Mystery." While working on this book, I have incurred debts in several languages. Professor Chikako Takeishi of Chuo University, Tokyo, guided me, as good as blind, through early editions of Motoori Norinaga and scrupulously supervised and edited my use of Japanese texts generally. Dr. Michael Thurman reviewed and translated Dutch sources for me. Their assistance was invaluable. But English was the language in which I needed most help. My students—the first, captive, audience of this book—tried, however gently, to draw my attention to potential problems and made numerous helpful suggestions, among them syntactic. (In this context I must mention in particular Oliver Benoit, Oyeshiku Carr, Zana Citak, Jonathan Eastwood, and Rosanne Felicello—members of the 1998–99 Modernity Seminar—as well as Peter Tamm.) Jonathan Eastwood heroically took upon himself the exclusive responsibility for the correct use of the tricky *the*'s and *a*'s (in addition to helping with references and index); Irina Ostrovskaya did her best to correct whatever he left uncorrected. At the eleventh hour Michael McKernan stepped in to cross the remaining t's and dot the remaining i's, including, specifically, in the notes. I am certain these collective efforts made the book more readable than it would have been otherwise.

Faced with the alternative of cutting out the notes altogether and urged by the press to economize wherever possible, I throughout the text combined references originally spread over several pages. The resulting composite notes, as a rule, and unless otherwise indicated, list specific references in the order in which material cited appears in the discussion. I apologize for any inconvenience this may cause the reader, but I believe that including the notes, however compressed, in the book is preferable to posting them on the Internet.

The Introduction and Chapter 1 incorporate portions of my articles "The Worth of Nations: Some Economic Implications of Nationalism" and "The Birth of Economic Competitiveness," published in the *Critical Review,* 9:4 (Fall 1995) and 10:3 (Summer 1996), respectively. I am grateful to the editor, Jeffrey Friedman, for valuable comments.

The spirit with whom I communed while writing *The Spirit of Capitalism* was that of the great Max Weber: the borrowed title of this book makes evident its inspiration. But I would be remiss not to acknowledge the contribution of an anonymous reviewer for *The Economist* (March 27, 1993), who pointed to the economic lacunae in my book *Nationalism: Five Roads to Modernity,* then newly published. That comment was the immediate reason for my decision to focus on the links between nationalism and economic growth.

Belmont, Massachusetts
March 2001

The Spirit of Capitalism

Introduction

This book attempts to answer two questions: (1) What was the direct cause of the emergence of modern economy; that is, what explains the *sustained* orientation of this economy, which distinguishes it from all others, to growth? (2) What made the economic sphere so central in the modern, and in particular American, consciousness that our civilization can in truth be called an "economic civilization"; that is, what persuaded millions of men and women, contrary to much of the historical experience and intimations of their own self-knowledge, to put their trust in economic growth (seen as natural) as the necessary and sufficient condition of social progress and political felicity? The focus is on the immediate motivating causes, or reasons, rather than conditions: on *why*, rather than *how*, modern economy and "economic civilization" came about. The emergence of the new economic orientation in England, France, Germany, and Japan—the first and, with the exception of France, particularly impressive cases of modern economic performance—provides the empirical basis for the answer to the first question. To test the argument, I also analyze the intriguing case of the Dutch Republic, which some scholars consider to be one of the first modern economies, and which could have been one (for it had all the conditions for this), but was not. The second question is examined in relation to the United States of America—the birthplace of the "economic civilization" and the site where it has flourished.

My central thesis is that the factor responsible for the reorientation of economic activity toward growth is nationalism, and that the unprecedented position of the economic sphere in the modern consciousness is a product of the dynamics of American society, in turn shaped by the singular characteristics of American nationalism. The concept of nationalism in this book is based on the arguments of my earlier work, *Nationalism: Five Roads to Modernity* (Harvard University Press, 1992), which analyzed the nature and traced the development of this vastly important phenomenon in England, where it was created, and then in France, Russia, Germany, and the United States. Since (however painful this is for the author) it is quite possible that the reader will

1

not be familiar with that earlier study, and since the text of the present one should not be encumbered by reiteration of propositions developed and substantiated elsewhere, I must define some of the concepts with which I operate here. For those interested chiefly in the economic significance of nationalism, they will provide a point of easy reference.

Nationalism is a unique form of social consciousness which emerged in the early sixteenth century in England and subsequently spread, first to the English settlements in America, then, in the course of the eighteenth century, to France and Russia, and in the course of the last two centuries conquered the rest of Europe and the Americas, the antipodes, much of Asia, and some of Africa. At the core of this social consciousness lies a compelling, inclusive image of society, referred to as the "nation," an image of a sovereign community of fundamentally equal members. National consciousness is inherently democratic: egalitarianism represents the essential principle of the social organization it implies, and popular sovereignty its essential political principle. These two principles, however, may be interpreted in radically different ways, giving rise to sharply different social and political arrangements. The interpretation depends on whether the nation is seen as a composite entity or in unitary terms, and on whether the criteria of national membership, that is, nationality, are civic or ethnic. In practice, these variables (which theoretically may exist in four combinations) yield three types of nationalisms with their corresponding forms of nations and national identities: the *individualistic-civic* type, the *collectivistic-civic* type, and the *collectivistic-ethnic* type.

In the *individualistic-civic* type, which was the original type of nationalism, the composite definition of the nation, that is, the idea of society as an association of individuals, is combined with the civic concept of nationality. It is because the individuals who compose the nation are regarded as equal and free that the nation is considered sovereign: it reflects the qualities of its members. The civic nationality, in turn, is equated with citizenship, that is, with the, in principle, conscious acceptance of certain rights and obligations; membership in the nation in this case ultimately depends on one's will to be a member, and nationality, similarly to religion, may be both acquired and lost. While all nationalisms imply democracy, individualistic-civic nationalisms imply individualistic, or liberal, democracy. The will of individualistic-civic nations is the will of the majority of their citizens: their governments are representative in fact as well as in principle; they cherish individual, human, rights and foster institutions which safeguard them.

In distinction, collectivistic nationalisms envision the nation as a collective individual, possessed of its own will, needs, and interests, which take precedence over the wills, needs, and interests of the human individuals who compose it and are not to be gauged from those of the majority. The national will must be divined by a specially qualified elite. Such an elite is, obviously, self-appointed, and at the same time its members sincerely believe that they represent the will of the nation. Modern dictatorships are invariably products of collectivistic nationalisms; the democracy to which all of them pledge allegiance is socialist, or popular, democracy.

The most common variety of collectivistic nationalism (the most common variety of nationalism in general) is *collectivistic-ethnic* nationalism. It combines the unitary definition of the nation with the ethnic concept of membership, that is, the view that nationality is an inherent, genetic, characteristic, transmitted by blood and independent of one's will, a trait which can be neither acquired if one is not born with it, nor lost if one is. The ethnic element in collectivistic-ethnic nationalism reinforces the authoritarian implications of its collectivistic element, the quasi-biological (ultimately racist) idea of nationality facilitating the image of human individuals as but biological members, or cells, in a greater ideal organism of the nation, and thus denying them every shred of individual liberty. The liberty or sovereignty of the nation, in this framework, is redefined as freedom from foreign domination.

In contrast to the individualistic-civic and collectivistic-ethnic types of nationalism, the elements of which reinforce each other, the combination of the unitary definition of the nation with civic criteria of nationality creates an ambivalent, cognitively problematic type. The social and political institutions and traditions of *collectivistic-civic* nations reflect a sort of double vision. The first such nation was France, whose turbulent history attests to the irreconcilable inconsistencies between its national ideals.

The type of nationalism (namely, the type of social consciousness and identity) represents the blueprint of social reality in a nation, to a large extent shapes this reality, and so directly and perceptibly affects those who happen to live it. The experiences of individuals in individualistic and collectivistic, civic and ethnic nations may differ dramatically. Still, in one crucial respect these experiences are similar: the inclusive nature of nationalism and its core principles of fundamental equality of membership and popular sovereignty (however interpreted and implemented) give people with a national identity a sense of dignity, which was unknown to most people in earlier periods. It is this sense of dignity that lies at the basis of national patriotism and commitment to national causes, which often strike outside observers as irrational. I emphasize this because dignity has much to do with economic growth.

In *Nationalism: Five Roads to Modernity* I focused on the process of formation of nationalism in general and of the five specific nationalisms in the particular cases chosen for their importance in modern politics. To the extent the book dealt with the effects of my *explanandum,* it was in passing and mostly with its political effects. A central premise of the book, however, was that nationalism is the constitutive element, or the organizing principle, of modernity, and I expected the impact of its nature, both general and particular, to be felt in every sphere of a nation's life. The present study, focusing on the links between nationalism and modern economy, is an indirect continuation of the project begun there.

Who Says It's All the Economy?

The relationship between nationalism and economics is usually seen in terms of the so-called structuralist approach which has been dominant in the social sciences in the last half century. It regards economic processes, such as industrialization, commercialization, the growth of capitalism, as fundamental and everything else—social relations, political institutions, and culture, that is, the ways people perceive things—as secondary, reflective, or at the least dependent on these fundamental processes. On the principle that all secondary things are created equal but some are nevertheless more secondary than others, culture, as a rule, is believed to be the farthest removed from the material objectivity of economics, and therefore the least important. In the words of a famous author, it has "no history, no development" independent of economic processes. As an epiphenomenon, culture represents a projection of the economic development in the mind, something like a shadow cast by an architectural structure—with definite forms of culture corresponding to each stage of economic progress, or, alternatively, called forth as functional requirements of such stages by the systemic needs of each economic system to facilitate the realization of their economic potential. Nationalism, being essentially a matter of perception and thus culture, and corresponding chronologically to the development of capitalism and industrialization, is therefore seen as either a reflection or a functional prerequisite of economic modernization.[1] Put crudely, it is believed to be *caused* by capitalism and industrialization.

This position has some intriguing implications which today probably deprive its proponents of sleep. These implications follow logically from the postulation of nationalism's dependency on economics: if nationalism is a product of a certain stage of economic development—that, presumably, of early capitalism and industrialization—then the passing of this stage must imply the passing of nationalism. Today, it is claimed, we live in the period of late capitalism, and possibly in the postindustrial society; yet nationalism, unfortunately, is not gone, nor does it show any signs of being gone soon. This refusal of humanity to listen to the reason of its most respected social scientists and to abide by the laws in which they place such faith is shocking in many respects, not least because it demonstrates exactly how irrelevant the social sciences have become in their hard-nosed and supposedly scientific materialism to the real world in which most of us live. Of course, the structuralist position has not gone unchallenged. Max Weber opposed it in the past; so do, emphatically, some distinguished authors in the present.

Still, the paradigm remains dominant—among other reasons, because it corresponds so well to the preeminence of the economic sphere in the lives of modern Western societies, particularly the United States. Generally speaking, Americans and, to an extent, other Westerners, who could not care less for social scientists, do regard prosperity as the cause of happiness, and economic development as the foundation of all other social processes—an unmitigated good, the necessary condition of a just society. We came to believe that if only a certain satisfactory level of economic development were achieved, all else would follow automatically, thereby making economic development the focus of our care and concern. This view shapes our private lives as much as it does foreign policy. (Why else would we push Russia, against the will of its people, and despite obvious political costs, to adopt market reform if it were not for our firm conviction that market reform today means liberal democracy tomorrow?) One hundred and fifty years ago this was a revolutionary view.

How this view gained ascendancy and how the economic sphere came to occupy such a central place in our thinking and experience are questions very rarely raised. Economists and economic historians discuss endlessly the reasons for the relative prosperity of nations, for their success or failure in the industrial race, but they do not ask why such a race exists at all and why nations should want to enter it. This they regard as self-evident. But there is nothing self-evident about it. In most historical societies, economic activities held the place occupied by classes which participated in them—the bottom of the social ladder and value hierarchy. They did not connote status and therefore did not attract talent. Prosperity was better than destitution, to be sure, but it rarely stood alone as a goal in life, and was far from being equated with happiness. In fact, it was often seen as an obstacle: Saint Matthew, as is well known, suggested that "it is easier for a camel to go through the eye of the needle, than for a rich man to enter the kingdom of God." In our time—and in our society—this has obviously changed.[2] But only a linear and deterministic view of history, assuming a succession of stages and uniform systemic needs corresponding to them, and oblivious to the empirical differences between cultures and the contingent nature of the historical process, would justify regarding such change as natural. This deterministic set of assumptions is called "historical materialism"; it is history according to Marx.

Curiously, Marxism, abandoned in the lands traditionally dedicated to its propagation and proved wrong by experience, is remarkably similar to the dominant Anglo-American view of the world. The two positions differ in regard to the nature of economic processes and forces (whereas Marxism stresses "forces of production," our "economism" may put an emphasis on the interplay between supply and demand); but in terms of their ontological and anthropological presuppositions—namely, ideas about the constitution of social reality and human nature—there is very little disagreement. Moreover, though Marx was among the first to postulate the principle of the centrality of economics in social life, the idea did not originate with him. It appears now that the immediate reason he turned his attention to economics was the publication in 1841 of *The National System of Political Economy* by his contemporary Friedrich List, also considered today, in some circles, to be a major economic theorist. In turn, List was inspired by the reading (or, rather, the common misreading, as we shall see later) of Adam Smith's *Wealth of Nations*, which was a central point of reference for Marx as well. Therefore, "in the final analysis," as Marx would say, the springs of the economistic view of society are to be sought in Britain. And to arrive at them one must first explore the far more significant, and perhaps more mysterious, problem of the rise of modern economy, to which we now turn.

Do We Know Why Economies Grow?

Why modern economy emerged represents the central question of both economic history and economics. To answer it is to explain what caused economic growth in the first place and to understand what sustains it in some cases and arrests it in others. In contrast to the phenomenon of the distinctive economism of modern consciousness, which scholars in the field unanimously neglect, it is thus a subject of a vast body of specialized literature. Both economic historians and economists, however, have been rather more successful in explaining how modern economy emerged, that is, in describing what happened—in the economies that have accomplished the so-called "take-off into self-sustained growth"—when the transformation took place. The literature has focused on the conditions and the process of the economic revolution, not on its causes. The reason may have been the centrality of the economic sphere in the modern experience (to which I alluded earlier) and the paramount, and unquestioned, commitment to economic growth, which made it an article of faith. From Marx to Simon Kuznetz, wrote David Landes in a 1991 review of the state of scholarship on the subject, economists and economic historians considered economic growth to be destiny—natural, inevitable, and self-explanatory. "Because of this, there was no real effort to probe the sources of the wealth of nations. Rather, the process of growth was taken for cause and explanation; the how stood in for the why." "This confusion of the what and the how for the why, of process and effect for cause" Landes called "the economists' sympathetic fallacy"—the tendency to substitute "what you know and like for what you need [to know]."[3]

Caught within a professional paradigm that has been a central element in the worldview of modern society, the students of the economic revolution have nevertheless been aware of the limited nature of their conclusions on the subject. They have generally agreed that the *conditions* for sustained growth (or the environment in which it occurs) include growth of population, the development of financial mechanisms and institutions encouraging capital accumulation, market expansion, and the development of a body of scientific knowledge capable of producing a steady flow of technological inventions. But they have also agreed that, while the obstacles to economic growth posed by the absence of these demographic, financial, commercial, and intellectual factors—stagnant or declining population, the lack of capital or mechanisms for its transfer, markets, and technical means of production—are obvious, the nature of their positive effect (that is, the exact manner in which they stimulate sustained growth where it has not as yet occurred) and the fact that they indeed have such a positive effect, or play a *causal* role, is not as clear. To quote from surveys of the literature in the field, in presumably the first and, therefore, best-studied British case, population growth "was so closely interwoven with economic expansion that [it is] exceedingly difficult to distinguish cause from effect in the pattern of development," while in the developmental cycles of traditional economies, it often formed the Malthusian barrier to economic expansion. An increase in the availability of capital "at best . . . is a trend which permits growth to occur. It is not in itself a cause of growth unless it can be argued that a shortage of capital has previously inhibited growth." Markets have been known to expand in many settings without leading to sustained growth, leading instead to the conclusion that "there is no natural or irresistible movement" from one to the other. And even science and technology, the factor which, to many an economic historian, "distinguishe[d] the world since the industrial revolution from the world before," can only be claimed with certainty to have contributed "to the progress" of economic modernization; their role in the origins of the latter is much harder to determine, the level of scientific achievement was not necessarily reflected in the comparable level of technological invention, invention did not automatically lead to innovation, and the wide availability of technology failed to accomplish economic modernization where it was not taking place for other reasons.[4]

To exemplify the problem identified by David Landes—the substitution, insofar as the question of growth is concerned, of descriptive analysis for explanatory theory in economics and economic history—one can turn to the work of W. W. Rostow, which is likely to be familiar to the reader with a general interest in the subject. Like most economists and economic historians, Rostow assumed the natural and fundamental character of economic processes, and specifically of the process of growth, which might be impaired by a hostile environment or promoted by a friendly one, but was inherent in the historical process. Its timing and pace, and especially its failure to occur, were thus regarded as problematic and in need of explanation, but the fact of its occurrence was seen as self-evident. (For this reason, Rostow began his account of the origins of modern economy with an explanation of why traditional societies *did not* generate self-sustained growth.[5] Putting the question this way is not different from asking how come Shakespeare did not write *Oliver Twist* or Michelangelo did not paint *Guernica*.)

Guided by these assumptions, Rostow identified stages of growth, which were analogous to ages of an organism. "Take-off into self-sustained growth," that is, the emergence of modern economy, represented the third stage, and required "all three of the following related conditions: 1) a rise in the rate of productive investment from, say, 5% or less to over 10% of national income; 2) the development of one or more substantial manufacturing sectors, with a high rate of growth; 3) the existence or quick emergence of a political, social and institutional framework which exploits the impulses to expansion in the modern sector." Interestingly, the first two conditions were conditions of, rather than for, takeoff: these were descriptions of what happens when it happens, of states that occur when takeoff is taking place. The only condition for takeoff was the third, which pertained to the wider social, and especially political, context of the economic process. The addition of the political dimension did not add to the explanation but raised additional questions. Since economic growth was natural, favorable political conditions (specifically, as Rostow specified elsewhere, nation-states oriented toward economic modernization, that is, interested in takeoff) only cleared the ground for takeoff, eliminating obstacles to further development, as revolutions did in the Marxist deterministic scheme. But Rostow was not an explicit, or consistent, determinist. He admitted that nation-states had independent agendas and might "be turned in any one of several directions [including] outward to right real or believed past humiliations suffered on the world scene or to exploit real or believed opportunities for national [political] aggrandizement."[6] In other words, the alliance of the state and the economy, the choice by the state of the path of economic modernization, is not a given; it is not explained when it is postulated or described. The recognition in an exogenous, political factor of a necessary condition for economic growth redefines the problem of economic growth. The crucial question becomes why certain states develop an interest in it. An answer to this question, however, would presuppose a project altogether different from the ones attempted in economics and economic history (as well as much of the discussion of the relationship between the state and the economy): it would require a study of motivations and would properly belong to the sphere of the history of ideas and the sociology of culture.

Rostow's central metaphor, and, along with "industrial revolution," the central metaphor of the field—the "take-off"—also pointed to the crucial importance of these "ideal factors" which, with one exception, he accorded no more than a passing mention. The metaphor, significantly, suggested an analogy with technology or engineering—"an aeroplane taking off from the ground"[7]—which, unlike the biological idea of "growth," inevitably presupposed the existence of spirit behind the matter. Airplanes, after all, no matter how perfectly equipped for the action, do not take off of their own accord. Neither do they represent natural phenomena, whose development is independent of human will and perceptions. They are constructed for the purpose of carrying out the former and in accordance with the latter; and however complete our understanding of how the airplane is constructed, how it builds up speed and sustains itself in flight, however extensive our knowledge of the physical laws operating at every stage, we cannot understand what causes these laws to operate, why the plane takes off, and why it was constructed in the first place unless we account for the concrete guiding and creative intelligence, human intelligence, behind the process.

The exception to Rostow's general disregard of the directing motives was, significantly, nationalism. Throughout his work he emphasized the importance of international competition and "reactive nationalism," that is, nationalism "reacting against intrusion from more advanced nations" in fostering economic growth. He proposed, among other things, that "reactive nationalism . . . has been a most important and powerful motive force in the transition from traditional to modern societies, at least as important as the profit motive." Such emphasis is both revealing and problematic. It is revealing of the salience of nationalism in the economic process, which an empirically sensitive historian cannot avoid noticing, however little it fits into one's theoretical scheme. It is problematic because nationalism (if only reactive nationalism, which raises a host of questions in regard to nationalism which is not reactive and painfully piques one's curiosity by its unaccounted appearance on the modern economy's launching site) did not fit Rostow's theoretical scheme indeed, but in fact unnecessarily burdened and undermined his argument. Reactive nationalism, Rostow observed, was especially important in the diffusion of economic growth after the British takeoff, accounting for "a good deal of European economic history in the nineteenth century." But the logic of his argument dictated that "the preconditions for take-off were slowly being built up from the fifteenth to the eighteenth centuries, from London to St. Petersburg [sic], from Stockholm to Madrid," making it reasonable to "assume that sooner or later the forces at work would have yielded a take-off elsewhere in Europe (or in the United States), if Britain had not led the way."[8] If, however, the process of economic development resulting in the takeoff into sustained growth was endemic—that is, natural or inherent in history—the leadership of Britain could have no greater causal significance than the blooming of the first flower in a flower bed ready to bloom, and the stimulus of reactive nationalism was needless and wholly superfluous in explaining the takeoff of other economies. The prominence of reactive nationalism among the factors responsible for bringing about the post-British takeoffs was an anomaly for the theory and suggested that the process was contingent on subjective perceptions and interests, again focusing attention on the question of motivation.

The purpose of this discussion is not to criticize Rostow or to diminish the significance of his very valuable contribution to the study of modern economy. With his concept of "take-off into self-sustained growth," he put a finger on its central distinguishing characteristic, and his analysis of stages presented a clear and articulate picture of the process of economic modernization. The purpose of the foregoing discussion is, rather, to point to the inescapable limitations of attempts to explain social (including economic) phenomena while disregarding human agency and the element of motivation. Immediate causes of social action are always the reasons of social actors, and the omission of this crucial link in the chain of social causation keeps even the best, empirically grounded, scholarship on the level of description. Unlike some of his numberless followers, Rostow has been aware of the built-in limitations of his approach, writing, among other places, in the 1990 edition of *The Stages of Economic Growth* that "the approach to growth via mainstream economics is misleading [because] cultural, social, and political factors are all at work as well as economic factors; and . . . the process of growth is inherently interactive, yielding not only changes in the parameters but even in the rules of behavior. In a sense, there can be no formal theory of growth of the kind held up as a goal by [Robert] Solow until there is a unified theory of both human beings and the societies they construct out of their multi-dimensional complexity."[9] He felt, however, that students in the field were professionally unprepared to tackle problems outside their disciplinary purview and had to fend as well they could within the bounds of established paradigms.

The *Protestant Ethic* Controversy

Changes in the rules of (economic) behavior—specifically, the transformation in the orientations or motivation of economic action, leading to the emergence of modern economy capable of sustained growth—were not entirely disregarded in the literature on the subject. In fact, they have been the focus of one of the most famous and lasting controversies in the social sciences. I refer, of course, to the controversy around Max Weber's *Protestant Ethic and the Spirit of Capitalism,* a deliberate and so far unsurpassed attempt to transcend the limitations of the necessarily descriptive research, exclusively focused on "real factors," and capture the most elusive aspect in the "multi-dimensional complexity" of economic modernization. Often interpreted as an argument with the ghost of Marx and an idealistic alternative to Marx's materialism, *The Protestant Ethic,* like all of Weber's work, was, rather, a challenge to deterministic and unilinear theories of all kinds. Its purpose was to explain the shift in social attitudes to economic activity, and the nature of new attitudes, which, in the then existing conditions of material development, pertaining to the state of markets, financial institutions, technology, population, and agricultural capacity, oriented the economy toward, and were responsible for the definition of, growth as socially desirable, making it a value and thereby promoting its institutionalization. The argument did not by any means imply that these cultural factors produced the capitalist economic system in its entirety or were responsible for any of its elements except one. The scope of the explanation was strictly limited to the motivations which channeled economic action—to the extent allowed by the current development of commerce, finance, and technology—toward growth. In the absence of these material conditions, the spirit of capitalism would have had no body to animate; it would have been economically useless. Yet only its presence could lend to the economy what we recognize as its modern character.

Weber referred to the orientation of the economy toward growth as "the spirit of capitalism," and he called the economy oriented to and capable of growth "capitalism." The reason he chose this notoriously vague concept might have had to do with its prominence in the discussion in which he was participating, specifically its use in Werner Sombart's 1902 *Der Moderne Kapitalismus,* which had already raised the problem of "the spirit of capitalism." It is clear that the term as such greatly contributed to the confusion about Weber's argument and was responsible for some of the reaction against it. But though he may not have been sufficiently sensitive to the symbolic significance the word "capitalism" had acquired or was to acquire in the first decades of the twentieth century, Weber made an effort to define the meaning he wished to attribute to it and offered his readers the means to avoid the kind of misunderstanding that his critics have most commonly exhibited.

In the introduction to his essay, Weber explicitly distinguished the modern economy or capitalism, which he was trying to explain (in the body of the argument he used the two terms interchangeably), from other types of economic and capitalistic activity, and specifically defined his *explanandum* as an expression of a particular degree and, more important, a particular form of what he perceived as the fundamental social process and historical principle—"rationalization." He wrote:

> The impulse to acquisition, pursuit of gain, of money, of the greatest possible amount of money, has in itself nothing to do with capitalism . . . One may say that [this impulse] has been common to all sorts and conditions of men at all times and in all countries of the earth, wherever the objective possibility of it is or has been given . . . Unlimited greed for gain is not in the least identical with capitalism, and still less its spirit . . . But capitalism is identical with the pursuit of profit, and forever renewed profit, by means of continuous, rational, capitalistic enterprise . . . So far as the transactions are rational, calculation underlies every single action of the partners . . . But these are points affecting only the degree of rationality of capitalistic acquisition . . . Now in this sense capitalism and capitalistic enterprises, even with a considerable rationalization of capitalistic calculation, have existed in all civilized countries of the earth, so far as economic documents permit us to judge—in China, India, Babylon, Egypt, Mediterranean antiquity, and the Middle Ages, as well as in modern times . . . [T]rade especially was for a long time not continuous like our own, but consisted essentially in a series of individual undertakings. Only gradually did the activities of even the large merchants acquire an inner cohesion . . . In any case, the capitalistic enterprise and the capitalistic entrepreneur, not only as occasional but as regular entrepreneurs, are very old and were very widespread.
>
> Now, however, the Occident has developed capitalism both to a quantitative extent, and (carrying this quantitative development) in types, forms, and directions which have never existed elsewhere . . . a very different form of capitalism which has appeared nowhere else: the rational capitalistic organization of (formally) free labor. Only suggestions of it are found elsewhere . . . [T]he concept of the citizen has not existed outside the Occident, and that of the bourgeoisie outside the modern Occident. Similarly, the proletariat as a class could not exist, because there was no rational organization of free labor under regular discipline . . . Hence in a universal history of culture the central problem for us is not, in the last analysis, even from a purely economic viewpoint, the development of capitalistic activity as such, differing in different cultures only in form: the adventurer type, or capitalism in trade, war, politics, or administration as sources of gain. It is rather the origin of this sober bourgeois capitalism with its rational organization of free labor. Or in terms of cultural history, the problem is that of the origin of the Western bourgeois class and of its peculiarities.

Granted the unfortunate choice and somewhat inconsistent use of the term "capitalism" (specifically, its application to both modern and pre-modern types of economic activity, and to continuously as well as sporadically rational acquisition), it is quite clear what Weber's focus is and what is, consequently, the nature of his question. Modern economy—the "capitalism" of *The Protestant Ethic*—is distinguished by the type and degree of the rationalization, and by the institutionalization, or the societal character, of the acquisitive drive, two separate though related qualities (there is a possibility of rationalization without institutionalization), both of which represent necessary conditions for sustained growth.

"Rationalization" is another problematic concept, also defined only by the many varied contexts in which Weber uses it. "By this term," he writes,

> very different things may be understood . . . There is, for example, rationalization of mystical contemplation, that is of an attitude which, viewed from other departments of life, is especially irrational, just as much as there are rationalizations of economic life, of technique, of scientific research, of military training, of law and administration. Furthermore, each one of these fields may be rationalized in terms of very different ultimate ends, and what is rational from one point of view may well be irrational from another. Hence rationalizations of the most varied character have existed in various departments of life and in all areas of culture. To characterize their differences from the viewpoint of cultural history it is necessary to know what departments are rationalized and in what direction.

The general meaning of "rationalization" which emerges out of, and allows its application in, such widely differing "departments of life" as mystical contemplation and economy is that of "articulation and organization, primarily cognitive, of an area of experience." The need for rationalization arises from the inherently disorderly nature of reality to which human beings are born (in distinction to other forms of life that emerge fully equipped with detailed blueprints and the means for organizing their environment, in effect carrying order in their genes) and the fact that the responsibility for introducing elements of order into it falls to themselves. "Rationalization," in other words, refers to the fundamental process of the ordering of reality, or its cultural construction. It represents a biological imperative, because without it reality would be unmanageable and the survival of the species impossible, and, as a result, it goes on all the time, in every society, and in all spheres of life. In this Weberian framework, to claim that one society is more rational, or "rationalized," than another would be an absurdity; it would be tantamount to claiming that it is more of a society, or more human. "Rationalization" is not necessarily a cumulative process, and the differences between societies (or spheres of activity in a society) in this respect are likely to be not quantitative but qualitative: while they cannot be more or less rationalized, they are, as a rule, rationalized in different ways.

Modern economy, or modern Western capitalism, which Weber sought to explain, was in his view a product of "the specific and peculiar rationalism of Western culture," which manifested itself, in addition, in Western music, architecture, science, and law. In all these areas, rationalization resulted in the formulation of general principles and the types of organization which were endlessly adaptable (or, at least, appeared so at the beginning of the twentieth century) and capable of endless ramification and therefore internal development. It was this potential for growth (which communicated to these Western cultural phenomena a quality of living entities) which prompted Weber to claim for them a "universal significance and value."[10]

To conceptualize the central organizing historical process as "rationalization" is to recognize it as an essentially mental process. As such, "rationalization" goes on in the minds of individuals, and in the overwhelming majority of cases, the significance of particular rationalizations is strictly limited. Some rationalizations, however—those that organize recurrent experiences shared by members of numerically or otherwise influential groups—acquire the character of social processes: their articulation becomes a matter of collective effort with benefits extending far beyond the circle of those who actively participate in it. When the reality that is being rationalized endures over time, rationalization may become the basis of institutionalization. In this case the society commits itself to a particular rationalization—that is, a particular way of organizing a certain area of experience or a particular image of order—and, putting its weight behind it, makes subscribing to it normative, thereby incorporating it as, and into, the social structure. It is as part of social institutions that rationalization (in its diverse forms) exerts its most profound and lasting influence and acts as the organizing force in society. When Weber speaks of the "specific and peculiar rationalism of Western culture," whether in music, science, law, or economy, he is referring to precisely such a social force. For all the attempts to represent him as an idealist, he is in fact interested not in disembodied ideas or "rationalization" as such but in the socially significant, that is, institutionalized rationalization that transcends its original individual character and acquires societal character. Consequently, the problem he poses in *The Protestant Ethic* and other works is necessarily twofold: one must explain the evolution of a particular form of rationalization and its institutionalization, which does not automatically follow.[11]

Most of Weber's critics, whether or not they understood the nature of his question, focused on the central empirical proposition of *The Protestant Ethic*, which related the emergence of the new norms of economic behavior, "the spirit of capitalism," to Protestantism, specifically to the Calvinist dogma of predestination and interpretation of the idea of the "calling." This proposition was based on the observation, not seriously disputed in his time or later (however tentative the agreement on its significance), that economic action was visibly reoriented in northern Europe, specifically in England, somewhere around the seventeenth century. The reorientation, in particular, concerned the attitude toward the accumulation of profit (thus growth) which, though for centuries condemned as leading to the perdition of the soul and pursued only erratically, was now practiced systematically and with a confidence that bespoke not just toleration but encouragement by the society at large. To prompt a positive reinterpretation (and institutionalization of such a reinterpretation) of the pursuit of profit at that time and place, a congenial cultural environment, a new moral code, had to emerge in the period immediately preceding it. Since that happened to be the period of religious revolution which affected all of western Europe, but specifically north European societies, the explanation naturally suggested itself.

This sensible hypothesis has not been corroborated by subsequent research. It has been repeatedly pointed out that Weber's interpretation of the Protestant ethic, which was to explain the spirit of capitalism, was based on the very documents which formed the basis of his idea of the spirit of capitalism. Systematic examination of the writings of the leading early Protestant divines, which represented the foundational texts of Protestant theology, revealed them as economic traditionalists, as suspicious of enterprise and hostile to profit making (and, therefore, growth) as any medieval Schoolman, if not more so, and so most unlikely godparents of economic progress.[12] This examination, bringing into sharper focus such Protestant theological principles as the ideas of predestination and "calling," also cast serious doubt on, if it did not contradict outright, Weber's interpretation of these principles. At the very least, as R. H. Tawney was to conclude, Weber had attributed to them greater significance and consistency than the sources warranted. Weber's almost exclusive concentration on Puritan England, which he chose as the clearest example of the religious origins of the spirit of capitalism, and especially his leaving out of account the equally Calvinist Netherlands, whose economic prowess was both not sustained and, at its zenith, apparently infused with a different spirit, further weakened the argument.

A refutation of Weber's hypothesis regarding the relationship of Calvinist Protestantism to the spirit of capitalism, however, was nothing Weber could not expect and reconcile himself to in advance. For while he proposed that the ethic of modern economy (the set of economic orientations and norms of behavior implying and encouraging growth) was related to this particular religious ethical system, he also suggested, significantly, that this ethical system could have a functional equivalent and was not the only possible system of thought to have had such an effect. This suggestion made explicit the tentative, provisional, or hypothetical character of the central empirical thesis of *The Protestant Ethic*, entirely consistent with Weber's *Wissenschaftslehre*, specifically, his conviction that the price of scientific progress and improved understanding was the continuous suppression of older hypotheses by new and more accurate ones.

Moreover, to prove Weber wrong on this point was to prove him wrong on a relatively minor point of his theory, the essence of which consisted in the claim that the emergence of modern economy presupposed—that is, could not have occurred without—a new set of motivations and a new system of ethics. This was a theory predicated on the realization that society represented an aspect of life of the thinking species, endowed with prodigious symbolic capacity but insufficient genetic regulation, and thus distinguished by the propensity and the necessity for rationalization. The distinctive characteristic of (human) social action, which made it essentially unlike the behavior of other species, even those capable of highly sophisticated cooperative action, was its meaningfully intentional character. This principle in turn implied that, for meaningful and intentional social action to be consistently channeled in a particular direction, such action had to be invested with a positive meaning: it had to be an object of social approbation, defined as legitimate and morally commendable. In other words, it had to find support in a certain system of ethics. An enduring reorientation in a particular type of social action (for instance, economic) implied its reinterpretation and the development of new motivations and intentions among the participants, which presupposed an emergence of new ethical standards. An invalidation of the proposition that the cultural environment of capitalism was a product of the Protestant Reformation not only did not negate this general and far more important theory, but, as such, contributed very little to the solution of the problem in question (the reorientation of social action and the emergence of modern economy). Such invalidation eliminated one conceivable explanation—that is all. To stop there, to focus on whether or not Weber was right in claiming this dramatic role for a particular religious teaching, would be to beg the question. Yet this is exactly what most of Weber's critics did.

The fruitlessness of the debate over (or, rather, preoccupation with) *The Protestant Ethic*, which by now has lasted almost a century, providing an eloquent testimony to the compelling nature of its argument, should, no doubt, be attributed to the fact that Weber's opponents concentrated their efforts on the refutation of a relatively minor point as an end in itself. They failed to appreciate the broader sociological significance of Weber's essay and meet the challenge, specifically, of his contribution to the understanding of the central problem of modern economic history—the origins of economic growth. This failure is most conspicuous where it is of greatest consequence, in the writings of economic historians, and, among them, in Tawney's trend-setting and in many respects representative *Religion and the Rise of Capitalism.*

The very title of Tawney's book reflected his misunderstanding of Weber. The focus on religion was misplaced: as Tawney himself convincingly demonstrated, on closer examination Protestantism turned out to be an unlikely doctrine to promote the ethos of the modern economic system which Weber called the spirit of capitalism (and nobody ever suspected its major religious alternative of such sympathies). One had to look for the source of this ethical reorientation in a wider cultural context. Instead, Tawney redefined the spirit of capitalism itself, equating it with nothing less than "conscienceless individualism," thereby identifying capitalism with the egoistic pursuit of one's material self-interest, uninhibited by moral scruples and social concerns. (That individualism is identical with the spirit, or, as it has been lately referred to, the "culture," of capitalism—which in turn stands for modern economy and even, specifically, industrialization—is now a common assumption that lies at the basis of much contemporary economic history. It is but a reformulation of the fundamental proposition of laissez-faire economics to the effect that economic growth is a function of greed or natural acquisitive impulse—the very notion which, Weber suggested, should be extinguished in the kindergarten[13]—and its roots, like the roots of laissez-faire economics, go back to the vulgarization of Adam Smith's idea of the "invisible hand" and the substitution for his complex view of man as the bearer of moral sentiments the surreal but simple image of the self-interested, rational egoist, representing the embodiment of the propensity "to truck, barter, and exchange." The misunderstanding of Weber thus is directly linked to the misunderstanding of Smith.)

Having thus redefined his *explanandum,* Tawney resolved the problem of the inconsistency between the ethical principles of Protestantism and the values of modern economy, and was able to retain the *explanans.* The question was no longer that of the emergence of a new system of social norms and ethical standards, a cultural system of "the peculiarly Occidental rationalism" actively orienting social action, but that of the relaxation of ethical standards which had existed before and the emergence from under the ideological rubble of a self-directed (and inherently rational) natural system. The specific character of the ethical standards that were relaxed was of no importance. What mattered was the fact of relaxation and, perhaps, the process that brought it about. Protestantism, Tawney claimed, did indeed play a role in the emergence of the new "commercial civilization," but it played this role despite what it represented and because of what happened to it. Its economic function was due primarily not to the nature of the faith, as Weber had suggested, but to the circumstances in which it was put, which ironically led to the loss of faith and resulted in "the abdication of religion from its theoretical primacy over economic activity and social institutions." "The elements which combined to produce [the modern] economic revolution," Tawney wrote, "are too numerous to be summarized in any neat formula. But, side by side with expansion of trade and the rise of the new classes to political power, there was a further cause . . . It was the contraction of the territory within which the writ of religion was conceived to run."

Tawney therefore professed partial agreement with Weber's thesis, conceding that "Puritanism [was] a potent force in preparing the way for the commercial civilization which finally triumphed after the Revolution." In effect, however, he substituted for Weber's theory an entirely different argument that can in all fairness be characterized as reversion to orthodox Marxism. He concluded that Calvinism, and in particular English Puritanism, eventually grew less disapproving of the pursuit of profit, more tolerant toward economic motives, less restrictive in respect to enterprise, and able to regard business life in general with greater equanimity than it was originally and than was the case with other currents within Christianity. It thus released "the magnificent energy which changed in a century the face of material civilization" and made economic progress possible. But, he claimed, such friendliness to economic development on the part of the Protestant creed was itself the effect of this development's "corroding march" on it. "The 'capitalist spirit,'" Tawney wrote,

> is as old as history, and was not, as has sometimes been said, the offspring of Puritanism . . . At first sight, no contrast could be more violent than that between the iron collectivism . . . the remorseless and violent rigours practiced in Calvin's Geneva and preached elsewhere . . . by his disciples, and the impatient rejection of all traditional restrictions on economic enterprise which was the temper of the English business world after the Civil War . . . Like traits of individual character which are suppressed till the approach of maturity releases them, the tendencies of Puritanism, which were to make it later a potent ally of the movement against the control of economic relations in the name either of social morality or of public interest, did not reveal themselves till political and economic changes had prepared a congenial environment for their growth . . . in the late sixteenth and early seventeenth centuries, had come the wave of commercial expansion—companies, colonies, capitalism in textiles, capitalism in mining, capitalism in finance—on the crest of which the English commercial classes, in Calvin's day still held in

leading-strings by conservative statesmen, had climbed to a position of dignity and affluence . . . The collectivist, half-communistic aspect [of Puritanism] which had never been acclimatized in England, quietly dropped out of notice . . . [T]he individualism congenial to the world of business became the distinctive characteristic of Puritanism which had arrived, and which, in becoming a political force, was at once secularized and committed to a career of compromise . . . Given the social and political conditions in England, the transformation was inevitable.

The "wave of commercial expansion," the "commercial classes" (whose rise Weber considered the problem of the cultural history of economics), the "world of business" apparently appeared of themselves or were, like the spirit of capitalism, as old as history, and therefore did not require an explanation. This argument essentially reversed Weber's thesis regarding the relationship between economic development and religion. To Tawney, it was economics that gave rise to "the Protestant ethic," picking out and cultivating one of several currents in the doctrine, and selecting, or in effect constructing, an appropriate ideology for economic development.

The role that Protestantism was forced to play consisted in leaving economics alone, letting individualism take the place of the collective consciousness, and thereby "liberating economic energies" or allowing free play to Adam Smith's (misunderstood) invisible hand. Ideological controls were lifted, all shackles removed, and man could pursue his rational interest.[14] The rest was natural, automatic, self-evident. The argument made sense only on the assumption of the "objective rationality"—thus natural character—of the pursuit of material self-interest, namely, gain, and the resulting economic process. When man's nature is defined as objectively rational, rationality, by definition, becomes the essential expression of nature, or an equivalent of instinct. The trouble with this assumption is not just that it reduces humanity to the level of dumb beasts with their genetically programmed reality and eliminates with one fell swoop the grand problem of order and the need for social sciences, but that the modern economic process and the behavior that lies at its basis are neither natural nor rational in this sense. Weber stressed this repeatedly, writing in his definition of the spirit of capitalism:

In fact, the *summum bonum* of [the capitalist economic] ethic, the earning of more and more money, combined with the strict avoidance of all spontaneous enjoyment of life, is completely devoid of any eudaemonistic, not to say hedonistic, admixture. It is thought of so purely as an end in itself, that from the point of view of the happiness of, or utility to, the single individual, it appears entirely transcendental and absolutely irrational . . . Economic acquisition is no longer subordinated to man as the means for the satisfaction of his material needs. This reversal of what we should call the natural relationship, so irrational from a naive point of view, is evidently as definitively a leading principle of capitalism as it is foreign to all peoples not under capitalistic influence.[15]

The fact that the spirit of capitalism is not in itself natural and rational, yet is obviously regarded as such, means that it was at some point defined (or interpreted) as natural and rational, and makes it imperative for us to approach the emergence of modern economy as a problem in the cultural construction of reality.

If one assumes that the orientation of modern capitalism—to profit making and thus to growth—is natural in the sense of being objectively rational and fundamental, one has to account for the recency and the unevenness of its institutionalization and the fact that for millennia it was allowed only sporadic manifestations. To attribute this to artificially imposed ethical (ideological) restraints would not suffice, for the two indisputably fundamental orientations of human nature—namely, the hunger and sex drives—though always ideologically regulated and often "repressed," have, after all, never been reduced to the level of deviant behavior (for centuries the status of profit-oriented economic activity), but, on the contrary, have always been provided with institutionalized channels for systematic expression and gratification. The comparison with the natural drives is edifying. Every society invests food and sex with some degree of cultural significance and makes them an object of moral, ethical interpretation. Even the alimentary and sexual experiences are therefore, to a degree, culturally constructed. But the extent of their genetic determination ensures their fundamental moral indifference, in the sense that, on the level of whole societies, these drives neither can be effectively suppressed nor, more important, do they require cultural, ethical stimulation for sustained and robust manifestation. For this very reason, however, these fundamental natural drives have no history; like animal societies, they are not historical phenomena. History, including economic history, exists precisely because social (and economic) reality is genetically indeterminate, not natural in that very weighty sense of the word.

We return to the fundamental thesis of Weber's sociology. *History is the march (or, rather, ramble) of rationalization, the endless succession of disconnected attempts to introduce order into experience which does not carry it within itself.* The process of rationalization is natural, as is humanity, but man-made things are, by definition, artificial, and so are the products of rationalization—specific orientations of social action, interpretations, ideals, and images, those various "rationalisms" peculiar to one or another culture which Weber tried to delineate, if not to explain. There is nothing inevitable about them, they do not occur of themselves, they are not self-evident. It is the un-naturalness, irrationality—and historicity—of "the peculiarly Occidental rationalism" that makes it impossible to grasp fully the dynamics of the modern economic process without understanding its cultural origins and necessitates that we find the ethical system which transformed an erratic individual propensity into a social norm and ideal to be systematically pursued. And if Puritanism, Protestantism, and religion in general prove not to be that ethical system, we have to cast our net wider.

I have spent this much time on "the Weber thesis" because my argument in regard to nationalism and modern economy derives directly from the premises of *The Protestant Ethic,* and I want to make clear what exactly are the points on which I agree with it and why, and where I dissent and go my own way. In my disagreement with Weber, as much as in my agreement, I believe I follow the principles of his approach. Credit should be given where it is due. Though the meagerness of returns on a most considerable expenditure of effort in the case of the social sciences reveals that, unlike the natural sciences, and unlike the modern economy, they have not yet reached the stage of take-off into self-sustained growth, Newton's metaphor for scientific progress applies to us too. If ever we see farther than our predecessors, it is only because we stand on the shoulders of giants.

Why Nationalism?

And now—*revenons à nos moutons.* The question I have posed may bear repeating. It is a question of motivation, and it falls within the domain of the sociology of knowledge. I am asking why the historically exceptional inclination for ever-increasing gain, characteristic of certain individuals in societies which regarded it at best with suspicion, became defined, on the level of the individual, as rational self-interest, constitutive of man's very nature and, on the level of society, as common good and paramount collective interest. I claim that behind this shift of societal attitudes in regard to the acquisitive drive and its dramatic valorization stood a new secular form of collective consciousness (thus a new system of ethical standards): nationalism. This makes nationalism the source of "the spirit of capitalism"—the orientation of modern economic action—and a crucial factor in the emergence of modern economy. But this does not make it "the sole agency" in this process. No account of why something happens is complete unless supplemented by the account of how it happens; it is one thing to explain why economic growth became a desired goal, quite another to elucidate the conditions and mechanisms that have allowed for its realization. I deal only with desire and leave the question of capability to economists and economic historians. They have been sharpening the tools of their analysis for a century and delved so deep into the minutiae of economic development as to make scrutiny of their findings by an amateur a hopeless and needless project. I do not doubt the soundness of their conclusions—insofar as they do not confuse (to quote Landes again) process with cause, and the what and the how with the why. For my part, I do not presume to provide a comprehensive, or an "alternative," explanation of the rise of the modern economy of growth, only to add to the existing explanation a missing—and essential—motivational dimension.

The relationship between the desire and the capability, as Weber had already argued in regard to the capitalist spirit and organization, is not one of necessary or simple interdependence. The two, he wrote, "may very well occur separately." Today, in particular, examples abound of ardent desire for economic growth even when no conditions exist for its realization, and even today there are cases (which one may assume to have been common in earlier periods) where an enormous potential for growth, that is, an undeniable capability, remains unrealized because there is no desire, as in Russia. The relationship, Weber suggests, is best conceptualized as that of mutual reinforcement of the essentially autonomous factors, with the attitude of mind finding its most suitable expression when the capability exists, and the capability deriving its most suitable motive force from the attitude of mind.[16] Both, therefore, should be taken into consideration in explaining modern economy.

Quite aside from its ubiquitous presence in the age of economic growth, several factors recommend nationalism to the attention of a student of modern economy. To start, it has the merit of fitting in perfectly in terms of the chronology of "the industrial revolution" broadly defined and, in particular, allows one to account for the dazzling—and otherwise perplexing—case of Britain. It should be remembered that the historical priority of Britain's take-off does not make sense in the framework of the "natural evolution" theory in economics and economic history. On the threshold of its economic supremacy, Britain was not the most advanced economy in the world. From the point of view of objective capacity (the buildup of preconditions for takeoff), as late as the end of the sixteenth century, the Dutch Republic, France, Germany, and even Spain or Italy might have been better positioned to assume the role that fell to Britain. It was exactly because it came from behind and overtook these more advanced economies that its rise was in the nature of a miracle. The fact that relatively backward England, and not the equally Calvinist Dutch Republic, was to accomplish the breakthrough and achieve lasting dominance in the modern economic system is a major anomaly for the "Protestant ethic" thesis as well. Bringing nationalism into the argument, however, resolves these anomalies.

Nationalism first appeared in England, becoming the preponderant vision of society there and effectively transforming social consciousness by 1600. More than a century had to pass before signs of similar transformations were felt elsewhere. In the Netherlands, in particular, perhaps because the society was so advanced—economically as well as politically—the development of national identity and consciousness was delayed still further and cannot be discerned until well into the nineteenth century. England, therefore, was the first to acquire a new spirit, which it was the only one to possess for some two centuries, and this spirit, this motive force, added to its relatively unimpressive resources an element that reoriented, transformed, and magnified them, inspiring it to undertake a journey for which other societies might have been better equipped and thus giving it a competitive edge over them.

Unlike Protestantism, nationalism necessarily promotes the type of social structure which the modern economy needs to develop. Being inherently egalitarian, nationalism has as one of its central cultural consequences an open—or class—system of stratification, which allows for social mobility, makes labor free (that is, able to shift between sectors), and dramatically expands the sphere of operation of market forces. Since it redefines the nature of social hierarchy, in the absence of countervening factors, it elevates the prestige of traditionally disparaged occupations, specifically those oriented to the pursuit of profit, and makes them a magnet for talent—the function Weber attributed to the Calvinist dogma of predestination and the idea of calling. Also, because of the members' investment in the dignity of the nation—that is, its prestige—which is necessarily assessed in relation to the status of other nations, nationalism implies international competition. This makes competitiveness a measure of success in every sphere which a nation defines as significant for its self-image, and commits societies which define themselves as nations to a race with a relative and therefore forever receding finish line. When the economy is included among the areas of competition, this presupposes a commitment to constant growth. In other words, the sustained growth characteristic of modern economy is not self-sustained; it is stimulated and sustained by nationalism.

While it is conducive to the development of a social structure of the type modern economy requires to exist, and while it stimulates international competition, creating a favorable environment for economic growth, nationalism actively promotes economic growth within this environment only when economic achievement, competitiveness, and prosperity are defined as positive and important national values. This in turn depends on the type and specific character of particular nationalisms. As a rule, individualistic-civic nationalisms, which define nations as associations of individuals, will value economic achievement simply because of its significance, and the importance of economic activity in general, for large numbers of individuals. Therefore, they are likely to include economic growth among national interests. In the framework of collectivistic nationalisms (either civic or ethnic), national interests are defined independently from the interests of individuals and may not include economic interests at all, or consider them to be of secondary importance. In ethnic nationalisms where economic activity is not particularly valued, it is often the minorities who become prominent economic actors, and this may stigmatize both the minorities and the economic activity. For that reason, it is likely that economic activity, and growth, in ethnic nations will be more valued in ethnically homogeneous societies.

The initial predisposition of the individualistic-civic English nationalism to value economic activity and achievement was reinforced by certain idiosyncratic features which led it to select the economy (significantly, along with science) as a particular area of national superiority. English nationalism thus directly and actively promoted economic growth. The spectacular economic success of Britain, and its rise to superpower status in general, were major stimulants of economic competitiveness, ensuring that many a reactive nationalism also focused on economics, and greatly contributing to the formation of the modern "economic civilization."

The ability of English nationalism to contribute to the British, and then worldwide, "economic miracle" is explained, in the first place, by the fact that the British (as later American) "sense of identity" evolved from the conceptual framework, and on the basis of principles, provided by the original English nationalism, and, second, by this contagious nature of the British example. What is of utmost importance here is that this effect of nationalism was not simply an effect of a cultural factor, but that it was ultimately a cultural effect. It was owing not to the fact that nationalism liberated natural economic energies from the constraining tutelage of ethical considerations and social concerns, and therefore, unlike other ideological structures, such as traditional Christian teaching, did not inhibit economic growth, but, on the contrary, to the fact that it provided a new set of ethical considerations and social concerns that invested economic growth with a positive value and focused naturally diffuse social energies on it.

Nationalism is a form of social consciousness, a way of cognitive and moral organization of reality. As such it represents the foundation of the moral order of modern society, the source of its values, the framework of its characteristic—national—identity, and the basis of social integration in it. The fact that the original, English, nationalism, to which we owe the forward aspiration of modern economy and its insatiable yearning for ever greater material power, was (and to a large extent is at the place of its birth, as well as where it was transplanted, for instance, in the United States or Australia) a form of philosophical and moral individualism in no respect contradicts and should not obscure that. As a principle of social solidarity, individualistic nationalism has proved to be very effective, perhaps more effective than nationalism of collectivistic types, if the exceptional political stability of individualistic nations, underneath the constant ripple of conflict, and the unusually low rate of emigration from them despite the lack of legal impediments, are an indication. This is not surprising if individualism is understood, as in this case it must be, as a moral ideal, which directs and controls natural appetites, rather than as moral laxity allowing them free rein. The definition of the individual as the highest social value and the fundamental moral unit of society—that is, as an independent moral actor—adds dignity to the national identity and, taking much farther the commitment to egalitarianism which every nationalism preaches, makes its practice in individualistic nationalisms much more consistent than in nationalisms of other types, thereby increasing national commitment.

Individualism (as a moral and philosophical position) and nationalism (as a form of social consciousness and collective solidarity) may be perceived as contradictory only if the moral primacy of the individual is believed to be a reflection of the empirical or natural primacy—a notion, curiously, which is met only in individualistic societies—that is, if the original, or natural, individual is believed to be presocial. While perfectly consistent with the anthropological and sociological presuppositions of contemporary economic theory (also mostly flourishing in individualistic nations), this belief runs counter to all we know of the life of other sociable species, knowledge that the philosophers from economics, given their naturalistic bent, might be expected to take into consideration. A natural individual organism is not an individual in the sense we ascribe to the term, of an independent moral agent. Such individuality is a product of culture, not of nature; it is necessarily an aspiration, a projection of an ideal image, which nature can only approximate, and thus of an image of society—of social consciousness, of a type of rationalization. Already Durkheim recognized the individual as a social construction, specifically a product of organic solidarity. He thought individualism was the way modern society "represented" itself in the minds of its members and made them worship it and obey its commands. It was for him the central element of the moral and cognitive complex he called "conscience collective," the core of a directing, compelling ethic of the kind Weber thought to have found in Protestantism.

This individualist ethic is the core and distinguishing characteristic of that communal identity, that type of nationalism, which provided the original inspiration for the economics of sustained growth. But while modern economic theory assumed the principles of this individualistic type of nationalism, and would be inconceivable if it were not individualistic, modern economic practice drew inspiration from nationalism as such. England devel-

oped economic nationalism because its national consciousness was individualistic, but, as demonstrated *inter alia* by the protracted debate around the
idea of economic freedom (of which free foreign trade was only one prominent aspect) and the time it took to associate, as a matter of course, private
with public interest, early economic nationalism in England was focused exclusively on the common good of the nation, to which the good of its individual members was, as it would be for the opponents of economic liberalism
several centuries later, held to be subservient.

I | Another Take on How It All Began

1 | The Capitalist Spirit and the British Economic Miracle

Adam Smith, as is well known but systematically forgotten, was not an economist but what was then called a "moral philosopher." Neither was he an economist, with an emphasis on the last syllable: in his philosophy, the economic sphere did not occupy the paramount place it held, for example, for Marx. In his first great book, *The Theory of Moral Sentiments,* which was the cornerstone of his system, Smith was preoccupied with issues fundamental to the modern discipline of sociology: the constitution of society, the mechanisms of social integration, or, as it is often called, the problem of order—the all-important question of how separate individuals come to transcend themselves and constitute aggregate entities which give the impression of unity, and how they develop moral, that is, social (contributing to social integration) sentiments.

Smith's basic argument was that human beings were by nature predisposed to form hierarchical and cohesive social structures because they were driven in life by a desire for social approbation, which expressed itself in the willingness to submit to norms of propriety and in relentless status seeking. This desire was essentially of a non-material nature, and material self-interest was entirely subordinated to it. Social order was based on a systematic sacrifice of material advantage to propriety or social convention. Status, the respect of others, rather than greed or will to power, was the primary mover of history. It was status, Smith wrote, that was "the end of half the labours of human life" and "the cause of all the tumult and bustle, all the rapine and injustice, which avarice and ambition have introduced into this world." Even "people of sense" could not afford to despise it, and only that man had no "desire for superiority" who was either raised very much above the ordinary standard of the human nature or sunk so very much below it as to become "habituated to the idea of his own meanness" and to drown "in slothful and sottish indifference."

The faculty underneath the desire for social approbation, the mechanism through which it operated, was "sympathy"—our ability to identify with the situation of another, to put ourselves into another's shoes. It was through "sympathy" that we were able to perceive how others judged our actions, through "sympathy" that we constructed a composite image of the other, who became our constant companion, a "man within [our] breast," and as such kept a tireless watch over our conduct. "Sympathy" made us amenable to socialization; only because of it were we able to receive guidance. Being at the center of attention—eminence (or, again, status)—thus was the innermost need of human nature, and obscurity the darkest misfortune, far more debilitating than poverty: it connoted that truly benighted state in which one was deprived of guidance and, being unable to form a notion of the judgment of others because nobody cared to judge one's actions, was doomed to vegetate on the margins of social integration and morality, leading only a marginally human existence.

"Two different roads," suggested Smith, led "to the attainment of this so much desired object [to deserve, to acquire, and to enjoy the respect and admiration of mankind]; the one, by the study of wisdom and the practice of virtue; the other by the acquisition of wealth and greatness." Moreover, "the great mob of mankind" were "the admirers and worshippers," and at that "the disinterested admirers and worshippers" of the latter road. For that reason, in the context of the problem of order, it was helpful to explore the dynamics underlying the pursuit of wealth.

In the concluding paragraph of *The Theory of Moral Sentiments,* Smith announced his intention to undertake such a study as one of the several projects related to his central theme. He wanted, he said "in another discourse [to] endeavour to give an account of the general principles of law and government" (by which he meant "the general principles which ought to run through and be the foundation of the laws of all nations"), "and of the different revolutions they have undergone in the different ages and periods of society, not only in what concerns justice, but in what concerns police, revenue, and arms, and whatever else is the object of law."[1] That he regarded his magisterial *Inquiry into the Nature and Causes of the Wealth of Nations* as a partial fulfillment of this intention, and thus as a contribution to the larger project of *The Theory of Moral Sentiments,* is indicated in the author's "Advertisement" for the sixth edition of the latter work, published in 1790, where he referred to its last sentence and wrote, "In the *Enquiry Concerning the Nature and Causes of the Wealth of Nations,* I have partly executed [my] promise, at least so far as concerns police, revenue, and arms."

These considerations help to place Smith's relation to modern economics in a new light, making it evident that he would not want to be held responsible for its birth. Economics is a child he simply could not have conceived. Indeed, if we insist on his paternity, it would be an unnatural and pitifully crippled creature, emerging out of the brain of its progenitor in the manner of Athena springing out of Zeus' head, but unlike that other goddess, taken out forcibly and piecemeal, with its own head—*The Theory of Moral Sentiments*—thrown out as useless, and with no legs to stand on, since Smith did not have the chance to complete his creation. It would be all stomach, and its imagination would be limited to the digestive process; it would be a discipline driven to conclude that man is what he eats. In other words, if Adam Smith is to be credited with the birth of economics, we have to regard it, from his point of view, as an unfortunate accident; had he been interested in intellectual fatherhood and able to carry his offspring to term, economics would be a part of sociology.

Given that *The Wealth of Nations* was but a giant and brilliant appendix, one of a series of intended appendices, to *The Theory of Moral Sentiments,* its interpretation out of this context was bound to be a misinterpretation. In fact, its intention was almost immediately misconstrued, and the author, transformed into a straw man, was credited and blamed for claims he was equally innocent of advancing and would have been disturbed to be associated with. One accusation, leveled early against his alleged economic theory by critics in Germany (notably List, for this reason hailed as "the first major critic" of the Scotsman), in turn elevated into a doctrine and later embraced by Smith's American admirers as the hallmark of his "science," was that Smith disregarded nationality.

Of List's ideas on Smith, which led an English editor to wonder whether that German theorist had read Smith himself or had only "taken for granted the *Smithianismus* bandied around in popular pamphlets," this was surely one of the least warranted. Smith's thought was suffused with appreciation of the idea of the nation, inspired with nationalism, and none of his statements, beginning with the title *The Wealth of Nations* itself, can be properly understood outside the framework of English (in the eighteenth century, British) national consciousness. After all, in 1776 there was only one nation in the world for certain—the one of which Smith was a member—while two more were struggling to emerge: the United States and France. In the Germany of the time, the idea of the nation was still regarded as "a political monstrosity."[2] The fact that Smith wrote of the wealth of *nations,* when most of his contemporaries recognized none but dynastic realms, private individuals, and humanity, was eloquent proof of the salience of nationality in his mind and evidence that he saw the world through its prism.

Defining a society as a nation implied a radical transformation of social consciousness, nothing less than a conceptual revolution. It presupposed the image of an inclusive, sovereign, and in essence egalitarian community, which stood in sharp contrast to the hierarchical and compartmentalized image of the feudal *society of orders* in which nationalism first arose. This image was closely related to the idea of man as a rational being. It was as such that man was created in the image of God, and it was because men were created in the image of God that they were equal to one another in the most significant aspect of their being and, as a result, free, capable of self-government, and therefore of participation in the government of their community. The community of such rational, equal, and free men was a nation by definition. The English concept of the nation originally referred to a composite entity, the essence of which inhered in the nature of its elements—the individuals. In the English of the eighteenth century, the word *nation* (similarly to other related terms) was plural; it corresponded to plural pronouns such as *we* and *they*, not to the singular *it* or *she*. List berated Smith for seeing no nations but "merely" numbers of individuals dwelling together, and was wrong and right at the same time. The existence of nations was obvious for Smith, but the nation was defined as individuals—rational, equal, and free—dwelling together.

Nationality was not a corrective or an addition to Smith's vision of society, or even its central element; it was the very framework of this vision. The reasoning in both *The Theory of Moral Sentiments* and *The Wealth of Nations* reflected the eighteenth-century English national consciousness. Smith's sociological imagination was limited by the image of society that was defined as a nation, in the sense in which that was understood in England. This type of society—a new species of social life as yet unfamiliar anywhere but where Smith lived—was the one he knew, and he considered it ordinary and natural. Seeing the world through the prism of his experience, he was not able to appreciate, or to conceive of deep reasons for, variation among societies. So unquestioning was his acceptance of nations, so thorough the penetration of the idea in the British soil, that he simply could not imagine societies that were not nations, and, needless to say, it did not occur to him that nationality could be a product of cultural construction. For Smith, all societies were open societies that allowed social mobility; the dynamics of ambition and envy on which he focused in his first book, and of supply and demand which formed the lasting contribution of the second, were both expressions of this central structural feature. Thinking them universal, Smith looked for universal psychological regularities to explain them. But social mobility was, par excellence, the feature of *nations*, perhaps the most consequential expression of *nationalism* in social structure. Smith presumed a uniformity in the most significant cultural element of societies—the ways in which they defined their identities—and for that reason was able to analyze social and economic processes as if they took place in a cultural vacuum. This inattention to culture was culturally determined: it was a consequence of Smith's untroubled national consciousness. If anything, he should have been accused of taking nationality too seriously.

As often happens, the popularity of his second book—and it was immensely popular—had less to do with what it actually offered than with what its readers believed they had found in it: a way to account for one of the most startling and incomprehensible phenomena of the age, the tantalizing spectacle of the British economy, its salience in the British society, its sheer grandeur, its evident political and military implications, and its unquestionable contribution to British national prestige. In the history of European civilization there had never before been a society in which the economy enjoyed such superior status, nor one whose status among others was so obviously and profoundly affected by the glowing state of its economy. For the first time in this history, therefore, an economy—the British economy—became the focus of envy and admiration.

What was the secret of this new reality? *The Wealth of Nations,* so intriguingly titled and coming, as it were, from the horse's mouth, seemed to provide the answer: the economy was ascendant because of man's natural and rational propensity to truck, barter, and exchange, and the British economy was ascendant because of free competition. Of course, this answer raised some questions, such as what had concealed human nature, which was not created yesterday, from sight before the coming of Adam Smith, or why competition in Britain was in some respects freer than in other countries. But, overwhelmed by the apparently sudden rise of a previously unnoticed sphere of social life to such dazzling prominence, those (from across the Channel) who witnessed it were not in a condition to look for deep causes. They were easily satisfied that the cat was out of the bag, and eager to believe it a common pet. For many, the misunderstanding of *The Wealth of Nations* made reality, which for a while had escaped the grip of comprehension, understandable again. It is this unintended contribution to the peace of the collective mind, no doubt, that suggested to it—against fact or logic—the year of the book's publication, 1776, as the birth date of modern economy. But Smith's *Inquiry* signified the culmination rather than the beginning of the process, which, in 1776, had been going on for nearly two centuries.

Economic nationalism emerged in England as early as nationalism in general: it was, to begin with, a refraction of national consciousness in the consciousness of particular—economically active—strata. It would be wrong to say that members of these strata perceived nationalism as instrumental to their (given, economic) interests. Rather, superadded onto their occupational and estate identities, national identity changed the nature of these other identities, changed the meaning—and potential importance—of belonging to these strata (transforming their "class" consciousness and the very nature of the "trading" or "commercial class"), and thus necessitated the formation of new interests, which were perceived at once as the interests of these economically active strata and as national interest.

There are clear signs of a reorientation on the part of economic actors in England and the emergence among them of a new—competitive, assertive, and nationalistic—spirit very early in the sixteenth century. Foreign trade provides the most dramatic example of this. At the beginning of the sixteenth century, English foreign trade was dominated by the merchants of the Hanseatic League. The Hanseatics had been granted special privileges by the English kings, who, from Richard II to Henry VIII, turned to them in their hour of financial need. Their *Kontor* in London occupied the Steelyard, the site of the London standard weighing balance, and their centrality in the English economy was reflected in that even English currency, the "pound *sterling*," was believed, perhaps mistakenly, to be derived from their nickname in England, the "Easterlings." The privileges of the Hanseatics in England were a reflection of their wealth and capacity to finance the English Crown, but this capacity was sustained by the privileges, which perpetuated their superiority over the native merchants. No group of English merchants could compete or hope to compete with the League while these privileges lasted, and unless a community of interest was perceived to exist between the struggling English merchants and the Crown, they would not be revoked. Such a community of interest was perceived by both the merchants and the Crown as soon as England was defined as a nation; and while it might be possible to claim that such perception was, objectively, in the interest of the merchants (which, in fact, was not so), it was clearly not in the interest of the Crown.

In 1505, Henry VII granted an extensive charter of privileges to a fellowship of cloth merchants with chapters in several English port cities and incorporated them as the Company of Merchants Adventurers. The fellowship, which had existed since the thirteenth century as a loose organization, similar in principle to the Hanseatic League or Dutch trading companies, became the first *national* trading company, in the sense of being centralized in fact as well as in principle; and from 1564 its members called themselves "Merchants Adventurers of England." Like the Hanseatic League and other organizations of the time, the Merchants Adventurers sought to monopolize the trade in which they were engaged and saw nothing wrong with measures which would facilitate their commerce and inhibit that of their competitors; but, unlike other trading companies, who were satisfied with procuring privileges from rulers of the countries in which they traded, the Merchants Adventurers tried to secure the support of those they perceived as their "own" (that is, English) rulers in the first place. In addition, they accepted only native-born Englishmen and insisted on their marrying English women.

The commercial policies of the English state, at least until the reign of Elizabeth, were not consistent. Henry VII favored the English merchants over their foreign competitors in general, and imposed a heavy penalty on the Hanseatic merchants for selling cloth in the traditional market of the Merchants Adventurers. Henry VIII, who constantly appeared to be in financial straits, was somewhat uncommitted, and might have helped the Hansa to strengthen its presence in England. By that time, however, the Merchants Adventurers were already exporting twice as much cloth (which was the main English manufacture, "the credite and Creame of the Kingdome")[3] as the League. English nationalists would not be satisfied with this state of affairs. They exaggerated the share of the Hanseatics and complained that that of the English merchants was too small. Under Edward VI they set out to terminate the Hanseatic privileges.

The immediate reason for this is revealing. The initiative came from Sir Thomas Gresham, the founder, for "the publique good oth'Nation,"[4] of both the Exchange and the college that cradled English science. As the financial agent of Edward VI in Antwerp, Gresham was entrusted with liquidating considerable debts left there by Henry VIII to his minor son and was determined to do so without further loans from foreigners. If the Merchants Adventurers, already a formidable economic organization, were relieved of the competition from the Hanseatic League, they could be relied on for the necessary funds. In 1552 a court of the king's Privy Council revoked the special privileges of the merchants of the Hansa, putting them under the heavy duties imposed on all other foreign merchants. Export trade of the Merchants Adventurers increased dramatically as a result, but whether the members of the fellowship felt much improvement in their individual situations is questionable, for much of the company's profits from that point on went on financing the state. The arrangement was clearly in the interest of Gresham, who was a nationalist, but, unless the Merchants Adventurers, as well as the Crown, also identified their interests with the interest (in this case, the financial independence and dignity) of the nation, it could be argued that they acted against their interest.

Some of the Hansa's privileges were reinstated under Mary. But the accession of Elizabeth signaled the beginning of their end and of the no longer interrupted economic ascendancy of England. Gresham was the queen's financial adviser, and the advice he proffered (and she, we are told, followed unswervingly) contained points such as "not to restore Steelyard [the Hansa] to their usurped privileges; to come in as small debt as you can beyond seas; to keep up your credit, and especially with your own merchants, for it is they must stand by you at all events in your necessity."[5] Here we have a stark example of nationalism being made an explicit foundation of the economic policy of the state, and of a nationalist educating—and guiding—the state.

By 1558 the Merchants Adventurers dominated the cloth export trade. When the revolt of the Netherlands destabilized their traditional market, they invaded the traditional market of the Hanseatics. The reason they were able to do so was that, unlike themselves, the league of the Hansa towns was indeed instrumental only, and faced with an opportunity to advance one's particular interests at the expense of the other member cities, none of them, unless pressured, thought twice. In 1564 the Merchants Adventurers of England, flaunting their identity, were allowed to trade in Hamburg, which, four years later, against the opposition of the League, offered them a ten-year contract of privileges as extensive as those previously held by the Hanseatic merchants in England. Somewhat later, counting on the invincibility of the Spanish Armada and the restoration of the status quo ante, Hamburg withdrew its welcome, and an imperial mandate was drafted with the purpose of exiling the Merchants Adventurers from the territory of the empire as a monopoly. It was not made effective for fifteen years, during which the Hansa repeatedly and unsuccessfully attempted to force Elizabeth into reinstating them in their privileges, while the Merchants Adventurers continued to operate in their markets. The decree was finally issued in 1597. In response, Elizabeth exiled all Hanseatic merchants from England, leaving English merchants in control of the lucrative English cloth export trade.

It was a victory for the nationalist principle in commerce. Both the queen and the Merchants Adventurers agreed that it was in the interest of the nation. But it was not in the "objective" economic interest of the English people, including the individual members of the Merchants Adventurers, or of the state. In the words of G. B. Hotchkiss, who studied the commercial warfare between the Merchants Adventurers and the Hanseatics:

> The interruption of trade with Germany obviously could not prove a benefit to English industry . . . [I]t aggravated the depression from which the business of the country was already suffering as a result of the long war with Spain. Not only was the Spanish market cut off, but the Mediterranean trade-routes were still dangerous for English shipping. Capital had been withdrawn from legitimate trade to be invested in privateering expeditions, gold-seeking explorations, and other speculative enterprises . . . It may truly be argued that this bold and brilliant period of English history not only produced great heroes and great literature, but incubated great schemes that were later to enrich the nation. Out of it came the great East India Company . . . and the companies formed to

colonize America. But these enterprises brought no dividends for a long time to come . . . [These] were lean years for most of the people who lived through them. Prices were high and many workers were unemployed. The triumph of the principle of English trade by Englishmen was a fine thing for English patriotism, but it brought no immediate gains to English purses.[6]

What reaction this sacrifice of the purses for the sake of a patriotic ideal aroused among the general public may be gleaned from a play, *English-men for My Money, or A Woman Will Have Her Will*, written by William Haughton and produced by Philip Henslowe in 1598. It poked fun at foreign merchants—a Frenchman, an Italian, and a Dutchman (that is, a German),[7] especially the last—and clearly celebrated the (Pyrrhic) victory of the English over the Hanseatics. The foreign merchants vainly attempt to win the hearts of three English sisters, and are supported in their efforts by the girls' father, an English merchant, but of Portuguese birth; the girls themselves, however, all native-born English maidens, prefer Englishmen as suitors. (Among other things, the play suggests that it did not take long at the time to become English, and demonstrates that English nationalism, even when accentuated for dramatic effect, lacked an ethnic dimension; belonging was not to be understood in terms of blood.)

The Birth of Political Economy

If there was an adverse reaction to the material plight brought upon the English by their new ideal commitments, it expressed itself in the sentiment against monopolies and regulated companies and for free trade in England, meaning the liberty of all Englishmen to trade. It was this sentiment which apparently induced the secretary of the Merchants Adventurers, John Wheeler, to issue an apology for the company, *A Treatise of Commerce,* in 1601. The book was "the first example of commercial publicity on behalf of a private profit-making organization," and one of the earliest, if not the earliest, of English apologies for commerce in general, that is, attempts to defend or justify economic activity in terms of prevailing ethical ideals, to articulate its relationship to these ideals, and to present it as an inherently just, ethical activity. Because of its early date and the significance of its subject, *A Treatise of Commerce* is a document which deserves a most careful study. It is made all the more remarkable by the almost total absence of references to religion and a total absence of what might be seen as religious sentiment.

The moral ideal to which Wheeler relates commerce, instead, and the sentiment to which he appeals exclusively are the national ideal and national sentiment. The merits of commerce in general and the way it is carried on by the Company of Merchants Adventurers lie in the "benefits and commodities arising by [them]" to the English "State and Commonwealth." The preference for regulation over free trade is justified by *"Experience[,] the surest Doctor in the School of Man's life,"* which teaches that regulation does greater good to the commonwealth of England, while free (or, rather, "dispersed, straggling, and promiscuous") trade at best benefits a few "private English," who, in their disorganized ways, make "vile the principallest commodity of the Realm," namely, cloth, "embasing that excellent Commodity [to] the discredit of our Nation." Rather than being "private gain and lucre seekers" (which, Wheeler thinks, the company "by no sound reason or argument can be charged to be"), in their various undertakings the Merchants Adventurers are "moved in duty toward her Majesty and their Native Country." The organization of the Company, specifically, has the purpose of

> the seemly and orderly Government and rule of all the members, parts, and brethren of the said Company wheresoever in their trade and feat of Merchandise. Secondly the Preservation of Amity, and the Intercourse between the Realm of England and their Neighbours and Allies, and the Preventing of Innovations, griefs, wrongs, and exactions contrary to the same. Thirdly, the great Vent, Advancement, and keeping in Estimation of English Commodities, and the bringing in of foreign Commodities good cheap. Fourthly, the Maintenance of Navigation. Fifthly, the Increase of Queen's Incomes and Customs. Sixthly, and lastly, the Honor and Service of the Prince and of our State and Country, at home and abroad.

It should be noted that in this list political and prestige-related benefits take precedence over the strictly economic. The last chapter of the book, building to a climax Wheeler's apology and making explicit his clinching argument—introduced, however, very early in the text and running through it—indeed stresses the contribution of commerce, and the Merchants Adventurers in particular, to the honor, or prestige, of England. The merchants represent the nation in foreign lands. They serve, literally and metaphorically, as its ambassadors. If they look good, it looks good. A large, regulated company, representing England officially, as its very title, "Merchants Adventurers of England," indicates, obviously makes a greater impression than a "straggling" private Englishman here and there. The concluding chapter contains a detailed description of the care they take to show off "at the change of Princes and receiving in of new, at triumphs for victories and coronations [proving that] the said Company have not forgot the honour of their Prince and Country, but have spent and laid out great sums of money this way." The display at the entry of Philip of Spain into Antwerp in 1549, for instance, had cost them over two thousand French crowns: the governor of the company and thirty merchants riding in a livery of purple velvet "and paned hose embroidered full of silver waves like the waves of the sea," with doublets of satin and hats with fair brooches, "and each of them a chain of gold about his neck of great value," and more and more, including threescore and six beautifully clad lackeys and three pages on horseback, "in which their doing they showed themselves for the honour of their Prince and Country nothing inferior to the merchants of other nations, namely the Germans, Easterlings, Italians, Spaniards and Portugals, and surmounting some of them in costly apparel, furniture of themselves and their horses, and in other preparation to entertain the said Prince, whereby they won great honour and commendation to themselves and the whole English name."

As commendation of the Merchants Adventurers brought honor to the English nation, so too did any injury to them mean an insult to England. Since Elizabeth fully concurred in this perception, Wheeler was able to represent the rivalry between his company and the Hanseatic League, to the history of which he devoted about a third of his *Treatise,* as a "controversy between her Majesty and the Hanses," or a political conflict between two nations, England and Germany (even though the latter at the time was truly an "imagined community" in the sense that it existed solely in the imagination of the English). Hanseatic merchants were portrayed as England's ill-wishers and "favourers" of the preeminent national enemy, Spain, which, in their efforts to undercut the trade of the Merchants Adventurers, they knowingly assisted in the plot "to set strangers over us, and to reestablish Popery, and so lastly, bring the whole English people and subjects of her Majesty into miserable slavery of body and conscience, under an ungodly and superstitious Nation, from which the Almighty God in mercy keep us and our posterity." (The extremity of the civic peril in this case apparently justified the very unusual, for Wheeler, concentration of religious references and a most exceptional appeal to the Almighty God.) "The Hanses," Wheeler tells us, after all "were sore insensed, not only against the said M.M. Adventurers, but also against the whole English name." The end of the imperial mandate, for which they were responsible, "a blind man may see to be none other than through the sides of the M.M. Adventurers to hurt and wound the State of England," and the intention behind its publication fifteen years later was to cause "greater and more enormous injury and reproach of her Majesty and her Highness' actions and of the Company of M.M. Adventurers, as no doubt their meaning was, that were the authors and doers thereof, and consequently to make the whole English nation and name the more odious and condemned by all men."

The expulsion of the Hanseatic merchants from the English export trade was a triumph for the English nation, and whatever inconveniences resulted from the loss of extensive imperial markets in consequence had to be borne cheerfully by "all the well-willers and lovers of the Commonwealth and State of England and all the good subjects of her Majesty . . . lest unawares they join hands with the common enemy." Happily, such patriotic exertion was required only briefly. Before long, Hanseatic towns—Stade in 1607 and Hamburg in 1611—animated by commercial good sense rather than considerations of communal dignity, broke ranks and opened the German market to the Merchants Adventurers. The Merchants Adventurers became "the dominant commercial organization in the world" and "the most famous company of merchants in Christendom," the title they were to hold until "the lusty English giant," the East India Company, in a way their own progeny, rose to claim it.

An important aspect of Wheeler's *Treatise of Commerce* was the defense of commerce in general, to which he devoted the first chapter of the book. In it he introduced some important ideas which were to become commonplace in the discourse on economics and Western thought in general, but were clearly radical in his time. For example, he was of the opinion that "there is nothing in the world so ordinary and natural unto men, as to contract, truck, merchandize, and traffic with one another," a thought that Adam Smith, who was credited with it, was to repeat almost verbatim in 1776. Of course, the definition of the propensity to "truck, barter, and exchange" as natural did not in itself lead to its commendation; it led Catholic Schoolmen, as Tawney demonstrated so convincingly, rather to condemn it. Wheeler, however, went farther. He defined commerce very widely, including in it "all that a man worketh with his hand or discourseth in his spirit" and all manner of exchange, whether of goods or services, oriented to a material end, even "selling words," and meaning by it, probably, something we would call an "economic system." This economic system, he claimed, was the foundation of civic life and on a par with government. To this effect Wheeler quoted a Latin maxim, one of many that were interspersed throughout the *Treatise* and that, whether this was his intention or not, contributed to the impression that the author was a learned, sophisticated man, which could only serve to elevate the "estate of Merchandise" he represented in the eyes of the readers among whom the several thousand copies of the book were distributed. To elevate this estate, the classes of people engaged in economic activity, was indeed Wheeler's express goal. The economic propensity, he wrote, was a universal human propensity, found in "both high and low, yet there are of the notablest and pricipallest traffickers which are ashamed and think scorn to be called Merchants." This, he believed, was an unacceptable attitude, for indeed merchandise which is used by way of proper vocation, being rightly considered of, is not to be despised, or accounted base by men of judgment, but to the contrary by many reasons and examples it is to be proved that the estate is honorable, and may be exercised not only of those of the third estate (as we term them) but also by the Nobles and chiefest men of this Realm with commendable profit, and without any derogation to their Nobilities, high degrees, and conditions. With what great good to their States, honor, and enriching of themselves and their Countries, the *Venetians, Florentines, Genoese,* and our neighbours the *Hollanders,* have used this trade of life, who knoweth not? Or having seen the beauty, strength, opulency, and populousness of the abovesaid Cities and Provinces wondereth not thereat?

In his introduction to the modern edition of the *Treatise,* Hotchkiss comments that "although [Wheeler's] defense [of the commercial estate] suggests that in his time a defense was needed, its tone is not humble."[8] Indeed it was a reflection of the new national consciousness, which attached little importance to the distinctions between nobles and commoners and presupposed a fluid and open, that is, egalitarian, conception of social stratification. Wheeler was the first to spell out and draw attention to the implications of this egalitarian national principle for the status of the trading classes. Not everyone was equally perceptive, and this might have been the reason for the efforts of those numerous champions who defended the dignity of commerce over the next two centuries. Their "apologies," however, were even less humble than his, and with time grew openly boastful. Their tone, in fact, suggests that in these later cases, the defense was often undertaken not because it was needed but because it was sheer fun.

Wheeler's *Treatise of Commerce* started the public discourse on economic matters in England. Its publication in effect marked the beginning of the tradition of business literature in general and political economy in particular, which, by imperceptible stages, was to transform our idea of economic activity from something that needed justification in terms of extraneous values to something that was the foundation of all values, and thus to transform our thinking about society. In the Stationers' Register for 1600, we are told, "the only title that seems to suggest business is Shakespeare's *The Merchant of Venice.*" "Books dealing in any way with business [before 1601] had been few and far between," writes Hotchkiss; "most of these few were dramas or other forms of entertainment, or else criticisms by clergymen and landowners." Like the first swallow announcing the coming of spring, Wheeler's *Treatise* signaled the arrival of a new mindset, and soon similar books were pouring in. Moved, like Thomas Mun (or Munn)—a merchant of the East India

Company and the author of the very influential "England's Treasure by Forraign Trade"—by the "Zeal to the Common-wealth," one concerned writer after another exhorted business-minded Englishmen to exert themselves for the benefit of their nation. They strove to teach their readers "how to love and serve [their country], by instructing [them] in the duties and proceedings of sundry [economic] Vocations," and in the process developed what B. E. Supple calls "doctrines which have subsequently been labeled mercantilist." They all discussed economic issues in the light of the good that might come from them to England, and so presented economic power (or wealth) as a very important tool, but a tool nevertheless, for the achievement of the ultimate goal of national prestige and political and military might.[9]

Some of this literature consisted of apologies—advertisements—for private corporations, written by members whose aim was to garner public support for a particular business or way of doing business. A considerable portion, however, was written by men who were men of affairs only occasionally and could be regarded as disinterested propagandists, moved solely by altruistic, nationalist concerns (though, obviously, they identified the interest of the nation with their own). Among such authors was Sir Walter Raleigh, who, in 1605, "provoked," as he claimed, by "my love and bounden duty to your Majesty and my country," came out with *Observations touching Trade and Commerce with the Hollander, and other Nations . . . wherein is proved That our Sea and Land Commodities serve to inrich and strengthen other Countries against our own*. The attitude of Raleigh's book was different from that of Wheeler's. Raleigh's goal was not to ensure the dignity and independence of English trade (to which he added manufacture) as such, but to ensure that England did better than others. He was openly jealous of foreign merchants, Hollanders in particular, and saw them as England's economic rivals and competitors, but, as a matter of fact, these foreign merchants did not impinge on the *existing interests* of English merchant companies and were not in direct competition with them; Raleigh envied them their success. Here was the national competitive spirit (which animated and fortified Merchants Adventurers in their conflict with the Hansa) in the abstract, which made it a far more powerful motive and vastly increased the scope of its application.

Raleigh was offended by the fact that, though England was far better situated and endowed with natural resources for the role of the world's greatest commercial power, this role belonged to the little, enterprising Holland, which had no such resources. Holland's greatness was an injury to England, a detriment to English prosperity and honor, and this made Holland England's enemy, in thought as well as in deed. The language Raleigh used to describe the effects of the Dutch trade on England left no place for any other interpretation. "They suck our commonwealth of her riches," he wrote, "cut down our merchants, and decay our navigation; not with their natural commodities, which grow in their own countries, but the merchandises of other countries and kingdoms . . . they beat us out of trade in all parts with our own commodities." England was partly to blame for that, however. It was a shame to the nation, he admonished King James, tending "to the great decay of your kingdom, and impoverishing of your people, discredit to the company of merchants, and dishonor to the land, that any nation that have no corn in their own country growing, should serve this famous kingdom, which God hath so enabled within itself . . . that any nation should carry away out of this kingdom yearly great mass of money for fish taken in our seas and sold again by them to us . . . must needs be a great dishonor to our nation, and hindrance to the realm." And yet, he insisted, "all [they do] we may do better than they," and would, if only the king introduced the right policies. "They outgo us in all kind of fishing and merchandising in all countries, by reason they spare no cost, nor deny no privileges that may encourage advancement of trade and manufactory." England needed to follow this example; it had to turn the stream of trade "to the good of this kingdom," which would "prevent the deceivers, ingross the commodities of the ingrossers, inrich ourselves, and increase our navigation, shipping, and mariners, [and thereby] make all nations to vail the bonnet to England." To this end, among other things (such as encouragement of shipbuilding and fishing, cultivation of manufacture, and protection of trade), Raleigh advised the king "to allure and encourage the people for their private gain, to be all workers and creators of a commonwealth."[10] This was undoubtedly a proposition validating material self-interest, but it was clearly advocated only as a means to a higher, collective end.

National Reasoning behind Economic Competitiveness

The new economic consciousness matured quickly. In the course of its development, new elements were added to its early articulations, while others grew more robust and assertive. In the seeming confusion of the Civil War, ostensibly animated by the spirit of religion, the new secular spirit of the age crystallized, its premises were made explicit and distinct, and its nature became unmistakable. Nationalism was this new spirit, the cognitive and ethical framework which gave meaning to reality, and it was no longer conceivable that economic matters, among others, could be evaluated and made meaningful in any but its terms. In 1663 Samuel Fortrey perceived "the genius, and disposition of the times, to study more the Interest and Improvement of the nation, than usually heretofore," and offered to the reader a work which faithfully reflected this preoccupation of the age in its title as well as contents.

Englands Interest and Improvement, thought Fortrey's contemporary Josiah Child, was "a most rational and admirable Treatise" and "hath done more for [the] Country than would have been the Gift of some millions of pounds sterling, into the Publique Exchequer." It was, apparently, quite influential, directly affecting commercial policies and specifically inspiring the protective anti-French legislation of 1678–1688.

Fortrey opened the treatise with a new and radical claim, that "Englands Interest and Improvement consists chiefly in the increase of store and trade." Economic strength and prosperity were not simply an aid to but the foundation of national greatness. And since two things were "chiefly necessary to make a nation great, and powerfull; which is to be rich and populous," and in respect to these two things England "not onely equal[ed] any neighbour countrey, but far excel[led them] in all profitable advantages," it could "expect to become the most great, and flourishing [nation] of all others." To realize this natural potential, Fortrey recommended the adoption of a liberal immigration policy; cutthroat competition, supported by protectionist measures, with neighbor nations who might harbor similar aspirations; and subordination of private interest to public under all circumstances.

England would do well, he wrote, to give permission "to all people of foreign contreys . . . freely to inhabit and reside within this kingdom with liberty to buy or sell lands or goods, to import or export any commodities, with the like privilege that *English* men have, [for] it might very much increase, both the riches and power of this nation." Specifically, "by this liberty to foreiners," he thought, "we should quickly attain to the perfection of those manufactures, which now we so highly value and purchase so dear from abroad." For their part, foreigners, Fortrey was confident, would want to become Englishmen, because England was naturally "as pleasant, or more pleasant, healthful, fruitful and temperate than any other" country; it was, as a political community, "far better than any other, for the ease, quiet, peace and security of the people"; and it had a superior economic potential, so that, if it were realized, and "our trade and manufactures were but improved to that advantage, as they are capable of, there would be no country in the world, where industrious people might improve their estates, and grow more rich, than in this." The hope of gain, he thought, was a natural proclivity and bore "so great a sway amongst men, that it [was] alone sufficient to prevail with most."

Still, England had another advantage, which, if the first three were not sufficient, would make its appeal irresistible: it was "the most eminent and intire countrey of all others, that profess the Protestant Religion." The Protestant religion was preferable because it was "free from vain and superstitious beliefs and ceremonies [and] the only model of true piety and vertue," but its chief recommendation consisted in that to profess it, to the exclusion of other creeds, for England was "a matter of greatest policy and prudence." The alternative (besides return to the vain and superstitious Catholicism, which was not to be considered) was internal division and strife—all too real a possibility in 1663—the thought of which indeed led some to wonder whether "a strict uniformity in Church-government" was not the only means to prevent it from materializing. Fortrey conceded that the thought was valid, but stipulated that, were such uniformity made a policy, care should be taken "that what is so imposed, be onely such things as are barely necessary and such as may agree best with the quiet and preservation of the State." In this philosophical and frankly utilitarian approach to religion, nonchalantly expressed virtually on the morrow of the Puritan Rebellion, there is no reflection of the soul-scorching sacred fires kindled by the dread of eternal damnation which alone could empower Protestantism to beget the spirit of capitalism. Far from serving as the validating moral standard for secular behavior, religion is itself validated by its contribution and correspondence to an emphatically secular end: the interest of the nation.

This interest, the nation's greatness, according to Fortrey, was directly dependent not simply on England's economic strength and prosperity, but on its economic supremacy (we would call it competitiveness) relative to other nations. In fact, such relative supremacy was the measure of prosperity. The context of Fortrey's argument was essentially comparative, and not for a moment, while he discoursed of England's interest and improvement, did he lose sight of the relevant others. For his readiness to embrace "all foreigners" who would become Englishmen, and his complete indifference to the ethnic origins of his compatriots—an indifference which has indeed been an integral part of the English national consciousness—coexisted with anxious and aggressive suspicion of all foreigners still united in their separate political communities, which characterized the English national consciousness in this early period.

The guiding principles of Fortrey's economic theory were few: "The art is when we deal with strangers, to sell dear and to buy cheap; and this will increase our wealth"; and to take care "that we impoverish not our selves to enrich strangers" (the danger of which, apparently, far surpassed that of impoverishing ourselves with no benefit to strangers). All other economic policies and ideas were assessed in the light of these axioms and subject to change in accordance with circumstances. To gain the upper hand over foreigners, Fortrey advocated raising cattle at the expense of wheat and the selective, pragmatic use of free trade and protective tariffs. He wrote:

> Our care should . . . be, to increase chiefly those things which are of least charge at home, and greatest value abroad; and cattel may be of far greater advantage to us, then corn can be . . . for what we should in-

crease in the room of it of greater value by exportation, would not onely bring us home as much corn as that land would have yeelded, but plenty of money to boot . . . [W]e may also by our singular advantage, in the increase of those cattel, have the sole trade, being able so far to exceed our own wants, as to furnish all our neighbours, who must be forced [nota bene] to good rates . . . And might we freely have the liberty to export them, or so much of them as may be fitting, we should need no laws to hinder the exportation of corn . . . [C]oncerning our trade abroad . . . when any commodity is raised to the greatest height it is capable of, it should be free for exportation, under so reasonable customs, that the merchant may afford his commodities abroad, as cheap as others, or else he would not be able to vent it . . . [A]ll foreign commodities whatsoever, that are onely usefull to be spent within the nation [and thus cannot contribute to its economic improvement and competitiveness], and that have already all their perfection, as fruits, sugars, wines, linen cloth, laces, silks . . . such commodities should pay extraordinary customs.

This neighborly philosophy in principle applied to all countries with which England maintained trade relations, but the significant other for Fortrey was France. France was the chief supplier of luxury commodities such as silks, lace, and wines, for which the English, to Fortrey's chagrin, had developed an "unnatural" taste and on which they were wasting "at least sixteen hundred thousands pounds a year." He could not think without consternation about "the vast sums of money the *French* yearly delude us of; either by such commodities as we may as well have of our own, or else by such others, as we might well in great part be without," and exhorted Charles II, freshly restored to the English throne, to stop mimicking French fashions and set a better example to his people:

Hereby it may appear how insensibly our treasure will be exhausted, and the nation begger'd, whilst we carelessly neglect our own Interest, and strangers abroad are diligent to make their advantages by us. But most of these evils would be easily prevented, if onely his Majesty would be pleased to commend to his people, by his own example, the esteem and value he hath of his own commodities, in which the greatest Courtier may be as honourably clad, as in the best dress, *Paris,* or a *French* Taylour can put him in; besides it seems to be more honourable for a King of *England,* rather to become a pattern to his own people, than to conform to the humours and fancies of other nations.

Fortrey advocated state intervention in economic affairs in general. "Private advantages," he wrote, "are often impediments of publick profit . . .

whereby it may appear, how necessary it is that the publick profits should be in a single power to direct, whose Interest is onely the benefit of the whole." The interests of individuals were to be subordinated to the interest of the nation, which was not necessarily the same. For example, enclosures were in the interest of the nation, but individuals, misguided by "the many several Interests" could not agree that they would result in the "properest use, and best advantage" of the land, in consequence of which selfish blindness "much land [was] tilled . . . to the increase of nothing but beggery in this nation." Fortrey dismissed arguments that enclosures led to depopulation:

As to depopulations by inclosures, granting it increases plenty . . . how increase and plenty can depopulate, cannot well be conceived; nor surely do any imagine that the people which lived in those towns they call depopulated, were all destroyed, because they lived no longer there; when indeed they were onely removed to other places, where they might better benefit themselves, and profit the publick . . . And if the manufactures and other profitable employments of this nation are increased, by adding thereto such numbers of people, who formerly served onely to waste, not to increase the store of the nation, it cannot be denied, but the encouragement of inclosure, where every mans just right may be preserved, would infinitely conduce to the increase and plenty of this nation.

He argued similarly in defense of the recent Acts of Navigation (which did "wisely provide [for the shipping of this nation], by ordering that no foreigner should bring any commoditie hither, but what was the growth of their own countrey; Whereby the *Hamburger* and *Flemming*, that run hackney all the world over, were a little stayed from coming hither crowding so thick"), and regulated companies. Against the former some claimed that the English carrying trade raised the cost of commodities it carried for Englishmen. "[If] the same commoditie brought hither in any of our own vessels, cannot be afforded so cheap as what might be brought by others," countered Fortrey, "by reason indeed, that our shipping is much more chargeable, and better manned than any other . . . this being rightly considered, it is rather an advantage than a prejudice to the publick . . . and whatever it costs the dearer to the purchaser here, is no prejudice to the publick, when our nation receives the profit of it; especially it being by the increase of that, in which consists the greatest honour and safety of the kingdom [i.e., shipping]." The argument for the regulation of trade (namely, "concerning Merchants, associating themselves in companies") was structurally identical: "It is true," wrote Fortrey, it is opposed by many, conceiving the free liberty of trade [who say] if the trade were free, our own commodities having more chapmen, would sell at better rates, and what is brought home in return, would be distributed at much cheaper prices amongst the people . . . In truth our commodities are sold the dearer to strangers [by companies, because they exercise a monopoly], and foreign commodities brought much cheaper; when both would happen contrary in a free trade, where each will undersell the other . . . and the prejudice that may happen by them to the workmen, or home chapmen, is fully recompensed by the clear profit they return to the publick; of which they are members as well as others.[11]

Tawney to the contrary, the new commercial mentality evidently implied not the emancipation of material self-interest from the tutelage of collective ethic and social consciousness, but the imposition on it of a new but, from the economic point of view, much more productive social harness.

Interestingly, the very same argument—that what served the interest of the individual did not always serve the national interest, and that, in the case of discrepancy, the latter was to be preferred to the former—could be used in defense of the policies of free trade. It was so employed, for instance, by Nicholas Barbon, a medic, businessman, and politician, in the 1690 *Discourse of Trade,* which led at least one student of economic thought to perceive in it "the ablest refutation of the [mercantilist] theory of balance of trade previous to Hume and Adam Smith" and place Barbon as an economist above Locke. Barbon considered prohibitions, along with high interest, to be the two chief impediments to the growth of commerce, and believed that while protective tariffs could advance some special interests, in the long run they hurt the nation. "If the Suppressing or Prohibiting of some sorts of Goods," he wrote,

should prove an Advantage to the *Trader,* and Increase the Consumption of the same sort of our Native Commodity: Yet it may prove a Loss to the Nation. For the Advantage to the Nation from *Trade,* is, from the Customs, and from those Goods that Imploys most Hands. So that, tho' the Prohibition may Increase, as the Consumption of the like sort of the Native; yet if it should Obstruct the Transporting of other Goods which were Exchanged for them, that Paid more Custom, Freight, or Imployed more Hands in making; the Nation will be a loser by the Prohibition.

By 1690 England had achieved that economic supremacy relative to its neighbors which was still only an aspiration for Fortrey in 1663. Gregory King opened his technical tract, *Of the Naval Trade of England [around]*

1688 and the National Profit then arising thereby, with the statement of "this great Fundamental Truth[:] That the Trade and Wealth of England did mightily advance between the years 1600 and 1688." London was already without doubt "the Largest, Richest, and Chiefest City in the World, for Trade." Barbon was aware of this, and his *Discourse* reflected it. Confident of his nation's economic superiority and of its role in England's destiny, he was far less concerned to ward off dangers that might arise from foreigners' efforts to better themselves than to elucidate the principles of *economic growth* which made England great. He wrote in the preface: "Notwithstanding the great Influence, that *Trade* now hath in the Support and Welfare of States and Kingdoms, yet there is nothing more unknown, or that Men differ more in their Sentiments, than about the True Causes that raise and promote Trade." His position was that of a political economist, rather than of an economist proper, for he was mainly interested in "how [trade] may be most Profitable to the Nation." The extensive literature on the subject that had already existed in his time, he thought, failed to address it adequately, because it was "byassed with Private Interest," even though, he noted parenthetically (thus proving the central point of this chapter), all the authors claimed that their arguments that ran "contrary to one another, as their Interest[s were] opposite . . . would be for the Advance of *Trade,* and Publick Good of the Nation." Despite such statements, he was far less suspicious of self-interest than Fortrey, and perceived a far greater degree of natural correspondence between it and general interest, in some statements anticipating Smith's notion of the "invisible hand." He also showed somewhat greater concern for the well-being of individuals, considering "the Benefits of *Trade,* as they Relate to Mankind," such as "the Inhabitants in general [being] well Fed, Clothed and Lodged," alongside "those that Relate to Government."

With Barbon's *Discourse of Trade,* economic discourse in England reached a degree of theoretical sophistication, which would make it an important landmark to consider in the history of economic thought. Insofar as it relates to the development of English economic nationalism, of which it was an expression, it was very much a part of what was already a mighty current and does not stand out among other contributions. For the purpose of the present discussion, it might be worthwhile to mention just one other point he makes, arguing, in effect, the inconsistency of the Protestant ethic with economic advancement. Barbon maintained that "prodigality is a Vice that is prejudicial to the Man, but not to *Trade,*" while its opposite, that is, saving rather than spending money, which he called "covetousness," "[is] prejudicial both to Man and *Trade,*" so that "a Conspiracy of the Rich Men [not to] spend, would be as dangerous to a Trading State, as a Forreign War; for . . . they would make the Nation poor, and the Government great Losers in the

Customs and Excises that ariseth from Expense." For this reason he advocated conspicuous consumption and believed that fashion was "a great Promoter of *Trade,* because it occasion[ed] the Expence of Cloaths, before the Old ones are worn out." It was, he said, "the Spirit and Life of *Trade.*" And since fashion kept "the great Body of *Trade* [i.e., the economy] in Motion," it was most unreasonable to exclaim against its vanity; instead, Barbon advised that "the Promoting of New Fashions, ought to be encouraged, because it provides a Livelihood for a great Part of Mankind." Not everyone was of this opinion, however, and Barbon took to task Thomas Munn, in particular, for commending "Parsimony, Frugality, and Sumptuary Laws as the means to make a Nation rich."[12] Thus some of Barbon's contemporaries apparently did agree with Weber's notion of the character congenial to the development of modern economy and may have practiced, as well as preached, this-worldly asceticism.

The Forerunner of Adam Smith

No account of English economic nationalism prior to the Industrial Revolution is complete without a discussion of the place in it of Daniel Defoe. One of the greatest writers of the period, and perhaps the most popular, Defoe was an economic nationalist par excellence, in whose numerous writings on commerce the various elements of this vigorous trend of thought received their fullest expression and acquired additional power to influence, excite, and spur on the people already tense with collective economic ambition and set on a course of constant "improvement." He was also a preeminent example of the effortless, straightforward transformation of the English into British nationalism, and, though this expansion of an identity (which for some involved its modification) was certainly more problematic for many of his contemporaries, for this reason represents a very important case for any analysis of late seventeenth- to early eighteenth-century English and British nationalism in general.

From 1704 to 1713 Defoe published the *Review,* "admittedly the most significant periodical of his time," the first of its kind, a "journal of opinion . . . which taught the masses in Queen Anne's reign what to think upon important political and social questions."[13] It was originally conceived of as a commentary on the war with France in which England at the time was engaged, but its scope grew broader, as was reflected in the title of the third volume, *A Review of the State of the English Nation.* In volume four, number twelve, the title was modified again and became *A Review of the State of the British Nation.* In his writings on commerce, among others, after the Union (which Defoe, in a small way, helped to bring about with his public addresses in Scotland as well as in England), he used the terms "English" and "British" interchangeably and often employed them explicitly as synonyms in phrases such as "English, or British, nation [interests, trade, and so on]." The ease with which Defoe himself metamorphosed from an Englishman into a Briton was consistent with his portrayal of a model "true-born Englishman" as an immigrant, and may have had to do with the fact that he, as is well known and important to keep in mind, was himself an Englishman of foreign extraction and rather recent immigrant stock. G. M. Trevelyan, however, characterized him as "the typical man of his day,"[14] and such openness to people of other ethnic origins, and readiness to incorporate them in the nation, was indeed a central characteristic of English nationalism.

For Defoe, there was no longer any doubt that the economic dimension had become fundamental in social life, and that political power and national greatness, or prestige, had come to rest on it. He was aware that this was a recent change. He put the thought forward on many occasions, on at least one of them introducing the now famous phrase with which we associate the birth of modern economics. "The Power of Nations," wrote Defoe in volume two, number twenty of the *Review,* "is not now measur'd, as it has been, by Prowess, Gallantry, and Conduct. 'Tis the Wealth of Nations that makes them Great." He was also aware that something had changed in the very nature of the economic process, and that the evident and indisputable economic preeminence of England (or Great Britain) owed to the fact that English "Trade"—still the conventional term for "the economy"—epitomized this change. He saw England, in distinction to other countries, as, essentially, "an improving nation," "improvement" being a contemporary equivalent of "progress"; its economy, already "an immense and almost incredible Thing," exhibited an unusual inherent capacity for growth. This capacity, Defoe knew, did not exist before. Introducing the subject "Of the first Rise, Growth and Encrease of the Commerce of England" in *A Plan of the English Commerce,* Defoe stressed the historical recency of this change and resorted to a set of very suggestive metaphors to elucidate its nature.

It is something difficult to adjust the Terms of our first Part of this Work . . . the Rise, Growth, and Encrease of our Trade, all which Words, as they imply a Progression, they necessarily imply a stated Period, like an Epocha of Time, from whence the Motion might be said to begin like the starting Post, or Place of a Race, where all that run, set out exactly upon an Equality, whatever Advantage is obtain'd afterwards, being the Effect of the Strength and Vigour of the Racers . . .

I suppose all Nations had some Trade, and all People some Dealing with one another from the Beginning. [But to focus on that] would lead us back into dull Speculations of the Nature and Original of Commerce; a dry useless Subject, and therefore carefully avoided in my Title, where it may be observ'd, that I do not call this Work a History of Trade, or a History of the *English* Trade; but a History of the *Rise, Growth, and Increase* of it [i.e., of economic growth or of modern economy only]; by which I mean as above, from the Time . . . when standing upon the Square with the rest of the World, *England* gave it self a Loose, and got the Start of all the Nations about her in Trade; and having held it ever since, her Commerce is by that Means arriv'd to that Prodigy for Magnitude, which it appears in at this Time, and in which 'tis acknowledg'd by all her Neighbours, she out-does all the Nations in the World.

The clarity of Defoe's vision—of nations racing against one another for economic supremacy, that is, of international competition as the framework of the economic process, of the exceptional nature of this process in economic history, and, finally, of England's "take-off"—is astonishing. The author of *Robinson Crusoe* shows himself far more historically conscious than many of today's economic historians and more perceptive of the springs of economic development than many a later theorist. Nevertheless, "Trade" remained for him a "half-known thing," and all his life, alongside his many other projects, he strove to penetrate its "hidden Mystery," the "Dark Gulph of General Negoce." He thought that in England, in particular, no effort was too great to achieve such understanding and lamented his countrymen's ignorance in the area of such paramount national importance: "In a Nation rais'd as we are by Trade, fam'd for carrying on the most extended Commerce in the World, and particularly prosperous in the greatest Undertakings, whether for Improvement at Home or Adventure Abroad, nothing is more wonderful, than to see how ignorant the Generality of our People are about it."[15] He wrote *The Complete English Tradesman* with a view of contributing to the correction of this deficiency and the explicit purpose to describe the "*English* or *British* product" and "to lay down [the] general maxims" of proper economic behavior for the benefit of the businessman.

Among the principles of business ethics Defoe advocated was patriotism in commercial transactions, and specifically the importance of preference for the native commodities over foreign importations. An admonition on the subject was very much in order, since it was "so much the humour of the people of this nation (more perhaps than of any other in the world) to despise the growth or product of their own country and give the most extravagant prices for foreign manufactures, whether better in kind or not." As an example, Defoe described a typical scene in the shop of a silk merchant, stocking excellent creations of English artisans, which he bought very cheaply, but, knowing the taste of his customers for all things French, selling these English silks as French imports and for an exorbitant price: "The first question the ladies ask is, If they are really *French?* The mercer makes no scruple to affirm they are, and that perhaps very solemnly; but fails not to add another black article, *French!* yes, madam, your Ladyship may depend on it, *they are* French; *we can make no such things as these in England.*'"

"There are two direct falsehoods by way of preliminary," fumed Defoe, "besides laying a scandal upon his country, as if we were not able to come up to the *French,* or any other nation, in the perfection of the manufacture; whereas this known we now go beyond them in every branch of the trade, and in every particular article of the performance." Besides being ethically objectionable, this was most impolitic behavior, for it gave a bad name to business and in the end was bound to turn against the unethical merchant himself:

> Here is general trade propagated by a double crime; the *first,* against *man,* in the foolish depressing a useful home manufacture, discouraging trade, depriving the poor of our own country, and affecting the labours of foreigners; and the *second* against *truth,* and the Author of truth [it did not hurt the matter to call the wrath of God on the sinners' heads], in pushing on business at the expense of our morals . . . Who would be a rich man at this price? and how do these things give life to the general scandal upon business, *That a tradesman cannot be an honest man* . . . indeed, in such cases, this little better than the *devil* driving the trade, and the tradesmen being the *devil's* journeymen . . . thus the *tradesmen* get the *money,* and the *devil* gets the *tradesmen.*

Honesty, advised Defoe, which equaled patriotism, was the best policy. It had the triple advantage of underselling the French (without in the least hurting the material interest of the merchant), preserving the reputation of businessmen from blight, and advancing the productive capacity of the country. "Would the mercers act the honest part of their country," he urged,

> and to the manufacture wrought at home, as they really ought to do, and propagate our own manufactures with their utmost endeavour, refusing universally to sell any *French* or foreign silks, which really and *bona fide* there is no manner of need of; and would they, at the same time; tell the ladies plainly, that *France* cannot furnish any thing finer, richer, more beautiful, or more agreeable than is made by our own weavers, and that all these charming patterns, fine colours, rich brocades, etc. are made at home, and are inimitable from abroad, as is most true: Would they do thus . . . they would soon effectually suppress the foolish

humour of despising our own manufacture, which is so general among the people, and our own weavers would soon advance their improvements to such a degree, as to send their wrought silks abroad, even to *France* itself.

And as ethical imperative in this case evidently conspired with common sense to bring the desired result, he left the subject "upon the minds of the buyers and sellers too, to regulate their conduct by it for the future, as the profit of the one, and the conscience of the other, and the honour of the kingdom to them both, may induce them." Defoe's trust in the "invisible hand" might not have been blind, but he trusted it nevertheless.

Several chapters in the manual were intended to teach businesspeople proper self-respect. Such self-respect was justified by the centrality of commerce among the factors that made England great and by the position of the commercial classes in the social stratification of the English nation, which Defoe saw as a prominent national trait. With the help of extracts from the genealogies of "illustrious Families of our *English* Nobility," he proved the literal nobility of tradesmen in England, showing "abundantly . . . the near Relation . . . between many of our principal Nobility, and the eminent Traders of *England*," not the least of his design being with such proof "to inspire citizens on one part, with a noble emulation, and a resolution to do nothing unworthy of themselves; and the Nobility on the other, with a desire of cherishing and protecting . . . the trade and commerce of this nation, to which they are so much indebted for their high distinctions in life." He then devoted to the subject a further chapter entitled explicitly "Of the Dignity of *Trade* in *England* more than in other Countries."

"Besides the benefit which we reap by being a trading nation," he wrote, "which is our *principle glory,* trade is a very different thing in *England,* than it is in many other countries, and is carried on by persons who, both in their education and descent, are far from being the dregs of the people." On the contrary. King Charles II "used to say, *That the Tradesmen were the only Gentry* in England: His Majesty spoke merrily, but it had a happy signification in it." The memory of the king's half-joking recognition led Defoe to a somewhat non sequitur panegyric to the nation at large, which deserves to be quoted in full, for its charm if nothing else. "I make no scruple to advance these three points in honour of our country," he admitted:

1. That we are the greatest trading country in the world, because we have the greatest exportation of the growth and product of our land, and of the manufacture and labour of our people; and the greatest importation and consumption of the growth, product, and manufacture of other countries from abroad, of any nation in the world.

2. That our climate is the best and most agreeable to live in; because a man can be more out of doors in England than in other countries.

3. That our men are the stoutest and best; because, strip them naked from the waist upwards, and give them no weapons at all but their hands and heels, and turn them into a room, or stage, and lock them in with the like number of men of any nation, man for man, and they shall beat the best men you shall find in the world.

Because in England businessmen were not, "as it generally is in other countries," of the meanest sort of people, "nor is trade itself in *England*, as it generally is in other countries, the meanest thing the men can turn their hand to." Rather, it was a magnet for talent, "being the readiest way for men to raise their fortunes and families; and therefore . . . a field for men of figure and of good families to enter upon." In thus stressing what "value we put upon Trade and Tradesmen in *England*," Defoe believed he was doing "a particular piece of justice to ourselves," that is, the nation. Indeed, England being defined as "a trading nation" and its "whole glory and greatness . . . being . . . raised by Trade . . . which is the only fountain from whence we all, *take us as a nation*, are raised, and by which we are inriched and maintained," showing respect for trade became pure patriotism, upholding national dignity and self-respect.

Trade inspired patriotism and boosted England's self-respect in other ways as well. It increased the power and greatness "of the British nation" through navigation and discoveries, populating colonies "as well in the islands as on the continent of America . . . entirely [with the people] from *Great Britain* and *Ireland*," replacing and making unnecessary such traditional means of empire-building as war and subjugation of foreign peoples (this was a common idea, developed, among others, by Barbon). And, unless they removed to the said colonies, it increased the attachment of British citizens to their native island, "where they are multiplied to that prodigious degree, and do still continue to multiply in such a manner, that, if it goes on so, time may come that all the lands in *England* will do little more than serve for gardens for them, and to feed their cows, and their corn and cattle be supplied from *Scotland* and *Ireland*." Conspicuously few English, claimed Defoe, relative to other nations, emigrated and sought service in other countries, the reason for which, he thought, was nothing "but Trade, the increase of business at home, and the employment of the poor in the business and manufactures of this kingdom, by which the poor get so good wages, and live so well."

The prosperity of the people, of the trading and laboring classes, had indeed become another distinctive national trait, and the point was so remarkable and so worthy of every recognition that, in Defoe's opinion, no amount of repeating would make it trite. He therefore belabored it endlessly, writing in *The Complete English Tradesman,* among other places, that

> the same trade that keeps our people at home, is the cause of the well-living of the people here; for as frugality is not the national virtue of *England* [*nota bene* another missile in the direction of the Protestant ethic argument], so the people that get much, spend much; and as they work hard, so they live well, eat and drink well, cloath warm, and lodge soft: in a word, the working manufacturing people of *England* eat the fat, drink the sweet, live better, and fare better than the working poor of any other nation in *Europe;* they make better wages of their work, and spend more of the money upon their backs and bellies, than in any other country.

This general prosperity, created by the economic growth, in its turn contributed to the expansion of the home market, greatly increasing overall demand and allowing, in particular, for "the expense of the poor," that is, the working classes, which caused "a prodigious consumption both of the provisions, and of the manufactures of our country at home," and thus stimulated further economic growth.

The definition of prosperity as a national characteristic and an object of national, patriotic pride marked an important stage in the understanding of the nature and significance of the economic power or "the wealth of nations." Defoe's interpretation of it was far more democratic than that of his predecessors among English economic nationalists as late as Barbon and fully anticipated Adam Smith's individualistic conception. "The wealth of the nation," wrote Defoe, "undoubtedly lies chiefly among the trading part of the people," which was the wealthiest class. This meant that the wealth of a nation in general was the wealth of the members of the nation, a sum or aggregate of their individual fortunes, and not the economic resources of the state. Or, rather, the power of the state to command economic resources and harness the wealth of the nation to political and military goals was a function of the wealth of the masses of the nation's members (and their willingness to part with some of it). To those who might doubt that this was in fact so, and that the economy, in consequence, was indeed the foundation of the nation's power, glory, and greatness, Defoe retorted: "And by whom have the prodigious taxes been paid, the loans supplied, and money advanced upon all occasions? By whom are the banks and companies carried on? and on whom are the taxes and excises levied? Have not the trade and tradesmen borne the burden of the war? And do they not still pay four millions a year interest for the public debts? On whom are the funds levied, and by whom the public credit supported? Is not Trade the inexhausted fund of all funds, and upon which all the rest depend?"[16]

This was not an apology, but frank and confident glorification. Defoe added his clear and exuberant voice to the hymn of praise which his compatriots had begun to intone in the sixteenth century and which was to burst into a mighty hallelujah in the "noisy cult of commerce" of his own age.[17] It was this cult, whose supreme deity was the nation and whose credo held that economic interest equaled the national interest, that inspired its enthusiasts to incessant activity which made them rich and gave them "the magnificent energy to change in a century the face of material civilization."

The effect of nationalism on the economy in England was prodigious, for it was the redefinition of the English society as a nation which allowed the economy's emergence from its traditionally subordinate position in relation to political and religious institutions and its establishment—or institutionalization—at the top of the value hierarchy. The redefinition of the English society as a nation, which implied the fundamental equality of all Englishmen, freed economic occupations, specifically those oriented to the pursuit of profit, from the stigma attached to them in traditional Christian thinking. Birth declined in importance as the basis of status, and occupational prestige became, in a large measure, a function of the expected service to the common good of the nation. Since the nation was defined as a composite entity, it had no will but that composed of the wills of its members and no interests beyond their interests. The common good, therefore, was the greatest good of the greatest number. Obviously, this was originally mostly a matter of theory, because nobody cared to ask what exactly the greatest number considered their good. But the growing respect for the common man, implied in the idea of the nation, was necessarily reflected in greater attention to the needs of the population at large. This spurred economic activity, and eventually both the resulting prosperity and economic growth were included among the distinguishing characteristics of the English nation. To be prosperous and usefully employed became a matter of patriotic duty, adding a certain spiritual satisfaction to the material comforts of the former and compensating for certain unavoidable disadvantages of the latter. The contribution of commerce and industry, in particular, to England's power and prestige further reinforced this trend, making profitable and useful trades highly respectable and bestowing on the economy that social approbation which alone would enable it to attract talent. "Merchant" was a term of derision in much of Christian Europe; in England it became an honorable title, and commerce was an occupation of choice for many able and well-positioned people who could have, and in France or Germany of the time would have, done something else with their abilities. In England gaining wealth went hand in hand with gaining status, and men who were animated by the desire for rank and eminence, as Smith so perceptively noted, were content to satisfy it by way of making themselves rich, thereby turning wealth into a foundation of status.

It was of course this quite exceptional circumstance which motivated

Smith to turn his attention to the wealth of nations as he was examining the stratagems people employed in their insatiable search for honors. As they climbed the ladder of success, these Englishmen, empowered by their proud nationalism, accomplished several things. They made their economy boom and prepared the ground for the Industrial Revolution; they made their country the envy of the world and provoked wave after wave of reactive nationalisms, among them nationalisms that were economic, thereby leading other countries to focus on their economies; and they purged filthy lucre of its filth, making it worth striving for for reasons that had nothing to do with greed, stressing the altruistic element in material self-interest, and elevating the economy to the place of honor it holds in our collective imagination today.

I said before that nationalism was the source of the spirit of capitalism. I would like to rephrase this now: the spirit of capitalism was nationalism. Nationalism was the ethical motive force behind the modern economy of growth. The economic process was reoriented very soon after the emergence of national consciousness, and if the modern economy was not as robust at birth as it was to become two centuries later, neither, one should remember, are babies, which is no reason to confuse a birth date with a moment of maturity. To what extent nationalism contributed to the industrial transformation of this modern economy and was the motivational lever of the Industrial Revolution as well is a separate question which should not concern us here. The important point is that when the Industrial Revolution began, the British economy was already consciously oriented to, and capable of, sustained growth.

2 | "The Great Seventeenth-Century Exception"

It is generally agreed that the transformation of the British economy was the first of its kind, breaking through the cycles of growth and decline, characteristic of the premodern economic reality, and making growth "a normal condition," and that Britain, specifically England, therefore was the site of the world's takeoff. But this priority is not entirely unchallenged. A few economic historians point to the fact that before Britannia ruled the waves, the scepter belonged to its unprepossessing neighbor in the Low Countries, and that the United Provinces of the Netherlands, rather than the United Kingdom, was the first world economic hegemon. Indeed, the rise of the Low Countries was in the making already in those economic dark ages, when England still tarried aimlessly upon the Square, little minding its mean renown as "an economic backwater" and having no intention of starting a race. It coincided with the rise of Europe and with the onset of economic globalization over which that previously benighted continent was to preside for the next (now past) half millennium. For globalization—which had at long last caught the eye of academic experts by the end of the twentieth century—was proceeding apace from the time when "the European age in history" is said to have dawned, in 1500.[1] With Europe as the center, the world began uniting into one economic system.

The "Global Village" in the Sixteenth Century

Economic links between continents were not altogether absent before that time. But by and large, economies were landlocked, and the links that existed were relatively few, limited in importance, and difficult to maintain. The most robust economies of the period were all Asian. The foremost of them was that of Ming China, whose population of more than 100 million was larger than that of Europe as a whole. In the Middle East, the Ottoman and Safavid empires were rapidly emerging as economic powers. The overlapping trade networks of these commercial giants extended from the heart of Africa to

Central and Southeast Asia to Europe, from the Pacific to the Indian Ocean, and to the Atlantic.

Italy was the economic center of Europe. Several Italian cities had populations as large as one hundred thousand, equaled north of the Alps only by Paris; in their hour of financial need, rulers and feudal lords everywhere in Europe turned to the banking houses of Florence (of which in 1460 there were thirty-three); Genoa had extensive trade connections, while the routes of the Venetian merchant fleet took it to the ports of North Africa, the Middle East, and northern Europe. It took a galley from Venice thirty-seven days to reach Constantinople, sixty-five days to reach Alexandria, eighty days was the time required to get from Venice to Damascus. Travel across Europe was, on the whole, less time-consuming, but still a journey from Venice to London or Valladolid would last about a month, to Nuremberg three weeks, to Lyons two, and to Lisbon a month and a half. Yet travel the merchants did.

The northern counterpart of Venice's commercial empire was the Hanseatic League. As its name indicated, it was a merchant guild, a business organization created for the protection of its members' interests. By the end of the fourteenth century it was a political power and waged wars with princes. The army that the League raised was formidable enough to defeat that of Valdemar IV of Denmark, who challenged Hansa's influence in the Baltic, and, for a while, to impose the will of the organization on his kingdom. Its headquarters was in Lübeck, and its members were drawn from some one hundred mostly German (speaking) towns. It was not the towns, however, as civic communities, that united in the League but only their merchants, and the army was in their service. The League was coordinated by occasionally convened assemblies which, like representative bodies that played a minor part in the political process of the German(ic) Holy Roman Empire, were called "diets."

Agencies of this powerful corporation—in fact colonies—existed in about twenty towns which were not members, eight of them in England (which testified to the importance of English cloth), one in Scotland, three in the Netherlands (where the League, in addition, had member towns), and four in eastern Europe (where it had associated members too). The sites of the chief *Kontor* were Bergen, London (the Steelyard), Novgorod, and Bruges—the major entrepôt that drew merchants from every region in Europe. Bruges was literally an international trading center, because companies which had agencies there were referred to as "nations." (This explicit commercial connotation might have prevented people in the area from perceiving the political and quasi-religious significance which the word acquired in the age of nationalism, and made it more difficult for them than for others to conceptualize civic sentiments, perhaps quite similar in nature to those which elsewhere were labeled nationalist as such, or to "recognize" and objectify them in general, thus preventing their internalization and development.) One such "nation" was Hansa; it was considered distinct from the German "nation" that, apparently, transiently united merchants from German towns not admitted to the League. Other merchant "nations" bore the names of their cities: thus there were Florentine, Milanese, and Venetian "nations," as well as the Genovese—the last to be constituted, that is to say, granted privileges. Still others were named after principalities—Aragon, Biscay, Castille, and Navarre among them. Finally, the commercial "national" identity of a minority corresponded to the political national identities that were to develop in the future, in the majority of cases rather distant; English, Scottish, Danish, and Swedish merchant "nations" would know such political reincarnation.

In Bruges, merchants from all over Europe assembled, interacted, traded, and exchanged money year round. This could be done at the "Bourse," so called after the owner of the premises, a merchant named van der Burse: thus the French and the Russian, among others, modern name for "an exchange." The Hansa *Kontor* there was aptly referred to as the "Assemblies." In addition to Bruges, they were brought together at various periodic fairs which since the twelfth century had served as centers of exchange between northern staples (especially cloth) and luxury goods brought by Italians from the Orient. In the fifteenth century the most important fairs were those at Lyons, but major fairs were also held at Besançon and Chambéry, Geneva, Villalón, Medina de Rioseco and Medina del Campo, Piacenza, Frankfurt, and Leipzig. By the end of the fifteenth century, fairs at Medina del Campo attracted as many as 2,500 merchants, who came twice a year for fifty days at a time to trade goods as well as settle outstanding accounts. Credit was advanced by the means of bills of exchange, cleared at the fairs. This Italian invention of the previous century allowed transfers of large amounts of money without the inconvenience and danger attendant on their physical movement.

Clearly, even at that early period before the conventional cutoff date of 1500, world economic integration was advanced to an already considerable degree. Europe, west of Novgorod and Kiev at least, functioned as one economic system, and represented part of a sprawling commercial network, woven by Chinese, Muslim, and Italian merchants, which connected the continent to Asia and Africa. Still, the momentous changes that occurred at the turn of the sixteenth century justify the view of the age as the beginning of a new era in economic history, permitting us to identify it as the time when a truly global economy was born and, "aside from some sparsely inhabited wastelands," every part of the world became incorporated into the Europe-centered *Weltwirtschaft*.[2]

The majority of these changes could be characterized as quantitative: the density of commercial interactions, including intercontinental commerce, and the volume of trade dramatically increased. So did the capital assets of major banks: whereas in the mid-fifteenth century the fortune of the Medici bank in Florence equaled 1,750 kilograms of silver (already ten times the amount owned by the Peruzzi a century earlier), the assets of the Augsburg house of Fugger in the 1540s equaled 13,000 kilograms. The larger sums of money involved were reflected in the greater financial sophistication of the system: already in the 1520s, at the quarterly fairs of Piacenza, representatives of a hundred or so commercial firms and fifty merchant banks were transfering among them sums totaling some 15 million Spanish gold crowns, and yet moved less than 150,000 crowns in cash. Quantitative changes of such magnitude could be easily perceived as a fundamental, qualitative transformation, but it was in fact a qualitative transformation that lay at their basis.

At the turn of the century, Columbus, searching for a sea route to India, chanced upon America, and Vasco da Gama discovered that route, which led the Portuguese to Brazil, as well as deep into Asia. These Iberian explorations brought into being a new, larger, and, less obviously, much more adaptable world. A direct result of the discoveries was a rapid and sustained growth of population around the globe. Despite setbacks, such as lasting religious wars and the plague, in Europe the population increased almost threefold in three centuries, from 70 million in 1500 to 190 million by 1800. What made this growth possible was the intercontinental diffusion of food plants: wheat, from Eurasia and Africa, where it was already common, to the Western Hemisphere; rice and sugar cane from Asia to everywhere else; and maize and potatoes from America eastward. Prompted by the growing domestic demand, European commerce not only extended to the new markets opened by the discoveries but also diversified, creating markets for new goods both at home and abroad. The luxury trade with the Orient (mostly spices and silks) continued and remained important, but the staples of the "triangular trade" which now connected Europe to America and Africa consisted of less refined commodities: European rum, cloth, and metal manufactures shipped to Africa; African slaves sold in America; and American bullion, sugar, and tobacco brought back to Europe.

For a while, political globalization went hand in hand with the economic. A child born in 1500 in Ghent happened to be the grandson—and the heir—of four of the greatest territorial lords of the time: on his father's side the Habsburg Maximilian of Austria and Mary of Burgundy, and on his mother's their Catholic Majesties Isabella of Castille and Ferdinand of Aragon. Upon the death of Ferdinand, the child was crowned King Charles I of Spain, with which kingdom came the colonies overseas. Upon the death of Maximilian, he became the archduke of Austria, aquiring with the lands historically in the

Habsburg possession the Burgundian Netherlands and the kingdom of Naples. In 1519 he made a bid for the Holy Roman Empire and had the good fortune of being backed by Jakob Fugger the Rich against the French Francis I. Fugger's generous contribution of close to 544,000 guilders (to the total election expenses of 852,000) allowed Charles to buy enough German electoral votes to secure his success and become Emperor Charles V.

Having thus seen to the realization of Habsburg interests, Jakob the Rich, whose motto was "I want to gain while I can," turned to the equally global concerns of his own dynasty. The 544,000 guilders he advanced Charles was a loan; it was to be repaid by the exclusive rights to mercury and silver mines at Almadén and Guadalcanal and the collection of the Maestrazgo taxes. The house developed numerous mining interests in central and eastern Europe (mostly in the territory of the Holy Roman Empire) and in America; soon it also controlled all the Spanish customs. The holdings of this intercontinental concern "stretched from Danzig to Lisbon, from Budapest to Rome and from Moscow to Chile."[3]

When Jakob Fugger died in 1525, he left to his nephew and successor Anton a capital of more than 2 million guilders. In the next twenty years Anton Fugger doubled this capital. But things were no longer going well. The rulers' need for credit all over Europe was insatiable, and to advance loans the bank had to borrow elsewhere. At Anton's death in 1560, its assets amounted to 5.6 million guilders and its liabilities to 5.4 million. As looking after the family fortune was proving too much trouble, the family turned from making money to spending it. Proud of the nobility acquired by Jakob the Rich (who was created count by Maximilian I) and made little of by Anton, later Fuggers enjoyed the fruits of their predecessors' good work, and preferred not to work themselves. Most of them, from the late sixteenth century on, lived a life of idle refinement on the central European estates left to them by their world banker ancestors, and collected books rather than mines. By that time, though, the global empire of Charles V was also beginning to crumble, and while the firm that helped create it, however weakened, survived for another hundred years, this experiment in globalization politics had lost its most prized possession and lay in shambles as the first century of globalization drew to a close.

The Rise of the Low Countries

While Europe emerged as the center of the new, global, economic system, the center of economic activity in Europe moved north from the Mediterranean; the area to succeed Italy as the economic powerhouse in the age of global economy was the Netherlands. So the Netherlands were the first to achieve world economic primacy. The Netherlands were a unity (if ever they were a unity) of very recent creation. The name "Netherlands" entered political discourse only in the later half of the sixteenth century, referring to the seventeen provinces that swore allegiance to Philip II on his accession to the Spanish crown (which Charles V, his father, transferred to him in 1555) and then participated in the rebellion against their sovereign. These provinces were assembled piecemeal. The last of them, Gelderland, the territory of the counts of Egmont, was added by Charles V to his possessions only in 1543. The richest, arguably the most important, of these provinces by the time of the Revolt was still Flanders, which contributed close to one third of the revenues the Crown collected in the Netherlands as a whole. In the Middle Ages, however, Flanders was a fief of the French kings. When the latter temporarily lost their grip on their extensive territories, it became virtually, though briefly, independent, the count of Flanders joining the neighboring princes (formally vassals of the Holy Roman Emperor, but in fact enjoying perfect freedom to do what they pleased) in their incessant brawl for regional supremacy.

Some of the quarreling provinces were united around the turn of the fifteenth century by the Valois dukes of Burgundy, who in 1378 acquired Flanders through marriage and in 1404 inherited Brabant. The duchy continued to grow, in the 1430s adding Holland, Zeeland, and Hainaut by treaty and other territories by marriage, purchase, and even gift, and emerging by the 1470s as one of Europe's greater powers. Duke Charles the Bold, however, being a little too bold for his own good, in 1477 lost, in addition to his life, all his French fiefs (including Boulonnais, Ponthieu, Amiens, Vermandois, and Burgundy itself) to Louis XI. The rest of his possessions passed to his daughter Mary and her Habsburg husband, whose son, though "born and bred in the Dutch-speaking Netherlands," became, having married the daughter of Ferdinand and Isabella, the king of Castille, and thus "prepared the unnatural [according to Pieter Geyl] connection of the Netherlands to Spain."

In retrospect, this connection does not appear to be any more unnatural than that between Flanders and Holland, which soon were to go their separate ways, or between Holland and Zeeland, which Charles V inherited from his Burgundian line, on the one hand, and Friesland, Groningen, Overijssel, Utrecht, and Gelderland, which he acquired by purchase, negotiation, or conquest between 1523 and 1543, on the other. Since their separation at the end of the sixteenth century, Flanders and Holland, both Dutch-speaking, have been provinces of different states. The language spoken in Friesland remains distinct from Dutch, and Gelderland and Groningen (whose people western Netherlanders called "Overlanders") produced a different literary language, apparently nipped in the bud upon unification. But whatever their natural affinities, for fiscal and administrative purposes Charles V treated the seventeen provinces he assembled in the area as a unit, and it was this unit which became the center of industrial and commercial activity at the dawn of the "long sixteenth century."

Before the Revolt, the southern provinces of Flanders and, increasingly, Brabant dominated the economy of the Netherlands. Flanders retained its place as the preeminent industrial (specifically, textile-producing) country, though its preeminence was already contested by England. Brabant united the administrative center, Brussels, with the "commercial metropolis" of Antwerp. Antwerp replaced Bruges, whose harbor silted up by the late 1400s, as the economic hub of the system and its entrepôt market. It kept the "multinational" character of its predecessor, offering hospitality to numerous "nations" or colonies of foreign merchants. But it grew more rapidly, swelling from 47,000 inhabitants in 1496 to 100,000 by 1560, a growth that reflected the greater intensity of economic activity in it. The increased volume of trade, as elsewhere earlier, led to greater financial sophistication. The "multi-national merchant community used negotiable checks as well as discounted and endorsed bills of exchange. For the first time, credit replaced cash as the principal medium of exchange and interest rates in the city fell from 25% around 1500 to 9% in the 1550s."

Despite numerous continuities which connected Antwerp to commercial centers that preceded it, it was a phenomenon unique in economic history, because the period during which it was the center was a unique and brief one. "For the first time in history," wrote J. A. van Houtte, there was "a world market, in the sense that the bulk of certain commodities was traded in one spot." Jonathan Israel emphasizes that Antwerp was "the first general entrepôt," as against regional ones, among which one should include Bruges. While Antwerp reigned, the northern provinces were establishing themselves as economic powers in their own right, the "steady growth of the trade in Holland and Zeeland" being, according to Geyl, another "one of the most noticeable phenomena in the economic history of the first half of the sixteenth century." It was Hollanders and Zeelanders who owned most of the Dutch ships in the merchant fleet doing the business of Antwerp, and there is no doubt that the shipping industry in the two maritime provinces profited from this proximity. But Holland had already in the fifteenth century established itself as "the leading 'carrying' nation of Europe," and had long dominated the Baltic bulk trade (bringing English and Flemish wool, French and Rhine wines, Iberian salt, some American silver, and Dutch herring to the Baltic, and grain, timber, and naval stores back), which was recognized as the pillar of the province's economic strength and called its "mother-trade" *(moedernegotie).* The relative prosperity of the provinces was reflected in the quota system of taxation, established under the dukes of Burgundy and in use during the Habsburg period. According to it, the province of Brabant paid one-sixth less of the variable tax, consisting of the so-called ordinary and extraordinary subsidies, imposed on Flanders (which, as was mentioned earlier, paid one third of the entire amount collected), whatever the amount was. Holland paid half of Brabant's tax, Zeeland a quarter of what was asked of Holland.[4]

Interests behind the Revolt

The rising fiscal pressure and exploitation of the Netherlands' prosperity by the Habsburgs in the interests of dynastic policy that was of marginal concern for the provinces were among the major causes of the Revolt. This pressure exacerbated, focused, and (by forcing the provincial Estates to meet more often to vote for and ensure the collection of requested subsidies) offered possibilities for expression and formulation to the sense of, a more general discontent. This general discontent was aroused by Charles's, and then Philip's, attempts at centralization, which undermined traditional privileges of the towns and the nobility.

Demands for money began to mount in the 1540s when Charles V had to respond in kind to the building of French fortifications on the Flemish border. The site chosen by the French king for the new episode in the Valois-Habsburg conflict placed his adversary in an advantageous position. Owing to the (civic and physical) geography on either side of the border, the new French fortresses left the French territory relatively unprotected while posing little threat to the Spanish interests in the Netherlands, which were very well protected by their dikes, city walls, and rivers. The realization that this was so led Charles to conceive of the Netherlands as the "bridle" of France, a military fortress in its own right, and money was needed to keep it in a state of constant readiness. The emperor's native city, Ghent, apparently opposed this conception and rose in revolt, which Charles suppressed, suppressing in addition, as punishment, the city's privileges. The rest of the Netherlands, for the time being, acquiesced. The States of Holland, indeed, favored some of Charles's military initiatives, such as the annexation of Egmont's Gelderland, and were sincerely willing to support them.

Prospering provinces with advanced financial infrastructure such as Holland, Brabant, and Flanders were able to meet the exactions of the 1540s without straining their resources. Some of the "new measures" instituted to do so in fact aroused considerable enthusiasm among the population. These were the interest-bearing *renten,* or bonds, which many saw as a welcome opportunity for investment. So long as the public who paid the interest on the *renten* appeared solvent, individuals composing the public were willing to buy them. The interest was paid through excises on beer, herring, salt, and wine, which were also included among the "new measures" *(middelen)*. In addition, there was a direct tax on wealth.

The very facility with which the Netherlands raised the needed funds in the 1540s, as Jonathan Israel points out, was bound to be used against them, as it "was all too apt to encourage" the government in Spain, which met with such facility nowhere else, to ask for more, and to create "an unhealthy financial, logistical, and strategic dependence of the Habsburg Crown on its Netherlands provinces." This understandable tendency to regard the Netherlands as a bottomless chest was reinforced by the war with France, which began in earnest in 1552, dramatically increasing the Spanish need for resources. The Crown "representatives were everlastingly pestering the States with requests for money." As "finance became ever more [the] predominant care" of the government, the Dutch public, already "grumbling about heavy charges," grew much less tolerant toward other centralizing (and globalizing) initiatives of its sovereigns.

The main irritant was the upsetting of traditional corporate privileges—specifically, those of the nobility and the towns, that is, the urban elites—which was an unavoidable effect of absolutism, and to which at least the nobility in the Netherlands reacted rather like the other nobilities whose experiences were similar. The discontent of that proud estate became manifest after the government was transferred to Philip II. Charles V was careful to placate the nobles, appointing them stadtholders (or viceroys) of individual provinces, uniting the more influential in the Council of State, and consulting them on important policy matters. Besides, they regarded the Ghent-born emperor as one of their own. Philip, however, had been born in Spain. When he arrived in the Netherlands in 1555, "he could not even speak French, let alone Dutch."[5] The nobles did speak French and found such linguistic deficiency on the part of their future sovereign reflective of an inadequate commitment to their interests; as they swore allegiance to him and said good-bye to Charles, eyewitnesses recorded they shed tears.

Their suspicions proved justified, though, already familiar with the thrust of royal absolutism as they were, they did not wait for such proof and opposed Philip's policies almost immediately upon his accession. For his part, desperately in need of money for the ongoing war with France, the king at first tried to humor the locals and lavishly distributed honors among the Netherlands aristocracy, appointing new stadtholders, Knights of the Golden Fleece, and Councillors of State. The logic of the regime commanded, however, that such honors be dissociated from any real power. The nobles were reduced to the role of figureheads and, as they enjoyed considerable respect among the populace, were expected by their association to bestow legitimacy on policies in which they had no hand. They refused to cooperate. What they resented most, it appears, was not that the new government was attempting to abuse their popularity or even that it was depriving them of real influence, but, as was the case in conflicts between aristocracies and absolutist monarchs elsewhere, that power was delegated to "servants [kings] had raised from nothing."[6] The focus of the aristocratic displeasure in the period directly preceding the outbreak of the Revolt was a certain Antoine Perrenot de Granvelle, a clergyman from Besançon, who was placed in the Council of State (along with the prince of Orange) by Charles V and became Philip's most trusted adviser.

Philip arrived in Brussels in September 1555 and as early as March 1556 suffered his first major defeat, when the States General, led by Brabant, refused him the subsidy of the staggering sum of 3 million guilders to finance the war. After two years of deliberations they agreed to it, but on conditions that were far from satisfactory to Philip. By that time a new conflict was brewing. It had to do with the establishment in the provinces of new bishoprics, which would eliminate both foreign and local ecclesiastical authority, reserving the right of nomination to the Crown, and increase the numbers of bishops to aid in the fight against heresy. The new bishops were to take the place of the abbots of Afflighem, Marienweed, and Tongerloo at the States and would be funded by the revenues of the abbeys; in addition, they were to be actually learned in theology, which made it impossible to use the positions as sinecures for uneducated sons of the nobility. Granvelle—already a bishop, educated at the theological faculties of Padua and Louvain—was made archbishop of Mechlin, a cardinal, and "the Primate over the whole Netherlands Church." As could be expected, "resistance was violent. All classes—the nobility, the clergy, and the towns—made a great outcry about the violation of their rights." Philip had to give in, in 1564 ordering Granvelle to relinquish his posts and leave the Netherlands.

Granvelle was at that time the virtual head of the royal administration, which Philip left in his hands in 1559, when problems in the other parts of his global empire called him to Spain. Formally, however, the power belonged to Philip's half-sister Margaret of Parma, who was instructed to rule with the Council of State and in consultation with its preeminent members from the nobility—in particular William of Orange, appointed stadtholder of Holland, Zeeland, and Utrecht, and count of Egmont, stadtholder of Flanders and Artois. It was, predictably, the prince of Orange, the wealthiest and most influential nobleman of the area, who found Granvelle's authority especially irksome. "The early motivation," writes Israel, for Orange's opposition to

Granvelle "was probably just the usual one amongst great noblemen of the sixteenth century—the ambitious pursuit of power and prestige" and the desire to "substitute [his] own preponderance for that of the bureaucrats."[7] The prince made it easy, however, to identify his personal motives, whatever they were, with the religious aspirations of the populace, which provided another important cause for the Revolt, for a long time considered its main cause. As a result, eventually, William of Orange emerged as the leader of the insurrection against Spain.

The Religious Question

The beginnings of economic globalization under the aegis of western Europe coincided with the Reformation and, consequently, the fragmentation of the Respublica Christiana, which had previously united western Europe into one ideological space and, despite differences in language, which separated its lower classes, and dynastic divisions, made it in essence one civilization. The institutions which reflected this unity were the church and the universities in which men of the church were prepared for their vocation. The Holy Roman Empire, which was conceived of as its political framework, by the end of the Middle Ages no longer performed its original function, but though politically splintered, the cultural space—the manner in which people imagined, and thus constructed, their world—remained one. The disintegration of this cultural space presented no obstacle at all to its economic integration; while the latter was powerless to make people think alike and—despite what many like to believe today—in no way contributed to the "understanding" among those it turned into business partners, it may actually have been catalyzed by the "misunderstandings" that existed and facilitated by the diversity of (and divergences between) mentalities. By contrast, political integration, while not entirely dependent on cultural unity, was nevertheless inherently linked to and could not be accomplished without it. The global empire of Charles V, fortuitous though its coming into being was, thus was exceptionally badly timed; in the conditions of profound religious discord attendant on its birth, it was doomed to dissolution.

By the mid-sixteenth century the Netherlands had a long indigenous tradition of religious dissent. The church was not popular with the towns, which believed their privileges threatened by its extensive and growing control over landed property. As elsewhere, the many failings and abuses of the Catholic clergy attracted much attention. Toward the end of the fourteenth century, a dissident form of worship—the modern devotion—spread from Deventer in Overijssel across the Burgundian Netherlands and beyond, into the adjoining regions of Westphalia and northern France as well as distant Spain and Italy.

It was a form of pietism which emphasized inner faith over ritual and dogma and idealized primitive, or original and therefore true, Christianity. Its followers organized in Societies of Brothers (and Sisters) of Common Life, which was a life of chastity, personal poverty, humility, and obedience to communal rules and an elected rector. Some members were clerics, but the majority were laymen from all social classes. All had to work to contribute to the common fund and—in contrast to the monasteries—to work in the world. Many of the Brothers taught in schools attended by members of the larger community, and their influence was very widespread. Modern devotion was sometimes called "Reform before the Reformation," but it was a religious current within the Catholic Church.

In the early sixteenth century this mildly dissident form of Christianity was carried on in Biblical Humanism—another movement native to the Netherlands—whose leader was Erasmus of Rotterdam. Biblical Humanists, many of whom were educated in the schools of Brothers of the Common Life, believed in the reformative potential of "good letters," that is, classical learning, which, unlike orthodox theologians, they saw as congenial to the spirit of Christianity. On the whole, however, Biblical Humanists were little interested in theology, and this made their own spirit very different from that of Catholic and Protestant zealots alike. A biographer wrote of Erasmus that he "was in his own age the apostle of common sense and of rational religion. He did not care for dogma, and accordingly the dogmas of Rome, which had the consent of the Christian world, were in his eyes preferable to the dogmas of Protestantism . . . From the beginning to the end of his career he remained true to the purpose of his life, which was to fight the battle of sound learning and plain common sense against the powers of ignorance and superstition, and amid all the convulsions of that period he never once lost his mental balance." The sixteenth-century adage that "Erasmus laid the egg and Luther hatched it" therefore reflected a misconception. But "the convulsions of that period" led to the identification of ignorance and superstition with religious intolerance, and, forced to take sides, many followers of Erasmus did in fact become Protestants, however little it was in their character.

The Habsburg Netherlands experienced religious intolerance in a particularly oppressive and alienating measure, not at all commensurate with their reserved Erasmian enthusiasms, almost from the moment Luther nailed his Ninety-five Theses to the door of All Saints Church in Wittenberg. True to his imperial role as the protector of the Holy Catholic Church, Charles V undertook to make his patrimony an example of orthodoxy and in 1522 established a special Inquisition to reinforce and supervise the Episcopal Inquisition that existed everywhere. As municipal and provincial governments opposed it on the grounds that it trespassed on their traditional privileges, he used his sovereign prerogative to pass anti-heresy edicts, which culminated in the 1550 "edict of blood" and placed the heavy responsibility of persecution on the shoulders of secular authorities. Two Augustinian monks in Brussels had been burned at the stake in 1523, and many people were frightened enough to emigrate. The majority obviously stayed in place but, instead of duly learning their lesson, were outraged by Charles's didactic methods and grew sympathetic to the suspected heresy. "This sort," a contemporary noted in regard to numbers of Protestants in the Netherlands, "is fast growing among the Dutch and Walloons."

Until the 1550s the majority of these Protestants were Baptists, and it was they who bore the brunt of Charles's concern for the salvation of his subjects' souls. *The Lord's Sacrifice*—as the Dutch *Book of Martyrs* was called—collected the stories of those most tangibly affected by this concern; it was published almost simultaneously with Foxe's masterpiece in 1562. Most of these people, as in the English case, were simple citizens, but the tenor of their last testaments was rather different. According to Pieter Geyl, they were meek and unwilling to judge the powers that persecuted them, and so on account of the "gentleness and individualism" of their faith, the account of their fate did not have the incendiary effect produced in England by the story told in the *Acts and Monuments*.

At the time of the publication of *The Lord's Sacrifice*, however, Baptism had already been replaced as the main brand of Protestantism in the Netherlands by Calvinism, which reached the provinces in the 1550s. The creed of "this-worldly asceticism," it was more politically minded and activist, and rather than abstaining from judgment of secular authorities, condemned rulers who interfered with the freedom of (Reformed) religion as unrighteous and justified rebellion against them. Many of the nobles who opposed Granvelle—at once the representative of centralization and Inquisition, of attack on their secular interests and of religious intolerance—embraced these political implications of Calvinism, if not its theological presuppositions, and encouraged Calvinist religious sentiments among the population. Some of these nobles, such as William of Orange, were related by marriage to the Protestant nobility in Germany and, however indifferent to questions of doctrine themselves, were sincerely distressed by the forcible imposition of Catholicism. In the majority of cases, however, the nobility, and, more important, the towns, saw the religious policies of the central government as an intolerable affront to their traditional privileges. It is significant that the Inquisition and anti-heresy decrees were detested by Catholics possibly as much as, and certainly with more effect than, by Protestants, for the majority of the population took an Erasmian position and saw no reason to leave the fold of the church into which they had been born. The establishment of the new bishoprics in particular—and with much justification, for it aimed and was bound to destroy existing networks of patronage and therefore influence—was regarded by the nobility, the towns, and large sectors of the Catholic clergy as an infringement on their immediate interests. In Overijssel towns the new bishops were branded "heretic-hunters and inquisitors" (which they were as a matter of fact). But lampoons in Flanders and Brabant openly decried the violation of provincial privileges, declaring it a breach of contract between the Netherlands and their sovereign, which justified resistance to his policies on legal grounds.

The high nobility, which stood at the head of the opposition at this stage, in general refrained from focusing on the material issues which would necessitate an attack on the king's authority. Upon the dismissal of Granvelle, as Egmont was leaving for Spain for further negotiations with Philip, William of Orange insisted in a speech before the Council of State that the issue at stake was freedom of religion. "The King errs," he said, "if he thinks that the Netherlands, surrounded as they are by countries where religious freedom is permitted, can indefinitely support these sanguinary [anti-heresy] Edicts. However strongly I am attached to the Catholic religion, I cannot approve of princes attempting to rule the consciences of their subjects and wanting to rob them of the liberty of faith." Philip's dismissal of this admonition radicalized the opposition and temporarily transferred leadership to the hands of the lesser nobility, "Protestant and crypto-Protestant." Count Hendrik van Brederode, who stood at its head, in late 1565 organized the League of Compromise (whose carefully chosen name revealed the organization's optimism and peaceful intentions). In April of the following year, between two hundred (according to Israel) and four hundred (according to Geyl) of these noblemen marched to the residence of Margaret of Parma in Brussels and presented her with the Petition of Compromise. The petition also focused on the Inquisition, but it stated in uncompromising terms that the latter "would deprive the States of this country [that is, the social orders represented in assemblies] of all freedom to express their opinions, do away with all ancient privileges, franchises, and immunities, and not just make the burghers and inhabitants of this country miserable and perpetual slaves of the Inquisitors, who are worthless people, but even subject magistrates, office-holders, and all nobles to the mercy of their investigations."[8]

It was on this occasion that the witticism of a courtier who put the Leaguers down as "beggars" (obviously in French: *gueux*) was adopted as the new party name, and it was this name that later became the name of the Revolt. Soon afterwards the events acquired their own momentum, and within a year the vacillating opposition, ostensibly aiming at the "religious peace" and originally bent on compromise, was pushed to an all-out war against the

Spanish rule. This war lasted eighty years, and before it was over the Revolt of the Beggars ushered onto the stage of history by far the most successful European economic system of any that had existed previously and the first economic system to achieve world primacy.

The First Economic Miracle

The combination of the name of the rebellion and its outcome is not the only feature of that momentous event to strike an observer as paradoxical. Seventeen provinces rose against Spain, and seven of them formed the Dutch Republic: Holland, Zeeland, Friesland, Utrecht, Groningen, Overijssel, and Gelderland. Yet, this dramatic diminution in size (in effect, wrote Johan Huizinga, the region almost wholly responsible for the greatness and glory of the Netherlands was "not much more than sixty miles square"), and the exclusion from the Habsburg intercontinental commercial network, led not to the contraction in size of the Dutch economy, including the size of its domestic and foreign markets, but to its phenomenal expansion. "Except for Britain after around 1780," writes one observer,

> no one power in history ever achieved so great a preponderance over the processes of world trade as did the Dutch . . . That any one nation, or state, particularly one lacking the early start and past imperial grandeur of [others] should have achieved so prolonged, and constantly renewed, a capacity to dominate the world economy is, in itself, sufficiently amazing. But what makes it still more astounding is that at the time of its maritime and commercial greatness the Dutch Republic was the smallest of the major European states in territory, population, and natural resources.

Moreover, rather than being weakened by the war, the Republic grew stronger with every year it lasted, emerging in 1647, when the hostilities finally ceased, as a major European political power and the global economic "hegemon." "In 1650," wrote Braudel, for the sake of the argument zeroing in on the precise point in time as well as in space, "the center of the world was tiny Holland, or rather Amsterdam."

The sudden rise of the Dutch economy was, it appears, the first of the events to which economic historians refer as "economic miracles." And contemporaries, at least in England, where they watched it closely, clearly saw it as such. "[It] seems a wonder to the world," wrote Thomas Munn in 1621,

> that such a small countrey, not fully so big as two of our best shires, having little natural wealth, victuals, timber or other necessary ammuni-

tions, either for war or peace, should notwithstanding possess them all in such extraordinary plenty that besides their own wants (which are very great) they can and do likewise serve and sell to other Princes, ships, ordnance, cordage, corn, powder, shot and what not, which by their industrious trading they gather from all the quarters of the world: in which courses they are no less injurious to supplant others (especially the English) than they are careful to strengthen themselves.

In 1668 Sir Josiah Child expressed the same sentiments more succinctly. "The prodigious increase of the Netherlanders," he wrote, "in their domestick and forreign Trade, Riches and multitude of Shipping is the envy of the present and may be the wonder of all future generations."

The achievement of the United Netherlands was indeed prodigious. The period roughly between 1580 and 1670, called the Dutch "Golden Age," was one of continuous and astonishing growth affecting all the sectors of the economy, though not uniformly throughout the provinces. There is some disagreement among economic historians as to what was the source of this economy's strength, but it is clear that it experienced a "boom," some aspects of which amounted to a revolution. Unfortunately, it appears to be impossible to estimate the rate of growth of the Dutch economy in the Golden Age. The authors of the comprehensive Dutch economic history *The First Modern Economy* (1997), Jan de Vries and Ad van der Woude, conclude that "the most basic information needed to express that growth in quantitative terms is unavailable." "But," they insist, "real growth of per capita income there was, of that we are confident. The evidence for it is found (1) in the agricultural sector, where our rough estimates suggest a near doubling of labor productivity between 1510 and 1650; (2) in the substantial augmentation of physical capital and energy sources in industry; (3) in the reduced manning rates per ton of ocean shipping volume; and (4) reflecting these productivity gains, in the increased real wages." They estimate the Dutch "national income" in the late seventeenth century to have been 30 to 40 percent greater than that of England, Scotland, and Wales combined.[9]

Cheese and Herring

Other facts augment this picture. Between 1540 and 1715, 364,565 acres in Holland, Zeeland, and Friesland were reclaimed from the sea, and another 84,638 acres from inland lakes, nearly half of this land reclamation taking place between 1590 and 1650. In this sixty-year period the acreage drained per year increased annually, reaching 4,450 acres in 1640. Most of the lakes in Holland, such as Hugowaard, Purmer, Schermer, Wieringerwaard, and

Wormer, as well as twenty marshes, altogether more than 120,000 acres, were drained between 1612 and 1640. Indeed, one was fully justified in saying that "God created the world, but Dutchmen made Holland."

The newly reclaimed land reinforced the trend toward specialization in agriculture, which, in the beginning, could possibly be attributed to the efficacy of the Dutch Baltic trade. Specifically, the reliable supplies of Baltic grain, the imports of which grew fivefold in the first sixty years of the sixteenth century, made unnecessary the degree of concentration on cereal production then characteristic of most of Europe and allowed Dutch farmers to "diversify . . . into other, and now more profitable, products, especially dairy foods, meat, wool, flax, hops, and fodder crops." This resulted, among other things, in a nutritionally superior "Republican diet" of the Dutch population, which had more in common with the high-calorie intake of the indiscriminate present-day glutton than with the austere bread and beer regimen of most of their contemporaries. This also brought about a dramatic increase in the production and export of butter and, more important, cheese—"the most successfully commercialized of the various kinds of agricultural produce." A Frenchman living in the Netherlands in the 1660s personally saw more than 150,000 pounds of cheese being delivered one fine day on a thousand peasant carts to the market at Hoorn to be weighed. At this time Edam was exporting five hundred tons of its cheese annually, lending some justification to the envious French and English characterization of the Netherlands as a "nation of cheesemongers." Meanwhile, the agricultural sector as a whole, employing less than 40 percent of the total labor force, made of the Netherlands "almost a net food exporter."

The rest of the labor force was available for work in other sectors. This nonagricultural labor supply grew at the rate of 3 percent per year during the half century between 1570 and 1620, and at 1 percent annually between 1620 and 1660. Throughout this period wages rose too, registering their most significant increases in 1572–1583 and 1592–1616, but continuing to rise steadily until 1665. The demand for this extraordinary supply existed in fishing, in trade, and in industry. According to Paul Zumthor, fishing was "the point of departure for Dutch prosperity," which began in 1385, when a Zeeland fisherman invented the process of curing and barreling herring— "the patriotic fish"—at sea. (In 1621 Thomas Munn agreed: it was "not the barren Netherlands," he claimed, "but the rich fishing, which gives foundation, trade, and subsistence to those multitudes of Ships, Arts and people.") This invention was implemented thanks to the "herring buss"—"an unprecedentedly large fishing vessel, often carrying fifteen or eighteen crew, more than many of the Baltic grain ships [and] designed to weather storms and stay at sea for long periods, and to carry large stocks of salt." The quantum leap in efficiency that this implied transformed a purely local occupation into "a vast international trade." In the seventeenth century the centers of herring fishing were Enkhuizen (whose connection to the trade was reflected in the three herrings on its coat of arms) and Rotterdam; the collective herring fleet of these two large and many smaller ports consisted of five hundred busses and generated annual revenues of 10 million guilders.

In addition to employing some seven thousand men at sea, the expansion of this "chiefest trade and gold mine" of the Netherlands called for the establishment of numerous subsidiary industries on shore. These included secondary pickling (since the original process of curing and barreling at sea was no longer sufficient after herring became a staple of Dutch international trade and had to be preserved for longer periods), salt refining, herring packing, cooperage, and net making, as well as shipbuilding, sailcloth weaving, and food provisioning, also related to shipping in general. These industries were widely spread among Dutch towns and villages, including Amsterdam. Thus, there was some truth in Marshall's obviously exaggerated (though unoriginal) statement that Amsterdam was built on a bed of herring bones.

The major Dutch industry was shipbuilding. Naval dockyards in Zaandam were the place to acquire mastery of "pegging, joining, carving, squaring, planing, drilling, sawing, cutting planks and knot-burning"; it was there that Russia's Peter the Great went to learn these skills at the end of the seventeenth century. By the time of the tsar's stay, thirty to thirty-five new ships left Zaandam every year. A major invention in shipbuilding was that of the *fluyt* (which was first built in Hoorn in the 1590s). This "flute-ship," "fly-ship," or "store-ship" was particularly well suited for bulk freight, simple and relatively cheap to build (between 800 and 1,400 pounds, depending on the size), and required no more than nine or ten men to operate. English and French critics found the design wanting, but the *fluyt* was to a large degree responsible for the low Dutch freight rates.

Holland alone had around 1,800 seagoing vessels as early as the 1560s—a telling comparison, as Israel points out, with Venice, which had no more than 300 ships in 1450 at the height of its seafaring glory. In 1655 Colbert feared the number of Dutch ships had increased to fifteen or sixteen thousand, which would amount to 75 percent of all European ships (of which France owned but a few hundred). The actual number of Dutch vessels was closer to 20 percent, with the carrying capacity of the fleet growing at the annual rate of 1 percent in the previous century: the great minister must have been deceived by the ubiquity of Dutch carriers which reigned over international commerce.

The Baltic bulk trade was dominated by the Dutch as early as the fifteenth century, and even before the Revolt they could be said to have had a "trade empire" characterized by "the vast and unprecedented size of its stock of merchant shipping, its incomparably low freight charges, and its unrivalled capacity to transfer bulky goods cheaply and in large quantity." In the 1590s, however, the new Republic entered the much more profitable trade in luxury goods, or "rich trades," and it was this new venture, itself explained by the new circumstances created by the Revolt, that, at least according to some scholars, propelled it to the position of primacy in the world economy it was to enjoy in the course of its Golden Age. The growth of Dutch foreign trade in the next several decades, write de Vries and van der Woude, was "explosive." Its annual value reached at least 225 million guilders by 1625 and perhaps as much as 400 million by 1650. "The established trade routes [were extended], connecting Iberia with the Baltic to the Mediterranean, the White Sea, and ultimately to Asia, Africa, and the Western Hemisphere, [and multiplying and enriching] the flows of commodities that reached the ports of Holland and Zeeland." "The trade of the Hollanders," marveled an English contemporary, Charles Davenant, "is so far extended that it may be said to have no other bounds than those which the Almighty set at Creation."

Before the introduction of the first English Navigation Act in 1651, the Netherlands virtually monopolized international trade in northern and western Europe. Ten Dutch cargo ships left for England for every English vessel carrying goods to the Dutch ports. The Dutch share of the Baltic trade continued to grow: 55 percent of the ships sailing to Russia and Sweden in 1600, and 67 percent in 1615, were Dutch. The value of Dutch trade, however, increased with distance, and this, among other things, explains the exceptional importance of the East India Company (VOC) in the Dutch economy. "Europe's first effective joint-stock company" was formed in 1602 with a capital of 6,424,588 guilders, contributed by 1,800 investors. Its first dividend in 1610 was paid in spices, amounting in value to 125 percent. By 1650 its capital returns were 500 percent. The VOC was the single largest employer in the Republic, in the 1660s expending more than 3 million guilders annually on payroll, close to 1 million in the Republic itself, and the rest at sea and abroad (where the great majority of its employees, until the end of the seventeenth century, were Dutch). In addition, during the same period, the Company yearly spent 1.2 million guilders in domestic commodity purchases, including trade goods, shipbuilding materials, and provisions. Export trade was of relatively minor importance in the activity of the VOC; nevertheless, in the 1660s the value of its exports amounted to a million guilders annually, and continued to rise. Though some of these exports, such as wine and lead, consisted of goods imported from other European countries, the Company provided an important stimulus for certain domestic industries (for example, textiles) even when not directly related to shipping. Including taxes, dividends, and interest, the Company pumped into the domestic economy "steadily rising amounts": in the eighteenth century from 3 to nearly 5 million guilders in wages and 1 to 2 million in orders for supplies. No wonder that it "had come to assume a central place in both the Republic's trading system and its domestic economy."

It is unnecessary to dwell on the many other achievements of this economy; they have been recorded with meticulous care elsewhere. Almost every single aspect of it—be it "highly capitalized peat-digging" which supplied urban industries "with a level of per capita energy consumption unsurpassed until the British Industrial Revolution," or the creation of the sprawling network of public transportation via canals and wagon trails which by the mid-seventeenth century "blanketed" the Republic, "connecting small places to regional centers, and regional centers . . . to major cities, offering a predictable, regulated service for the domestic distribution of goods"—provides a striking contrast to other economies of the time and far exceeds their standards.[10] One sector, advanced to a degree astonishing even by comparison to the other parts of this exceptional economic system, however, must be briefly discussed. It is finance.

Finance

The Dutch Republic undoubtedly was the first political entity to experience "financial revolution"—England's, for which the term was coined, occurring in the wake of the Glorious Revolution of 1688. The concept connotes, in particular, government finance by means of direct and indirect taxation and public debt, expedients practiced in the Netherlands on the municipal level as far back as the fourteenth century. This obviously presupposed the existence of sophisticated instruments and techniques, the result of an evolution, in private finance as well.

The Dutch economy was exceptionally highly monetized from early on. Gregory King in 1688 estimated the Dutch money supply at 9 million pounds, which meant that per capita money supply in the Netherlands was around twice the amount in England and three times the amount in France. Until the end of the seventeenth century this money supply was decentralized and would strike today's observer as chaotic. Fourteen independent mints in cities and on noble estates were authorized by the ancient imperial privilege to mint coin. During the government of the earl of Leicester at the end of the sixteenth century, the work of the mints was coordinated to a minor extent, with only the larger ones minting the silver Rijksdaalder and Leeuwendaalder and the gold dukaat for heavy trade, and others restricted to smaller coins for everyday domestic use. But since, in addition, foreign coins, especially German, circulated freely, the situation remained confusing. It was this confusion which, among other things, prompted the creation of the Bank of Amsterdam in 1609. A savings and giro bank, whose credit was guaranteed by the city of Amsterdam, it provided the merchants with both a most efficient means to settle large accounts and with security which at that time (and for the next century) could be matched by no other institution in the world. By the end of the seventeenth century, the vaults of the bank contained around 10 million guilders—close to 1 million pounds sterling—in coin, and its daily transactions amounted to several million guilders. "It grew . . . to become the clearinghouse of world trade, settling international debts and effecting transfers of capital. Moreover, it did this on a continuous basis rather than at long intervals, as had been the practice of the old fairs."

The services provided by its Wisselbank, which had already made Amsterdam the financial nerve center of the world, were further augmented by the regular flow of information available only there. By 1611 Amsterdam had correspondents stationed in Antwerp, Cologne, Hamburg, Wesel, Münster, Ghent, Lille, Tournai, Valenciennes, and Lisbon who regularly reported on news of commercial importance. In 1613 the brokers' guild began publishing biweekly bulletins of price and exchange rate quotations. The first such *Price Courant* was issued as early as 1583, and in the first decade of the new century exchange rates were already available for ten major centers: Antwerp, Cologne, Danzig, Frankfurt, Hamburg, London, Nuremberg, Paris, Rouen, and Venice. In 1618 to these sources were added newspapers—two columns of quarto paper, coming out up to three times a week, "the passion for reading [which] became as widespread as the use of tobacco." (The use of tobacco was very widespread indeed. "A Hollander without a pipe," it was said, "is a national impossibility, akin to a town without a house, a stage without actors, a spring without flowers. If a Hollander should be bereft of his pipe of tobacco, he could not blissfully enter heaven." And a French observer noted with disdain: "Holland is a country where the demon gold is seated on a throne of cheese, and crowned with tobacco.") Within three decades all six large cities in Holland had their "gazettes," some—*Gazette d'Amsterdam*, *Gazette de Leyde*—in French.

The development of the institutional infrastructure of Dutch finance coincided with the rapid accumulation of prodigious stocks of capital. Much of it, according to de Vries and van der Woude, was owing to the explosive growth of Dutch foreign trade, the profits of which were repeatedly reinvested. In the latter part of the Golden Age, at least as important appear to be the changes in government finance, in particular, measures taken to finance the Revolt. In the last three decades of war, the annual budget of the Republic's military expenses, reconstructed by Marjolein 't Hart, stood at about 24 million guilders. The "financial revolution," which would, paradoxically, make the Netherlands "embarrassingly" rich, consisted, as she argues, in shifting this burden onto the Dutch public. This shift was accomplished with the help of two innovative strategies: imposition of direct and indirect taxes, and the creation of a public debt. Direct taxes on wealth—or *capital* in Dutch—may be the source of our concept "capitalism." One of the earliest such taxes was introduced in Holland in 1585: named the *capitale impositie*, it was, in fact, a forced loan affecting the affluent. In 1621 special registers, drawn for the purpose of levying extraordinary property taxes, created a category of those whose taxable property amounted to more than two thousand guilders; they were referred to as "capitalists"—*capitalisten*. Four years later another tax category was added, "semi-capitalists," or *halve capitalisten*, those worth from one thousand to two thousand guilders. Those who had less were exempt from taxes of these kinds; in the vocabulary of the time and place, they were not capitalists at all. "Capitalists" thus meant "wealthy," "rich," while "poor," by inversion, meant "not capitalist." But "capitalism" was certainly not the only invention the Dutch of the Golden Age bequeathed to us. In the field of taxation proper it seems to have been they who first introduced excise taxes. The English believed so, at least, referring to excises, which they adopted in 1689, as the Dutch fiscal "invention."

The Union of Utrecht, a mutual defense pact concluded by the seven provinces—the "allies," as they called themselves—which served as the fundamental law of the Republic, stipulated that the taxes to finance the war were to be collected "equally in all the United provinces, and at the same rate," but it never worked that way. Instead, the levies were based on the modified quota system, inherited from the Habsburg period. Holland, which was by far the wealthiest and the most populous province, had its quota fixed first at over 60, then at 58 percent of the total. But its relative contribution to supporting the public debt was greater still. The States of Holland were the first to overcome the reluctance of private lenders, and it was Holland that secured the Generality bonds, the *renten*, which began to be sold in 1596. Holland also paid 96–98 percent of the interest on the Generality debt in the ordinary budgets between 1621 and 1647. Its good credit—and its credit market—grew together with the economy as a whole. The English ambassador to the Netherlands in the 1660s, Sir William Temple, estimated that Holland's public debt was held by some 65,000 individuals, which, with one per household, would include almost 30 percent of the province's households. By 1640, some 60 percent of Holland's taxes went on servicing this debt, although in the next thirty years the service charges were reduced thanks to ingenious management techniques and required only 50 percent. The debt itself, which in 1640 stood at 95 million guilders, by 1668 grew to 125 million.

The immediate result of this fiscal policy was the accumulation of spectacular amounts of capital in the hands of the Republic's bondholders. After the end of the war in 1647, they received some 9 million guilders a year in interest, with total accumulation amounting to between 33 and 99 million guilders in the period 1646—1689. "The owners of the Republic's public debt," say de Vries and van der Woude, "were awash in cash." They were practically swimming in money—this was a major case of *overvloed* so masterfully depicted in Simon Schama's iconographic study of seventeenth-century Dutch culture. Such was the rentiers' level of income that they could "wallow in luxury and [still] reserve large sums for investment," and, as they "sought to place their interest earnings and redemptions in comparable debt instruments abroad," Amsterdam emerged as "Europe's foremost supplier of short- and long-term credit"—an international capital market of unprecedented proportions.

Dutch merchant bankers had a long tradition of lending to foreign governments. In 1688, however, an entirely new page in foreign lending was turned, as Dutch private investors began participating in the English public debt and acquiring stock of English joint stock companies. The ratio of foreign investment to the economy of the Dutch Republic has never been exceeded; at the end of the eighteenth century it was more than double the value of de Vries and van der Woude's "guesstimate" of the Dutch GNP. Its foreign government lending in 1780 stood at 380 million guilders—with at least 200 million invested in English bonds—and rendered 16 million a year in interest. By that time the Republic had been the financial center of the world for well over a century, and finance, for at least a century, had been the major part of its economy.

Finance seems to have become the business of choice in the Netherlands rather early, and swimming in money, when the level of capital made this possible, was clearly preferred to sailing the high seas. But already in the sixteenth century the precocious development of business imagination and technique had attracted Dutch grain and herring dealers to "speculative" (that is, guesswork), or air, commerce; they were trading in futures as early as 1550, buying and selling grain that had not yet been harvested and fish that had not been caught. Charles Kindleberger finds this "impressive."[11] Indeed, we must be impressed: in the practices of these early Dutch entrepreneurs we cannot but see ourselves. We still engage in—and consider the acme of business finesse—the *windhandel* that they invented and mastered to perfection half a millenium ago. In many ways, Amsterdam was an early version of today's Wall Street.

The First Modern Economy?

The question is: Was this advanced and successful economy modern? Or, in other words, was modern economy born in the Dutch Republic rather than England, as is commonly thought by those insufficiently acquainted with the Dutch experience? Some authors answer these questions with a firm yes.

Since this answer is nowhere more extensively substantiated than in de Vries's and van der Woude's study *The First Modern Economy,* the argument of their book deserves to be considered at some length.

Appearances

Many features of the Dutch economy "give a distinctly modern impression," say de Vries and van der Woude. It grew under conditions that appear to them "early expressions of . . . an open bourgeois society," manifesting, in distinction to most societies of the time,

> the diversified character of landownership and land use; the weakness or absence of collective institutions such as open fields and guilds; the open relations between town and country; the strongly nuclear household structure of the population and its implications for the character of family life; the occupational flexibility that made possible, for instance, the integrating of farming, fishing, and seafaring; the pluriform religious life made possible by a relatively high degree of toleration and space for personal freedom; the strong attachment to local autonomy; and the jealous protection of vested rights and privileges.

Some of these features may not strike the reader as characteristically bourgeois; for de Vries and van der Woude, however, they combine to form a species of "proto-modernity," which they see as related to an exceptionally high level of urbanization. Already in 1525, they estimate, 31–32 percent of the population of the Republic as a whole (and 45 percent in Holland) consisted of urban dwellers. By the end of the Golden Age, around 1675, the urban population of the Republic had reached 45 percent. How precocious this was becomes apparent if one compares the Netherlands to England, where the urban population did not approach this level until 1850, and as late as 1800 was only at 20 percent.

The exceptional features of Dutch society, argue the co-authors, "contributed to the development of mentalities and social structures that were especially suited to the rapid emergence and intense prosperity of a modern economy." Mentalities such as freedom, individualism, and market orientation, they say, in fact characterized this society "long before the end of the Middle Ages." It appears that already under the Burgundian dukes, the northern Netherlands possessed the same "culture of capitalism" that Alan MacFarlane discovered in thirteenth-century England. As for structures, besides those already mentioned among the conditions, these included occupational specialization so "far in advance of the rest of Europe" that not even England reached a similar level before the end of the eighteenth century; a system of education capable of producing high levels of literacy and numeracy and in general fostering a rational approach in life and thought; and an "anti-absolutist political regime, sensitive to the interests of the citizens."

This very impressive list of facilitating conditions, immediate and twice removed, however cannot in itself justify the claim that the Dutch economy of the Golden Age was a modern economy. The very fact, which de Vries and van der Woude constantly stress, that England lagged behind the Republic in so many respects, even at the time when its economy became the standard of modernity, contradicts it. If England could achieve a modern economy without rates of urbanization, occupational specialization, or capital available for investment at levels comparable to those in the Netherlands at the time of their primacy, this means that none of these conditions are essential for determining the modern character of an economy. Indeed, de Vries and van der Woude's rationale for defining the Dutch economy as modern is not clear. Sometimes it appears that it is so defined simply because its emergence was rapid and its prosperity intense, that is, because of the spectacular character of its achievement. At other times their argument seems to be based on certain similarities between the experiences of that economy and the economies of the present, as, for example, when the authors remark that "the eighteenth-century Dutch labor market exhibited several strikingly modern features: high wages, probably the highest in Europe, together with substantial unemployment and, at the same time, seasonal labor shortages and a dependence on migrant labor from a neighboring society with a much lower standard of living." Present-day economies, however, are not modern because they exist in the present; nor is their modernity a reflection of the fact that some of them may indeed combine high wages with substantial unemployment and seasonal labor shortages. Basing a classification of economic systems on such characteristics is akin to classifying lifelike dolls or robots together with human beings whom they superficially, albeit perfectly, resemble. The fact that the Dutch economy looked like a modern one, or—to quote de Vries and van der Woude again—that it "gave a distinctly modern impression," does not mean that it was a modern economy, in other words.

In the interest of fairness, it must be said that de Vries and van der Woude do not rest satisfied with this rationale for their claim either, and, toward the end of the book, propose yet another one. "The United Provinces," they say,

> can lay claim to being the first modern economy by virtue of continuity (it has been a modern economy ever since) and by virtue of its leadership in establishing the conditions of economic modernity over much of Europe. It became not only the commercial entrepôt for Europe; it also achieved Europe's highest overall level of total factor productivity for

the better part of the seventeenth and eighteenth centuries. That is, it became the first . . . "lead country," operating nearest to the technological frontier and doing most to define that frontier, until it was dislodged from that position by Great Britain . . . Britain, in turn, ceded this place at the technological frontier to the United States.

Leaving aside the proposition regarding the continuity of Dutch modernity, which is a tautology, this statement bases the claim to modernity of the Dutch economy on the fact of its world economic primacy. The logic of the argument is, "The Dutch Republic had the place occupied by England before England; therefore it was like England: modern."[12]

Absolute versus Relative Decline

De Vries and van der Woude are not the only ones to regard the Dutch and the English economic experiences as strictly comparable. Charles Kindleberger also treats them as more or less equivalent chapters of the same story in his 1996 *World Economic Primacy, 1500—1990,* which deals with economic growth and decline, "whether absolute or relative." Kindleberger approaches these as different phases in the natural cycle of a country's "economic vitality"—a cycle, he proposes, analogous to the human life cycle. Economies, Kindleberger says, mature and age, like a person, and though the outcomes of these processes can be affected by exogenous events, the processes themselves are endogenous, inherent in the nature of things. In this natural cycle, which the iron hand of inevitability bends into an S-curve, economic sectors, industries, and national economies go through stages as immutable in their fundamental character and order of succession as puberty and menopause. A slow start is followed by "speedup, slowdown in the rate of growth, steady growth, and then decline, usually relative to other industries, sectors, regions, or economies."

Global economic development appears similarly predetermined. "In due course" the political framework of economic systems changes: "city-states come to dominate their surroundings and grow into provinces, which in due course join others to form nations." "In due course, financial institutions develo[p], such as banks dealing in bills of exchange, insurance, standard money, standard weights and measures, and governmental protection against piracy, privateers, and interlopers who tr[y] to invade government-assigned monopolies." "In due course" Mediterranean galleys give way to sailing ships. "Slowly but relentlessly" the technology of sailing grows, stimulating improvements in navigation and cartography. "In due course . . . this produc[es] the Age of Discovery, led by the Portuguese."

"Economic primacy," says Kindleberger, belongs to those concepts "that cannot be defined rigorously, but most people know what is meant by them." How economic primacy is related to the cycles of economic vitality is also not entirely clear. Nevertheless, it appears that Kindleberger equates it with the phases of speedup through steady growth on the S-curve and with the relative "age" of an economy. One "lead economy" succeeds another "in due course," so to speak, as do generations. But, fundamentally, the very same process of growth and decline happens in every (economic) generation. Indeed, Kindleberger does not distinguish sharply (if at all) between relative and absolute decline; therefore, there is no need to draw a sharp distinction between relative economic vitality (economic primacy) and absolute vitality, which is conceivable out of all comparison with other economies. The successive primacies are conceptually identical: to interpret one is to interpret all of them; they simply occur at different times—and under different economic conditions—in different places. The seventeenth century was the time of the Netherlands; by the end of the eighteenth century, when the Dutch economy had already "aged," Great Britain was reaching its prime.[13]

Relative and absolute decline—or vitality—however, are phenomena of a completely different nature. A decline which is relative to the performance of others, in fact, may not be a decline at all. Consider a runner who is steadily winning races until encountering a faster runner and losing. Can the victory of the new champion be regarded as the decline of the former one? No, the term can be used in this context only metaphorically. Moreover, the explanation of this metaphorical "decline" has to do exclusively with the new champion: its causes lie not with any change in the swiftness of the first runner (there may not be any change), but with the superior agility—or perhaps motivation—of the one who overtakes him. What about a decline which is relative to one's own prior performance? This is also only a metaphor. A decline is the opposite of growth; it is synonymous with diminution, deterioration, and decay; it implies a downward turn. A teenager who was growing an inch a month in the previous year and is at present growing an inch every two months is not in decline. The learning capacity of a student whose foreign vocabulary increased at the rate of a hundred words a week in the first months of study and later, being quite extensive, is augmented only occasionally and by a few words is not in decline. Declining health is health that is failing rather than improving, however slowly, or simply remaining stable; a declining economy is an economy which is contracting rather than growing at a rate less impressive than before. It follows from this that if the decline of the Dutch economy was absolute, and the decline of the British one relative, which we know was the case, these are not at all comparable, and the primacy each in its time enjoyed in the world economy, rather than being two successive chapters in the same story, is in each case a story in its own right and must be explained differently.

The decline of the Dutch economy was absolute. The evidence presented by de Vries and van der Woude to this effect is unequivocal. The signs of the decline appeared soon after 1648—"the acknowledged high point of the Golden Age." Already in the 1650s the investments in land reclamation "lost their profitability and . . . stopped." The expansion of peat canals ceased at the same time, and "after a spectacular growth in the first half of the 17th century, output [of peat production] fell by half in the second half," causing the revenue from Holland's excise tax on peat to decline "by nearly 20% between the 1660s and the 1680s." The construction of *trekvaart*—canals equipped with towpaths—ended in 1665, as did the "process of infrastructural investment" in general. "The extensions of such cities as Haarlem, Groningen, and Amsterdam . . . were finished in the 1670s and languished, only partially occupied, until the 19th century," among other things, because demographic growth stopped too and after the mid-seventeenth century was replaced by "stagnation or even decline." While between 1500 and 1650 the population of the Republic "had doubled, and that of the coastal provinces nearly tripled[,] after the mid-seventeenth century . . . in the coastal provinces, the population growth came to a full stop . . . [I]n North Holland and Friesland . . . it fell absolutely." "Especially noteworthy" in this respect, comment de Vries and van der Woude, was "the absence of renewed population growth after 1750, when this became general everywhere else in Europe." Depopulation was accompanied by de-urbanization. The urban population of the Republic, which stood at a remarkable 45 percent in 1675, was 42 percent in 1750, and fell further, to 38 percent by 1815: "Only four cities (Amsterdam, Rotterdam, The Hague, and Schiedam) had larger populations in 1795 than in 1622. All the other cities of Holland possessed, in the best cases, the same population, or, more commonly, but a fraction of their 1622 population." At the same time, the character of the numerically declining labor force was changing for the worse. Between 1575 and 1648, the tiny Republic founded five universities, with the numbers of university-educated men soaring as a consequence: in the seventeenth century, twenty-five out of every one thousand young men (ages eighteen and up) went to a university. In the eighteenth century only half that number achieved similar levels of education. The wages of labor, exceptionally high during the Golden Age, "were literally frozen for at least 150 years after 1650." De Vries and van der Woude speculate that "the total income of the Republic as a whole must have experienced a significant downward pressure."

The persistent government demand for more loans and the preference among the public for investments in bonds after 1689 led to the withdrawal of capital from commerce, industry, and agriculture. The continuing increase in the public debt resulted in "the state's fiscal exhaustion": by 1713, the wealthiest of the provinces, Holland, in the words of Secretary of the Council of State van Slingelandt, was "burdened to the point of sinking." The owners of government debt, who also invested heavily in foreign loans, continued to reap profits, but this was "accumulation without growth." In the eighteenth century, the seventeenth-century marvel of economic vitality was "a rich but stagnant economy," "a machine for the maintenance of a colossal public debt." The English no longer looked at the Dutch Republic with envy but regarded it with self-satisfied condescension. James Mitchell, a traveler, remarked around 1800 à propos the Dutch system of public transportation, which had aroused so much admiration a century earlier: "Their mode of travelling seems to afford a fair example of Dutch arrangements generally: it is economical of money, but expensive of time . . . While a Dutchman travels three miles in an hour, an Englishman travels six or eight, and this is nearly the difference between the spirit and energy of the two nations."

A few decades after its prime, the most powerful economy in the world, the first one to achieve world economic primacy, was but a shadow of its former self. By 1806 it was of no greater importance than an "entrepôt de la contrebande." There is no misreading the indicators. "The growth potential of the investment strategies of the preceding century fell to zero," only "very few" industries—among them, the slave trade—escaping the fate of the rest. The East India Company expanded, but this was "profitless growth." The period was one of "continuing deindustrialization." "The per capita gross national income stood at a lower level in the 1740s . . . than it had in the 1660s." The industrial towns were increasingly characterized by "idle resources," and the position of Dutch traders in many European markets became marginalized. "The last quarter of the seventeenth century," conclude de Vries and van der Woude, "almost certainly brought absolute decline to the total output of the Dutch economy."[14]

A Modern Decline

How do de Vries and van der Woude reconcile this record with their insistence on the modernity of the Dutch economy? They reject sustained growth as an element of the definition of modernity. "The presumption of sustained, even unending, growth," they write,

> adheres to the definitions of modern economic growth, while the economic history of the Republic was clearly one of growth followed by stagnation, something approximating an S-shaped, or logistic, curve.

Instead of persisting exponential growth, our study describes a society whose growth eventually moved asymptotically toward a limit, rather as the classical economists predicted. [But] the Republic's growth did not decelerate because of the supply constraints of inelastic energy sources, but because of economic circumstances that limited demand. [There is] an implicit claim about modern economic growth. It is not self-sustained, exponential, and unbounded . . . [M]odern economic growth is no process of growth without end but rather tends at some point toward deceleration and stagnation. A first cycle of such growth, crisis, and stagnation was pioneered by the Netherlands between the 16th century and 1850 . . . [T]he situation in which the old Republic found itself in the early 18th century seems in many ways illustrative of the problems of today.

But what then, one may ask, distinguished this "first modern economy" from the economies before it, which also went through cycles of growth and decline? What exactly did the Netherlands pioneer? To these questions de Vries and van der Woude have a ready answer: "The Republic suffered a 'modern decline.'" It is the character of its decline, they say, that allows us to qualify an economy—and its growth—as modern.

What made the decline of the Dutch economy modern? The fact that theories used to explain the decline of earlier economies do not apply to it. This includes the Malthusian model—"an indispensable basis for the analysis of economic life" during the preindustrial period, subscribed to by most influential economic historians. "The essence of Malthusian interpretations of economic history," de Vries and van der Woude explain, "is the belief that population and economy interact in the form of negative feedback loops, such that any impulse toward growth is, in time, reversed—checked—to restore equilibrium. In an economy dominated by Malthusian forces, economic expansion is necessarily limited, episodic, and stunted." But, they say, "by the end of the [sixteenth] century, a conventional Malthusian model is no longer adequate to account for the economic and demographic dynamics of the new Republic . . . Strong positive feedback loops, where an impulse toward expansion stimulates further growth, now made their appearance in the Dutch economy, significantly weakening the influence of Malthusian forces." When the Dutch economy did decline, its decline was not a Malthusian crisis but "an altogether modern problem," pertaining to the management of an excessive public debt. An additional proof of the modernity of the Dutch economic decline, and therefore of its growth and character in general, is that its significantly delayed industrialization was not predicated on characteristics similar to those of other late industrializers. No less an authority than Alexander Gerschenkron, the authors say, "argued that delayed industrialization was a symptom of backwardness, which in turn signified the absence or imperfection of institutions and ideologies needed to mobilize economic resources effectively . . . [But when Dutch] industrialization finally did get underway, it possessed none of the characteristic 'late industrializer' attributes predicted by Gerschenkron. The reason for that is not hard to uncover: the Netherlands was not backward."[15]

But surely there are other reasons one can think of: for example, that Gerschenkron was (at the very least partly) wrong. Like most economic historians of his generation, Gerschenkron believed that industrialization was a natural process, a developmental stage which every society would sooner or later inevitably reach. Delayed industrialization, by definition, then became a function of general retardation, or backwardness, and since backwardness was defined as the presence of structural and cultural factors associated with delayed industrialization in the limited number of cases Gerschenkron studied, the argument was not too hard to substantiate. But what if industrialization is not inevitable? What if, like almost anything else of importance in human society, it is a matter of historical contingency, thus an accident of history? Then the concepts of both "delayed industrialization" and "backwardness" lose their meaning, and late(r) industrializations, as well as earlier ones, need a different explanation.

One can even muster enough courage to question the authority of the Malthusian interpretation. No matter how many influential historians believe in it, no theory should be indispensable for analysis. Analyses are indispensable for the construction of theories. Theories aid us in making sense of the empirical evidence. And when a theory is contradicted by the empirical evidence to which it is expected to apply, one's first response should be to reexamine the theory rather than redefine the evidence. If the concept of modernity in the economic sphere is to have any meaning, it must capture economic reality which is significantly—that is, qualitatively—different from economic realities that are not modern. Its correspondence to existing theories is a matter of secondary importance; it should not be manipulated to fit them.

As a characteristic of decline, the concept of modern economy is meaningless: to define a particular species of economic reality in this fashion is similar to defining the human species by the specifics of the physical decay experienced by humans in old age and death. Such a focus can contribute very little (and nothing of significance) to our understanding of the processes of life itself (whether economic or human), and, presumably, it is these processes that are of interest. In both cases one must focus on growth. And, in the case of economies, it is the character of this growth, the fact that it is sustained, which allows us to distinguish modern economy from others. The Dutch economy, prodigiously successful during the Golden Age, but one which later experienced absolute decline, does not fit this meaningful concept of modern economy. Therefore, it was not a modern economy. To say this is not to diminish its great achievement or to classify it as a failure in the transition to industrialization. To use a simile from the previous chapter, to do so would be akin to considering Michelangelo a failure in the transition to cubism. Economic modernization is not a stage in a unilinear and inevitable social evolution known ahead of time. It is a matter of choice. The Dutch of the seventeenth and eighteenth centuries did not choose to become modern. They did not make a fetish of ever-continued growth and did not develop the orientation, the spirit, that was to become the mark of the "peculiarly Occidental rationalism." They remained economically rational instead, embodying the ideal of *Homo economicus* so rare in modern economic reality and so dear to economic theory. In other words, they were not a nation.

The Identity of the Dutch Republic

To some students of the Dutch seventeenth century, this statement may appear surprising, if not absurd. For Simon Schama, the period was "the springtime of [Dutch] nationality," and he claimed the Dutch "nation" as the subject of *The Embarrassment of Riches*. Johan Huizinga, whose "Dutch Civilization in the Seventeenth Century" was the standard text in Dutch culturography before the publication of Schama's resplendent opus, was of the same opinion. Though, in his view, "only fifty years before Rembrandt's birth, there was no Dutch nation," he believed that, after the Union of Utrecht, "there it suddenly was," and his treatment suggests that he considered its existence thereafter as utterly unproblematic. Similarly, Pieter Geyl, the original title of whose *Revolt of the Netherlands* was *The History of the Dutch Race,* insisted that national consciousness and identity existed in the Netherlands even before the Eighty Years' War, inspired and given a distinctive coloration as, in his view, it was by the fact that the dynasty against which the provinces rose "was of alien origin." Like Schama, Geyl considered the revolt to be a struggle for national liberation.

These and similar views are contested. De Vries and van der Woude question the soundness of the very orientation of early modern European historiography, and in particular economic history, to the idea of the nation, and the treatment of the political, national, system, on the one hand, and the economy, on the other, as necessarily coextensive, because "in this theoretical context, the Dutch Republic stands as a great exception." The Dutch economy, they claim, was not "encompassed by the national frontiers," and it is dubious whether it can be "treated as a national economy at all." The Dutch economy was not a single integrated economy: the economic fortunes of various provinces and fifty-seven cities with voting rights within them differed, often dramatically; despite the provisions of the Union of Utrecht, numerous internal tariffs persisted; the competition between the provinces and towns was brutal, cooperation rare and reluctant, and few of them, "least of all Holland, resisted the temptation to discriminate between 'foreign' (i.e. non-provincial) and domestic goods" and interests. Neither was this economy given coherence and direction by the power of a (centralized) territorial state.

The political organization of the Dutch Republic was the very opposite of a centralized state. All real power resided in the provinces and the municipalities; the Generality lacked effective means of coercion and wholly depended on their good will. This is also the point emphasized by Marjolein 't Hart. "It seems misplaced to speak of a strong state or to point to shared national feelings," she writes:

> Israel, Schama, and Wallerstein [who do so] overlooked the contradictions among the multiple mercantile and entrepreneurial factions within the Netherlands. No powerful central institution existed which acted as an arbiter deciding what . . . "vital interests" [of the Republic] should look like, and Dutch policies—although they may have had the appearance of quick-wittedness for outsiders—were determined by continuously changing coalitions of provinces, cities, and factions . . . Bargaining and coalition-making dominated the republican state-machinery. Despite central meetings at The Hague, little of a conscious national feeling emerged. In the end, the Estates General, or Their High Mightinesses, as they came to be called, were composed of delegates of the seven northern provinces. They represented their province first, and the Republic only secondarily . . . With virtually no independent funds for the war against Spain, it was necessary to obtain the willing support of all cities and provinces in order to dispose of the available resources. To secure that support, provinces had to remain sovereign, with autonomous financial institutions.

Yet "that which was administratively and politically fragmented possessed an informal unity based on economic relations." Indeed, Pensionary de Witt argued that "through commonalities, association, and consultation in commercial and other matters . . . the reciprocal possession of property, customs, and other things, they [the provinces] are so fastened to and interwoven with each other that it is almost impossible, except by great violence, to tear them apart." De Vries and van der Woude accept this quasi-Durkheimean argument (a truly Durkheimean argument would stress the fundamental importance of "pre-contractual elements," without which even the most developed division of labor is unable to produce the feeling of solidarity) and state in an evident contradiction to their earlier contention: "The economy was a practical reality before it became a political reality." That is, the Dutch economy preceded the formation of the political—national—framework within which it was supposed to develop. That it was one economy, they claim, is reflected in the consistently high correlations in price fluctuations among the provincial markets, and in the integration of the markets for commodities as well as for capital and labor. At the same time, they emphasize that "in many cases, those strong ties extended far beyond the borders of the Republic." This leads them to conclude, rather despondently (for this conclusion effectively eliminates their subject): "Clearly, the Dutch economy became much larger than its land area and native population could support. But, if this is so, where does one draw the line between the Dutch economy and the European, indeed, the world economy?"[16]

Strictly speaking, the arguments (and supporting evidence) advanced by de Vries and van der Woude and by Marjolein 't Hart do not contradict the position regarding the existence of Dutch nationality, represented by Schama and others, for the two views are predicated on different notions of what nationality is. The former view (that the Dutch of the seventeenth century did not form a nation) is based on the idea that a nation is a type of social formation (or possibly a stage of social evolution) which reflects or is constituted by—to stay within the Durkheimean vocabulary—a very high volume and density of interaction (in turn reflecting an advanced stage in the development of communications and leading to a high degree of division of labor), which volume and density of interaction are significantly, discontinuously, higher than those that characterize interactions between members of the nation with nonmembers. This view belongs within the fold of that sociological structuralism embedded in philosophical materialism which finds its quintessential expression in Marxist economic determinism. In its explicit formulations, the theory of nationalism, reflecting this paradigm (which is only implicit in the claims of de Vries, van der Woude, and 't Hart in regard to Dutch nationhood, since the nationality of the Dutch Republic represents a side issue for these authors), holds that national organization of a society, as well as national consciousness and identity, is a function and a direct accomplishment of the modern—that is, centralized and bureaucratic—territorial state, which is, in turn, a function or a systemic requirement of a particular, capitalistic, stage of economic development. Capitalist economy and centralized territorial state, according to this theory, represent the objective—structural and material—conditions for the development (and at the same time attributes) of the nation, without which the latter is inconceivable. The fact that, in the Dutch case, the requisite economy existed without producing a "modern" state creates a problem for the theory and is an anomaly, if ever there was one, for the structuralist paradigm as a whole. Unfortunately, neither de Vries and van der Woude nor 't Hart ponder the far-reaching, possibly invalidating implications of their findings for the paradigm. Instead, they affirm the absence of the state and deduce from this (assuming the validity of the theory) that any talk of Dutch national consciousness in the seventeenth century can only "impede the clarity of vision." However regrettable, such deductions are perfectly normal for "normal" science.

While de Vries, van der Woude, and 't Hart focus on the structural factors, allegedly representing "objective" conditions and attributes of a nation—the centralized state, the relative degrees of integration within the system and between it and outside elements—Schama, Huizinga, and Geyl choose as their subject cultural factors, both "objective" and subjective, believed to be such conditions and attributes: shared consciousness and a sense of specific Dutch identity. Their understanding of what constitutes a nation is embedded in an approach for obvious reasons more appealing to those who study concrete historical personalities and events than to economic historians and social scientists dealing in general trends and "social forces." But their assumptions are equally untested and, in their own way, equally deterministic and ahistorical. All these authors equate national identity with identity in general (that is, they fail to see the specificity of national identity vis-à-vis other identities) and thus necessarily (even though in Schama's case only implicitly) regard identity as a psychological function or reflection of certain objectively present conditions, such as cultural, linguistic, for Geyl even racial, affinities which unite particular populations in an in effect natural community: the nation. The nation is constituted by such affinities irrespective of the wills of human agents involved; human individuals, in fact, cannot be seen as agents, but only as vehicles for the action of forces behind them. The nation is not a historical construction, reflecting the ideas and choices of these individuals, but, as with determinists of the structuralist-materialist variety, a function of objective realities, in this case language or race. The question of Dutch nationality in the seventeenth century, specifically, becomes one of whether the Dutch Republic constituted an "area of cultural affinity" and whether people in the Republic were aware of such affinity.[17] A positive answer to this question is perfectly consistent with the negative one to the question whether the Republic possessed a centralized bureaucratic state and whether markets within it were significantly better integrated among themselves than with those across its borders. Both these questions, however, are only marginally related to the problem I wish to address here, that is, whether or not the Dutch Republic was a nation. The evidence regarding political and economic integration tells us somewhat more about it (indeed suggesting that in the seventeenth century it was not) than does the information, fascinating as it is, on the cultural affinities between various united provinces and widespread Dutch consciousness, though not for the reasons de Vries, van der Woude, and 't Hart would adduce.

Objectively existing cultural commonalities do not automatically translate into shared identities (as the situation in the former Yugoslavia so poignantly attests), and the absence of such cultural commonalities does not necessarily prevent the formation of a shared identity (as can be well seen in the examples of immigrant nations such as the United States and Australia). An identity, any identity, is not a Pavlovian response to external stimuli, whatever they are. Instead, it is a result of creative interpretation, thus construction, of social reality, which may be in a certain part—but never more than in part—stimulated by an external situation. The character of an identity does not reflect the situation by which it may be inspired; it reflects the creative interpretation of this situation. And because creativity is the capacity to put existing materials to unpredictable uses, because innovations cannot be foreseen, no specific identity can be deduced from or assumed to exist, given certain conditions: it can be ascertained only in retrospect.

An identity represents, in effect, a map of social reality (or a particular slice of reality) for its bearer. It places the bearer in social life and provides the bearer with a set of directions: legitimate actions, legitimate expectations, expectations that others may legitimately have, legitimate reactions to these expectations and attitudes in general. To provide such guidelines in the inherently chaotic, uncharted social world may be called the general function of identity. (This is also the function of the consciousness which corresponds to each identity and reflects a particular image of reality or of a slice of reality. Consciousness and identity, in this context, are complementary concepts, which, depending on the situation, may be used interchangeably.) Every identity represents a particular perspective on reality, and as such focuses on a particular aspect of it, organizing the rest of it around that aspect. As a result, there exist gender, political, territorial (local, regional, continental), occupational, class, ethnic, racial, religious, ideological categories of identities. These categories are distinguished according to the aspect of reality serving as a defining characteristic within an identity, but each one of them allows numerous interpretations of the defining aspect (consider the religious identity of a Christian, a Muslim, and a Jew) and may be ascribed various degrees of importance (for instance, religious identity in sixteenth-century Europe was far more important than the same identity in Europe today).

Communities have one identity at a time, and the change of identity signifies a change in their character, but individuals within them invariably hold numerous identities. These numerous identities are often integrated into systems of identities (though occasionally several identities may coexist independently of one another and even work at cross-purposes; in such cases one talks of a conflict of identities). When several identities are integrated, one serves as the focus and the organizing, defining element of the entire system, and subsumes and overrides the demands of the other identities. This central or "fundamental" identity is the one with the widest area of application: that is, it defines one's place in the social world in general, rather than in any limited sphere of social life, and as a result is believed to define the very essence of its bearer. For much of humanity, for most of human history, the "fundamental" identity was religious identity. One was a Christian first, and a speaker of Dutch, a woman, a merchant, or the subject of a king only second. And it was one's religion that, in principle, defined the community to which one owed supreme allegiance. Today the place of religion is taken by nationality: in the modern world it is considered one's central and essential identity; it prescribes the rules of behavior in the widest variety of social contexts, and it defines the community to which one owes supreme loyalty—the nation. But even today there are exceptions to this rule: there are societies whose identities are not national. In the seventeenth century, however, the exceptions were societies in which national identity existed. National consciousness was a novel—revolutionary—consciousness at the time, and though all existing communities obviously had some identity, only one was redefined (and reconstructed) as a nation for certain: England.

National identity belongs to the political category of identities: it focuses on the political aspect of social reality, namely, on relations of authority, making the community constituted by these relations, a polity defined as a nation, the object of supreme loyalty. This does not imply that the nation necessitates the prior existence of a centralized state; as a matter of historical fact, the state develops as a result of the emergence of national consciousness. What it implies is that national identity and national consciousness redefine specifically the nature of political reality, offer a new image of political order, and thus construct a new political order.

Obviously, not every political identity (or consciousness) is national, as not every religious identity is Christian. Political identities existed long before national identity first emerged: such were, for instance, identities of subjects of kings and of vassals of feudal lords. These identities were, arguably, less important for their bearers than national identity has become, for they were part of the essentially religious system of identities. The image of social order they reflected was dramatically different from that implied in the national identity. This latter image, as defined earlier, is one of an inclusive (that is, embracing all social strata within a population) sovereign community, whose members, despite being stratified, are considered fundamentally equal. It is such a community—a very peculiar community if compared to other social formations—which is defined as a nation.

The general function of identity is to cognitively organize reality, which is inherently disorderly. Different specific identities fulfill this function with different degrees of success and, in doing so, also fulfill different additional functions, which quite often answer needs these identities themselves generate. Religious identities, for instance, provided their bearers with hope which reached far beyond their physical existence and "made suffering sufferable."[18] Rigid status identities, such as those of caste or estate, matched aspirations to probable achievements, expectations to what was possible, and thus saved their bearers from anomic insecurities and made their world stable and predictable. National identity gave up on hope beyond this world (in fact, losing interest in the transcendental realm) and dispensed with stability, opening wide the possibilities for social mobility (fundamental equality of membership in the nation made it silly to stay where one was born if one did not fancy the place). But with the burden of responsibility for one's destiny, and with the anomie which flooded society as the dams of social distinction were burst, nationality brought its bearers a sense of dignity and control over one's own life unknown to most of humanity whose consciousness and identity were different.

The dignity of the national identity—which is a distinctive characteristic of the national experience—lies at the basis of the commitment to the nation, that is, to the common good, among the member population, and specifically contributes to the emotional investment in the dignity of the nation, or national prestige, on which the sense of dignity of individual members is at least in part dependent. It is this commitment and investment, as I argued in the previous chapter, that are of particular importance from the point of view of modern economic history, for it is they that stimulate international competition and explain the reorientation of economic activity toward growth. The general good, and specifically the prestige, of the nation is the ultimate value that justifies, and renders both ethical and rational, the unending striving for ever-increasing wealth.

There was no national consciousness in the Dutch Republic, the identity of the Republican Dutch was not national, and the Republic was not a nation. This is undoubtedly so, despite the fact that Geyl is most certainly right in maintaining that the northern Netherlands in many respects represented an area of cultural affinity, as is Schama in asserting that a "fresh," "special and particular" Dutch "communal identity" did develop during the republican period, or even in claiming that there existed a particular Dutch, republican patriotism. Though the most common patriotism nowadays is national patriotism, the existence of patriotism in general is no proof of underlying national sentiments. Patriotism refers to one's civic commitments and attachments, and widely different sets of such commitments are possible. One can be a patriot of the village where one owns a country house (a local patriot of sorts) and a patriot of the European Community, for instance. These patriotisms are independent from, yet consistent with, national patriotism, but there are ones which are inconsistent with national sentiments altogether. An obvious example is the Christian patriotism of the High Middle Ages, which denoted devotion to the *patrie céleste* to the exclusion of all earthly commitments. The classical patriotism of the polis, though the accepted model of today's national patriotism, is also inconsistent with it, for it presupposes a fundamentally different image of the cosmic and social order.

The Dutch identity and patriotism of the Golden Age were probably of the diffuse nature of today's European identity and patriotism. The Dutch identity had its place among many other equally or more important identities, perhaps modifying some of them to a certain extent; but the consciousness of Dutchness, of participation in the community of the Dutch Republic, clearly was not the element that defined the essence of the individual Hollander or Brabanter from the Generality lands, nor the prism through which one viewed reality. To begin with, whatever the supreme loyalty of such a Hollander or Brabanter was focused on, it was not focused on the Republic. The Republic was an instrumental association of provinces jealous of their separate communal sovereignties, concluded to fight a formidable enemy "whom Brabant, Holland, Zeeland, Flanders, Henegouwe and Artois together would better resist than one land alone."[19] But, unlike the other famous "union concluded by necessity," that of the American colonies, and then the states, it had never developed a presupposition of a natural and indivisible community of destiny on the republican level, whether because such thinking was alien to it or because it simply ran out of time before such a presupposition could emerge.[20]

More important, one cannot, in the case of the Dutch Republic, speak of an investment in the dignity of this common polity and possibly of concern with collective prestige at all. For most of the time, according to Schama, the spokesmen of the Republic "refrained from utterances of sinful pride." Such modesty, he suggests, was "in keeping with the national character," but, apart from the fact that behavior of this nature goes against the very essence of nationalism, it seems rather to reflect the vagueness of existing notions of what this character—whether or not it was national—consisted of. The Dutch, it appears, were uncertain of their political ideals and relied on foreigners to reveal, analyze, and even extol them. In regard to some of these ideals, such as republicanism, it seems, they were for a long time in virtual denial. Not only did they go to some lengths to find a new king for themselves after their relations with Philip of Spain were strained beyond repair, offering sovereign authority over themselves to Elizabeth I, among others. But also, having failed in this monarchist pursuit and reconciled themselves to being a republic (which, E. H. Kossmann argues, was no "moment of triumph for the republican idea but rather one of resigned acceptance of a no longer disputable fact"), they seemed to be embarrassed to be so distinguished among communities presided over by crowned heads and, whether consciously or not, attempted to obfuscate this fact. "Dutch diplomacy," writes Kossmann,

> was generally not eager to underline the republican character of the state it represented. Treaties were made by the States General of the "Vereenighde Nederlantsche Provincien," or the "Vrije Vereenighde Nederlanden," etc. In the text of the treaties the country was often called "this State," "the State of these countries," or even simply "the State." Only in treaties with other republics was the word "republic" used with any regularity. In a treaty with the "Serenissime Republique van Venetien" of 1619 the expressions "both republics" or "this republic and the other one" occur frequently, but the contracting parties were indicated as on the one hand the Republic of Venice and on the other the States General of the United Netherlands Provinces. In the treaty of 1654 ending the first Anglo-Dutch War it is the States General of the United Provinces which make peace with the lord protector of the republic of England, Scotland, and Ireland. Although the text of the treaty contains the expressions also used in the Venetian one ("both republics," "this republic and the other one," etc.), the United Provinces were never called "The Republic of the Netherlands" or "The Dutch Republic."

Only by the second half of the seventeenth century, as the Republic was nearing its decline and as the sense of its "singularity," that is, its separate identity, according to Schama, was already becoming "diluted," was it possible to say that republicanism had clearly "become an integral part of components held to constitute 'Dutch freedom.'"

This "embarrassed self-consciousness," to borrow one more bon mot from Schama's inexhaustible repository, was even more pronounced in regard to another one of the Republic's distinguishing characteristics, which its citizens could justifiably be proud of but were not: its astounding prosperity. Busy amassing their legendary riches, the Dutch of the Golden Age rarely took time to articulate their attitude toward wealth in terms of their general worldview and moral code, but when they did, it appears—on the basis of the evidence presented in such abundance by Schama, among others—that, on the collective level, this attitude was negative. For all the material advantages and power wealth brought, it made the citizens of the world's economic "hegemon" feel uncomfortable. It did not sit well with the emergent Dutch identity: it did not fit the Dutch image of order and rendered precarious the place the Dutch believed the Republic occupied in it. "Wealth," Schama writes, "so far from being the reassuring symptom of the predestined Elect, as Weber argued, acted on contemporary consciences as a moral agitator. Without it the Republic would collapse; with it, the Dutch could fall prey to false gods, Mammon and Baal, and engineer their own downfall."

The separate Dutch communal identity was "fresh" in the sense that it reflected the emergence of a new geopolitical entity: the Dutch Republic. (Its novelty, therefore, was of a nature quite different from the novelty of the national identity in England, France, or any number of other societies which developed this identity later, where it reflected, rather, a new worldview, a new form of social consciousness, and where it thus helped to reconstruct society within the existing geopolitical entities or even create, as in the United States, wholly new geopolitical entities.) But this "fresh" identity was an identity of an old type. As Schama convincingly argues, it was basically a religious, specifically Christian, identity with an appreciable "dusting" of Calvinism, however moderated by the native Erasmian tradition. In other words, the Dutch community was imagined—in a manner fundamentally different from national imagination, which is essentially secular—as an integral part of a transcendental order, responsible to and bound by the rules emanating from a sovereign source beyond this world.

It was a proud religious identity, constituted by a special bond between God and the Dutch community which Calvinists in its midst, at least, believed was His Chosen People. The sign of their collective election was His unremitting attention, itself reflected both in the many ordeals through which the community was put, whether by water or by the Spanish sword, and in its repeated ability to triumph over these formidable foes, which was nothing short of miraculous. God, obviously, had His own reasons for so distinguishing the United Provinces among other of His "children below," and they were far from the hubris of ascribing His choice to their native advantages over these latter or otherwise examining His actions. Instead, they meekly accepted all the blows He dealt them and credited Him with their many victories. In 1668, when in England religion, for all intents and purposes, was already dispatched to the dustbin of history and by no stretch of the imagination could be considered a viable competitor to the vigorous secular spirit, confident of the earthly powers of the nation and willing to recognize no authority outside of it, a certain Jacobus Lydius thus accounted for the achievements of the Dutch in the second Anglo-Dutch War. "When men ask," he wrote, "how the Netherlanders, with such little power, could overcome their enemies on land and destroy them at sea and on so many occasions snatch victory from the jaws of defeat . . . we can only say that this could only have come about through the eternal *covenant* made between God and his children below [*Nederkinderen*]."

The providential purpose of this new Jerusalem was to serve witness to the glory of God, to present a view of "a commonwealth, the most holy and exemplary in all the world because its author and founder was not mortal but immortal God." It was certainly not amassing wealth. The Republic's very success in this enterprise portended disaster. Wealth was temptation, and giving in to it could not but displease the jealous Sovereign watching His *Nederkinderen* from above. Indeed, it was to such displeasure that the preachers who specialized in spelling out this philosophy attributed the natural calamities that befell the Republic with frustrating regularity, as well as its political or military setbacks. Given this general view of reality and the fact that most of the time the Dutch heartily enjoyed their prosperity (thus living in sin), each such event could logically be interpreted as "an outbreak of God's wrath, a rod of punishment for [the inhabitants of the Republic] and for their lust for riches."[21]

Though in the short run a blooming economy appeared to be unaffected by this explicitly antimaterialist *Weltanschauung,* in the long run the implications of the character of Dutch identity on economic development were tremendous. Defined as it was by its special relationship to God, the Dutch Republic as an entity was not economically (or otherwise) competitive. It was not competitive not in the sense that it lacked the capacity to do as well as, or better than, neighboring societies, but in the sense that the idea of these societies as competitors, and of international (to use, for lack of a better term, one which would be an anachronism in application to any seventeenth-century society but England) relations as a race—ideas which to the English mind at the time already appeared self-evident—in the framework of the Dutch consciousness did not make much sense. It was, after all, immortal God, not the aspirations of their mortal members, who placed various societies where they were placed, and His inscrutable will which determined whether any particular society fared better or worse than others, not their efforts. It did not make much sense to suspect the English or the French of malicious designs, entertained by virtue of their being English and French—of which the nationalist English and, to a lesser extent, the French, who were slowly developing national consciousness, constantly suspected the Dutch— simply because these designs could not matter much: *l'homme proposes et Dieu disposes.* When such designs existed as a matter of undeniable fact, they were interpreted as another test to which God wished to submit His chosen *Nederkinderen,* using this or that earthly power as the instrument of His will, and had to be taken in stride.

As a result, while the English and, to a lesser extent, the French heaped abuse on the Dutch Republic for the insufferable offense of becoming the world's most successful economy, the Dutch—at least according to the secondary works which prove their reliability by meticulously recording this one-sided abuse as evidence of Anglo-Dutch or Franco-Dutch competition—did not respond in kind. This was not because the Dutch were made of a different stuff, but because they saw the world differently. It is this difference in perspective, in the nature of identity, that explains, among other things, why every one of the four Anglo-Dutch trade wars was initiated by the English, why there was no counterpart to the Navigation Acts, and why the Dutch rather consistently (though, obviously, not with absolute consistency, which would have required the existence of an economic ideology which they lacked) advocated free trade in the face of perfectly consistent protectionist (or "mercantilist") measures their neighbors directed against them.

The Costs of Economic Liberalism

Not being competitive as a unit, the Dutch Republic lacked the motivation necessary to sustain economic growth over a long period. The Dutch economy, however, was not even in the short run oriented toward growth. This, in the first place, was an implication simply of the lack of a Dutch economic ethic—or collective economic orientation—altogether. The Dutch *conscience collective* was anti-economic; it placed economic activity—activity aimed at the production of wealth as such—outside of the sphere of moral and socially approved conduct, and refused to see any properly economic goal as ethical. It is revealing that the Dutch of the Golden Age contributed virtually nothing to the development of economic thought in general,[22] and nothing at all touching on the problem of growth in particular, and that later "the innovative economic thinking in the Netherlands," according to de Vries and van der Woude, "was not focused on the wellsprings of the 'wealth of nations'; it focused instead on the problem of poverty and its relief . . . Correspondingly, they had little to say about stimulating economic growth, but much to say about reforming poor relief to restore economic and social health." Unlike the present-day United States, for instance, which defines economic health as economic growth and considers social health as inseparable from the economic health so defined, the first society to achieve world economic primacy apparently viewed economic growth and economic and social health as entirely separate and possibly contrary objectives.

But the Dutch collective conscience was vague and for the most part eclipsed by provincial and municipal particularistic identities. If it did not set for the Republic any economic goals worthy of collective effort, it could not act as an effective ethical constraint on economic activity either, and could not deflect its members from economic goals they set themselves. The singularity of the Dutch case—the fact responsible for its not fitting easily either with traditional economies actually controlled by religious ethics or with modern economies oriented by nationalism (which, however, does not at all make it a "transitional" economy)—consisted in the fact that these goals were in effect set in an ethical vacuum.

The Revolt of the Netherlands, which brought into being the Dutch Republic, with its diffuse and socially ineffective common consciousness and identity, also undermined the two institutions which were the main carriers of traditional ethics: the nobility and the church. The social standing of the nobility suffered irreparably as a result of the rebellion for which it provided the leadership. Its representation in the provincial and general estates was drastically reduced as that of the cities grew. And its characteristic values—the ideal of noble (that is, idle) living, the ideal of honor, which implied contempt for money, commerce, and calculation in general, in any case never as influential in this "land of towns" as, for instance, in France, where they served as a bridle on economic development well into the eighteenth century—lost all influence.

At the same time, in keeping with the practice of toleration and the native spirit of "Erasmian evangelism," with its suspicion of the discipline of any church and implicit recognition of "each man's right to follow his own path to perfection," the influence of organized religion was greatly diminished too and limited to certain spheres from which the economy was quite explicitly excluded. The social and political power was left in the hands of urban patriciates, the regents—an economic elite whose status was a function of its members' wealth. This made Republican politics a function of economics, while general economic good was defined in terms of private economic interests. (In this sense the Dutch Republic was more like a giant business conglomerate than a political community.) Economic activity was emancipated from all extraeconomic influences and placed in a unique, improbable situation in which none but the considerations of rational economic actors—the economic individuals of the theory—applied. Private economic interests, as we know, prevailed over the collective political ones even during the war against Spain, and "even to the rejection of the rule that one does not trade with the enemy"—which, incidentally, was approved of by Grotius as implying "the highest degree of reason and profit." Collective dignity was made equally subservient to self-interested economic considerations. This was put starkly by Grotius's near contemporary Pieter de la Court, who in *The Wealth of Leiden* argued against quality control of its textiles by the city, advocated to maintain the reputation of Leiden's products, on the grounds that "for the subsistence of this city and of the merchants in particular reputation is not worth a straw if there is, or will come, no profit of it; for first one has to look for a living and then be reputable."[23] A Wheeler or a Defoe, with their concern for "the whole English name," simply would not have understood this reasoning.

As for the Dutch view of collective economic interest, it was best reflected in the Republic's extraordinary record of foreign investment. That to their nationalist neighbors across the North Sea this view appeared nothing less than unnatural may be gauged from a comment by David Ricardo. Ricardo was a national patriot of recent origin; his father, Abraham Ricardo, a Dutch businessman of Portuguese Jewish descent, moved to London in 1760, joining in the general England-bound exodus of Dutch bankers as the sun was setting on Amsterdam. The irony of this detail of his family history, however, must have been entirely lost on the great economist, who was obviously animated by the spirit of the English nation when, in regard to capital flows, he observed:

> Experience . . . shows that the fancied or real insecurity of capital, when not under the immediate control of its owner, together with the natural disinclination which every man has to quit the country of his birth and connections, and intrust himself, with all his habits fixed, to a strange government and new laws, check the emigration of capital. These feelings, which I should be sorry to see weakened, induce most men of property to be satisfied with a low rate of profits in their own country, rather than seek a more advantageous employment for their wealth in foreign nations.[24]

A *Homo economicus,* motivated solely by self-interest and rational in the sense of strictly economic rationality, however, could not be attracted to profit for profit's sake—which, we are reminded by Weber, "from the point of view of the happiness of, or utility to, the single individual [must appear] entirely transcendental and absolutely irrational"—and thus could not find the idea of economic growth reasonable. A rational economic actor would wish to subordinate economic acquisition to his material needs. He would strive to increase pleasure and decrease pain: eat well, clothe warm, enjoy the comforts of a good home—and spend less rather than more effort in achieving all this. It is precisely this strictly economic rationality that we see reflected in the history of the Dutch economy. There is nothing remotely similar to Weber's this-worldly asceticism in the Dutch culture of the Golden Age. The protagonists of Schama's story were no strangers to addiction, but they certainly were no workaholics. Astute businessmen, quick to perceive new opportunities and to use old structures, unafraid of risks, and with a vision unclouded by the chimeras of a binding collective imagination, they grew very rich salting herring, shipping goods from continent to continent, and blazing financial pathways. But then they discovered a less tiresome way of making money—and as this money was more than enough to satisfy all their wants, they, rationally, turned to clipping coupons. Their rents bled the Republic dry. But what of it? To be bothered by this would be letting in extraeconomic, ethical considerations. And then they would not be rational economic actors.

Dutch capitalism thus was Tawney's kind of capitalism and the capitalism of the reigning disciplinary paradigm, a "conscienceless individualism" uninhibited by moral scruples and social concerns. The Dutch Republic, not England or Britain, most closely corresponds to the theoretical ideal of this thinking. Were its understanding of the wellsprings of modern economy correct, the history of all modern economies would be a replay of Dutch economic history. These economies would not be oriented toward growth and thus would not be capable of sustaining it—and, like de Vries and van der Woude, we would have to redefine modernity. In fact, the Dutch experience is exceptional: the near-perfect economic freedom, the ethical vacuum in which the economy of the Golden Age developed, is a most unlikely occurrence in human history. And it is an exception that proves the rule. It proves the irrelevance of "economic rationality" to sustained growth and the inability of conditions that allow an economy to grow to induce it. Above all, this very successful economy that lacked the spirit of nationalism—a negative case—proves the crucial importance of this spirit for modern economic development.

The Dutch Republic possessed all the conditions for the "take-off" into sustained growth: it was demographically, commercially, financially, and technologically capable of it. It even had the requisite social structure—open and fluid owing to the original weakness of feudalism in the Netherlands and consequences of the Revolt—and thus a "free" labor. It was, to return to Rostowian metaphor, a fine-tuned and well-equipped plane. Had this magnificent economic machine taken off, economic historians would have no difficulty explaining how it did so and what kept it going. But it lacked the reason to do so—the spirit to focus its many strengths on a collective goal and give it direction. And in the absence of this essential intangible, the logic of economic rationality led it to spend these strengths and dissipate the economic energies which its history, improbably, liberated from traditional ideological constrains.

One could say that the Dutch Golden Age was intended as a lesson to obstinate economists who refuse to believe in the importance of spirits. But, as we know, history has no purpose.

II | The Spread of the New Economic Consciousness on the European Continent

3 | The First Convert: France

Where it developed, the new economic consciousness—the competitive and forward-oriented collective spirit of capitalism—followed closely upon the heels of the nascent nationalism. At least, before the twentieth century this was invariably so. In the twentieth century, the economic consciousness has reigned supreme; with the economic sphere presumed to be fundamental, it stands on its own and can spread without being in every particular case grounded in a change of identity and overall social consciousness that this implies. In fact, the only societies which remain impervious to it today are those whose nationalism explicitly rejects the new economic spirit as irrelevant or opposed to the national ideals.

Mercantilism

Before it had achieved its current hegemony and acquired the status of a natural and rational proclivity, the spirit of capitalism needed the support of the broader nationalist spirit and was inconceivable without it. The new economic consciousness, put simply, was the expression of nationalism in the economic sphere: the spirit of capitalism was born as economic nationalism.

The true identity of the infant, which was soon to be revealed as such a prodigy, however, has been long obscured by the name that was given to it some two centuries after its birth, when, for reasons of an accidental connection, first the French Physiocrats and then Adam Smith baptized it the "mercantile system." This name, later shortened to "mercantilism," sharply distinguished between the early spirit of capitalism and its mature incarnation in classical economic thought, at the same time fusing it in the theoretical imagination of many generations of economists with earlier and contemporary forms of consciousness with which it had little in common.

Both the Physiocrats and Adam Smith regarded the focus on commerce as the source of the nation's wealth, and protectionism, as central principles of mercantilism. Both were sharply critical of these principles and considered the English economic policies in the previous two centuries (the sixteenth through the eighteenth) and those of Colbert in France (1661–1683) as chief examples of their implementation. But the meaning they imputed to the term (and their reasons for selecting the name) were, most probably, different. The Physiocrats were newly converted nationalists, which after the Seven Years' War meant Anglophobes, perhaps even greater Anglophobes than other groups of nationalistic philosophes of the time; they resented the English, considering them mean-spirited rather than simply misguided, and were likely to intend any characterization of typical English behavior and thought as a put-down. In a culture which regarded commerce as ignoble, and never so explicitly as in the years when the Physiocrats were writing, labeling the English economy the "mercantile system" fit the bill to perfection: it underscored the baseness of the proponents, as much as any theoretical element of their position. As for Colbert, he was an upstart son of a merchant, never forgiven this mean beginning by the aristocracy and the intellectuals who wanted to be aristocrats, and the Physiocrats blamed him for the disastrous condition of French agriculture in the century following his death.[1]

Though believing the "expedients" of the "mercantile system" to be "mean and malignant," Smith, for his part, was driven by no such animus. "Mercantile system," for him, meant simply the theory of economic behavior which focused on commerce, rather than agriculture or manufacture, as the source of the nation's wealth. He referred to it otherwise as "a system of commerce" and opposed it to the "agricultural system" (among whose modern proponents he included the Physiocrats) as its only historical alternative. Taking Smith as an example in this as in other respects, "classical" economists followed the same principle in identifying their own position as the "industrial system." Since Smith's opinions carried the day, he should be considered at least partly responsible for constructing (the idea of) mercantilism as it exists today.[2]

Smith devoted to the criticism of the "mercantile system" almost the entire book four of *The Wealth of Nations,* clearly regarding it and his own position as mutually exclusive and believing a most comprehensive refutation essential for the success of the right economic principles. He viewed it as the dominant theory of his time, presumably accepted universally (though best understood in Britain) and impossible to dismiss in a short chapter as a plaything of a small sect of intellectuals that has "never been adopted by any nation [and] never has done, [nor was likely to] do any harm in any part of the world," which is what he did with the Physiocrats. Neither would Smith, as in the case of the "agricultural system," recognize that some of its "disagreeable metaphysical arguments" might be compensated by its "liberal and generous" character, the ingenuity of its authors, or any other merit. But while he regarded mercantilism as "the modern system," and while the brunt of his criticism was directed at seventeenth-century English economic thinkers, beginning with Thomas Mun, he traced its origins deep into history, finding signs of it even "where we should least of all expect to find it, in some old Scotch acts of parliament," as well as in all the different nations of Europe.

The errors of mercantilists, in Smith's opinion, were indeed of ancient origin. They proceeded from the mistaken identification of wealth with money and with precious metals from which money was coined. The original form of mercantilism was bullionism, which presented a country's economic objective to be the conservation and augmentation of its stores of silver and gold, and advocated prohibitions on their export. Though some of Smith's seventeenth-century compatriots (among whom he included Locke) subscribed to this primitive notion, he recognized that most of them moved beyond it. The change occurred, Smith argued, when a country became commercial, at which point its merchants found the prohibitions on the exportation of coin "extremely inconvenient [and] remonstrated, therefore, against [it] as hurtful to trade." They claimed, on the one hand, that such exportation might, in fact, increase the quantity of precious metals at home, "because, if the consumption of foreign goods was not thereby increased in the country, those goods might be re-exported to foreign countries, and being there sold for a large profit, might bring back much more treasure than was originally sent out to purchase them . . . [an] operation of foreign trade [comparable] to the seed-time and harvest of agriculture." On the other hand, they also believed that prohibitions could not effectively prevent the exportation of gold and silver in any case, "which on account of the smallness of their bulk in proportion to their value, could easily be smuggled abroad . . . this exportation could only be prevented by a proper attention to, what they called, the balance of trade." Such attention implied an emphasis on foreign commerce as the chief source of the nation's riches, at the expense of domestic commerce, agriculture, and industry, and protection of home industries from foreign competition with the help of tariffs and duties at the expense of the freedom of foreign trade. This change in economic thinking, Smith contended, meant no improvement:

> The attention of government was turned away from guarding against the exportation of gold and silver, to watch over the balance of trade, as the only cause which could occasion any augmentation or diminution of these metals. From one fruitless care it was turned away to another care much more intricate, much more embarrassing, and just equally fruit-

less. The title of Mun's book, England's Treasure in Foreign Trade, became a fundamental maxim in the political economy, not of England only, but of all other commercial countries. The inland or home trade, the most important of all, the trade in which an equal capital affords the greatest revenue, and creates the greatest employment to the people of the country, was considered as subsidiary only to foreign trade.

This should suffice to give one a pretty clear idea as to what views and policies Smith defined as the "mercantile system." It is important to note that he did not object to government intervention as such (under certain conditions, indeed, he advocated it, for instance justifying the Navigation Acts), and that he assumed that the purpose of the mercantilists' efforts was, like his own, to promote the wealth of the nation, understood first and foremost as the prosperity of the people. It was the nature of government intervention which the mercantilists advocated and the way they went about achieving that prosperity that he found unacceptable. His brand of economics was very much a political economy, "a branch of the science of a statesman or legislator," and the "mercantile system" was for him an (erroneous) approach to that—political—science.[3]

Most of the later critics of mercantilism belonged already to the new breed of apolitical economists, and for them "mercantilism" came to stand for a phase in the development of the science of economics—a sovereign perspective focused exclusively on the reified ideal of the rational individual and claiming universal validity and applicability. As such, it was judged in comparison to the, supposedly Smithian, reigning—true—paradigm, which, naturally, held politics to be foreign to the economic domain and for this reason allowed no place for it. The political engagement of mercantilism, whether its reliance on the state or its focus on the wealth of the nation, thus appeared both as a central feature of that superseded, and therefore wrong, theory and as its most egregious sin. This change of perspective affected analyses of economic historians as well, even though they knew better and had to treat mercantilism in its political context. Their definitions followed Smith's as far as the understanding of strictly economic concepts, such as wealth or economic growth, but parted ways when it came to political motivations behind economic process, which Smith took for granted. Thus they also, and with lesser justification, lumped together, as Smith had done implicitly, views and policies informed by completely different visions of reality and people moved by vastly different motives, and helped to further obscure the revolution in economic consciousness occurring in the very period the concept of mercantilism was supposed to illuminate.

That this rendered the concept itself exceedingly vague and unwieldy was clearly recognized. "Mercantilism," Eli Heckscher opened his classic study, "never existed in the sense that Colbert or Cromwell existed. It is only an instrumental concept which, if aptly chosen, should enable us to understand a particular historical period more clearly than we otherwise might." The question of whether it was aptly chosen, however, remained open. In Heckscher's book, the concept was to stand for "a phase in the history of economic policy," which was more easily defined in terms of dates, however approximate, within which it was enclosed ("the time between the Middle Ages and the age of *laissez-faire*"), than substance. Since this definition was not acceptable, Heckscher set out to provide a more meaningful one, which in large part he pieced together from definitions offered by his predecessors. It contained five heterogeneous elements: (1) mercantilism as an agent of unification; (2) mercantilism as a system of power; (3) mercantilism as a protectionist system; (4) mercantilism as a monetary system; and, finally, (5) mercantilism as a conception of society. Of these, the fifth point was supplemented by Heckscher himself; the emphasis on protectionism and monetary doctrine, underscoring the nature of mercantilism as an economic theory, was taken from Adam Smith; and the elements of definition which represented it as a political phenomenon came from Gustav Schmoller (mercantilism as an agent of unification) and from William Cunningham (mercantilism as a system of power.) This broad conception of a generously delimited phase in the history of economic policy, considered in its political and sociophilosophical, as well as strictly economic, aspects, was bound to result, in the hands of such a conscientious and careful historian as Eli Heckscher, in a monumental, comprehensive study, which remains a gold mine of valuable information for anyone interested in anything pertaining to the economic development between the Middle Ages and the age of laissez-faire. But the very breadth of this conception prevented Heckscher from noticing and thus focusing attention on what was arguably the most important aspect of this development: the emergence of a new economic spirit.

It is significant that Schmoller and Cunningham, on whose work Heckscher relied, but who, unlike him, based their views of mercantilism on the experience of, respectively, Germany and England, developed more precise definitions of the phenomenon. For Schmoller, mercantilism was "nothing other than state-formation . . . state-formation in the modern sense of the word, to make the community that forms the state into an economic society and so to give it increased importance." Thus the thrust of mercantilist policies was "the total reconstruction of society and its organization, as well as of the state and its institutions, by substituting for the local and provincial economic policy that of the state and the nation." Writing at about the same time, Cunningham emphasized the motive behind policies he considered mercantilist rather than their effects (indeed, Germany was in greater need of unification, economic and otherwise, than England). This motive was "the patriotic duty of strengthening the nation": "The politicians of the sixteenth, seventeenth and greater part of the eighteenth century were agreed in trying to regulate all commerce and industry, so that the power of England relative to other nations might be promoted."

This was the view of other authors discussing English mercantilism as well. Lawrence Stone saw sixteenth-century English mercantilism as "a system of economic nationalism," and J. W. Horrocks, for whose *Short History of Mercantilism* the English and British variety furnished the central case ("partly because any common tendency of the spirit of nationalism, as of other impelling forces, can be best apprehended from the shape which it has assumed in one's own land, and partly because, independently of that general consideration, from the history of no other country is there to be obtained so clear an understanding of the Mercantile System . . . as that which the British record renders possible"), observed: "Mercantilism has presented an almost invariable association with the growth of national self-consciousness and egotism. It has stood for national power as a necessity for defence and offence, as something to which the economic interests of the people must be subordinated and which they must be made to subserve, and which in its turn must be used to safeguard and advance those interests as distinct from, and even opposed to, those of other peoples. It has stood for economic nationalism or patriotism of the exclusive and aggressive types." And though not every nationalist doctrine in economics, such as, for instance, List's *National System,* included all of the distinctive features of historical mercantilism (as it developed in sixteenth-century England), mercantilism warranted the definition as "a regime of economic nationalism."

If those scholars who studied mercantilism elsewhere disagreed, this was because what stood for mercantilism in England was not what passed for it elsewhere. There was no reality behind the concept; no common principle corresponded to superficial similarities of policy (such as prohibitions, for instance, which have been common to mercantilism and the phases of economic history before and after it). These superficial similarities, significantly, had to do with the understanding of specifically economic realities, for example, the nature of wealth. Horrocks explains why first the bullionist and then the balance-of-trade conception was favored. He writes:

> The later Middle Ages are marked on the one hand by a growth of commerce and spread of money economy, and on the other hand by a dwindling in the supply of the precious metals by which that economy must be supported, and the cities and States of Europe were much concerned to maintain their stock even if they might not hope largely to increase it.

The want and lust of gold and the hope to make or find it played their part in causing debasement of coinage, encouraging the vogue of alchemy, and stimulating exploration. It also influenced the nature of the relations that were being evolved between one country or State and another. Both Aristotle and the canonists had condemned exchanges between individuals where, as they held, one man's gain must mean the other man's loss. The view was now extending that the same principle held good in the commerce of nations and other communities, but it was accepted as a fact without condemnation, and it was felt that as money was urgently needed, care must be taken that the gain, which was estimated in terms of money, should be on the right side. The forbidding of the export of the precious metals was a crude expedient for conserving the country's supply. The devices by which it was sought so to control individual transactions with foreigners that no money should leave the country were more complicated, but still did not rest upon any general idea concerning the country's trade as a whole. But the balance-of-trade doctrine was conceived at any rate as early as the later part of the fourteenth century, and the great influx of precious metals from the west in the sixteenth combined with the expansion of commerce to bring increasingly forward in the policy of States, even where it was not consciously formulated, an idea which connected the procurement of treasure with the proper development and management of foreign trade.

Spain could obtain bullion direct from the mines. But countries with no such resources must obviously get what they wanted by indirect means.

This economic paradigm—a view of relationships ostensibly obtaining in a certain sphere of reality—might have been erroneous, but it was value-free, and as such could coexist with any number of value orientations. The economic policies and "theories" between the Middle Ages and the age of laissez-faire in England, France, Spain, Germany, the Netherlands, and elsewhere in Europe reflected different value orientations, as well as the common view of the economic reality, and this explains the great differences between English, French, Spanish, German, Dutch, and other "mercantilisms." Whether or not the paradigm with which these different value-orientations coexisted was indeed erroneous is for economists to decide. J. M. Keynes believed that the position, rooted in common sense, contained an important "element of scientific truth" and was, instead, critical of the classical school, whose "*theoretical* foundations" he considered inadequate and whose "extraordinary achievement," in his opinion, "was to overcome the beliefs of the 'natural man' and, at the same time, to be wrong."[4] But whatever one thinks is the best way to stimulate home investment and the role rates of interest, liquidity preference, and the quantity of money play in it, from the point of view of the cultural history of economic development (and the question *why* modern economy was born is a question of cultural history), the value orientations corresponding to similar practices make all the difference. Insofar as the motivation of economic actors is concerned, it is one thing when broad sectors of the population become committed to the development of their country's industry, in which they have a vested interest for nationalistic reasons, and quite another when such development is the interest of one powerful minister. And if English economic policies and thought in the sixteenth and seventeenth centuries—routinely recognized as an expression of economic nationalism and reflecting the birth of a new consciousness, a new societal attitude to economic activity—are to be called mercantilism, there seems to be little reason, if any, also to so classify economic policies and thought in those countries where they merely perpetuated traditional practices and habits of thought in different economic conditions or reflected the increasing activism of absolutist governments.

Early Mercantilist France

No example demonstrates better than France, on the one hand, the independence of economic policies and specialized opinion, interpreted as mercantilist, from the general social orientation in the economic sphere and, on the other, the tight connection between the emergence of the modern economy of growth and the change in this orientation under the impact of nationalism. France was the first society to join England in the vanguard of economic development. "England and France," wrote François Crouzet, "were, the one the pioneer of industrial revolution and modern economic growth, the other the first to follow suit."[5] It followed suit, however, only after the "mercantilist" period was already over.

One cannot think of French mercantilism without thinking of Colbert. The minister, wrote Adam Smith, "had unfortunately embraced all the prejudices of the mercantile system, in its nature and essence [of] a system of restraint and regulation." Colbert's "beliefs and efforts so well exemplified the mercantilist tenets that Colbertism has become a synonym for mercantilism." But, though he certainly "gave the new policy coherence, and made mercantilist principles his guiding star," in 1660, when Colbert assumed his responsibilities, the policy had been rather consistently resorted to for more than half a century by the previous administrations of the dynasty he served, and the principles behind it were articulated and debated in French for at least a hundred years.[6]

As elsewhere, the vast majority of the French population had from time immemorial been engaged in economic activity, and, from time to time, those who engaged in it only marginally and had leisure to think gave it some thought. The oldest economic treatise in French, which appeared in the 1450s, already, to some extent, presupposed the mercantilist view of economic reality. Titled *Le Débat des Hérauts d'Armes de France et d'Angleterre*, it must have aimed at reestablishing the self-confidence of France after the hundred years of devastation at the hands of its insular rival, whom at long last the French succeeded in pushing back beyond the Channel. To achieve this aim, the author drew a broad comparison between the two kingdoms, from which France, as could be expected, emerged as the winner. While dwelling on such advantages of his native country as its greater numbers of beautiful maidens, valiant knights, and holy relics, he also devoted attention to its greater economic potential, specifically—and most significantly in the present context—in distant trade.

Though at the time of the writing the French king had no ships with which to ply it, the author of the *Debate* claimed that he had all that was needed to build a large number of them, including vast resources of timber. England, in distinction, was so poor in this respect that its people had to use coal for heat; thus its naval superiority was certain to be short-lived, even beyond the fact that its shipping could easily be undermined by French protective regulations. The herald of England was relatively taciturn, possibly having little to say in response to such overwhelming evidence of French superiority. But among the things he did say was the following boast of England's successful commercial policy:

> There is an ancient ordinance in England that the merchants never carry abroad out of the said kingdom either gold or silver, or very little, but mostly carry goods which they sell for gold and silver, and they bring these to their houses and their kingdom, and thus they sneakingly draw and carry into their houses and kingdom the money of their neighbor countries . . . When foreigners as merchants bring wines or other goods into England, the English let them sell their goods but never tolerate that they take out money, but must by necessity buy the goods which they barter for those of England. It is no wonder that there are great riches of gold and silver in England, for one always brings them thither and is never allowed to take any out.[7]

The French economic consciousness thus already contained some mercantilist ideas in the fifteenth century. Such ideas became widespread in the next hundred years. The economic propositions of the Estates General which assembled in Tours in 1484 were both bullionist and protectionist. The three orders agreed that money was the lifeblood of the body politic and compared the loss of coin in foreign payments to the bleeding and purging of the monarchy. To put a stop to sanguinary depredations of this sort and revive native commerce, the Third Estate recommended abolishing domestic customs and establishing more of them at the frontiers, making life difficult for foreign merchants, prohibiting the importation of silk cloth, taking strong measures against contraband, and employing the royal marine for the protection of the merchant ships. Unfortunately, notes one commentator, hardly had the Tours deputies returned to their homes when the rulers of France, to whom their recommendations were addressed, were diverted by the Italian wars, so that during the Renaissance, amid innovations in every sphere of life, "le *cahier de la marchandise,* si admirablement pensé qu'il fut, était destiné à rester lettre morte." Still, however attenuated, mercantilist ideas persisted and "after the middle of the 16th century the value of a large supply of bullion was an almost axiomatic basis of argument in France. Sometimes explicit, more often not, it colored French economic thought for generations."

The thought that the bullionist considerations colored was that of the administrators responsible for the economic policy of the realm, which explains why these considerations, for the most part, remained implicit—in the edicts they issued and measures they resorted to (frequently for fiscal, rather than properly economic, purposes). Very rarely did economic issues of any kind enter the public discourse: economics was not a subject that preoccupied the otherwise most fertile French mind in the sixteenth century. It is all the more remarkable that one thinker who did address it, however marginally, Jean Bodin, was on the forefront of economic *theory* and far ahead of his time. In a response to a pamphlet presented by a financial official to Charles IX, Bodin in 1568 outlined the quantity theory of money, as well as advancing some precocious free trade opinions in both this work and in his 1576 *Les six livres de la république.* But although his ideas were not "altogether peculiar to him," they clearly failed to engage public attention.[8]

The First Sprouts of Political Economy

One has to wait for the seventeenth century to see the first works in French to focus exclusively on economics. Even then, they remain very few and are, as before, written by and/or for members of the royal bureaucracy. The *Oeconomies royales* of Sully, the trusted minister of Henry IV, the "treatises," pamphlets, and reports of Barthélemy de Laffemas, and the *Traicté de l'oeconomie politique* of Antoine de Montchrétien should be included among these. Only the latter two authors can be characterized as mercantilists.[9] Theirs, however, is an ideal-typical, articulate mercantilism, and, not coincidentally, these two Frenchmen are often singled out as early spokesmen for the doctrine.

The official position of Barthélemy de Laffemas was that of a *valet de chambre* to Henry IV, whom he had loyally served as tailor and Keeper of the

King's Silver in Henry's earlier days as king of Navarre. His responsibilities, obviously, extended far beyond the royal household proper to include the entire royal patrimony, the household—the *economy*[10]—of France. In 1601 Henry formed a commission to examine the commercial propositions of Laffemas, later transforming it into a permanent Council of Commerce, which Augustin Thierry was to call "sorte d'États généraux de l'industrie." Laffemas was appointed its president and Controlleur Général du Commerce, or, in modern American parlance, secretary of commerce. Under his leadership the Council labored to formulate an economic policy that would keep money and augment its stores in France, precious metals being "the nerve and the foundation of kingdoms and monarchies."

As things stood, more treasure was going out of than coming into the kingdom, and the chief reason for that, thought Laffemas, was the decline and poor quality of French manufactures (for which he blamed "the laziness and carelessness of the French") and the willingness of French merchants, moved by self-interest rather than considerations of the common good, to bring goods from abroad. To correct this lamentable state of affairs, he proposed the establishment and regulation of native manufactures, especially silk, and the prohibition of all imports of manufactured goods, "whether it be cloth of gold; of silver; textiles; serges; leathers gilt and tooled, or in the form of gloves, or otherwise; iron; steel; copper; bronze; watches; clocks; and in general all products whatsoever used as furniture, ornaments, and clothing, of whatever quality they may be and for whatever purpose they may be employed." (Interestingly, he excepted from this prohibition *bons livres* and works of art made during or before the reign of Francis I.)

The emphasis of these measures, both positive and negative, was on luxury goods. Love of luxury among the French nobility and the better-off bourgeoisie was also among the factors Laffemas considered responsible for the drain of money out of France. This was a sin that the overwhelming majority of the French population could not afford, but the majority of the French population clearly little interested this early secretary of commerce. Laffemas also wished to involve the impoverished nobility in manufacture and trade, proposing that nobles be forced to grow mulberry trees and advocating special concessions to the glass industry, in which a nobleman could participate without losing status *(sans déroger)*.

There was much opposition to many of Laffemas's propositions, which ran counter to the existing practices and commercial interests. "So that the *grands* and others could know" the truth, he fought it valiantly, in prose, in verse, and occasionally—as in *The treasures and riches of France* [*intended*] *to render the state splendid and show truly the ruin of the French by the traffic and commerce of strangers,* which he finished with a prayer put to music—even resorting to song. He was conscious of the revolutionary implications of his own efforts, and compared himself to Columbus, equally misunderstood before being vindicated by history. Consequently he accused his opponents of selfishness and lack of good sense, branding them "enemies of [both] themselves and of this country," and proposed such means as banishment and confiscation of property, or—if everything else failed—the gallows, to make them see the light.

Laffemas did, however, from the start have the king's ear, and at least some of his suggestions were put into practice and before long bore fruit. This was literally so in the case of mulberry trees, which signaled the beginning of the flourishing silk industry. To set an example for his reluctant subjects, Henry had them planted in all the royal gardens, starting with the Tuileries, and later ordered each diocese in France to establish a nursery of fifty thousand trees and then distribute seeds and seedlings to the clergy, nobility, and common entrepreneurs in the vicinity. Already in 1604 Laffemas had reason to boast of some very impressive achievements, for which the policy he masterminded was responsible. Silk culture was established and manufacture began, saving France "more than six million *écus* each year," which before had had to be "exported" abroad, "without the return of any goods or commodities except musk, perfumes, feminine luxuries and all sorts of poisons of the body and of the spirit." Silk manufacture nevertheless still needed encouragement to prevent the French from buying fabrics "at excessive prices from foreigners." Numerous other manufactures were introduced, including Bologna crepes, Milan gold thread, gilt leather hangings, fine iron products, better steel, white lead, and better lead pipes. In addition, French apprentices were forced upon Italian glassmakers and Flemish tapestry weavers; the silk and wool stocking industry was regulated, a more efficient flour mill introduced, and fishing conditions improved in the Seine.

This was a very distinguished record. A nineteenth-century historian spoke of these years as "a veritable industrial renaissance [for all of France] which manifested itself toward the end of this splendid reign by the least equivocal signs of domestic prosperity." The king took justifiable pride in the improved state of his economy, accounting for it in a manner that was very much in keeping with the original (etymological), as well as mercantilist, managerial understanding of economics. To a foreign ambassador, who marveled at the suddenly flourishing condition of his kingdom, he explained: "Now that the father of the family takes care of his children, they prosper."[11] But Henry IV, an excellent husband in the economic sense of the word, yet one notoriously wanting in conventional matrimonial virtues, was murdered while dreaming of illicit pleasures, and for a long while France was left at the mercy of impersonal economic forces without a hand to guide it and manage them for its sake.

It was Henry's widow and minor son, Louis XIII, to whom Montchrétien addressed and dedicated his *Traicté de l'oeconomie politique* in 1615. The remarkable title of this work, which marks the first time the phrase "political economy" was used, justifies the proud claim of its author's compatriots to the invention of the discipline: the statement that "l'économie politique est née en France" is literally true.[12] In fact, the phrase reflects no alteration in the understanding of economic reality. The idea behind it is the one also captured in the title of Sully's *Oeconomies royales:* the extension of the notion of the private household to the royal/public domain. What changes is the size of the plant, the *oikos,* to be managed, not its nature. Economics, therefore, remains the craft of management. What makes Montchrétien's title appear striking in its historical context is rather the substitution of "political" for "royal," even though the phrase *politia nostra* in reference to France was employed as far back as the fifteenth century.

Montchrétien, as his few biographers agree, was a much more colorful personality than Laffemas. Son of an apothecary, he lived "nobly" by his sword and pen, becoming a playwright of some repute and acquiring the fame of a rogue and a duelist. The most important fact in his biography, in the context of the present discussion, is that, following a duel in which he killed his opponent, he fled to England and spent several years there. It was there that he became interested in economic questions, giving up the notion prevalent in France that such an interest was undignified, and it was upon his return (with King James I, no less, interceding on his behalf) that he wrote the *Traicté*—an ardent plea for royal intervention in the economic development of his native land.

Public utility should preoccupy them above all, Montchrétien instructed his sovereign addressees, and he interpreted public utility in a way which already deviated from the conventional French notion: "Those who are called to the government of states should have their glory, increase, and enrichment as their principal goal." Even though glory and increase in territory came first, the *increase* in wealth was included among the principal responsibilities of the government. Sound politics necessarily comprised an economic element, which, moreover, could be considered fundamental:

> Private vocations make the public. The house is prior to the city; the city to the province; the province to the kingdom. In the same manner, the art of politics depends on the economic . . . for the good domestic government, if well understood, is the teacher and the model of the public.

In making this argument Montchrétien relied on the classics. Aristotle and Xenophon, he reminded their Majesties, were of the opinion that "one could not separate the economy from the polity without dismembering the principal part from the whole, and as the science of acquisition of riches, which they name thus, is common to republics as well as to families." It was therefore the prince's duty to govern, or manage, his realm's economy, specifically by efficiently allocating its resources and assisting his subjects in finding a proper application for their energies, for their activity languished "as if suffocated in the absence of such assistance."

Unfortunately, lamented Montchrétien, France altogether lacked the necessary understanding of the need for management, and, as a result, its resources were squandered:

> This is the reason that so many of our people are forced to seek elsewhere employment and work—some in Spain, some in England, some in Germany, some in Flanders [the politically—and economically—significant others]. How many more, moreover, roam among us, able, robust of body in the flower of their years and health, wandering day and night from one place to another, with no occupation nor permanent roof above their heads, everyone sees this daily with astonishment.

And yet France was a country of infinite riches, and one that could be entirely self-sufficient (or perfectly independent from the economic point of view). Perhaps this was not apparent. "Your majesties possess a great estate," admonished Montchrétien,

> agreeable in its situation, abundant in riches, prolific in people, powerful in good and strong cities, invincible in arms, triumphant in glory . . . France alone can forgo all that she has of the neighboring lands, but none of these lands can do without her. She has infinite riches, known and yet unknown . . . France alone can be [for itself] the whole world . . . [T]he least of the French provinces furnishes your majesties with its crops, its wines, its salt, its cloths, its wool, its iron, its oils, [making the country] richer than all the Perus of the world . . . but of its greatest riches the greatest is the inexhaustible abundance of its people—for one who would know how to manage them.

While its abundant workforce wandered unemployed, foreigners cheated France of all its riches, creating among its citizens a wholly unwarranted sense of dependence. "We ordinarily make greater ado over foreign things than our own, and . . . seek far away that which we have near." "I want to make your Majesties understand," Montchrétien argued passionately, "that France, your one love and your most cherished delight, is full of those fine arts and useful crafts of which the foreigners who practice them like we do, would like forever to cheat us, usurping against all right the native and legitimate industry."[13]

Unlike Laffemas, Montchrétien was fierce in his dislike of foreigners: there is not a trace in his political economy of that cooperative Christian spirit—related to the certainty that God must have had a good reason for making different nations dependent on one another—which moved Bodin to advocate free trade. Foreigners never had the interests of France in mind, and instead were always plotting how to cheat her out of her birthright and render her dependent on them for the necessities of life. They were nothing but

> leeches who attach themselves to this great body, suck out its best blood and gorge themselves with it, then leave the skin and detach themselves. They are ravenous lice who suck its juice and feed to bursting on it but who would leave it if it were dead. To speak clearly and without metaphor, they amass the gold and silver of France and take it away, some to Seville, some to Lisbon, some to London, some to Amsterdam, some to Middleburg. They even use us when they are among us for this purpose, make us as it were the pipes of a fountain, which get no good from the water that they carry and conduct. What more? Since everything must be told, we pay for their feasts and gluttony. It is at our expense that they live so well and regale themselves on such delicacies. We ourselves put the decoy in their hands so that they may lure and entrap us.

Such tirades were more in tune with the English economic writings of the time than French intellectual production of any kind, but, in contrast to English economic nationalists—whose xenophobia was as a rule focused on a particular group of foreigners, fueled exclusively by economic concerns, and represented an occasional rather than chronic condition of the spirit—Montchrétien's sentiment was of a more fundamental and general nature. He did not like foreigners as such, for not being born French. It did not matter to him if they came to France to settle (thus ceasing to be foreigners in the English understanding): the Jews, who had "slipped into France of late," for instance, were contaminating France with their repulsive habits. Originally "so pure, so clean [, it was becoming] a bilge, a sewer, a cesspool for other countries." And Montchrétien was not at all more accepting toward Christians. His judgment was sweeping and unequivocal: "What is foreign corrupts us." He found foreign accents "barbarous," foreign faces "strange." Foreign ideas were poisonous. For this reason, he specifically included books among commodities whose importation he recommended to prohibit. Of course, there were economic reasons too, but Laffemas did not think them sufficient justification for such prohibition. "I do not doubt," wrote Montchrétien,

> that if the importation of foreign books was forbidden the printers and booksellers would soon become rich. And to say frankly what I think, this prohibition could only be for the good and safety both of the rulers

and the subjects [of France]. The foreign teachings poison our minds and corrupt our manners. By them a way has been found to make many of our men degenerate and to seduce them from their legitimate obedience. Bad seed has been sown in the tenderest hearts, and in them has been planted the vine of Sodom and Gomorrah. In short, monsters have been created in France which was undefiled by them before.[14]

Montchrétien's fierce xenophobia reflected his ardent love for France, which, in its intensity as well as character, also reminds one more of the English, rather than the French, political economy of the day. France was as yet unfamiliar with national discourse (French nationalism would hardly be imagined for almost another century and a half), and Montchrétien lacked the vocabulary to express his national patriotism. But though he did not use the new concepts such as "nation" or "people," and his language reflected the classicist preoccupations of his intellectual milieu, the national character of his *amor patriae* is unmistakable. He addressed his treatise to the king and the queen mother, and he had to make all the requisite overtures, but the king was no longer the focus of his loyalty and concern, even though he did constantly speak of their Majesties' glory. This focus was, instead, the *patrie,* which he explicitly separated from the person of the sovereign and in which, by emphatic use of the possessive case, he claimed to share. His motives were revealed in the first sentence of the dedication, where he begged their Majesties to kindly receive "from the hand of those who are devoted to your glory and to the augmentation of their *patrie,* all that God had given them of action, thought, and speech." These are the motives of a citizen of a nation rather than a subject politically defined by his relationship with the prince. Montchrétien admitted that his place was to obey rather than to instruct the prince, the only one with the right to command; but he found justification for his action, which in the France of 1615 must have appeared presumptuous, in the conviction (which reads more like an admonition) that since in any case the general good was the foremost preoccupation of his intended readers, they would look favorably upon any proffer of help in achieving it. It was this conviction, he said, "that led me, first, to write this work and then lay it at the feet of your Majesties with the humblest supplication to receive it as a testimony of my devotion to your service and to the good of my country." Respectful enough but for the last discordantly proud note, which sounds so English.

Not surprisingly, it was the English, the source of Montchrétien's precocious nationalism, whom he singled out as the most pernicious of all foreigners. In manufacture they undermined the French metal industry. (Metalworking was uppermost in Montchrétien's mind among other things because, upon his return from England, he set up a metal workshop, producing scythes, knives, and other tools. Unlike Laffemas, he devoted much less attention to luxury manufactures.) Profiting from the French wars of religion, which tore France apart and arrested her industry, England replaced France as the preeminent metal manufacturer in Europe. It learned the secrets of the craft from French emigrants ("It is to them alone," said Montchrétien, "that she owes the manufacture of all sorts of arms, guns, locks, cutlery") and now was reaping profits which were in truth due to France. The same was true of the woolen industry. Having first learned the craft from the French, the ingrate insularies were now supplying France with their shoddy products (apparently they did not learn well), while French workers went unemployed and had "for the most part to take up another trade or very often to beg for their bread." When some French cloth—of better quality—reached England, it was seized and destroyed. In trade relations, in general, the English behaved despicably. "In a word," Montchrétien summarized their commercial policy vis-à-vis France, "they prohibit all goods as it pleases them and when it pleases them, while on the contrary everything is free for them in France except contraband goods . . . It is not possible to take there a hat, a sword blade, a purse, a belt, a thing which causes great loss to this kingdom." Not that other foreigners, the Dutch and the Flemings, the Spaniards, the Portuguese, were much better. They were all trying (and, lamentably, succeeding) to cheat France of its due, and all were vile Scythians to France's Greece.[15]

To cure all the ills created by foreign scheming and assure France a prosperous economy and superiority in manufacture and commerce, commensurate with its natural riches and dignity, Montchrétien prescribed a perfectly mercantilist remedy. Briefly, sound political economy meant following the English example. Import of foreign manufactures was to be prohibited and domestic manufactures, thus protected from competition, actively supported and their export encouraged. Export of raw materials, however, should be heavily taxed. Not only would such a policy drive away idleness, providing Frenchmen with employment, but it would fully compensate France for the absence of gold and silver mines, fallen as these were by a trick of fate into the unworthy hands of the Spaniards: French-wrought iron would become gold and France's linen industry a mine, forcing Potosi to "disgorge almost all of its silver" for it. Native commerce should be encouraged in general: the interests of the French merchants should be protected, the trade of foreigners in France restricted and made uncomfortable with special taxation. Montchrétien also advocated the development of a powerful French fleet— the merchant marine, the navy, and fishing vessels—and overseas colonization in America, which would add to the riches of France itself by supplying it with needed raw materials and offering new markets for French manufactures. As to the Asian trade, he assured their Majesties, "Asia awaits you and the ocean opens its arms to you." The only thing that was needed was a French East India Company, built on the Dutch and the English model.

In his summary of Montchrétien's ideas, C. W. Cole, a leading authority on French mercantilism, wrote:

> To call the *Traicté* a complete presentation of early mercantilism is not unfair, for in it are lacking only those elements which were to come into prominence later in the seventeenth century. The most notable omission is the failure to develop explicitly the doctrine of the balance of trade. It is present implicitly in most of the measures which Montchrétien advocated, but never in so many words does he urge an excess of exports, over imports, as the chief desideratum. He was, perhaps, a little too skeptical of the ultimate value of gold and silver to be a full-fledged mercantilist, yet for 1615 he was a remarkably good one.[16]

This assessment is fully justified. Still, it was not Montchrétien's economics that made him, in 1615, stand out among his compatriots, but the ideological framework of his presentation—the precociously nationalistic use to which economics was put. He was the only one on the Continent—perhaps in the world—already converted to the new, secular, faith which inspired economic writers in England, and animated by the new spirit which in France, too, would be the spirit of capitalism.

One cannot expect French nationalism, a century and a half before it was to be articulated and even *begin* its conquest, to be as assertive vis-à-vis the traditional image of social order, which it was to replace, as was its fully entrenched English counterpart. Indeed, it was not. Its lack of self-assurance was evident in Montchrétien's attitude to the status of economic activity, the encouragement of which he so passionately urged. He begged their Majesties not to disregard his work for the reason of the meanness of the subject treated in it ("la petitesse des choses qui semblent y êstre traictées"). It was true, he admitted, that "the principles that I propose are not of the most obvious or lofty." But, if developed, he was certain they had the potential to become very imposing. His discourse, Montchrétien argued further, did not at all concern the two upper orders of society, the clergy and the nobility: "these parties [were] delicate" and required direct royal attention. It concerned solely the last, the popular, order. Though it appeared "the most negligible," Montchrétien said, this order, which included the entire French work force, all the millions of Frenchmen engaged in economic activity, was in fact "rather considerable." After all, it formed the base which allowed the upper orders to survive and from which they drew their subsistence. It could be likened to a nourishing spring at which all the rest of society gathered to drink.[17] Economic activity, Montchrétien insisted, was very important, but he made no attempt to present it as dignified. Manufacture and commerce could add to the glory of France, but, as in the colonies, which could do that too and which were to be exploited specifically with this end in mind, there was no dignity in them.

Changing Body—Unchanging Spirit

Yet, it was precisely the dignity with which nationalism invested economic activity (as part of its general redefinition of social stratification) which attracted talent to it in England, and it was the nationalist elevation of the working population (first of all the urban working population, such as merchants and artisans) to the dignity of an elite which ensured the commitment of this population to the nation and the identification of private interests with the public. None of this would happen in France for another century and a half, and, as a result, for another century and a half the old economic orientation—to subsistence, consumption of wealth, and private gain—would persist there. This old orientation coexisted comfortably with the mercantilism of the successive administrations of Richelieu and Mazarin, both of whom, however otherwise engaged, pursued the same sort of policies that would characterize the vigorous mercantilism of Colbert and shared the latter's economic philosophy. Colbert was not a nationalist (and, by implication, not an economic nationalist): he was body and soul dedicated to the service of the absolute king who claimed "l'État c'est moi." He identified his interest with the interest of this king—this state—and for the sake of this king he tried to change the existing economic orientation. He wanted French merchants, whose rapacity and taste for quick profits had cost French foreign trade its reputation, to be guided by considerations of the general good; he wanted French industry, in so many areas nonexistent, to become self-sufficient; he wanted wealthy Frenchmen to risk their fortunes in new ventures at home and abroad, establishing new businesses and settling colonies, unwilling to accept Sully's diagnosis that "the acquisition and maintenance of such conquests are inconsistent with the nature and mentality of the French," who had "neither the perseverance nor the foresight necessary for such things."[18] Unfortunately, the glory of Louis XIV's France was not enough of an incentive for such a dramatic alteration of behavior on the part of his subjects, and despite all of Colbert's efforts—and he spared none—despite his many achievements, the economic spirit did not change.

After his death, Colbert's prodigious contribution to France—to its power and glory—was recognized and honored by the rare epithet "le Grand" and an exquisite funerary monument, the work of Coysevox, in St. Eustache. This was rather a sign of relief than regret, for the minister was not appreciated during his lifetime. He was feared for his power and hated for what he did with it. His selfless motives were misunderstood, attributed to his vile—mercantile—origins. At least one reason for this misunderstanding was that Colbert fought the spirit of the age without having anything to replace it with. He might have been unaware of this. For while the societal orientation to economic activity stubbornly resisted change, economic consciousness now reflected on a rapidly changing economic reality, adapting to it through modification of some old notions and incorporation of some new ones. With England and the Dutch Republic rising to the position of superpowers in the span of one generation on the sheer strength of their economies, threatening France and periodically engaged in wars for economic supremacy before the eyes of a stupefied world which had never before considered commerce a respectable casus belli, money at that time was beginning to be appreciated in France in quite a new way. A certain B.-F. Barrême captured this appreciation—underscoring its recency in the opening line—in the following "éloge de l'argent," perhaps intended as a satire, but too clearly awestruck to carry out this intention successfully:

> L'argent fait aujourd'hui le destin des humains;
> L'argent est une force à laquelle tout céde;
> L'argent sans s'émouvoir pousse les desseins;
> L'argent est aux malheurs un souverain remède;
> L'argent est le pivot des banquiers, des marchands;
> L'argent est le recours des bons et des méchants;
> L'argent est des auteurs le premier des points de vue;
> L'argent est un objet où visent tous les arts;
> L'argent fait traverser les murs et les hasards;
> Et l'argent est l'agent qui fait que tout remue.
> L'argent seul peut changer un misérable sort;
> L'argent est une clef d'une douce puissance;
> L'argent dans le péril nous peut ouvrir le port,
> Parce qu'il charme tout lorsqu'on en fait l'avance.
> Dans ce vaste univers chacun lui fait la cour;
> L'argent tient sous ses lois et l'honneur et l'amour:
> Pour l'honneur et l'amour il brise les obstacles.
> L'argent gagne les coeurs dans un chaste dessein;
> L'argent rend beau le laid et malade le sain,
> Et l'argent en un mot fait presque des miracles.

L'argent a tout pouvoir sur la terre et sur l'onde;
L'argent sauve la vie et délivre des fers;
L'argent ouvre les cieux et ferme les enfers;
L'argent fait tout le bien et tout le mal du monde.[19]

It must have been the shock of discovery and the novelty of the idea that led M. Barrême to such a wild exaggeration of money's powers for both good and evil. It was much more important in his day than it was before, surely, but, in itself, it did not make the world go round, certainly not in the France of Louis XIV, and did not perform miracles. Indeed, many of Colbert's problems derived from the fact that, in trying to put France to work, he could offer only money as a reward.[20]

In his Herculean efforts to reform—and in many areas create—French industry and commerce, Colbert relied mainly on administrative controls by means of edicts and regulations, counting, perhaps, on custom to become second nature, and forced practice, in time, to beget the kind of motivation that was needed to make the French economy flourish. One of his collaborators, though, Jacques Savary, most likely with Colbert's encouragement, tackled the problem of motivation differently, attempting to reeducate French merchants and teach them to think in the way Colbert ordered them to act. With this goal in mind he wrote *Le Parfait Négociant ou Instruction générale pour ce qui regarde le commerce des Marchandises de France et de pays étrangers*. The book enjoyed wide popularity, remaining the essential work of reference in business for more than a century. The first edition appeared in 1675; by 1679 the work had already been reissued with the supplement of *Pareres* (or recommendations on specific matters) in a second edition, dedicated to Colbert; apparently three more appeared before Savary's death in 1690, while the book was also translated into German, Dutch, English, and Italian. The seventh edition, by the author's son Jacques Savary de Bruslons, himself the author of the famous *Dictionary of Commerce*, was published in 1713 and, in turn, reissued again with biographical supplements in 1721, 1757, and 1777. The last edition appeared in the year VIII after the Revolution. This continued popularity suggests that Savary's views resonated with the views of his many readers for the entire period between Louis XIV and Napoleon, but it is especially interesting as an expression of attitudes toward commerce in the immediate entourage of Colbert—where in the seventeenth century they could be expected to be the most sympathetic.

Savary (1622–1690) was born into a family that was originally noble, but which had engaged in commerce since the fifteenth century and, as a result, had lost its former status and the privileges associated with it. Apprenticed to a mercer, he became master of the guild and was apparently successful enough in his business to marry well and soon after that, as was the custom, quit it, which he did at the relatively young age of thirty-six. At this time, with the help of Fouquet, the brilliant Superintendent of Finances, whose downfall was engineered by Colbert, he purchased an "office," with which came a higher status and, possibly, a nobility of some sort, though his lean biography does not mention this. The disgrace of his patron entailed no major perturbations in Savary's comfortable situation, because Colbert, recognizing in his rival's "creature" a kindred spirit, decided to patronize him in turn. The great minister particularly liked Savary's views on the deleterious effects of merchants' self-interest on the state of French commerce. In *Parfait Négociant*, Savary was to write: "Isn't it astonishing and altogether shameful that French merchants could have destroyed and ruined their Levantine trade in cloth, one of the chief French manufactures, by their dishonesty, and all because of the greed for great gains and the desire to make their fortunes by wicked means [and] quickly, and without thinking that this would cost the Nation its reputation[?]" Consequently, Colbert set his new collaborator to work on the Reform Council, which was entrusted with the formulation of "l'ordonnance sur le commerce," to be signed by the king in March 1673, whose official title announced it as "Regulations capable of assuring among the merchants good faith against fraud," though unofficially it was to become "Code Savary."

During his work on the Council, Savary began his *Parfait Négociant*, envisioning it as a "practical commentary on the regulation of commerce." His explicit intention was pedagogical and rather modest: "to lay down the maxims to the youth who would want to enter commerce, so that they could conduct themselves well in their business, and avoid the characteristic misfortune of this profession." He therefore had the interests of future merchants in mind, and not of French commerce, or commerce as a profession in its entirety. The character of his intended audience made it unnecessary for Savary to vaunt the advantages of this profession and insist on its importance. Unlike Wheeler's *Treatise* or, even more appropriately, Defoe's *Complete English Tradesman*, both of which were written for the general public, *Le Parfait Négociant* was not an apology, but a manual. All that Savary had to say regarding his subject's general significance, therefore, could be said in a short preface, barely half a page in length, and it was hardly original. The paragraph bore the title "De la necessité et utilité du commerce," and essentially reproduced Bodin's formulation of the conventional medieval position. "From the manner in which God had arranged things on earth one well sees that he wished to establish unity and compassion among all men, for he imposed a kind of necessity [on them] to always need each other. He did not want that everything necessary for life would be found in one place; and dispersed his gifts so that people would have to trade." God's will was not to be argued with: commerce was a legitimate enterprise, and to state this was to speak enough in its favor.

True, this modest praise of commerce—which sounds cool, to say the least, in comparison with the dithyrambs sung to it at that very time across the Channel—might have appeared to Savary's readers as unusually enthusiastic, for the general attitude to their trade in France was plainly derogatory, even among merchants themselves. In addition, Savary insisted that commerce was not a proper occupation for "dull-witted and stupid" fellows, which was contrary to the common opinion. (French parents apparently considered it the outlet for the least bright of their children in the seventeenth century, notes an economic historian, writing in 1925, as much as in the nineteenth, and perhaps even the twentieth.) Instead, he clarified, it demanded intelligence and rich imagination, as well as a robust physique—to handle heavy packages and endure arduous travel—and an attractive appearance, to appeal to customers. Children who had these important qualities Savary advised to apprentice early, recommending for them an educational program which consisted of writing, arithmetic, bookkeeping, and modern languages, among which, interestingly, he emphasized Italian, Spanish, and German (but not Dutch or English). He also suggested that they read history and travelogues to learn about the customs of the countries in which they might have to trade and the nature of their supply and demand. He did not believe it desirable for a merchant to be too educated, and advised against teaching children who prepared for a career in trade Latin, grammar, rhetoric, or philosophy. What we may call "high culture," he thought, was not conducive and even counter to commerce, and he believed that trade was so little developed in France because culture was developed all too much. Colbert apparently shared his views on the matter, as did, before him, Richelieu. All three probably were right in their assessment, though not for the reasons they adduced. If colleges were attracting better people than trade guilds, this was due to the fact that, while culture in the seventeenth century was rapidly rising in prestige, commerce still had absolutely none.

The social elite—the nobility—professed a decided aversion to trade, firmly convinced that business was undignified and inconsistent with their sense of honor. Savary attempted to argue with this notion. He recommended Italy and England as models. In Italy, he wrote, "the nobility considers commerce an honorable thing, particularly in Genoa, Venice, and Florence, there being numerous gentlemen who own galleys for trade on the Mediterranean sea. In England, commerce is believed to be so respectable that nobles of the highest rank do business in wool and cattle." It was silly, he suggested, for impecunious cadets of French noble families, who depended on the charity of their elder brothers, to fear to dishonor themselves by practicing a profitable trade which would free them from such dependence.

But Savary was not convinced that commerce was in fact honorable enough for the nobility to engage in. It was not altogether dishonorable, and if one had no choice (as in the case of an impecunious cadet), one could practice it without shame, yet this was a somewhat halfhearted recommendation. Indeed, one of the qualities that made commerce a good career choice, in his view, was that success in it could be a way into the nobility. Mercery, for instance, was a business in which Savary had known families who began with five hundred livres and made a fortune enabling their heirs to rise to "the most desirable offices of the Robe [judiciary nobility]." Commerce could, in other words, upgrade one's status. But the corollary of this was that one whose status was already noble degraded oneself by stooping to commerce. Savary could not help admiring this transformative ability of business, even as he regretted it, for he clearly understood and stressed how harmful were its economic effects in France, where all too many successful businessmen abandoned their business the moment it could afford them a letter of nobility. "The moment a merchant in France acquires great wealth in commerce," he wrote, "far be it that his children follow his profession; on the contrary, they enter public offices." That was the reason why wealth in Holland, for example, was so much more productive, and someone just starting a business of his own often had more capital at his disposal than the richest merchant in France about to leave commerce for some prestigious "office."

Savary's feeble attempts to interest the nobility in commerce underscored his low regard for it. For instance, he argued that wholesale commerce had nothing in it that was "mean or abject." The nobility could engage in it without losing their dignity, especially if they did so "en commandité," as backers or silent partners. *Commanditaires,* after all, he wrote, "do not ply commerce and do not but give their money to merchants who, trading under their names, afford them participation in the profits and losses . . . [A]s they take part neither in the purchase nor in the sale of goods, one cannot say that they engage in any servile or plebeian action which could dishonor them . . . [A]ll this does not at all detract from their nobility or their station." In other words, if one did not, in fact, do anything, doing business did not degrade.

Within the wholesale trade, haberdashery, Savary's own former profession, was the most genteel. In it, "the owners of business do not work at all and do not make anything with their hands, unless it is to embellish things which are already wrought and manufactured such as trimming gloves, attaching ribbons to coats and other clothes, and similar decorations." The apprentices in this trade were treated "nobly," "it is being forbidden to them by the statutes to make or manufacture anything, but to embellish as mentioned above." In distinction, other types of trade involved and savored of menial work: there was "something of the mechanical arts about [them]," Savary noted regretfully. And he could not bring himself at all to recommend to the nobility commerce in retail; the nobility never engages in retail trade, he postulated, "because there is something servile in it, while in the wholesale trade there is none but the respectable and the noble."

In comparison to the proudly and increasingly assertive paeans to commerce, in particular, and trading classes, in general, of his English counterparts—beginning with Wheeler, who wrote three quarters of a century before Savary—the humble picture presented by him strikes one as archaic. This premodern character of the *Parfait Négociant* is evident in other respects as well. There is no national, and therefore not much of a competitive, spirit in the book, even though, in accordance with the mercantilist economic doctrine, Savary regarded foreign trade as the most important (indeed, only those engaged in it merited the title of "perfect merchants"). There is no sense of a common undertaking, of working toward the achievement of a general good. The performance of French merchants, which left so much to be desired in every respect, including moral, reflected on France as a whole, and therefore on the king of France, and Savary did his best to help French merchants improve their performance. Nevertheless, it is clear that he saw commerce chiefly, if not exclusively, as a career for certain individuals, not particularly well placed to begin with, rather than a matter of public concern and great social importance, an economic arm of the nation. He had some harsh words to say about foreign merchants with whom the French did business. The Russians, or rather the Muscovites, did not, he said, "inspire confidence." They were proud, disloyal, and treated foreigners badly. They were quite able in matters of commerce, but stubborn, and did not keep their promises. The difficulties of trading with them were exacerbated by interference from the Dutch, whose successful propaganda led Russians to distrust the French, but in this undercutting, unfortunately, they were helped by the French themselves, "qui n'ont pas toujours toute la modération qui serait à souhaiter." The ubiquity of the Dutch was distressing, and Savary, writing three years after Louis XIV's invasion of the Republic, was familiar with Colbert's sentiments toward them: they were the "mortal enemies" of the Sun King. It is probable that he shared in these sentiments. But he did not conceal his admiration for the commercial prowess of this tiny people, who had nothing of their own to sell but some "beurre et fromage," and yet ruled world trade. "There are no better businessmen in all of Europe than [the Dutch]," he said.

Savary's harshest judgment was reserved for the English. "This nation," he wrote of them, "is avaricious and greedy of gain." They were "suspicious and attached to their own interests." The "cruel and barbaric temper of *ces insulaires*" in relation to foreigners, and particularly Frenchmen, was fearsome. Indeed, they treated French merchants very badly, making English trade—the most important for France—oppressively difficult with innumerable exorbitant tariffs and exactions. "One would have well shocked Savary," wrote an early twentieth-century reviewer, "if one suggested to him that England was to become the cradle of free trade. The England of his time, which was the first to build mercantilism into a system and completed it by the Acts of Navigation, aspired to be fully self-sufficient, and made life difficult for foreign merchants." But, then, Savary was critical of his compatriots too, berating them, for instance, for not having a mind for commerce.

Unlike his English contemporaries, and unlike Montchrétien, Savary did not regard patriotism to be a relevant consideration for business. The ethical *maximes* he offered his readers were strictly traditional: "The first thing the apprentices should have on their mind is the love and fear of God, without which God will never bless their work and they will never succeed in their endeavors." Therefore he suggested that, "if they can, they must go to holy mass every day."[21]

The English Challenge and the Quarrel over Commerce

The transformation in the traditional attitudes to commerce, which would result in the reorientation of economic action and the birth of the spirit of capitalism in France, occurred in the eighteenth century. It followed on the heels of the nascent national consciousness, with its dramatic alteration of the entire image of the social order, unmistakably representing an element of it; and, like the development of the national consciousness, it was tortuous and slow, lasting about fifty years. The change first became noticeable around 1750, precisely at the time when national discourse first reached the French public. In 1754 the marquis d'Argenson—to whom we owe, among other things, the famous dictum "laissez faire"—noted, "Never before were the names of Nation and State evoked as often as today. These two words were never pronounced under Louis XIV, and one hardly knew what they meant."[22] As these unfamiliar terms entered polite conversation, crowding out every subject which could not be adapted to accommodate them, the salon society became interested in economic questions, in particular commerce. In 1756 Abbé Coyer, the author of timely essays on the word *patrie* and the nature of the "people," published *La Noblesse commerçante*. He wrote there: "Let no one say anymore that we love only pleasant and frivolous things: The serious and the significant are taking hold of us. Commerce, for some time already, occupies some good pens and a number of readers. If it weren't for our disputes over religion, apparently more necessary, it would become almost the fashion to converse about it. I even heard some courtiers vaunt its advantages."[23]

The rise in the social importance of commerce evidently took place as part and parcel of the ongoing redefinition of French identity. As in many other cases, this redefinition, and the rise of French nationalism, was a response to a crisis in the situation of the French elite—the nobility and the groups aspiring and likely to be ennobled, such as the intellectuals. This elite was suffering from an acute status-inconsistency resulting from its methodical disempowerment at the hands of absolutist rulers, to whose program of centralization the nobility was, not surprisingly, hostile, and impoverishment, which left the elite status of this estate virtually hanging in the air, lacking material support, and increasingly insecure. The redefinition of identity, therefore, was, to begin with, the redefinition of the noble identity—specifically, the position of the nobility vis-à-vis the sovereign (that is, the royal power) and the people. The nobility accomplished it through the redefinition of the nature of sovereignty and the people, importing the idea of the nation from England, and placing itself (as a class) at the apex of the new, national, social pyramid by right of its superior contribution to the well-being of the new social whole. In doing so, it necessarily reinterpreted—and thus reconstructed— the system of social stratification. The egalitarian character of this reconstruction, implicit in nationalism, emboldened and empowered those outside the nobility to carry it further—eventually to the exclusion of the nobility from the national community, which occurred during the Revolution. Initially, however, the redefinition of every other element of French society (whose positions in the system—status, and therefore identity—would change with the change of the system as a whole) was articulated in relation to the nobility. Thus economic discussion in the 1750s focused on the question of noble participation in commerce, and it was this discussion that marked the beginning of the shift in societal attitudes toward economic activity.

Abbé Coyer's *Noblesse commerçante* was not the first work to broach the issue. Marquis de Lassay, who died in 1738, but whose *Réflexions* appeared in 1754, claimed there that "one hears *incessantly* that the nobility should be allowed to engage in commerce." Nevertheless, *Noblesse commerçante* was a major event in French intellectual life, which is to say in the life of the French public—the society of the salons—and produced a storm. It went through four editions within a year of its publication, was praised to the skies by the authoritative *Année littéraire,* and was declared by the *Journal de Trévoux* to be pioneering in its argument, if not the subject, "the work that spawned a flourishing of pamphlets and essays which came to support or to undermine the theory of Coyer." One of his critics—Chevalier d'Arcq, an illegitimate grandson of Louis XIV—attacked him with a brochure pointedly titled *La Noblesse militaire ou le patriote français*. In response, Coyer came out with a development of his original thesis, *Développement et défense du système de la Noblesse Commerçante*. This in turn inspired another series of contributions from its defenders and (mostly) critics. The so-called "querelle" over the *Noblesse commerçante* lasted four years, and after it was quelled, the question was not resolved but continued to trouble the public, in particular intellectuals who were busy rethinking French society.[24]

At the time the debate took place, the commonly held view regarding the relationship between nobility and economic activity was that commerce (which included manufacture, but not local trade in agricultural produce) took away the nobility—"le commerce déroge à la noblesse." This view, it was believed, reflected the law of "dérogeance," which many considered fundamental to the monarchy. In fact, the law was of relatively recent origin, dating back only to a fifteenth-century order of the duke of Brittany and an edict of François I, issued in 1540, and, as Coyer explained, was a temporary military exigency. Moreover, numerous later edicts, beginning with Richelieu's declaration of 1629 and continuously reiterated on such occasions as, for instance, the establishment of the Compagnie des Indes in 1719, qualified this original law, limiting its application only to retail trade, and explicitly excepting from *dérogeance* both wholesale and foreign commerce, as well as manufactures, at least if they were "considerable and greatly useful to the State." In Brittany, even retail trade, legally, no longer carried the penalty of the loss of status; gentlemen practicing it simply "let their nobility sleep" for the time that they engaged in business; when they left it (which it was assumed they would do), they and their families automatically regained all their rights.

All this had no effect on the way the public viewed the matter. Commerce—of whatever kind—was held in very low esteem in France. To prove that its practice did not tarnish noble dignity, Chevalier Eon, writing after the publication of the first series of permissions in 1646, had to develop arguments even longer than the title of his *Commerce honorable ou considérations politiques contenant les motifs de necessité, d'honneur et de profit qui se trouvent à former des compagnies de personnes de toutes conditions pour l'entretien du négoce de mer en France*. They too were to no avail. It is true, the nobility at the court showed lively interest in the Compagnie des Indes orientales, but Colbert was the sole cause of this interest, having recommended it "d'un ton impératif," and it died together with Colbert.

The public opinion was unequivocal, and it was that commerce and nobility were incompatible. No less an authority than Montesquieu, writing in 1748, declared himself in full agreement. "It is contrary to the spirit of commerce," he asserted in *L'Esprit des Lois,* "that the nobility in a monarchical state engage in it . . . It is contrary to the spirit of monarchy that the nobility in it engage in commerce . . . The practice of this country is very wise: its merchants are not nobles, but they may be ennobled . . . [T]hey have no surer means to leave their profession than by practicing it well or practicing it with honor . . . The possibility to purchase nobility with money encourages many merchants to put themselves in the position to do so." Commerce was related to nobility only as a means to an end, and the end was to leave it as soon as one could.

It was this contempt for commerce, for business activity in general, that Coyer set out to undermine in his *Noblesse commerçante.* The front page represented the visual image of the thesis to follow: a nobleman laying down his escutcheon and titles of nobility (with a superscription, "What use is this vain pile of worthless glory?") and welcoming a merchant vessel. The engraving was accompanied by an explanation: "The gentleman whom one sees here, tired of living in poverty and idleness, points to the signs of his nobility . . . the gifts of birth from which he derived no fruit. He rejects them and prepares to set sail in order to serve his country by making himself rich in commerce." It was the good of the nation that was Coyer's main concern, and commerce offered the nobility (at the time, from the national point of view, useless) an opportunity to contribute to it.

Coyer's point of departure was that the French economy—distant trade in particular—was in a bad way, and that a large portion of the nobility was languishing in poverty. The two problems were connected: business earned no respect because the nobility spurned it, and the nobility was poor because it refused to enter business. The nobility had to change its attitude to commerce: this way it would improve its own situation, while at the same time raising the prestige of business activity and helping the economy. Only in the second place did Coyer appeal to the self-interest of the nobility: it had to change its attitude to business for patriotic reasons. It was "for the *patrie*" that he exhorted nobles to become "the nurturers of its lands, the life of the arts, supporters of the population, pillars of the navy, the soul of our colonies, the nerves of the state, and the instrument of the public wealth." Even if much of the nobility was not poor, he declared, "I would still urge it to engage in commerce for the good of commerce itself, that is to say, for the good of France." The fact was that, *recently,* commerce had become "the basis of the greatness of kings and of the happiness of peoples. Commerce ha[d] become *the soul of the political interests and of the balance of power.* It [was] no longer a private business, [but] a service of the State." This was so, among other things, Coyer explained in a vein similar to today's theorists of "state-building," because "money, this tyrant of the world, has extended its empire since the invention of gunpowder and firearms. War has become more an expense of money than an expense of men . . . [O]ne cannot arm without immense sums; and as commerce is the source of riches, all of Europe make it their chief object . . . [*T*]*he balance of commerce and the balance of power are now one and the same thing.*" But French commerce—and therefore French power and prestige—was underdeveloped and deteriorating. By comparison to its former state, it was "much diminished or completely lost"; but in comparison to other nations, its pitiful condition appeared truly unacceptable. Even tiny Holland was doing better than France, and Holland was no longer the great commercial power it had been. It was England that preoccupied those who had the interest of France at heart: "We couldn't take a step in the sphere of commerce without bumping into England: her famous *Navigation Act* puts us at a constant disadvantage in our dealings with her merchants: she has closed to us Portugal; in the Levant, she sits in ambush behind us; there is no part of the world where we are safe from her pursuit." Coyer's equation of economic strength with political power and prestige necessarily introduced into his political economy an element of relativity and therefore made it competitive.

England was already regarded as the chief rival of France in every respect, but for Coyer it remained first of all its chief model. He evoked the example of England incessantly. It served as proof of the importance of commerce for a great nation and of the perfect compatibility between commerce and nobility. The English nobility saw nothing demeaning in business, and the result was that business in England was respected in a way simply inconceivable in France. The consequences of this were plain for everyone to see: no one any longer disputed the supremacy of England in world politics. In addition to presenting the model of the most sensible social attitudes, England was an epitome of sound economic thinking. Coyer was a mercantilist and a firm believer in the principle of balance of trade, but his was a new kind of French mercantilism, far removed from the hands-on ministerial management of Colbert and indeed approaching the English economic nationalism of the time with its insistence on the *liberty of trade* (understood as the liberty of every Englishman to trade). The interpreter of Coyer's economic work, Edgar Depitre, calls this "neo-mercantilism" or "purified commercialism . . . which . . . loudly declares the grand principle that *liberty is the soul of commerce.*" Coyer insisted, "Commerce befits every estate that can make use of it: it is an element as common as air, and it must be as free." This general principle, however, was consistent with demands for "a Navigation Act similar to that which supports England" and prohibitions on the importation of foreign luxury goods (on the familiar grounds that it took money out of France), as well as for the abolition of guilds and other restrictions on business practice in France. The common thread which tied these heterogeneous measures into a system—and lent them authority—was the impressive fact that they worked in England. "England," intoned Coyer, "says to all its navigators, pointing to the colonies: Go and come back to the ports that best serve your interests; France says to but some of hers: Go and come back, but only to the same port from which you left. England allows all its subjects the commerce of the Levant; France allows it only to those from Marseille . . . England offers its manufacturers instruction; France [issues] penal ordinances."[25]

Some of Coyer's critics objected as much to this unending eulogy of England, whose superiority was painfully evident as it was, as to his insistence that lowly merchants were of more use to the nation than the idle nobility (and by implication, unconscionable as it was, deserving of greater respect). The first offense was likely to be interpreted as an expression of Anglomania—a widespread disease of the spirit, an "épidémie philosophique" that afflicted the French *monde* of that generation, which was, unbeknownst to its victims and diagnosticians alike, a common condition of infant nationalism.[26] England was all the rage. "Mature men studied and envied the English laws. Young people would have none but the English horses, jockeys, boots, and coats." "None but the glory of Voltaire," confessed Mlle. de l'Espinasse, "could console me for not being born English." In economics, specifically, every author of note—Vincent de Gournay (the proto-Physiocrat and a friend of Coyer), Secondat, Guy de Malves, Butel-Dumont, Forbonnais—"more or less liberally" translated Child, Tucker, Gee, King, Decker, and Cary. A twentieth-century observer commented: "The sudden taste for commerce . . . was in France one of the forms of Anglomania." One constantly compared the records of the two societies in every area of life, constructing parallel tables of their respective advantages and disadvantages. France did not fare well in these tables.[27]

On the question of nobility and commerce, already de Lassay had complained, "One constantly hears that it should be permitted to the nobility to trade as in England."[28] D'Arcq, who slyly warned the reader he would attack Coyer's propositions "with the zeal of a patriot and the naiveté of a soldier who says what he thinks"—a veritable d'Artagnan opposing Colbert[29]—protested: England was an inappropriate model for France. England was a limited monarchy, which is to say, a republic in disguise. France was a monarchy. It was sensible to wish for a development of commerce in a republic, whose purpose was internal prosperity. But in a monarchy, whose purpose was glory, military glory in the first place, commerce did not play an important political role and was of necessity confined to a secondary rank among concerns of the government. The "military spirit" of the monarchy, reflecting the nobility's sense of honor, was naturally opposed to the commercial "spirit of calculation," informed solely by interest. Moreover, development of commerce obfuscated social distinctions, of which republics were, in any event, intolerant. But monarchy rested on these distinctions; social inequality, "far from being pernicious," d'Arcq maintained, "[was] necessary for its conservation." Participation of the nobility in business activities as in England, however, would break down the barriers between orders of society, ruin "l'inégalité harmonique des classes," and threaten with destruction the monarchical government. The country would become richer, true, but it would lose in every other respect: with honor forgotten and interest ruling the day, there would be no one to protect it from its poorer, but more powerful neighbors. "French nobles," he appealed to his audience, certain of the response, "do you want to become rich? Renounce that luxury that degrades you . . . Your ancestors, your virtues, the services you render to the state—that is your true greatness."

The "harmonious inequality of orders" preoccupied many in mid-eighteenth-century France. D'Alembert of the *Encyclopédie* asked as late as 1779: "Is a great effort of philosophy necessary to understand that . . . especially in a large state, it is indispensable to have rank defined by clear distinctions, that . . . the superiority of birth and position commands our deference and our respect? And how could men of letters envy or misconstrue the so legitimate prerogatives of other estates?"

It was this concern that formed the crux of the matter, "le vrai champ de bataille," in the quarrel over the noble participation in commerce. The disharmony, the breaches, the structural inconsistencies in the system turned the nobility to England and to nationalism for a solution, but nationalism, with its essentially egalitarian, demotic vision of society, destroyed this system altogether. The nobility's ship was sinking, but those on it were still hopeful that the holes in it could be tarred, and resented the vaunting of advantages of the merchant marine. Champions of commerce wished ill the nobility and the social order of which it formed the cornerstone, that is, France as it was: such was the claim, often implicit, of Coyer's numerous critics. And they too invoked England as proof: "The result of all the English policies has been to weaken the nobility by making it easy for its members to become rich, and to lay it low by diminishing the consideration it [had] enjoyed."

This conservative position was a natural, but the least convincing, response to the English challenge. Inherent in the nascent French nationalism, this challenge could not be evaded, or, rather, the only way to evade it was to pretend that it did not exist. England was the source from which France imported the idea of the nation, the new—national—form of its consciousness, and the vision of society to which it corresponded; England, therefore, was by definition a model for France. The moment the French (that is, the French elite, or public) began thinking of themselves as members of a nation—the moment, in other words, they acquired a national identity—their eyes were focused on England; they had to compare themselves to it and try to become like it. When the quarrel over *La Noblesse commerçante* broke out, France was already in the throes of the conceptual revolution, of which the great conflagration of the French Revolution thirty years later was only the most dramatic aftershock; the critics of Coyer—d'Arcq and others—as much as Coyer himself, were already nationalists. However confused about the implications of their new identity (which they, obviously, did not experience as new), they already thought of their society as a *nation,* of themselves as members of this *nation,* first and foremost, and were animated by *national* interests. Thus they were also exposed to the English challenge: obfuscation of social distinctions, commerce, and all. They preferred to deny the relevance of English practices and values: with its "Aristocratico-Democratico-Monarchique" confusion of a government, England was no example for the properly monarchical France.[30]

Anglomanes and the Ennoblement of Commerce

The other responses, probably more prevalent, certainly more influential, eschewed such escapism. They were fundamentally of two kinds. One was to accept English ideals (and therefore the challenge), while also temporarily admitting England's superiority in their implementation, and urge France on to catch up with—and surpass—its model and rival in firm confidence that such catching up and surpassing were neither too difficult nor very time-consuming. This attitude of competitive emulation, inspired as it was by nascent nationalism, was a major stimulant for the development of the contents of French *national* consciousness (and thus national culture and character) and, among other things, was behind the development of the spirit of capitalism in France.

The response of the second kind was to accept English ideals (some of them, as in the other case), while denying their English origins and insisting that English practice systematically contradicted these ideals, which implied defining England as the anti-model. This response reflected a painfully felt sense of national inferiority and resentment (or, rather, *ressentiment,* for it was an existential and continuous experience) against England, in turn related to the lack of confidence in France's ability to compete successfully with its neighbor, and as a rule involved a transvaluation, or reinterpretation, of the appropriated English values. It also exerted considerable influence on the formation of national consciousness—though perhaps less profound, in the long run, than its alternative—and had inspired, specifically, the original theoretical tradition in French economic thought, namely, Physiocracy.

French nationalism, even when fully developed, retained the original ambivalence which reflected the coexistence of these two activist responses to the English challenge and incorporated both of the often contradictory attitudes to which they gave rise. But, in the eighteenth century, the former was more characteristic of the earlier, Anglomaniac, period (until about the Seven Years' War), while the latter characterized the years leading to and during the Revolution, logically identified as the period of "Anglophobia in France." However different in their effects, Anglomania and Anglophobia represented closely connected tendencies in the formation of the French nationality, or the way the French defined themselves as a nation.[31]

The leading Angloman was, unquestionably, Voltaire. England—the first nation and the new superpower, which within living memory had paid court to France but now dictated its will to the world—was bound to capture the imagination of the French public with or without him. Still, it is undeniable that his *Lettres philosophiques* (or *anglaises*) contributed to the sway of Anglomania over French salon society, making the admiration for the English way of life highly respectable, and, to a significant extent, defined the nature of this respectable admiration, focusing it sharply on the great national ideals of liberty and equality.

In this there was something fortuitous. Had Voltaire not been at odds with the authorities in Paris, he might not have arrived in England so clearly prejudiced in its favor, and so eager to rub the nose of French society in its own defectiveness, or might not have traveled to England at all. Had the banker upon whom he had bills of exchange not gone broke, he might never have resorted to the hospitality and become a friend of the kind Mr. Falkener, who happened to be not only a merchant (the sort of company with which few French intellectuals would associate on their own initiative at the time), but also a brother-in-law of Sir Peter Delme, a former mayor of London, and thus a veritable mine of information on economic matters. But, as it happened, Voltaire did travel to England and did write his panegyric to English society with the intention of teaching his countrymen a lesson, and did stay with Mr. Falkener, probably learning more in his company about the English economy than he ever expected. As a consequence, the *Lettres anglaises* contain a letter "On Commerce" which endorsed it in the strongest possible terms, stressing that English superiority in trade and military, especially naval, power were closely related, presenting economic enterprise as an ally of political liberty, and depicting with admiration the dignity of English merchants.

Voltaire wrote:

Commerce, which has brought wealth to the citizenry of England, has helped to make them free, and freedom has developed commerce in its turn. By means of it the nation has grown great; it is commerce that little by little has strengthened the naval forces that make the English the masters of the seas. At present they have nearly two hundred warships. Posterity may learn with some surprise that a little island with nothing of its own but a bit of lead, tin, fuller's earth, and coarse wool, became, by means of its commerce, powerful enough by 1723 [1726] to send three fleets at one time to three different ends of the earth—one to guard Gibraltar, conquered and kept by its arms; another to Portobello to dispossess the King of Spain of the treasures of the Indies; and the third to the Baltic Sea to prevent the Northern Powers from fighting . . .

All this makes the English merchant justly proud, and allows him boldly to compare himself, not without some reason, to a Roman citizen; moreover, the younger brother of a peer of the realm does not scorn to enter the trade . . .

This custom . . . appears monstrous to Germans infatuated with their quarterings. They are unable to imagine how the son of a peer of England could be only a rich and powerful bourgeois, whereas Germany is all Prince: there have been at one time as many as thirty Highnesses of the same name, with nothing to show for it but pride and a coat of arms.

In France anybody who wants to can be a marquis; and whoever arrives in Paris from the remotest part of some province with money to spend and an *ac* or an *ille* at the end of his name, may indulge in such phrases as "a man of my sort," "a man of my rank and quality," and with sovereign eye look down upon a wholesaler. The merchant himself so often hears his profession spoken of disdainfully that he is fool enough to blush. Yet I don't know which is the more useful to a state, a well-powdered lord who knows precisely what time the king gets up in the morning and what time he goes to bed, and who gives himself airs of grandeur while playing the role of slave in a minister's antechamber, or a great merchant who enriches his country, sends orders from his office to Surat and to Cairo, and contributes to the well-being of the world.

Coming from the pen of Voltaire, this brief, incisive essay did perhaps more to raise the prestige of business in the eyes of salon society than anything else in French letters. It was certainly greatly responsible for focusing the attention of the enlightened public on the economy as a foundation of national prestige and an important area of international competition, and thus for adding an economic dimension to French nationalism.

Voltaire's contributions to reforming his country's (anti-) economic spirit—and therefore to the development of modern economy in France—did not end there. His dedication of *Zaire* to "M. Falkener, marchand anglais" undoubtedly exerted some influence as well. It was, in the appreciative words of a British critic, "not only a fitting honor to a deserving friend, but a noteworthy departure from tradition, no French work of art having been dedicated to a simple merchant before." But Voltaire's acceptance of the new spirit coming from England, and his championship of new bases for social status, insouciant of the consequences their adoption would have—inevitably—for the existing regime in France, reflected his easy confidence in the potential of his nation. He could admit with equanimity that the French were "in many things the disciples of England," for he had no doubt at all that they would "end by being equals of [their] masters."[32]

The intellectual legitimation of the interest in business, its inclusion in the national consciousness as a support for liberty and a road to national power and prestige, and, more generally, the endorsement of English values and practices by the "enlightened" sector of the elite, which was dominant, gave a tremendous boost to economic activity in France. It was then that the French commercial classes, the bourgeoisie—so often and so wrongly reviled or belauded by historians as the revolutionary force, but in fact, before the era of nationalism, wholly lacking in the spirit of adventure and resigned to the place of no importance assigned to it in society—accepted "le défi britannique," and "reactive" nationalism could, for the first time, exert that "modernizing" influence to which Rostow attributes "the entire course of European economic history of the 19th century."

Summarizing the vast literature on English and French economic development in the eighteenth century, François Crouzet concludes that, "as regards the global growth of the two economies . . . the growth in average real output and income per head might . . . have been roughly of the same order of magnitude in both countries—and possibly faster in France." Though during the "post-1630 seventeenth century . . . France was clearly outdistanced by England," after 1730 the growth there appears to have been "general and quite fast." For instance, "the value of French foreign trade was by 1715 markedly lower than that of the English, [but] by the eve of the Revolution [it] had reached about the same level." In fact, we learn from Guy Palmade, the volume of French foreign commerce was then four times what it had been in 1715. In some areas of international trade the French actually achieved a dominant position: they were the main suppliers of manufactured goods to Spain and the Spanish American colonies; they wrested from England "most of the entrepôt trade in colonial produce," and French European trade "was growing almost as fast as total trade, certainly faster than that of England with the Continent." Before collapsing in 1793—in the midst of an immense political conflagration—French foreign trade reached a record level, with a value of over a billion francs.

Granted, this was "the most flourishing sector of the French economy."

But in France, as in England, as Crouzet had emphasized, commercial expansion was a strategic factor in the growth of the industry, and, indeed, there was a parallel development in French industrial production, which "increased at much the same pace [as the English] between the early eighteenth century and the French Revolution." There was considerable growth in textiles, including cotton, and in mining and metalworks. Coal production, though obviously at a lower level than in Britain, by the time of the Revolution was growing "very fast": it "seems to have increased," Palmade estimates, "by 700 to 800 percent," while French output of pig iron stood at between 130,000 and 140,000 tons, "as against only 60,000 in England," increasing by 72 percent since the early eighteenth century. "As regards *volume of output*," writes Crouzet, "French industrial performance up to the Revolution compares not unfavorably with the English. France was producing less coal, non-ferrous metals, ships and cotton goods than Britain, but more woollens, linens, and silks, as well as more iron. French total industrial production was appreciably higher than the English, but production per head remained smaller, as it had already been in the seventeenth century." Some industries were adversely affected by the agricultural depression of the 1780s, but "the stagnation of old industries . . . was in part compensated by the fast rise of new industries—cotton in particular, but also coal, iron, glass, and chemical products."

There was a noticeable shift in social attitudes toward economic activity: the nobility was no longer "uninterested in business." The *noblesse d'épée* had a controlling interest in coal mining, and there were many "gentlemen iron-masters and glassmakers." Palmade gives a long list of noble families in business: the duke of Croy, the marquess of Cernay, the Castries, the Solages, the dukes of Humières, of Aumont and of Charost, the count of Artois, the duke of Orléans, Lameth, Gouy d'Arsy, Castellane, Gallifet, Talleyrand, Cardinal de Rohan, and so on. "The fact was that the nobility, and often the highest-ranking nobility, simply because it was wealthy and up-to-date in outlook, did not brush capitalism aside."

Aristocratic participation was most pronounced in the new sectors (perhaps because they did not carry the odium of the *roture*), which were most technologically advanced and grew most rapidly. "On the eve of the Revolution a number of *grands seigneurs* like the Duke of Orleans and the Count of Artois were active in enterprises concerned to introduce English technology into France." Technology, Crouzet asserts, subscribing to a very common view, was "the fundamental difference between the two economies": "Britain was the place where all the basic inventions which created modern industry—the spinning machine, the flying shuttle, the power-loom, the printing drum, the coke furnace, puddling, and most revolutionary of all, the steam engine—were made, perfected and introduced into industry." He regrets the lack of a similar outburst of inventiveness in France, which, given that the French economy was growing at a pace similar to the British (even though it was obviously far behind owing to a much later start), cannot be explained in purely economic terms.

But there was a dramatic upsurge in French technical inventions and innovations which the government—in the spirit of "Colbertism"—encouraged with prizes and pensions, and various voluntary associations, in addition, with dignity that reflected the status of their members, many of whom belonged to exalted nobility. Members of the first such association included twenty scions of the old military nobility—the topmost rung within the aristocracy—not counting four ladies of the same standing, and another nineteen representatives of the powerful *noblesse de robe*. It bore the name of "The Free Society of Emulation for the Encouragement of Inventions Which Tend to Perfect the Application of the Arts and Trades in Imitation of That of London," which requires no commentary. It was founded in 1776 in Paris by Abbé Beaudeau, a Physiocrat. In addition, French businessmen traveled to England to learn, invited English workers and technicians to teach them, and imported English machinery. It is possible that at this stage, very early in the development of both French nationalism and its modern economic consciousness, when essentially everything in French business life was an innovation, French entrepreneurs felt less of an incentive to invent or less interest in native inventions precisely because England was considered the sole and unquestionable authority on all matters of economic importance.

When French inventors turned their attention to industrial technology, the competitive, nationalistic, motive took precedence over economic considerations. In his study of French inventions in the eighteenth century, Shelby McCloy stressed:

> In our own century, due in no small degree to the writings of Karl Marx, a reader might easily jump to the conclusion that the economic motive was paramount. With not a few of the inventors it must have been. It is probable, in fact, that most of them hoped to realize some financial benefit from their inventions. This is far from saying that the hope of economic gain was the paramount motive, or indeed that it was the original driving force. Few inventors benefited appreciably from their inventions; a much greater number squandered their inheritance and savings on their inventive activity. The largest return to most of them was a government pension, usually modest. Some received no reward whatever. As a matter of fact, some inventors were so indifferent to monetary returns that they renounced claim to economic exploitation of their in-

ventions . . . With these men patriotism and humanitarianism burned brightly. Even more brightly burned the desire for achievement and fame; this was the dominant motive of the French inventors. Economic returns were of secondary consideration, and humanitarianism and patriotism were seldom absent.

The same was no doubt true of business activity in general. Nationalism altered the significance of economic pursuits, making them a sphere where one could satisfy one's desire for achievement and fame. Finally—finally—material success did not just afford one some "soap for scum," but furnished a basis for social status. Competition with England elevated the self-effacing French bourgeois to the dignity of his rivals, the respected English merchants who could with good reason compare themselves to Roman citizens, and placed him on a par with other French patriots whose talents contributed to the glory of the nation: the man of letters, the statesman, the military leader. National consciousness—and the new economic consciousness—redefined his daily actions and gave them a nobler purpose. Guided by the spirit of capitalism, the French businessman could confidently wave aside accusations of greed and egoism and take pride in his way of life: he served the *patrie* "by making himself rich in commerce."

As 1789 approached, Crouzet writes, "English industry had a clear superiority, but was only just entering the stage of fast growth and widespread revolutionary changes. France was not disastrously behind, and the Industrial Revolution might have taken off there with only a few years' delay in relation to England. But the 'national catastrophe' which the French Revolution and the twenty years' war meant to the French economy would intensify the discrepancy." There is no doubt that these political events postponed French "take-off," which occurred between 1830 and 1860. Nevertheless, even in these fateful years the French economy experienced no absolute decline. Instead, during the alleged lull between 1789 and 1815, "the change from trade to manufacture proceeded apace . . . Production had certainly increased in general and in the newest sectors it was spectacular. Cast iron production seems almost to have doubled between 1789 and 1796, and almost quadrupled between 1796 and 1811. Production of spun cotton nearly quintupled between 1806 and 1812."

It was also during that period (in 1800) that the Bank of France was established in Paris, aiding in the organization and systematization—at least in the capital city—of the circulation of capital. For one must keep in mind (especially since the present thesis is likely to be accused of not doing so) that the birth of the spirit of capitalism and new economic consciousness could not, in and of itself and thin air, produce advanced economic structures. The lack of this spirit inhibited their emergence in France, and time was needed for their creation. In the eighteenth century, while its development was rapid, the French economy suffered from "a relative scarcity of capital due to insufficient accumulation [which], in turn, aggravated the weaknesses from which it sprang." What one saw in France suggests Palmade, "was a kind of precapitalism, or capitalism in its infancy." The commercial law was archaic. Lending for interest was still frowned upon, defined as usury, and therefore a sin, an attitude explicitly reaffirmed in the Papal Bull *Vix Pervenit* as late as 1745. Far from disregarding such ultramontane instructions, the Parlement under Louis XVI (i.e., several decades later) also condemned "every kind of usury forbiden by canon law." Though then as now astute businessmen found ways around the law, the necessity to do so resulted in certain cumbersome practices: for example, to borrow money, for business as well as for individual needs, one would resort to settlement of an annuity. Credit arrangements were further complicated by the fact that paper money remained uncommon, with transfer of large payments taking the tragicomic form of "carriers bending under the weight of their bulging money-bags, running—in Paris—on the 10th, 20th, and 30th of the month between 10 o'clock in the morning and noon, as if an enemy was about to take the town by surprise." "Such a practice," summed up Louis-Sebastien Mercier, who painted this picture for us, "showed our inability to establish an acceptable and reputable token to replace metal coins."

Historians agree, however, that "requirements of a capitalist system [began to appear] during the feverish years of the reign of Louis XVI [and] Parisian business . . . certainly assumed a new dimension and new vitality." In the late 1770s and 1780s a new group of financiers—including, notably, Swiss descendants of French Huguenots—became active, establishing public companies, such as the Compagnie des Eaux de Paris, the first insurance companies, and, most important, the Caisse d'Escompte—a bankers' bank, which dealt in issue and discount, and was to become the foundation of the Bank of France. (The Compagnie des Eaux de Paris contracted to supply water from the Seine, by means of steam engines, to Parisian homes. Its chief engineers, the brothers Perier, issued a "Prospectus" to attract shareholders and customers, which used an argument that was sure to appeal to the patriotic ambition of the enlightened public. It both began and ended with a comparison between London and Paris highlighting the technical superiority of the English capital and the shameful experience of the French: "Several French citizens, having seen, with a jealous eye, the city of London freshened and supplied with water as plentiful as it is cheap for any private person, and suffering upon their return from finding Paris almost entirely deprived of that element most necessary for the salubrity of the air, the cleanliness of the city, the health and well-being of the citizens," realized the necessity of establishing a similar system at home. The engineers Perier called on their compatriots to sponsor such a system "at long last, its construction, too long neglected [in Paris], being for almost a century, to our shame and before our eyes, so successful in London.")

A period of *agiotage*—speculation on the stock market—followed, unseen in France since the crush of John Law's "Système" sixty years earlier. It was the best game in town and attracted most prominent people. Talleyrand, who was apparently an especially adroit player (Palmade called him "un agioteur-né"), explained the temptation: "J'ai toujours été riche; il faut être riche." "In this way," says Palmade, "Paris experienced a business fever which swept away traditional restrictions." Not less than the first examples of "mammoth industry," these new market structures and atmosphere "bore witness to the birth of a new ethos which seemed to augur an imminent industrial upsurge."[33]

The Économistes

Given its late start, the advances made by French capitalism by the end of the eighteenth century were very impressive. Perhaps it was unrealistic to expect more even in the absence of the Revolution, and its occurrence at the time when the new economy was just coming into its own, its interruption and redirection of every trend of which it was not a direct continuation might have been a sufficient explanation for the fact that the industrial upsurge did not occur then. In no sense was the French Revolution a bourgeois one. Its leaders came from the ranks of the nobility and intellectuals aspiring to be seen as nobility; the origins of some of them may have been within the bourgeoisie, but they did everything within their power to conceal and forget them and felt no solidarity whatsoever with the class they defined as vile and detested all the more for coming from it. The Revolution certainly was not bourgeois, if the bourgeoisie is equated with the capitalist or business class, in the sense we attribute to the term today. The dramatic difference between the two classes is obscured by Marxist periodization, which even those of us who have serious doubts as to the validity of the theory often take as axiomatic (the period of the French Revolution, textbooks teach, was the period of the bourgeois revolution, in which the productive forces of capital burst the fetters of the feudal society), and by the misunderstanding of the nature of social stratification, rooted in Marxist theory. But the fact is that these two classes had nothing in common (or, at least, as little as any two different classes in society): one was docile, interested in security, ashamed of its social position; the other adventurous, achievement-oriented, and self-assertive. Their collective tempers, their interests, outlooks, and styles of life—everything that could characterize them as communities, that is, classes in a meaningful sense—were different. Moreover, in distinction to the bourgeoisie, which was many centuries old, the capitalist class was only emerging in France in the late eighteenth century. It evolved out of the bourgeoisie, it is true, but also out of sectors of the nobility, and, in any case, like other new social groups, such as the intellectuals, it did not cultivate collective memory that would emphasize its genetic lineage; there was a break in continuity. It was a new social construction, a new reality, in fact so new that its members could hardly have been aware of its existence as a class, and it could not, as such, have taken a significant part in the preparation and shaping of the Revolution.

It has been argued—in line with the Marxist view of "objective" or "really real" historical process—that, whatever the bourgeoisie's actual involvement in the Revolution, the Revolution was nevertheless bourgeois, that is, capitalist, for the simple reason that it organized "a new social order in harmony with the ideas as well as with the interests of the victorious bourgeousie," that its "results were favorable to capitalism because they fitted in with the *bourgeois* notion of property and therefore of society." But the results were favorable to capitalism because capitalism was consistent with nationalism, and the Revolution, which owed to nationalism its character, direction, and the very fact of its occurrence (though not timing), established nationalism as the foundation of the social order.

Still, when the industrial upsurge did occur, it was, in some views, less of an achievement than eighteenth-century auguries—or the potential of France, in general—could lead one to expect. France has been called "a perpetual challenger": it never quite made it to the winners' circle; the growth of its economy was sometimes "so slow as to justify the term 'stagnation'"; it was an economic "laggard" and occupied a minor place in the economic world. It is useless to speculate whether, without the Revolution, the situation would have been the same. Some scholars, however, have attributed the relative weaknesses of French capitalism to the deficiencies of French "entrepreneurial psychology," the mentality and social values of its capitalists. Crouzet is unhappy with this argument, claiming that "such observations are primarily descriptive and quite superficial, leaving the differences in the two mentalities [French and English] unaccounted for."[34] The present analysis eliminates this objection: there are weighty reasons for such differences in the nature and process of the formation of French nationalism.

The ambivalence of the French national tradition and the vagaries of its gestation caused the French spirit of capitalism to be born with a serious handicap—or an (economically) evil twin who was the very spirit of anticapitalism. Of the two activist reactions to the English challenge, which together stimulated and shaped the character of emergent French nationalism, the An-glophobe reaction, fueled by *ressentiment,* was more aggressive and appeared more dynamic. In the decade immediately preceding the Revolution, with the desire for reform among the elite becoming ever more urgent and radi-cal, it was this reaction that became dominant. The social philosophy inspired by it denied every claim England might have to superiority in respect to the realization of the ideals—specifically those of liberty, equality, and reason—which France had imported from England and now appropriated, and im-plied a thoroughgoing reinterpretation of these ideals. This reinterpretation, in turn, necessarily affected the views of economic reality and actors, in gen-eral downplaying their significance in social life, and, in particular, rejecting profit-oriented capitalist activities as both useless and immoral.

The traditional contempt of the nobility for industry and commerce was carried on and turned into a veritable phobia in the writings of intellectuals, among whom Rousseau was the most prominent. The ferocity of their vitu-peration against money and men of money—capitalists—would be mind-boggling if their motives for adopting this anticapitalist stance were not so obvious: the intellectuals, as a group, were in the process of self-definition, competing with the men of money for entry into the elite; they needed to distinguish sharply between themselves and this competitor, in many respects better endowed, and make as clear as possible the latter's worthlessness. Thus it is not all that surprising that the views of the radical Rousseau, who was a brilliant casuist, echoed statements of the simple-hearted (on his own testi-mony) conservative Chevalier d'Arcq. Rousseau, too, opposed wealth to the military virtue, writing in *Government of Poland,* "Rich peoples, in point of fact, have always been beaten and taken over by poor peoples," and appealed to the Polish nobility, as d'Arcq did to the French: "Poles, do this for me: let the others have all the money in the world . . . Systems of finance produce ve-nal hearts." As one who had "the knowledge of the human heart," Rousseau assured his eastern European readers that interest in "pecuniary gain [was] the most evil [of all interests], the most vile, the readiest to be corrupted, though also . . . the least important and compelling." His message to the French public, in *The Social Contract,* was similar. "The word *finance,*" Rous-seau asserted there, "is a slavish word." And he confessed, "I hold enforced labor to be less opposed to liberty."

Views such as this made the concept of capitalism odious; though of Dutch origin, it acquired its negative meaning in prerevolutionary France. Louis-Sebastien Mercier's *Tableau de Paris* gave the word "capitalist" as a deroga-tory term currency in French. An 1804 dictionary considered Mercier the in-ventor of this neologism and sought to capture the meaning he attributed to it in its definition. *Capitaliste,* it stated, was a word "known only in Paris, and

. . . describe[d] a monster of wealth who has none but monetary affections [*des affections metalliques*]. When people talk about land taxation the capitalist jeers at them: he has not an inch of land, so how can he be taxed? Like the Arabs of the desert, who, having robbed a passing caravan, would bury their loot, out of fear of being robbed in their turn by other brigands, so our *capitalists* hide away our money." Capitalists were thus monsters and brigands who robbed people of their money and cunningly avoided bearing their share of the common burden of taxation which supported the state. Indeed, they were accused of being unpatriotic: "capitalists," professed Linguet in 1789, "are inspired by love of money rather than love of country." This was a rather general view, propagated, among others, by the Physiocrats. Marquis de Mirabeau, in fact, went further and denied capitalists social sentiment altogether. His opinion was that "stockholders [were] naturally antisocial," with interests opposed to the well-being of humanity: "The capitalist aims for the highest possible interest, a state of affairs which is bound up with public misery."[35]

The opprobium which attached to wealthy men—and this was the most general definition of "capitalist," if one was not a nobleman—by association stained wealth itself. Thus a correspondent of Rousseau would write in self-congratulation, "I am neither a great lord nor a capitalist, I am poor and happy," certain of the master's approval. Being rich, as in earlier times, became a moral disability and reflected discredit upon one's character. The nature of wealth was also redefined, bringing about a profound reinterpretation of political economy. This was mainly the work of the Physiocrats, the first group of men identified as "economists." Though some mercantilists (such as Forbonnais) were still active, the tide in France had been turning against mercantilism for quite some time when the revered father of the school, Quesnay, published his *Tableau Oeconomique,* but the Physiocrats dealt the dominant "system" a death blow in the mind of their compatriots, thereby inaugurating the era (or the rhetoric) of "laisser faire."

It was a curious school, in many respects archaic, which combined the medieval economic vision of its founder—who was, apparently, a deeply believing Catholic and, in social philosophy, a follower of the teachings of Aquinas—with the revolutionary, nationalistic, and essentially modern, radicalism of his disciples, whose contribution to the theory lay entirely in the interpretation and popularization of Quesnay's ideas. The purpose of Physiocracy, stated Mercier de la Rivière, was "the establishment of the natural and essential order," which at the time of his writing, as it seems, existed nowhere in the world, with the possible exception of China, regarded by Quesnay as an ideal. What the natural order looked like was supposed to be established on the basis of its *evidence,* which, paradoxically, struck only particularly perceptive intelligences, fortunately characteristic of the Physiocrats, who were capable of detecting the laws of nature under the thick layer of artificial arrangements that concealed them from the view of ordinary people. The laws of nature were the foundation of the natural rights of men, which, according to Quesnay, could be "vaguely defined as the right[s] which man has to things appropriate for his enjoyment," that is, the rights to things which answered man's natural needs, presumably such as food, clothing, and shelter. The natural economy was an economy based on agriculture. It was the only source of real wealth, in turn defined as things to which man had a natural right. Agriculture, therefore, was the only "productive" sector of the economy, since other sectors, by definition, did not create real wealth. Manufacture served only to earn the subsistence of craftsmen; it was, consequently, "sterile" activity; only in certain conditions, if it employed superfluous agricultural resources, did it augment national wealth. In distinction, most commerce and all finance were not simply sterile but unnatural and, as a result, immoral: they militated against the laws of nature and infringed on man's natural rights.

The annual income of the nation equaled its *produit net*—the yield of the land and its cultivation. This income was to be taxable and thus provide the revenue of the state. It was calculated on the basis of the "just price" at which the agricultural, productive, classes—proprietors and cultivators—offered their products to the consumer, in the "sale from the first hand," under the natural, namely, unrestricted, conditions of exchange. In other words, the price was just and the exchange moral only in a free market. The free market in agricultural goods encouraged competition and increased demand (by bringing in foreign buyers), and this resulted in prosperous agriculture and ensured the wealth of the nation. It was in this context that Quesnay availed himself of d'Argenson's felicitous phrase, advising the king—for *Tableau Oeconomique* was written specifically for Louis XV—to "laisser passer, laisser faire," and urging him not "to govern too much" or fix the prices (of corn), since "only competition can regulate prices with equity."

Direct transactions between producers and consumers of agricultural goods constituted legitimate commerce. When transactions involved merchants, however, their role was legitimate only if they bought from the cultivators their surplus to sell on a foreign market, thereby contributing to the wealth of the nation. In all other cases, merchants' activity represented traffic and was reprehensible. Instead of adding to the wealth of the nation, such merchant-traffickers *(marchands-revendeurs)* wasted it, raising prices above the just level to cover their expenses and secure their profits. Since merchants created no value, the rise in price was not justified, and the productive classes ultimately were left paying the difference. The nation, in effect, grew poorer by the riches of its merchants, whose interests were antithetical to the national interest. Naturally, then, merchants were "strangers in their land," their money knew "neither king nor country," and together they constituted a "universal republic of traders"—a community which was both unnatural and antinational. Therefore, Quesnay recommended establishing a low maximum price on the services of merchants; in services there was to be no free market.

The very same principles that regulated relations between consumers and producers in one country applied to exchanges between countries. There was to be free trade in agricultural produce and manufactures which utilized its surplus; such free trade, which was natural—implied in the very distribution of natural resources in the world—would benefit all the participants, destined as they were to exchange what they had in abundance for what they had in short supply. A country with more plentiful agricultural resources and population was bound to come out of these transactions richer, having a more flourishing economy. For instance, France was bound to become wealthier than England, whose current agricultural superiority was "not in the nature of things." This was so, explained Le Trosne, because "the territorial extent of France is more than double that of England, and the population three times greater. Husbandry is good enough in England itself; it is quite inferior in Scotland and Ireland; and France has provinces as rich as the richest in England." But since all the parties to free international exchanges benefited from them equally (in the sense of satisfying their respective natural needs), there was no justification for a country whose inescapable—natural—fate was to end up poorer to resent its more fortunate neighbor. However important competition was in the agriculture of any one country, the Physiocrats apparently believed competitive spirit had no place in international commerce. Moreover, all policies designed to undermine the preponderance of the naturally wealthier nation were certain to ricochet against the nation which adopted such policies. First, it would not be able to satisfy its natural needs; more important, it would be promoting the selfish pecuniary interests of its necessarily disloyal merchants at the expense of its national interests; finally, aiming to increase its stock of money, it would uselessly dissipate its energies, for money was not real wealth.

Mercantilist policies were not only unsound; they trespassed on the natural rights of man and were immoral. Thus the Physiocrats did not sympathize with England, obviously a victim of its merchants; they condemned it. England in their view was the nation of merchants; mercantilism was in its blood; it was, in its entirety, moved solely by avarice and love of money. It was a country "where not only the colonies, but even the provinces of the metropolis, are subjected to the laws of the carrying trade . . . where the interests of the soil and of the state are subordinated to the interests of the merchants; where commerce in agricultural products, the ownership of the land, and the state itself are regarded merely as accessories of the metropolis, and the metropolis as composed of merchants." In short, it was the domain of capitalism.[36]

Whatever its intrinsic value as a contribution to economic theory—and the doctrine long retained the respect of French economists—Physiocracy performed a valuable psychological service for its audience. Like Rousseau and his followers, it bolstered Anglophobia (which otherwise might appear inspired by envy) with rational and moral arguments, thereby ennobling and legitimating it, and at the same time reassured Anglophobe French nationalists as to the potential of France in economic competition with England, whose superiority it explained away, making it much easier to cope with. Yet, from the point of view of economic growth, this service was probably a disservice, for in developing its peculiar economic liberalism (which, it should be stressed, was combined with most authoritarian ideas in politics and a social philosophy that was essentially aristocratic, and made a travesty of the ideas of liberty and equality) and in redefining the nature of wealth, the Physiocrats perpetuated traditional—pre-mercantilist—attitudes to business activity, discrediting and discouraging precisely those forms of enterprise that were needed to sustain rapid economic growth in France.

How significant the ambivalence of the French national tradition with regard to business was is hard to say, since business in France had very little credit or encouragement before nationalism. But it is certain that this ambivalence retarded the spread, if not the rise, of the spirit of capitalism in France. It slowed down the development of that aggressively competitive mentality which historians found lacking in French "entrepreneurial psychology" and was at least partially responsible for the somewhat disappointing economic performance of France in the nineteenth century.

4 | The Power of Concerted Action: Putting the Spirit of Capitalism to Work in Germany

There are many reasons why Germany deserves attentive study as a case in the history of nationalism, though German national consciousness developed relatively late and the idea of the nation was conspicuously imported from the outside. In the history of *economic* nationalism, however, the country broke new ground and is, therefore, of especial interest. The development of the new economic consciousness—the competitive spirit of capitalism—in both England and France was part and parcel of the development of national consciousness there: the refraction of the principles of nationalism as such and of the type of nationalism emerging in each of these countries, respectively, in the consciousness of the economically active strata and the mind of leading participants in the national redefinition of the community. Economic nationalism was neither more central (in France, clearly, less central) than other elements of nationalism nor more fully articulated; the reorientation of economic action reflected the changed and pervasive image of the entire social order. In distinction, in Germany, economic nationalism, owing to the history of the formation of German national identity, had a privileged cognitive status within national consciousness because it was presented as, and enjoyed the added authority of, a scientific theory. As a result, it was made far more explicit than in either England or France and was backed at first by the universities, the intellectual elite, and an extremely influential group of reform-minded officials within the upper echelons of the bureaucracy, and after the formation of the Zollverein, by the entire apparatus of the Prussian and then German state. Thus it could affect popular attitudes and reorient societal action even before general principles of nationalism became deeply ingrained, and its power—its impact on behavior—was greatly augmented. It is commonplace (so commonplace that it is commonplace to note that it is commonplace) to note that German economic growth, after a relatively late start, was astonishingly rapid, placing the nation, within two generations at most, firmly among the greatest economic powers of the modern world. The ef-

154

ficacy of the overt economic nationalism as a motive force was at least one reason for this spectacular rise, and not the least important one.

The Background: Character and Development of German Nationalism

"Time has had no share in producing industrial Germany," argued the French economic historian Henri Hauser in a somewhat plaintive lecture on German industry as a cause of World War I, delivered before the Société d'Encouragement pour l'Industrie Nationale in 1915; "like nearly everything else in modern Germany it is an upstart." Indeed, half a century earlier, similarly, without a sign of warning or development, German nationalism emerged, full-grown, as if awakened from a deep sleep by Prussia's crushing defeat at the hands of the Revolutionary French. Of course, it was not awakened: nationalisms are not animals that hybernate, and a "sleeping nationalism" is simply nationalism that does not exist. To realize this helps one to appreciate how striking was the appearance of German nationalism on the historical scene. In 1800, in 1805 even, the few Germans who busied themselves with questions of identity were convinced cosmopolitans. Then, as John Clapham eloquently put it, Jena.[1] And by 1810, nationalism—ardent, militant, fiercely particularistic and xenophobic, possessed of all the characteristic features which would distinguish it in Germany—reigned supreme in the heart of every German alert to a civic passion. In 1813 Germany's intellectuals, the idealistic, otherworldly dreamers of a few years before, apolitical and insensible of state borders, rose in the War of Liberation against the foreigner whom so recently they had been eager to welcome as a liberator and with whom they identified, and their enthusiasm roused the country.

The French army gone, it became clear that nationalism had failed to take hold of the people's psyche: the peasantry, the bourgeoisie, and even the nobility of various German lands—the three main classes of the German society—remained largely unstirred by it. Only a small bureaucratic elite and the marginal group of middle-class intellectuals, the "educated bourgeoisie" (Bildungsbürgertum) as they were called in Germany, were fully converted. But the influence of these two groups was enormous and grew as that of the other elites diminished. As professors, journalists, preachers, authors of popular and, significantly, children's literature, the intellectuals found themselves in control of the cognitive formation of their compatriots, with both an opportunity and a will to propagate their views. It so happened that the bureaucrats who shared these views were soon to have the power to back them by decree—a method of persuasion which quickly broke the resistance of those unresponsive to subtler means of indoctrination. The new, united, German nation, therefore, was brought into being in 1871 fully equipped with a robust national spirit, and this spirit was precisely the one born miraculously in the aftershock of the Jena debacle.

Sudden and unexpected as it was, German nationalism did not appear out of nowhere. In fact, every feature of the new image of social reality had been minutely articulated before it was named *national*. What was taken to be a birth of a new consciousness, in other words, was only a baptism. This new consciousness was a creation of German intellectuals and essentially represented a response to the oppressive structural situation—the condition of psychologically intolerable status-inconsistency—in which the educated middle class found itself in the last quarter of the eighteenth century. The status-inconsistency of intellectuals reflected the contradiction between the rigid social structure of German societies—which remained, fundamentally, that of the "society of orders," legally defined and separated from one another and admitting of no social mobility—and the new spirit of the German Enlightenment, the *Aufklärung,* which defined educated reason as a supreme social value and thus an important, if not the only true, basis for high social position, and which in many German lands, and, in particular, in the Prussia of Frederick the Great, had the status of the official ideology. Lured by the promise of Enlightenment, talented young people from the lower classes, the bourgeoisie and the peasantry, flocked to high schools and numerous German universities, where, often at the price of great material hardship and humiliation, they acquired degrees which were supposed to throw the doors of high society open to them—only to find that they were bolted. In the meantime, the schools and universities taught them self-respect, further inflated their social expectations, and developed their sensitivity to indignities with which the status of a commoner was associated in Germany, making a return to their social origins inconceivable. They were caught between the strata from which they came and those to which they wished, but could not, gain admittance, in a society which did not recognize anything between these strata—thousands upon thousands of the most talented, intelligent young men, utterly marginalized, deprived of identity, and often very poor.

For their misery they blamed the promise of Enlightenment, and, as they had all the time and analytical skill to ruminate on it, in their attempt to make their collective situation bearable, they developed a compelling anti-Enlightenment *Weltanschauung,* which was destined to become the framework of the German national consciousness. The original form of this consciousness was Romanticism, which Henri Brunschwig correctly identified as a type of mentality (rather than only a literary or artistic style, which it is, as a rule, erroneously taken to be). In constructing their Romantic *Weltanschauung,* the German intellectuals used two independent traditions—the *Aufklärung* against which it was a reaction, but whose principles, nevertheless, the Romantics internalized in the course of their studies, and Pietism, a mystical, fatalist, and emotional adaptation of Protestant orthodoxy, which in Germany had wide appeal in every social class, to whose teaching many of these unhappy "educated burghers" were exposed before university. The union of these two tacitly contradictory systems of ideas proved remarkably fruitful and produced, among other things, an impressive social philosophy. A detailed analysis of its principles and evolution may be found elsewhere.[2] But, as some of these principles would impact directly the character of economic theory and practice, they must be discussed here.

The central value of the philosophy of the *Aufklärung* was reason, and it was this value that the Romantics turned against. They undermined it with the help of the notions of "totality" and "individuality." These, at first, expressed the contention that reason was not the fundamental faculty of human nature but only one of equally important faculties, and that, specifically, emotion was at least as great a virtue, but ultimately led to the rejection of the value of reason altogether, and its redefinition as an evil. Beginning from a position of cultural relativism (the claim that reason was a cultural rather than universal value, and that irrational cultures were as valuable as rational), Romanticism quickly replaced it with a new—antirational—absolutism (which held that rationalism was a cultural and moral aberration).

Any social entity (a culture as well as a person) was to be judged by the degree to which it expressed the totality of its individuality, that is, its nature. In accordance with the Romantic absolutism, the notion of "totality" was soon defined to refer to the faculties of *human* nature, and individual cultures and people were judged, regardless of their "individuality," according to whether or not they allowed the expression of all human faculties. Then "individuality," too, was reinterpreted and ended up as the very opposite of what it was originally: instead of denoting what was unique about each individual or culture, it now meant that which they all held in common. It followed that cultures (or individuals) which emphasized one quality—for instance, reason—at the expense of others lacked individuality and were incomplete or crippled. This could apply to cultures which overstressed feelings and senses, or to emotional and sensual individuals as much as cultures that put value on reason and individuals who were overly rational. The Romantics, however, confined their verdict to reason alone, exempting everything else from the logical implications of their argument, and condemned reason as the weapon of mutilation, the means of destroying the totality and individuality of human nature, and, therefore, of rendering both societies and men unnatural. In terms that they would bequeath to their followers in the nineteenth and twentieth centuries, they defined it as the instrument of alienation.

The corollary of this in social philosophy was the rejection of the "enlightened" or "modern" society which venerated and institutionalized reason. Though various German societies in which the Romantics developed their theories were, clearly, too "enlightened" for their taste, they saw not Germany but France and (to a lesser extent, at first) England as the representative examples of modernity, and though it was their personal unhappy experience of marginalization in Germany that was reflected in their gloomy social diagnosis, they constructed their theoretical models on the basis of vague ideas they had of these two foreign countries. They believed that rational, modern society constricted human nature, splitting natural, wholesome personalities into one-dimensional shadows of human beings, who were "half-thinkers and half-feelers; moralists who are not doers, epic poets who are not heroes, orators who are not administrators, artistic legislators who are not artists."[3] The division of labor was evidently opposed to the principle of "totality." And where this principle was opposed, man was marginalized and isolated by definition and could not escape alienation. Their own loneliness was a proof of that.

To this cruel and unnatural society Romantics contraposed an ideal image of community, which they believed to be natural, but which was even further removed from any existing society than their abstract model of modernity, for, in distinction to it, the only basis for this ideal image was this abstract model. Nevertheless, it has had a lasting appeal. The original Romantics were aware of the irreality of their ideas, even though they did not sharply distinguish between fantasy and reality, and referred to their ideal community as "the Kingdom of God." Their followers forgot this, and its realization became the goal of many a secular political movement of the nineteenth and twentieth centuries, in Germany and elsewhere. The realization that it was a goal of the Bolshevik Revolution in Russia and of National Socialism helps one to appreciate the grave significance of Romantic broodings, which might otherwise seem esoteric to a businessman or a policy maker.

The social ideal that the Romantics envisioned and of which they thought as the Kingdom of God was that of a totalitarian society. Nobody in it would be isolated and uncertain of one's place, as they were; there would be no private sphere where one would be able to retire from the joys of participation. Of course, no totalitarian society ever existed: societies exerting total control over the lives of each of their members are a practical impossibility, but it is certainly possible to imagine them, and it was in the Romantic spirit to aspire to an unattainable goal. What aided the Romantics in the formulation of this aspiration was a twofold conceptual confusion—itself a mark of their deliberately irrational reasoning—which allowed them to believe that totalitarianism was a natural human condition. They equated "society" as a particular social entity with "society" as social reality in general, and they identified "society" in both senses with a particular state.⁴ The portentous political implications of this conception were articulated by Adam Müller, the political philosopher of Romanticism, who was one of the first and most vehement critics of Adam Smith in Germany.

Müller began with an unproblematic assumption that man was a social being, and that human life, in any meaningful sense, was impossible outside society. Therefore, he concluded without further ado, human nature equaled the state. The next step in his argument, in which pathos substituted for logic, was a claim that being true to one's human nature, or one's universal "individuality" and totality, which was defined not simply as a natural inclination but as a moral imperative, was possible only through the fusion in one's—concrete—state. Man overcame alienation, became whole with himself (and wholesome), and thus an individual, only by letting his self dissolve in his state's higher individuality. It was morally reprehensible to wish to remain oneself; as a punishment one was denied individuality and thus humanity.

The individuality of the state appears to have had a greater reality, certainly greater significance, for the Romantics than that of a human individual. In their imagination, the state became a living, breathing being. Müller intoned: "The state is not a mere factory, a farm, an insurance institution or mercantile society [the reader may surmise what was on his mind when he was saying that], it is the intimate association of all physical and spiritual needs, of the whole physical and spiritual wealth, of the total internal and external life of a nation into a great, energetic, infinitely active and living whole." In a characteristically circular fashion he argued: "If one regards the state as a great individual encompassing all the small individuals, then one understands that human society cannot be conceived except as an august and complete personality."

The purpose of the state, like that of the human individual, was the realization of its individuality and totality. To think that it was a means to the well-being or prosperity of its members was a mistake. Therefore, the Romantics believed the state should be intolerant of self-interest or independence on the part of its members, of "anything which was exempted from its authority," and Müller asked rhetorically (continuing his battle against none other than the alleged father of modern economics): "How is it . . . possible . . . to tolerate . . . a domestic virtue which is entirely opposed to civil virtue . . . an inclination of the heart which is completely antagonistic to external obligations, a science whose work is contrary to all nationality, a religion of indolence, of cowardice and of isolated interest, which completely destroy the energetic spirit of political life?" "This," he thought, "was worse than the state within the state." Created in the image of status-starved intellectuals, states were animated by a "powerful striving for the possession of importance and splendour" and thus naturally competitive. The chief means in this competition were wars, "great institutions for the refinement of the idea," which revealed the "inner destiny of the human race." It was in wars that the individuality and the totality of the state were achieved most effectively.

To this totalitarian idea of the state corresponded equally ominous concepts of liberty, equality, and political leadership. The first of these, obviously, could not be defined in terms of individual freedom, and, in fact, referred to its very opposite. Liberty was the ability to realize one's individuality, that is, to give up one's liberty and subject oneself entirely to the authority of the state. No sacrifice was involved in this, of course, since the state was "nothing but the articulation of the concept of freedom," "that form of reality in which the individual has and enjoys freedom; but on the condition of his recognizing, believing in, and willing that which is common to the Whole." It went without saying that to accept this condition was a moral obligation.

In distinction to liberty, which was drastically redefined but retained as a value, equality was rejected for the sake of inequality. Such rejection was a logical consequence of the original meaning of "individuality"—namely, individuality as what distinguished one individual from others. As a distinguishing characteristic, one's social position was to be cherished, whatever it was, for in attempting to change it one alienated a part of, and sinned against, one's "individuality" and "totality." Interestingly, the very same conclusion in regard to equality was reached when "individuality" was defined as its opposite, what was common to all men. It was Hegel who performed the magic trick that made possible the reconciliation of patently irreconcilable propositions. A person, Hegel claimed, could achieve individuality (in the sense of becoming conscious of one's universality) only as a member of a particular social class, which represented a "specific particularity" where the sense of the general particularity, or individuality of the state, stopped as it trickled down from the higher individual to the lower. It followed that the preservation of social distinctions was imperative.

Equality had no appeal to the *Bildungsbürger* for psychological reasons: they craved status and wanted to be treated as superior, that is, unequal, to the strata from which they came. Their claim to superiority was justified by their intellectual abilities (that reason the value of which they denied), and to support it they developed concepts of "art" and of "genius," which tied these mental powers to "individuality" and "totality," and postulated the natural and sovereign authority of their possessors. The Romantic idea of political leadership also came to rest on the concepts of "art" and "genius." "Artists make mankind an individual," pronounced Friedrich Schlegel, who also advised, in accordance with the early Romantic indifference to politics, that "the artist should have as little desire to rule as to serve. He can only create, do nothing but create, and so help the state only by making rulers and servants, and by exalting politicians and economists into artists." "A true prince," declared his friend Novalis, "is the artist of artists." It was implied in the Romantic concepts of "art" and "genius" that a true artist, who was a genius by definition, was above all law, including the dictates of tradition and reason. By defining political leaders as artists, the Romantics placed them above law as well, and created an authoritarian ideal whose claims to power and obedience were unlimited and extended far beyond those of absolutist kingship even where, as in the case of Prussia's Frederick the Great, it was exceptionally unhampered.[5]

An external event, the victorious advance of the French Revolutionary armies, transformed the Romantic mentality into German nationalism, eventually making it the German mentality. Until the collapse of Prussia in 1806, the idea of the nation, which was by that time long known, had no appeal in Germany. The upper classes, whose discontent was the reason for the development of nationalism in France and Russia, for example, were in Germany perfectly satisfied with their lot, enviable indeed, and the discontented intellectuals, who could have an interest in redefining their community along nationalist lines, were in no position to demand such a redefinition without the support of the nobility and the bureaucracy. Thus they, too, remained indifferent to the radical notions of people as an elite, of popular sovereignty and equality of communal membership, which struck fire in men's hearts and inflamed political imaginations across the Rhein. The French attack, which was directed specifically against the upper classes—the beneficiaries of the "old regime"—alerted them and the intellectuals to the merits of these notions. Identifying the humiliation of the upper classes as a national humiliation justified their appeal to the population for support, placing the latter under an ethical obligation, and offered the intellectuals an opportunity to be of essential, inestimable service to the elite. They were given a sympathetic hearing, and their fraternizing advances—as Germans to Germans, irrespective of social status—were graciously tolerated and for a while perhaps even welcome. Psychologically, at least, they finally gained an entrée to the status to which they had so long aspired, and, with the consent of the powers that be, for the purpose at hand, Germany was declared a nation. It did not matter that, from a geopolitical point of view, its violated body had long been divided between a multitude of sovereign territorial principalities; the lack of a common state framework presented no problem and was not even contemplated. What mattered was that this national redefinition of the disjointed and defunct Empire constructed a community where none had existed and made the French operation—which otherwise might be praised as a not at all unusual but especially adroit exercise in *Realpolitik*, or what some did praise it for, a liberated people's selfless help to one still in bondage—clearly appear as a brazen, criminal, and intolerable aggression.

This transformation of the Romantic mentality into nationalism, however fortuitous, entailed no substantive reconceptualization. France was already seen as the prime example of an unnatural "enlightened" society and as such condemned. Now its revolting enlightenment was attacked as proof—if any was needed—of its inherent criminality. The Kingdom of God was lowered onto earth and made to take up residence in Germany, though in the past or future Germany rather than the one that existed in the present. "Individuality," "totality," all the qualities characteristic of the naturally social man were attributed to the German people. The totalitarian ideal of the state and the corresponding ideals of liberty, equality, and political leadership were made German ideals. The articulation of the national consciousness was left entirely in the hands of the Romantic intellectuals. Obviously, the nationalism they constructed was very different from the English or French nationalisms, but it was nationalism nevertheless, and, as a collective ethic, it was at least as powerful and inspiring.

Economics as Statecraft

Keeping a German House

Originally, the Romantics were oblivious of the economy, though it is revealing that Schlegel thought politicians *and economists* equally deserving of being exalted as artists. Interest in economic questions, which emerged in Germany much later than in England or France, was until the end of the eighteenth century limited to a handful of academics, *Bildungsbürger* for whom education paid off and who were lucky to obtain positions most coveted among aspiring commoners—professorships in territorial universities, which were very few relative to the number of aspirants, even though the universities were many. They were fully conscious of their luck and grateful to Fate, and to the earthly powers representing Fate in Germany, the rulers of the various states. Professors in Germany were civil servants; they knew which hand fed them, and to a degree their preoccupation with economics, which probably attested to a largely disinterested identification with the interest of the masters, could be attributed to the vested interest in making themselves useful and keeping that hand bountiful.

German economic thought developed as a part of the "administrative sciences" or *Kameralwissenschaften* (from *Kammer,* the political cabinet of the prince). The economy was conceived of clearly, more so than in France, as a dimension of political reality and a matter of policy. The idea that it was such a matter derived from two sources, one theoretical, or, rather, doctrinal, the other empirical. Already Erasmus, in the *Institute of a Christian Prince,* which he dedicated to a fellow Hollander, Charles Habsburg, the German emperor, included care and regulation of his subjects' material welfare among the responsibilities of an ideal prince, a *pater familii* on a large scale. Included among the means to assure such material welfare was some advice along the mercantilist lines, for instance, to raise treasure by taxing foreign merchants, which, it seems, Charles was eager to put into practice, though forestalled by the unruly towns and their selfish commercial interests. German Reformers offered the same paternalistic ideal to territorial princes, who were busy dismembering the Empire. The definition of a "foreigner" changed, but the mercantilist—and managerial—tone of practical advice did not. In fact, it became more pronounced, and economic life was placed firmly under princely control.

The empirical factors that drew attention to economic questions came into play later and had to do with the growing fiscal needs of the territorial states, in particular the military expenditure in Prussia, which from the late seventeenth century was increasing dramatically. As in many other areas of German history and thought, which it was beginning to dominate, Prussia provided the most conspicuous example of emerging economic attitudes, and put them in bolder relief than other German principalities, but the approach was characteristic of all the lands and can be discussed as a general phenomenon.

Economic vitality assumed importance as a means to traditional ends of dynastic government: glory and power. Schmoller thought that this was made "perfectly evident" by the 1722 "Political Testament" of Friedrich Wilhelm I, king of Prussia and the father of Frederick the Great. The objective of his entire policy, Schmoller wrote, was "the internal and external strength of the state. For this a good and large army [was] necessary, together with orderly administration; neither [was] possible without flourishing management and much money. And these presuppose[d] an increasing population and flourishing manufactures." The king's son, preparing to assume the reins of power, similarly asserted in *Anti-Machiavel:* "The might of a state does not at all consist in the extent of its lands, nor in the possession of vast wastes or immense deserts, but in the wealth of its inhabitants and in their number. The interest of a prince is thus to populate a country, to make it flourish."[6]

The first works by German authors that addressed economic subjects essentially belabored this theme, providing rationalizations for the inclusion of the economy among the functions of government. The way they went about it reinforced the original managerial aspect of economic discourse and was to leave a profound imprint on the character of German economic culture.

Since the economy was a new field of interest and the discussion of it broke new intellectual ground, the first thing to do, if one wished to be systematic, was to define it, which they did by literally translating *oeconomia* from Greek into German—*Haushaltung*, "keeping house." In contrast to the first English economists, who dispensed with definitions altogether and for two centuries did without a specific term, and in distinction to the French ones, who adopted a transliteration of the Greek word and used the original Aristotelian concept only as a metaphor or a simile (as in Montchrétien's title *Économie politique* and discussions of "économie"), the German authors thus carried the original meaning of the Greek term over and actually identified (rather than compared for heuristic purposes) the head of a state with the head of a family.

This conception gave rise to the so-called *Hausväterliteratur* (the *pater familii* literature), which flourished in the late seventeenth and early eighteenth centuries. Among its titles were *Oeconomus prudens et legalis or the Generally Prudent and Judicious Hausvater* by F. P. Florinus (published in 1702), Becher's *Kluger Haus-Vater* of 1714, and *Teutscher Fürsten-Staat* (The German Princely State) by von Seckendorff, who became the first Chancellor of the University of Halle in 1692. Written in 1656, while he was a state official, this work posthumously earned Seckendorff the name of "the Adam Smith of Cameralism." The "high point" of this primitive stage of Cameralism is considered to be the 1682 work by von Hohberg, *Georgica curiosa*, which he opened with a declaration that *Wirtschaft* or "Oeconomia is nothing else than a prudent carefulness to happily conduct a *Hauswirtschaft*, to direct and to maintain." The German word was chosen advisedly, the root *Wirt* denoting a private or public housekeeper, and the original meaning of the derivative *Wirtschaft* being a "public house" or inn. Three things were necessary to run the *Wirtschaft* properly: God's blessing, "without which nothing of use or good can be done" (in this Hohberg's views were similar to those of his near-contemporary Savary); and a *Hausvater* who would (a) know his resources and (b) have good managerial skills, including "people skills." Some works in this genre were general housekeeping manuals, including house plans, disquisitions on agriculture, and even medical and culinary advice. But, on the whole, it represented a genre of political theory, since the ideal *pater familii* to whom this literature was addressed was the prince. "The ruler," wrote the author of "The Princely Treasure—and Revenue-Cabinet," "is in fact the same as a *Hausvater*, and his subjects are, in respect of their having to be ruled, his children."

The subjects *had to be* ruled for their own good, implying mutual responsibilities on the part of the ruler and the ruled. The problem with the subjects was that they had various material needs, which had to be satisfied if they were to be made useful for the prince, but lacked sufficient acumen and integrity to satisfy these needs on their own. The needs were determined by one's social position, or *Stand,* though, apparently, some (perhaps most) people were unaware of this and desired what they did not need. The state of satisfaction of socially appropriate (*standesmässig* or *standmässig*) needs was called "happiness." The furtherance of popular happiness was the responsibility of the ruler by default, because it could not be left to the devices of lesser men. A foremost representative of Prussian *Aufklärung,* Christian Wolff, explained in his 1721 *Politik:*

> If all possessed the same degree of understanding and virtue, so would each contribute fully and voluntarily to the common welfare [and their happiness], according to his powers and capacities: but unfortunately, since the greater part of mankind possesses little of either, not only does one hinder the happiness of others where he should be furthering it, in part openly and unabashed, in part on the pretext of doing good, that harmful interests might be concealed; but also many, in striving to promote the welfare of the land, fall victim to the evil assaults of ignorance and foolishness.[7]

Happiness was, clearly, a social, rather than an individual, condition—the term denoted as much a good order as an experience of well-being—and thus, given the unreliability of human nature in general, depended on regulation. To achieve happiness, people had to be managed—and such management was government. It was only just that in return for the invaluable contribution the prince made to his subjects' happiness, they were expected to provide him with a sufficient tax base and, in general, the material means for the realization of his goals: the internal and external strength of the state.

"Cameral Sciences" as an Academic Discipline

In the first decades of the eighteenth century the *Hausväterliteratur,* whose authors were, by and large, administrators, was taken over by academics, and consequently replaced by a closely related genre, the focus of which was on the need and means to train future administrators for the service in the prince's *Kammer.* This literature argued for the desirability of the state's having professors able to contribute to or teach it; it was implicitly self-promoting, which may explain the growing interest in its subject in academic circles, reflected in the increasing production of publications. In the attempt to persuade their audience—that is, territorial rulers—of the merits of their position, these Cameralists proposed several new definitions of economics which significantly added to its importance as an area of discourse.

For instance, a certain J. H. G. claimed in 1713 that "the science of Oeconomie is essential to the Cammer, thus the teachings of Oeconomie is the genuine and proper founding principle upon which the whole state, from the highest to the lowest, rests." This, in effect, postulated that economics was the foundation, rather than one aspect, of politics. The ideal Cameralist or state official, accordingly, was defined as "an experienced, good and prudent Oeconomus or householder." Becoming one, in J. H. G.'s opinion, involved a lengthy education. An aspiring economist (for what else was "Oeconomus" in modern parlance?) was advised to concentrate on languages at school; then, before entering the university, employ a tutor in writing, calculation, oratory, composition, history, and geography, as well as in mathematics, astronomy, and architecture, though these latter subjects were to be studied in less depth. The development of skills in sketching, dancing, fencing, and riding, less demanding intellectually, were not to be neglected either, and, if one expressed particular interest, it was desirable to get a basic idea of some crafts and handiwork. The course of studies at the university, which followed this comprehensive preparation, was to consist of theology, law, veterinary sciences, anatomy, and surgery, the mastery of theoretical principles acquired there to be supplemented by a residency in the administration and courts, and the whole process rounded off by travel in Germany, Holland, Brabant, France, England, Italy, and the Baltic countries—no more, no less. This program was the German equivalent of the one Savary proposed in *Le Parfait Négociant;* Defoe significantly omitted such advice from *The Complete English Tradesman*. It is interesting to contemplate the reasons for and implications of the differences between these texts.

Unlike in either England or France, the ideal-typical economic actor envisioned by German Cameralists was a theoretician rather than a practical man of affairs. This was, among other things, related to the fact that, throughout the eighteenth century, the economy, which was discussed, remained very much an area of discourse and not of activity. One author after another proposed a plan for a course of its study, defining it this way and that, discussing its relation to better-established areas of specialization or ones that were as novel and unformed, and reflecting on the profound question whether it represented a science or an art. It was eventually agreed that it was a science—a *political* science with a focus slightly different from that of *Polizei*. (The nature of *Polizei*, unfortunately, was unclear, one of the exponents of economic science, J. C. Dithmar, writing: "Police Science deals with Policey affairs, but what is understood by this is not agreed by all, in that some range under this only food, drink and human clothing, others, however, far extending it and opposing it to the judiciary.") One author suggested in 1716 that the new discipline should focus in the first place on acquisition and production of goods, concerning itself with administration in addition. Essentially the same definition was adopted in 1731 by Dithmar: "Oeconomic science or the art of house economy and householding teaches the manner in which livelihood and wealth, promoting temporal happiness, might be achieved through the industry of country and town."

In 1744 there already was a "General Economic Dictionary," *Allgemeines Oeconomisches Lexicon*. It was compiled by G. H. Zincke and contained baffling entries of the sort: "To pursue the business of subsistence [or nourishment, sustenance—*Nahrungs-Geschäfte*] with property, or to use the same is called *wirtschaften* [to engage in economic activity?]. When however a property is prudently employed with application and labor, such that not only the necessities and comforts of physical life . . . but also wealth are adequate . . . then this is called *gut wirtschaften* [to engage in economic activity well?]" or "*The art of householding or the art of keeping house,* oeconomy, oeconomic science, is a practical science, wherein the wisdom, prudence and art of nearly all learned sciences are applied to the end of the rightful concern for the business of subsistence or householding [*Nahrung-oder Wirtschaffts Geschäffte*] so that one can recognize the true nature and condition of on the one hand in general the objects, purposes and specific conduct of such affairs, on the other the assistants, tools and advantages, partly the therein included affairs of subsistence." Consultation of the *General Lexicon* was certain to leave the reader thoroughly bewildered in regard to every particular point but one: the exceptional importance of the mysterious discipline of economics, the beneficiary as it was of the wisdom of all the learned sciences. And both, the bewilderment in regard to particulars and the realization of the significance of the matter under consideration in general, could stimulate the desire for further study, and thus advance the immediate goal pursued by the would-be economists penning these cumbersome works—the establishment of professorships in the new field they were attempting to define.

Their efforts were crowned with success. In 1727 Friedrich Wilhelm I had issued a decree to the effect that Simon Peter Gasser, who had impressed the king with his work in the administration, be appointed to a new chair in "Oeconomie, Policey und Cammersachen" at the University of Halle. Then as now, the faculty resented appointments by administrative fiat, and opposed Gasser, but they were no match for the king of Prussia. Gasser assumed his newly established post and taught in the area of his expertise, namely, on "buildings, cattle, fields, milling, duties and taxation, forestry and hunting." The same year Dithmar, a historian, was appointed to the chair of "Kameral-Okonomie und Polizeiwissenschaft" at Frankfurt an der Oder. There in 1731 he published the textbook quoted earlier. But so great was the hunger for instruction(s) among aspiring Cameralists that, despite the fact that two distinguished universities offered courses in the field, "the need for a suitable compendium," we are told, "was still bemoaned in 1728."[8] At that time England had long since given "it self a Loose" and, not bothering with university chairs or compendia, was racing ahead, daily increasing the distance that separated it from the rest of the world.

Staatswirtschaft

In the following years, more and more German universities created programs in Cameral studies, and more and more professors, from jurists and historians to specialists in veterinary medicine, crossed over into the new field and taught—among other things—what today we would call "business administration" and what they increasingly referred to as *Staatswirtschaft*, or "state economy." Zincke, too—one thinks with sympathy of his students—taught Cameralism at Leipzig between 1740 and 1745. With the discipline thus officially recognized and accorded a definite position within the existing structure, it was time to pay closer attention to its content, which was promptly done, with the Cameralist paradigm (if one may call it such) firmly in place by the middle decades of the century.

It was chiefly the work of two men: Johann Heinrich Gottlob Justi (who added the preposition *von* to his name) and Joseph von Sonnenfels (to whose name it had been officially added in the previous generation). Though it might have been the definition-churning Zincke who actually coined the term, Justi seems to have introduced the concept of *Staatswirtschaft* into general academic discourse when he made it the title of his authoritative statement of Cameralist principles. The book—which, together with Sonnenfels's later work, according to Keith Tribe, was to achieve canonical status—first appeared in 1755 and ran to 1,245 pages. Apparently the ideas of eighteenth-century German professors in regard to appropriate weekly assignments differed from ours, for in the preface to the second, "augmented" edition, published in 1758 after the first one sold out, Justi explained that he had tried to keep the original text short so that it could be used as a textbook. Justi's Cameralistic ideas were developed while he taught eloquence and Cameral sciences (fiscal, financial, commercial, and industrial administration) in the Theresianum school for the nobility in Vienna. There, too, Sonnenfels taught at the university: failing in his quest for a Chair in Eloquence, he was appointed in 1763 to the Chair in *Polizei* and Cameralism which he had been instrumental in founding. Sonnenfels's book, the 1765 *Principles of Police, Commercial, and Financial Science*, was also conceived as a textbook, judged necessary for the reason of the lengthiness of Justi's *Staatswirtschaft*, and therefore exceeded the latter in the number of pages.

As could be expected, the treatment of a nonexistent body of doctrine at such length resulted in "a phenomenon of unwavering repetition," but did wonders: when Justi and Sonnenfels were done, the murky principles of Cameralism were clear as glass. Cameralism was identified with economics, which was a political science concerned with government or management of material resources. "We call the sciences dedicated to the government of a state the economic as well as Cameralistic sciences," wrote Justi,

> or the economic and Cameralistic sciences. Economics or *Haushaltungskunst* [the art of keeping house] has for its aim to teach how the means of private persons are to be preserved, increased and reasonably applied. What economics attempts to do in connection with the goods of private persons, the governmental sciences aim to do in the case of the total means of the state. Hence they properly bear the name of the economic sciences. We give them the name Cameralistic sciences, however, because the high Collegia which the sovereigns have established, to manage the preservation, expansion and use of the means of the commonweal, are usually called Cammern or Cammercollegia.

Later he reiterated:

> All the affairs of a state may be included under two main headings: they all aim either at maintaining and increasing the wealth of the state, or using and managing it wisely. Hence arise naturally the two main divisions of all the sciences devoted to the government of the state. In the first division we have to consider accordingly the business of maintaining and increasing the wealth and power of the state and the ways and means concerned with this. The principles and rules for this are contained in political science [*Staatskunst*], in the science of commercial policies, and in economy, or household management; for all these sciences have no other aim than to make clear the principles according to which the wealth of the state can either be maintained or increased.

The wealth of the state was, at the same time, its strength, which, Justi declared—anticipating, as it happens, the argument proposed by Francis Fukuyama—"consists principally in common trust and love, which a wise ruler and happy subjects of a considerable state have for each other, so that the property of the state can be continually maintained and increased with united powers." The trust and love on the part of the subjects, however, appeared to be a mere flourish of speech, for they were obliged to put their shoulders to the common effort and could not withhold their assistance, even if they mistrusted and disliked the ruler, because they—and their powers— were considered the property of the state. One read in *Staatswirtschaft*, "The persons . . . must to a certain extent be reckoned to the property of the state," while the second edition articulated: "To the means and powers of the state belong not only all sorts of goods, both fixed and movable, within the boundaries of the country, but also all the talents and abilities of the persons who reside in the country. The reasonable use of all these things, then, and the prerogative of such use, is therefore the supreme power." *Guten Wirthschaft*, that is, "the proper use" of their powers and property, was a duty of the subjects, for otherwise, Justi claimed, "they would be useless inhabitants, and incapable of paying their dues to the state."[9]

Of course, the "ultimate purpose" of the state, and of the subjects' obligation to render themselves economically useful, was the subjects' happiness. But Justi dispelled any hedonistic illusions one might harbor in that regard by ruling: "I understand here by happiness of the subjects the good order and condition of a state such that each is able, by his own efforts, to attain those moral and temporal goods which are necessary for a pleasant life according to his respective *Stand*." In fact, maintaining the various *Stände* in their "requisite relationship" (that is, in the "harmonious inequality" so valued at exactly the same time by d'Arcq and d'Alembert in France) was one of the primary duties of the state. Since wealth could only be enjoyed in peace, the prince had to make sure that it prevailed and the state was secure from external attack and at peace within its borders. Internal security—the focus of *Polizei*—referred precisely to keeping everyone, in every respect, in one's place; it involved the regulation of the subjects' moral and religious life, as well as of their outward conduct, including fashion and diet. This definition of the purpose of the state economy as the maintenance of the established social order, with material demand held constant by the norms governing consumption in each class, presupposed a fundamentally static conception of the economic process. *Staatswirtschaft* was not supposed to be a growing economy.

It has been pointed out many times that Cameralism, though "a species of the genus Mercantilist," was "much more" than Mercantilism and did not perfectly correspond to Smith's minimalist idea of the "mercantile system." Since this is true of every mercantilism that had actually existed—the target of Smith's critique being a polemical construction that united into a system certain disjointed notions about economic reality, which Smith held particularly objectionable—this is obvious. Like other mercantilists, Cameralists were primarily preoccupied with politics rather than what we would regard as economics. (According to Tribe, who thoroughly studied their writings, one has to plough through two thirds of the bulky first volume of Sonnenfels's canonical *Principles* before getting to a discussion of any remotely economic matter.) In addition, unlike other mercantilists, they were explicitly and systematically engaged in the development of a political *science*. Yet, as regards their idea of economic reality proper (the nature of wealth and the ways of producing and augmenting it) and the specifically economic policies they advocated, they were mercantilists who "fit quite naturally into Smith's conception" and (from the point of view of equally ideal laissez-faire philosophy) displayed all the requisite fallacies: "special attention to domestic production rather than the comparative advantages of trade, concentration on flows of bullion, and, of course, the whole supportive apparatus of legislative measures." Like all mercantilisms, Cameralist mercantilism was not entirely consistent. For instance, Justi argued regarding the nature of wealth:

> Wealth . . . consists really of those goods, which in accordance with the existing constitution and manner of living of the world are used for food, clothing and shelter and all other forms of human need and comfort; and if it were possible that a country produced within its own boundaries all these goods in sufficient amount, and had with other people no relations or business, which make the importation and exportation of certain goods necessary, we would of course have to call such a country wealthy, although no trace of gold or silver were found in it. But no country, especially in our part of the world, is so constituted.

This, as well as some of Justi's pronouncements in regard to the importance of agriculture or Sonnenfels's opinion that the validating principle of every measure tending to the promotion of happiness was each measure's contribution to the increase of population, is reminiscent of Quesnay (though Physiocrats, of course, spoke of natural human needs, which were quite independent of society, while the Cameralists explicitly equated need with social norm). But such pronouncements did not prevent them from maintaining that "only foreign commerce can increase the wealth of a land" and that "the first principle of advantageous commerce with foreign nations is that more gold and silver shall come into the country as a result than goes out," with all the consequences for trade policy that followed from this. On the whole, at a time when, in France, Physiocracy had already replaced mercantilism as the dominant mode of economic thinking, and in Glasgow Adam Smith had already conceived *The Wealth of Nations,* the German vision of economic reality was still conventionally and contentedly mercantilist and showed no indication of changing.[10]

The Prussian Colbert

Such complacency in intellectually turbulent times was in part explained by the fact that—to borrow from Macaulay's treatment of Frederick II—German scholars had on their side illustrious examples and popular prejudice. Grievously as they erred, they erred in good company. The company was, first and foremost, that of the great monarch himself, as well as of the other German princes. Frederick, in particular, was a most consistent mercantilist, a Prussian Colbert a century after Colbert.

In some respects, the economy—the household—that he had to manage was less developed than Colbert's France. The country was overwhelmingly agricultural, and rural life, of which the relationship between the lord and the peasant represented the social centerpiece, was still feudal in character. The majority of peasants were serfs, though the definition of servile status differed between the lands east of the Elbe and west of it. On the vast Junker estates in the east, serfdom took the particularly oppressive form of *Gutsherrschaft*, which, as in Russia, approximated chattel slavery, in rare cases being practically identical to it in the sense that serfs could be sold. Under this system the peasant belonged to the lord's estate and in every aspect of life was subject to his authority. For the right to till the plot of land he held from the lord, the peasant owed the latter numerous services, as well as payments in kind, which in the eighteenth century were increasingly converted into money rent.

Originally his bondage—however incongruous it is to say so—had a silver lining: the peasant could not leave the land, but the lord had an obligation to support him if he fell on hard times and provide him with certain necessities, such as wood from his forests for construction and fuel. The peasants, in fact, attached great value to this safety net, and to maintain it were willing to put up with myriad indignities and the generally wretched existence associated with their status. This is clear from their opposition to the government's attempts at their emancipation. But even this perk of their pitiful position was taken from them as the Junkers grew relaxed in regard to their own part in the traditional contract which connected the lord and the peasant in a relationship of mutual obligations and began treating their serfs as tenants at will. No wonder the peasants, "soil-bound, but evictable," were not a happy lot and presented an observer with a picture of a "gloomy, discontented, coarse, slavish . . . hapless missing link between a beast of burden and a man."

In the west the situation of the peasants was somewhat better. The principle of *Grundherrschaft* which applied to them meant that they were tied to the land, but not to the estate or a particular noble family, and while the law, which stipulated their rights, imposed on them numerous duties toward the landowner, they were not subject to his arbitrary authority. The smaller estates resulted in greater specialization, and this in turn produced a more affluent economy. The life of the western peasant was not pleasant, but neither was it as harsh as that of the rural population in the east.

In the eighteenth century, the rulers of most German states were becoming uncomfortable with serfdom, and many were "feeling their way towards emancipation." Prussia offered the most conspicuous example of this tendency, the determined attack on the institution, according to John H. Clapham, commencing there "where most Prussian stories begin, with Frederick." Friedrich Wilhelm I, however, was concerned with the condition of the peasants as well. Between 1719 and 1723 he emancipated the domain serfs in Prussia, Kammin, and Pomerania, and would have wished to see serfdom abolished on private estates, but neither the lords nor the peasants shared this wish. He also tried to improve their lot in bondage, forbidding physical punishment in 1738, and the next year instituting the policy of *Bauernschutz*— the protection of peasants from eviction. In the actual work of liberation Frederick was hardly more successful than his father. In 1748 he allowed Silesian serfs to buy themselves out, but they could not afford it, straining their financial capacities to the utmost as it was to pay the money rents that the landlords now demanded instead of payments in kind. Fifteen years later he issued an edict on the emancipation in private estates and cities in Pomerania. It was staunchly opposed by the Junkers, who tolerated absolute rule only so long as it was in absolute accord with their interests and operated on the principle "Und der König absolut/Wenn er uns den Willen thut." The king's good intentions, therefore, remained largely unrealized.

Nevertheless, agriculture was considerably improved. Again, Friedrich Wilhelm had begun to introduce the new style of hands-on royal management, which throughout the eighteenth century remained the most potent economic factor. His "Haushaltungsreglements" (or "Economic Regulations") of 1732 aimed at making agriculture more efficient and represented a detailed manual elevated to the status of a law. Frederick went beyond instructions. He introduced into Prussia potatoes—against strenuous opposition— and merino sheep, and established spinning schools for girls to take care of the wool. He instigated and financed huge works in land reclamation, using the famed Prussian army to expedite them and establishing some 1,200 new settlements, "une nouvelle petite province," as he put it, elegantly, and obviously in French, "que l'industrie conquit sur l'ignorance et la paresse." It was added to the hundred thousand hectares reclaimed between 1718 and 1722 on the initiative of his father. He established three agricultural credit banks and made grants and loans to landowners for the improvement of their properties. He experimented with new agricultural techniques on his domains—a third of Prussian territory, no less—and made serf tenure on them hereditary, thus increasing peasants' interest in improvement. He encouraged the introduction of tobacco, and invited Dutch farmers to settle in Prussia and make their famous cheese and butter there; and so on and so forth.[11]

The Hohenzollern industrial and commercial policies were equally energetic, though "agriculture was the chief industry of the country" and the main economic preoccupation of the householder-kings. As in agriculture, Frederick built on the foundations laid by his father, who, in turn, modified but left standing, and in some instances reinforced, the traditional system of industrial production and trade. To prevent conflicts between the guilds and journeymen's unions, which affected manufactures everywhere in the Empire, but whose frequency in the textile industry of the New Mark caused particular concern in Prussia, Friedrich Wilhelm I, between 1732 and 1736, revised the regulations governing the guilds, letting in a modicum of the individual freedom of trade (in the sense of the choice of occupation and initiative) and at the same time eliminating every shadow of independence from the control of the state on the part of the guilds. The new regulations, among other things, allowed a greater range of activity to merchants, making possible the development of the domestic system and laying the foundations for the accumulation of native capital. The guilds were, in effect, undermined, and were eventually forced to organize production along new, factory lines, while the newly developing industries dispensed with the guild structure from the outset. At the same time, these measures instituted virtual industrial serfdom for journeymen, leaving them completely dependent on the guilds. "No journeyman could travel beyond the confines of Prussia. Strikes and rebellion were forbidden. In addition to certificates of age and training, a passport stating previous location, length of service there and good behavior was required. A journeyman without such a passport was a man without a country and treated accordingly."[12]

Frederick's economic leadership spurred the sluggish German industry on. He encouraged existing trades and, like Colbert, founded new ones. The Prussian silk and porcelain industries were his "artificial" creations, and he jealously watched over their progress, taking umbrage against criticism which was delivered too boldly. (An official of the State Department of Manufactures and Commerce, who, in the course of an investigation, made on the king's command, of the causes of the 1765–66 depression in silk production, dared to point to the shortcomings of the policy of royal patronage, paid for this by a term of imprisonment in the fortress of Spandau.) He also protected these pet industries in proper mercantilist fashion with high duties on foreign imports. The woolen industry was similarly protected and supported. The large domestic market, which included the clothing of Frederick's formidable military establishment, was reserved for it and its export abilities systematically cultivated. To facilitate exports of woolens into Russia, a special company had been established in 1734; eventually the uniforms for both the Prussian and the Russian armies were made of Prussian cloth. In pursuit of "self-sufficiency," Frederick heavily taxed both the export and the import of raw materials, and so regarded cotton manufacture, which depended on imports, with less favor than other textile industries. But it also benefited from his solicitude for domestic production.

It was under Frederick that the first insurance agency began operating in 1765 and the Royal Bank of Berlin opened with the initial capital of 8 million thalers. The establishment of Seehandlung, or the Overseas Trading Corporation, in 1772, was the king's major contribution to the development of Prussian foreign trade. He insisted that Prussian goods be carried in Prussian vessels and wished to have a merchant marine capable of handling all of Prussia's foreign trade. By the time of his death in 1786, Prussia had 1,200 merchant ships, and such was almost the case. This king's wish, indeed, was his subjects' command.

The disadvantage of an economy in which the manager was all-important, the other side of the coin that, on the whole, functioned very well in eighteenth-century Prussia, was that it could not "create that initiative necessary to the development of an active middle class and an active industrial life which accompanies it . . . [T]he spirit of enterprise did not exist."[13] Not that people were strangers to good old-fashioned greed (although governmental regulation of consumption made one of its most attractive functions—flaunting one's wealth—unattainable) or that native commercial ability was lacking. Both were in as ample supply as in any other genetic pool—one must assume this, if racist explanations of economic performance are to be rejected. But the culture did not favor these natural propensities; economic action was not oriented toward growth.

A Sad Tale of a Patriotic Merchant

There existed individual entrepreneurs on a heroic scale (one had to be an entrepreneur on a heroic scale in Frederick's Berlin to be an entrepreneur) whose exceptional personal histories demonstrate the impossibility of a business career, in the sense of "a course of continued progress" in business activity, in this society. One of these epic figures, the Berlin merchant Johann Ernst Gotzkowsky, told his story in *Geschichte eines patriotischen Kaufmanns* (A History of a Patriotic Merchant),[14] which he published in 1768, seven years before dying in poverty and oblivion. And a sad tale it was.

A son of an impoverished Polish nobleman who died soon after the child's birth, this "leading merchant, financier and entrepreneur" was brought up in Dresden and at age fourteen was apprenticed to the Berlin merchant house of Adrian Sproegel. When Gotzkowsky turned twenty (in 1730), Sproegel's business burned down, and he joined in business his brother, already established as a haberdashery and jewelry merchant, soon becoming quite successful on his own. Already at this early stage his exports, he claimed in his auto-biography, contributed considerably to the Prussian treasury, and indeed such was his reputation that Frederick, then still the Crown Prince, made him his buyer at the Leipzig Fair (an expression of trust no doubt provoked, among other things, by Gotzkowsky's noble origins, for Frederick was noto-rious for his contempt for the bourgeoisie).

When the prince became king, Gotzkowsky was the person with whom he shared his commercial and, especially, industrial hopes. Almost immediately upon assuming power, Frederick confided in him his desire for the establish-ment of new trades in Prussia, for which, he thought, foreign artisans would have to be brought in to settle. Taking this as a hint, Gotzkowsky promptly persuaded his father-in-law, K. F. Blume, to establish a velvet workshop in Berlin, previous attempts to develop luxury fabrics industry in Prussia having been unsuccessful and declared nonviable by the Department of Commerce and Manufactures in 1744. It was Herr Blume, however, who proved non-viable, dying before the workshop opened and leaving the management in Gotzkowsky's hands. To be able to give it his full attention, Gotzkowsky in turn left the running of his own jewelry business to a partner, recruited for-eign artisans, and in 1748 had sixty looms and 244 workers.

These were not auspicious times. The price of raw silk from Italy rose, and Prussian consumers had not as yet acquired the taste for domestic manufac-tured product. The State Silk Warehouse, which Frederick established in Berlin, stored raw silk bought in Italy by royal agents and sold to Prussian manufacturers on credit. The king also issued orders prohibiting the impor-tation of silk fabrics to protect the industry from unpatriotic consumers, but these measures were not effective. Gotzkowsky was attacked by the wholesal-ers, who objected to the fact that he not only produced but also marketed his merchandise. Such practice went against the principles of the division of labor sanctioned by the guilds and was seen as undermining legitimate wholesale business. In 1750 the dealer was sufficiently hard-pressed to turn to the king for help. Frederick gave him 10,000 thalers, plus another failing silk work-shop, the looms and the house previously belonging to the former master in-cluded. It had only ten workers; Gotzkowsky soon employed eighty. His out-put per year reached the value of 100,000 thalers. He improved the style of his fabrics, and his sales grew. He became the most influential of the silk mer-chants and manufacturers in Prussia, and used his influence in trying to talk other moneyed Prussians into opening silk works and foreign artisans into moving to Berlin. He also was behind much protectionist legislation related to the industry.

His labors on behalf of Prussian silk were rewarded by a royal loan—which turned to be a gift—of 18,500 thalers and a commission to furnish art for the new Sans Souci palace. This inspired Gotzkowsky to diversify his business interests to include art dealership. Toward the mid-1750s his various businesses engaged more than a thousand workers. The earthquake in Lisbon, that "unfortunate disaster [that] had such repercussions on commerce that all large merchant houses have closed their books and have called in their debts," caused another downturn in his affairs, and in late 1755 he was obliged to ask the king for help again. Frederick ordered an examination of Gotzkowsky's accounts, but then, apparently satisfied with the results, lent him 40,000 thalers. His Majesty's kindness and this new mark of confidence, Gotzkowsky wrote in his *History,* affected him so much that during an audience a few days later, he clasped the king's knees and wept in gratitude. He thought this showed better than words how he felt.

Gotzkowsky was back on the horse again. But in 1756 the Seven Years' War broke out and his affairs suffered. While Frederick added Silesia to his dominions, Prussia was overrun by enemies. The debasement of coinage, necessitated by wartime exigencies, brought in its train across-the-board inflation. Gotzkowsky was particularly incommoded by the fact that, while Prussian law obliged him to accept devalued money from his debtors, his foreign creditors (in Amsterdam and Hamburg) demanded payment in sound silver coin, a difference which cost him 200,000 thalers in lost money. He did not publicize this loss, but rather borrowed more and kept afloat, in fact increasing his investment in silk works, the industry about which Frederick cared in particular. In 1759 Gotzkowsky added to his enterprises the twenty-loom taffeta manufacture of Samuel Schwartze (the workshop, as well as Schwartze's house, was a gift from the king), and within months put in operation fifty-five more looms.

The hour of Gotzkowsky's true glory struck in the fall of 1760, during the second occupation of Berlin by the Russians, led by a one-time Berliner, General Tottleben. The occupying force demanded 4 million thalers for the promise to abstain from looting. In unofficial negotiations, Gotzkowsky, known to another German general in the Russian service, was able to reduce the sum to 1.5 million thalers, with only 500,000 thalers, collected among the city's merchants, payable immediately in prewar coin. This induced Marquis d'Argens, a correspondent of Frederick the Great, to write to his royal pen pal: "Gotzkowsky is a splendid fellow and a fine citizen. I would wish that many such men were numbered among your subjects." But Gotzkowsky's services to the city in this time of distress were not limited to cutting its ransom by the considerable sum of 2.5 million thalers. In addition, he stored the valuables of other merchants (who did not believe in Russian promises, however dearly bought) in his house, certain to be off-limits to brigands, for Tottleben's adjutant was staying there. When the German command of the Russian army had an idea to take the two Jewish bankers Ephraim and Itzig hostage to squeeze money from the Berlin Jewish community, Gotzkowsky intervened on their behalf and was able to persuade Tottleben to get the payment without taking hostages. He also saved several Berlin journalists from flogging, to which they were condemned for being critical of Russia's policy. Finally, using bribes, deceit, and flattery, he prevented much of the damage to the royal manufactures, all of which Tottleben had specifically been instructed to destroy (such being the meaning of competitiveness at the time).

When the occupants, frightened by the news of Frederick's march on his capital from the newly conquered Silesia, departed, Gotzkowsky went to Meissen to see the king and inform him of the results of his negotiations with the Russians. Frederick presented him with 150,000 thalers, one third of which could be interpreted as a token of appreciation (according to Gotzkowsky, 100,000 was in payment of an outstanding debt for some paintings he acquired for the Sans Souci palace). The king also shared with him his interest in porcelain, for which Meissen was famous, and which he wished could be made in Berlin as well. Again, Gotzkowsky lost no time in transforming the royal dream into reality. Upon returning to Berlin, he found a porcelain master, paid him 10,000 thalers for his trade secrets, and convinced him—for 1,000 thalers a year and free lodging—to start a workshop in one of the houses he had earlier received from Frederick. For another 2,000 thalers he hired a miniaturist, and by 1762 employed seventy workers and eighty apprentices.

Frederick was delighted. But Gotzkowsky was buried in debt and knew that neither his silk nor his new porcelain business was going to help him to get out from under it. His situation was aggravated by a number of risky and unsuccessful transactions undertaken to patch things up, and in 1763 "a general crash" on the Continent delivered the final blow. The king was willing to buy Gotzkowsky's porcelain manufacture and paid for it 225,000 thalers. But neither this nor Gotzkowsky's genius for bargaining, which brought his creditors to agree to be fully satisfied with only a 50 percent repayment, could land him back on his feet. In 1764 he had to tell Frederick that he had no means to keep his silk businesses running. Frederick, who by this time thought he had bailed out his industrialist friend once too often, confined himself to comments on the merits of hard work and disciplined management. And so, in 1765, Gotzkowsky sold his velvet, silk, and taffeta establishments.

In 1767 he was bankrupt once again. No one wished to remember the shrewdness and subtlety of his dealings with the Russians, which had saved

Berlin from industrial and financial ruin only seven years before. No one cared that his pioneering efforts did in fact establish the silk and porcelain industries in Berlin. Pestered by creditors, he was left to write his book. He concluded it ruefully: "Ich kann diese Geschichte mit Recht mit den Worten aus einer bekannten Fabel schliessen: 'Mit Undank lohnet die Welt.'"

Such was the fate of an enterprising patriotic merchant in eighteenth-century Prussia.[15]

Borrowed Wisdom

It is a testimony to the economic marginality of Germany—including Prussia, by the end of the eighteenth century the largest and most powerful German state—that Adam Smith did not mention the quintessentially mercantilist practices of its rulers (or the equally mercantilist theories of the Cameralists) in his discussion of the "mercantile system." It is a testimony to the marginality of the economy in Germany, including Prussia, that Cameralists, as well as rulers, paid hardly any attention to the developments in Britain. It was France that set cultural standards for the *Aufklärer,* and the fact that this applied to economic thought as much as to literary taste was yet another reflection of the essentially theoretical nature of economic interests in Germany—the definition of the economy as an academic discipline, an area of discourse, rather than an autonomous and increasingly important sphere of reality.

Some German authors on economic matters, such as Bielfeld, since 1747 curator of all Prussian universities, who left us the definition of politics as "the knowledge of the means best fitted to rendering a state formidable and its citizens happy," wrote in French. His *Institutions Politiques,* virtually indistinguishable from the proliferating tracts on *Staatswirtschaft,* is judged by Tribe as "by no means part of the tradition of [German] Cameralist writing [but of the] French tradition of writing on politics" with an economic tinge. Sonnenfels considered the Parisian *Journal de Commerce* the epitome of economic wisdom and contemplated publishing a journal of translations from it. When asked for a list of particularly important contemporary works on economics, he pointed, in addition to Justi's *Staatswirtschaft,* to Melon, Forbonnais—and the French translation of Hume's *Political Discourses.* One of the most important Cameralistic educational establishments, the Kameral-Hohe-Schule zu Lautern, founded two years before the publication of *The Wealth of Nations,* included French, but not English, among its offerings, though by 1780, English was apparently added. The school's library, catalogued in the 1790s, reflected a similar bias in favor of France, even if it contained only nine works by the Physiocrats. Its English holdings were limited to a few manuals on pig husbandry and the cultivation of carrots, with the addition of Young's *Experimental Agriculture,* the French translation of Hume's *Political Discourses,* and a German one of Steuart's *Inquiry into the Principles of Political Oeconomy.*[16]

The Age of Smithianismus

James Steuart, who spent some time in Germany and was a mercantilist, was widely believed in Cameralist circles to be the most important and influential of contemporary British economic thinkers. This did not prevent German "economists" from recognizing the significance of Adam Smith's implicit attack on his famous compatriot (though it is doubtful whether they had ever understood it fully), which might even have been the reason why *The Wealth of Nations* gained their attention so quickly. The first German translation of the book appeared in Leipzig in 1776, the very year it was published in Britain. The translator, a certain J. F. Schiller, though a German, resided in London, and therefore perhaps even more remarkable was the appearance of the first German review—in *Göttingische gelehrte Anzeigen* in March 1777. (The University of Göttingen, located as it was in the electorate of Hanover, the patrimony of the English royal house, was in many ways a seedbed of British influences, which reached it earlier than other German universities, owing to the considerable number of British students, and which, owing to its stature—with Halle and Leipzig it ranked among the three best schools—it helped to spread.)

The author of the review, a professor of philosophy, J. G. H. Feder, was judiciously enthusiastic. Smith's work, he said, was "a classic; very estimable both for its thorough, not too limited, often far-sighted political philosophy, and for the numerous, frequently discursive historical notes." But there also was much in it that was "open to objection, especially in the latter part" (which, the reader will recall, was devoted to the critique of mercantilism). Indeed, though sympathetic, Feder found problems with the "free trade" argument. "Too great competition" inside a country, he thought, was bound to produce shoddy goods and deceptions, as well as to force under "many an able man, especially if he is likewise honest," while liberty of occupational choice might tempt many to "choose attractive but unprofitable trades" which would bring about their ruin—all "evils," he concluded, "that outweigh any gains of such complete freedom." As to laissez-faire principles of international trade, Feder thought them "valid only at a certain stage of industry, wealth and enlightenment" and did not believe they could "be incorporated in the universal principles of state." Thus the very first published assessment of Adam Smith's economic ideas in Germany sounded the note of historicism that, in the nineteenth century, would become characteristic of "scientific nationalism" in particular and German economics in general. Skepticism in regard to individual freedom reflected the distrust of the (common) individual's intellectual and moral capacities, which underlay *Hausväterliteratur* and permeated German mercantilism, and also anticipated developments in economic thought informed by the new national sentiment, which would reinforce this old attitude.

It seems that there were altogether three reviews of the original translation, the other two appearing in Nicolai's *Allgemeine deutsche Bibliothek* and Iselin's *Ephemerides der Menschheit,* which openly drew inspiration from Baudeau's Physiocratic organ. The two reviewers indeed misinterpreted Smith as a Physiocrat and welcomed him to the club with some grandiloquent rejoicing, the one in *Bibliothek* exclaiming, "Blessed be the Briton, who thinks so justly and wisely!" After that the initial interest died out and no more extensive treatments of *The Wealth of Nations* appeared in print until the last decade of the century.[17]

In the privacy of their studies, however, some German intellectuals were developing a deeper admiration for the Scottish philosopher (whom they clearly identified as such). Some of them admired him for reasons that might strike us as somewhat unrelated to the conceptual revolution which his monumental opus effected. For instance, Friedrich von Gentz believed that the work deserved "unrestrained praise" chiefly because "in respect to method and literary art [it was] one of the most complete and perfect books, that exist in any science." "In respect to style," he wrote in a letter to Christian Garve, whom he wished to undertake the translation, "I confess that I consider Smith the most perfect English prose writer . . . Of German writers there is only one, in whose literary art I find any similarity, and indeed in many points, and he is Garve."

Garve was a dedicated man of Enlightenment, a minor priest at its shrine, who worshipped by translation. He translated from English, as well as French, Latin, and Greek, and had already helped German readers to become acquainted with Ferguson and Burke. Although berated by his friend for being insufficiently excited about *The Wealth of Nations* in 1790, he was swayed by his flattery, shameless because it probably was sincere and reflected a genuine lack of intellectual discrimination, and was to say in the introduction to his translation in 1794 that the book "attracted me as only few books have in the course of my studies through the number of new views which it gave me not only concerning the actual object of [Smith's] investigations, but concerning all related material from the philosophy of civil and social life." The depth of Garve's understanding of Smith can be measured against his views regarding the economic policies of Frederick the Great. "It is really fortunate for an author in the Prussian states," he wrote, "that in respect to many points in state economy he is able, in any general investigation of what should be done, to agree with those rules which form the basis of the actions, or at least of the views, of his prince."

However that may be, Garve's translation was an important step in the development of economic thought and policy in Germany, for the translator was held in such great esteem that it could not fail to convince the readers of the virtues of the author who merited the distinction of his application. Its appearance reinforced Smith's new popularity, the main source of which, again, was Göttingen. There, a disciple of Feder and now a young professor of history, Georg Sartorius, taught Adam Smith's doctrine in 1792, and in 1793 contributed another review to *Göttingische Anzeigen,* focused on the additions to the third English edition of 1784, and answering the concerns expressed by the German publisher who was bringing out their translation. "While this work is of undoubted importance," wrote the publisher anxiously, "the sales with which the translation has met in Germany have been for so many years so moderate that we have . . . long been dubious of whether the publication of the additions and revisions would pay the effort of translation and the cost of printing." "Smith will not remain long on the shelves," Sartorius assured him, "for reason will assert itself in the end." In a review of Garve's new translation the next year, however, Sartorius admitted that, so far, Smith "had no influence on the alteration of the doctrine of state economy in our Fatherland . . . If here and there one finds a note of this book, it is as if [Smith] has never been read."

Considering this unacceptable, Sartorius in 1796 published an exegetical *Handbook of State Economy,* based on his lecture notes. He faithfully presented Smith's arguments, but criticized him for making mistakes in detail, saying rather dismissively: "Many historical data referring to the continent are of course false; even some conclusions of his theory seem to lack solidarity." Sartorius went on to teach Smith, all the while cognizant of "the undying services of this excellent man to science," yet the better acquainted with his work he became, the more critical was his assessment. He still held that "Smith's views on the effects of trade and his examination of the Mercantile system are excellently done," but disagreed with the Scotsman "on the unconditional application of the principle of free disposal of industry and capital, on the harmony of individual and social interests, on productive and unproductive labor, on taxes, and on certain other points," namely, on virtually everything that was new in Smith's work and distinguished it sharply from Cameralist/mercantilist orthodoxy. The farthest he would go was to stipulate that the "cooperation on the part of the government in advancing the national wealth, aside from protection against foreign enemies, the administration of justice at home, and the development of certain institutions, is also to be recommended, provided it remains within proper boundaries." (Since it was exactly on the definition of what boundaries were proper that Smith disagreed with the mercantilists, this was not much of a concession.)

A colleague of Sartorius at the University of Königsberg, Christian Jakob Kraus, was upset by the publication of the *Handbook* and disputed the priority of the Göttingen historian in alerting the new generation to Smith's importance. Himself a professor of Practical Philosophy and Cameralia, Kraus did not publish much, but in a 1797 letter to a friend fulminated against Sartorius's "saying that he was the first to give academic lectures on Smith in Germany, when I, right in the midst of threatening storms, have for six years past and recently entirely without subterfuge not only presented the only true, great, beautiful, just and beneficial system [of Adam Smith], but have been able to inspire with it some fine fellows."

Kraus was a man of extraordinary range of interests (besides state economy and practical philosophy, his courses at Königsberg included ones on Greek classics, history, mathematics, and Shakespeare) and of peculiar intellectual abilities, buttressed by an exceptional capacity for learning by rote. Intrigued by English literature, he undertook in 1776 to master the language, and, according to his biographer, accomplished this, starting from scratch, by memorizing a dictionary. In 1777 his English was good enough to allow him to translate Young's *Political Arithmetic,* which, however, he understood so little that, piqued, he then decided to turn to a systematic study of political economy. Apparently, understanding was Kraus's weak spot, perhaps because his intellect was overpowered by all the information he forced it to process. In 1902 a critic wrote unamiably: "Kraus . . . was not capable of expressing a single thought without immediate recourse to an authority . . . [A] scholar of reputation [he] was not only incapable of intellectual production or even of outlining of ideas, but . . . had exceptional difficulty in detecting something certain and correct in the range of opinions and counteropinions before him." But Kraus was a great teacher—at the time only Kant surpassed him in popularity at Königsberg—and, more important, he had great students, who were to become Prussia's leaders during the period of its reforms. Already in 1795 one of them, von Schroetter, then minister of the Provincial Department of Old Prussia and New East Prussia, decided that Kraus should certify everyone entering the civil service in positions requiring expertise in economic matters. The professor was jubilant, rhetorically asking: "But tell, how does it come that so many counts are turning to the study of Cameralia, which so far as I know has never happened before . . . Is law losing its former position of honor? Have the Cameralia risen in power and glory?"

Another former student of Kraus, von Auerswald, published two posthumous collections of his notes, one on the subject of *Staatswirtschaft*, in five volumes, the other, a miscellany, in eight. The first four tomes of *Staatswirtschaft* had to do with Smith and represented, essentially, a compilation of paraphrases—and often verbatim quotations—from *The Wealth of Nations*. There was little rethinking and even less critical interpretation. Smith was allowed to speak to his German audience almost directly. The fact that he spoke through a teacher held by his students in reverence could only make his arguments more compelling, especially since it is likely that Kraus would from time to time add his own voice to that of the great author, whose vicar he was, to emphasize the importance of the teaching. His opinion was that "the world has seen no more important book than that of Adam Smith; certainly since the times of the New Testament no writing has had more beneficial results than this will have, when it has become better known and has penetrated further into the minds of all who have to do with matters of state economy," a deeper study of which "for us Prussians of today is more necessary than ever." He thus compared *The Wealth of Nations* to the word of God, while stressing its patriotic significance. *Smithianismus,* a cult of Smith that existed among German state economists in the last years of the eighteenth century and first decades of the nineteenth, was a natural response to such encomiums.[18]

From *Staatswirtschaft* to *Nationaloekonomie*

Of course, *Smithianismus* had other sources as well. In his detailed study of the academic economic discourse in Germany during the century between 1750 and 1850, Tribe stresses the importance of the reinterpretation of the notion of Natural Law, and specifically of Kant's Critical Philosophy, in making Cameralists receptive to the liberal ideas of Adam Smith and preparing the ground for the transformation of the Cameralist *Staatswirtschaft* into the tellingly christened *Nationaloekonomie*. There is no doubt that these intellectual developments, with their emphasis on the properties and capacities of the individual human being, the needs and reason, which were independent of one's social position, were of great moment. They reinforced, and to a certain extent reflected, a far more general phenomenon—the penetration into the wide sectors of the German public (if not yet the population in its entirety) of the idea of the nation.

The stage was set for it by the French Revolution, which alerted the German educated classes to the advantages nationalism could have for them, revealing its implications for their status, and, several years later—in the late 1790s—by the Revolutionary wars, when the nascent national consciousness was fortified by the change of sentiment toward France. The idea of the nation transformed the image of social order that was, among other things, the foundation of the concept of *Staatswirtschaft;* it was no longer possible to conceive of the economy as a grand "house" passively awaiting the care of the princely *pater familii*. The society was no longer conceived of in terms of territory; it was a living, natural entity (which in its German interpretation would soon be reified and emerge as a collective individual), an animate, pulsating mass of natural energies, not somebody's inert possession. Economics, as an area of discourse, was reconceptualized as the study of these natural energies, and the concern with *Haushaltung,* management and managers, necessarily receded into the background. It became possible to conceive of the drawbacks of excessive control and the advantages of letting nature regulate itself. This was the premise of Wilhelm von Humboldt's *Limits of State Action*. Significantly, his and similar advocacies of economic freedom were not rooted in the ethics of individualism and did not imply the elevation of the individual—or individual liberty—to the apex of the social value scale. The individual was validated as the vessel for the self-expression and self-realization of the nation, which carried its energies in much the same way the vessels of an organism carry blood. The regulation of the economy by the state was harmful to the extent that it sapped these national energies by preventing their materialization; if it helped to tap them, it was all right.

Nevertheless, the emphatically individualistic liberalism of *The Wealth of Nations* bore a certain superficial resemblance to the "new economics" which the nationalist reconceptualization of the social order had inspired in Germany, and, on the face of it, might seem closer to it than the old Cameralist thinking it was replacing but perpetuating in spirit. This allowed the generation of German "economists," who taught and published in the late 1790s and the early 1800s, to identify with Smith while subscribing to ideas which were diametrically opposed to his. They recognized that Smith's criticism of the "mercantile system" applied to the Cameralist theory in the bosom of which they had been brought up, but they had no difficulty accepting this, for they too rejected the idea of money as the foundation of national wealth (which was, they thought, what "mercantilism" chiefly meant) and were convinced of the superior importance of industry. In principle, they argued against the forcing of economic action by the state, for it was now a matter of consensus that, *ceteris paribus,* nature was best left to its own devices.[19] But it was perfectly acceptable for the state to instruct men what these devices were, "and so," suggested C. D. H. Bensen, professor of Cameralia and Philosophy at Erlangen in 1798, "the highest power should, in accordance with the purposes of the state, take requisite care of the culture of the citizen, that is, for his *enlightenment and morality*. It should *facilitate* . . . his cultural advance." That same Professor Bensen, who otherwise most decidedly opposed state intervention in the economy, and was in general agreement with the liberal view, would also write—and in the very same paragraph the gist of which was "pas trop gouverner!"—"The nation should gradually see itself as a single family; all individuality, with all due regard, should vanish."[20]

There is no doubt that some of the appeal of Smith's theory, which was generally misunderstood, in Germany during these years can be attributed to the eye-opening, striking title of his book: *The Wealth of Nations*. In the context of nascent nationalism (which was anti-French, and thus by default increased the appeal of all things British), this focus on the nation suggested a ready framework for the reinterpretation of economic reality and the reorientation of economic discourse, necessitated by the adoption of national consciousness. It was only a peg, really, on which to hang a vision that was entirely independent of Smith's; but he provided the peg, and German "economists" seized on it. The redefinition of *Staatswirtschaft* as *Nationaloekonomie* allowed the emergent image of the economy to congeal within years or even months and put everything in its place.[21]

The new name made its appearance in 1805, when two authors, L. H. Jakob and F. J. H. von Soden, both reacting to Smith, used it independently in the titles of their books: Jakob's *Grundsätze der National-Oekonomie oder National-Wirthschaftslehre* and von Soden's *Die Nazional-Oekonomie*. Jakob's influence was felt clearly in the flood of books on national economy which appeared in the next decade, when, finally, economics became a *fashionable* subject in Germany. He distinguished between the state and the nation, and between *Staatswirtschaft* and the *National-Oekonomie*. His focus was on "how is wealth formed in a nation?"—the question which was the province of the latter, new discipline. *Staatswirtschaft* was defined narrowly: according to Jakob, it dealt only with the management of state, or public, property, of which the rulers were the *Wirte*. It was thus properly divided into *Polizei* and finance. By contrast, "the expression *National-Oekonomie* or *National-Wirtschaft*," he wrote, "appears to me most appropriate to characterize a system of concepts in which the entire nature of popular wealth, its origin and dissipation [distribution?], thus its Physik, should be analyzed." Or elsewhere: "*National-Oekonomie* or *National-Wirtschaftslehre* investigates the means through which the populace, under the protection of the government, achieves its end, namely the acquisition, increase and enjoyment of its property; the manner in which national wealth arises, is distributed, consumed and reproduced or maintained; and the influence which all circumstances and events in the state have upon this." This brought the national economy back within the sphere of influence, if not the activity, of the state, and thus within the fold of the political sciences.

As a form of political economy, the "new economics" in Germany remained dubious of the universal validity of Smith's principles and, by and large, denied that they had such validity. Indeed, "*Nationaloekonomie* explicitly adopted [the] principle of variability of economic circumstance and need as a central tenet which marked it off from developments in France and Britain."[22] Certain authors were willing to admit the existence of universal laws, though their operation in the case of every particular economy was mediated by variable historical circumstances. To examine these circumstances was the task of *Staatswirtschaft*, while the universal laws, first expounded in *The Wealth of Nations*, were, by association with Smith's work, referred to as *Nationaloekonomie*. This interpretation, which attempted to combine the idea of economics as a set of natural, universal principles, independent of human volition, with its Cameralist opposite, stressing the defining role of the human (managerial) will, later bore the brunt of the attack on *Smithianismus*.

Nationalism and Economic Liberty

It is safe to assume that more courses on economics were taught in late eighteenth-century Germany than in Britain and France combined, and that the number of pages devoted to the subject in numerous "handbooks" written to accompany these courses far exceeded the total output of British and French authors. But while the learned professors of Cameral Sciences surpassed one another in producing ever more elaborate definitions, very little was happening in Germany in the way of economic development. After the death of Frederick, Prussia experienced its "twenty inglorious years." The economy, which drew all its energy from management, lost whatever momentum it had when the great manager was gone, and coasted placidly, "moderately prosperous" but stagnant. The infant industry, unable as yet to stand on its own, experienced absolute decline: between 1789 and 1791 the industrial work force shrank from 177,925 to 159,700 workers, and the total value of products remained stationary at 34 to 35 million thaler, despite a considerable rise in prices. The agricultural sector, or rather the landowners, fared better—because of the rapid economic development in England, whose industrialization made the country dependent on foreign grain. The Junker estates in Prussia, especially in the Baltic provinces, were natural suppliers and profited from this demand, which was magnified when England was drawn into the Napoleonic Wars.

The agricultural boom, not unexpectedly, resulted in widespread misery in the countryside, as the landowners, given a taste, quickly acquired a robust appetite for money and consolidated their estates without any regard to the state policy of *Bauernschutz*. Thus the emergence of the rural proletariat accompanied the commercialization of agriculture, which proceeded apace. To the increase in agricultural exports corresponded an increase in industrial imports, those from England constituting the bulk and rising ten times in value between 1792 and 1814. But the balance of trade remained in Prussia's favor, and the resulting growth in specie contributed to the rise in prices and speeded on commercialization. In a way, Prussia of the 1790s resembled Russia two centuries later: production was stagnant or declining and financial infrastructure lacking, but it was easy to become rich in speculation.[23] Other German states also grew rich (with a resulting rise in speculative activity) thanks to the rising output of silver mines and English and French bribes, or "subsidies," to various princes. England alone "subsidized" Germany to the tune of some 200 million thalers (or 35 million pounds) between 1793 and 1815, on top of 21 million paid to Hesse and Brunswick for mercenaries at the time of the American war.

Political concerns, as elsewhere, focused on France. Though drawn into the conflict with the Revolutionary state in 1792, Prussia deftly disengaged itself three years later, leaving the other Germans to fend for themselves, and for most of the period stayed out of it. Indeed, it greatly profited from its newly established friendship with the victorious champions of liberty, equality, and fraternity, who reserved for it the largest—if not the best—cuts of land, as they redistributed the territory of the defunct Empire among the newly formed or reconstructed German states. It had to give up some too, surrendering to France 1,075 square miles of the left bank of the Rhine with its 125,000 people, but got over four times more in exchange: 4,700 square miles with 500,000 former subjects of other rulers. King Friedrich Wilhelm III, whose head, it was said, "was inferior to his heart," but whose heart, judging by his actions, also left much to be desired, could be content—and was—even though his augmented domain was cut in two by the independent state of Hanover.[24]

The fact that Hanover belonged to England made it, in the conditions of aggravating tensions between Britain and France, a particularly problematic spot, which had been made clear already in 1803, when hostilities between the two superpowers reopened and Napoleon occupied it. Friedrich Wilhelm, believing that the fate of Hanover was Hanover's business, did not consider this occupation a sufficient reason to break off his friendly relations with France, which might have given the French a mistaken impression of his patience and encouraged General Bernadotte (precociously sovereign in his movements) to march through part of Prussia on the pretext that this was the most direct route from point A to point B of his itinerary. This Friedrich Wilhelm did not like at all and, in protest, made Prussia a party to the Austro-

Russian coalition against Bonaparte. Unfortunately for Prussia, his action was badly timed, even though, as it happened, signing the treaty entailed no military action, for Napoleon promptly defeated the Russians and the Austrians at Austerlitz and was now waging war by other means. For breaking its neutrality, Prussia was forced to give up Anspach (the province through which Bernadotte rode to his engagement) and to take Hanover—which placed Prussia in direct conflict with England. It also had to close its ports to English trade, which was certain to affect its own grievously, and in reaction to which England appropriated the four hundred Prussian ships at the time moored in English ports. Despite that loss, Friedrich Wilhelm appeared not to mind being in a state of war with England, probably considering his newly acquired province well worth it. He grew so fond of Hanover, in fact, that, upon being informed that Napoleon contemplated returning it to England, he challenged the emperor of France to a battle. Napoleon gave him two—Jena and Auerstädt—and Prussia collapsed.

The "lame and impotent conclusion" of its military venture had grave consequences for Prussia's economy. Its territory was cut by roughly half; French troops—10,000 between 1806 and 1808 and 500,000 in 1812—were stationed in the remainder and had to be supported; and a staggering indemnity of originally 120 million francs, which was constantly increased, was imposed on the vanquished state, whose military machine had only recently been believed invincible. *Vae victis!* Altogether, between 1806 and 1813, when their fortunes were reversed, the French drew from Prussia as much, perhaps, as 1.5 billion francs. Add to that the disastrous effects of the Continental Blockade on Prussia's foreign trade and its faltering industry (whose loss, however, turned into a gain for some other German provinces), and it becomes evident that no stopgap measures, such as international borrowing or panhandling, sale of the crown lands, or extraordinary taxation—to all of which the government of Friedrich Wilhelm III indeed resorted—were going to restore to the state its former prosperity and, more important, its stature, or even to tide it over until better times. What was needed was a thoroughgoing reform of the entire social, political, and economic system, nothing less than a revolution from above.

And so "the great reform period of 1807–1819 in Prussia, associated with the names of Stein and Hardenberg, was a direct result of the military collapse of the Prussian armies before Napoleon at Jena and Auerstädt." In the inspiration of the reformers, the aspirations of young and vigorous German nationalism, which emerged fully formed from the Romantic dreams of the Heavenly Kingdom, combined with the particularistic interests of the Prussian state, producing, among other things, an economic policy which was very much in keeping with the disquisitions of *Nationaloekonomie* and appeared to reflect certain ideas of Adam Smith. The logic behind the reforms was, in the words of a sympathetic observer, the following:

> All the Prussian reformers were united in the belief that the Frederician state . . . had been a "machine state," in which the individual was to function as a cog in a mechanism . . . But the disregard of the moral character of man had also undermined the foundations of the state. The apathy with which the population had gazed at Prussia's collapse and the eagerness with which people had adjusted themselves to foreign domination, as if the events from Jena to Tilsit had been but the king's personal misfortunes, were the logical outcome of a governmental system which had demanded blind obedience from its subjects instead of gaining the loyalty of free citizens. Now, the individual's free development was proclaimed one of the government's fundamental objectives, as was his education for participation in public life.

And, as regards specifically the economy:

> Just as natural laws controlled the movements of celestial bodies, so the instinct of self-preservation governed the acts of men. Pursuing their own interests, they created a new order from which they expected a maximum of prosperity. State interference was condemned as obnoxious. *Laisser faire* was proclaimed as a rule of the State. The less State interference was felt the better. The more free play that was given, the greater the prosperity that would result. There would be a natural harmony between the interests of the individuals and the general welfare.

Posterity declared them liberals, but the reformers' trust in economic freedom was perfectly compatible with frankly illiberal political and social ideals, even when these were of a radical revolutionary nature, and, in some cases, coexisted peacefully with militant reactionary conservatism. The sweetly named Professor Theodor Schmaltz, the first rector of the progressive University of Berlin, in his 1797 *Encyclopaedie der Cameralwissenschaften* seconded Smith's critique of regulation and defined men as rational economic actors, whose activity, directed to the satisfaction of their individual needs, created in the process the common wealth, but in 1815, at the time of the so-called *Demagogenverfolgungen,* railed against the German nationalist "Jacobins" (the champions of German unification, then identified with liberalism), decrying "those insensate orations about the union of all Germany under one government (in a parliamentary system, as they call it . . .), in favor of which allegiance to the several dynasties is to be extinguished in every German breast by means of derision and agitation . . . They preach German nationalism, as formerly the Jacobins preached cosmopolitanism, to make us forget the oaths which bind each of us to his sovereign."

In general, the radicalism, if not liberalism, of the reformist vision corresponded to the intensity of the reformers' nationalism and, specifically, commitment to the ideal of one Germany. Vom Stein, who was a Prussian only by occupation, stated unequivocally: "I have but one fatherland, and that is Germany . . . [T]o it, and not to any part of it, I am wholeheartedly devoted. I am completely indifferent, in this historic moment, to the fate of the dynasties . . . So far as I am concerned you may do with Prussia what you like, you may dismember it altogether." Gneisenau, Scharnhorst, and for some time Humboldt were animated by a similar deep and fervent German national sentiment. Others, such as von Schön and von Boyen, were Prussians first. Still others were not certain where Germany ended and Prussia began: Niebuhr, the scholar-politician, who was not born Prussian, argued that Prussia held a special place for all Germans (with the implication that its interests were Germany's interests). "It is the common fatherland of every German who distinguishes himself in the sciences, in arms, in administration," he claimed. The "smooth and diplomatic Count Hardenberg," a consummate politician, played both the German and the Prussian cards, as circumstances required. Economic issues were not the chief interest of any of these men, but all of them were exposed to and in varying degrees accepted the modish propositions regarding the natural economic energies of the populace, and knew (at least of) and deferred to the author of *The Wealth of Nations*. The most dedicated and radical Smithian in the group, however, was the student of the venerable Professor Kraus, von Schön, who did not appear to be a particularly zealous nationalist, though he was, by all accounts, a Prussian national patriot.

Under the impact of the French Revolution and invasion, the bureaucracies and rulers in all of Germany recognized the potency and utility of the idea of the nation, and many converted to nationalism. The geopolitical objects of their national loyalties varied, for national consciousness as such presupposed no particular political unit. Germany certainly was not the only conceivable framework for a German national identity. Newly formed states appealed to the "national" spirit of populations which Napoleon placed under their governments and attempted to instill in them national patriotism. To a certain extent this was true of Prussia as well. The reformers, wrote Hajo Holborn, "wanted most immediately to transform the Prussian state into a 'nation.'" But Prussia was the state of Frederick the Great, which had known international prominence and was "deeply imbued with a sense of European power."[25] It could not reconcile itself to the position of a vassal territory, an insignificant satellite of France, which it considered an equal. To battle Napoleon alone, as its experience so pointedly demonstrated, was no longer within its ability. For the moment it seemed that it could reassert itself and regain its former ascendancy only if German states united against the aggressor; thus its leaders were especially receptive to the ideals of German nationalism and tended to define the narrower Prussian concerns in its terms.

Nationalism, whether German or Prussian, entailed a reconstruction of the image of the social order and political community. Sovereignty, if only in principle, had to be vested in the people, and estates, frozen in rigid separation, had to be blended into a society of equal members. It was neither a liberal democracy nor an egalitarian society as such that was the goal of the reformers—they never conceived of these as objects of their actions—but the idea of the nation implied popular sovereignty and equality under the law, and no nation could either be imagined or elicit popular support without these qualities. In what is considered "the best single source for Stein's reform program," the great statesman defined his purpose in 1807 as "the reawakening of a spirit of community and civic pride, the employment of dormant and misapplied energies and of unused knowledge, harmony between the views and desires of the nation and those of the administrative authorities of the state, the revival of patriotism and of the desire for national honor and independence." Later he reiterated: "My desire is that Germany shall grow large and strong, so that it may recover its independence and nationality and maintain them against both France and Russia." To accomplish this, it was necessary to emancipate the peasants, to instill an unfamiliar sense of dignity and independence in the meek and unambitious bourgeoisie, to curb the pride of the nobility and destroy its caste privileges. The reformers wanted to turn the "machine state" of the enlightened despots into the organic community of the Romantics and to transform the individual from a cog in a mechanism into a living cell. From the economic point of view, these measures translated into a regime of economic freedom. Prussians were taught by their kings to obey; now Germans would be forced to be free.

The most important expression, in terms of its economic consequences, of this liberalism by decree was the so-called Edict of Emancipation, or the Reform Edict of October 9, 1807. It was issued eight days into Stein's second ministry, but was in preparation for some time, with Hardenberg initiating the discussions of the question of serfdom, and Schön and Schrötter drafting the proposed laws. Not all of their suggestions were included in the final document, signed by Stein and Friedrich Wilhelm, but the edict was radical enough. In the name of the king, the preamble announced:

Since the establishment of peace, we have been concerned above all with relieving the depressed condition of our loyal subjects and with the quickest possible revival and greatest possible improvement of the situation. We have considered that because of the widespread want, the means at our disposal would not be sufficient to assist each individual, and even if they were sufficient, we could not hope to accomplish our purpose. Moreover, in accordance with the imperative demands of justice and with the principles of a wise economic policy, we should like to remove every obstacle which, in the past, has prevented the individual from attaining that prosperity he was capable of reaching. We have further considered that the existing restrictions, both on the ownership and enjoyment of landed property and on the personal status of the agricultural worker, are at odds with our beneficent desires and serve to handicap a powerful force that might be used in the restoration of agriculture. Not only do these restrictions have a prejudicial influence on the value of landed property and the credit of the owner, but also they diminish the value of labor. It is our desire, therefore, to reduce both restrictions insofar as the common welfare demands.

Having thus abdicated his *Hausvater* responsibilities and made known to his subjects his desire—based as it was on the demands of justice and principles of a wise economic policy—that they become independent and pursue their own interests and common prosperity, the king proclaimed freedom of exchange of property, from which it followed that "the noble . . . may own not only noble, but also non-noble, citizen [burgher], or peasant lands of any kind, and the citizen and peasant may own not only citizen, peasant, or other non-noble, but also noble tracts of land without the necessity, in any case, of acquiring special permission for any acquisition whatsoever. However, from this time on, as before, every change of ownership must be reported to the authorities. All privileges possessed hetherto by noble over citizen are completely abolished"; and free choice of occupation, which "allowed [every noble] from this time on, without any derogation from his status, to engage in citizen [burgher] occupation [and permitted every burgher] to pass from the citizen into the peasant class or vice-versa." An article on the abolition of serfdom declared that "from Martinmas, 1810, there shall be only free individuals, such as is already the case on the royal domains in our provinces—free persons, but still subject, as a matter of course, to all the obligations which bind them, as free persons, because of the ownership of an estate or because of a special contract."

In the spirit of economic freedom, the faithful Smithian von Schön had originally proposed that *Bauernschutz*, the policy of peasant protection, be abolished simultaneously with serfdom. The East Prussian minister von Schrötter, who had to deal with the Junkers, was concerned that the introduction of economic freedom might offend the nobility and anxious to include in the edict some provisions to protect their dignity. As he put the finishing touches on the law, Stein rejected both suggestions, refusing to pander any further to the nobility, anyhow emerging as the chief beneficiary of the new legislation, and insisted that *Bauernschutz* be kept. Both Schön and Schrötter also suggested the abolition of guilds, but it was decided to leave this to another decree. Referred to as Prussia's "habeas corpus," the law of October 9, 1807, was "the first expression [there] . . . of the principle of freedom of ownership and occupation, a cardinal principle of Smithian economics. Through the terms of this edict the bonds of the feudal caste system of the Frederician state were loosened and the way was prepared for further reforms. It was not a reform in the field of agriculture alone."

The letter of the law, however, lent itself to a variety of interpretations, and Prussian economic liberalism—historians actually refer to the complex of policies adopted to rebuild Prussia and fight the liberating influences of the French Revolution by that name—took on some rather curious forms. Stein's efforts to imbue the bourgeoisie with national patriotism and the spirit of initiative failed, the good burghers being unwilling to submit even to the privileges of self-administration which the minister tried in vain to impose on them in the *Städteordnung* of November 1808. Some of them made haste indeed to take advantage of the newly granted right to purchase noble land—this was a way of moving into the nobility—and joined the Junkers in their pursuit of economic interest along the lines of capitalist agriculture. But the capital they sank into the landed estates added little, if anything, to the growth of agricultural production, and, from the point of view of the general good, might have been better spent elsewhere. Neither the burghers nor the nobles, however, showed any interest in industrial activities; they were astute enough to know where profits were to be got with the least expenditure of effort and risk.

As regards the peasantry, its situation hardly improved, and whatever energy was stored up in its midst had to be, as before, squandered on eking out a miserable living. Stein's attempts to undermine the social arrangements associated with serfdom were crushed against the wall of noble opposition. Thus "only after the revolution of 1848–49 was patrimonial jurisdiction wrested from the nobility, while the exemption from the land tax was only lifted in 1861, and self-government of the rural communities according to Stein's principles was first introduced in 1891. Another significant prerogative of the country squire, his rights as patron of the parish, was abolished only after the revolution of 1918."[26]

It took time to accomplish a revolution from above. Hardenberg's edict of 1811 specified the price one had to pay for freedom: it was one third of the peasant's holding for those who had hereditary use of the land, and one half of it for those whose tenure was nonhereditary. The Declaration of 1816 took the principles of economic liberalism further, abolishing *Bauernschutz* and limiting the rights of peasant proprietors, as defined under the 1811 edict, to the *spannfähig* peasants, the lucky owners of draft animals. The rest were left to the whims of fate, eventually becoming landless laborers. Their land—between 46,000 and 54,000 farms and 70,000 small plots—added about a million hectares (2.471 million acres) to the Junker estates. Liberty might have been worth it, but the peasants were not granted liberty. Serfdom, abolished de jure, was reintroduced de facto in the draconian *Gesindeordnung* of 1810, which prohibited any agricultural worker or domestic servant to resign, declared striking a crime carrying a prison sentence, and reinstituted "paternal discipline," which the enlightened despot Friedrich Wilhelm I had considered an abomination in 1738. This ordinance also remained in force until 1918. Hardenberg, both more comfortable with authoritarian government than Stein, and more resolutely faithful to the principles of economic liberalism, pursued a policy of increasing economic freedom in city industries, and, unmoved by burghers' cries of protest, deprived the guilds of their remaining privileges. He also attempted a fiscal reform that would bring town and country closer together by devising a general tax system; but the nobility was more protective of its privileges than the bourgeoisie, and, in the face of its stiffer opposition, the chancellor had to back down. The economic effects of all these measures were negligible.

Altogether, the period of Prussian reform was brought to a close in 1819 with the repressive Carlsbad decrees, drawn up by Metternich and ratified by the Diet of the four-year-old German Confederation, which were directed specifically against the spirit of German nationalism, illiberal and totalitarian as it was, whose tremendous revolutionary potential the perspicacious Austrian minister clearly saw. In Prussia, Friedrich Wilhelm III, long wary of the nationalist aspirations of his advisers, who saw in his kingdom only a means to the achievement of a German goal, in which the king had no interest whatsoever, sighed a sigh of relief. The overzealous councilors—Humboldt, Boyen—were let go. Hardenberg conveniently died in 1822. According to Friedrich Meinecke, this was the first of "the three tragic turning points of modern German history." The defeat of Napoleon made nationalism, the commitment to which among the territorial rulers was often only instrumental and therefore halfhearted, irrelevant again, and the reforms in social, economic, and political arrangements that it implied no longer appeared justifiable.

First Shoots of Economic Nationalism

Economic liberty was inextricably bound to nationalism in the minds of the Prussian reformers, who saw in it both a reflection of and a means to the development of national patriotism. Romantic nationalists, however, were already turning away from this English invention, *Smithianismus* coming under attack precisely at the time when the Anglophile Stein was attempting to make its ideals reality. General anti-economic opinions, consistent with the Romantic ineptitude—and therefore contempt—for the mundane, had been voiced before. The attack on Smith, though, led by Adam Müller, rather than rejecting the importance of economics, anticipated German economic nationalism.

Müller's popularity coincided with the heroic spurt in German economic development at the end of the nineteenth and the beginning of the twentieth centuries, long after he died in 1829. The son of a Prussian official, he was educated in Göttingen, where he made friends with von Gentz and, probably, took courses taught by Sartorius, for in his early days he was a Smithian. When, with many others, he renounced the delusions of his youth and became the most outspoken critic of Smith's theory in Germany, Müller nevertheless referred to Smith as the "august Adam Smith" and considered him "the great and wise and good man." Neither did he deny all merit to Smith's theory. He was perfectly willing to admit—as did German "Smithians" before him and Friedrich List later—that it applied to England, whose specific situation justified and perhaps necessitated unlimited economic freedom. But Germany was not England and could not follow England as its model: it went its own way and was morally obligated to remain true to it. He also granted that Smith's system had the arguable advantage (for those, that is, who saw virtue in disciplined reasoning, which Müller did not) of general coherence and would be unassailable if it were not based on faulty assumptions. The chief of these assumptions was the idea of the individual as an independent (economic) actor, which contradicted Müller's conviction that human life was possible only in and through the state. Since the autonomous individual was the foundation stone of Smith's theoretical structure, its elimination not only caused the entire edifice to crumble but also revealed the latter's inherent immorality, for to insist on the principles of economic liberalism in its absence was to go against the very source of all morality: human nature. The essence of economic liberalism was in fact (and in this Müller was right) its individualism, but man was a social being, to present him as an independent actor was to alienate from him that which was central and constitutive in him; Müller did not use the term "species-being," but this was precisely what he meant.

Constructions that derived from the idea of the individual as an independent actor, such as private property, had the same alienating function. Private property, as envisioned by economic liberals, was "nothing but a spasmodic clinging to the isolation *(Einzelheit)* of things which nature gave us for the purpose of separating and dividing them for transformation into sexual [reciprocal] interrelationships." In addition to alienating man from his nature, it also alienated him from the society of other men by withdrawing what was meant for all from the public sphere, and therefore was not real, enjoyable, but dead property, for "whatever is excluded from the reciprocity of production and consumption . . . is to be judged as dead." As far as economic *life* was concerned, in other words, communism was the natural and desirable condition. "Property in the real meaning of the term," Müller explained, was "only possession in common; private property is only usufruct and transitoriness." Only objects of individual consumption constituted private property. All other kinds of properties were communal, either corporate (family, village, and so on) or state, and the individual at any moment had to "be prepared to share his property, even that consisting in his person, with others, or to transfer it to the state."

Land, which was "the permanent, in fact the eternal, heritage of the whole immortal state-family," was a property above all others; therefore neither its sale nor mortgaging was permissible. But obstruction of free land transfers implied severe limitations on the freedom of labor, and indeed Müller was all in favor of serfdom (which presumably connected both the lords and the peasants to their species-being and allowed fullest expression to their innermost nature), and thought that freedom of trade in industry and commerce should be tolerated only within narrow limits and in a system of guilds and regulations. Unlimited economic liberty was inefficient and counterproductive—"an unregulated activity of everybody, where one wave of industriousness devours the other, instead of the rule of incessant work." Freedom of contract, for its part, destroyed the traditional—natural—relationships of reciprocity, and thus also was but a "false liberty."

Adam Smith's system was, in short, an "allegedly liberal" system, and it threatened "to engulf the entire natural order of things in Europe." Its individualism—"the most general manifestation of [modern] anti-social spirit, of arrogant egoism, of immoral enthusiasm for false reason and false enlightenment"—stripped all social relations of their warmth, converting them into mere money relations. It increased alienation and polarized society, relieving the upper classes of their traditional responsibilities and exacerbating the exploitation of the poor. It reduced the worker "to a mere wage-laborer to be thrown on the dump-hill when no longer useful to the big economic machine." By pretending to liberate man from the "omnipresence of a common will," it deprived him of real liberty and made him a slave to the vagaries of the market—prey to insecurity, instability, and competition. (Here it is no longer the *Nationaloekonomie* that one is reminded of but the feverish cadences of *The Communist Manifesto* or *Slaves without Masters* of our own George Fitzhugh.)

Economic liberty was a yoke, and what internal freedom of trade did to

man, international freedom of trade was bound to do to the great and beautiful individual of the state. It stood in the way of individuality and totality, it
prevented self-realization. Such principles could make a society rich, but they
could not make it wealthy, for the true wealth of nations was "wealth that
guarantees itself," reproducing its "organic" uniqueness. "The mere existence of wealth," Müller insisted, "is not enough; by its political and social
conditioning it must have the power to individualize itself as the wealth of a
definite person, of a definite 'estate,' or of a definite state; that is it must be
able to defend and maintain itself against the whole covetous world."

So defined, wealth could not be measured and had little in common with
quantifiable notions of riches, prosperity, and even material subsistence (for
Müller objected to quantification). A parallel idea of productivity, and therefore productive forces, corresponded to it. To these forces belonged, first and
foremost, "national moral capital" *(geistiges National-Kapital)*, as well as the
labor, including the mental or spiritual labor, of past generations. "Adam
Smith," Müller argued in his second lecture in *Elements of Politics,*

> in spite of all his eminence, [was] never able to understand how, in fact,
> the products of the minds in the state must be taken into consideration
> together with the more solid products of the earth and of manufac-
> ture[.] He had no idea how to fit scholars, statesmen, actors or clerics
> into his purpose; only if they produce a tangible product, e.g. if the phi-
> losopher produces a book, in short, only if their industry is really materi-
> ally productive and if what they produce takes the form of a real ob-
> ject for trade, only then are they, in his opinion, of any importance to
> the state. He wanted to draw an absolute boundary to production, he
> wanted to give a fixed concept of national wealth; in order to satisfy this
> *concept* the most fruitful thoughts of the statesman, the most stimulating
> discourses of the scholar or cleric had to be excluded from the sum of
> the productive work of the state. It was a matter of being able to grasp
> something, to seize hold of it physically; for Adam Smith, the product
> was the touchstone of productive work.
>
> The problem, however, of understanding production is far more in-
> teresting, for production is that great movement of the minds and hands
> which is profoundly complex and yet so simple, under which national
> wealth is in the process of continuous growth. Anyone who wishes to
> consider this movement can no longer exclude the powerfully active in-
> ner or spiritual forces of man . . . As soon as we draw a boundary around
> abstract pure products in order to answer absolutely and finally the one
> question "what is wealth?" we are forced, like Adam Smith, to erect an
> absolute and insurmountable wall between the physical and moral, be-

tween real and ideal possession, and then we can no longer depict movement and growth.[27]

Some influential economists, including in America, were to advance very similar ideas later, in our own day reflected in such concepts as "cultural," "social," and "human capital." Some of Müller's other ideas, particularly his castigation of economic freedom as an instrument of exploitation and alienation, as was pointed out earlier, were taken up by Marx, in whose able hands they became potent weapons of revolutionary propaganda. All the economic implications of Romantic nationalism, which were to find their place in Marxism (the definition of wealth as an organic totality, of private property as dead, and of communism as the natural, thus healthful economic condition), were already revealed by Müller. But Marx had combined these ideas with the principles of economic liberalism in an ingenious historicist scheme, presenting them as stages of world economic development, itself the foundation of historical process (from primitive communism, through individualistic economic liberalism, a.k.a. capitalism, to communism as the culmination of history) and making the presumed triumph of economic liberalism, which Müller anticipated and lamented, the very means of its own inescapable destruction. The spring of history was the total natural energy of the "whole," or completely social, human being, and its compression in alienation, effected by the division of labor, private property, and self-interest, was to bring about the explosive revolutionary release of the communist apocalypse. Economic determinism thus added to the economic implications of Romantic nationalism the promise of the realization of the Kingdom of God on earth—its innermost aspiration. Moreover, it was to be fulfilled through the agency of the Smithian invisible hand, which slyly guided self-interested sinners to prepare their own punishment, and without the slightest effort on the part of the just. The meek—those who lacked economic ambition and initiative—would inherit the earth; the have-nots would have all, and all they had to do was sit and wait.

Friedrich List: The Reorientation of Economic Action

It was List's economic nationalism, rather than Marx's economic determinism, which carried the day in Germany, however. As regards its specifically economic aspect, the Marxian promise appealed to those who were willing to sit and wait because they did not assign much importance either to prosperity or to economic competitiveness, or (as was sometimes the case in the twentieth century) to those who had no other choice, even if they considered these values important. Germans were no longer prepared to wait at the time it was sounded; they had other choices, and they were impatient for economic greatness.

List's 1841 *National System of Political Economy* was the first authoritative formulation of economic nationalism. When he wrote it, List was fifty-two and approaching the end of a lifelong career of nationalistic agitation. He was born in 1789 in the Württemberg city of Reutlingen to a tanner's family, and at an early age became a clerk and then entered the government civil service. By 1816 he was promoted to the post of ministerial undersecretary of finance in the Württemberg Ministry of the Interior. The minister liked him well and soon appointed him professor of Practical Administration *(Staatspraxis)* at the University of Tübingen, even though List did not have a university degree. As the faculty resented this appointment, and the minister himself soon lost favor with the king, by 1819 List had to resign, having been simultaneously kicked out of the civil service for espousing revolutionary political views.

For being a nationalist at that time in Germany was revolutionary. List advocated the establishment of a German national parliament, army, and judiciary, as well as cultural institutions, which obviously went against the interests of the rulers of the thirty-eight independent states united at that time in a loose German Confederation. He also agitated against the customs barriers separating these states, in 1819 becoming the president (or *Konsul*) of the Association of German Merchants and Manufacturers founded in Frankfurt to abolish them and establish a "universal German system on the principle of retaliation against foreign states." From the politically correct point of view this was a serious transgression, and when List was elected representative from Reutlingen to the Württemberg National Assembly, his election "was canceled by Ministerial veto." Elected again, he was expelled from the Diet and sentenced "for demagoguery" "to 10 months imprisonment in a fortress, with hard labor," having to pay the costs of the proceedings against him. List fled to Strassburg and then to Baden, both of which he was ordered to leave, then, forced to cross the German border altogether, went to Paris. There he met Lafayette, who took a liking to him and, therefore, invited the German fugitive to . . . the United States. (The dashing marquis, a French nationalist and the author of the idea of the United States of Europe under the leadership of France, loved the United States of America at least as much as he detested England.)

But List did not want to go; "his intense love of his native country urged him to return to Württemberg and appeal to the mercy of the king." The king, however, used the opportunity to seize List and immure him in another fortress. He was freed only after several discouraging months and solely on the condition of immediate renunciation of his Württemberg citizenship. He went to Strassburg again and was again kicked out, returning again to France. But this time, at the request of the vengeful Württemberg sovereign, he was kicked out of France too. So, *volens nolens,* he went to the United States and was met there with open arms.

Lafayette introduced List to some influential Americans, then quite agitated about English economic superiority, and these Americans invited him to express himself on the subject of the unfairness of Great Britain's trade policies, which he did. His opinions first appeared in the German-language newspaper which he published, but were later reissued as a collection of letters by the Pennsylvania Association for the Promotion of Manufacturing Industry. In these letters List attacked Adam Smith, advocated protectionist policies, and praised the so-called American system (moving a defender of free trade in the House of Representatives to remark, "We appear to have imported a Professor from Germany, in absolute violation of the American system, to lecture upon its lessons").

This defense of American economic interests against England earned List the gratitude of his American friends, and, as they knew that Germany was foremost on his mind, he was appointed U.S. consul in Hamburg. Hamburgers, still under the impression that he was a dangerous revolutionary, would have none of that. He was fated to go to Paris again and then, briefly, back to the United States. Finally, however, he returned to Germany as American consul in Leipzig, where he was able to render some very valuable services to the duchies of Weimar, Gotha, and Meiningen, whose gratitude improved his position in Germany generally.

List completed the first part of *The National System of Political Economy* in Augsburg. The book was immediately attacked for its exclusive preoccupation with German interests, but went through three editions in several months, also appearing in French and Hungarian translations. In the last part, titled "Politics" (1844), List, in addition to inveighing against the "crafty and spiteful commercial policy of England," and arguing for the development of all-German communications, proposed the adoption of a common German flag, the establishment of German colonies overseas, and a national emigration policy. The numbers of his admirers grew. Even the king of Württemberg decided to bury the hatchet, and, having invited List to an audience, said: "My dear List, I bear you no ill-will. What a pity it is that 24 years ago we had not learnt to know each other as well as we do now!"[28] This was, however, too little too late: in 1846, his spirit broken by twenty-four years of frustration, List committed suicide.

Unlike Marx—who, as behooves a true Romantic, lived in and wrote about the world entirely of his imagination, and was (par excellence) a theorist in that proud sense of the word which emphasizes the independence of theory from cumbersome reality—List lived in the real world and was a man of practice. For lack of an alternative, as well as perhaps by inclination far more engrossed than Marx in the quotidian business of earning a living, List was not a philosophical materialist and did not believe economics to be the end-all of human endeavor. Like all Romantic nationalists, List thought that the world was naturally divided into nations, and that nations, rather than individual human beings, were the real (that is, significant) actors in history. Both individual human beings and humanity as a whole depended on nations and could find realization only through them. The nations were hierarchically ranked and could be divided into the important and unimportant in accordance, fundamentally, with the level of their cultural development and potential, in turn determined by nature; in List's opinion, they were ultimately defined by climate. Nations of the so-called "temperate zone," which corresponded to Europe and North America, he believed, were inherently superior to the nations of the area he termed "torrid," and, as a result, were justified in attempting to use the resources of the latter in the service of their own national self-fulfillment. Individual members of the nation could also be legitimately used for this purpose: the interests of individuals did not necessarily combine into the interests of the nation and, under all circumstances, were subservient to these. The root interest of every nation was the interest in national self-realization. Self-realization could be obstructed by the efforts or lack of cooperation of other nations, each set on its independent course by the same desire to realize itself. This presupposed a state of permanent international competition.

While Marx presented the competition between nations in terms of a universal economic struggle, whether or not it actually took the form of economic rivalry, with List, while still presented as competition between nations, it acquired an economic dimension. List's ideas therefore provided an alternative outlet for nationalist energies, channeling them into economic pursuits with eventually dramatic effects. Like Marx, List believed that Germany compared unfavorably with some other European nations. The main reason for such unfavorable comparison, in his view, however, was the underdevelopment of its industry, and for that reason he saw as his nation's chief rivals not only England and France but also Holland. Still, England was at the center of his attention: it was by far the greatest economic power of the time, and List thought that Germany's economic inferiority could be in a large measure attributed to England's imposition on its partners of the policy of free trade—which, under the conditions that then prevailed, served to maintain England in the position of unrivaled exporter of manufactured goods. List therefore concentrated his efforts on trying to convince his countrymen of the benefits of protective tariffs against English imports. List was not in principle opposed to freedom of trade and did not have a principled commitment to protective tariffs, but he was of the opinion that, the circumstances being what they were, freedom of foreign trade was bad for Germany and protective tariffs were in its interest. Arguing for protection against foreign industrial imports, he at the same time insisted on the necessity of abolishing all tariffs within Germany, that is, customs barriers between various German states, and praised the benefits of internal free competition for the development of the economy. That such competition could prove deleterious to individuals and large groups (such as the industrial proletariat) within Germany, and that the ability to buy foreign goods cheaply meant greater comfort for large numbers of Germans, appeared to him irrelevant. He was at no point concerned with the prosperity of his fellow men, but was devoted single-mindedly to the ideal of a powerful and prestigious Germany, holding a place in the international community commensurate with its cultural achievement and potential. This was a cultural or, at most, political rather than economic ideal: the development of national economy was not an end in itself, but only a crucially important means toward its achievement. Vigorous industry, in List's view, was "a tonic for the national spirit"; without it Germans would be unable "to soar to national greatness." It implied superior conditions for political and cultural development and was indispensable as a condition for national prestige. Inattention to questions of economy was perilous: to say nothing of their inferiority vis-à-vis England, it could leave the Germans "far behind the French and North Americans, nay: far behind the Russians," a state of obvious degradation, the prospect of which would frighten any patriot out of his wits.

Because so much depended on it, the development of the national economy was too important a project to entrust to the invisible hand operating through individual economic interests. The economic interests of merchants aroused List's particular suspicion: he thought them inherently deficient in patriotic spirit, ready to pursue their selfish ends "at the expense of the nation's productive powers, and indeed of its independence," and for that very reason enamored, together with "robbers, cheats, and thieves," of the principle "Laissez faire, laissez passer." Merchants, in his view, however, were less important to the national economy than "producers," that is, entrepreneurs and managers engaged in the manufacturing industry, but also all those who contributed to the nation's "productive power" or its "power of producing wealth" through education, administration, and planning, as well as through generally raising its cultural and intellectual level. In fact, he believed "the mental labours of those who maintain laws and order, and cultivate and promote instruction, religion, science, and art" to be among the primary causes of wealth, "instructors of youth and of adults, virtuosos, musicians, physicians, judges, and administrators [being] productive in a much higher degree," and thus more important for the nation's business, than businessmen as such. But in the case of "producers" too, List was convinced that "only where the interest of individuals has been subordinated to those of the nation . . . the nations have been brought to harmonious development of their productive powers." This made the national economy the business of the state, while the involvement of the state provided ample opportunities for the participation of farsighted patriotic intellectuals.

One of the features which made List's approach to economics appealing is its intellectual indeterminism and, therefore, activism. The economic dimension was obviously very important to him as a basis for cultural and political development, but it was clearly not the *Unterbau* of social existence it was for Marx, and was, in its turn, dependent on cultural and political processes. List remained open with regard to the question "whether the material forces exert a greater influence over moral forces, or whether the moral outweigh the material in their operation; whether the social forces act upon the individual forces the more powerfully, or whether the latter upon the former." His view of social causality was multidirectional, admitting and accepting "this much [as] certain[:] that between the two there subsists an interchanging sequence of action and reaction, with the result that the increase of one set of forces promotes the increase of the other, and that the enfeeblement of the one ever involves the enfeeblement of the other." The economic and non-economic factors were interdependent. This implied the importance of people's commitments and gave one the possibility of, even required, active participation (with its accompanying responsibilities and potential sense of accomplishment) in the social process. The appeal of List's ideas has been at its strongest in times when the laws of history or the invisible hand failed to bring the desired results unaided and people grew impatient with them. It is this impatience which drew so many European intellectuals in the 1920s and 1930s from Marxist socialism to fascism and which may have been the reason behind the attraction of state interventionists, right and left, to List.

List's objections to Adam Smith, however, did not focus on the "invisible hand" argument. In his view, the theory exalted by champions of *Smithianismus* suffered from graver problems. "True political economy," List wrote, was "that policy which each separate nation had to obey in order to make progress in its economic conditions," or "*national* economy." But with it Smith "concerned himself little." "The system of the school" exhibited

> three main defects: . . . boundless *cosmopolitanism*, which neither recognizes the principle of nationality, not takes into consideration the satis-

faction of its interests . . . a dead *materialism,* which everywhere regards chiefly the mere exchangeable value of things without taking into consideration the mental and political, the present and the future interests, and the productive powers of the nation . . . a *disorganizing particularism* and *individualism,* which, ignoring the nature and character of social labour and the operation of the union of powers in their higher consequences, considers private industry only as it would develop itself under a state of free interchange with society (i.e. with the whole human race) were that race not divided into separate national societies. Between each individual and entire humanity, however, stands the NA-TION, with its special language and literature.

Smith, List argued, "[nullified] nationality and . . . State power [and exalted] individualism to the position of author of all effective power." He conceived of a nation merely as "a community, i.e. a number of individuals dwelling together [who] know best for themselves what branches of occupation are most to their advantage, and . . . can best select for themselves the means which promote their prosperity." This, List insisted, was "nothing more than . . . a mere shopkeeper's . . . theory—not a scientific doctrine showing how the productive powers of an entire nation can be called into existence, increased, maintained, and preserved—for the special benefit of its civilization, welfare, might, continuance, and independence. [It regarded] everything from the shopkeeper's point of view."

At the same time, List claimed that Smith's theory of free trade served the interests of English industry, maintaining its near-monopoly on the market and keeping other nations at a competitive disadvantage. Smith's cosmopolitanism, in other words, was a subterfuge (an "ideology" in Marxist terms), and a tool of English nationalism. The results of the operation of free trade under the existing political conditions, List thought, were predictable. "The Britons," he wrote,

as an independent and separate nation would henceforth take their national interest as the sole guide of their policy. The Englishman, from predilection for his language, for his laws, regulations, and habits, would whenever it was possible devote his powers and his capital to develop his own native industry, for which the system of free trade, by extending the market for English manufactures over all countries, would offer him sufficient opportunity; he would not readily take a fancy to establish manufactures in France or Germany. All excess of capital in England would be at once devoted to trading with foreign parts of the world. If the Englishman took it into his head to emigrate, or to invest his capital elsewhere than in England, he would as he now does prefer those more distant countries where he would find already existing his language, his laws, his regulations, rather than the benighted countries of the Continent. All England would thus be developed into one immense manufacturing city. Asia, Africa, and Australia would be civilized by England, and covered with new states modeled after the English fashion. In time a world of English states would be formed, under the presidency of the mother state, in which the European Continental nations would be lost as unimportant, unproductive races. By this arrangement it would fall to the lot of France, together with Spain and Portugal, to supply this English world with the choicest wines, and to drink the bad ones herself: at most France might retain the manufacture of a little millinery. Germany would scarcely have more to supply this English world with than children's toys, wooden clocks, and philological writings, and sometimes also an auxiliary corps, who might sacrifice themselves to pine away in the deserts of Asia or Africa, for the sake of extending the manufacturing and commercial supremacy, the literature and language of England. It would not require many centuries before people of this English world would think and speak of the Germans and French in the same tone as we speak at present of Asiatic nations.

"True political science," he concluded, "regards such a result of universal free trade as a very unnatural one; it will argue that had universal free trade been introduced at the time of the Hanseatic League, the German nationality instead of the English would have secured an advance in commerce and manufacture over all other countries. It would be most unjust, [therefore] even on cosmopolitical grounds, now to resign to the English all the wealth and power of the earth."[29]

List, claimed Louis Kossuth, as he welcomed "the fiery Swabian" to the Budapest *Komitat* in 1844, was the man "who has most clearly revealed to the nation its true economic interests." So important—and so novel—was this message that Kossuth, the great Hungarian nationalist, was willing to disregard the fact that the only nation for whose economic interests List had any concern was a unified Germany (which, in his mind, included Austria, to the fight against which Kossuth dedicated his life). A century later his grateful countrymen would recognize in List "the most important predecessor of Bismarck," and an American historian, Louis Snyder, singled him out from thousands of thinkers and activists, alongside a handful of others, as one of "the great representatives of German national consciousness." List's "work was vital," Snyder wrote, and, as a prophecy of German nationalism, "takes a place alongside [that of] the poet Ernst Moritz Arndt, the philologists Jakob and Wilhelm Grimm, the historian Heinrich von Treitschke, and the composer Richard Wagner. List's unique contribution to German nationalism was the first expression of a systematic content of the national concept at the economic level."[30] But the economic significance of List's work, if anything, exceeded the importance of his contribution to German national consciousness, for what he did went far beyond simply fixing the attention of his fellow Germanophones on matters economic (which was no small achievement in itself, given that before him these matters had aroused very slight interest) to, in fact, projecting and focusing nationalism on them. Thereby this one ardent and unhappy man, unrecognized and unrewarded for much of his life, added a powerful, and heretofore lacking, ethical dimension to economic activity and reoriented it toward international competition and growth.

At the time List began his propagandist activity on behalf of the German economy—in early 1819—German nationalism had already become a formidable political force, and it was its recognition as such by Metternich and other German rulers that led to the crackdown and the onset of reaction later that year. But though it burned brightly in the hearts of Romantic intellectuals, students, and university-educated bureaucrats, it had not yet reached deep into the masses of the German people, whether in the cities or in the countryside, and become a significant motivation in their everyday lives. Economic activity, in particular, had not yet been affected in the least, which is to say, it was still ethically unmotivated, and the fact that the only motives that spurred it on (as opposed to containing it within traditional boundaries) were the motives of individual self-interest, that it lacked the stimulus of social approbation, goes a long way in accounting for the general sluggishness of the German economy in the first half of the nineteenth century.

It is clear that very few of even the most active merchants or manufacturers, otherwise richly endowed with entrepreneurial spirit, were moved by national sentiment in those early days and interpreted their business interests, or those of their class, in the light of the broader interest of the nation. They were obviously unaware of the enormous implications of such an interpretation for the advancement of business interests and for their own social standing. They did not see beyond the advantages or disadvantages of an immediate situation and used their business sense to navigate in the limited economic space created by various political and fiscal arrangements, trying to benefit from the former and avoid the latter. It was such narrow concerns that led to the formation of the German Union of Merchants and Manufacturers (Deutscher Handels-und Gewerbsverein) in Frankfurt am Main in April 1819, which offered the first opportunity for List's pan-German nationalist agitation.

The specific grievance which the union was supposed—and List, as its chosen spokesman, was requested—to address was the added costs of commerce between parts of Germany which resulted from the institution of the 1818 Prussian tariff. Aiming to eliminate archaic customs barriers within the many Prussian territories, and true to the dictates of free trade, the new law exchanged all internal tolls for very moderate duties at the frontiers, which were levied by weight rather than value. As a result, the tariffs were higher on cheaper goods, especially when imported in bulk, than on more expensive ones. Since it was from its German neighbors that Prussia bought the former, and from other foreigners, such as the English, the latter, German merchants and manufacturers had to pay the price for Prussian liberalism of which others reaped the profits. They were also particularly affected by duties levied on traffic through Prussian territories, having no other way to get their products to German markets in the other states. "In the transit dues," wrote Clapham, "the new Prussia had got hold of a most formidable economico-political bludgeon. From the first there was a howl against this blackmailing of German trade."

But it was not the discrimination against German merchants by the Prussian tariff, or the tariff as such, which was the focus of the petition to the Federal Assembly which List prepared ostensibly on their behalf. Instead, he focused on the necessity of surrounding all of Germany (in which, incidentally, like Engels later, he wished to include Holland and Denmark) by a tariff wall, "based on the principle of retaliation against foreign nations," while abolishing all the duties between German states. The petition thus inaugurated a lifelong work of propaganda for German economic unification, eventually contributing to the formation of the *Zollverein* in 1834. The purpose of List's activity, again, was immediately perceived by Metternich, who by June 1819 had already registered his unhappiness with the "cabal of the new, highly dangerous confederation [which] was attempting to expand its idea of Germanness into the circles of German practical revolutionaries."

The role of List's "plan of economic unification" and of his subsequent lobbying in bringing about this landmark development, which represented a necessary condition for modern economy in Germany, was crucial. Arnold Price ranks it as the second among the four factors to which the Customs Union owed its establishment. "He was to a great extent responsible," writes Snyder, "for setting the chain-reaction into motion which led to the formation of the *Zollverein*. He was the irritant, the hair-shirt, the catalytic agent." But, clearly, *Zollverein* was also in the interest of Prussia, and it was, once again, the coincidence between German nationalism and Prussia's particularist designs that promoted the cause with which both temporarily identified.

In Prussia *Zollverein* was first conceived of as *Zollanschluss*, namely, a fiscal conquest rather than a fiscal union, but so long as it dictated the terms, Prussia was willing to conduct business under any name. Prussian ministers, beginning with Hardenberg, whose support List attempted to recruit in November 1819, therefore showed themselves receptive to the idea of a wider union (although they disagreed with List in respect to the advisability of a protective or "retaliatory" tariff) and even encouraged the Union of Merchants to pursue the matter further at the Federal Ministerial Congress which was soon to take place in Vienna. Yet "*Zollverein*, paradoxically, was originally a device utilized by Prussia to prevent a general German economic union. The Prussians were understandably concerned lest any such economic union achieved through the German Confederation might result in Austrian hegemony in Germany." Prussia, we learn,

> had no consideration for the welfare of other German states and no desire to see a customs union worked out by common consent. Instead, the Prussian economic administrators . . . began the process of economic amalgamation of their own territories, which lay scattered throughout the Germanies. Slowly but surely, economic pressures forced other German states one by one into the Prussian system, whose economic power and the political interests behind it proved to be too strong for any other German state or combination of states. Both the South German states and the Central German states desired the benefits of enlarged customs unions of their own without giving up their economic independence to Prussia, but they were eventually drawn into the Prussian orbit."[31]

None of the German states had any consideration for the common welfare, and the ultimate success of Prussian policy should be attributed, in addition to economic pressures, to the skillful diplomacy of Prussia's representatives.[32] When the time was ripe, they made use of the nationalist arguments supplied by List: in the middle of the nineteenth century in Prussia, it was still possible to believe that it was safe to inject the masses with the national sentiment at will, for the government could control and contain its spread. When it came into being, *Zollverein* was the realization of the Prussian aspiration of *Zollanschluss* and "was a very different organization from the one envisaged by List. It was not established by the German Confederation as List had proposed. It was founded by Prussia and its members accepted the Prussian tariff which List regarded as far too liberal to give German manufacturers adequate protection against foreign competition."

But List's economic nationalism was a double-edged sword, which served as a weapon in the hands of the industrialists clamoring for protection as well. And so, as soon as the Customs Union was founded, the duties on manufactured goods, in particular English pig iron and cotton yarn, exhibited a tendency "to become a good deal heavier." The history of the *Zollverein*, therefore, was "unhappily that of a gradual departure from the sound principles on which it was originally based." The main reason for Prussia's preference for a moderate tariff was political. Austrian economy was still managed in accordance with mercantilist/*Staatswirtschaft* principles of protection and prohibition: the economic liberalism of the *Zollverein* made membership in it less attractive for Austrian manufacturers, and Prussia wanted to keep Austria out, because Austria still had the power to wrest the leadership of the union—and the Confederation—from Prussia's hands. With the entry of Hanover and Oldenburg in 1854, which finally opened for the *Zollverein* access to the North Sea, and the demise of Austria in the next decade, this reason disappeared and Prussia was ready to accept List's teaching.

List's concern for German "infant industries," which required protection by means of what he termed "educational tariffs," was rooted in his conviction, which could only be inspired by the example of England (though it was reinforced by like-minded Americans with whom he came in contact during his sojourn in the Western Hemisphere), that the economic strength of a nation ultimately rested on its industry, rather than agriculture or commerce. A critic of Smith, he nevertheless firmly believed in the "industrial system." This emphasis on industry, in the bucolic conditions of early to mid-nineteenth-century Germany, perhaps more than any other aspect of List's thought, revealed him as a visionary: there was nothing in the German reality that justified such outlandish ideas. They appeared all the stranger, since List very early recognized and insisted on the importance of industrialization in the sense of the introduction of machinery. As late as 1844, during his visit to Austria and Hungary (this time to garner support for his railway schemes and plans for the Austro-German colonization of the Balkans), he had to argue against the disbelief of his audiences that industrialization was indeed "a means of promoting economic growth."[33] The argument was still controversial. Obviously List, who was willing to, and in fact did, accept martyrdom to make his message heard, was not a person to shy away from unpopular opinions.

His propagandist activity was an important factor in bringing railways to Germany. He claimed that he had become convinced of the importance of a railway network of communications as a means of national economic development as early as 1824, while traveling in England, though his biographers consider this unlikely, since the only railway he could have seen at that date was the Wandsworth-Croydon line, which was horse-drawn. But a seer may see things hidden from other mortals and is aided by more than the physical faculty of sight in interpreting their significance. However that may be, List started his agitation for the construction of railways in Germany in earnest in 1830. In 1831 the lack of interest among his countrymen plunged him into "mental depression" and he confessed to a correspondent in Munich that he had "given up hope of achieving anything in Germany" and was forced to consider promoting railway construction in France. (This was depressing in itself, given that List saw himself as "a spokesman for Germany's national interests" rather than being simply a railway enthusiast.) He did not allow human frailty to divert him from what was clearly an apostolic mission, however, and soon was concerned with raising capital to establish a Hanseatic-Bavarian railroad company. An American consul in Leipzig since 1834, List neglected the responsibilities (and undoubtedly used the authority) of his position to advance the plans for the construction of the Leipzig-Dresden line, "the first German railroad line of major consequence," which was opened in 1837. "Without his vigorous propaganda in favour of the scheme," writes W. O. Henderson, "and his tireless work on the committee which made the preparations for the establishment of the railway company, it may be doubted whether the line could have been built at the time."

His labors were recognized in a grant of 4,000 thalers, but his application for the post of the railroad manager, and a steady income, was rejected. Though disappointed, in 1840 he was planning railways in Thuringia and successfully negotiated an agreement on construction between the principalities of Saxe-Coburg-Gotha, Saxe-Meiningen, and Weimar. This time his reward was one hundred Friedrich d'or and an honorary degree from the University of Jena. As Treitschke already pointed out, it was the railroads that "first dragged the German nation out of its economic stagnation." It was the railroads that transformed "the area of the German customs Union into a common market. The wide and greatly intensified exchange of goods quickened industrial production . . . Only in conjunction with the railroads did the customs Union become a powerful, dynamic influence on German economic life."[34] But the construction of the German network was, in the early days of the industry, obstructed by the lack of cooperation among various German governments and the weakness of national sentiment among private entrepreneurs. To a very significant extent, it was List's tireless activity which aroused this sentiment in the business class and was responsible for overcoming the obstacles to the expansion of the railway system in Germany.

In our age of social science placing all of its faith in grand and impersonal social forces (which includes economics and economic history), it is difficult to comprehend how a private individual, a man without position or wealth, constantly preoccupied with making ends meet, could have exerted such a tremendous influence on the economy of a vast and politically heterogeneous geographic area as to become, in effect, a central factor in its material development. The explanation lies in the transforming powers of his message, which were truly magical—touched by nationalism, no aspect of reality looked, and was, the same—and in the nature of his preferred method of delivery. Most of his working life List was a journalist, and in the middle decades of the nineteenth century in Germany, as contemporaries clearly perceived and as many authors today recognize, journalism was "a major form of political activity." The singular efficacy of List's propaganda had to do with the fact that, owing to the economic orientation of his nationalism, he targeted an audience to whom the nationalist message had not been specifically addressed before: the uneducated bourgeoisie, whom lofty Romantic definitions of Germanity in fact slighted. List's ennoblement of the economic sphere (through the broad definition of productive forces and the insistence on the centrality of the economic dimension in the totality of national self-realization) drew the bourgeoisie into the purifying and ennobling charmed circle of the national community, revealing to the timid burghers the breathtaking implications of nationalism for their self-image and social status. They learned that the success of a business could have a wider patriotic significance, that a commercial venture or, more so, an industrial undertaking had an element of the heroic—that there was dignity, in other words, in the activities they pursued, for lack of choice, in order to make a living. Thus through List the Romantic nationalist message reached the economically active middle class.

It is a testimony to the authority of the printed word in early nineteenth-century Germany that, when he returned to Europe in 1830, List was already known as a "revolutionary," "Jacobin," "Republican," and "demagogue" (though, as Treitschke emphasized later, "a demagogue only in the noblest sense"). His influence on public opinion, however (in distinction to the effect of his ideas on the many officials whom he personally lobbied), was exercised mainly through publications to which he contributed in the last sixteen years of his life (1830–1846). Among these, one should mention first the Augsburg *Allgemeine Zeitung,* an old and respected paper with a wide circulation, which broadcast List's gospel to a general audience. Rotteck and Welcker's *Staatslexicon,* which was launched at List's suggestion in 1833 and in which he published several important articles on machinery, banks, and transport, was another highly visible forum, since, according to William Carr, it "soon became the bible of theoretical liberalism," that is, defined the political (which, as we remember, included economic) vocabulary of everyone who was not a reactionary.

In 1834, with two prominent Leipzig publishers, List founded a popular family weekly with the ambitious and self-explanatory title *The National Magazine* [and then in smaller print] *for Commerce and Industry, for Home—and General Economy* [*Haus—und Landwirthschaft*], *Statistics and Transport, New Inventions and* [in large print] *National Undertakings.* On the cover of the third issue were depicted representatives of the clearly respectable public on board something that looked like a locomotive; and indeed, the *National Magazine,* according to List's plan, already announced in his "Appeal to the People of Saxony concerning a Railway between Dresden and Leipzig," published simultaneously with the first issue in March 1834, consistently included essays on railways. The journal was attractively illustrated and, alongside serious articles on economic subjects, carried stories of a more frivolous nature, for instance, on Dick Whittington and his cat. The original number of subscribers was quite substantial: twelve thousand, rising to twenty thousand in less than half a year. Another half year later, however, owing to friction between the partners, the journal ceased publication, and List—who sold his share in the venture—without, it appears, skipping a beat, continued his propaganda in a new periodical, which he founded and ran himself. This was the *Eisenbahn-Journal und National Magazin,* which, as the title indicated, focused on railways. It survived for two years, but then was banned in Austria—no doubt because clear-sighted Metternich was convinced of the revolutionary implications of anything published by List—and closed. List left for France, where he wrote, among other things, the work that would assure his immortality, but upon returning to the Fatherland resumed his journalistic activities. In January 1843 he began publication of the *Zollvereinsblatt,* contributing to it some 650 articles in the three years remaining until his death. Its editorship was later assumed by Theodor Toegel, a Göttingen professor, wholly devoted to List's principles, who collaborated with him on the magazine and acted as his deputy during List's absences. Under Toegel's leadership, *Zollvereinsblatt* changed its title to *Vereinsblatt für deutsche Arbeit* and became the organ of protectionism.

It may be wrong, as Tribe suggests, to regard List as an economist in general, for he was clearly "an agitator and no professor," and as a German economist, in particular, because of the deep affinities between his ideas and those of American authors on economic matters, with whose work he was acquainted, as well as because he lacked thorough knowledge of the native academic tradition and was unaware of the fine distinctions between *Staatswirtschaft* and *Nationaloekonomie.* Yet the publication of *The National System of Political Economy* did establish him as the leading German author on economics, whose ideas were taken at least as "seriously in the 1840s by major German economists of the stature of Rau and Hildebrand" as his "genius, experience, and . . . political influence" were by Prussian bureaucrats.[35] Thus, to the inherent appeal of his nationalist message and to the contagious power of his enthusiasm was added the weighty authority of science.

In 1845 a French economist, Henri Richelot, wrote that List was "a power to be reckoned with in Germany." In the decades following List's death his influence only grew. True, certain political considerations (such as the desire of Prussia to keep Austria out of the *Zollverein*) for some time prevented the implementation of the economic policies he suggested, and in the 1860s it appeared that Germany had been forever converted to Smithian principles, that is, the principles of the German supporters of free trade, conveniently led by a certain J. P. Smith. But this was not for love of economic liberty and, as it happened, directly contributed to the German unification under Prussian "hegemony" that would ensure the decisive victory of Listian economic nationalism in the next generation. Considered a disaster by Metternich, German unification—and German nationalism—had long been viewed favorably by Prussian conservatives, who harnessed it skillfully to their interests. In 1851, in the context of negotiations which were to bring Hanover into the *Zollverein*, Bismarck wrote: "The consolidation of the healthy North German elements by means of the bond of material interests . . . would not fail to advance the conservative cause in our own internal politics and would justify us in regarding Federal political developments with greater composure."

Though the protectionist movement would not regain strength until after the unification, many of List's other ideas, less dependent on the support of the government, were being realized: coordinated by the Union of German Railway Administrators, formed a year after his death, railroad construction proceeded apace, and all over Germany industrial enterprises were springing up in the 1850s and 1860s. A new edition of *The National System* appeared in the 1860s, as well as translations into major European languages. At the University of Berlin, Dühring proclaimed that List was the greatest genius of the century, whose views were "the first real advance" in economics since *The Wealth of Nations* (a statement which was bound to upset Karl Marx). The stage of apotheosis was reached in the late 1870s, when *The National System* became "the most popular handbook" in Germany. Bismarck owned a copy and shared many of the views—but not the frustration—of "Germany's frustrated Colbert."[36]

The Spirit Triumphant

German nationalism, articulated by Romantic intellectuals and adapted for the use of the economically active middle classes by List, became a mass sentiment in the 1830s. In the early 1840s, provoked by Thiers's unwisely publicized designs for the Rhineland, it reached a fever pitch, moving a youthful Friedrich Engels to call for war against the insolent French and giving a new meaning to the expression "Teutonic madness." The genie was finally out of the bottle. At the same time, the first signs of economic growth appeared, "perceptible from about 1835, and conspicuous from about 1845."

To which extent this could be attributed to the formation of the *Zollverein* is debatable. According to some experts, the economic significance of the Customs Union was greatly exaggerated owing to its political importance. As with the factors that accompanied economic development in other cases, it is evident that the *Zollverein* facilitated growth, especially after the onset of the railroad age in the 1840s, but its causal role, if any, is unclear. In general, the timing of the German takeoff did not seem to have been affected by forces, spiritual and material, believed to be responsible for the birth of the modern economy. *Smithianismus*—that is, economic liberalism in its vulgar form— ruled supreme in the universities, which trained state officials, and guided economic policies of governments throughout Germany in the early decades of the nineteenth century, but released no Tawneyesque magnificent energies. The Rhineland—thanks to the French occupation—was traversed in all directions by "not only good, but luxurious roads" (as an English traveler marveled in 1845), which, Clapham suggests, could have been "a real assistance to industry and trade ever since 1815," but were not. Similarly, the exceptionally rich German coal resources (the lack of which is thought to have significantly slowed down development in France) were largely unutilized until the 1840s and produced no accelerating effect on the German economy.

Historians agree that, by any standard, "the economic and social forces that determined the forward course of English and French history in the first half of the nineteenth century had no counterparts in Germany." "The states which were eventually to become Imperial Germany showed an exceedingly low level of industrialization in 1815, and a level very little higher in 1850." In the 1850s, however, "all the forces tending to industrialization had struck Germany at once," and, to quote Sombart, "modern capitalism was definitely made the basis of the national economy." Railroads, which between 1850 and 1860 grew from 3,639 to 6,891 miles of track, were the leading industry and provided the rest of the German economy, literally and metaphorically, with the "locomotive of history," a powerful engine which pulled other sectors behind it. The first German-made railroad engine, built on an American model by August Borsig, left his Berlin workshop only in 1841; seven years later Borsig was capable of meeting the demand of almost the entire railway system in Prussia. By 1855 his factory and those of Maffei in Munich, Kessler in Karlsruhe and Esslingen, and Henschel in Kassel were exporting railroad machinery. The output of the coal, iron, and steel industries tripled between 1850 and 1860; the production of consumer goods, such as textiles, doubled; so did capital. The demand for it necessitated new financial institutions. Darmstädter Bank, modeled on the French Crédit Mobilier, was founded in 1853 by Gustav Mevissen (a follower of List as regards protection), and David Hansemann, with some French capital, established the largest bank in Germany for a long time to come, the Diskonto Gesellschaft. By 1857 Germany had twenty-nine banks of issue—twenty more than only six years earlier—which operated in the smaller states.

Already in 1860 Germany was producing more coal than either France or Belgium, both of which had been significantly ahead in the 1840s; by 1871 German output, which more than doubled in the decade, was larger than the French and Belgian yields put together (29.4 million metric tons as against 13.3 million French and 13.7 million Belgian). This was just coal, but in addition, Germany, alone in western Europe, was lucky enough to possess rich deposits of brown coal, or lignite, not as powerful a fuel, perhaps, but a far more accessible one, and thus at least as efficient, and in 1871 it was turning out 8.5 million metric tons of it. Over the next forty-three years its production of coal expanded more than sixfold, dwarfing the French output, which trebled, and the Belgian, which increased only about 1.7 times. In 1913 Germany was producing 191.5 million metric tons of coal, and with its 87.5 million additional tons of lignite was following close upon the heels of Great Britain, whose yield was 292 million tons of coal at the time, "almost ready at the last to challenge England on England's chosen ground."[37] It became a major coal exporter, selling to France, Belgium, Holland, Switzerland, and Austria, among others, to the tune of 30 million English pounds a year around 1912, but still imported some 9 million pounds' worth from Britain.

The development in the iron industry was similar. In 1845 it barely existed, and in 1850, while the French output of iron ore was 1.821 million tons and the British around 6 million tons, all of Germany, with its enormous resources, was producing 838,000 tons of iron ore, the situation being almost the same insofar as pig iron was concerned. By the 1860s France had been surpassed, and in the early 1870s, significantly, the German "infant" industry—for it was but a baby in comparison to its counterparts—experienced a postbellum boom, with more iron and engineering works springing up in Prussia between 1871 and 1874 than in the entire period between 1800 and 1871. The acquisition of the iron-rich and developed Lorraine was important, but Keynes was wrong when he suggested that "the German Empire was built more truly on coal and iron than on blood and iron," for the belief in blood and iron helped even more. On the night Metz surrendered, a Prussian commander is reported to have said, underscoring the profound affinity between the motives behind Germany's military and economic projects, "We have just conquered in the military sphere: our task is now to fight and conquer in the industrial sphere." The postbellum years happened to be the period of immense advance on the part of the nascent chemical industry as well, and in this case, too, the connection did not escape contemporary notice.

"The German Soldier," wrote a British observer, "established the political Empire; the German Chemist of the early Seventies went far to do the same for the industrial State. No happier point could have been devised for the beginning of a Great Industry than the moment when Germany, flushed with victory, and glorying in her new-found strength, went forth to conquer the world in trade, as she had conquered France in arms."[38]

The British competition, encouraged by the liberal tariffs which the empire had to accept with the rest of the Prussian trousseau, proved a more formidable adversary than the French military, and with British iron and steel gushing in, in 1876, 210 of the German blast furnaces were standing idle. But then some British imports, for instance, the Thomas and Gilchrist method of steel production from phosphoric ore, worked to Germany's benefit, while Bismarck quickly gave up on liberalism, the attachment to which for him, as for most Prussians, was strictly instrumental in any case. As a result, from 1880 the German output of both pig iron and steel increased by leaps and bounds. By 1910, when France was no longer in the race, Germany—with close to 15 million tons of pig iron and 13 million tons of steel—left Britain far behind (the figures for the latter being 10.172 million and 7.613 million, respectively).

And so it went. Germany became a major exporter of iron and steel goods of all sorts; it developed, virtually from scratch, a powerful modern shipbuilding industry; there was a prodigious development in textiles, which made it "a very large exporter of wool[, the] fourth in the great groups of her exports in 1913; just below coal and coke; rather further below machinery; far below iron and steel goods other than machinery; but . . . far above any other single group. A mighty industry, not one-fourteenth part of whose raw material came from Germany or from any German colony or protectorate." The process of industrialization in cotton was exceptionally swift, even by German standards, but this achievement was dwarfed by the "singularly rapid development" of the chemical and electrical industries. In both of these, English observers had to admit, by the 1890s Germany was ahead of Great Britain. "Beyond question," declared Clapham in 1936, "the creation of [the electrical] industry was the greatest single industrial achievement of modern Germany. The world had before it a new group of scientific and economic problems. In the handling of those problems Germany, now a fully equipped industrial nation, took the lead. She led too in all the specialized applications of electricity during the early years of the current century."[39]

Within at the most two generations of acquiring national consciousness, a backward, sluggish economy with no conception of economic growth was poised to overtake the world's economic front-runner.[40] A "people which forty years ago scarcely counted at all in economic geography" was competing with Great Britain for industrial leadership. Suddenly, Germany took notice of its tremendous resources (for it was indeed exceptionally well endowed)—the "gifts of nature," such as coal and iron, and "almost unique deposits of potash salts," but also the boon of the well-schooled population, in every sense of the word and on every level—and learned to utilize them with astonishing speed. The abrupt character of its economic takeoff in the 1880s paralleled the suddenness of the nationalization of its identity in the 1840s, when nationalism, long confined to the universities and intellectuals in and outside the bureaucracies, spread like wildfire, burning to ashes the traditional humility of the German bourgeoisie and setting its spirit ablaze with economic ambition. The transformed burghers were fully conscious of the nationalist essence of this ambition and knew to honor the memory of the unrewarded laborer who kindled the first spark of it in their hearts. Germany's rise to the position of an industrial superpower was the fulfillment of List's dream. In 1904 Karl Lamprecht wrote in a book devoted to Germany's recent history and focused on the economy: "Today every nerve is strained to maintain the position of *Deutschtum* in the world, and to advance it. This requires that our economic life should be united, all its forces acting as a whole, 'like an army' . . . List's prophecy is realized: the sea must no longer be merely a highway for our commerce and a nursing-mother of our national economy, but a battlefield in our struggle with the nations and a cradle of a new freedom."[41]

War by Other Means and Simply War

The view of the economy as a battlefield in the struggle for national supremacy was widespread. It reflected the common belief that, like a strong army, business was power (the amalgam of *Staatswirtschaft* and Romantic notions to the effect that economics was a business of the state whose natural and optimal state was war) and was reflected in the systematic pursuit of *Handels- und Machtpolitik,* or the policy of business and power. Economic growth was an equivalent of military expansion, and, conceived in military terms, it justified and called for military tactics. One such tactic was the infiltration of enemy positions. It was employed in several ways. For instance, in June 1914 the *Deutsche Export Revue* carried a piece of information headed "The aims of German national economy: a syndicate to supply news abroad." The announcement was worded somewhat undiplomatically for the taste of the Imperial Office of Foreign Affairs, which issued instructions not to reproduce it, but it was quite accurate and, in fact, belated. It referred to the formation, several months earlier, of a society, subsidized by the said Imperial Office, and composed, in addition to its representatives, of companies such as the Norddeutscher Lloyd, the Hamburg-Amerika, the Deutsche Bank, the Diskonto Gesellschaft, the Allgemeine Elektrizitäts Gesellschaft, Siemens-Schuckert, Krupp, and so on, with the purpose of promoting the manufacturing prestige of Germany abroad. The chosen method of promotion was to plant information favorable to Germany, ready-made in the respective native languages, in the foreign press, while rewarding those receptive to such information (by offering them reduced charges for German cables, for example) and imposing economic penalties on those less receptive. The actual printing of the information supplied was to be done by gullible native personnel. As the *Deutsche Export Revue* cheerfully but imprudently commented, "It is better to choose men already connected with the various journals, who will serve German interests without attracting so much attention."

Another method of infiltrating enemy territory was by establishing German companies there under native names. For instance, the Compagnie parisienne des couleurs d'aniline turned out to be a branch of Meister, Lucius, and Bruning of Hoechst. Henri Hauser writes that another German dye company, Badische Sodafabrik, "under a French name, provided the madder-dye for the red trousers of the French army, and possibly it even inspired the Press campaign, conducted with the support of sentimental arguments, in favor of a colour which was dangerous from a military point of view." Giovanni Preziozi, in a series of articles published in 1914 under the ominous common title "La Germania alla conquista dell'Italia" (Germany on a Conquest of Italy), described German banks operating in Italy and calling themselves "Banca . . . italiana" that "act as a pump which pumps out of Italy and pumps into Germany." At about the same time, the Swiss *Gazette de Lausanne* reported on several German pseudo-Swiss companies which looked remarkably like today's multinational corporations. The staff of the Neuchâtel-based Société ânonyme pour l'industrie de l'aluminium included eight Germans, one Austrian, and six Swiss; the Zurich Banque des chemins de fer orientaux eight Germans, one Frenchman, one Belgian, one Austrian, and five Swiss; the Banque pour entreprises électriques, also in Zurich, fifteen Germans and nine Swiss; the Basel Société des valeurs de métaux ten Germans, five Swiss. The share capital in all these companies was in German hands, but the debentures were offered in Switzerland. Thus "the money of the Swiss debenture-holder," commented the *Gazette,* served "to support German undertakings competing with Swiss manufactures in our own country."

From war tactics in economic conquest one easily arrived at the idea of war as a tactic, or, rather, the economy now offered another reason for war, which was a good in its own right. A popular booklet, *Deutschlands Stellung in Weltwirtschaft* (Germany's Position in World Economy), explained to its audience in 1908 that with Germany's growing dependence on foreign markets, war was inevitable, but complemented this gloomy prognosis with the following comforting consideration. "No doubt, if we wish to be and remain a great people, a world power, we expose ourselves to serious struggles. But this must not alarm us. There is profound truth in the dictum that man degenerates in peacetime. The call to arms is often needed to rouse a world benumbed with apathy and indolence. Those who can look far and deeply into things see that warfare is often a blessing to humanity." Such inspirational speeches resonated harmoniously with the deeply embedded notion that economy was war by other means and reinforced the military spirit which permeated the German economy. "The spirit of discipline," wrote the historian von Below proudly in *Militarismus und Kultur in Deutschland,* "which reigns in the German army, is also the spirit to which we owe the economic growth which has drawn on us the hatred of England. Militarism is the school of our working classes."[42]

The Clear and Present Danger

For the German industrial empire, daily growing more powerful, England took the place France had occupied in the imagination of its enfeebled and dismembered predecessor several generations earlier: it was the enemy. A German economist warned in 1913: "Most of the present problems, national alliances and international events, are found to have their ultimate origin in the competition of England and Germany." This was also the impression of the authors of the 1884 Report of the Royal Commission on Technical Education, which stated: "Every step taken for the improvement of German industries was influenced mainly by the desire to strengthen their position with regard to the rivalry of England. They magnify the industrial advantages of England, and consider it impossible to compete with England on equal terms."

England, however, was for a long time oblivious to this competition, regarding the prodigious economic advances of the Continental latecomer with self-confident benevolence (which reminds one of today's American solicitude for the progress of its potential rivals). But by the 1890s the challenge Germany mounted to British industrial supremacy began to cause some concern. This concern helped to remind the public in England what was at stake in its racing economic light years ahead of the world: it was not the prosperity of the individual Englishman but the prestige of the nation, its relative position vis-à-vis the others, which was damaged if the distance was not at the least maintained. Thus it revealed the nationalistic wellsprings of the British dedication to growth, obscured in Weberian routinization, which was made possible by decades of unproblematic leadership. The goal for Britain was "to retain our position as the wealthiest nation," Ernest Edwin Williams spelled out in his very popular 1896 polemic *"Made in Germany."* "A man with a thousand pounds is a rich man," he explained, "as long as none of his neighbours have more than a hundred; but if *they* increase their possessions to ten thousand a-piece, *his* thousand spells poverty. If, then, he would maintain his position he must increase his wealth." This was Adam Smith's old idea of the significance of wealth—that of a tool in the all-important pursuit of status.

In an attempt to explain Germany's stupendous gains, British commentators at once drew attention to the economic impact of German nationalism, pointing, among other things, to the "overt jingoism of [the] ruling classes," which was not noticed before. The role of the growth of national feeling in general, and the excitement which accompanied the victory over France in particular, for instance, were the first in the list of factors emphasized by the article in the *Saturday Review* of December 19, 1885, which contained apparently one of the earliest discussions of German industrial progress in the press. Sir Charles Oppenheimer of the Foreign Office, in a report of July 1894, called on "the great industries of England" to "draw the lesson for her own mode of proceeding from [this] increased zeal" and stressed "the enthusiasm of the German industrial party," which, he suggested, "may be regarded as an expression of the increased feeling awakened within them of the need of expansion." Williams underscored the "practical patriotism" of German businessmen, which was "of peculiar importance" in view of Germany's economic development, for "here [in Germany] patriotism goes hand in hand with economy." "This zeal," he complained, "has eaten us up." It was this "German-made patriotism" that was behind the country's determination "to conquer the world of industry"—the "push" which Williams considered "perhaps the biggest part of Germany's success." It was the extinction of this "push" among businessmen in England that made it so "difficult for the English patriot to keep patience with the English manufacturer."[43]

Most concerned English patriots (they appear to have been a minority until just before World War II, if not later, for the majority of patriots refused to believe that England could lose its lead and therefore were not concerned), who, after the old British fashion, were firmly convinced materialists, however, sought explanation and remedy among more tangible factors, such as government protection and technical education. (Williams considered these also very important, but not the most important reasons for the momentum of German development.) Government intervention and the education of the work force thus became the focus of the Movement for National Efficiency, whose members Austen Albu characterizes as "Imperialists of one sort or another," which is to say that they included conservatives such as Joseph Chamberlain, liberals such as Rosebery, and socialists such as the Fabians Sidney Webb and George Bernard Shaw.

At least Shaw was at first vehemently opposed to Williams's advocacy of protectionist policies, and the movement attracted proponents of free trade as well as tariff reformers. Nevertheless, the feeling that regulation had much to recommend it was quite widespread, and there was a certain weakness for the hands-on managerial style of running the economy. "The Germans," the vice president of the council in the Conservative administration, Sir John Gorst, wrote wistfully in 1902, "are governed by skilled experts: we by ill-informed amateurs." The well-ordered German "household" had a competitor for the admiration of the British public in Japan, making one marvel how history repeats itself. The Webbs considered the Russo-Japanese War to be "a triumph for collective regulation and action over the *laissez-faire* creed," apparently because the Russians were the natural champions of the latter, while Haldane found endearing "the fierce disciplinarianism" of the Japanese army and Rosebery lauded, significantly, the nation's "universal and practical patriotism."

But, on the whole, the methods of *Staatswirtschaft* were alien to the individualistic British, and it was these methods—like everything else, from human aspirations to natural resources, reoriented by the spirit of nationalism and put to the service of interests it defined—that lived on in the German economy of the industrial age and lent it its peculiar character. None of the singular features of this wonderfully successful economy—not the surviving guilds in the handicrafts, actively promoted and defended by the state; nor the powerful cartels in the great modern industries, which, between the 1870s, when the first twenty of them were formed, and 1900, spread "over a much wider field than might have been anticipated" ("evidently," as a leading historian suggests, being "suited [to] the temper of the German business man"); nor the early and expert organization of labor in the mass socialist movement and labor unions, which carried nationalism beyond the bourgeoisie and adapted it to the needs of the industrial proletariat; nor the consistent and massive intervention in every aspect of economic life by the state, which remained true to its anciently arrogated role of the supreme manager and *pater familii* and as such, among many other things, protected labor against unemployment with the same thorough care which characterized its protection of the industries from foreign competition—none of these features, admirable in their efficiency, aimed at releasing the forces of individual initiative or cultivation of individual self-reliance.[44] Rather, they all reflected the Romantic horror of self-interest; their guiding principle was its abnegation; and they stamped out both every trace of individualism where they could find it, and those allegedly "healthy and natural" processes that British opinion associated with economic liberty—as cartels, whose explicit purpose was to restrict competition at home, the better to compete abroad.

But then it was not individualism that made Britain the economic superpower in the first place, and it was not the collectivistic and authoritarian managerial methods of *Staatswirtschaft* which gave Germany the ability and the spunk to challenge it. It was the transforming spirit of nationalism, which in one case worked in tandem with individualism and in the other harnessed to its goals the methods of *Staatswirtschaft*. This spirit turned dead matter from the bowels of the earth into a living force fostering growth: it had no difficulty altering the deadening grip of the state into a life-affirming and reassuring caress. Nationalism was like the magic wand that changed Cinderella's pumpkin and mice into a gilded coach-and-four. It could not create a coach from nothing, but it seems that it did not matter much what the something was to which its powers were applied: presumably a melon or a large grapefruit would do just as well.

III | The Asian Challenge: The Way of Japan

5 | Japanese Nationalism

However miraculous was the economic transformation effected by nationalism in Germany, however astounding the speed with which this great country—lying in the middle of Europe, at the crossroads of centuries-old European trade routes, steeped in European traditions of inquiry and discourse, possessed of enormous natural resources—rose to economic preeminence, its development appears plodding and plausible when compared with the meteoric and entirely unexpected emergence of modern Japan. Though perhaps this was not immediately realized by contemporaries (as it was too shocking to be realized), Japan's modernization—namely, its transformation into a novel, modern type of society, with the inclusive membership of legally equal individuals, cutting across class distinctions; with a legal-rational political order and, in principle, impersonal government; with an economy consistently oriented toward growth—took less than twenty years. In 1868 the young samurai who led the Meiji Restoration overturned the government presiding over the Japanese society of orders. By the mid-1880s not only was the entire traditional social structure disassembled, but the new one was established as well and smoothly functioned in its place, and the economy, much of it created by political fiat in the previous decade, industrializing at a breathtaking pace, was ready to take off.

So fast and successful a modernization in either the social or economic sphere had no precedent and set a record that so far has not been bested. Naturally, it has baffled observers, who, by the time Japan took its place among the world's most powerful industrial societies, came to see economic modernization in terms of the post-1776 European experience. Though warned by Sir George Sansom against applying "to the study of Far Eastern history the terms of a conventional analysis which may, or may not, be valid for European history," Western students of Japan continued to do so and, as Sansom predicted, before long were led "to error and confusion." Edwin Reischauer tried out seemingly unassailable historical categories, but was forced to conclude that "to call the Meiji Restoration a bourgeois revolution is more confusing than helpful . . . To compare Japan's transition to the triumph of absolutism in early modern Europe is even more inaccurate . . . [and] to call the Restoration a counterrevolution is equally misleading." He summed up: "No European precedents are very useful" in explaining modernization in Japan, a situation apparently accounted for by the singularity and the inherent difficulty of the case.[1] The first reaction is almost invariably to blame the data for the inadequacy of a theory.

In fact, the Japanese case is neither more nor less difficult to explain than any of the other cases discussed in this book. Japan's story is unique, as is the story of any other society; but the emergence in Japan of a modern economy, oriented to growth, and, more generally, the emergence of the modern society is not, and neither are the forces and the processes which brought it about, although obviously they operated in a different setting and took on, as in every other case, a singular coloration reflective of different initial conditions.

The explanation for the remarkably speedy and successful modernization of Japan—that is, for the reconstruction of Japanese society, including the economy, along the lines of the novel, modern, type of society—lies in the equally remarkable, speedy, and successful articulation and spread of Japanese nationalism. The history of its formation follows very closely the European pattern of the development of national consciousness and identity. As in all the other cases, with the exception of the English, nationalism in Japan is imported, but it is imported and later takes root, as in every society where it develops, for indigenous reasons. Structurally, these reasons are exactly the same as, for instance, in France, Germany, or Russia. Cultural differences, pertaining to the indigenous pre-national traditions, and circumstances of the importation account for the differences in the end results—in this case, for that which makes Japanese nationalism Japanese. The structural and cultural conditions for the development of nationalism (the reasons for the receptivity to the imported ideas and the native terms in which they are appropriated) evolve, in Japan as well as elsewhere, over the course of a long time—several generations, perhaps as much as a century and a half. As in Germany, when nationalization of consciousness occurs, triggered by an exogenous, unforeseen event, the mold for nationalism in Japan is ready. Only in Japan, the work of preparation is concealed from the European view: the conditions which make possible the immediate absorption of the revolutionary idea of the nation, brought from the West, gestate in the bosom of the Tokugawa society that is sedulously protected against prying eyes and all manner of contact with foreigners. Indeed, the impression of the discontinuity in Japan's development, created by the truly astonishing rapidity of its modernization, is reinforced by the fact that the commencement of the process coincides with the abandonment (under duress) of its two-centuries-old policy of isolation.

Tokugawa Japan: The Womb of Japanese Nationalism

Tokugawa Japan was not a backward or "underdeveloped" society by any standard. It enjoyed exceptional political stability, a flourishing and, in some views, "even brilliant" culture, and a greater prosperity "in per capita terms than any other Asian people," Asia not being worse off than Europe at the time. "Intellectually and institutionally," we are told, "the Tokugawa period was the most vigorous of Japan's historical eras." In the eighteenth century, "probably no contemporary European community was more civilized and polished." This was the period of "Great Peace throughout the Realm"—*tenka taihei*—lasting for a quarter of a millennium. The country was punctiliously and, on the whole, competently governed: a closer approximation to the *Aufklärung* ideal of a "well-ordered police-state" than any of the then-existing absolutisms in Europe. ("There is not a land better governed in the world by civil police," noted an English seaman, Will Adams, in 1611.) It was "a happy society as human societies go."[2]

Early European visitors—even before the establishment of Tokugawa rule in 1600—recognized the superiority of the Japanese civilization to most contemporary societies with which they were familiar. Christian missionaries who worked there in the course of Japan's "Christian century" (1549—1639), in particular, clearly perceived that Japan was different from all the other pagan countries. A saint (Francis Xavier) believed the Japanese to be most worthy material for conversion, confessing: "These people are the delight of my heart." Father Louis Frois, who came to Japan in 1563 and gained the trust of Oda Nobunaga, thought them "as gifted a nation as any in Europe." Cosme de Torres wrote:

> These Japanese are better disposed to embrace our holy Faith than any other people in the world. They are as prudent as could be desired and are governed by reason just as much as, or even more than, Spaniards; they are more inquisitive than any other people I have met. No men in the wide world like more than they to hear sermons on how to serve their Creator and save their souls. Their conversation is so polite that they all seem to have been brought up in the palaces of great nobles; in fact, the compliments they pay each other are beyond description. They grumble but little about their neighbors and envy nobody. They do not

gamble; just as theft is punished by death, so also is gambling. As a pastime they practice with their weapons, at which they are extremely adept, or write couplets, just as the Romans composed poetry, and most of the gentry occupy themselves in this way.

The characteristic sense of propriety (which would satisfy Adam Smith's exacting standard), the concern of the Japanese with decorum, which contrasted sharply with their indifference to material comforts and even security, attracted the most attention. "They spend all their money on dress, weapons, and servants, and do not possess any treasures," observed Saint Francis Xavier. Thirty years later, around 1580, Alessandro Valigniano commented:

> They are very prudent and discreet in all their dealings with others and they never weary anybody by recounting their troubles or by complaining or grumbling as people do in Europe. When they go visiting, their etiquette demands that they never say anything which might upset their host. And so they never come and talk about their troubles and grievances, because as they claim to suffer much and always show courage in adversity, they keep their troubles to themselves as best they can. When they meet or go to visit somebody, they always appear cheerful and in good spirits, and they either do not refer to their troubles at all, or, if they do, at most they just mention them with a laugh as if they did not worry about such unimportant matters. As they are so opposed to every kind of gossip, they never talk about other people's affairs or grumble about their princes and rulers . . . For this reason (and also in order not to become heated in their dealings with others), they observe a general custom in Japan of not transacting any important or difficult business face to face with another person, but instead they do it all through messages of a third person . . . As a result they live in such peace and quietness that even the children forbear to use inelegant expressions among themselves, nor do they fight or hit each other like European lads; instead, they speak politely and never fail to show each other respect. In fact they show such incredible gravity and maturity that they seem more like solemn men than children . . . They are also moderate in their emotions . . . Husbands do not beat or shout at their wives, neither do fathers [beat] their sons, nor masters their servants. On the contrary they outwardly appear very calm and deal with each other either by the messages that they send or by the cultured words that they speak; in this way, even though they may be exiled, killed, or thrown out of their homes, everything is done quietly and in good order.
>
> Finally, although two men may be deadly enemies, they will both smile at each other and neither will fail to perform any of the customary

courtesies towards each other. Their conduct in such cases is beyond both belief and understanding; things reach such a pass that when they are most determined to take revenge or kill somebody, they show him much affection and familiarity, laughing and joking with him. Seizing their chance when he is completely off his guard, they draw their heavy swords, which are as sharp as razors, and so attack him that generally he is killed by the first or second blow. Then they replace their swords quietly and calmly . . . and do not give the slightest indication of passion or anger . . . And thus they all give the impression of being very mild, patient, and well disposed, and it cannot be denied that they are superior to all other peoples in this respect.

Will Adams, as becomes an Englishman, summed it up in a few words: "courteous above measure."[3]

Absolutism and the Society of Orders

The founder of the Tokugawa dynasty, Ieyasu, who gained control over Japan in the battle of Sekigahara in 1600 and in 1603 took the title of shogun, continued the policy of centralization, begun and already greatly advanced by his two predecessors, Oda Nobunaga and Toyotomi Hideyoshi, in the last four decades of the sixteenth century. These policies roughly corresponded to those pursued since the beginning of that same century by the kings of France, who also attempted to substitute a strong central power for the endemic disorder of feudalism. The central power triumphed in the two countries at about the same time—in 1594 in France and 1590 in Japan. But the political system that replaced feudalism in Japan—the *baku-han* system—was far more effective, and could with greater reason be called absolutist, than the absolute monarchy established in France. In fact, the *baku-han* system bore a close resemblance to the Russian autocracy: the shogun was not, like the king of France, the first gentleman of the realm, in principle required to abide by the rules that governed the conduct of the nobility, but an all-powerful ruler before whom the subjects of all classes were equally slaves.

THE ARISTOCRACY Purposefully aiming not simply to break the resistance but to destroy the very habitat of the feudal aristocracy (in clear contrast to the French kings, who never pursued this goal systematically), the centralizing warlords, beginning with Hideyoshi, adopted a strategy virtually identical to the one used by the Muscovite princes—in particular Ivan III and Tsar Ivan IV, "the Terrible"—as part of their policy of territorial aggrandizement and incorporation of the previously independent Russian principalities.

Like the early Russian tsars, who replaced the hereditary estates of boyars and appanage princes with service estates in other territories, thus undermining both their power base and the hereditary principle in general, obviating the distinctions between formerly sovereign rulers and the service nobility, and making everyone completely dependent on the will of the autocrat, the *bakufu* confiscated and reassigned the domains *(han)* of the feudal lords—the *daimyo*—tying continued possession to satisfactory behavior. In an edict of 1595, Hideyoshi declared marriages between the *daimyo* families contingent on his explicit approval; prohibited all feudal unions and contracts between the *daimyo*, as well as vendettas, essential to the feudal structure; and, with the exception of several individuals, including Tokugawa Ieyasu, forbade the use of a palanquin to able-bodied *daimyo* under the age of fifty (transforming a symbol of superior social status into a convenience indicative of bodily weakness). Earlier, in 1587, though most less exalted personages for the time being were allowed the choice of religion, he had prohibited the *daimyo* to convert to Christianity, warning them against influencing people on their domains—which, it was stressed, were entrusted to them on a temporary basis—to convert. Such influence was considered "a most unreasonable illegal act." The law articulated: "If a *daimyo* who has a fief over a province, a district, or a village, forces his retainers to become followers of the padre, he is committing a crime . . . This will have an adverse effect on the country. Anyone who cannot use good judgment in this matter will be punished."[4]

Tokugawa Ieyasu further limited the *daimyo* freedom of action and methodically used co-optation and the principle of "divide and rule" to break the barons' habit of independence. To start, he divided the *daimyo* into three classes: the *shimpan*, or "related" *daimyo*, who belonged to the Tokugawa extended family; the *fudai*, or "hereditary" *daimyo*, the families loyal to Ieyasu before the battle of Sekigahara; and the *tozama*, or "outer" *daimyo*, families who had attached themselves to Ieyasu later. After the redistribution of the domains, one quarter of all agricultural land, as well as all major cities, ports, and mines, became the property of the shogun. The rest of the country was allocated to the *daimyo*, of whom there were 295 at the time, with *fudai* getting about the same quantity of arable land (as measured in *koku*[5] of rice produced) as the shogun, *tozama* receiving immense estates, amounting to more than a third of the land, which were situated in the western and northern regions, and *shimpan*, related to the shogun anyway, having to content themselves with a mere eighth of the rice-producing territory. Only the "hereditary" *daimyo* were systematically involved in the *bakufu* bureaucracy, which contributed to their vested interest in the regime and thus their loyalty to the Tokugawa. The "outer" *daimyo* were legally barred from the central government, while the "related" families kept away from it as a matter of custom, though, when the ruling shogun died without a direct heir, these families ensured the shogunal succession.

Though the *daimyo* were theoretically autonomous so far as the administration of their domains was concerned, it was closely and constantly supervised by the central government through the agency of special inspectors (the *metsuke*, not unlike the French intendants) instituted for this purpose. The assertion of independence in practice was prevented by frequent, and always expected, relocations: in the first fifty years of Tokugawa rule, 281 *daimyo* were reassigned from one *han* to another. Transgressions against the law of the *bakufu* were punished by confiscation, which was a misfortune that could befall an innocent lordly family as well, in case it failed to secure an heir who satisfied the demands of the central government: the *bakufu* had the last word in the wills of the *daimyo*. To make sure that their wills did not contradict that of the shogun, the more important *daimyo* were reined in before the question of succession came up by means of marriage alliances with Tokugawa family. Still, 217 *daimyo* lost domains for one reason or another between 1600 and 1650.

In 1611, to ensure the compliance of the *daimyo* with his regulations, Ieyasu imposed on them an oath of fealty, phrased in the language of feudal obligations and putting the feudal code of behavior in the service of his antifeudal undertaking. This oath, the first document which articulated the duties of the aristocracy in the *baku-han* system, was signed jointly by the *daimyo* in Kyoto on the sixteenth day of the fourth month of the sixteenth year of Keicho. It appealed to tradition, as well as to the *daimyo* interest, its opening clause declaring: "We will respect the laws and formularies established by the *bakufu* for generations since the time of General of the Right [1192–1199]; out of concern for our own interest, we will strictly obey any regulations which may be issued by Edo thereafter."

But Ieyasu did not trust his *daimyo* even when they married women of his clan, accepted the interference of his inspectors, and solemnly swore obedience to his regulations. To render them absolutely impotent, therefore, he instituted the ingenious system of "alternate attendance"—the *sankin kotai*—which was nothing less than a systematic and comprehensive policy of hostage taking. This arrangement, which by the 1630s had become compulsory, required that each *daimyo* spend several months a year in attendance at the court in Edo, which Ieyasu received as part of his domain from Hideyoshi and made the site of the shogunal government. "It is now settled," pronounced the 1635 amendment to the 1615 Laws of the Military Households, "that *daimyo* and *shomyo* (lesser lords) are to serve in turns *(kotai)* at Edo. They shall proceed hither *(sankin)* every year in summer during the course of the fourth month . . . The roads, post horses, ferries, and bridges must be carefully attended to ensure continuous service. Do not permit any impediment to efficient communication." When the *daimyo* returned to their domains, their wives and heirs remained at Edo. Officers of the *bakufu* kept a watchful eye over travelers to and from the court, instructed to prevent "outward women and inward guns," since to smuggle out the former and in the latter would be a plotting *daimyo*'s natural desire.[6] Checking stations were established exclusively for the supervision of processions related to *sankin kotai:* indeed, they had no other business, since all communications between *daimyo* domains were discouraged to the point of prohibition. The effect of the system on the feudal aristocracy of Japan was rather like that of Versailles on the French nobility: it was emasculated. The *daimyo* were turned into absentee lords, which undermined their political influence and effectiveness as administrators, and became courtiers, which weakened them psychologically and financially. Unlike in France, however, the policy was pursued with such forethought and skill, and was so successful, that after 1650 the shoguns no longer had to concern themselves with the *daimyo* at all.

THE PEASANTRY The reorganization of the rest of Japanese society to promote political centralization was carried out with similar dispatch. Hideyoshi began by disarming the peasantry, legally and sharply separating between the military and agricultural classes. In 1588 he issued an Edict on the Collection of Swords, like many Japanese edicts formulated as an argument, and so appealing to the reason and interest of its intended audience and its concern for the common—largely the *bakufu*'s—good, rather than blind obedience. It read:

1. Farmers of all provinces are strictly forbidden to have in their possession any swords, short swords, bows, spears, firearms, or other types of weapons. If unnecessary implements of war are kept, the collection of annual rent may become more difficult, and without provocation uprisings can be fomented. Therefore, those who perpetrate improper acts against samurai who receive a grant of land must be brought to trial and punished. However, in that event, their wet and dry fields will remain unattended, and the samurai will lose their rights to the yields from the fields. Therefore, the heads of provinces, samurai who receive a grant of land, and deputies must collect all the weapons described above and submit them to Hideyoshi's government.

2. The swords and short swords collected in the above manner will

not be wasted. They will be used as nails and bolts in the construction of the Great Image of Buddha. In this way, farmers will benefit not only in this life but also in the lives to come.

3. If farmers possess only agricultural implements and devote themselves exclusively to cultivating the fields, they and their descendants will prosper. This compassionate concern for the well-being of the farmers is the reason for the issuance of this edict, and such a concern is the foundation for the peace and security of the country and the joy and happiness of all the people. In China, in olden days, the sage ruler Yao pacified the country and converted precious swords and sharp knives into agricultural implements. But there is no precedent for such an act in this country. Thus, all the people must abide by the provisions of this edict and understand its intent, and farmers must work diligently in agriculture and sericulture.

The decision, worthy of a prudent householder, to beat the swords into nails and bolts rather than ploughshares, as was done in China, was justified by appeal to native tradition, as well as to the best interests of the peasants, who would benefit from it forever and ever. Hideyoshi's compassionate concern for the farmers reminds one of the *hausväterlich* German princes of a hundred years later, and indeed his idea of the people's happiness corresponded closely to the one developed in late seventeenth- and early eighteenth-century *Hausväterliteratur*.

As in Germany, a stable social order was believed to be the foundation of "the joy and happiness of all the people" in Japan, and a "stable social order" presupposed a clear hierarchy of classes. The care for the implied "harmonious inequality of ranks" was expressed in Hideyoshi's 1591 Edict on the Change of Status, which provided that no samurai should assume the status of a townsman *(chonin)* or farmer, and no townsman the status of a farmer and vice versa (that townsmen and farmers could assume the status of a samurai was, apparently, inconceivable). The punishment for transgressions of this edict was severe. "The townsmen and farmers must see that this order is carried out," it declared:

If [any samurai who assumed a non-samurai status] is kept concealed, the entire town or village shall be held responsible and punished accordingly. If any farmer abandons his wet and dry fields and engages in trade or offers himself for hire for wages, not only is he to be punished, but also his fellow villagers. If there is anyone who neither serves in the military nor cultivates land, it is the responsibility of the deputies and other local officials to investigate and expel him. If they do not take action, those local officials shall be stripped of their posts on account of negligence. If a townsman is disguised as a farmer, and that fact is concealed, that country or town shall be regarded as committing a culpable crime.

Insofar as the peasants were concerned, this amounted to the institution of serfdom: they were tied to the land and had no right to leave it. (Obversely, the *daimyo* were instructed that, from the eighteenth day of the sixth month of the fifteenth year of Tensho—1587—"the sale of persons in Japan [was] forbidden," and it was illegal to sell Japanese people to China, to the South Seas, or to Korea as slaves.[7] The Japanese rulers were clearly more possessive than their counterparts in some other parts of the world.)

The peasants' status was further defined—down to the fabrics of their clothes and grains in their meals—and the machinery of collective responsibility, devised for its maintenance, perfected under Ieyasu. Collective responsibility was a particularly effective method of social control (as the Soviet authorities so well realized closer to our time) and made it so constant, thorough, and inescapable that the need for supervision was virtually eliminated. Payment of taxes (the burden of which, with the exception of extraordinary levies, lay on the shoulders of the cultivators),[8] as well as the conduct of every individual, became the responsibility of "groups of five," the *goningumi*, into which every village was divided. With the help of this cunning device, the peasants, who constituted 80 percent of the Japanese population, could be managed from a distance. The already rigidly limited sphere of the peasant's freedom was limited still further. What he (or she, for women too were members of the groups of five) had to endure is illustrated by the instruction issued for the benefit (no doubt it was conceived of this way, given the compassionate concern of the Japanese lords for their people) of his peasants by the *daimyo* of Echizen in 1632:

> If there is anyone in the group of five who is given to malfeasance, that fact must be reported without concealing anything. If there is anyone in the group of five who fails to pay his annual taxes or perform the services required, other members of the group must quickly rectify the situation. If there is anyone in the group of five who runs away, those who are remaining must quickly search for and return him. If the return of the runaway cannot be secured, the group of five will be rendered culpable.

In comparison to these draconian exactions, the *bakufu* indeed appeared compassionate. It recognized that the life of a peasant could be made truly intolerable and was willing to treat the behavior of the domanial lord as an extenuating circumstance in the case of runaways. If a farmer left the domains because of wrongdoing by the masters, declared the commissioners of Edo and Kanto, he would be sent back only upon due investigation into the reasons for his action. Of course, the farmer would have to pay all outstanding taxes, but "once that payment of the tax is completed the farmer may be permitted to reside elsewhere." Moreover, the *daimyo* were cautioned that it was forbidden to kill farmers "without cause." Even if a farmer did commit a crime, his guilt had to be ascertained by the magistrate's office before an execution could take place.[9]

Whatever protection against the loss of peasant life such intervention from above afforded, so long as it lasted, the life of the Tokugawa cultivator was barely mitigated misery. The farmers' regimen was that of convict laborers in penitentiaries interested in the productivity of slave labor rather than the rehabilitation of the prisoners—nothing like the relative comforts enjoyed by the residents of the Amsterdam House of Correction, with its grim discipline, drowning cell, and all;[10] beasts of burden had it better. The purpose of the peasants' existence was work, and they were expected—and forced—to pursue it single-mindedly, stopping only for the barest necessities, a little sleep and minimal nourishment. Every day and night had its quota, and every instinct was manipulated to keep one going. In the domain of Aizu, in 1619, the rules were the following:

> During the first five days of the new year, pay respect to those around you in accordance with your position. Within the first fifteen days, make more than enough ropes needed to perform your major and minor public services (corvee labor for the year). After the first fifteen days, when mountains and fields are covered with snow, accumulate all the firewood needed for the year. Use a sleigh to put nightsoil on the fields. At night make sandals for horses. Daughters and wives must sew and weave China-grass to make clothing for their menfolk . . . During the fourth month, men must work in the fields from dawn to dusk and make furrows as deep as the hoe can penetrate. Wives and daughters must make meals three times, put on red headbands and take the meals to the fields. Old and young alike must put the meals in front of the men who are soiled from their work. By seeing the wives attired in red, men, old and young alike, can be so encouraged [as to forget] their fatigue. Once men are home after dusk, give them bath water, and let them wash their feet. Sisters-in-law and female cousins must put the chapped feet of the man on the stomach of his wife and massage them. Let him forget the toil of the day.

The wife was used as an incentive throughout the year, and while in the fourth month it was the anticipation of her soft (with her Spartan diet could it have been soft?) belly under his tired feet at the end of the day that kept his motivation strong, at the end of the year it was the fear of losing her—and thus the prospect of not only additional sensual deprivation but social disgrace as well. The injunctions to the peasants of Aizu were explicit:

> During the twelfth month, if there is a notification from the fief holder or magistrate about a tax overdue, quickly make the payment. For this favor he renders you, send a bowl of loach fish soup accompanied by a dish of fried sardines. Although according to the regulations, all that is expected of a farmer on such an occasion is a bowl of soup and a dish of vegetables, the ones [just suggested] are more appropriate. If no tax is paid after the due notice, you can have your precious wife taken away from you as security. Do not forget that in your master's house there are many young minor officials and middlemen who may steal your wife. To make sure that kind of thing never happens to you, pay all your taxes before the end of the eleventh month. Take heed that this advice is adhered to. You are known as a man of a lowly origin. But even so, you do not wish to see your precious wife exposed to wild winds (misfortunes), being taken away from you, and stolen by younger men. In this fashion you may lose the support of the way of heaven, come to the end of the rope, be scorned by your lowly peer group [*nota bene*], and regret the incident forever. Always remember that such a misfortune can befall you. Be diligent in delivering your annual tax rice and in doing work for the magistrate. Once all the annual taxes are paid, prepare for the coming of the new year. Make the remaining rice into rice cake, brew some *sake,* buy some salted fish, and add another year to your life happily.

It is possible that the disgrace associated with the loss of a wife to other men (as a fine for overdue tax) weighed more, at least with the author of the injunctions, than any other sentiment one might assume under the circumstances, because he rather nonchalantly recommended divorce if the wife was not hardworking enough and made "excessive amounts of tea to entertain others." "Even if a man has a child with her," he admonished, "that kind of woman must be sent away."

And in 1643 the *bakufu* deprived the peasants, already deprived of everything else, of their sake and rice cake (possibly setting the precedent for other zealous governments seeking to protect populations entrusted to their care, who are not to be trusted to take care of themselves, from harmful substances which people tend to enjoy). The brewing of sake, as well as its consumption, was prohibited in the villages, and a special clause in the sumptuary law of the year enjoined: "Do not go to the market to drink freely." At the same time only grains other than wheat and rice were deemed appropriate for the farmers' diet. "Rice especially," the law declared, "must not be consumed indiscriminately" (i.e., by all classes). This was ironic, since growing rice was the farmers' particular responsibility, but the irony was lost on the legislators. The purpose of the 1643 regulations, stated in the characteristic effort to make their reasoning clear, was preventing the "wasteful use of the five grains." For good order, and thus happiness, consisted in everyone being *standmässig,* and "even in the matters of Buddhist ceremonies and religious festivals, overindulgence beyond one's status [was to] be avoided."[11]

Thus the peasants were kept frugal and hardworking, though to what extent this was owing to the internalization of the values that their masters tried to instill in them, rather than the harshness of their circumstances, remains a question. The way they were kept in this virtuous state rendered meaningless their theoretical position in the social hierarchy immediately below the samurai nobility—an equivalent of the upper-middle class in our terms. It is unclear that the farmers were aware of this distinction and doubtful whether it made any difference in their existence. Certainly, status-inconsistency, which could have been created by the contradiction between theory and experience, was not among their troubles (requiring leisure to have an effect). This modern misery had been spared them: they were not plagued by anomie. I am not aware of the suicide statistics among early Tokugawa peasants, but if any of them did commit it, it would probably have to be classified as "fatalistic"—caused by the absolute inability to escape their place, which they knew only too well, rather than by the sense of being lost in the social space.

THE SAMURAI The shoguns dealt skillfully with the two potential sources of challenge to the centralized political order, the feudal aristocracy and the peasantry, but they faced a much harder problem with the military class of the samurai—the equivalent of the European lower nobility. The samurai constituted about 7 percent of the Japanese population, thus being a very large upper class: in France, for instance, at most 2 percent of the population belonged to its counterpart. Moreover, it was a class of warriors, whose fighting spirit was kept alive and whose military skills were honed by constant practice in the conflicts of their feudal lords, which for centuries tore Japan apart. In 1550 Saint Francis Xavier noticed the value a society attached to weapons and the profession of arms. "The Japanese," he wrote,

> have a high opinion of themselves because they think that no other nation can compare with them in regard to weapons and valor . . . They greatly prize and value their arms, and prefer to have good weapons, decorated with gold and silver, more than anything else in the world. They carry a sword and a dagger both inside and outside the house and lay them at their pillows when they sleep. Never in my life have I met people who rely so much on their arms. They are excellent archers and

fight on foot, although there are horses in the country . . . They are very warlike and are always involved in wars, and thus the ablest man becomes the greatest lord.

Yet after the power fell to Tokugawa Ieyasu, the ablest man of the moment, the *bakufu* put an end to feudal warfare and found on its hands a large military class that had no reason for existence. It could neither disempower this class through co-optation, gifts of land, and direct and constant supervision, as it did the three hundred or so *daimyo*, because the samurai were too numerous, nor disarm them, as it did the hapless and meek peasantry. So it left them their right to bear swords and warrior pride but attempted to reeducate them, gently nudging this bellicose group to redefine itself as a cultural elite. (Again, one is struck by the singular similarity between Japan and European cases. In England, France, Russia, and Germany the value of learning dramatically increased in the century leading to the establishment of the national consciousness in them; in France and Russia, where the architects of nationalism came from the aristocracy, the nobility was redefined as a cultural elite.)

A year before his death, in 1615, Ieyasu issued the already mentioned Laws of the Military Households *(Buke Shohatto)*, which opened with the following surprising injunction: "The study of literature and the practice of military arts, including archery and horsemanship, must be cultivated diligently." The command was presently justified with reference to tradition: "'On the left hand literature, on the right hand use of arms' was the law of the ancients" (the left being considered more important than the right). But, aware that cultivation of the intellect was in itself a double-edged sword and thus could give to the samurai, already armed to the teeth, the powerful weapon of independent thinking, the legislators took the precaution of clearly defining the sphere where reason, the development of which they recommended, was to be applied, before it got out of hand. "Law is the foundation of social order," they declared. "Reason may be violated in the name of the law, but law may not be violated in the name of reason. Anyone who violates the law must be severely punished." The law instructed the samurai to keep a watchful eye over those of their kind who might overstep the bounds of reason by placing too much trust in it—"If innovations are being made . . . in a neighboring domain, it must be reported immediately"—and appealed to the common sense of its audience: "Why must one engage in [meaningless] innovations, instead of obeying old examples?"[12]

The intellectual framework of the Tokugawa's vision of the social order, based on the teachings of the twelfth-century Chinese neo-Confucian Chu Hsi, was suggested to Ieyasu by his adviser on education and foreign affairs Hayashi Razan, the principal author of many of the early Tokugawa laws.

Chu Hsi divided society into four hierarchically arranged orders: the scholar-rulers; the peasantry, who were the primary producers of wealth; the artisans, secondary producers; and the largely useless and parasitic order of merchants. In the Japanese version of this social philosophy, the military nobility took the place—and with it the characteristics—of the scholarly ruling class. The social order was a part of the cosmic order, which dramatically increased the consequences of any potential disturbance in the former. Hayashi explained:

> Heaven is above and earth is below. This is the order of heaven and earth. If we can understand the meaning of the order existing between heaven and earth, we can perceive that in everything there is an order separating those who are above and those who are below. When we extend this understanding between heaven and earth, we cannot allow disorder in the relations between the ruler and the subject, and between those who are above and those who are below. The separation into four classes of samurai, farmers, artisans and merchants . . . is part of the principles of heaven and is the Way which was taught by the Sage (Confucius) . . . To know the way of heaven is to respect heaven and to secure humble submission from earth, for heaven is high above and earth is low below. There is a differentiation between the above and the below. Likewise among the people, rulers are to be respected and subjects are to submit humbly. Only when this differentiation between those who are above and those who are below is made clear can there be law and propriety. In this way, people's minds can be satisfied.

There is no doubt that the minds of the people within the *bakufu*, as well as of the samurai, were satisfied. Chu Hsi's argument so well served the interests of the former group, and so explicitly flattered the latter, that they must have found its logic irrefutable. The status of the samurai, sanctioned by the authority of heaven, was safeguarded from encroachment. Like the nobility in France, they were separated from the hoi polloi by the theoretically impermeable division, constituted by their birth or, rather, family affiliation (for one could become a samurai by adoption), into a different, superior species of human beings. Secure in the consciousness of their social superiority, they did not particularly care which of the symbols of their status—the swords, which they had the undisputed right to carry, or the education which they were encouraged to acquire—was to be considered central, and responded with increasing enthusiasm to the government's preference for the latter. Confucian philosophy equated a perfect man, a true gentleman, and a sage; so be it, decided the samurai. Confucian schools for the nobility proliferated, the first founded in 1630 by Hayashi in Edo as a private establishment, but soon transformed into the official *bakufu* school, Shoheiko. The *daimyo* followed suit, and within several decades, most samurai could polish their classical Chinese and become experts in Confucian philosophy in their own *han*. By the eighteenth century, writes Reischauer, "an illiterate warrior samurai was a rarity," so much so that the shogun Yoshimune, who came to power in 1716, thought that "the substitution of learning for military discipline" had gone too far and sponsored "great hunting parties, which were in reality military exercises." The problem now was "how to maintain discipline and fighting spirit among men" whose will and sense of duty had atrophied for lack of use and who were spoiled by the abundance of leisure (somewhat like the tenured faculty in modern universities). It may be for this reason that one could observe, as did Sansom, "particularly from the beginning of the eighteenth century, a deliberate policy of ethical propaganda [whose] most obvious result is to be found in the formation of the cult known as *Bushido* or the Way of the Warrior."[13]

The Order Unravels

Learning was still encouraged. But it no longer needed encouragement. Clearly, the samurai had developed an appetite for it and, while willing to incorporate *bushido* into their Confucianism-based class ethic—which they had no difficulty doing, since the values the two emphasized were largely the same—were not to be diverted from their intellectual interests by hunting parties. The initial immersion in the doctrines of Chu Hsi led them in many directions, some of which proved quite subversive for the Tokugawa regime and later provided building blocks for the Japanese national consciousness, though none, it must be stressed, contributed to it directly.

In recommending neo-Confucianism to Ieyasu, Hayashi pointed to the affinities between Chu Hsi and the native Shinto tradition, juxtaposing it to the widespread Buddhism, which (like Confucianism) was of foreign origin. He argued in the characteristically non sequitur manner:

> Our country is the country of gods, Shinto is the same as the [Confucian] Way of the King *(odo)*. However, the rise of Buddhism made the people abandon the Way of the King and Shinto. Someone may ask how Shinto and Confucianism may be differentiated. I respond by saying that according to my observation the Principle *(ri)* is the same, but only its application differs.
>
> In comparing the books on the age of gods in the *Nihon Shoki* (Chronicles of Japan) with Master Zhou's [Zhou Dunyi, 1017–1073] *Taiji tushuo* (Diagram of the Supreme Ultimate Explained), I have yet to find any discrepancy in substantive matters. The Way of the King trans-

forms itself into Shinto and Shinto transforms itself into the Way. What I mean by the term "Way" is the Way of Confucianism, and it is not the so-called alien doctrine. The alien doctrine is Buddhism.[14]

In this manner a native cult, consisting of seasonal rituals, administered by a lay (often female) priesthood, which, though important in the lives of the rural communities, lacked a body of doctrine and even basic scripture, and thus had no intellectual prestige, was made a venerable object of learning. Before long, educated neo-Shintoists were declaring that Shinto was in every respect much better than Confucianism, and that Confucianism was in fact an alien doctrine. Made intellectually legitimate by association with Confucianism, Shintoism turned in the hands of intellectuals, within a century, into an expression of Sinophobia.

KOKUGAKU: PRE-NATIONAL SENSE OF JAPANESE UNIQUENESS
In 1728 the lay priest at the Inari Shrine in Kyoto, Kada Azumamaro, submitted a memorandum to the shogun Yoshimune in which, in the ornate and most formal Chinese style ("Respectfully submitted, craving your bountiful favor . . . I bow my head in awe and trepidation; vile and base as I am, I abjectly offer my words") and with constant references to Chinese classics, he asked for the privilege of creating a school of native learning—*kokugaku*. He began by presenting an idealized image of the current state of affairs, some elements of which were patently untrue but are particularly interesting exactly for this reason:

> [Since Ieyasu's time] enlightened rulers have successively ascended to power, and the literary pursuits have grown increasingly splendid; their refulgence shines even farther. The military arts are more perfected than ever; how noble and accomplished they are! Could the love of the Kamakura rulers for sobriety compare to this? Could the respect of the Muromachi family for literature be mentioned on the same day? In keeping with this age of great peace, Heaven has sent us a generous and benevolent ruler. No talented men are without employ; the court is thronged with upright men. Above he respects the emperor and devotes himself to effecting a government without deceit. Below he cherishes the *daimyo*, who offer him tribute. Because his policies are perfected and he has leisure for other pursuits, he has turned his mind to ancient studies; when the teachings in them are not complete he gives profound study to the rule of the men of old. He buys rare books for a thousand pieces of gold. The celebrated scholars of the country, following his example, search for rare and forgotten books. Visitors of unusual talent from all over the world flock to his court.

Of course, by 1728 Japan had been closed for about a century, and its foreign contacts were limited to a trickle of Chinese and Dutch traders who (the latter in particular) were kept in veritable confinement off the shores of Japan. How the *daimyo* were cherished we have heard. The emperor and his court in Kyoto were allocated a miserly 187,000 *koku* of rice a year—around five hundredths of 1 percent of the total yield, of which the *bakufu* appropriated one fourth—and were treated with marked disrespect. And the fact that the overwhelming majority of talented and well-educated men could find no employment in the structure built by Yoshimune's predecessors was to turn into the biggest problem for the regime and eventually bring it down. But Kada did not notice any of that. So far as he was concerned, he lived in the best of all possible social worlds, whose only imperfection was the neglect of native learning; therefore, prostrate, he beseeched Yoshimune to give him a quiet tract of land, where he could open a school.

When *kokugakusha*—the school of native learning—was founded, there was no more prostrating oneself before shoguns. Instead, the Shintoist scholars attacked the existing order with vehemence worthy of biblical prophets, without the usual Chinese flourishes, "in almost pure Japanese." They rejected its rationalism, its glorification of (Chinese) book learning, and opposed to it spontaneous emotion, which they believed characteristic of the native Japanese tradition and thought inherently superior to ratiocination as a moral guide. The anti-intellectualist temper of their discourse resembled that of the German Pietists and, even more, Romantics; some of their arguments, based on immersion in Japanese classics, had a certain resemblance to the Dutch *devotio moderna*. Submission to the intellectual authority of Chinese sages, they claimed, caused Japan to swerve from its god-given and natural Way—the ethical code that was the sign of Japan's election, placing it above all other societies, and guaranteed its well-being. "The True Way," wrote, for instance, Motoori Norinaga, one of the leaders of the Shinto revival and first explorers of the Japanese history and literature, "is one and the same, in every country and throughout heaven and earth. This Way, however, has been correctly transmitted only in our Imperial Land." This was so because of the direct descent of the imperial line from the Sun Goddess, which meant "that ours is the native land of the Heaven-Shining Goddess who casts her light over all countries in the four seas. Thus our country is the source and fountainhead of all other countries, and in all matters it excels all the others." If one accepted the first premise of this uncomplicated syllogism, the conclusion followed. Nevertheless, to clinch his argument, Motoori adduced further evidence. "It would be impossible," he suggested,

> to list all the products in which our country excels, but foremost among
> them is rice, which sustains the life of man, for whom there is no product

more important. Our country's rice has no peer in foreign countries, from which fact it may be seen why our other products are also superior. Those who were born in this country have long been accustomed to our rice and take it for granted, unaware of its excellence. They can enjoy such excellent rice morning and night to their heart's content because they have been fortunate enough to be born in this country. [Little did he know. Or perhaps he did not take into account the 80 percent of the Japanese population who were peasants, because it was not the peasants to whom his homilies were addressed.] This is a matter for which they should give thanks to our shining deities, but to my great dismay they seem to be unmindful of it.[15]

Hirata Atsutane was even more explicit, if somewhat repetitive, in arguing for Japanese superiority. The only proof he resorted to was the existence of consensus on the matter worldwide, and his world was wide indeed, including such otherworldly entities as Holland and Russia. In his *Summary of the Ancient Way (Kodo Taii)*, written in 1811, he asserted:

People all over the world refer to Japan as the Land of the Gods, and call us the descendants of the gods. Indeed, it is exactly as they say: our country, as a special mark of favor from the heavenly gods, was begotten by them, and there is thus so immense a difference between Japan and all the other countries of the world as to defy comparison. Ours is a splendid and blessed country, the Land of the Gods beyond any doubt, and we, down to the most humble man and woman, are the descendants of the gods . . . Japanese differ completely from and are superior to the peoples of China, India, Russia, Holland, Siam, Cambodia, and all other countries of the world, and for us to have called our country the Land of the Gods was not mere vainglory. It was the gods who formed all the lands of the world at the Creation, and these gods were without exception born in Japan. Japan is thus the homeland of the gods, and that is why we call it the Land of the Gods. This is a matter of universal belief, and is quite beyond dispute. Even in countries where our ancient traditions have not been transmitted, the peoples recognize Japan as a divine land because of the majestic effulgence that of itself emanates from our country.

And yet, people in Japan were unmindful of their good fortune; they exchanged their Way, the best way of all, for the ethical code concocted by alien sages; they neglected—even ridiculed, *horribile dictu*—their native deities and worshipped at the shrine of reason. It was for this, above all, that *kokugaku* scholars blamed Confucianism. It made men far too clever for their own good. And so grievous did they find this offense that they were willing to embrace and exculpate from the accusation of foreignness Buddhism, which left people's natural stupidity intact. One of the earliest representatives of "native learning," Kamo Mabuchi, wrote in 1765:

> Japan in ancient days was governed in accordance with the natural laws of Heaven and earth. There was never any indulgence in such petty rationalizing as marked China, but when suddenly these teachings were transmitted here from abroad, they quickly spread, for the men of old in their simplicity took them for the truth. In Japan there had been generation after generation, extending back to the remote past, which had known prosperity, but no sooner were these Confucian teachings propagated here that . . . a great rebellion occurred . . . Some people speak ill of Buddhism, but since it is a teaching which makes men stupid, it does not represent a grave evil; after all, rulers do not prosper unless the people are stupid.

"Sages are superior to other people only in their cleverness," argued Motoori tautologically. "The fact is that they were all impostors." Adulation of human reason deprived people of their innate moral sense and destroyed social order, knowledge was inherently corrupting, therefore *kokugaku* scholars believed its possession had to be limited to the select few. "Ever since man impetuously decided that knowledge would be of use to him," asseverated Kamo, "evil motives of every kind have sprung up among people, and have finally thrown the world into turmoil . . . It might be desirable if just one or two men in the world had knowledge, but when everyone possesses it, what a dreadful chaos ensues, and in the end the knowledge itself is useless." Lack of knowledge, consequently, was something to be proud of, and the surest indication of the purity of soul. Thus Hirata inveighed against the Confucian scholar Dazai Jun. Dazai claimed, apparently, that before exposure to Confucianism, the Japanese lacked an ethic—a Way—for there were no native Japanese expressions for concepts such as humanity, righteousness, decorum, music, filial piety, and fraternal affection. "The majority of the Confucian pedants and other scholars partial to things Chinese," wrote Hirata in a tellingly entitled opus *Indignant Discussion of Chinese Books,*

> are overjoyed and infatuated with the idea that China possesses the teachings of a Way, and proclaim that in ancient Japan there were no teachings like those of China. But however much they may heap indignation on Japan, all that they assert is utterly in error. Humanity, righteousness, filial piety, and the rest are all principles governing the proper

conduct of man. If they are always automatically observed and never violated, it is unnecessary to teach them. If they are the invariable standard
of behavior, what need is there for a "Way"? . . . The ancient Japanese all
constantly and correctly practiced what the Chinese called humanity,
righteousness, the five cardinal virtues and the rest, without any need to
name them or to teach them. There was thus no necessity for anything
to be especially constituted as a Way. This is the essentially Japanese
quality of Japan, and one where we may see a magnificent example of Japan's superiority to all other countries of the world. In China, as I have
already had frequent occasions to mention, there were evil customs from
the outset, and human behavior, far from being proper, was extremely li-
centious. That is the reason why so many sages appeared in ancient times
to guide and instruct the Chinese . . . From this we may see that the very
fact that in ancient Japan there was no Way is the most praiseworthy feature of the country, and that it is the shame of a country if it has had to
invent a Way for the guidance of the people.

The values of *kokugaku* bear a striking resemblance to those of early German Romanticism, a trend with which it was almost contemporary. Both de-
nounced civilization and extolled the virtues of the primitive, "natural" way
of life; both castigated rationalism and showered praise on freely expressed
emotion; both identified the present society with evil and idealized the immemorial past; both blamed whatever ailed them on the foreigner. There
were differences, of course: instead of primitive Christianity, *kokugaku* derived its ideals from Shinto, and Confucian China occupied in the mind of
the Japanese scholars the place held by the modern Western society, especially
France, in the thought of the Romantics. Nevertheless, certain pronouncements of the neo-Shintoist theorists correspond almost word for word to
those of their German counterparts.

Take, for instance, the Romantics' glorification of poetry as the most perfect form of human knowledge (expressed famously in the "Athenaeum Frag-
ment" number 116). On the condition that Japanese poetry substitute for
the Romantic, Kamo Mabuchi would agree: "Japanese poetry has as its subject the human heart. It may seem to be of no practical use and just as well
left uncomposed, but when one knows poetry well, one understands also
without explanation the reasons governing order and disorder in the world."
The Romantic detestation of all rational discourse and intellectual discipline—reflected in Hamann's dismissal of reason as "unnatural," in Adam
Müller's principled rejection of clear concepts in favor of the vague, cryptic
"Idea," in Herder's declaration that "all learning is of the devil," and perhaps
most vividly in his Ossian essay, where he proclaimed that "the *wilder*, i.e. *the*

more living, more fully active a people is, the wilder, i.e. more living, more sensuous, freer, fuller of lyrical action must be its poetry," thereby identifying cultural superiority, and life itself, with irrationality—also had a *kokugaku* equivalent. Kamo believed that "things which are explained in terms of theories are as dead. Those which operate together with Heaven and earth spontaneously are alive and active." As Romantic excesses were inconsistent with the Japanese love of decorum, he tried to moderate this unequivocal opinion, but the attempt was, obviously, halfhearted. "I do not mean to say," he claimed disingenuously, "that it is a bad idea to have a general knowledge of all things, but it is a common human failing to tend to lean excessively in that direction . . . [D]octors often study and master Chinese texts, but very seldom do they cure any sickness. On the other hand, medicines which have been transmitted naturally in this country with no reasons or theoretical knowledge behind them, infallibly cure all maladies. It is good when a man spontaneously devotes himself to these things." And in regard to material civilization more generally (which the Romantics, too, accused of destroying the natural state of bliss): "In ancient times words and things were few. When things are few the heart is sincere, and there is no need for difficult teachings."

Similarly to the German Romantics, the *kokugaku* intellectuals, when it suited them, were relativists: at times it appeared that they could be satisfied with proving the equality of the native culture with the Confucian tradition generally considered superior. On the principle that "the perfection of a thing is its reality" (for the Romantics, formulated by Herder), they, too, were prone to claim that a society was happiest when it followed its unique individuality, or nature, and that therefore, however beneficial was Confucianism for China, it simply was not appropriate for Japan. But, as with the Romantics, this cultural relativism promptly gave way to a new moral absolutism, and claims to inherent superiority replaced claims to equality. In the light of this development, continued support for Confucian theories was not only erroneous but morally reprehensible as well. Motoori argued seamlessly:

Leaving aside for the moment the question as to which is superior, let us first make a distinction between the Chinese and the Japanese views. From the Chinese point of view, the Japanese view is wrong, and from the Japanese point of view, the Chinese view is wrong. But the objector advances only the Chinese view and attempts to universalize it, even denying the antiquity of our Imperial Land. Is this not prejudiced and arbitrary? To this he might reply that the universe is one, that there is no distinction between a Chinese and Japanese point of view, and that narrow partiality lies in attempting to make such distinctions. However, the ob-

jector, in advancing only the Chinese view and casting doubt on the antiquity of our Imperial Land, himself makes such a distinction and shows
partiality to China . . . Even if there were no distinctions among the
countries, it would still be proper for the various countries of the world,
each with its own traditions and its point of view, to maintain their views
according to their own traditions. Our Imperial Land in particular is superior to the rest of the world in its possession of the correct transmission of the ancient Way, which is that of the great Goddess who casts her
light all over the world. It is treasonable malice to urge that we discard
that transmission in favor of a senseless foreign view which, moreover,
insists that our ancient transmission is a fantasy and a fabrication.

Kamo Mabuchi preferred teaching by gentle analogy, but reached the same
conclusion. "Just as roads are naturally created when people live in uncultivated woodlands or fields," he wrote, "so the Way of the Age of the Gods
spontaneously took hold in Japan. Because it was a Way indigenous to the
country it caused our emperors to wax increasingly in prosperity. However,
the Confucian teachings had not only repeatedly thrown China into disorder,
but they now had the same effect in Japan. Yet there are those unwitting of
these facts who reverence Confucianism and think that it is the Way to govern the country! This is a deplorable attitude."

The instrument of Confucianism's destructive work was the cultivation of
reason. People acquired confidence in their ability to decipher mysteries of
the universe, and it sowed doubt in their hearts. Because they could not understand the actions of the gods, they lost their belief. Kamo complained:
"Japan has always been a country where the people are honest. As long as a
few teachings were carefully observed and we worked in accordance with the
Will of Heaven and earth, the country would be well off without any special
instruction. Nevertheless, Chinese doctrines were introduced and corrupted
men's hearts." Motoori echoed him: "The people of antiquity never attempted to reason out the acts of the gods with their own intelligence, but
the people of a later age, influenced by the Chinese, have become addicts
of rationalism."[16] Thus they abandoned the Way of their forefathers and
plunged their society into turmoil; in the end, kokugaku was a form of social
criticism.

Paradoxically, like German Romanticism, which owed so much of its intellectual sophistication to the rationalism of the Aufklärung, against which
it revolted, kokugaku derived its methods from Confucianism. Preoccupation with ancient Japanese literature, and, even more important, language—
which formed the very basis of kokugaku studies—reflected the nominalism
of the Chu Hsi doctrine. Explorations of native history (the most notable of

which was the *Dai Nihon shi* of Tokugawa Mitsukuni), another central element, were obviously first encouraged by the Confucian emphasis on history.[17] Like the first German Romantics, who were men of Enlightenment before they turned against it, the *kokugaku* scholars were Confucians before they became anti-Confucians. Inevitably, their Confucianism- (and therefore *bakufu-*) inspired interests in philology and history led them to a focus on the emperor and the criticism, initially implicit, of the Tokugawa regime. Kamo Mabuchi intoned:

> Confucianism made men crafty, and led them to worship the ruler to such an excessive degree that the whole country acquired a servant's mentality. Later it even came about that an emperor was sacrilegiously driven to an island exile. This occurred because the country had become infected with Chinese ideas . . . Our country in ancient times was not like that. It obeyed the laws of Heaven and earth. The emperor was the sun and moon and the subjects the stars. If the subjects as stars protect the sun and moon, they will not hide it as is now the case. Just as the sun, moon, and stars have always been in Heaven, so our imperial sun and moon, and the stars his vassals, have existed without change from ancient days and have ruled the world fairly. However, some knaves appeared, and as a result the emperor is diminished in power.

The Sinophobia of the *kokugaku* scholars and their insistence on the inherent superiority of Japan should not be interpreted as a sign of the nascent national consciousness, even if only among a few intellectuals. What, besides sheer academic interest, led these individuals to stress Japanese native tradition and in the process to articulate a sense of a unique Japanese identity (which does not, as such, equal nationalism) was a professional problem, similar indeed to the one faced by German intellectuals who became Romantics. The respect for learning in Tokugawa society made education an avenue of upward mobility, perhaps the only one for a samurai to excel in and gain an official position and respect, commensurate with his theoretically elite status, since high administrative posts in the *bakufu* were limited to certain high-ranking families and were insufficient in number even for them. Confucian scholars in the government-sponsored tradition of Chu Hsi, however, were overproduced, and the competition among them must have been quite brutal. *Kokugaku* provided a professional niche, where one could escape this competition and had a better chance of success. In fact, some "unfriendly critics of Motoori have insinuated that he took up the study of National Learning because it offered easier chances of recognition than the already overcrowded field of Confucian studies." It is significant that the editors of

Sources of Japanese Tradition, from which I have quoted in this discussion, while evidently sympathetic to Motoori, bring this "insinuation" up.[18]

Neither the sentiment that moved these intellectuals, nor the nature of the unique identity they articulated, was national: there was no place for popular sovereignty in their thought, and though they clamored for equality with Confucianism (and insisted on the superiority) of their school, a suggestion that they were essentially equal to Japanese peasants, or, worse still, merchants, would have outraged them. Their image of society was very different from the one nationalism implies, and they surely would have found the idea of the nation incomprehensible.

DUTCH STUDIES: A GLIMPSE OF THE WEST   The interpretation of *kokugaku* as an attempt at intellectual product differentiation, provoked by the overproduction of orthodox, Chu Hsi Confucians, is supported by the fact that it was only one of several heterodox intellectual trends that developed among the samurai at the time. Some Japanese philosophers chose to follow the introspective teaching of a later Chinese thinker, Wang Yang-ming (in Japanese, Oyomei, who lived between 1472 and 1529). This trend also bore a certain resemblance to Pietism and Romanticism (which reflected the similarity between Chu Hsi Confucianism and the *Aufklärung*), opposing as it did intuition and action to book learning and theoretical speculation. It stressed the natural moral sense and self-control, the qualities also extolled by Zen Buddhism, which was the preferred philosophy of the feudal warrior, and so had numerous adherents among "the best sort of samurai." Its early exponents included Nakae Toju in the first half of the seventeenth century and Kumazawa Banzan in the second half. Many of the leaders of the Meiji Restoration were influenced by it.

Of far greater moment was "Dutch learning"—the *rangaku*,[19] which introduced Japanese intellectuals to Western science and eventually Western thought in general. Some students of Japanese intellectual history trace the origins of *rangaku* to the publication in the early eighteenth century of two works by Arai Hakuseki, a mentor and adviser of the shoguns Ienobu and Ietsugu, which dealt with the geography and social conditions of Western countries and were based on Arai's talks with the Dutch on Dejima and a Sicilian missionary, Giovanni Sidotti, who somehow managed to visit Japan in 1708. There was some interest in Western knowledge at the time, but it was limited to a few especially audacious or well-placed thinkers. A dissenting Confucian of great renown, Ogyu Sorai, protested against the ban on Western books, arguing that it defeated the purpose for which the *bakufu* introduced it. "Owing to these prohibitions nobody knows what Christianity teaches," he wrote. "But the officials should not leave us in ignorance on this subject, since we ought to know whether it is good or bad . . . Buddhists, Shintoists and Confucianists should be in a position to prove that it is errone-ous or harmful, but they cannot do this unless they are allowed to see the books." In 1720, Yoshimune, having to resort to an astronomical encyclope-dia compiled for the Chinese court by a Westerner, in an emergency (he was in need of an astrologer's advice, and the Japanese calendar, on which it was to be based, was believed unreliable), lifted the ban. Western literature, with the exception of books propagating Christian doctrine, was allowed into the country, and this created conditions for the emergence of a more general in-terest, which focused on military technology, especially gunnery, medicine, and astronomy. The lack of minimal acquaintance with Western languages, however, presented a major difficulty: the first teach-yourself manual (for Dutch, as could be expected) did not appear until 1783.

Sugita Gempaku, one of the founders of "Dutch learning," indeed, dates its emergence to the end of the eighteenth century, specifically to the spring of 1771, when he, personally, was presented with irrefutable evidence of the superiority of Western science to Chinese philosophy. The substitution of the authority of facts for that of the acclaimed authors of books, the realization that empirical evidence could be used as a standard of intellectual judgment, the definition of actually existing reality, rather than texts about it, as a legiti-mate object of learning, transformed the nature of knowledge and with it one's entire perspective on the world. It was an earth-shaking experience, similar to a religious revelation, a cognitive shift, an innovation of far greater proportions than those implied in any of the other currents with which *rangaku* coexisted, and a much more formidable challenge to the suprem-acy of Confucianism. Sugita left a memoir, *The Beginning of Dutch Studies (Rangaku Kotohajime)*, which captures beautifully the sense of discovery, liberation, and excitement associated with this transformation, and his story deserves retelling.

Sugita was a surgeon, trained in traditional medicine. He had heard about Dutch medical science and often discussed its alleged excellence with his friends. "As we have learned," they would say to one another, "the Dutch method of scholarly investigation through field work and surveys is truly amazing. If we can directly understand books written by them, we will bene-fit greatly. However, it is pitiful that there has been no one who has set his mind on working in this field. Can we somehow blaze this trail? It is impossi-ble to do it in Edo. Perhaps it is best if we ask translators in Nagasaki to make some translations. If one book can be completely translated, there will be an immeasurable benefit to the country." But for a long time, all they could do was to deplore "the impossibility of implementing our desires."

Then "somehow, miraculously" Sugita obtained a Dutch book on anatomy, *Tabulae Anatomicae*. He wrote: "It may well be that Dutch studies in this country began when I thought of comparing the illustrations in the book with real things." The opportunity presented itself when, several months later, he was invited to witness a postmortem examination of the body of a condemned criminal. A dream he had nursed for at least twelve years was realized:

> At one time my colleague by the name of Kosugi Genteki had an occasion to witness a post-mortem dissection of a body . . . After seeing the dissection first-hand, Kosugi remarked that what was said by the people of old was false and simply could not be trusted. "The people of old spoke of nine internal organs, and nowadays, people divide them into five viscera and six internal organs. That [perpetuates] inaccuracy," Kosugi once said. Around that time (1759) Dr. Toyo published a book entitled *Zoshi (On Internal Organs)*. Having read that book, I had hoped that some day I could witness a dissection. When I also acquired a Dutch book on anatomy, I wanted above all to compare the two to find out which one accurately described the truth.

Excited about "this unusually fortunate circumstance" and believing that it would be selfish to "monopolize this good fortune," Sugita invited two friends to share in it. In preparation, the companions leafed through the Dutch book and found that the illustrations of the heart did not look like its descriptions in the Chinese medical books, but, wisely, postponed judgment. "None of us were sure until we could actually see the dissection," wrote Sugita.

The ninety-year-old butcher performing the postmortem was a healthy old man.

> He had experienced many dissections since his youth, and boasted that he dissected a number of bodies. Those dissections were performed in those days by men of the *eta* class . . . That day, the old butcher pointed to this and that organ. After the heart, liver, gall bladder, and stomach were identified, he pointed to other parts for which there were no names. "I don't know their names, [he said.] But I have dissected quite a few bodies from my youthful days. Inside of everyone's abdomen there were these parts and those parts."

After consulting the Dutch anatomy chart, Sugita realized that he had seen an arterial tube, a vein, and a suprarenal gland. The coroner-butcher told the companions that every time he performed a dissection, he pointed out to the physicians who were present the mysterious parts, but not a single one of them questioned what they were. They then "compared the body as dissected against the charts [in the *Tabulae Anatomicae*] and could not find a single variance from the charts." The Chinese notions proved to be sheer fantasy. "The Chinese *Book of Medicine (Yi jing),*" wrote Sugita,

> says that the lungs are like the eight petals of the lotus flower, with three petals hanging in front, three in back, and two petals forming like two ears and that the liver has three petals to the left and four petals to the right. There were no such divisions, and the positions and shapes of intestines and gastric organs were all different from those taught by the old theories. The official physicians, Dr. Okada Yosen and Dr. Fujimoto Rissen, have witnessed dissection seven or eight times. Whenever they witnessed the dissection, they found that the old theories contradicted reality. Each time they were perplexed and could not resolve their doubts. Every time they wrote down what they thought was strange. They wrote in their books, "The more we think of it, there must be fundamental differences in the bodies of Chinese and of the eastern barbarians [i.e., Japanese]." I could see why they wrote this way.

After the dissection was over, the companions decided to "examine the shape of the skeletons left exposed on the execution ground." They collected the bones and compared them against the illustrations in *Tabulae Anatomicae*. "Again," recalled Sugita, "we were struck by the fact that they all differed from the old theories while conforming to the Dutch charts."

They discussed their "marvelous" experience on the way home, excited and bitter at once. "It is a shame," they said, "that we were ignorant of these things until now. As physicians who serve their masters through medicine, we performed our duties in complete ignorance of the true form of the human body. How disgraceful it is." But, their mental horizons vastly expanded from the day's discoveries, they were filled with the desire to learn more and felt a new confidence in their powers. "Somehow, through this experience," they told one another, "let us investigate further the truth about the human body. If we practice medicine with this knowledge behind us, we can make contributions for people under heaven and on this earth . . . Somehow if we can translate anew this book called *Tabulae Anatomicae,* we can get a clear notion of the human body inside out. It will have great benefit in the treatment of our patients. Let us do our best to read it and understand it without the help of the translators." One of Sugita's friends, Ryotaku, confessed that he had wished to read Dutch books for some time, but found no one to share his interest. Thus, he "spent days lamenting it." "If both of you wish," he suggested, "I have been in Nagasaki before and have retained some Dutch. Let us use it as a beginning to tackle the book together." Sugita responded:

"This is simply wonderful. If we join our efforts, I shall also resolve to do my very best."

And so the next day they assembled in Ryotaku's house. "When we faced that *Tabulae Anatomicae*," remembered Sugita, "we felt as if we were setting sail on a great ocean in a ship without oars or a rudder. With the magnitude of the work before us, we were dumbfounded by our own ignorance . . . At that time I did not know the twenty-five letters of the Dutch alphabet. I decided to study the language with firm determination, but I had to acquaint myself with letters and words gradually."

The translation took our determined friends three years, "at the rate of ten lines a day." Its appearance in Japanese print in 1774 marked the very beginning of translations of Western works in Japan. Indeed, the second *rangaku* book to be published was the Dutch self-instruction manual of 1783.

Clearly, in their quest for Western knowledge, people like Sugita Gempaku were driven by a personal passion, the urgent need to satisfy their curiosity, though Sugita's memoirs suggest that social ambition was not entirely absent from his considerations. In any intellectual *movement* or *trend,* which, by definition, attracted more than a few exceptional individuals, social motives, concerns with status above all, were bound to predominate. Most of the *rangaku* adherents, Sansom noted, "were in the first place attracted to Dutch studies because they afforded opportunities of advancement that were not open to them so long as they confined themselves to the routine" studies or duties of a rank-and-file samurai.[20] Like *kokugaku,* it was a professional niche, which protected those in it from the increasingly strenuous competition resulting from overcrowding and improved their chances of success. It was, obviously, less concerned than the "native school" with the nature of Japanese identity, but it too provided one of the important building blocks for Japanese nationalism which was to emerge in the late nineteenth century. "Dutch studies" forced Japanese intellectuals to compare themselves to the West and develop a sense of cultural inferiority with respect to it. Later, this would contribute to the establishment of the West as the significant other and the model for Japan, and stimulate the fierce competitiveness it would develop as a nation.

STATUS-INCONSISTENCY AND ELITE DISAFFECTION The emphasis on education and the prestige of learning reflected the desire of the Tokugawa government to divert the attention of its warrior nobility from their more traditional and dangerous pursuits, which could easily lead to mischief, and to provide them with something respectable to do instead, and the strategy, initially, was successful. But as time passed, the new habit of thinking became second nature to the sword-flaunting samurai, and some of them, at least, were no longer satisfied with thinking only what they were taught. Moreover, what they were taught in fact led them to certain unanticipated discoveries that threw new—and unflattering—light on the Tokugawa regime which had inspired them to think and learn in the first place. In the meantime, the social situation also encouraged critical reflection, which was articulated by dissenting intellectuals and emboldened them.

The reduction in the number of feudal domains under Ieyasu implied a proportional reduction in the number of positions available for retainers, as well as the breakdown of numerous ties of vassalage, on which samurai depended for employment. A huge group of déclassé samurai emerged as a result: 400,000 persons were *ronin*, or unattached, masterless samurai, as early as 1650. It was equal in actual numbers to the entire French nobility, according to the highest estimate of the latter's size in the 1750s, when it was particularly numerous, but was proportionally much larger, for the population of Japan in 1650 was about 15 million and that of France a century later 20 million. As samurai, the *ronin* retained the honorific distinctions of their class, for their legally defined status was unaffected by their circumstances, but their duties and, therefore, rights and relations with those around them, in general, were unclear, and they had no regular income. Some of the *ronin* traded their social superiority and tiresome leisure for the ignoble but gainful occupations of peasants or burghers, though this was prohibited by law. Some earned their living as itinerant intellectuals. Kumazawa Banzan, who came from a *ronin* family, found food for thought and comfort for his soul in Chu Hsi and Wang Yang-ming Confucianism, becoming an accomplished scholar by his twenties. As for food to nurture his body, however, sometimes to him "it seemed as though, embracing my mother and my sisters and brothers, I might die of starvation." Having made a name for himself, he escaped this fate with the help of an administrative appointment in Okayama. It sustained him for ten years, providing, among other things, much valuable knowledge for his later writings on economics. In 1657, in his late thirties, he left Okayama and supported himself by teaching and writing. His was, of course, an exceptional case. If they wandered the countryside, *ronin* who did not have Kumazawa's talents did so not because they chose to. Many became vagrants and even bandits. All of them, the more and the less lucky, existed in a condition of extreme status-inconsistency, forming a large pool of armed, bitterly disaffected men, always available to support opposition to the existing order.

The situation of the rest of the samurai was not much better, although their problems did not become evident until the eighteenth century. They were kept on stipends of around twenty *koku* of rice per year, paid from the revenues of the *bakufu* or feudal domains, where they occupied various clerical, managerial, and overseer posts. But, despite the reduction of their numbers by 40 percent (which the 400,000 of those who became *ronin* must have represented), they were still too numerous to guarantee meaningful employment—namely, such that entailed at least certain responsibilities—for each of them. The majority constituted a leisure class of domanial court towns and swelling cities such as Kyoto, Osaka, and Edo, free to immerse themselves in Confucian (or anti-Confucian) studies, practice their swordsmanship, or frequent the famous entertainment districts, where naughtiness combined with untrammeled creativity to produce an exquisite lighthearted culture, which would be unique if it did not so closely resemble—in its aesthetic conception, focus, and the character of its audience—the Dutch culture of about the same time.

Though generally useless, the existence of the samurai was not carefree. Twenty *koku* of rice per year was not much in the best of times. As the eighteenth century began, and "the period called *Genroku* [1688–1704, which might] be looked upon as the zenith of Tokugawa prosperity" ended, the times were, clearly, not the best. A hundred years of rigidly enforced *sankin kotai*, which required the *daimyo*, gradually turned into a class of courtiers, to maintain costly establishments in Edo, created a constant demand for money among them and stimulated commercialization and monetization of the economy. They would now convert their rice into cash, making it a commodity to be traded rather than the all-important item of immediate consumption. The arrangement was also the chief factor in the prodigious growth of Edo (which, with over a million inhabitants in 1700 and close to a million and a half by 1750, was probably the most populous city in the world), and, indirectly, in urbanization in general. Kyoto, the old imperial capital, and Osaka, which became a great trade center, had 300,000 residents each, while altogether some 15 percent of Japan's population—more than in England at the time—lived in urban areas. Prices of real estate in the cities skyrocketed. The value of Ogyu Sorai's family home, for instance, increased forty times within one generation. "My grandfather," he remembered, "owned a piece of land in Ise which had been cultivated for generations by his ancestors. He sold it and bought a house in Edo for only 50 *ryo*. I understand that the house was sold in my father's time for a sum of more than 2,000 *ryo*."[21]

Urbanization, in turn, further promoted commercial development. For the samurai this had direct and calamitous implications. In an effort to extract more money from their crops, many *daimyo* cut the stipends of their retainers, often as much as in half, leaving masses of samurai to survive on the miserly amount of ten *koku* of rice a year. To provide for the needs of their families, these ten *koku* now had to be sold. But the prices of rice, in the years of good harvest, were falling, while during the frequent famines, one was obliged to keep it for food, yet it was impossible to live in the cities on rice alone. In his *Political Proposals (Seidan)*, composed in the 1720s, Ogyu Sorai lamented:

> In olden days, the countryside had hardly any money and all the purchase was made with rice or barley but not with money. This is what I experienced while living in the countryside. However, I have heard that from the Genroku period on, money economy has spread to the countryside, and they now use money to purchase things . . . Nowadays, samurai are forced to live in castle towns in discharge of their duties. Living away from home, in a manner similar to travelers seeking lodging, requires cash for sustenance. They must sell rice for cash, and purchase their daily needs from merchants. In this way, merchants become masters while samurai are relegated to the position of customers, unable to determine prices fixed on different commodities. In olden days when samurai lived on their own lands, they had no need to sell their rice. Merchants came to buy rice, and under such circumstances, samurai remained masters and the merchants their customers. Prices of different commodities were dictated by the samurai class. This is the law that was established by the ancient sage [Confucius] in his infinite wisdom. It must remain inviolable through the ages. One recommendation I have is to charge an exorbitantly high price for the rice and force the merchants to eat grains other than rice.

But this was not to be done. Paralleling the plight of the French nobility, but far more severe and common, the impoverishment of the samurai continued unabated. They tried to cope: married merchants' daughters, which in France was referred to as "manuring noble land," only samurai had no land to manure; adopted merchants' children or children of affluent farmers for money, which the biological parents were willing to pay, for it assured their offspring the samurai status, still valued more than prosperity among prosperous commoners and the society at large; a few, like the *ronin* of the seventeenth century, gave up their nobility for the ability to support themselves and their families and became merchants. But, as Sansom stresses, "the majority fell into an indigent state." No wonder they were demoralized, preoccupied with pecuniary worries, and unable to keep up the true samurai spirit or the warrior skills which made their grandfathers so feared and therefore respected. "Seven or eight out of ten bannermen and retainers," Sugita Gempaku wrote contemptuously, "are effeminate. They are mean-spirited and behave like shopkeepers. Those who profess a taste for military arts do it for the sake of worldly success and to get appointments . . . If on taking a test they are lucky enough to hit a two-foot target and to dismount safely after bestriding a horse as tame as a cat, they are promoted for their exploits and after that they put their accomplishments on the shelf." Were it so easy to be promoted!

The most serious problem for the Tokugawa regime, as was to become clear with time, was its inability—only partly explained by unwillingness—to promote men of talent. The system, as in Germany in the age of Enlightenment, with its stress on education and the Confucian definition of the ruling class as the cultural elite, overproduced such men, and, as in Germany in the age of Enlightenment, could not put to use the abilities whose development it encouraged or satisfy the ambitions it bred. The number of positions of responsibility and influence commensurate with these people's aspirations in the *bakufu* was obviously limited, and these positions, moreover, were open only to persons of specific rank. Even the select families, whose scions were eligible for appointment to these coveted posts usually produced more qualified candidates than could be satisfied, and this, as Reischauer points out, "gave rise in time to contending reformist and conservative cliques vying for power by winning the *shogun*'s backing," or, in other words, led to competition and discontent within the topmost echelon of Tokugawa society.[22] The *daimyo* administrations could not compensate for the *bakufu*'s inadequacy in this respect, although they did provide valued employment, and with it peace of mind and a kinder view of the society in general, for several exceptionally talented individuals who were important in Japan's intellectual and political development. Exceptional ability, combined with exceptional luck, could bring one to the attention of the shogun or high-placed officials and change one's destiny, but this was not to be counted on, and very few of the capable, well-educated, and ambitious samurai were exceptionally talented or lucky. Thus a condition of jarring status-inconsistency was perpetuated, which affected the brightest and the most articulate group in society, best qualified to rationalize, broadcast, and garner support for its discontent.

It was perceived early that the problem might have dire consequences. In his *Political Proposals*, Ogyu Sorai analyzed the principle limiting positions of influence to the aristocracy of birth, concluding that it was illegitimate in the framework of Confucian doctrine, as well as dangerous for the Tokugawa regime, and urged the government to abandon it. He argued:

It is a general and lasting principle of the natural order that old things should pass away and new things be brought into existence . . . [I]n accordance with [it] that which is below rises step by step to a superior position and, when it has reached its zenith, falls into decay and is in turn replaced from below . . . But in the matter of government it is characteristic of human nature that the families of men who rendered services to the state in the past should be cherished and their succession assured as long as possible . . . This means that there is a conflict between the principles of the natural order and the normal workings of human nature, for what is old must pass away, no matter how much we may wish to hold onto it. To conclude that it is best that all old things should be swept away at once is to carry wisdom to excess, and is not in accordance with the Way of the Sages [Confucianism]. But merely to attempt to preserve what is old is to carry folly to excess and is also not in accordance with the Way of the Sages [which] does not consist in unthinking adherence to what is generally accepted.

Because of the principle in the natural order which I have mentioned, [sometime famous families have become extinct]. The ancestors of the present *daimyo* were men of insignificant social position who rose to power as a result of their services in the field . . . But if men in high positions try to postpone the time when they should give place to others, and are so foolish as to attempt to keep things as they are by laying it down that the families which are in a superior position and those which are in an inferior position shall remain in that state forever, they will be acting against the principle of the natural order. As a result of this, persons of ability will disappear from among the upper class and in the course of time an age of disorder will come, in which men of ability will appear among the lower classes and overthrow the dynasty. The Sages were aware of this principle, and in order that their dynasties should last as long as possible they instituted a system of "rewards and punishments," encouraging and promoting to office men of ability from the lower classes, and removing men from the upper classes as the mind of Heaven willed it, either by their dying without direct descendants, or as a result of their committing some offence. When government is carried on in this way all men of ability are in positions of authority and those who have no ability are in positions of subordination, and because this is in accordance with the principles of the natural order the dynasty remains in power for a long time.

"It should be realized," Ogyu warned transparently, "that if a ruler neglects this correspondence with the natural order, and is not conversant with the principles governing the totality of Heaven, Earth and Man, his rule will not be in accordance with the mind of Heaven, and will not be true government." It would, in other words, be illegitimate, and both invite and justify rebellion. Nor did he stop at pointing to the inconsistency between rule through an aristocracy of birth and the laws of heaven: he explained why the laws of heaven were reasonable (and therefore appealing to and recommended by the Sages):

When the members of the lower orders who possess ability are promoted, the will of those above is diffused throughout the lower classes in
a way similar to the descent of the spirit of Heaven. But if good men
among the lower orders are not promoted, the feelings of the lower orders are not made known to the upper class, as happens when the spirit
of Earth does not rise. The upper and lower classes are then disunited
and separated from one another as when Heaven and Earth are not
united in harmonious combination, and the state declines in the same
way in which all things wither and decay in autumn and winter.

The reason for the fact that after a long period of peace, good men are
to be found among the lower orders while the members of the upper
classes become more and more stupid, is that all human ability is produced by suffering difficulties and hardships. [A man who had experienced these] is particularly well-suited to government because he has
acquired his intelligence in the course of being knocked about as a member of the lower orders, and is therefore well acquainted with the life of
the common people. In the Way of the Sages, too, one is commanded
to "raise up the worthy and talented," that is to promote men from below . . . All the ancestors of those who for generations have received
great emoluments and have occupied high offices acquired intelligence
from the hardships which they suffered in the course of life-and-death
struggle of civil war. Hence they did great deeds and obtained great
emoluments and high office. But their descendants have enjoyed great
emoluments and high office by hereditary succession; they occupy their
superior position by reason of their birth, and since they undergo no
hardships at all they have no opportunity of developing intelligence . . .
They receive respect on the account of their birth, and, believing that
this is merely what is due to them, are not disposed to be deeply grateful
for the benefits which their superiors have conferred upon them, while
in personal conduct they act in an arbitrary fashion and think of their social inferiors as so much vermin.

Ogyu insisted: "In the Way of Sages the first thing spoken about is the promotion of talent from below, while 'seikan,' that is the occupation of important offices by successive generations of the same family, is strongly depreci-
ated." And yet there was nothing revolutionary in what he had in mind; he
would be satisfied by a very moderate reform. "Acceptance of the principle of
promoting men of worth and talent," he counseled the *bakufu,*

does not imply driving out all those who have held positions in the past
and reversing the position of rulers and ruled. If only two or three, or
even only one or two, men of worth and talent are promoted from the
lower classes, the hitherto unbroken precedent of hereditary succession

will be destroyed and everyone will adopt a new attitude, each working with great diligence in imitation of the men who have been promoted, and thus by one stroke the entire country will be transformed into a better state.

But Ogyu was wrong. The promotion of one or two gifted people would not satisfy the rest of the equally gifted samurai but only increase their frustration, as in fact it did, for one or two were promoted from time to time. It would be better if no one was promoted ever, so that the rigidity of the system would appear in principle unyielding, than to compromise it, give rise to false hopes, and dash them. Hope of fulfillment generates desire; hope of promotion, paradoxically, may make a perfectly comfortable position appear unacceptable, and a situation that is less than comfortable downright intolerable, while dashed hopes breed anomie, which, when applied to men of ability in sufficient numbers, has been known to undermine the seemingly most stable systems. The situation and attitudes of the lower educated samurai, from Ogyu's days on, indeed closely parallel the experience and views of the members of the Russian nobility who, by the end of the eighteenth century, began redefining themselves as the "intelligentsia." Ogyu's "Proposal for Employing Men of Talent" finds an almost exact counterpart (allowing for obvious differences in the historical setting) in Denis Fonvisin's famous "Questions," addressed to Catherine the Great in the 1770s. In the Russian case, the systemic frustration of the ablest group within the nobility by the turn of the nineteenth century led to the transformation of the Russian identity (the emergence of nationalism) and by 1825 apparently could be endured no longer, expressing itself in the Decembrist Rebellion, whose suppression, if not the fact itself, "woke up" the revolutionary movement that was to topple the Romanovs' autocratic state a century later.

It took longer to arrive at the initial stage of this development in Japan—mainly because of the country's isolation from the West, which kept its emerging intelligentsia happily (for the *bakufu*) unaware of the revolutionary idea of the nation. The class clearly experienced a crisis of identity—inevitable given the condition of status-inconsistency in which it was placed as a result of the way the Tokugawa society was intentionally organized and its heightened sensitivity to inconsistency which came with intellectual training and sophistication. The stage, therefore, was set for a transformation of identity. But the direction of this transformation was uncertain; each of the intellectual currents reviewed here offered a different one; and in the meantime the rare expressions of samurai discontent were couched, by the participants and onlookers alike, in terms of the traditional samurai worldview.

The most important of these incidents, the only one in the more than two and a half centuries of the Tokugawa shogunate, according to Reischauer, to shake the entire country, was "the affair of 47 *ronin*," which took place between 1701 and 1703. The forty-seven *ronin* in question were left masterless as a result of the involuntary suicide of their *daimyo* and confiscation of his domain. The unlucky *daimyo* was ordered to take his life as punishment for transgressing against the Edo etiquette: taunted beyond endurance by a high official, he struck him within the castle grounds. The *daimyo*'s retainers, at once and through no fault of their own deprived of a respectable situation and means of livelihood, were obviously upset and would not let it go. On the principle that "revenge is a dish best tasted cold," they waited for two years and then, when the *daimyo*'s enemy lowered his guard, broke into his home and cut his head off. Public opinion was on their side, so much so that they were allowed, upon consideration, to die an honorable death by their own hand. They were hailed as martyrs to the cause of chivalry and made the subject of legends, but the real reason for such general approbation might have been the sad fact that any samurai could identify with them. They were all *ronin*, all *déclassés* in some way, never secure that they would ever achieve the status they believed they deserved (when they believed so), always in danger of losing the one, often beneath their dignity, they had, as well as the income that came with it.[23]

THE FLEETING, FLOATING WORLD OF THE TOKUGAWA MERCHANTS AND THE MIXING OF RANKS   On top of it all, as the samurai were sinking into the obscurity of poverty and political insignificance, the life of another class—the base and despised merchants, the lowest rung on the social ladder in the Confucian scheme, below which one could not fall—acquired increasing luster. The rise in demand for their services, the consequence of *sankin kotai*, in the first place, made them wealthy and led to a rise in their influence. Some of them served as advisers to the *bakufu*, acquired semi-samurai status, and were even allowed to bear swords. They affected the manners of the nobility, cultivated refined tastes in food and clothing, and showed themselves capable of and eager to experience ever higher pleasures. In the late seventeenth century in Osaka, according to the writer Ihara Saikaku, a typical representative of the beau monde was a self-made man of money, which was easily converted into the gentleman's education and style of life. "Gradually as opportunities offer, he acquires the elements of Chinese and Japanese verse composition," wrote Ihara of such a typical nouveau riche, "kickball, archery, the flute, the drums, incense blending and the tea ceremony, and by associating with the best people he even loses his old vulgarities of speech." (The sad corollary of such marvelous transformations was that they were as likely in the opposite direction. "In life," concluded Ihara philosophically, "it is training rather than birth which counts, and it is not un-known for the unwanted offspring of noble families to earn their living by hawking home-made paper flowers.")[24]

It was the merchants who composed much of the market for *ukiyo-e,* that essentially urban and urbane art of the "fleeting, floating world" and "the world's first art for the masses,"[25] thus supporting its painters, many of whom were of samurai origin. They made up the greater part of the audience for Ka-buki theater and the plays of Chikamatsu Monzaemon—another *ronin.* They formed a mass reading public, perhaps also the world's first, with an insatiable appetite for the poems of Matsuo Basho, the humoresques of Ihara Saikaku, and the novels of Bakin and Kyoden. The latter was the author of the famous *Keisei-kai Shijuhachite* (Forty-eight Ways of Commerce with Harlots) which reminds one of *'t Amsterdamsch Hoerdom* and must have enjoyed in Edo a popularity similar to the latter's success in the Dutch metropolis, being, most probably, better illustrated. As in Holland, the literature of the *ukiyo* was "strikingly inferior to its painting";[26] it consisted mainly of *koshoku-bon,* or "sex books," which focused on erotic goings-on, real or imaginary, in Edo's many brothels. But, it is worth noting, these novels emphasized the qualities of chic *(sui)* and correct style *(tsu),* apparently considering good taste as im-portant in their limited area as in any other. Significantly, the appeal of classy brothels transcended class, and wealthy merchants there rubbed shoulders (oh, English!) with the nobility, not all of whom were down on their luck: in-deed, "it is said that more than half the visitors to the best-known establish-ments were samurai of all ranks, not excluding the highest."

City life, in general, blurred social distinctions. An incident from the biog-raphy of the novelist Takizawa Bakin in the early nineteenth century may serve as an example of the new "democratic" mores. To promote the sales of his works, Bakin was urged by his publishers to give a party at the great Manpachi-Ro restaurant in Yanagibashi. The over eight hundred guests, "both the elegant and the vulgar," included prominent authors and artists, Confucian scholars, paper merchants, booksellers and publishers, as well as high-ranking military nobles and courtiers. Geishas poured wine and sake (of which three barrels proved too little), and numerous attendants distributed tickets for food and drink. This must have been a lucky day for starving samu-rai. "Some people," Bakin described in a letter to a friend, "in the confusion contrived to get three or even four meal-tickets, wrapping up the food and taking it home." "It was agreed that there had not been so successful a party for twenty years."

Some authors think it strange that "this carefree society should have ma-tured in an era when the nation as a whole was in the grip of calamity, for the wealth that was drawn into the cities to sustain it came from the countryside frequently ravaged by disaster and oppressed by bad government." But a society in which members of the upper stratum would take advantage of confusion at a who's who party to bring home a meal does not strike one as particularly carefree, and it does not appear surprising that, so long as business was good, city merchants did not consider the woes of the countryside their business. Their mood, reflected in the exquisite art and the earthy literature of *ukiyo*, was "one of satisfaction with the existing order" in which they prospered, however often reminded that prosperity, like everything in life, was fleeting.[27]

Of course, a merchant's life in Tokugawa Japan was not without its aggravations. The government, *daimyo*, and samurai, all insolvent, constantly borrowed money, which the merchants could neither refuse to lend nor expect to see again, causing one of these involuntary gift-givers to quip, "While the townspeople were at one time rudely cut down by samurai swords, nowadays they are politely ruined by samurai borrowings." (This was a play on the words *kiritaosare* and *karitaosare* and probably sounds amusing in the original.) The merchants also bore the brunt of extraordinary taxation to which the *bakufu*, whose financial difficulties eventually became chronic, turned with increasing frequency, in addition being inconvenienced by repeated debasements of coinage, which became the main element in Tokugawa fiscal policy, at times relied on to contribute the bulk of state revenues.[28] Their business activities were subject to sporadic interference of the government—as during the administration of the especially hostile to the merchants Mizuno Tadakuni around 1840, when in a bout of unexplainable economic liberalism, of which it could not have been aware, the *bakufu* abolished the guilds—as well as to its regular attempts to fix prices (most particularly of rice), which more often than not contributed to their further destabilization. And still, merchants were generally satisfied with their lot—the only class that was satisfied with its lot in the end. The levies, and the loans that would not be repaid, and the meddling of incompetent bureaucrats were all part of business as usual; merchants learned to live with these nuisances so long as their wealth grew and they could enjoy their *koshoku-bon* novels, develop their *ukiyo-e* collections, and be entertained by their sophisticated mistresses, coveted by the samurai of rank—they, theoretically the most despised class of the Tokugawa society. Their position was becoming ever more comfortable, as that of the others was growing increasingly less so. As a result, unlike the rest of Japan, merchants were not ready for a revolution and did not survive it. When it happened, they disappeared—were defined out of existence as a class—with the *bakufu*.

Samurai begrudged merchants their prosperity and blamed their own misery on it. Kumazawa Banzan, for instance, attributed the poverty of both the warrior nobility and the peasantry to the commercialization of the economy, which at once made merchants numerous and filled their pockets. These were the reasons for the impoverishment of the samurai and the peasants, he argued:

> Firstly, in big cities and small alike, on land by the rivers and sea which is convenient for transport, urban areas are being built, and luxury is growing day by day without check. Merchants grow rich while warriors are impoverished. Secondly, the practice of exchanging grain for other goods is steadily disappearing, and gold, silver and copper alone are being used. Prices are becoming high and the country's gold and silver are flowing into the hands of merchants. As a result, great and lesser samurai are lacking in finances. Thirdly, when proper social customs are abandoned, [economic] affairs become more complex. Samurai exchange their rice stipends for gold, silver and copper coins, and so buy goods. If the price of rice is low and the price of goods is high, they are short of money . . . When the samurai are in distress, the amount which they take from the people doubles.

But, on the whole, it was not poverty which was the chief cause of their complaint. (It is important to realize that though many in the samurai class were truly destitute, those who did the complaining were, as a rule, and by definition when they did it, better off: one had to eat and be sure of the next day's meal before one could engage in social criticism.) The alleviation of peasant material distress, which was indeed extreme, would probably have diminished the number of rural rebellions. But it is doubtful whether the improvement of the upper class's financial condition alone would have sufficed to appease their discontent. Indeed, the *bakufu* tried periodically to lighten their burden with Acts of Grace, by which it freed the samurai (partially or completely) from the debts they owed to the merchants. But they were still incommoded by the necessity to approach these moneybags for more: it impinged on their pride that now they had to ruin townspeople politely, instead of rudely cutting them down with their swords, as was the practice in the good old days. It was the abandonment of the proper social customs that jarred them most. In fact, economic thought developed as part and parcel of commentary, usually critical, on the obliteration of social distinctions, the lowering of the high and raising of the low. For Ogyu Sorai the greatest evil was the loss of *reiho*—the quality of knowing one's place, being *standesmässig*, which he, like his German contemporaries, identified with social order and denoted with a word that may be translated as "propriety" or "etiquette." "All manner of propriety has disappeared," he observed ruefully, "and from clothing to houses and utensils, there is no way of distinguishing the noble from the common people . . . [T]here is no proper system of etiquette and the power of the merchants has increased."

Moreover, it was not only by merchants that the samurai saw their status threatened and degraded. There was a fundamental inconsistency between the Confucian identification of the ruling class with scholarship and intellectual ability and the powerless, marginal position of the best-educated samurai within Tokugawa society, excluded from a role in the government on account of their birth. The *bakufu* was not true to its own principles; it did not practice what it commanded to preach. In 1841 Sakuma Shozan, an accomplished Confucian, repeated in a program submitted to his lord, Sanada Yukitsura, then in charge of the *bakufu*'s coastal defenses, the plea Ogyu Sorai had addressed to the government a century and a half earlier in his "Political Proposals." "There must be established a system of selecting and employing men of ability in official posts," he urged.[29] The advice was not heeded, but by then it was anyhow too late for a gradual reform. By the mid-nineteenth century, the samurai had concluded that their situation had become intolerable, in the sense that they were no longer prepared to tolerate it. Their loyalty to the *bakufu* was a thing of the past, and discontent, brewing everywhere, was openly expressed. Only a spark was needed to cause a major explosion and an ideology to give direction to the ubiquitous but diffuse opposition and transform the inevitable revolt into a revolution. The West, moved by the understandable urge to spread its light (as well as the idea that drawing other parts of the world into its economy was in its interest), provided the spark and offered the requisite ideology: nationalism.

The Dawn of the Era of Nationalism

The West Plants the Seed

The growth of the opposition to the regime among the upper classes (it must be kept in mind that only the upper classes opposed the regime) coincided with stepping up measures on the part of Russia and two Western powers, Britain and the United States, to break Japan's policy of isolation. Those were the happy days when the liberal democracies on both sides of the Atlantic stood tall in their own eyes and those of the world exposed to their influence, cheerfully shouldering the white man's burden and confident in their manifest destiny and civilizing mission. Their none too delicate and (to an impartial bystander) obviously self-interested attempts to force their unwanted company on a great and proud civilization—of which they knew nothing, but which they nevertheless despised and believed pining for their attention—met with indignation among educated Japanese. Russia was already torn between a torturous complex of inferiority and megalomania, which were to motivate its political conduct until our day, but to the east it showed only the latter, and it was menacing in its very, ever-expanding, mass. Thus its overtures also aroused little enthusiasm. Yet it was the coincidence of this occidental harassment (it was never perceived as a military threat, really) with the domestic crisis—which was, essentially, a crisis of identity among the samurai, brought about by the internal inconsistencies within the Tokugawa social and political structure—that gave Western policies their immense significance as a factor in Japanese history and ensured that from that time on the history of Japan was in so many respects a history of modernization, or of *becoming like the West*.

As mentioned before, the crisis of identity among the samurai was a product of anomie, a structural situation in which, as Tessa Morris-Suzuki so well put it, "the dominant social theories [the image of the social order] are clearly out of kilter with reality." There are, fundamentally, two ways to deal with the inconsistency between the image of reality and its experience: to change reality and make the experience reflect the image, or to rationalize the experience in terms of a new image. Intellectuals, in particular, to quote Morris-Suzuki again, "may take one of two approaches: either they may argue that society should be made to conform to the ideals of existing theory, or they may try to modify theory to encompass existing reality." As a rule, they attempt both, on a trial-and-error basis, going with the method that leads them, personally, and the group which shares their predicament, out of the anomic impasse, and we have seen Ogyu Sorai and Sakuma Shozan try the former and fail. Now the West made available to the Japanese elite an image of social order that, while allowing the samurai to redefine themselves in a new and dignified way and freeing them from their estate identity (which only bred frustration), in the context of the impending standoff with the *bakufu*, offered them a powerful ideological tool for transforming reality. This image was nationalism.

Before the country was compelled to open up to the West, there was no national consciousness in Japan. Identity was defined, in the case of the samurai, essentially by class—and to a lesser extent by feudal allegiances, however altered in significance during the Tokugawa period—and religion; in the case of the peasantry, perhaps, essentially by religion. Even Delmer Brown, otherwise quick to diagnose as nationalism any sense of a particular identity or expression of xenophobia, recognized that the sixteenth-century efforts at Japan's unification were not motivated by a national sentiment, but were an implication of victory in a feudal power struggle. Indeed, Hideyoshi did not limit his aspirations to all of Japan. He had his eyes on China as well, planning, in the event of success, to establish his capital in Peking. Nor should the shoguns' change of heart regarding Christianity and the subsequent policy of seclusion be interpreted as a sign of national consciousness and identity. The fundamental egalitarianism of the Christian doctrine, however obfuscated in its institutionalization in Europe, to say nothing of the transoceanic loyalties of the faithful ("ultramontane" appears out of place in this geographical context) and the troubling tendency of the Spanish missionaries to be followed by troops, could easily make it appear subversive to the generals who no longer wished to fight and wished their new order to be established on a firm ideological basis which would keep everyone in his place, in spirit as well as in body. (To make his ideas clear beyond a shadow of a doubt, Hideyoshi expressed them memorably in 1597, ten years after issuing an edict which banned Christianity, deciding to enforce it by crucifying nine missionaries and seventeen converts. A symbolically curious gesture, given its intended audience, it could very well have produced the opposite of its intended effect.) In fact, the singular foreign policy of the shogunate would not even qualify as an expression of xenophobia: it reflected a sense of the perfect self-sufficiency of Japan, and therefore indifference to the outside world.[30]

Originally, the anti-foreign sentiment that characterized the elite in the nineteenth century was only a sign of the same engrossing preoccupation with internal affairs. It screened the opposition to the *bakufu* behind an attitude whose legitimacy in the framework of Japanese tradition was undeniable, thereby providing a ready justification for this opposition, and served as a pretext for its open expression. That is why the call to "expel the barbarians" *(joi)* was coupled with the older and much more compelling slogan "revere the emperor" *(sonno)*. Nominally, the emperor remained the sole and sovereign ruler of Japan throughout the Tokugawa period. Neo-Shintoist philosophers and *kokugaku* scholars emphasized this, but few dared to draw attention to the factual usurpation of imperial rule by the *bakufu*. The participation of the emperor in the government was limited to the ceremonial conferral of titles on the *bakufu*-designated officials, foremost among which was the appointment of the shogun himself. As the shogun's office was established during the wars with the Ainu, the "northern barbarians," his title actually was *se-i tai shogun*, which meant "commander-in-chief for quelling/fighting the barbarians," the appointment consequently implying strictly specified responsibilities in the area of foreign relations. The nominalism of Chu Hsi Confucianism, reinforced by the reverence for words in both the "classicism" of Ogyu Sorai and *kokugaku*, which invested old expressions with an almost legal authority, ensured that the educated classes would be immediately aware and critical of the discrepancy between the ideal and reality, the word and the deed, in a function as important as this. Fortunately for the Tokugawa, in the first century of their rule they fulfilled their "barbarian-fighting" role only too well, and until they entered their third century, contacts with foreigners were so limited that even if their vigilance slackened a bit, this could not give rise to any disapproval.

By that time, unhappiness with the regime among the samurai had already become quite widespread. It had nothing at all to do with foreigners, but reflected, as was argued earlier, the structural, and psychologically burdensome, conditions in which the upper class was placed in Tokugawa Japan. But in the framework of Confucian ethics and even dissenting intellectual currents, this unhappiness was illegitimate: it could not be justified in terms of traditional ideals. The determination of Western powers to make Japan part of their world and the evident inability of the *bakufu* to prevent the country from being imposed on made such justification possible. The samurai were, as before, upset by the impoverishment of their class, the debasement of their status owing to the simultaneous rise of the merchants in wealth and importance, the powerless and meaningless existence to which the great majority of them were condemned despite their many virtues. But they could now represent (to themselves as well as to others) these selfish worries as a selfless concern for the common well-being and raise their discontent to the dignified level of a legitimate dissatisfaction with the shogun's shirking of the job he was appointed to do by the emperor.

The scope and implications of the Western threat were magnified, at times assuming mythical proportions and character, and some of the authors who belabored the subject, at least, convinced by their own rhetoric, appeared really terrified by the prospect of relations with the red-haired and long-nosed creatures who sailed into Japan's pristine harbors enveloped by clouds of black smoke. Aizawa Seishisai, who first explicitly formulated the political position of the Mito school, and thus can be considered the author of the *sonno-joi* manifesto, for instance, had the lowest opinion of the moral, intellectual, and physical qualities of the occidental barbarians and did believe that Japan was in real and imminent danger of contamination, if nothing else, and had to be made ready for a life-and-death confrontation. In his *New Proposals* of 1825, he mapped the situation in no uncertain, frightening terms, all the more persuasive for framing the argument in the characteristic form of a syllogism:

> Today, the alien barbarians of the West, the lowly organs of the legs and feet of the world, are dashing about across the seas, trampling other countries underfoot, and daring, with their squinting eyes and limping feet, to override the noble nations. What manner of arrogance is this! The earth in the firmament appears to be perfectly round, without edges or corners. However, everything exists in its natural bodily form, and

our Divine Land is situated at the top of the earth. Thus, although it is not an extensive country spatially, it reigns over all quarters of the world, for it has never once changed its dynasty or its form of sovereignty. The various countries of the West correspond to the feet and legs of the body. That is why their ships come from afar to visit Japan. As for the land amidst the seas which the Western barbarians call America, it occupies the hindmost region of the earth; thus, its people are stupid and simple, and are incapable of doing things.

The natural simplicity of these dregs of humanity, however, coexisted with astounding craftiness on their part when it came to insinuating themselves into nobler communities, the chief methods of such insinuation being Christianity and commerce. In the past, wrote Aizawa, those who disturbed the order in Japan

> and confused the thinking of the populace with their improper teaching have only been people of our own realm. But now we must cope with foreigners of the West, where every country upholds the law of Jesus and attempts therewith to subdue other countries. Everywhere they go they set fire to shrines and temples, deceive and delude the people, and then invade and seize the country. Their purpose is not realized until the ruler of the land is made a subject and the people of the land subservient.

Only because of the provident isolation policy of its rulers had Japan escaped such a fate in the past two hundred years. But now the Western foreigners, "spurred by the desire to wreak havoc upon us," were daily prying into Japan's territorial waters. Was their dominance of the seas a sign of natural superiority in intelligence or bravery, asked Aizawa. Or did it reflect a more perfect and just society? His answer was: "Not so at all. All they have is Christianity to fall back upon in the prosecution of their schemes . . . When those barbarians plan to subdue a country not their own, they start by opening commerce and watch for a sign of weakness [among the people]. If an opportunity is presented, they will preach their alien religion to captivate their hearts." The people, unfortunately, lured by commerce, willingly let their hearts be captivated. "The people will be only too glad to die for the sake of the alien God," sighed the experienced historian.

> They have the courage to give battle; they offer all they own in adoration of the God and devote their resources to the cause of insurrection. The subversion of the people and overthrowing of the state are taught as being in accord with the God's will. So in the name of all-embracing love the subjugation of the land is accomplished. Though greed is the real

motive, it masquerades as a religious uprising. The absorption of the country and conquest of its territories are all done in this fashion.

It was imperative to nip this development in the bud, before it became too late. If timely precautions were not taken, warned Aizawa, the consequences would be terrible: "Our people will adopt such practices as eating dogs and sheep and wearing woolen clothing. And no one will be able to stop it."

To check "the harmful and weakening effects" of increased contact with the West and to prevent, as Aizawa put it, "the frost turning to hard ice," it was essential to strengthen the sense of loyalty and community among the people and eradicate self-interest. Ideological control and determined collectivism were the solution. "The means by which a sovereign protects his empire, preserves peace and order, and keeps the land from unrest is not the holding of the world in a tight grip or the keeping of people in fearful subjection. His only sure reliance is that the people should be of one mind, that they should cherish their sovereign, and that they should be unable to bear being separated from him." This suggestion was reminiscent of Novalis's ideal of a peasant who thanked heaven for allowing him to chew on moldy bread in his native land and treated with contempt the very idea of chicken and rice anyplace else. Aizawa's method of instilling such selfless commitment in the populace was also akin to the approach of the German Romantics: it was war, participation in the act of collective violence against the foreigner, as an end in itself. Whatever its outcome, war was a good in its own right, because peace, in fact, was an evil: it damaged collective morale. "Because of the prolonged peace [under the Tokugawa shogunate]," Aizawa argued,

> signs of weakness and sluggishness have appeared . . . [A]ll the people, high and low, are intent only upon their own selfish gain, with no concern for the security of the nation. This is not the way to preserve our national polity [or imperial land: *kokutai*].[31] When a great man assumes leadership, he is only concerned lest people be inactive. Mediocre leaders, thinking only of easy peace, are always afraid of the people's restlessness. They see to it that everything appears quiescent. But they let barbarians go unchecked under their very eyes, calling them just "fishing traders." They conspire together to hide realities, only to aggravate the situation through half-hearted inaction . . . If instead the shogunate issues orders to the entire nation in unmistakable terms to smash the barbarians whenever they come into sight and to treat them openly as our nation's foes, then within one day after the order is issued, everyone high and low will push forward to enforce the order.

This, Aizawa thought, was "a great opportunity as comes once in a thousand years [and] must not be lost," even though he was not at all certain that such a *levée en masse* would deter the barbarians. The material effects of war were immaterial: its advantages were expressive, not instrumental. The *sonno-joi* philosophy, indeed very similar to the German, was summarized in the following passage:

> In the defense of the state through armed preparedness, a policy for peace or for war must be decided upon before all else. If there is indecision on this point, the people will be apathetic, not knowing which way to turn. Morale will deteriorate while everyone hopes for peace that cannot materialize. The intelligent will be unable to plan; the brave will be unable to stir up their indignation. Thus day after day will be spent allowing the enemy to mature his plans. Waiting until defeat stares one in the face is due to an inner sense of fear that prevents resolute action . . . "Put a man in a position of inevitable death, and he will emerge unscathed," goes the saying. The ancients also said that the nation would be blessed if all in the land lived as if the enemy were right on the border. So I say, let a policy for peace or for war be decided upon first of all, thus putting the entire nation into the position of inevitable death. Then and only then can the defense problem be easily worked out.[32]

The ethical ideals which underlay the *sonno-joi* program, and much of the anti-foreign sentiment of the late Tokugawa period, were those of the *bushido*—the way of the warrior—which added to its significance as a reassertion of the samurai identity.

More sensible, and in the long run far more influential, was the position of Sakuma Shozan, whose disciples included such leading personalities of the Meiji period as "the father of the Japanese Navy," Katsu Kaishu, and whose motto "Eastern ethics—Western learning" provided the formula for Japanese nationalism in its early stages. Sakuma was active in the last decades of the Tokugawa regime, the years when Westerners in Japan's territorial waters became a much more familiar sight than they were in Aizawa's time, forcing Japan eventually to let them onto the shore and end the two-centuries-old policy of seclusion. As he formed his ideas of what these foreigners were about and what their intentions were with regard to Japan, therefore, Sakuma could rely less heavily than his predecessor on macabre fantasy, and these ideas were, in fact, quite sober. The danger that faced Japan, for him, was no longer the likelihood that the populace would develop a taste for mutton or woolen clothes; Sakuma might have accepted this with equanimity. It was, rather, the certain humiliation, the inevitable loss of face on the part of the entire community. For Sakuma harbored no illusions as to the native stupidity of the barbarians, however remote from the Land of the Rising Sun, and therefore low on the Shinto cognitive map. He realized that their knowledge, which Japan lacked, was power and, insofar as geopolitical status was concerned, placed them above Japan, so that, at least in this limited but very important sense and this moment in time, the Westerners were smarter than the Japanese. For this reason, he did not think that rushing into battle without a thought for the outcome and gloriously dying in it, while demonstrating Japan's military backwardness, would do much to defend its honor. Fighting, he believed, was at the moment out of the question. The only way to restore to the country its dignity was to learn from the West.

Sakuma's preoccupation with the dignity of Japan was inseparably connected to his sense of frustration in regard to the marginal and humiliating position of his class, the samurai, in Japan. The former, in fact, was a reflection of the latter. As in France, Russia, or Germany, it was the status-inconsistency of the native elite, specifically the cultural elite, which made the Western Other significant. The impression made by Perry's black ships; the imposition of the will of the American president, however courteously expressed, on the *bakufu;* the barbarians' disregard for Japanese sensibilities as they pushed and shoved and thrust themselves through Japan's gates gave Japanese intellectuals the possibility to reinterpret their humiliation at the hands of the *bakufu* as the humiliation of Japan at the hands of the foreigners. They were beginning to see their situation as representative of a broader problem that was of concern to everyone in the community, to identify their plight with that of the imagined distress of their country; in other words, *they were beginning to think in national terms.*

Imprisoned for supposedly encouraging one of his disciples, the patriotic martyr Yoshida Shoin, to stow away on an American ship in order to study abroad, Sakuma decided to preserve his thoughts for posterity and, when released, sometime in late 1855 or 1856, wrote a long memoir, entitled *Reflections on My Errors (Seiken-roku)* but actually representing a defense of his ideas and actions. One can observe in it the intertwining of the two themes, Japan and the West, and the samurai's position in Tokugawa Japan, as well as the evolution of a new, proto-national, image of society. The *Reflections* were numbered, the first nineteen apparently dealing with personal matters. Reflection 20 stated: "The gentleman has five pleasures, but wealth and rank are not among them." The thought, obviously, made a virtue out of necessity. The problem of the educated samurai was that they did not have wealth and rank; defining wealth and rank as not worth striving for solved this problem. Indeed, it would appear that the purpose of this reflection was to reconcile the samurai to reality. The first three pleasures, according to Sakuma, were desiderata of a private or inward nature, reasonable goals for someone whose social aspirations were curbed: marital peace, an ability to provide for oneself and one's family honorably, and the deep understanding and invariable compliance with the Way of the Sages. The two remaining ones, however, revealed him as a man of daring ambition:

> That he [the gentleman] is born after the opening of the vistas of science by the Westerners, and can therefore understand principles not known to the sages and wise men of old—this is the fourth pleasure. That he employs the ethics of the East and the scientific technique of the West, neglecting neither the spiritual nor material aspects of life, combining subjective and objective, and thus bringing benefit to the people and serving the nation—this is the fifth pleasure.

This implied that the modern samurai was in some important respects superior to those of the past and could take pride in this. He was more knowledgeable and better equipped for patriotic service. The problem was that Tokugawa Japan did not give him a chance to serve.

Reflection 28 picked up a related subject, revealing Sakuma's sense of national inferiority vis-à-vis the West. "The principal requisite of national defense," he reasoned,

> is that it prevents the foreign barbarians from holding us in contempt. The existing coastal defense installations all lack method; the pieces of artillery that have been set up in array are improperly made; and the officials who negotiate with the foreigners are mediocrities who have no understanding of warfare. The situation being such, even though we wish to avoid incurring the scorn of the barbarians, how, in fact, can we do so?

Mediocrities of rank were responsible for Japan's sorry state in the eyes of the world. In a vein very similar to Fonvisin's recriminations against the upper nobility, Sakuma continued this thought in Reflection 30, quickly arriving at the conclusion of his Russian counterpart, that aristocracy of birth should be replaced by meritocracy and that the true elite, the only one that could lead and defend the country, was the elite of patriotic virtue:

> Of the men who now hold posts as commanders of the army, those who are not dukes or princes or men of noble rank, are members of wealthy families. As such, they find their daily pleasure in drinking wine, singing, and dancing; and they are ignorant of military strategy and discipline. Should a national emergency arise, there is no one who could command the respect of the warriors and halt the enemy's attack. This is the great sorrow of our times. For this reason, I have wished to follow in sub-

stance the Western principles of armament, and, by banding together loyal, valorous, strong men of old, established families not in the military class [of the day]—men of whom one would equal to ten ordinary men—to form a voluntary group which would be made to have as its sole aim that of guarding the nation and protecting the people. Anyone wishing to join the society would be tested and his merits examined; and if he did not shirk hardship, he would then be permitted to join. Men of talent in military strategy, planning, and administration would be advanced to positions of leadership, and then, if the day should come when the country must be defended, this group could be gathered together and organized into an army to await official commands. It is to be hoped that they would drive the enemy away and perform greater service than those who now form the military class.[33]

In Sakuma's mind, the degraded, untenable position of the educated samurai—the Japanese intelligentsia—and Japan's inevitable loss of status in the eyes of the West, that is, its humiliation, even in the case of perfectly peaceful intentions on the part of the intruders (for the very fact of contact revealed the shameful and laughable state of the country's military preparations), were inseparably connected. It was impossible to tackle the latter, general problem without first solving the former, particular one. To save Japan's honor it was necessary to transform Japanese society. The fact that Western barbarians came and saw prompted the discontented samurai to contemplate a revolution.

The solicitude for the status of their country on the part of the Japanese educated elite was not a contrivance, resorted to to promote their particularistic interests. Intellectuals everywhere tend to identify with the culture, or civilization, which they represent (especially when it is clearly delineated by language and esoteric knowledge), and the samurai's experience of Japan's humiliation must have been painful and profound. Such identification of a particular disaffected group with the status of the country did not, in itself, imply the development of a national sentiment, but it made this group especially receptive to nationalist ideas. Nationalism was brought to Japan by the Americans, the British, and the Russians, for whom, in the 1850s, it was the natural view of the world, and who, using it unreflectively as their cognitive medium, could not fail to manifest it in every word and deed. Within years of opening the country, Japanese intellectuals were to encounter the same type of consciousness among the French and, significantly, the Germans, who, both because they were only recently converted to it and because of the Romantic nature of their nationalism, offered the most explicit and contagious example of the phenomenon. The Japanese got the idea very quickly, it appealed to them instantly and powerfully, and by the time of the Meiji Restoration, Japanese nationalism not only was born, but also was able to provide this revolution with its ideological direction.

The Character of Japanese Nationalism

As in France, Russia, and Germany, the receptivity to nationalism developed in Japan because of the condition of status-inconsistency which affected several successive generations of its noble and/or cultural elite. As in Germany, the mold for Japanese nationalism was fully prepared by the time of its arrival, shaped by the attempts of this elite to ease its social distress and, if nothing else, create an image of reality that would shield it from the corrosive and debilitating effects of anomie. When nationalism was imported, it was easily conceptualized in terms of neo-Shintoism and *kokugaku,* themselves simultaneously redefined and given new meaning in the light of its twin principles. It also fulfilled for the educated samurai several important functions. It refocused loyalty on the people, the community as a whole, and gave samurai grievances an altruistic, civic tint, representing their plight as a central element of a larger, national woe and justifying their disaffection from the *bakufu,* which could be accused of usurping the people's sovereignty and betraying its trust. The emperor became the symbol of the Japanese nation (connoting in his person the antiquity and the unbroken line of heavenly descent which constituted its unique character) and his virtual imprisonment in Kyoto (with an annual dole of 187,000 *koku* of rice for the upkeep of the entire imperial court and far from the seat of real power) the emblem of the usurpation of the nation's sovereignty and thus the iniquity of the Tokugawa regime. The national principle of the fundamental equality of membership, which allowed a cognitive and eventually institutional reconstruction of the system of stratification, minimized the importance of lineage as the basis of status (which for so long vexed lower-rank samurai) and made status dependent on merit, defined as the ability to contribute to the welfare—namely, status—of the nation. Since only educated samurai possessed such ability, this assured them a place at the top, which, in Tokugawa society, solicitous as it was for the exclusivity of the upper stratum, they were consistently denied. Certain of their superiority, they therefore eagerly embraced the egalitarian ideal and, within years of the Meiji Restoration, like the French nobility a century earlier, opted to self-destruct as a class.

Both the novelty of the social vision implied in nationalism and the spirit of selfless dedication the converted samurai brought to this new faith are readily apparent in the attitudes of the Meiji Restoration leaders. The most important popularizer of the new ideas and ideals was perhaps Fukuzawa Yukichi, who "proclaimed the gospel of a new civilization" in his books, which sold in the millions of copies, and the newspaper *Jiji-shimpo*, which he founded in 1882, thus being not without reason called "the apostle of Japanese Nationalism." As a translator and propagandist of Western ideas, especially those of British liberalism and utilitarianism, Fukuzawa should be credited with the creation of much of the vocabulary to be used in the new political (as well as economic) discourse: in fact, he probably was the inventor of the all-important term "nation"—*kokumin*, which, literally translated as "the people of a country," captured precisely the inclusive and demotic quality of the Western concept. A scion of an aristocratic family, Fukuzawa was proud to consider himself a "commoner," which, in the Meiji period, seems to have implied "a person without an official rank": he found political life distasteful and inconsistent with his sense of dignity and "clean living" and believed he would have greater freedom to express his opinions as a private citizen. The purpose of all his work, he wrote in his autobiography, was "to create in Japan a civilized nation, as well equipped in both the arts of war and peace as those of the Western world," and such a nation was predicated on the development of "independence and self-respect" among the people.

That "the people" in Fukuzawa's time was quite unfamiliar with sentiments of this nature is illustrated by the following incident he recorded. A peasant riding a horse, whom Fukuzawa met on one of his walks, got off his animal the moment he realized he was facing a person of a superior status. An interchange ensued. "I caught hold of his bridle and said: 'What do you mean by this?' The farmer bowed as if in great fear and began to apologize. 'No, no,' I said, 'don't be a fool . . . This is your horse, get back on it and ride on.' The poor fellow was afraid to mount before me. 'Now get back on your horse,' I repeated. 'If you don't, I'll beat you.'" Fukuzawa found the peasant's deference inappropriate, yet for him, too, egalitarianism was a new concept. On his first visit to the United States, in 1860, with the shogunate mission, he recalled "many confusing and embarrassing moments":

Things social, political, and economic proved most inexplicable. One day, on a sudden thought, I asked a gentleman where the descendants of George Washington might be. He replied, "I think there is a woman who is directly descended from Washington. I don't know where she is now, but I think I have heard she is married." His answer was so very casual that it shocked me.

Of course, I knew that America was a republic with a new president every four years, but I could not keep feeling that the family of Washington should be regarded as apart from all other families. My reasoning was based on the reverence in Japan for the founders of the great lines of rulers—like for Ieyasu of the Tokugawa family of shoguns, really deified in the popular mind. So I remember the intense astonishment I felt at receiving this indifferent answer about the Washington family.

He was similarly distressed by the newly egalitarian temper of Japanese society, though, apparently, not fully aware of the nature of his discomfort. He disliked, he wrote, "that rush and disorderly struggle for office which passed through the whole country at the beginning of the new government. Not only the samurai, who of course have been accustomed to holding offices, but even the sons of merchants and farmers—men with any kind of education at all were swarming together like insects around some fragrant food." This unseemly behavior on the part of the merchants' and farmers' sons was most probably a sign of the increasing independence and self-respect among them, and Fukuzawa's squeamish reaction an atavistic sentiment, obviously contradicting his professed ideals. It is therefore significant that he should have expressed it so unself-consciously as he was discussing the necessity of cultivating among the merchants and farmers the very virtues that filled him with disgust. Barely finished with the thought, he reiterated his principles on the subject: "The independence of a nation springs from the independent spirit of its citizens. Our nation cannot hold its own if the old slavish spirit is so manifest among the people." The arrogance of the hoi polloi, who presumed they could participate in the government just because they had any education at all, suggested that the slavish spirit was disappearing, however slowly, and its disappearance could not but sadden a samurai proud enough to lead his life (and exert influence) as a "commoner."

Another "perplexing institution" was representative government. Fukuzawa remembered his bewilderment when he first encountered it in England:

When I asked a gentleman what the "election law" was and what kind of an institution the Parliament really was, he simply replied with a smile, meaning I suppose that no intelligent person was expected to ask such a question. But these were things most difficult of all for me to understand. In this connection, I learned that there were different political parties—the Liberal and the Conservative—who were always "fighting" against each other in the government.

For some time it was beyond my comprehension to understand what they were "fighting" for, and what was meant, anyway, by "fighting" in peace time. "This man and that man are *enemies* in the House," they would tell me. But these "enemies" were to be seen at the same table, eating and drinking with each other. I felt as if I could not make much out of this. It took me a long time, with some tedious thinking, before I could gather a general notion of these separate mysterious facts. In some of the more complicated matters, I might achieve an understanding five or ten days after they were explained to me.

The idea of representative government as developed by the nationalist leaders of the Meiji Restoration—the low-ranking samurai from Satsuma and Choshu, such as Kido Koin, Saigo Takamori, and Okubo Toshimichi—allowed for no such internecine strife. The Japanese nation, unlike the English, in their view, was perfectly united in all the sentiments (that mattered), and its sovereignty was undivided and soon defined as indivisible. Kido Koin, who was to resign from the government over the issue of commutation of samurai stipends, was responsible for persuading the *daimyo* to *voluntarily* surrender their domains, which they held from Tokugawa, to the emperor, as a testimony to their national patriotism. He also framed the memorandum of the surrender, addressed to the emperor and explaining, in the name of the *daimyo,* and in a manner characteristic of Japanese legal discourse, the significance of and the reasoning behind the act. "We [the *daimyo*]," the text began,

> respectfully suggest that two things are essential to Your Majesty's administration. There must be one national polity [*kokutai:* literally, the body of the country] and one sovereign authority. Since the Imperial Ancestor founded the country and established a basis of government, there has been one imperial line for countless generations without change, making the farthest limits of heaven and earth its realm and all mankind its subjects. This is what is meant by the national polity. And the sole power of giving and taking away ranks and fiefs, by which the foundation is maintained, makes it impossible for a foot of ground to be held for private ends, or for one subject to be wantonly robbed. This is what is meant by sovereign authority . . . Now that we are about to establish an entirely new form of government, the national polity and the sovereign authority must not in the slightest degree be yielded to subordinates. The place where your servants live is the emperor's land, and those whom they rule are the emperor's people. How can these be made the property of subjects? [On the basis of these considerations, the *daimyo* respectfully begged his Majesty to be allowed to surrender their fiefs and asked furthermore] that the court lay down regulations regarding all things, from the administration of troops to uniform and military equipment, so that everyone in the empire both great and small shall be caused to submit to one [authority].

"Thus," Kido concluded, "in the future, in name and in fact our country can begin to take its place among the nations of the world." Both the land and the people of Japan were defined, essentially, as the property of the emperor, who was respectfully begged to assume absolute power over them and strictly regulate people's lives down to the smallest detail. This sounded more like the principles of German territorial states of the *Hausväterliteratur* period than the language of nationalism, and makes one wonder how serious was the intention of the signatories (and their spokesman) to establish an entirely new form of government. But "Meiji Restoration" was a euphemism, and despite Kido's emphatic verbal genuflection, a return to absolutism could not have been farther from his thoughts. The emperor was a symbol of a new awe-inspiring ideal, a sovereign people whose will he only represented.

Early in the Meiji years, the emperor proclaimed the Charter Oath, in whose drafting Kido also played a central role, which laid down the purpose of the 1868 Constitution and was to serve as its preamble. In his recollections of the occasion Kido wrote:

> The Emperor . . . pronounced an Oath containing five clauses, which was thereupon published throughout the empire, indicating to what end the Constitution should tend, and guiding the ideas of the people in one fixed direction. The heading of the Oath states: "By this Oath We set up as Our aim the establishment of the national weal on a broad basis and the framing of a constitution and laws." This led at last to granting the petitions for leave to restore the fiefs to the Emperor, which occasioned the abolition of feudal titles and the unification of the divided national authority. Is not all this consonant with the prevailing view in the powerful countries of the five great continents?
>
> However, in enlightened countries, though there may be a sovereign, still he does not hold sway in an arbitrary fashion. The people of the whole country give expression to their united and harmonious wishes and the business of the State is arranged accordingly, a department (styled the government) being charged with the execution of their judgments, and officials appointed to transact business. For this reason, all who hold office respect the wishes of the whole nation and serve their country under a deep sense of responsibility, so that even in extraordinary crises, they take no arbitrary step contrary to the people's will . . . [A]s an additional check upon illegal acts, the people have parliamentary representatives whose duty it is to inspect everything that is done and to check arbitrary proceedings on the part of the officials.

The purpose of every citizen's life, Kido continued in a still more revolutionary vein, was to preserve his *natural liberty*. One accomplished this by "exercising [one's] rights and [assisting] in carrying on the government by sharing its obligations." These rights and obligations were "therefore [presumably to make sure the citizens chose the proper means for the realization of their life purpose] specified exactly in writing and men [bound] themselves by a solemn promise to permit no infringement of them, but to act as mutual checks on each other in maintaining them." Kido's explanation underscored the novelty of the concept:

> These writings are what we call laws. The laws grow out of the Constitution, for the Constitution is the root of every part of the government, and there is nothing which does not branch out from it. For this reason, every country, when the time comes for changing its constitution, bestows on it the greatest care and the ripest consideration and ascertains to the full the general wishes . . . [T]he greatest care must be taken to ascertain them with accuracy, the internal conditions of the country must be profoundly studied, what the people produce must be taken into account, and, most important of all, policies must be suited to the degree of civilization of the people.

The last provision suggested that the people did not always know what their wishes were. Indeed, Kido's opinion was that "if the people is not yet sufficiently enlightened, it becomes necessary, at least for a time, that the Sovereign should by his superior discernment anticipate their unanimous wishes and act for them in arranging the affairs of the State." Such was the current condition of Japan. Therefore, unlike "those countries of Europe and America the conduct of whose governments embodies the will of the people," Japan was not yet ready—in 1868—for parliamentary inspection. This was, however, only a temporary state of affairs, which the Meiji leaders both expected and spared no effort to change quickly, and which in no way affected their idea of the nature of national polity and society.

Ito Hirobumi, the central figure in the leadership that succeeded to the "Meiji Triumvirate" of Kido, Saigo, and Okubo, articulated this idea in the many speeches he had occasion to deliver during his four terms as prime minister. His views were fundamentally identical to those of his immediate predecessors, but certain provisional elements assumed in them the rigidity of ultimate principles. The people was sovereign, but its sovereignty was concentrated in the hands of the emperor, who, however, symbolized the people and represented its true interests. There was a vast difference between this arrangement, based on the unanimity of the nation and the government, moved solely by its solicitude for the nation's well-being, and unenlightened and unacceptable absolutism of the sort that existed under the Tokugawa. Upon the adoption of the Constitution of 1889, Ito addressed this difference:

> I shall now proceed to discuss the subject of the participation of the people in the government of the state. It is only by the protection of the law

that the happiness of the nation can be promoted and the safety of the person and property secured, and to attain these ends the people may elect their representatives and empower the latter to deliberate on laws with a view to the promotion of their own happiness and the safeguarding of their rights. This, gentlemen, is enacted by the Constitution, and I think you will agree that it constitutes a concession to the people of a most valuable right. Under an absolute system of government the sovereign's will is his command, and the sovereign's command at once becomes law. In a constitutional country, however, the consent of that assembly which represents the people must be obtained. It will be evident, however, that as the supreme right is one and indivisible, the legislative power remains in the hands of the sovereign and is not bestowed on the people. While the supreme right extends to everything, and its exercise is wide and comprehensive, its legislative and executive functions are undoubtedly the most important. These are in the hands of the sovereign; the rights pertaining thereto cannot be held in common by the sovereign and his subjects; but the latter are permitted to take part in legislation according to the provisions of the Constitution. In a country which is under absolute rule the view of the sovereign is at once law; in a constitutional country, on the other hand, nothing being law without a concurrence of views between the sovereign and the people, the latter elect representatives to meet at an appointed place and carry out the view of the sovereign. In other words, law in a constitutional state is the result of a concord of ideas between the sovereign and subject; but there can be no law when these two are in opposition to each other.

The convoluted argument reflected a hopelessly contradictory position. It is evident that Ito was now and again losing the thread—and was in danger of being lost himself—between his propositions. Interestingly, the argument, and the propositions taken separately, survived this logical clash unscathed and lost none of their persuasiveness, owing mostly to the (by the end of the twentieth century undeniable) fact that it takes much more than a gross inconsistency for a gross inconsistency to be noticed, and to the never-failing ability of human beings to believe that white is black, if this is repeated often enough. Moreover, in their battle with logic, the Meiji nationalists did not stand alone: they followed in the footsteps of an ally who had already waged a similar war and emerged from it victorious—none other than the modern West—and they relied on its formidable authority.

The definition of Japan as a nation implied the acceptance of the Western societies, from which the idea was imported, as a model and involved Japan in a competition with them for status. The dignity of the nation, its prestige in the eyes of the reference group, was identified as the superior collective value, the essence of general good, and became an object of anxious concern on the part of the leadership. All Meiji nationalists felt that Japan's prestige at the moment was low. The forced intercourse with the West revealed to them their country's inferiority—moral and pertaining to political culture, as much as military, technological, and economic. Having included the masses in the entity with which the leaders identified, these samurai were ashamed of the downtrodden and "uncivilized" condition of their people at least as much as they were of Japan's obvious inability to defend itself. The task for them, therefore, became to raise the moral and intellectual level of the people, to "civilize" it. The humiliation of the nationalists was exacerbated by the absolute lack of regard shown to Japan by the Western powers, who treated the country with the unceremoniousness characteristic of a social superior, unmindful of the ferocious sense of pride of its upper stratum and, judging by the treaties they concluded with it, blithely oblivious of its very sovereignty. In light of this treatment, the attitude of the first generations of Meiji leadership toward the West appears the standard of self-restraint and moderation. Though from the outset opposed to the terms of the treaties, and using every opportunity to bring about their modification, they concentrated on internal reform, believing this the surest way to elevate Japan to equality with the countries whose opinion they valued, and showed remarkably little resentment. This was to come later.

The concern for national dignity was behind every effort of the leaders of the Restoration and the government of the Meiji period. Vowing a fight to the death against the practice of concubinage, Fukuzawa wrote: "I intend to work as long as I live for the abolition of this unhealthy custom. It does not matter whom I may have to encounter. I will attempt to make our society presentable if only on the surface." It was the fact that concubinage disgraced the nation in the eyes of Western observers (Fukuzawa was certain they were informed and cared about Japanese customs) that made it unacceptable to him. But if it were practiced less conspicuously, making Japan, on the surface, more presentable, it appears he would have had fewer objections. One must give him credit, however: on the whole, he was not satisfied with such surface repairs, and his most earnest desire was to elevate "the moral standards of men and women of my land to make them truly worthy of a civilized nation."

It was the concern for national dignity that inspired the slogan *fukoku kyohei*—"Rich Nation/Strong Army"—and which was the reason for the wish of Saigo Takamori (the patriot "selflessly dedicated to war," according to Tsunoda Ryusaku and his co-editors) to offer his life for the worthy cause of the otherwise unprovoked military campaign against Korea, a wish so fervent that when Saigo's friends in the government decided against the war, this most popular hero of the Restoration resigned and turned against his former comrades. He wished to be killed during an ambassadorial mission to Korea, to provide Japan a reason to open hostilities, and died leading a samurai rebellion, with which he identified only halfheartedly, if at all, against the national regime he had helped to establish. He was, obviously, indifferent to death, but this was not the end he wanted. While in exile off the coast of Kagoshima, he composed a poem, which, with characteristic succinctness, expressed the nature of his commitments: "I am a boat / Given to my country; / If the winds blow, let them! / If the waves rise, let them!"

Saigo's friend since childhood, Okubo Toshimichi, opposed the idea of a Korean war in 1873. But the motives of his opposition were identical to the considerations which moved Saigo to advocate the campaign. "The treaties our country has concluded with the countries of Europe and America," Okubo argued,

> are not equal, there being many terms in them which impair the dignity of an independent nation. The restraints they impose may bring some benefit, but there are, on the other hand, harmful aspects to these treaties. England and France, for example, on the pretext that our country's internal administration is not yet in order and that it cannot protect their subjects, have built barracks and stationed troops in our land as if our country were a territory of theirs. Externally, from the standpoint of foreign relations, is this not as much a disgrace as it is internally, from the standpoint of our nation's sovereignty? The time for treaty revision is well-nigh at hand. The ministers in the present government, by giving their zealous and thorough attention, must evolve a way to rid the country of its bondage and to secure for our country the dignity of an independent nation. This is an urgent matter of the moment which provides [one of the several reasons] why a hasty venture in Korea should not be undertaken . . . I consider such a venture entirely beyond comprehension, as it completely disregards the safety of our nation and ignores the interests of the people.

Ito was the most explicit. "The aim of our country," he reiterated incessantly, "has been from the very beginning, to attain among the nations of the world the status of a civilized nation and to become a member of the comity of European and American nations which occupy the position of civilized countries. To join this comity of nations means to become one of them." "The course which lies now before the Japanese empire is plain. Both ruler and ruled should apply their efforts smoothly and harmoniously to preserve tranquility; to elevate the status of the people; to secure the rights and promote the welfare of each individual; and finally, by manifesting abroad the dignity and power of Japan, to secure and maintain her dignity and independence." And even more ambitiously: "Since the Restoration it has been the aim of our government to excel the nations of the whole world."

The cultural superiority of the West was largely undisputed. "Our country's cultural standard is considerably lower than that of the countries of Europe," noted Kido as a matter of fact before outlining a program for a semiofficial newspaper with the view of bringing this standard up to a level of parity with the West. The leaders of the Restoration realized there was much to learn and had the patience and humility to take lessons. They learned very fast, however. As attentive students of comparative history, among other things, they soon saw that the achievements of Japan compared well with the records of their models. In 1898, as he was dictating his *Autobiography*, Fukuzawa Yukichi expressed his pride in the country's accomplishments. "The facts are these," he stated simply:

> It was not until the sixth year of Kaei (1853) that a steamship was seen for the first time; it was only in the second year of Ansei (1855) that we began to study navigation from the Dutch in Nagasaki; by 1860, the science was sufficiently understood to enable us to sail a ship across the Pacific. This means that about seven years after the first sight of a steamship, after only about five years of practice, the Japanese people made a trans-Pacific crossing without help from foreign experts. I think we can without undue pride boast before the world of this courage and skill. As I have shown, the Japanese officers were to receive no aid from Captain Brooke throughout the voyage. Even in taking observations, our officers and the Americans made them independently of each other. Sometimes they compared their results, but we were never in the least dependent on the Americans.
>
> As I consider all the other peoples of the Orient as they exist today, I feel convinced that there is no other nation which has the ability or the courage to navigate a steamship across the Pacific after a period of five years experience in navigation and engineering. Not only in the Orient would this feat stand as an act of unprecedented skill and daring. Even Peter the Great of Russia, who went to Holland to study navigation, with all his attainments in the science could not have equaled this feat of the Japanese. Without doubt, the famous Emperor of Russia was a man of exceptional genius, but his people did not respond to his leadership in the practice of science as did our Japanese in this great adventure.

Constructed on the Western model, Japan's system of constitutional politics was "without a rival in the East."[34] Its victory in the Sino-Japanese War of 1894, a veritable contest between David and Goliath, made the country of the "dwarfs"[35] the dominant Asian society. Ten years later it was to humiliate

Russia—a giant the Japanese considered Western—and emerge as a world power. In 1907 Okuma Shigenobu, the leader of the "progressive" opposition under Meiji, the founder of the Progressive Party and Waseda University (which was to provide early twentieth-century Japan with its most prominent journalists) and a radical Westernizing nationalist, reviewed the first "fifty years of New Japan." It is difficult not to be impressed by the picture he painted, as well as by the generosity with which he credited the West for the part it played in Japan's achievement.

> By comparing the Japan of fifty years ago with the Japan of today, it will be seen that she has gained considerably in the extent of her territory, as well as in her population, which now numbers nearly fifty million. Her government has become constitutional not only in name, but in fact, and her national education has attained to a high degree of excellence. In commerce and industry, the emblems of peace, she has also made rapid strides, until her import and export trades together amounted in 1907 to the enormous sum of 926,000,000 *yen* (£94,877,000), an increase of 84,000,000 *yen* (£8,606,000) on the previous year. Her general progress, during the short space of half a century, has been so sudden and swift that it presents a spectacle rare in the history of the world. This leap forward is the result of the stimulus which the country received on coming into contact with the civilization of Europe and America, and may well, in its broad sense, be regarded as a boon conferred by foreign intercourse. Foreign intercourse it was that animated the national consciousness of our people, who under the feudal system lived localized and disunited, and foreign intercourse it is that has enabled Japan to stand up as a world power. We possess today a powerful army and navy, but it was after Western models that we laid their foundations by establishing a system of conscription in pursuance of the principle "all our sons are soldiers," by promoting military education, and by encouraging the manufacture of arms and the art of shipbuilding. We have reorganized the systems of central and local administration, and effected reforms in the educational system of the empire. All this is nothing but the result of adopting the superior features of Western institutions.

But, he added, Japan was able to adopt these features because of her special susceptibility to the influences of foreign civilizations, a "peculiarly sensitive faculty" with which she had been endowed from the earliest days, and which, importantly, she complemented by the gift of "a strong retentive power which enables her to preserve and retain all that is good in and about herself."[36]

There was much that was good, and, toward the end of the Meiji period, some were beginning to feel that Western influences had been overemphasized. Ito defended feudal Japan and argued against "the very common illusion that there was no education and an entire absence of public spirit during feudal times," which, he thought, led superficial observers to claim "that our civilization is nothing but a hastily donned, superficial veneer." The very opposite was true, he claimed: the Japanese "have been enjoying a moral education of the highest type" for generations and centuries:

> The great ideals offered by philosophy and by historical examples of the golden ages of China and India, Japanicized in the form of a "crust of customs," developed and sanctified by the continuous usage of centuries under the comprehensive name of *bushido*, offered us splendid standards of morality, rigorously enforced in the everyday life of the educated classes. The result, as everyone who is acquainted with Old Japan knows, was an education which aspired to the attainment of Stoic heroism, a rustic simplicity and a self-sacrificing spirit unsurpassed in Sparta, and the aesthetic culture and intellectual refinement of Athens.

Moreover, Ito continued, in a vein strikingly reminiscent of the German Romantics: "We laid great stress on the harmonious combination of all the known accomplishments of a developed human being, and it is only since the introduction of modern technical sciences that we have been obliged to pay more attention to specialized technical attainments than to the harmonious development of the whole." *En passant,* he remarked that

> the humanitarian efforts which in the course of the recent [Russo-Japanese] war were so much in evidence and which so much surprised Western nations were not, as might have been thought, the products of the new civilization, but survivals of our ancient feudal chivalry. If further instance were needed, we may direct attention to the numbers of our renowned warriors and statesmen who have left behind them works of religious and moral devotions, of philosophical contemplations, as well as splendid specimens of calligraphy, painting, and poetry, to an extent probably unparalleled in the feudalism of other nations.

Having paid this tribute to the refinements of bygone days—in which Japan probably did surpass premodern Western cultures—Ito was able to disabuse foreign observers in reference to the present: "Thus it will be seen that what was lacking in our countrymen of the feudal era was not mental or moral fiber, but the scientific, technical, and materialistic side of modern civilization. Our present condition is not the result of the ingrafting of a civilization entirely different from our own, as foreign observers are apt to believe, but simply a different training and nursing of a strongly vital character already existent."

Sometimes praises of native characteristics contained more than a hint of a criticism of the Western mode of life. This was no longer the criticism of the *joi* variety, which dismissed the West as the hindmost part of the earth, poking fun at the low level of intelligence and repulsive countenance of its people and drawing for inspiration on wild fantasies and monster stories. Rather it was an expression of antimodernism—of the kind that had proliferated in the West, especially in Germany, since the eighteenth century. Nationalism, which was the consciousness, the cognitive medium, of modernity, was a package deal. It brought dignity and responsibility, freedom and anomie, equality and envy; and the Japanese, like the Germans, the Russians, to a certain extent the French before them, and like so many after, wanted to pick and choose; they wanted all the good parts and none of the bad.

Ito, for instance, lauded "one peculiarity of [Japanese] social conditions that [was] without parallel in any other civilized country" (though his reserve while doing so is worth noting). This peculiarity, extolled far more effusively in Russia and in Germany, where it also was considered a singular national characteristic, was the capacity and inclination to develop warm emotional relations with others in one's social environment, to treat society as family, which made it a true—natural and nurturing—community. This cozy communal propensity was intrinsically opposed to the cold, rational calculation, based on self-interest, which reduced every relationship, even family, to an artificial, temporary contract. The roots of this peculiarity in the case of Japan, in Ito's view—as in the other cases in the view of their respective spokesmen—went deep down to the country's feudal past. Ito explained:

Homogeneous in race, language, religion, and sentiments, so long secluded from the outside world, with the centuries-old traditions and inertia of the feudal system, in which the family and quasi-family ties permeated and formed the essence of every social organization, and moreover with such moral and religious tenets as laid undue stress on duties of fraternal aid and mutual succor, we had during the course of our seclusion unconsciously become a vast village community where cold intellect and calculation of public events were always restrained and even often hindered by warm emotions between man and man. Those who have closely observed the effects of the commercial crises in our country—that is, of the events wherein cold-blooded calculation ought to have the precedence of every other factor—and compared them with those in other countries, must have observed a remarkable distinction between them. In other countries they serve in a certain measure as the scavengers of the commercial world, the solid undertakings surviving the shock, while enterprises founded solely on speculative bases are sure to vanish thereafter. But, generally speaking, this is not the case in our country. Moral and emotional factors come into play. Solid undertakings are dragged into the whirlpool, and the speculative ones are saved from the abyss—the general standard of prosperity is lowered for the moment, but the commercial fabric escapes violent shocks. In industry, also, in spite of the recent enormous developments of manufactures in our country, our laborers have not yet degenerated into spiritless machines and toiling beasts. There still survives the bond of patron and protégé between them and the capitalist employers. It is this moral and emotional factor which will, in the future, form a healthy barrier against the threatening advance of socialistic ideas. It must, of course, be admitted that this social peculiarity is not without beneficial influences. It mitigates the conflict, serves as the lubricator of social organisms, and tends generally to act as a powerful lever for the practical application of the moral principle of mutual assistance between fellow citizens.

Ito recognized that, unless held in restraint, this salubrious characteristic of the Japanese identity could form an obstacle to the development of desirable features of modernity, promoting nepotism in the government, smothering free discussion, and making difficult "cool calculation of national welfare." Such cool but altruistic calculation, however, still seemed more compatible with the warmth of emotional relations between man and man in the vast village community of Japan than with the chilling image, presumably reflecting Western reality, of laborers as spiritless machines and toiling beasts in a world where ruled the cold-blooded calculation of (the unmentioned) self-interest.

It is not surprising that, as they shaped and articulated the values of the Japanese national consciousness, Meiji nationalists relied, of all foreign models, chiefly on the German one. The affinity between the ways of thinking in the two societies (or, rather, their intellectual and bureaucratic elites) was uncanny. Again, it was Ito who was most explicit and insistent regarding this philosophical kinship and the appropriateness of the German example—the corollary of which was the unsuitability of other Western models—for Japan. In 1881 he took his constitutional commission on another learning tour of the West (for him, it was the third) and was smitten by Bismarck's new Germany. Several years later, discussing the character of the Japanese Constitution of 1889, he was able to separate the sheep from the goats. "In explaining the nature of our government," he wrote,

> it must be said that . . . its control and operation rests on sovereignty, which, in our country, is united in the august person of the emperor . . .

In Europe at a time when controversy raged on the subject of sovereignty in the medieval period Montesquieu advanced the theory of the separation of powers. Separation of powers, as you know, is the division of the three powers of legislation, justice, and administration into three independent organs. However, according to a theory based on careful study and on actual experience and advanced by recent scholars [von Gneist and von Stein], sovereignty is one and indivisible. It is like the human body which has limbs and bones but whose source of spiritual life is the mind. Thus, present-day scholars who discuss sovereignty agree in general that it is one and indivisible. That this theory coincides with our interpretation of sovereignty based on our national polity (*kokutai*) is significant.

The Japanese, in other words, were practicing the organic theory of the state before the Westerners formulated it. The principles of German political science, the most elaborate and (academically) most advanced in the world, it appeared, were inherent in Japan to the same extent as the Way of the Sages.

Ito's conception of the parliament and its functions was unequivocally Teutonic. A parliament was a proper parliament, he argued in effect, only if it remained true to its origins in the forests of ancient Germania:

If we trace back to its origin the principle of a representative body, we find that it first manifested itself among an ancient German people. It has been, and still is indeed, affirmed that it is a growth of the English people, but it is not so in fact, for in an old German law, that in the levying of a tax the taxpayer should be consulted, we find the germ of the popular representative principle. The system prevailing in England must be an offshoot from the seedling that appeared in Germany, and from which the principle developed largely in later times in the west of Europe, though it never gained a hold in the central and eastern parts. Till about a century ago it was held that representative bodies should have a monopoly of the legislative right, and the theory of thus dividing the supreme right found much favor. But this conclusion has been held to be illogical by modern [German] scholars. They say the state is like a human body. Just as one brain controls the diverse actions of the limbs and other parts, so should one supreme power superintend and control all the other members of a nation, though such members may play various parts in the whole . . . [This] is sufficient to show the absurdity of the tripartite theory which maintains that the representative body should monopolize the right of legislation . . . [T]he sovereign may permit the representative body to take part in the process of practically applying the legislative right. Since the tripartite theory lost favor it has come to be recognized that the supreme right must be vested in one person and be indivisible.

In distinction to Germany, England had no example to offer Japan. For Ito, in fact, it came rather close to being an anti-model, a case to be studied in order to know what not to do and better appreciate one's blessings. To begin with, there was the disturbing incident of Magna Carta, the story of which Ito considered edifying enough to include in his celebratory speech on the occasion of the adoption of the Constitution of 1889. In England, he argued, unlike in Japan, there was no codified constitution, and the "so-called Great Charter" had been extorted from the king by the nobles (who, Ito thought, were still too numerous and too powerful for the nation's good) "at the point of the sword." "The case of Japan," he emphasized,

> is totally different. The most cordial relations prevail between the Throne and the people while our Constitution is granted. The position of our court cannot be at all compared with that of England when the Magna Carta was granted, for we know that our Imperial House has a single aim—the welfare and happiness of the nation. Not only were there no such discontented barons in this country, but our feudal lords, great and small, joined in requesting the Crown to take back the military and political rights which for centuries they had enjoyed. Could any two things be more radically different than the origins of the English and Japanese Constitutions? If the English people felicitate themselves on the influence exercised in promoting and developing the national welfare and interest, by a Charter given under such ominous circumstances as was theirs, how much more should we congratulate ourselves on having received from our benevolent sovereign, under the most happy and peaceful auspices, the Constitution of the Japanese Empire!

The originally individualistic concepts of liberty and equality, central to national consciousness everywhere and imported from the West as part and parcel of the idea of the nation, were reinterpreted in the light of this collectivistic and authoritarian vision and came to correspond closely to the form they assumed in the framework of other collectivistic nationalisms—in particular German, but also Russian and to some extent French. Liberty, not unexpectedly, was defined as self-abnegation, dissolution in the community, and a sense of duty to it. The "foremost apostle" of the ideal in Japan was the founder of the Liberal Party, Itagaki Taisuke, remembered as "a sort of Japanese Patrick Henry." Having been mortally wounded by an assassin, he is reported to have exclaimed: "Itagaki may die, but liberty will never die!" In 1882 he delivered before the members of his party an "Address on Liberty," which contained, among others, the following revealing statements. In feudal times, he asserted in a manner reminiscent of Marx's "sack of potatoes" argument, "the people were like slaves, so they felt remote from the nation and lacked the slightest sense of community among themselves. Even the samurai, though they enjoyed the status of citizens, conceived their sole duty as obedience to the commands of their lords, and ignored all other obligations. Each one harbored a spirit of individuality, and all were lacking in a feeling of community. They were aware of their own personal freedom, but they knew nothing of public freedom." The Japanese, Itagaki complained, "are deficient in community spirit; each holds to his own individuality"; but, he believed, by fostering the understanding that their public and private interest was one and the same and involving the people in the government, this unfortunate state of affairs could be altered. The purpose of the Liberal Party was to accomplish this. The instructions to his audience on the subject sounded more like a passage from Rousseau (or Adam Müller) than Patrick Henry. "In order for our party to organize a constitutional government and perfect the freedom of all," he said,

> each individual must cast away selfishness and assume the spirit of community. The people must become accustomed to banding together by depending on one another . . . [I]f a man wishes to enjoy liberty through the protection of his government he must strive to acquire a national liberty. If an individual can live satisfactorily in a state of isolation without caring for the common weal, he may be as selfish and extravagant as he pleases, without sacrificing any of his personal freedom. Nevertheless, people can only enjoy life by mixing with their fellows and depending on the community, and therefore their aim should be to secure civil liberty by making mutual concessions. The extension of national liberty is the means by which individual liberty is perfected and is the basis of social organization.

The discussion of equality in Meiji Japan—similarly to Germany and to a lesser degree France during the respective periods when national consciousness was articulated there—was both somewhat more meaningful and far more extensive. As in all nationalisms, the concept in general implied raising the status of the people and dignifying every social position, and, as in Germany in particular, it came to signify specifically the equality of obligations to the state. Each of the "Big Three of the Meiji Era"—Ito, identified with the Constitution; Okuma, who was the leader of the "public opinion"; and Yamagata Aritomo, the founder of the national army—insisted on equality as the supreme achievement of the Restoration and an invaluable gift to the people. In 1872, in the Official Notice which accompanied the Military Conscription Ordinance, Yamagata instructed millions of new soldiers, apparently quite incognizant of the great privilege that was about to hit them, as to what it implied. In ancient Japan, he pointed out, everyone was a soldier, but when the feudal conditions spread, "giving rise to indescribable evils," the warriors were separated from the peasants:

> Then came the great Restoration of the government . . . On the one hand, warriors who lived without labor for generations have had their stipends reduced and have been stripped of their swords; on the other hand, the four classes of the people are about to receive their right to freedom. This is the way to restore the balance between the high and the low and to grant equal rights to all. It is, in short, the basis of uniting the farmer and the soldier into one. Thus, the soldier is not the soldier of former days. The people are not the people of former days. They are now equally the people of the empire, and there is no distinction between them in their obligations to the State.

Some people might not understand why it was good for them to add to other burdens in their already burdened lives the hardship of compulsory military service. The notion that one had a stake in the well-being, and more than that, the prestige and international standing, of one's country, that the public and the private interest were one and the same, was so novel. Therefore, patiently and step by step, Yamagata explained:

> No one in the world is exempt from taxation with which the state defrays its expenditures. In this way, everyone should endeavor to repay one's country. The Occidentals call military obligation "blood tax," for it is one's repayment in life-blood to one's country. When the State suffers disaster, the people cannot escape being affected. Thus the people can ward off disaster to themselves by striving to ward off disaster to the State. And where there is a state, there is military defense; and if there is military defense there must be military service. It follows, therefore, that the law providing for a militia is the law of nature and not an accidental, man-made law.

The implication that "Occidental" meant "not accidental or man-made" but "natural" was somewhat out of tune with the culturally antimodernist tenor of the emerging Japanese nationalism, though in 1872 it was, obviously, less audible than ten years later. Nevertheless, Yamagata hastened to qualify his statement. "The Occidental countries established their military systems after several hundred years of study and experience," he said.

> Thus, their regulations are exact and detailed. However, the difference in geography rules out their wholesale adoption here. We should now select only what is good in them, use them to supplement our traditional

military system, establish an army and a navy, require all males who attain the age of twenty—irrespective of class—to register for military service, and have them in readiness for all emergencies. Heads of communities and chiefs of villages should keep this aim in mind and they should instruct the people so that they will understand the fundamental principle of national defense.

Not trusting the said functionaries to be persuasive enough, Yamagata included the same ideas in the Imperial Precepts to Soldiers and Sailors of 1882, which he then officially received from the emperor on behalf of the army. This time framed in the terms of immemorial Japanese tradition, rather than as a rational argument, and relying on the imperial, rather than Western, authority, the idea of equality in obligations was certain to have both a far greater significance and a clear appeal to the not yet sufficiently nationalized souls of its addressees. The imperial document proclaimed:

Soldiers and Sailors, We are your supreme Commander-in-Chief. Our relations with you will be most intimate when We rely upon you as Our limbs and you look up to Us as your head. Whether We are able to guard the Empire, and to prove Ourself worthy of Heaven's blessings and repay the benevolence of Our Ancestors, depends upon the faithful discharge of your duties as soldiers and sailors. If the majesty and power of Our Empire be impaired, you share with Us the sorrow; if the glory of Our arms shine resplendent, We will share with you the honor. If you all do your duty, and being one with Us in spirit do your utmost for the protection of the state, Our people will long enjoy the blessings of peace, and the might and dignity of Our Empire will shine in the world.

The meaning conveyed by these words was nothing short of revolutionary, and it was conveyed all the more efficiently because of the apparent archaism of the formula. Gently introducing the peasants to the organic theory of the state, the Precepts identified them with the emperor, the Japanese *tenno*—Heaven's monarch—and told them that he was dependent on them for the proper discharge of his duties, the keeping of the divine order. While his sorrows were their sorrows, they were to share in his honor, and the might and dignity of the empire, as much as the blessings of the peace, were made the immediate concern of the people. The dignity to which the people were thereby elevated was breathtaking. And if they had any sensitivity at all—if, that is, they were not so habituated, in Adam Smith's words, "to the idea of [their] own meanness, so sunk in slothful and sottish indifference, as entirely to have forgot the desire for superiority"—they would be converted into national patriots, ready "with single heart [to] fulfill [their] essential duty of loyalty" and firmly believing "that duty is weightier than a mountain, while death is lighter than a feather."

The prime minister delivered the same message as the minister of defense. In the 1899 Speech on the Restoration and Constitutional Government, Ito also stressed the connection between equality, duty, and dignity implied in the new, national, identity and social organization:

> From the standpoint of the sovereign power, that is, the emperor's prerogative to rule the country, the people are one and equal under the constitutional government. They are all direct subjects of the emperor. The so-called "indirect subjects" no longer exist. This means that the Japanese people have been able to raise their status and to achieve for themselves a great honor. They now have the right to share in legislative rights, which come from the emperor's sovereign powers, and to elect and send representatives. Having the right to send representatives they can, indirectly, voice their opinions on the advisability and the faults of their country's administration. Thus every member of the nation—be he a farmer, craftsman, or merchant—must become familiar beforehand with the merits and demerits of the questions of government. Not only on questions of government, but also on matters concerning his own occupation, the citizen must give due thought and become prosperous. When every man becomes wealthy, the village, the county, and the prefecture in turn become wealthy, and the accumulated total of that wealth becomes the wealth of Japan. The expansion of military strength and the promotion of national prestige depend upon the power of the individual members of the country. Therefore, in order to promote the development of military strength and national prestige, it is only proper and necessary to diffuse education so that the people can understand the changes and improvements with respect to their government . . . Since government is concerned with the administration of the country as a whole it does not follow that its acts are always favorable to all individuals. The nation's affairs, of their own nature, are not personal and concerned with the individual. They must be carried out according to the nation's aims, the nation's prestige, and the nation's honor. It is for this reason that the people have an obligation to understand the nation's aims. They must regard the nation as their own, meet the military obligation to defend it and to pay for the cost of defending it.

National identity implied the elevation of the populace to the dignity of an elite, and with the new dignified status came rights and responsibilities, or rights that were also responsibilities, the exercise of which contained its own reward. A member of the nation had the right and responsibility to know and participate in the electoral process; he had the right and responsibility to be prosperous, for the prosperity of the citizens combined into the wealth of Japan and undergirded its military strength and international prestige. The well-being of the nation was certainly connected to the well-being of its individual members, but they were the same thing only insofar as the individual was first and foremost a member of the nation. It was his responsibility to identify with the interests of the nation, for they were different from the interests of individuals as such. The nation's aims, the nation's prestige, the nation's honor always took precedence over individual needs, desires, and considerations, for it was a bigger and better individual than they. Unlike the English nation, the nation of Japan was conceived of as emphatically an emergent phenomenon: it was much more than an association of individuals, it could not be understood merely as a combination of its elements, and the laws governing the way it functioned could not be reduced to the laws of human nature. Ito realized that, despite its Western origins, national identity was not natural: it was an acquired characteristic, and people had to be educated, taught to develop it.

Perhaps most cogently, the views of Meiji leaders regarding the relationship between rights and obligations, general good and self-interest, and the blessings and banes of modernity were summarized by Okuma Shigenobu, who also offered the most explicit definition of the Japanese idea of the nation itself. It is to be found in his 1913 speech "Citizenship in the New World" on the occasion of the thirtieth anniversary of the foundation of Waseda University. Waseda students, Okuma claimed there, were the future leaders of the nation, its strength, and formed the foundation of its steady progress. They were destined to become "the vanguards of civilizing [i.e., modern] enterprises" and, as such, had to be model citizens. To be a model citizen, he explained, knowledge—understood specifically in the sense of Western science—was not sufficient. The reason for this was the following:

> According to the present usage, the term "nation" has two parts. The one is the state, the other is society. If society does not develop in an orderly way, the nation cannot be stable. And at the very root of this relationship is the family. The family is the basis of the state. Morality and ethics find their source in family life. Customs of behavior also spring from the family. Thus, the fundamental principle of education must be the cultivation of character. Man becomes self-seeking if he strives only to acquire specialized knowledge and ignores what I have said above. Moreover, the spirit of self-sacrifice among men for their country and for the world will gradually decline. This would be deplorable. It will be the curse of civilization. To avoid this curse and to acquire the benefits of

civilization is the responsibility of the model citizen. This is the essence of Waseda University's basic principles of education.

In April 1914 Okuma was appointed prime minister (for the second time: he had served as prime minister for several months in 1898) and about a year later gave the first address by a Japanese leader that was circulated as a recording. The address dealt with the danger of interparty squabbles and admonished the populace to exercise their political rights to control them. "The rights and duties given to the people by the Constitution," he expostulated, "are of great importance. The Constitution itself is the basis whereupon our nation is built. And the rights of the people as subjects, that is, the duties of the people given by the Constitution, are a matter of vital importance." He believed, Okuma declared, that "the power of public opinion controls the destiny of our country." If the public, the people, did not fulfill its obligations, Japan's "national destiny, her honor and her reputation" would be at risk.[37] Being recorded, this message that rights were duties, and that the nation's fate and honor depended on their conscientious discharge, could be endlessly replayed. The awesome modern medium through which it was delivered ensured that it reached deep and made an impression. The most exalted official in the government, talking to each one directly, told the people that they had great power and that it was up to them to increase it—by preserving and contributing to Japan's honor and reputation—or lose it. Naturally, they proved a receptive audience, and of course, whatever it took to keep, they would not give up what was once theirs.

6 | Racing and Fighting

Thirty-nine years after the publication of *"Made in Germany,"* in 1935, another book appeared at London bookstalls. Called *Made in Japan,* it was rather subdued in tone by comparison with Williams's patriotic tract, its German author, Günther Stein—"an economist of international repute," according to a brief introduction—determined to prevent his personal sentiments, whatever they were, from interfering with a scholarly discussion of the challenge that "the comet-like rise of Japan's export trade" posed to the British economy. Nevertheless, this challenge was by no means underestimated. The language of the opening pages of the book's first chapter, titled "The Danger Signal," was far from value-free, and enabled the author, with a minimal expense of words, to paint a picture certain to distress anyone who took British economic supremacy to heart. "A powerful stream of Japanese manufactures," stated Stein, "is *flooding* the markets of the world"; "established interests of the older exporting countries are *menaced* by a competitor whose prices are *absurdly* low and whose sale methods are amazingly successful." An analysis of this success, he promised, would contain lessons not without value "for the *harassed* manufacturers and traders of the West."

Stein reminded his readers that this was not the first time Great Britain had been "alarmed by the industrial coming of age of another great nation." About forty years before, "a new producer, demanding and finding markets, suddenly appeared in the international community of manufacturers, upsetting a delicate balance of supply and demand, and creating a scare which had much in common with the present fear of Japan." That producer was Germany. "The skill of German workers challenged that of the British; cheap German products began to force their way into all corners of the globe, pushing aside the manufactures of other countries. And Germany's competitors hoped to warn off potential buyers of German goods with the stamp 'made in Germany.'" Then as now, "people in England complained about incredibly low German prices; about low German wages . . . about the new competitor's dangerously effective pioneering enthusiasm. These grievances were dis-

299

cussed again and again in the House of Commons and in the Press; and the fathers of many of the present British unemployed may have lost their jobs because of German competition." As in Germany, Stein pointed out, the sudden success of Japan on world markets coincided with its political awakening: both countries were political latecomers, who tried to gain influence and power beyond their frontiers. This led our economist to a pessimistic conjecture regarding the political implications of Japan's "industrial coming of age," couched in the form of a hypothesis, and therefore all the more ominous. "The German scare gradually died down after the close of the century," he wrote.

> Or did the differences between goods "made in Germany" and those "made in England" and elsewhere help to develop the international atmosphere in which political ambitions, misunderstandings, apparent accidents and diplomatic mistakes could finally result in the World War? Was this World War perhaps fundamentally a struggle . . . though perhaps an unintentional one, between junior and senior participants in world trade?
>
> These questions arise when it is said that just as the German scare gradually abated towards the end of the century, the Japanese scare, too, will be "self-liquidating." "Such scares die a natural death." But perhaps they do not . . . unless all are given more room, far more room than they had before the World War, than they have to-day.

These considerations were followed by a dispassionate, but on the whole clearly sympathetic, comprehensive overview of Japanese business organization, methods of production, and work habits. Stein was obviously familiar with the country's recent history and society, and his analysis of its immense economic strength and the astonishing rapidity of its economic development was convincing. Certain statistics, adduced among other evidence, were particularly eloquent. "To-day Japan exports five or six times as many finished products as she did in 1914," wrote Stein, for instance. This brought its share in the world trade of manufactures to 10 percent, placing Japan directly behind "the four industrial Great Powers: Great Britain, the United States, Germany and France." The leaps and bounds by which Japan arrived at this position of the fifth-strongest commercial state heralded what was to come. With the exports of 1914 standing for 100, the index was 210 for 1920, 254 for 1928 (this despite the disastrous earthquake and fire in 1923, which destroyed the old Tokyo and Yokohama), 325 for 1932, and 555 for 1934, the last year for which Stein had figures.

In some products Japan had already overtaken its formidable rivals. It was the largest exporter of cotton fabrics, with a 40 percent share of world trade. "The British record, established shortly before the war," wrote Stein, "was 7,000,000,000 square yards of cotton tissues. At that time Japan was not a serious competitor." Still in 1928 Britain led, with exports of 3.866 billion yards, as against 1.419 for the Japanese. By 1934 the two countries had changed places: British exports of cotton tissues amounted to 1.995 billion yards and Japanese to 2.568 billion. Stein exulted: "Great Britain's exports of cotton tissues have gone back to the figures of the 'sixties, the time when feudal Japan was opened to international trade by force. At that time Japan had hardly any industry worth the name, and Japanese pioneers were coming to England to study Western spinning methods. And to-day Japan is ahead of Great Britain by 500,000,000 square yards!"

The nature of Japanese industrial exports was changing as rapidly as their volume. Within only two years, between 1932 and 1934, "non-textiles" rose from 37 percent of total exports of manufactured products to 52 percent, with both textile and total exports increasing substantially in 1933. Among the "non-textiles" exported to a value of at least a million pounds each were tinned foodstuffs, refined wheat flour and sugar, drugs and chemicals, dyes and paints, shoes, jewelry, paper, pottery, glass, iron rails, enameled ware, cutlery and nails, clocks and scientific instruments, lamps, and toys. Japan was also starting to export automobiles. It became "an all-round exporter of industrial products," commented Stein. Domestic production rose 52 percent between 1932 and 1934, much of it owing to the rise in the productivity of the Japanese worker. In this context, Stein quoted a 1932 statement by an English statistician, Colin Clark: "The Japanese worker had already reached 90% of the British productivity with his present working week. If the length of the working week were the same in the two countries his productivity would not be more than 66% of the British. For a productivity per annum of 90% of the British level he receives an annual wage of 38% the British wage." While these estimates were correct for the time when they were made, Stein believed that two years later "increasing rationalization has probably equalized the average productivity of the workers in both countries, and Japan, of course, continues to make up for her disadvantages by longer hours of work." Moreover, he added triumphantly, the average figure did not show that in the cotton industry, and perhaps in some others, the productivity of the Japanese worker was already greater than that of an English one "—even if the working hour and not the working day is used as a basis of comparison!"

Few would disagree with the conclusion Stein derived from this, that Japan was quickly moving to assume the leadership of the industrial world, that it was poised to overtake, one after another, the four industrial Great Powers, and that it was a delusion to count on the imaginary disadvantages of its oriental background to arrest this development. Things being as they were in 1934, it would surely continue, "not only as rationalization spreads to an increasing number of industries, but also as the Japanese worker becomes more experienced in his relatively new task." Japan already had much of what was needed to assert its parity with, if not superiority over, the world's strongest economies. "Technical and general schools in Japan are excellent," wrote Stein, "and we have already discussed the traditional skill of the Japanese. They are eager to learn, industrious and persistent, and existing industrial organization and customs in Japan give full scope to the ability of her workers. The legend of the industrial inferiority of the Asiatic races, at least as far as Japan is concerned, has been destroyed by reality."

It was all the more difficult, suggested Stein, to accept Japan's membership in the Superpower Club and its potential economic dominance, because its sudden prowess was utterly incomprehensible. Granted, several decades earlier Germany had provoked similar reactions, but, he argued,

> it was not difficult to understand why Germany succeeded . . . She was a country geographically near to England, and her inhabitants were a kindred people, though not as advanced politically or economically as the English. Japan, on the other hand, seems new and strange, and difficult to understand. The country is so far away, so little known. The Japanese are the first among the non-European races of the world to have achieved an independent industrial success. Japan is the first country in which industrialization seems to emerge directly from feudalism. Socially and economically she is as puzzling to Western observers as she sometimes appears in the political field.

The pleasure (and the headache) of solving this puzzle was left to the reader: after all, one could not expect a rational economic actor to waste effort on a labor-intensive task which promised only spiritual reward, if any.[1]

The emergence of a modern economy in Japan, where its capacity for sustained growth was so strikingly demonstrated as to create a scare among the great Western industrial powers, was, as elsewhere, a direct result of the rise of nationalism. To recognize this is not to deny that certain conditions for the emergence of a modern economy existed in Japan long before nationalism: Japan had been for many centuries singularly sophisticated, from the economic point of view, among the East Asian societies, probably as sophisticated as the most advanced premodern economies of the West. These conditions facilitated the process of economic reorientation inspired by nationalism and might have accounted for some of its rapidity. But their very antiquity is proof of their causal insignificance: in themselves they were impotent to produce the system the transition to which was eased by their presence.

Sophistication without Growth

Yamamoto Shichihei surmises that the first to notice the economic acuity of the Japanese and to give rise to the idea that the Japanese were "economic animals" were two Korean visitors, Song Hee Kyung and the envoy Park Shu Saeng. The former was astonished enough to report during his visit in 1420 that Japanese beggars preferred to receive alms in money rather than in kind, while the latter thought it deserved to be mentioned that money was all one needed to travel around the country with comfort, unburdened by bulky provisions. The early monetization of the Japanese economy clearly contrasted with the situation in neighboring countries. In fifteenth-century Korea, for instance, the use of money was unknown, even though King Sejong imported coin from China and, on the threat of severe punishment, prohibited the customary barter. His people could not understand what was wanted from them. The first person to suffer the consequences of this economic innocence, now defined as criminal, received a hundred lashes and was drafted into the navy. His wife and the mother of his little children, disconsolate and utterly bewildered, killed herself. This royal ferocity on behalf of economic progress failed to produce the desired effect: until late in the seventeenth century, Koreans remained oblivious to the advantages of the generalized medium of exchange and stubbornly clung to barter. They were not at all exceptional: in Vietnam money did not circulate widely until the eighteenth century.

In Japan, too, the money economy trickled down from the imperial court, which originally, as in Korea, attempted to encourage its spread by decree. In 708 the first coins were minted from native copper, of which Japan was a major producer. The populace did not cooperate, and the currency did not circulate. In 987 Emperor Ichijo made its use obligatory in payment for Buddhist services, in particular funerals, but, by and large, accounts were settled by means of rice, cloth, and silk, and taxes were collected in these commodities. The bureaucrats were likewise unsympathetic to the emperors' progressive ideas and used the dearth of mintable copper as an excuse for their economic conservatism. They were deprived of it when, in the twelfth century (1164), an influential samurai at the court suggested importing coin from China. For whatever reason, the people proved far more receptive to the Chinese money than they were to the native currency, with the result that "the imported money spread like wildfire throughout the country," fueling the economy, which in turn increased the demand for money. It has greased the wheels of Japanese commerce ever since.

For almost half a millennium, until 1637, Chinese specie fulfilled this important role for Japan. It was exchanged for gold, which in Japan was relatively abundant (indeed earning it the name of "the Land of Gold"), but used only for Buddhist statues and ornaments. In China, by contrast, the metal was in short supply, while the demand for it apparently was steady and strong—so much so that before long its insatiable appetite for the disgorgings of the Japanese mines resulted in a shortage of ready copper cash, and the Song government had to resort to paper money. "If China, therefore, was the first country in the world where paper money was widely circulated," comments Yamamoto with understandable excitement, "Japan was evidently responsible for that development, at least in part!" Chinese currency at that time could be used, in transactions between governments, throughout East Asia; very small amounts of gold (the value-in-use of which was nil) were sold for very large amounts of coin; and while wily Japan accumulated ever-increasing stores of this versatile medium, it quietly robbed China of it, using the Middle Kingdom almost as its own mint, for it paid for all Chinese imports with gold dust.

By the mid-thirteenth century the monetization of the Japanese economy had proceeded so far that special legislation was needed to counteract its deleterious effects on the feudal social structure. Feudal land was freely sold, creating a mass of "rootless" vassals who no longer had any income. In 1240 the Kamakura shoguns attempted to reaffirm the principles of feudal stratification by preventing the sale of samurai estates to commoners. The law to this effect, added to the first written code of samurai conduct, *Joei Shikimoku*, was for all intents and purposes identical to the one promulgated by the enlightened rulers of Prussia in the eighteenth century.[2] But money was lent at the exorbitant rate of interest of 100 percent on the principal, and though compound interest was prohibited and creditors' charges (after the introduction of another law in 1297) were not recognized in court, people who had any assets at all were eager to liquefy them and lend the cash at interest. The excessive cost of credit was the stimulus behind the creation, as early as 1255, of a primitive savings and loan associations or banks, the *mujin*. These associations, which, according to Stein, were still functioning in the 1930s, allowed a number of individuals to pool their funds and make loans to members, with their property serving as collateral. In 1239 the shogunate promulgated a law banning the circulation of money northeast of the Kanto area. The reason given for this action was the preference among the peasantry for paying taxes in cash, which led to a sad deterioration in the quality of silk cloth, tendered as tax previously. This law was intended as a corrective to an earlier decree of 1226 which ordered peasants of Musashi province to use copper coins instead of silk cloth in the payment of taxes. Musashi apparently complied and was promptly imitated by others. The shogunate was scared by its own success: monetization was getting out of control. It penetrated deep into the countryside, reaching every sector of the urban population, down to the humblest servants *(zonin)* and slaves *(nuhi)*. Even common thieves preferred the convenience of money in forays for their daily bread—or rice, as the case may be. Family and communal relations which were the pillars of feudal society were undermined and status distinctions eroded. But the economy remained stationary and, as before, passed through cycles of growth and decline, animated by the laws of economic rationality which dictated that effort should cease when one's material desires, limited by custom as well as the law of diminishing returns, were fulfilled.

Political Economy in Tokugawa Japan: "Physiocrats" and "Mercantilists"

The relatively advanced condition of the Japanese economy was reflected in the tradition of economic thought which, by the time of the Tokugawa takeover, went back many centuries, counting among its foundations thousand-year-old Confucian and Indian sources. This tradition was sophisticated and might strike some today as surprisingly modern. It included informed discussions of poverty and wealth, property, production and distribution, supply and demand, patterns of exchange, and the relationship of price, value, and quantity of money. But it was not a dynamic tradition. As the economy did not develop, caught as it was at a very high stage of economic organization for close to a millennium, neither did its interpretation. The conclusions of the sages of antiquity were faithfully transmitted from generation to generation, with the interests of each cohort of scholars defined by its circumstances, which tended to focus these interests alternately on growth and decline, prodding the scholars once and again to ruminate on the socially disruptive consequences of the former and ponder the causes and remedies for the material devastations of the latter.

In Tokugawa Japan, economic thought originally represented an aspect of Confucian philosophy. Since this philosophy was essentially political, its purpose being the discovery and formulation of the precepts of a perfect government, the economy was conceived of as a division of the ruler's administration. The conception was similar to the early idea of *économie politique* in

France and, in particular, that of *Staatswirtschaft* in Germany. In 1729 Dazai Shundai defined the idea of *keizai*, which means "economy" in Japanese, thus:

> To govern the whole nation [country] under heaven is *keizai*. It is the virtue of ruling society and relieving the sufferings of the people. *Kei* is wise statesmanship . . . *Kei* literally means "to control a thread." The warp of a piece of material is called *kei* and the woof, *i*. When a weaving woman makes silk cloth, she first prepares the warp . . . *Kei* is also "management" . . . When you construct a royal palace, you must first make a plan of the whole, and then you carry out the plan. This is *kei*.
>
> *Sai* means the virtue of salvation . . . literally . . . "to carry someone across a river to the farther bank" . . . It is also the virtue of bringing relief *(kyusai)*, which . . . means "to relieve people of their sufferings." Moreover, it may be interpreted as meaning "accomplishment" or "bringing to fruition." Therefore the term [*keizai*] has many meanings, but the essential point of those meanings is simply this: in short, to manage affairs and to bring these affairs to a successful conclusion.

Tessa Morris-Suzuki explains that "*keizai* was an abbreviation of the phrase *keikoku saimin* (or *keisei saimin*), which may be roughly translated as 'administering the nation [country: *koku*] and relieving the suffering of the people.'" Commenting on Dazai's definition, she says:

> The idea of *keizai*, in other words, has its origins in the Confucian world of public ethics with its paragon of the virtuous ruler . . . [*K*]*eizai* was a philosophical system inescapably bound up with questions of justice, law, and morality. It is entirely consistent with this tradition, therefore, that Shundai's *Economic Annals* [*Keizai Roku*, the work in which the definition of *keizai* appears] should contain sections on crime and punishment, geography, and education, for these matters were all integral parts of *keizai*. In the same way, Arai Hakuseki, the leading economic adviser of his day, would have made no distinction between his contributions to currency reform and trade policy and his advice on appropriate epitaphs for a deceased shogun. All of these tasks were equally concerned with *keizai*, the holding together of the social fabric of the nation.

Morris-Suzuki believes that this attitude distinguished Japanese economic thinking from contemporary trends in European economic thought, where "under the influence of Newtonian physics, [economics] came to present itself as a detached and objective science." But, in fact, German

Hausväterliteratur, as well as the later Cameral so-called "sciences," which invariably mixed economic discussions with *polizei,* reflected the very same attitude, and though in France and elsewhere economic thought progressed beyond the stage of Sully's *Économies royales* and was indeed, by the mid-eighteenth century, no longer regarded as a regular aspect of statecraft, nowhere, with the possible exception of Britain after 1776, did it become a science on the Newtonian model until very much later.

As there were numerous parallels between the Tokugawa and (Continental) European economies of the seventeenth through early nineteenth centuries, there were numerous parallels between Tokugawa and Continental European economic thought. Like Europe, Japan had its "mercantilists" and "physiocrats," its detractors and defenders of commerce, and its writers of business manuals for merchants as well as top (that is government) management—the counterparts of Savary on the one hand and Justi on the other. On the theoretical level, owing to the country's policy of isolation, it was the native "physiocratic" theory (what Adam Smith called "the agricultural system") that predominated, while the only form of mercantilism remained that of primitive bullionism rather than the more advanced variety focusing on the balance of trade. It is interesting that the French Physiocrats, who probably never gave much thought to Japan, but who were active at the time when things Chinese generally were in vogue, were aware of the affinity between their theories and Confucianism. They might even have believed in the Chinese origin of their central idea—that of the natural order—which would explain the references to Quesnay as "the venerable Confucius of Europe." Baudeau, for instance, referred to the Confucian idea of *li* when he wrote: "The single supreme will which exercises supreme power is not, strictly speaking, a human will at all. It is just the voice of nature—the will of God. The Chinese are the only people whose philosophy seems to have got hold of this supreme truth." Some believe that it was this idea which later found expression in Adam Smith's metaphor of the "invisible hand," which, whether or not this belief has any foundation in reality, certainly helps to appreciate the possible appeal of the notion of economics as an objective—Newtonian—science for a Confucian.

The similarity between Tokugawa "physiocrats" and the French Économistes, however, had mainly to do with the understandable emphasis on agriculture as the foundation of prosperity. In the seventeenth century, Kumazawa Banzan, preoccupied as he was with the plight of the impoverished samurai—the Japanese equivalent of the French *hobereaux*—defined grain as "the treasure of the people," and outlined the far-reaching implications of the recognition of this simple truth for the entire economy:

Gold, silver, copper and so forth are the servants of grain. They come after grain . . . The enlightened ruler stores grain plentifully for the people,
and, since all buying and selling is performed with grain, the people enjoy abundance . . . It is difficult to transport large quantities of grain, and
therefore, if grain is used [as a means of exchange], trade cannot be easily monopolized. So the price of goods is lowered and luxury does not
increase. Samurai and farmers are prosperous, while artisans and merchants also have secure fortunes.

The expression of concern, however dilatory, for the well-being of merchants was entirely disingenuous: Kumazawa detested them with the vehemence of Ulrich von Hutten, whose invectives against these creatures and
representatives of Mammon his own harangues indeed closely resembled. For
Kumazawa, too, as for the déclassé German knight, money was an evil: his
principle was *kikoku senkin*—"revering rice and despising gold."
While this was a majority view, there were important dissenters. Arai
Hakuseki, the shogunal adviser, thought that the country's wealth rested on
bullion, literally. "Gold and silver are made by heaven and earth," he argued.
"If we use the metaphor of the human form, we can say that they are like the
bones, while all other valuable products are like the blood, muscle, skin and
hair. Blood, muscle, skin and hair can be damaged and will grow again. But
bones, once they are damaged, cannot be regenerated. Gold and silver are
like the bones of heaven and earth. Once they have been removed, they cannot be recreated." This explained Arai's anxiety about the effects of Japan's
trade with the Dutch, which, though minimal, drained precious metals out of
the country. The Dutch brought in exotic birds for the wealthy, pencils and
eyeglasses for the bureaucrats, as well as some textile goods, spices, and herbs
for general consumption, but were, apparently, uninterested in native products. Arai was not bothered by the lack of exports, but thought that imports
unnecessarily taxed the economy. His ideal, like that of the early Continental mercantilists, was that of economic self-sufficiency, though he was willing
to make an exception for medicines and—like Laffemas a century earlier—
books, the latter being especially interesting since the ban on the import of
Western literature was not abolished until 1720.
The thinkers who were responsible for the elaboration of Tokugawa economic theory and, by the mid-eighteenth century, had contributed to it
most, if not all, of the concepts that defined contemporary economic thinking in Europe, like their European counterparts, were not economists in the
modern sense of the word but moral, that is, social, philosophers. Arai's mercantilism, apart from its theoretical originality, thus constituted a departure
from the system of ethics reflected in the dominant "physiocratic" views of

Kumazawa and others. In effect, Arai made the first step in legitimating commercial society. A few of the samurai intellectuals went beyond his acceptance of money and were willing to admit that commerce as such was a morally unobjectionable, even respectable activity. We find this attitude in the writings of Kaiho Seiryo, active in the later part of the eighteenth century and the beginning of the nineteenth. Like Coyer, whose near-contemporary he was, Kaiho championed the idea of *noblesse commerçante,* urging the commercialization of the domain economy and suggesting that the samurai should adopt some of the profit-seeking behavior of the merchants and pull themselves from impoverishment through trade (though, clearly, he was animated by the concern for his class and lacked the Abbé's patriotic inspiration). The arguments he used to defend this idea from attack by traditionalists who could be counted upon to retort that commerce was dishonorable for a samurai was practically identical to the one Coyer employed in the 1757 response to his detractors, where he claimed that, after all, preoccupation with monetary reward was no more present in commerce than in the ubiquitous among the nobility and perfectly respectable search for officers' commissions, making the army a business of sorts, and an officer a businessman as susceptible to the logic of self-interest as any other. Kaiho's argument differed from Coyer's only to the extent to which a Japanese translation of a proposition would be expected to differ from the French original. "From ancient times," he wrote,

> the relationship between lord and retainer has been like the relationship of the market. The retainer is granted a stipend, and gives his service to his lord in return. The lord buys from the retainer, and the retainer sells to the lord. It is a market exchange, and this buying and selling is a good and not an evil thing . . . All things between heaven and earth are commodities for exchange, and it is the law of commodities that they should produce other commodities. Without exception, fields produce rice and money produces profit.

This argument reflected a shift in the attitude toward the social significance of wealth: it was represented as a positive value, and striving for it appeared both natural and moral.[3]

Buddhist Pietism and the Way of the Merchant

By and large the samurai moralists *cum* economic theorists did not extend their approbation to those for whom commerce was a profession rather than an occasional activity, that is, merchants. The members of this humble class, however, were not left entirely without moral succor, for from early on in the Tokugawa period there existed a religious—Buddhist—ethic which offered them a place in the moral order and allowed them to find dignity in the way they earned their living. The precepts of this system of ethics were articulated by a Zen monk, Suzuki Shosan, a former retainer of Tokugawa Ieyasu, who fought by his side in the battle of Sekigahara and then served as an official of the *bakufu* in Osaka, but decided, and was exceptionally permitted, to take tonsure in 1620. The foundations of Suzuki's religious vision were laid down in the tract straightforwardly named "Anti-Christianity" *(Hakirishitan)*, whose polemical purpose may have been responsible for the systematic nature of his argument, uncharacteristic of Zen Buddhism. According to *Hakirishitan*, Buddha, the divine essence of all being, took on three forms, or aspects: the Moon, the Heart, and the Great Healing King. The Moon signified Buddha's reflection in the natural order; the Heart, the reflection of this natural order in the human heart, which was also a part of it. Thus, if one obeyed one's heart, doing what was natural, one lived in accordance with the dictates of the cosmic order, in unity with Buddha. If only everyone conformed to one's Buddhahood or original and true nature, peace and contentment would reign in society, for there would be no crime and no discord. The reality was different from this natural state of affairs, because men's hearts were filled with three "poisons": greed, anger, and discontent. An antidote was available: it could be administered by the Great Healing King, and a sincere desire to be cured, expressed in prayer to him and reflecting the faith in his powers, was the way to induce him to do so, and was instantly and invariably gratified. To desire to be cured was to be cured; to believe in Buddha was to become Buddha; the surest way to achieve contentment was to banish discontent: it was all quite easy and self-fulfilling, and the responsibility for making it work rested squarely on one's own shoulders.

Nevertheless, as the conception was rather novel, Suzuki in a later work, "Daily Life for the Four Classes" *(Shimin Nichiyo)*, formulated the rules for applying these abstract principles to the distinctive realities of the farmers, artisans, merchants, and samurai, thereby translating the religious vision of *Hakirishitan* into a versatile code of social ethics. Composed in the form of questions and answers, the work contained sections specifically relevant to each one of the major social groups, thus assuring everyone, irrespective of one's occupation, of the accessibility of the state of righteousness and bliss.

Shimin Nichiyo first considered striving for Buddhahood in peasant circumstances. An imaginary peasant was made to wonder:

We are taught that the next life is important and that we should not spare ourselves in Buddhist practice, but farm work keeps us so busy we do not have any time for practice. How unfair it seems that simply because we must make a living through menial labor, we are destined to waste this life and suffer in the next. How can we attain Buddhahood?

Suzuki countered:

> You must toil in extremes of heat and cold, spade, hoe, and sickle in hand. Your mind and body overgrown with the thicket of desire is your enemy. Torture yourself—plow, reap—work with all your heart . . . When one is unoccupied, the thicket of desire grows, but when one toils, subjecting one's mind and body to pain, one's heart is at peace. In this way one is engaged in Buddhist practice all the time. Why should a peasant long for another road to Buddhahood?[4]

In other words, performed with the right attitude, labor was ascetic practice, active piety, and the harder it was the better, for the right attitude consisted in cherishing one's pain, even seeking it. This was a very rational position (of course, not in the Western, economic sense of the word): not only did it make suffering, physical and inescapable, sufferable,[5] it made it meaningful and worthwhile as well.

The answer to the artisan's question was more generally applicable. "All occupations are Buddhist practice," assured Suzuki.

> Through work we are able to attain Buddhahood. There is no calling that is not Buddhist. All is for the good of the world . . . The all-encompassing Buddha-nature manifest in us all works for the world's good: without artisans, such as the blacksmith, there would be no tools; without officials there would be no order in the world; without farmers there would be no food; without merchants we would suffer inconvenience. All the other occupations as well are for the good of the world . . . All reveal the blessing of the Buddha. Those who are ignorant of the blessing of our Buddha-nature, who do not value themselves and their innate Buddha-nature and fall into evil ways of thinking and behaving, have lost their way . . . Above all you must believe in yourself. If you truly desire to become a Buddha, just believe in yourself. Believing in yourself is believing in the Buddha, for the Buddha is in you. The Buddha has no desires, its heart contains no anger, no discontent, no life or death . . . no right or wrong . . . no passions . . . no evil . . . Believe with all your heart. Believe.

Faith, its intensity and sincerity, above all, was instant salvation. The ability to perform one's task contentedly and yet without enthusiasm, attaching no importance whatsoever to one's success or failure, living one's life without caring for being alive, without joy, was the way to nirvana—the greatest happiness of all. How comforting it must have been for those who had no joy in life!

But merchants of early Tokugawa Japan were beginning to discover that life could be quite exciting. Their problem, if they had one as a class, was the contempt in which they were held by the society, the oppressive awareness that they were engaged in a loathsome, shameful, inherently sinful activity. Yet to them too, Suzuki held out the promise of salvation, as well as the possibility of seeing themselves in a different, more positive light. Like all the other occupations, commerce was a godly activity. It was "the function Heaven has assigned to those whose job it is to promote freedom [that is, convenience or easy access to goods] throughout the country." Not that the function itself was particularly valuable, but, like others, it offered an opportunity for ascetic practice. To an abject merchant, filled with the sense of his kind's unworthiness, who appealed to him, saying, "I ceaselessly pursue my humble trade in hopes of realizing a profit, but to my great regret I will never be able to achieve Buddhahood. Please tell me the way," Suzuki's advice was to forget the idea of profit. Use your business as a way to punish yourself, he urged:

> Throw yourself headlong into worldly activity. For the sake of the nation [country] and its citizens [people], send the goods of your province to other provinces, and bring the products of other provinces into your own. Travel around the country to distant parts to bring people what they desire. Your activity is an ascetic exercise that will cleanse you of all impurities. Challenge your mind and body by crossing mountain ranges. Purify your heart by fording rivers. When your ship sets sail on the boundless sea, lose yourself in prayer to the Buddha. If you understand that this life is but a trip through an evanescent world, and if you cast aside all attachments and desires and work hard, Heaven will protect you, the gods will bestow their favor, and your profits will be exceptional. You will become a person of wealth and virtue and care nothing for riches. Finally you will develop an unshakable faith; you will be engaged in meditation around the clock.

Making profits was not sinful; making them intentionally was. Fortunately for the merchant, according to Suzuki, it was also ineffective: the way to assure the success of an enterprise was not to care about it. It was the selfless man who best realized self-interest.

"Today we still instinctively sense that it is wrong to seek profit, but that profits that naturally result from labor are acceptable," writes Yamamoto Shichihei in his recent commentary on Suzuki. He also credits the Zen philosopher with being "most directly responsible for the development of capitalism in Japan." According to Yamamoto, Suzuki's variety of Buddhism represented a Japanese equivalent of English Calvinism, spawning an ethic which reinforced the values of hard work and frugality and thus performed for Japanese economy the Weberian function.[6]

It did no such thing. Quite apart from the fact, discussed in an earlier chapter, that the Protestant ethic was quite innocent of any involvement with the "spirit of capitalism," or that this "spirit" itself, in Weber's thinking, referred to the reorientation of the economy toward growth rather than to the traditional virtues of a businessman, the similarity between English Calvinism (the one economically significant variety of Protestantism, from Weber's point of view) and Suzuki's Buddhism is entirely superficial. Instead, with its emphasis on the process and studied unconcern for the end result, it is a form of Pietism and represents a counterpart of German Pietism of the eighteenth century, which also promised salvation irrespective of success and taught the faithful (all of whom were elect on that account) how to find solace in misery. Since redemption can be achieved in every position, depending solely on the sincerity and intensity of one's faith, both Pietisms, the Christian as well as the Buddhist, discourage mobility—or innovation—of any kind: one has to stay put where one was placed. In fact, staying put compliantly and ungrudgingly bearing every sort of misfortune demonstrates one's obedience to the will of God, thus faith, and constitutes active piety, unfailingly rewarded with *certitudo salutis*. All this is very different from the goal-directed, activist, adventurous spirit of Puritan Calvinism (whose experimental approach to predestination implies constant risk-taking) with its single-minded concern for the ever-renewed success.

A "Romantic" Apology for Commerce: Follow Thy Heart

If Suzuki Shosan's Zen Buddhism stands for English Calvinism—the source of the Protestant ethic—for Yamamoto, as well as for some other scholars, including the American sociologist Robert Bellah, the teaching of Ishida Baigan, *Sekimon Shingaku,* articulated in the early eighteenth century, represents the functional equivalent of the texts of the seventeenth-century religious moralists, such as Baxter and Bunyan, and Benjamin Franklin—that is, the Protestant ethic itself. Unlike Suzuki, Ishida, though of originally samurai stock, was born into a farmer's household and was as a child apprenticed to a merchant in Kyoto. Whether or not his employer cared for profit, he made none, being unable as a result even to provide for the boy the customary semiannual change of clothes, which, along with room and board, constituted the apprentice's pay. When Ishida, at the age of sixteen, visited his parents, he was wearing the same garb in which he had left home at the age of eleven. This sartorial deprivation did not affect the youth's sense of loyalty: he was supposed to—and did—treat his employer as his father. He never complained about his hardships and duly returned to his apprentice responsibilities when the vacation was over, but his parents believed the arrangement was not working out as expected and terminated it. Several years later Ishida joined another Kyoto business, working for a dry goods merchant. The times were tough: the prosperous Genroku period was over and a long-term decline set in. Without prospects of promotion (which, in better times, would have been automatic), Ishida became depressed. His concerned employer suggested that he let off some steam in a brothel. He obeyed, but concluded that the improvement in his condition was not worth his employer's money and turned to reading instead. He read voraciously, was never without a book according to tradition, reading even while attending to a customer or doing other work around the shop. It is not surprising that, with such clerks, his master was not one of Tokugawa Japan's success stories.

The books Ishida read belonged to the genre of *kanazoshi*—"popular science" literature of the times, ranging from guides to the tea ceremony or flower arrangement to lectures on Confucianism and Buddhism. Among others, Ishida came across the work of Suzuki Shosan. He became a disciple of another Zen philosopher, Oguri Ryoun, who died in 1729, when Ishida was just about to reach the age of retirement—forty-five—and, as a token of particular regard, left him his library, which signified his choice as a successor. Ishida left dry goods and opened a private school.

In distinction to the samurai Suzuki, Ishida was a merchant and was personally exposed to the scorn which society heaped on members of his class. His work, therefore, unlike that of Suzuki, was in fact an apology for commerce: he consciously attempted to save the profession from opprobrium. "People accuse only the merchants of being greedy and unprincipled, caring only for profit," he lamented. "People resent their activities and would like to curtail them. Why are merchants singled out?" The question was rhetorical; Ishida's apology implied an explanation, and it was clear that he held merchants themselves partly responsible for the prevailing social attitude in their regard. While this attitude was unjust, merchants' conduct could stand improvement, and it was their reformation in the first place, ahead of the reformation of society, that Ishida considered his mission. "Though I may be wandering about the town ringing a bell that no one can hear," he declared, "I must try to show them the Way."

His teaching, elaborated in a 1739 work, *Tohi Mondo* (Town and Country: Questions and Answers), was in many respects similar to Suzuki's. He, too, defined commerce as a proper "calling" (which corresponded to the Lutheran, rather than Puritan, idea of "calling" in the sense of divine appointment, irrespective of its compatibility with one's natural inclinations), essential to the social order and in keeping with the country's law, therefore exculpating the merchants from the accusation of peculiar self-interestedness. The merchant was not much different from the samurai, the artisan, or the farmer, he argued:

If there were no trade, the buyer would have nothing to buy and the seller could not sell. If it were thus, the merchants would have no livelihood and would become farmers and artisans. If the merchants all became farmers and artisans, there would be no one to circulate wealth and all the people would suffer. The samurai, farmers, artisans, and merchants are all of assistance in governing the empire. If the four classes were lacking, there would be no assistance. The governing of the four classes is the role of the ruler. Assisting the ruler is the role of the four classes. The samurai is the retainer *(shin)* who has rank from old. The farmer is the retainer of the countryside. The merchant and artisan are retainers of the town. To assist the ruler, as retainers, is the Way of the retainer. The trade of the merchants assists the empire. The payment of the price is the stipend *(roku)* of the artisan. Giving the harvest to the farmer is like the stipend of the samurai. Without the output of all the classes of the empire, how could it stand? The profit of the merchant too is a stipend permitted by the empire. To call this, which is only the profit of your own trade, greedy and immoral is to hate the merchants and wish for their destruction. Why hate and despise only the merchants? As for your saying not to give a profit for trade, if one pays and deducts the profit it will destroy the laws of the empire. As business is ordered from above, profit is received. Thus the profit of the merchant is like a permitted stipend . . . As for the Way of the samurai also, if he does not receive a stipend, he is not fit for service. If one calls receiving a stipend from one's lord "greedy" and "immoral," then from Confucius and Mencius on down there is not a man who knows the Way. What sort of thing is it to say, leaving samurai, farmers, and artisans aside, that the merchants' receiving a stipend is "greed" and that they cannot know the Way?[7]

Ishida's philosophy, however, as Yamamoto rightly points out, was of a deistic rather than—like Suzuki's—theistic variety and represented a step in the direction of the secularization of Buddhist ethics. To Suzuki's trinity of the Moon, the Heart, and the Great Healing King, which were the three aspects of the Buddha, Ishida opposed the three manifestations of "Goodness": Heaven, True Nature, and Medicine. Goodness was the principle of the cosmic order evident in all things; Heaven corresponded to its reflection in nature; True Nature, to the ideal human nature; and Medicine was what men had to use in case of deviation from the latter. The focus, as befit a system of ethics, was on human nature. To make Ishida's vision clearer, one of his disciples, Teshima Toan, substituted for his original term—True Nature—the concept of "true heart," *honshin*. The fact that this is what the teaching was about was captured in the name of Ishida's school, *Shingaku*—"The Study of the Heart."

"True heart," according to Ishida, was the basis of honesty and faith, and the foundation of the moral order. To have faith meant to believe in one's true heart, while to obey its commands meant being honest; honesty, in turn, was the essence of morality. "What I mean by honesty," Ishida explained, "is to follow the dictates of your compassion [emotion?] . . . Compassion as taught by revered sages is the true Heart, and it cannot be acquired by thinking or studying. It is a natural gift under the rule of Heaven." Honesty thus was sincerity and spontaneity, not devotion to objective truth. Commenting on Ishida's philosophy, Yamamoto notes that "at times [honesty] required lying to others, but Japanese find no contradiction there." He seems to consider this a peculiarity of the national character. But the Japanese are not the only ones who would lie to others with easy conscience, for they are not the only ones to define honesty as being true to one's own heart. The idea was embraced wholeheartedly by the German Romantics (Herder, for instance, writing, on one occasion, "Everyone's actions should arise utterly from the self, according to its innermost character; to be true to oneself: this is the whole of morality"), who also glorified spontaneous emotion and disparaged thinking and learning.

In pure form "true heart" existed only in a newborn baby, incapable of anything but breathing on his own, and willing nothing at all, for even this action was reflective rather than intentional. This led Ishida to define the newborn as the sage, the ideal human being, the epitome of *honshin* (and so the expression of the cosmic principle of Goodness). This conception closely resembles the German Romantic notion of *Wesenwille*—the "natural will," or what Marx called the "species-being." The "natural will" is the original human will, constitutive of the true community. It is opposed to the essentially destructive "rational will" (the *Kürwille*), which lies behind intentional, especially self-seeking, actions of individuals and represents the individual's self-assertion (against the community) or alienation. The Romantics, incidentally, also regarded children (though perhaps not newborn infants in particular) as quintessential embodiments of *Wesenwille:* the little tykes were, in the words of Goethe's Werther, "so unspoiled [by civilization], so whole."

Ishida was realist enough, however, to recognize that if grown-up men were as pure and natural—as honest—as babies, they would be as perfectly infantile, and society could not exist. As he was primarily interested in the constitution of the moral order, he felt compelled to extricate himself from this logical quagmire, and the solution he came up with brought him even closer to the Romantics. It consisted in the postulate "form embodies Heart," which could be interpreted as "to each his own *Wesenwille*." "We are part of creation," Ishida articulated in *Tohi Mondo.* "All things are born of Heaven. Could any Heart exist apart from things? Things themselves are

Heart . . . The form of a thing immediately reveals its Heart. Mosquito larvae in water do not sting humans. Once they become mosquitoes, however, they sting. Form determines Heart. Fauna are totally innocent. Their behavior is consistent with their form. All follow the laws of nature. The sage knows the laws." Buddhist in form, in its content (or Heart) the idea was identical to Herder's proposition in the context of the articulation of the master notions of totality and individuality that "the perfection of a thing is its reality" (though this identity made Ishida's idea untrue: at the very least the Heart was not unique to the form). More generally, it appeared to imply a kind of materialism, which Marx expressed in his classic and morally noncommittal axiom "Being determines consciousness." Indeed, the reasoning of the Tokugawa merchant had much in common with the deductions of the great critic of capitalism. Man, claimed Ishida, is what he does: one was defined by the manner in which one procured one's food—namely, labor. Man was *Homo faber*. To acknowledge, and willingly comply to, one's destiny was to know the Way (Marx declared that this was the essence of freedom). Such recognition of necessity, according to Ishida, put one in harmony with the Heart (one's innermost nature—Marx's "species-being") as well as the cosmic order, at the same time contributing to the maintenance of the social, moral, order, which was a part of it.

The Way (like freedom) was the same for everyone, but the destiny or necessity, the recognition of which revealed it, was not. One's "true heart" reflected the specificity of the labor one performed, one's profession: Ishida's was the Hegelian notion of "individuality." One's innermost nature, in other words—as in Marxism—was defined by one's class: *honshin* was "class consciousness." So long as one acted in accordance with it, one was an honest, moral person, and could not be rightfully accused of being self-interested.

It was, however, essential to obey the Heart, and follow the Way, as an end in itself, not as a means to some other, personal goal: there was to be no element of "rational will" in the thoughts of the virtuous. In the case of the merchants, whose salvation he particularly took to heart, Ishida therefore insisted on honesty and sincere concern for the good of the customer in business dealings. Profits were just so long as they were side effects of such concern. There is an enormous difference between this insistence on honesty as the mark of disinterested earnestness in the discharge of one's duty and Benjamin Franklin's instrumental maxim that "honesty is the best policy." The fact that the selfless dedication which Ishida recommended might in some cases actually lead to profits (his own case proved that it might not) is beside the point. *Shingaku* consciously strove to orient economic actors away from profits, insisting that the process itself was ascetic exercise and that *certitudo salutis* was to be found in it.

Similarly, the teaching's emphasis on frugality could have no effect comparable to that of the "this-worldly asceticism" which Weber discerned in the Protestant ethic. Of course, self-denial was an element of ascetic practice, but this practice was an end in itself rather than a means to continuous business success, achieved through ever-increasing investment. Ishida advised his readers to cut their profits each time they reduced their consumption costs; the ideal was to get from one's customers only as much as one needed for subsistence while providing them with service that was one's responsibility. Growth, very clearly, was not a consideration that entered Ishida's mind. Frugality was conceived as a moral discipline, an obligation essential for the maintenance of the social order because a central element in it, and shared by all classes of society; it was not an economic virtue per se. "I emphasize frugality," explained Ishida, "simply because with it everyone can go back to the honesty he or she had at birth." And

> if frugality is practiced with conviction, the household—and the nation [country]—will be in good order. Peace will reign throughout the land. Is this not the most fundamental ethic? Frugality is, after all, a means of moral training that helps people put their houses in order . . . [T]he most important concern for everyone, from emperor on down to commoner, is to attend to his moral cultivation. In moral training, should it matter whether one is warrior, farmer, artisan, or merchant? What is the subject of moral training? It is none other than the Heart.[8]

The conviction, the zeal with which one practiced virtue, was of far greater importance than any of the by definition unintended consequences of such practice or the extent of its actual effect on one's lifestyle. The proposition "It is the thought that counts" was, clearly, most congenial to the spirit of *Shingaku*. The discipline of self-denial it advocated indeed encouraged saving and could lead to the accumulation of capital—though only among non-merchants, for merchants were urged to cut their profits to the subsistence minimum. It was certain, however, to leave such capital idle and economically unproductive.

Of course, not all Tokugawa merchants found *Shingaku* convincing; in fact, few of them did. The teaching became quite popular after Ishida's death, but perhaps most of its followers were samurai. Samurai had an obvious interest in finding frugality meaningful and ennobling, thus making virtue out of what for so many of them was a necessity. The merchants, in distinction, especially successful merchants, seemed to be willing to take the risk of decreasing their chances of achieving the state of grace in the next life if it meant enjoying the comforts of gracious living in this one. They were bothered by the contemptuous attitude of the upper classes toward them and resented the lowly position assigned to commerce in their culture. But they found cunning and ostentatious display of wealth more therapeutic than honesty and self-denial. Not only was success the best revenge (this rule applied in Tokugawa Japan as well as in any other society), but in addition, cunning—in the sense of shrewdness, rather than deviousness—in business dealings allowed them to amass riches, and riches allowed them to leave the base world of commerce by becoming or, if not, taking on the airs of and posing as samurai. That such illicit change of identity was a very common occurrence is evident from the jeremiads of contemporary samurai moralists, such as Ogyu Sorai, known for their dislike of the trading class, as well as from the exhortations of ex-clerks in the *Shingaku* school, beginning with Ishida Baigan. On the whole, the Tokugawa merchants were a rational lot—sturdy economic men to gladden the heart of the most demanding theorist, who strove to maximize pleasure and minimize pain with the means that were available to them, and, untroubled by otherworldly desires, cared little for the sophistry of the philosophers, with which the latter tried to quench theirs. They worked hard, reaped their profits, lived frugally and saved; when they became rich enough, they stopped working and invested in status symbols. This made them a less interesting group for a historian than most others.

Exceptions

But in this exceptionally uninteresting group there were some remarkable exceptions. These were the merchants single-mindedly oriented to the increase of their family fortunes. They also were rational actors, but theirs was a rationality different from that of their self-interested brethren; and while they practiced asceticism, their motivation had little in common with *Shingaku*. The most prominent among the merchant families of this kind were those of Sumitomo and Mitsui. The founder of the Sumitomo commercial dynasty died three years before that of the Mitsui house was born, in 1652. His name was Masatomo, and in 1630 he opened a medicine and book shop in Kyoto, which was the beginning of the Sumitomo enterprises of today—alongside Mitsui, one of the largest *keiretsu*, or corporate groupings, in contemporary Japan—at about the same time laying down certain rules to be followed by members of his "household," which included both family members and employees. These rules, in which some see a precocious example of corporate philosophy typical of modern Japanese management, were simple and straightforward. "As in business," Masatomo advised,

likewise in all other things, exercise prudence in all respects.

1. Do not purchase an article offered below the prevailing market price, whatever it is, without knowing its origin. Regard such an article as stolen.

2. Do not give even one night's lodging to anyone, or accept in custody a property of another, not even a (simple) braided hat.
3. Do not act as a guarantor for another.
4. Do not sell anything on credit.
5. Do not become angry and speak intemperately and harshly, whatever the other party says. Whatever the subject, speak patiently, over and over again.

This was practical advice, of the kind one would find somewhat later in Savary's *Parfait Négociant,* but, like all such advice, it presupposed a broader philosophical framework. At first glance, this philosophy strikes one as almost sinister in its perfect, calculating rationality. The general rule is prudence above all: nothing should be done on the spur of the moment, nothing inspired by emotion. This rule translates into what appears to be a recommendation of pure egoism; one is cautioned against ever helping another, expressing sympathy, or having any fellow feeling at all. But this is not pure egoism, because the rules are addressed not to an individual but to a "household," a group of people related by mutual obligations as much as blood, and the strict limits placed on the members' relations to others—those outside the group—serve to emphasize its exclusive demand on their loyalty.

We must look elsewhere for the articulation of the philosophical premises on which Sumitomo's rules are based. One place to do so may be the ideas of Mitsui Takahira Hachiroemon, the founder of the most prominent commercial family of the Tokugawa period and possibly the greatest one of the handful that survived the Meiji Restoration and into our day. The foundations of the Mitsui family fortune were laid in 1683, when Takahira Hachiroemon established a "cash only" department store (in implicit agreement with Sumitomo's rule to sell nothing on credit). Rather than buy status, he left this fortune intact to his heir, warning him against such customary but unproductive use of capital—which, he believed, was one's to develop, but not to spend, as it was a family trust—and, apparently trusting little in the powers of intuition, added to the money a set of rules to be followed in business and a book, *Some Observations on Merchants (Chonin Koken Roku),* of his personal business philosophy.

Like *Shingaku* (which did not become popular until much later), Mitsui used the concept of "calling," but, it seems, only in the mundane sense of one's actual job and job-related responsibilities. (He probably knew it in the Calvinist or even modern secular sense of an inner aptitude and passion.) He did not believe that religion had any business mixing with business and even-handedly rejected Shinto, Buddhism, and Confucianism as irrelevant. His view of the proper attitude to customers was pragmatic, and he did not make honesty a fetish. The businessman was there to take care not of anyone's needs, but only those of his business, and was to respond to opportunities which presented themselves. This did not imply that taking advantage of one's customers was to be encouraged: Mitsui might agree that "honesty is the best policy." What he advocated was careful planning and policies which would bring long-term benefits; he dismissed speculation as a business strategy. Moreover, the use of one's business in one's personal interests, that is, the use that would be rational in the usual sense of the word as interpreted by economists, was equally rejected. One was to have no interest, in fact, but that of one's family, which, it appears, first and foremost meant the interest in the preservation of its good name or prestige. In promoting it, business acumen and forethought were of far greater importance than hard work and enthusiasm: Mitsui clearly preferred a cool head to a warm heart.

He also preferred content to form, all this advice being thrown together pell-mell, every sentence thoughtful but none elegantly expressed. If he enjoyed the process of writing, it did not show. But it was the result, not the process, that mattered, and Mitsui achieved that result, as we know. These were some of the instructions and thoughts he left to his successors:

> In Edo, some merchants take on building for the government or other speculative ventures and make a fortune at one mighty bound, but they only go to prove the common adage that "he who lives by the river drowns by the river." It is like a gambler's money, which, as everyone knows, finally is lost in the way in which it was made . . . In business bargaining, you should concentrate on following the opportunities of the times, and in observing the times, you should consider how they might change. If you do not give some thought to your business from time to time . . . your shop's business finally will fall off, and you will lose a good patrimony. Never waste your attention on matters which have nothing to do with your work. Merchants who ape samurai or think that Shinto, Confucianism, or Buddhism will preserve their inner hearts will find that they will only ruin their houses if they become too deeply engrossed in them . . . Remember that it is the family business which must not be neglected for a moment.

He had numerous stories about successful merchants, who thought they worked in order to live and squandered their wealth on luxuries and finery for their wives, starting "the decline of their families":

> Isoda, Iguchi, Ishiuchi, Horiuchi, Higuchi, the Fushimiya crowd, Kurata and Kinokuniya, merchants famous in Edo . . . have all crashed or, if still carrying on, might as well not be. Merchants always have been

in the position of having no fixed stipends, and so they grow rich through having a time of good fortune. However much wealth their children inherit, it is as though they were, thanks to their fathers' labors, holding in trust for a time money which is common currency. Thus, when the trustees fail to look after it properly, it immediately is dispersed.

He pointed to merchants' sons who, left in control of a large fortune, believe they no longer have reason to work and think nothing of enlarging it further:

They give themselves over to idleness, their behavior naturally deteriorates. Having no regard for reputation or appearances, they lose their sense of responsibility toward other people and carry on just as they please . . . They are not acting as human beings should . . . [A]bove all, human beings should seek their sustenance by working at their callings . . . To make one's own house prosperous, to nurture one's family property, to have a long life and to pass away with a clear conscience would be to be a living Buddha . . . Is it not true that things turn out as they do because people do not think highly of their calling or family?

Then there was a most edifying analogy between merchants and political rulers. What may be a virtue in the eyes of other people, Mitsui instructed his son, need not be such for the merchants:

When merchants become sages, their houses decline. In ruling the empire, there are the Way of the King and the Way of the Tyrant. Kings dislike fighting. They act not in their own interest but in the interests of the empire and the people. That is the Way of the King. Tyrants assume an outward appearance of benevolence but act in the interests of their families and themselves. That is the Way of the Tyrant. Realize that, from olden times, famous and clever generals have followed the Way of the Tyrant. To depart from benevolence for even a day is to be inhuman. On the other hand, however, to go too far in charity without counting the cost is stupid. You should understand this in a way which brings benefits in trade.

This, clearly, was neither cynicism nor pure economic rationality. It was an ethical system, but its ideas of right and wrong, of moral and immoral conduct differed from the prevalent notions of the time and such expressions of traditional morality as *Shingaku*. In some respects it was an ethic quite similar to the Protestant ethic, for, like the latter, it encouraged incessant labor and pursuit of profit. The conduct of men guided by this ethic was, therefore, irrational in the same sense in which all economic activity oriented to growth (rather than the satisfaction of man's needs) as an end in itself is irrational.

There was, of course, a logic to it—though one different both from the "Big Logic" (in the words of Eamonn Fingleton) of the modern Japanese economy and the "Small Logic" of American capitalism. To follow the metaphor, it was a "Medium Logic"—with the good of the family and its name (i.e., family spanning generations) as the purpose of economic effort, rather than the nation or the individual. Within this logical and moral framework, concrete business practices were very similar to those of the modern economy: they were perfectly rational in the sense of "instrumental rationality," making use of information, forecasting, and long-term planning to the full extent possible in the conditions of Tokugawa Japan.[9]

Though Mitsui dismissed Shinto, Confucianism, and Buddhism, his ethical system drew upon these religious traditions, the ideal of filial piety, core to all three, and related notions of ancestor worship obviously serving as its ultimate values. These traditional values made it possible for Mitsui (and a few people like him) to make sense of and justify—to rationalize in the Freudian sense of the word—a passion, a love for making money for its own sake. This love had nothing in common with greed. It was not love for money as such or for what money could buy, but an enjoyment of the creative process in business—a peculiar inner drive perhaps, but one not very different from any other, be it artistic inspiration or addiction to gambling. In fact, it made profit making an addiction, a sort of workaholism, which fulfilled an expressive rather than instrumental need. (Thus, despite himself, Mitsui followed *Shingaku*, for he was indeed obeying his heart.) But for an upstanding person, brought up in the morally saturated atmosphere of early Tokugawa Japan, which was unfamiliar with ethical neutrality, to give free rein to one's compulsions might imply an unacceptable lack of self-control. Such a person would sooner repress his natural inclinations than act immorally. Obversely, he would be predisposed to interpret them as moral. It was his passion which prompted Mitsui to reconstruct the traditional ethical system with the family as the pivot of the moral universe. This shift of emphasis, in turn, allowed him to indulge his passion and feel right doing so.

In Japan of the seventeenth and eighteenth centuries, people like Mitsui were very few: the society was unsympathetic to merchants who would be such by choice, even if not bound to commerce by the accident of birth, and left them entirely to their own devices. The system of ethics which he bequeathed to his heir corresponded in its implications to the "peculiar Occidental rationalism" behind the modern economy and was, like the latter, conducive to economic growth. But it could not gain the backing of Tokugawa society, which alone would make it a social ethic, capable of reorienting social action. It remained a personal, or family, ethic, and the scope of its influence was strictly limited. Later, the existence of this ethic, which could be easily adapted to the new, national, value system that had emerged for unrelated reasons, assured the smooth transition of Mitsui enterprises into the post-Restoration economy and allowed the corporation to assume and maintain in this economy a prominent place. It obviously contributed to Japan's development, but it played no role in the origins of its modernization.

Staatswirtschaft, Japanese-Style

In general, the culture of Tokugawa Japan favored a stationary economy. The ideal was stability (it was considered essential for the maintenance of the social order), and therefore there was no desire for growth. Moreover, in the framework of the prevailing conception of social reality, the expansion of the economy in its entirety did not appear possible. Throughout the Tokugawa period this conception had not essentially changed. Even thinkers well disposed to economic activity (a small minority), who recognized its importance in the functioning of a society and thought of wealth as a positive value, shared in it. One such thinker, Sato Nobuhiro, would write in the 1830s:

> Recently in every region the rich have come to be admired, and poor people are despised. This is a great mistake, for poor people cause little harm to a country, but where there are rich people the troubles of the country are increased. The reason for this is that, when rich farmers prosper, they absorb the property of several dozen families. As a result, troubles and distress push the small farmers deeper into poverty, and they sell their fields and houses to the big farmers and become beggars and vagrants.

This argument (not very different in tenor from the pronouncements of some late twentieth-century American moral economists) presupposed the view of the economy as one stationary pie, a zero-sum game in which whatever was gained by some was necessarily lost by others. Thus it was best to keep things as they were.

This consideration led Sato to the view of economics as the central aspect of police, or government administration, and inspired him to formulate a political-economic theory remarkably similar to the one developed by the German Cameralists. *"Keizai,"* he declared firmly, "means managing the country, developing its products, enriching [it] and rescuing all its people from suffering. Thus the person who rules the country must be able to carry out his important task without relaxing his vigilance even for a single day. If this administration of *keizai* is neglected, the country will inevitably become weakened, and both rulers and people will lack the necessities of life." In accordance with this definition, Sato articulated his economic doctrine in his *Confidential Memorandum on Government (Suito Hiroku),* in which he proposed, among other things, to divide the traditional four classes into eight occupational groups: farmers, forestry workers, miners, artisans, merchants, unskilled workers, mariners, and fishermen. Such occupational differentiation presumably would allow a more efficient allocation of tasks among the labor force, but it did not imply any relaxation in the rigidity of social relations. There was to be no mixing between the eight groups, and six separate ministries (modeled on an ancient Chinese example) were to keep them under close supervision. Four of these ministries, in addition to the ones of the army and navy, were specifically concerned with economic management and included the Ministry of Basic Affairs, or Agriculture; the Ministry of Development, or Forestry and Mining; the Ministry of Manufacturing; and the Ministry of Circulation.

The economy Sato envisioned was the ideal *Staatswirtschaft:* regulated, planned, and state-run for the sake of the citizens' happiness, understood as the preservation of the social order. The government was responsible for the optimal use of the collective resources, and to make it possible was expected to cultivate them employing the very methods Cameralists advocated in Germany: improvement of agricultural and mining techniques, land reclamation, cadastral surveys, and the like. It was to oversee the distribution of goods and to take care of the people's education. Like kindred spirits in Germany a century earlier, Sato, who devoted an entire chapter to the latter subject, emphasized moral education above all, and, as in Germany, education was to provide an avenue (the only legitimate avenue) of upward mobility for the especially talented, who would be selected and groomed for an office in the bureaucracy. Apparently, the investment in research and development (including that of human capital) would in a not so distant future enable the economy to function at the optimal level allowed by its resources, which, however abundant, were not perceived as unlimited: nothing indicates that Sato at any point imagined the possibility of sustained growth. But he considered the resources of Japan to be abundant indeed. And it might have been this optimistic assessment that explained his enthusiasm for foreign trade, unusual for the period. Writing at a time when the presence of Western ships in Japan's territorial waters had become quite common and awareness—if not knowledge—of the West was relatively widespread, Sato was conscious of the contribution economic strength made to the political power of Western countries and specifically the importance of commerce in promoting economic strength. He thought that Japan was in many respects similar to the greatest Western power of the time and was well positioned to follow its example and become even more powerful. "In the present-day world," he argued,

the country of England is militarily powerful and prosperous, and has control over a very large number of foreign nations [countries], so that the world trembles at its might. This country may be likened to Japan, but the English homelands lie between fifty degrees and sixty degrees north, and as a northern land it has a cold climate and its natural products are excelled by our Japanese products. However, because they have successfully sent ships out across the oceans and have traded with the nations of the world they have now become a most powerful and thriving people. Thus we can know that shipping and trade are important tasks for [Japan].

The superiority of Japan's natural resources and geographic location inspired in Sato certain hopes for his country that went far beyond the realization of its full economic potential. Giving free rein to imagination, he fantasized:

If we consider the whole nation [country] of Japan in terms of the geography of all other nations, we can see that it lies between thirty degrees and forty-five degrees north of the equator. The climate is mild, the soil is fertile and many natural products grow in great abundance. Our country faces the ocean on four sides and is unsurpassed among the nations for its ease of sea transport to neighboring countries. Its people are also superior to those of other nations in their courage, and its natural conditions are outstanding amongst all nations, and the country is perfectly equipped to control and advance nature and the world. By virtue of its superiority, this Land of the Gods, through conquering insignificant barbarians, would be able without difficulty to unite the world and dominate all the nations.[10]

The Shinto allusion notwithstanding, this aspiration, reflective as it was of the virtues of the country and its people, rather than the ruler, was strikingly modern (the reference to "insignificant barbarians," for instance, being reminiscent of Marx's comments on "unhistorical nations"). The nationalists who were to assume the guardianship of Japan within two decades of Sato's death recognized in him a kindred spirit and allowed his ideas to exert influence beyond the confines of the moribund society for which they were intended.

Nationalism and the Transformation of the Economy

Owing to the circumstances of its emergence, Japanese nationalism from the outset was focused on the economy and developed as economic nationalism in the first place. It was the awesome economic might of the West that was behind its military strength and that allowed Western powers to force themselves on Japan against its will. The vexing unequal treaties, agreed to under duress, which sanctioned the infringement on the country's sovereignty, made it evident that the political and the economic power of a nation were tightly linked and that its very independence was imperiled if not backed by a strong economy. It was also plainly demonstrated—the Western treatment of Japan allowing one no illusion—that economic frailty was taken as a sign of cultural backwardness, of being "uncivilized," and practically invited disrespect, and that national dignity, or prestige, was inseparable from economic performance. Nationalism, therefore, which was the greatest gift the West (to be sure, unwittingly) gave to Japan, and which, because of the indigenous conditions, was so gratefully and eagerly accepted, was brought to Japan in an economic package. This made economic achievement a central value in the Japanese national consciousness and an element of paramount importance for the way the Japanese—not just the so-called bourgeoisie, allegedly moved by economic interests under all circumstances, but everyone in whom national sentiment was alive—from now on would see themselves. National well-being, national freedom, national dignity: everything was interpreted in economic terms or at least had an important economic aspect. National existence itself, it appears, was unimaginable apart from economic considerations. In this, Japanese national consciousness resembled the American and, along with the latter, differed from all the other cases discussed in this book. Not even in English nationalism did the economy occupy such a prominent place. One momentous consequence of this economistic emphasis was the definition of the competition for national prestige (inherent in nationalism as such) as economic competition above all.

According to Sugiyama Chuhei, a professor of economics at the Tokyo Economics University, it is easy "to recognize that economic thought [of the new Japan] was inseparably fused with nationalism." His 1994 book, *Origins of Economic Thought in Modern Japan,* he thinks, could be as well titled "Enlightenment and Nationalism." The nationalist perspective radically transformed the image of economic reality. It was now viewed as essentially dynamic, capable of expansion and contraction but not of standing still. ("When there is no progress," wrote Fukuzawa Yukichi, "there is only digression, and when there is no digression, there is always progress. There is no such thing as stillness, which neither moves nor withdraws.") Modernity, to which Japanese referred as "civilization"—*bummei* (it was short for "modern Western civilization")—was identified with expansion, and constant growth, or progress, now easily conceivable, became the ideal. The new, economistic and dynamic, vision was reflected in the nationalist slogans of the Meiji era—*fukoku kyohei* (rich nation/strong army), *bummei kaika* (civilization and enlightenment), *shokusan kogyo* (encouragement of industries), and *oitsuke oikose* (catch up and pass)—and was ferociously competitive. How ferociously was reflected in the term for competition itself, *kyoso,* which could be literally translated as "running and fighting." It was a neologism, invented by Fukuzawa, for pre-national Japanese lacked a word for this new aspect of reality. It is significant that Fukuzawa chose not to look for an equivalent of the European euphemisms, which stressed the friendly nature or civility of the in fact brutal process (the English *competition,* like the French/German *concurrence/Konkurrenz,* and even the Russian *sorevnovanie,* means "striving—or running—together").

The economism of the Japanese national consciousness and the corresponding change in ideas about economic reality was apparent immediately. The view of the economy as fundamental became a matter of consensus within years. Shortly after the Meiji Restoration, Wakayama Norikazu, who happened to be Japan's first protectionist, announced that "according to Mr. Carey [that is, Henry Carey, the famous American protectionist], it is not force but wealth that brings about victory over enemies," thus both demonstrating his familiarity with Western economic thought and declaring his preference for the American brand. An official in the Restoration government, the Choshu samurai Inoue Shozo, was to play an important role in the establishment of the woolen industry in Japan. His interest in it was kindled on a visit to Germany, where he was sent in 1870 to study military science. Having changed his subject, he wrote in justification:

> I want to make our country the equal of Europe and America. Today even the small children of Japan talk of enriching the country and strengthening the military, and they call for civilization and enlightenment. But there are few men who really have attempted to discover the tree that has brought forth the fruit of civilization and enlightenment in Europe . . . After having read something of world history and geography in my search for the source of wealth, the military power, the civilization, and the enlightenment of present-day Western nations, I realized that the source must lie in technology, industry, commerce, and foreign trade. In order to apply these precepts and make the nation rich and strong, we must first of all instruct the people about industry. Then we can manufacture a variety of goods and export them, import those articles we lack, and accumulate wealth from abroad.[11]

"Civilization and Enlightenment" and the "Spirit of Independence"

Okubo Toshimichi shared these views. He also went to Europe, and, according to his biographer, returned with an "inferiority complex," provoked by the spectacle of Western economic achievement. The following year (in

1874) he urged the government to adopt a forceful policy of encouraging domestic industries: "Generally speaking, the strength or weakness of a country is dependent on the wealth or poverty of its people, and the people's wealth or poverty derives from the amount of available products. The diligence of the people is a major factor in determining the amount of products available, but in the final analysis, it can all be traced to the guidance and encouragement given by the government and its officials."

Though similar in its *Staatswirtschaftliche* trust in the managerial powers of the bureaucracy to the ideas of Tokugawa economists such as Sato and even Dazai, Okubo's argument had more in common with the contemporary German *Nationalökonomie*. The affinity was profound. "This is the most opportune time," Okubo argued,

> for the government and its officials to adopt a protective policy which has as its goal the enhancement of people's livelihood . . . Anyone who is responsible for a nation or its people must give careful consideration to the matters which can enhance the livelihood of the people, including the benefits to be gained from industrial production and the convenience derived from maritime and land transportation. He must set up a system suitable to the country's natural features and convention, taking into account the characteristics and intelligence of its people. Once that system is established it must be made the pivot of the country's administrative policies. Those industries which are already developed must be preserved, and those which are not in existence must be brought into being.

But it was England that Okubo recommended to the emperor, to whom his memorandum was addressed, as the example to be followed. Apparently oblivious of Adam Smith, he admired the wisdom of England's mercantilist policies, in particular the Navigation Acts:

> [The English] government and its officials have considered it the greatest fulfillment of their duties when they have made full use of their natural advantages, and have brought about maximum [industrial] development. In this endeavor the Queen and her subjects have put together their ingenuity and created an unprecedented maritime law in order to monopolize the maritime transportation of the world and to enhance her national industries . . . In this way her industries have prospered, and there has always been a surplus after providing the necessary commodities to her people . . . It is true that time, location, natural features and convention are not the same for each country, and one must not always be dazzled by the accomplishments of England and seek to imitate her

ability . . . However, our topography and natural conditions show similarities to those of England. What differs most is the feebleness in the temperament of our people. It is the responsibility of those who are in administrative positions in the government to guide and importune those who are weak in spirit to work diligently in the industries and to endure them. Your subject respectfully recommends that a clear-cut plan be established to find the natural advantages we enjoy, to measure the amount by which production can be increased, and to determine the priorities under which industries can be encouraged. It is further recommended that the characteristics of our people and the degree of their intelligence may be taken into account in establishing legislation aimed at encouraging development of industries. Let there be not a person who is derelict in performing his work. Let there not be a fear of anyone unable to have his occupation. If these goals can be attained the people can reach a position of adequate wealth. If the people are adequately wealthy, it follows naturally that the country will become strong and wealthy . . . If so, it will not be difficult for us to compete effectively with major powers.

Dissatisfaction with the people—a form of nationalistic self-criticism—is a common attitude in a nationalism provoked, or spurred on, by a sense of inferiority, and Okubo was not the only Meiji nationalist who found fault with the temperament of the Japanese. Fukuzawa was similarly concerned, expressing his anxiety in, among other works, an influential book, *Encouragement of Learning (Gakumon no Susume)*, which also appeared in 1874. Fukuzawa's opinions are of particular importance in this context because of the extraordinary range of his contributions to the Japanese economy (they included the creation of much of the vocabulary for the economic discourse; the penning of several popular books and countless articles on economic subjects; the introduction of classical economics to Japan through these works and numerous translations; the foundation of the first joint-stock company, Maruya & Co.; and, perhaps most important, the establishment of the Keio School, later University, focusing on economics, where he taught the first course in Japan on the subject) and the vast influence his multifaceted activities allowed him to exert. Like Okubo, Fukuzawa was oppressed by the evidence of Western economic superiority and the sorry sight Japan presented by comparison. "We are no more than crawling worms," he was to write in *Minkan Keizairoku* (Popular Political Economy, 1880), "whereas they have wings to fly with. How can we rival them with their industry and trade, with their forces and tactics? We have never been in greater danger." Unlike Okubo, however, Fukuzawa did not believe that the flourishing condition of the West could be attributed solely or even chiefly to wise management by government officials. It was the national sentiment of the people, he postulated, that brought it about. If this sentiment did not exist, the government could at best create a veneer of modernity, and the competition with the West—the very purpose of modernization—would be impossible. In Japan, in Fukuzawa's opinion, unfortunately, the national sentiment was very weak.

Essentially, for Fukuzawa, modernity meant the modern Western economy. Usually he referred to it as "civilization," using the word as a gerund, to denote the (largely economic) process of modernization rather than a cultural system. (Such usage led a later observer to conclude that "to Fukuzawa, or rather to the Japan of his day, the capitalist society of the West seemed to represent civilization itself.") According to him, things that "pertain[ed] to our civilization" included "commercial activities, legal debates, building of industries, agricultural works, as well as translation of books and publication of newspapers." The most important element in a civilization—the factor that was behind and animated the process of modernization—was the motivation of the people. "We cannot speak of any country's civilization," Fukuzawa argued,

by simply observing its outward manifestations. Schools, industries, the army, and the navy are all manifestations of a civilization. To formulate these outward manifestations is not too difficult. They can even be purchased by money. However, there is something which is invisible. It cannot be seen, cannot be heard, cannot be sold or bought, and cannot be lent or borrowed. When it is found in the midst of the citizens of a country, its power will be strongly felt, and without it, schools or any other outward manifestations of a civilization will be rendered useless. It can indeed be called the spirit of a civilization and it is its greatest and most important factor. What is it then? It is the spirit of independence among . men!

It would be a mistake to think that Fukuzawa—who did more than any other single individual to introduce to Japan the ideas of English Liberalism and Utilitarianism—was referring to individual liberty à la John Stuart Mill: such an interpretation, in fact, never entered his mind. His notion of "spirit of independence" was more akin to the German idea of freedom as national independence. As he explained elsewhere: "Independence does not mean merely non-reliance on others for the subsistence of life. It is more than an inner duty. There is an outer duty just as well, that is to say, the duty to exert oneself together with the rest of one's nation to make certain that one's country retains the state of freedom and independence." It was this—national—spirit of independence that was sadly lacking among the men of Japan. "In recent years," Fukuzawa complained,

> our government has been undertaking the task of building schools, encouraging industries, and establishing the army and the navy. These have provided a new outlook, which is essential to the outward manifestations of a civilized nation. Among the people, however, there is no one who is willing to assert our independence from foreign countries or willing to compete against foreigners in order to get ahead of them . . . In the final analysis, unless the people possess a spirit of independence, the outward manifestations of a civilization will become useless appendages to our country.

The responsibility for this distressing deficiency lay with the government. It was duty-bound to treat the people as a nation, that is, "to let everyone, regardless of the difference in rank or wealth or knowledge, think of one's country as one's own interest and do one's duty to one's own nation." The people had to be treated as equal, and equality had to be placed in the service of the national interest. Instead, in the past, the masses were not allowed the dignity of the national consciousness by their rulers because the latter lacked it themselves, while now the government was denying the people a sense of true membership in the nation because of its misguided patriotic zeal.

> The reasons for the lack of independent spirit may be found in our political system. For a thousand years, all powers resided in the government. It intervened in all sorts of things, including armament, literature, industry and commerce, as well as in the most minute of human activities. People blindly followed directions given by the government. The country was treated as a private preserve of the government, and its people as mere parasites. [Thus] they looked upon their country merely as their temporary dwelling, to which they had no sense of commitment. There was no opportunity of expressing their devotion, and the entire country was in a state of drift.
>
> How about today? There is something even worse than what I have just described . . . In the present-day Japan, the outward manifestations of civilization seem to move forward, but the spirit of its people, the very essence of our civilization, definitely moves backward . . . In the olden days . . . if people subjected themselves to the government, that was so because they lacked power to oppose it. It was not submission willingly entered into, but it was fear that led them into taking a posture of subjugation. Today the government possesses not only the power but also craftiness. It can deal with matters in a most timely fashion. Scarcely ten

years have passed since the Meiji Restoration, and we already have our school system and military completely overhauled. Railways and communication lines are constructed. Houses are built with cement, and iron bridges span over our rivers. In the decisiveness of its action, and in the beauty of its accomplishment, the government is to be commended. But the schools, military, railways, communication lines, houses built of cement, and iron bridges belong to the government. What credit is there to the people of this country? . . .

People feared the government of the olden days as if it were the devil incarnate. They worship the present-day government as if it were god . . . The government now has schools and railways. Must we not be proud of them as symbols of our civilized status? However, they are now regarded as ones established by the grace of the government, and people are inculcated with a feeling of dependence on the government . . . How can our people compete against foreign nations in building our own civilization? This is the reason why I say, unless we can instill in our people the spirit of independence, the outward manifestations of our civilization become merely its vain appendages.

So far, it followed, Japan was a pretend nation and modern society. It could not become real in either respect so long as its people lacked the "spirit of independence." This spirit, which was the spirit of civilization, thus the spirit of modern economy, was, underneath all these awkward new phrases, the national sentiment, the spirit of nationalism. And national spirit, in turn, was equated with competitiveness. Fukuzawa's conclusion was unequivocal:

From the above, we can infer that it is the task of private citizens to make a civilization meaningful, and it is the duty of the government to protect that civilization. A civilization belongs to its people who compete and fight for it and remain jealous and proud of it. If there is a significant accomplishment, the people applaud it with joy and fear only if the other nations go a step further than they have been able to proceed. Anything pertaining to a civilization is a means to enhance the vitality of its people. There is nothing in it that does not assist the independence of that nation. This is a condition that is exactly the opposite of what we find in our country.

Notably, Fukuzawa's emphasis on motivation, apart from being sociologically sound, reflected certain strictly economic considerations, pertaining to the dynamic nature of modern economy, capable of constant expansion. As early as 1875, in *Bunmeiron no Gairyaku* (An Outline of a Theory of Civilization), he analyzed the reasons for the disadvantageous position of Japan in trade with the modern countries, writing: "In economy the wealth of a nation depends far less on the surplus of natural produce than on the skill of human arts . . . [I]n trade between a manufacturing country and a growing [agricultural] country, the former makes use of *unlimited human power* and the latter the limited produce of land . . . This is exactly the case with the trade between Japan and foreign countries. We can only be on the losing side." These considerations, in turn, led to the increased emphasis on industry and trade as less dependent on limited natural resources than agriculture and allowing greater play to the expansive competitive spirit.

National sentiment was to express itself in competitiveness only in relations with foreigners, however. Fukuzawa's principle, formulated in a later work, *Jiji Shogen* (Current Affairs Briefly Discussed, 1881), was: "Peace inside and competition outside." In *Encouragement of Learning* he explained: though modernity implied economic liberty in the sense of free choice of occupation, this liberty had a particular collective purpose and was not to be abused in the pursuit of selfish ends. "It is up to us all to choose whatever profession we wish," he wrote. "All varieties of profession are open to free competition, but the competition is not for the sake of fighting against each other. On the contrary, the object of fighting, if not with one's sword but with one's intellect, is to confront foreigners. If we win in this intellectual fighting, then we shall improve the station of our country. If we lose, then we shall see it degraded."[12] This was consistent with his notion of the "spirit of independence," the conviction that the only rightful object of human striving was "[for people] to extend the right of their own nation, to enrich their own nation, to improve the wisdom and virtue of their own nation, and to glorify the honor of their own nation," and his ambivalence in regard to the value of self-interest, which never allowed him to accept fully the English economic liberalism he did so much to popularize.

War by Other Means

Yet another significant difference existed between Fukuzawa and his English teachers. Business for Fukuzawa was a warlike preoccupation, not a peaceful art. Rather than increase the understanding between (international) partners, the goal of engaging in commerce, broadly defined, was to increase the nation's power, extend its dominion, and triumph over the enemy. Economic competition was war by other means, an excellent substitute for war (but a substitute nevertheless) when war was impossible, the second-best means in realizing the nation's purpose. The enemy was the West. National spirit was a fighting spirit; it was hostile to the West by definition. At the same time it was not anti-Western in the usual sense of rejecting the Western model.

Fukuzawa insisted on the necessity to combine the hostility to the West with the admiration of Western "civilization." He was convinced that "the way to achieve greatness for our country" was to read "as many Western books as possible," and wished "to spread Western civilization rapidly in the country by reading, lecturing, or translating the books of the West, and thereby to increase the national strength." Yet, while discussing the bellicose intentions of Japan vis-à-vis its Asian neighbors, he declared: "We should be provident enough not to allow the Westerners to profit by the disputes between us Asians . . . Our powerful enemy now is in fact the Western countries. They are not an enemy in the military sense, but in the trading sense." The latter stipulation in no sense mitigated his animosity. At stake was the dignity, thus independence of the nation. Japan could not "achieve real independence unless it [stood] on an equal footing with Western countries," and "every step backward on our part necessarily [meant] a step forward on their part." This was a fair attitude, given that Western motives were hardly friendly—downright exploitative in fact. "It goes without saying," articulated Fukuzawa in the 1869 prospectus for Maruya & Co., "that the principal aim of foreigners in meeting our compatriots . . . is nothing other than making a profit out of the latter by means of trade. Therefore it would be contrary to our duty as Japanese if we stood idly by while foreigners kept the right of business and trade in this country in their own hands." Several years later he bitterly complained: "How do the foreigners live who reside in our trading ports? From where does their subsistence come? Riding beautiful horses, sitting in fabulous coaches, they spend millions or else take back the money to their home countries. That money . . . is nothing less than the outcome of the sweat of our brow. What else do we have to lament?"

Westerners were robbing the country; fighting them was no more than self-defense. But this fit Fukuzawa's general idea of world politics and international relations. In an 1874 "Prospectus of the School of Commerce," he characterized his time as "the age of battles by means of business" (in which "waging the war of trade against foreign countries" was "the public duty of merchants") and the following year, in his *Theory of Civilization*, no less, asserted, "The world as it presently stands may aptly be called the world of business and war," business being a kind of war. International relations meant constant struggle for financial and military preeminence, or power. In military conflicts, he said, they entailed "fighting with weapons," and during peacetime (so-called) "fighting with industry and trade."

It must be understood that economic competition was only a means in the struggle whose ends were political supremacy and international position, and that Fukuzawa's militarism went far deeper than his belligerent rhetoric (the immense importance of which should not be underestimated in any case). Japan, he believed, had "to fight against foreigners in trade and industry, in science and arts, and in all other spheres." War "with weapons" was by no means excluded; in fact, circumstances permitting, it was the preferred method. The difference between him and "the exclusionists of the old days," who rallied to the battle cry of *joi*—"expel the barbarians"—"lies only in that," he said, "postponing a military battle with foreigners to some future day, at the moment we merely want to fight a trade battle."[13] And indeed, as his changing opinions in regard to Japan's military involvement in China and Korea demonstrated, Fukuzawa's theoretical and rhetorical warmongering could be easily transformed into practical support for war, when the outcome looked promising.[14]

An observer of Japan's economic scene in the first post-Restoration decades would be wrong not to pay most careful attention to the utterances of "the influential Fukuzawa Yukichi," even were he alone in conflating military struggle and economic competition and regarding business as the best substitute for war: his, after all, was the most audible voice during this formative period. But Fukuzawa was not alone. Military imagery was characteristic of the spokesmen and leaders of Meiji economy in general and to a significant extent defined their thinking. The editorial in the first issue of *Tokai New Economic Review (Tokai Keizai Shimpo)*, associated with Mitsubishi, for instance, repeated Fukuzawa's comparison of the *joi* movement of 1860s with the businessmen of its own day, in 1880, almost verbatim:

> A decade or so ago we had in Japan those who advocated expelling the barbarians . . . Today, a decade later, there is still no disagreement . . . There is only one difference: those who wished to expel the barbarians of earlier times viewed the foreigners as animals and attempted to drive them away by force of arms alone. By contrast, we today view the foreigner as basically a man and an equal, and we attempt to fight him with economics—to do battle by means of trade.

Business school graduates going overseas to study Western economies were likened to "troops secretly reconnoitering the enemy positions"; prominent business leaders were "brilliant general[s] of commercial wars." Everywhere there was talk of "battle[s] of enterprise," of "the competition of foreign trade, which is peacetime war." As with Fukuzawa, the line between peacetime and actual war was not too carefully drawn: it was the line where the two merged rather than separated, enthusiasm for military victory adding zest to business activity and economic success kindling bellicose fantasies. It is of great significance that the "Japanese Industrial Revolution" is believed to have originated in the years immediately following the Sino-Japanese War.[15]

As in Germany, where similar inspiration was drawn from beating the French, it took a triumph on the battlefield to give Japan a final push to its Rostowian takeoff (both countries, one might say, had to make a killing before they broke the bank).

The New Business Class: Nation before Profits

The militarism and economism of the nascent but vigorous Meiji nationalism combined to produce a new class of entrepreneurs and a new, effective economic ethic. "The Tokugawa merchant class," as Byron Marshall points out, "gained remarkably little in power and prestige from the Restoration." In fact it gained not at all, for nationalism implied no shift in the attitudes toward it. Merchants (the truly great ones, Mitsui and Sumitomo, who opened their purses to the new regime, excluded) were despised as ever, perhaps more than ever. The samurai intellectuals, or men with samurai upbringing, who had led the revolution and now governed Japan, considered them a social dead weight—too stupid and morally deficient to participate, much less assume the leadership, in the process of modernization. "Sometimes we hear of a few who are reputed for cleverness, but they turn out to be men who rejoice in corruption, engage in speculation or monopolize profits," wrote two young government officials, Shibusawa Eiichi and Inoue Kaoru, in 1873, explaining why they felt compelled to leave their posts and become businessmen. "The worst of them ruin their business and lose their property by cheating, by fraud, and committing all sorts of dishonesty. Now it would be easier to expect a cock to crow in its eggshell than to see those [types] advance at once to the stage of civilization."

The fundamental lack of moral fiber that characterized this sector of the population expressed itself in particular in the constant concern for personal gain, which made the merchants unsusceptible to the noble feeling of patriotism. For this reason, Fukuzawa, in an 1886 article in his newspaper *Jiji Shimpo,* issued a call to "replace the old shopkeepers." In a similar vein, an 1895 editorial in *Toyo Keizai Shimpo* (The Oriental Economist) stated: "Examine the speech, appearance, attitudes, character, spirit, and habits of our merchants—all are shameful. They fight over trivial sums and short-range profits, and their only ambition is to feed themselves and their families. They know nothing of sovereign or country, nor are they concerned with the prosperity of the people or the good of society." In the periodical *Jitsugyo no Nihon* (Business Japan) at about the same time, a Confucian, Nishimura Shigeki, bemoaned the conduct of export-import merchants whose selfish immorality led them into "conspiracies with foreigners" and was certain to cost Japan's commerce its reputation. "Once their hearts have been seduced by the chance of immediate profit," he predicted, "Japanese merchants will no longer be trusted abroad." The man of commerce, being "the one who undertakes trade directly with the foreigner," Nishimura insisted, "must be a man of the highest quality and courage, completely different in character from the feudal merchant." Thus "feudal," or Tokugawa, merchants were crowded out, and a new group of businessmen, animated by the competitive spirit of nationalism, arose in their place for the specific purpose of leading Japan into economic modernity.

The new business class differed from the old one in background, in habits of thought and action, even in name. Its members were referred to as *jitsugyoka*, "men of affairs," not to be confused with the humble *suchonin*, or "shopkeepers." According to some sources, between 1868 and 1895, 46 percent—almost half—of the leading *jitsugyoka* came from samurai families, while 72 percent had a samurai education. The noble extraction of the "men of affairs," believed to be reflected in their character, was emphasized, *The Oriental Economist* enthusing in 1895:

> At present, samurai and those who have received a samurai education are in charge of, and make up the staff in, Mitsui, Mitsubishi, the Yusen Kaisha, the Bank of Japan, the [Yokohama] Specie Bank, the railroad companies, and the other large firms. Look at the leaders of our business world—are not the majority of them samurai who have been educated in *bushido*? Although a few are not, an examination of their conduct and character will reveal that none of them are without respect for honor, integrity, and fidelity to their word. Respect for these things is the true meaning of *bushido*.

This extraction, and the ethic which accompanied it, undoubtedly helped to elevate the status of the businessman and the prestige of the class as a whole, effecting what Joseph Ben-David, in a different context, called "role-hybridization."[16] Apparently, however, it did not raise this status as much as businessmen themselves believed desirable for altruistic as much as selfish reasons, and for a long time they continued to complain about it.

Shibusawa Eiichi was among their number. Yamamoto cites an adage about him: "Who was the man who built Japan's business community? If there is anyone who could say 'It is I,' this could only be Shibusawa Eiichi." Called "the patron-saint of Japanese enterprise," he took part in forming some five hundred companies, including the Dai-Ichi Kangyo Bank, one of the richest in the world today, served as president in a hundred of them, and lived, in the words of Fukuzawa, "two lives in one body." Born into a wealthy peasant family in 1840, he started his career as the follower of the *sonno-joi* movement and, filled with xenophobic zeal, in 1863 seriously intended to personally overthrow the *bakufu*. Persuaded by a relative to abandon this heroic but rash plan, he moved to Kyoto and was befriended by a retainer of the Hitotsubashi family, later entering its service as a samurai overseeing the domain finances. The *daimyo* of Hitotsubashi happened to be a "related" *daimyo*, and in 1866 Hitotsubashi Yoshinobu, whom Shibusawa served, became shogun. Shibusawa considered becoming a *ronin*, but precisely at the time Napoleon III invited Japan to participate in the Paris World Exposition, and Shibusawa was dispatched to France as a member of the official mission.

Not being, in the words of Yamamoto Shichihei, "one to cling blindly to unrealistic, outmoded 'principles,'" he approached his meeting with the West with an open mind. Aboard the French ship he already tried bread, butter, and coffee and found them "all very good," which, as one can well imagine, was indeed testimony to an adventurous and unprejudiced character. France impressed him immensely. "Western civilization is far more advanced than I had expected," he wrote in a letter, "everything I see amazes me. Maybe this is the direction in which the world is moving, a trend beyond our imagination." And

I had heard about the material wealth of Western civilization, and its wonderful machines, but when I saw these for myself I was even more surprised. The accounts that people do not pick up what has fallen in the streets and that pedestrians courteously make way for each other, are true. And the efficient means for using fire and water is wondrous; the underground of Paris is riddled with passages for fire and water! The fire is called "gas," which burns without any visible source. The flame is very clear, lighting up the night with a brightness like midday. The water in Paris bubbles forth in fountains situated all over the city, and people sprinkle the roads to keep the dust down. Citizens live in seven- or eight-story houses, usually made of stone, and more splendid than the residences of daymio or those of nobles in Japan. European ladies are like beautiful jewels, their skin fair as snow. Even an ordinary woman would cause the famed beauties Xi-shi and Yang-gui-fei of ancient China to hide in shame. I have come to this belief after comparing European women to a few Japanese and Chinese ladies I saw at the Exhibition.

His view of the national interest (and foreign policy) changed accordingly. "What we must do," he declared, "is form closer ties with foreign countries and absorb their strengths for the benefit of Japan. This may seem to contradict what I've said in the past, but it is unthinkable for Japan to remain isolated."[17]

In his 1937 autobiography Shibusawa recalled the state of opinion regarding business after the Meiji Restoration and his reasons for leaving the government for it:

> The business world around 1873, the year when I resigned my post at the Ministry of Finance, was one filled with inertia. That condition is hard to imagine from the standards we hold for the business world today. There was a tradition of respecting officials and despising common people. All talented men looked to government services as the ultimate goal of their lives, and ordinary students followed the examples set by them. There was practically no one who was interested in business . . . It was said that the Meiji Restoration was to bring about equality among the four classes of people. In practice, however, those who engaged in commerce and industry were regarded as plain townspeople as before, and were despised and had to remain subservient to government officials. I knew conditions such as these should not be allowed to persist. A rigid class structure should not be tolerated. We should be able to treat each other with respect and make no differentiation between government officials and townspeople. This was essential to our national welfare, as we looked forward to strengthening the country which required wealth to back it up. We needed commerce and industry to attain the goal of becoming a rich nation. Unworthy as I was, I thought of engaging in commerce and industry to help promote the prosperity of our nation. I might not have talent to become a good politician, but I was confident that I could make a difference in the fields of commerce and industry.

Traditional business methods, such as characterized the plain and despised townspeople, would not, in Shibusawa's opinion, advance the goals of the new Japan. It was necessary to follow the example of Western countries. "I felt," Shibusawa wrote in his autobiography, "that to engage in an individually managed shop would be going against the tide of the times, and it was necessary for small business firms to join their forces together. In other words, they have to incorporate, and I decided to devote my energy to this endeavor. As to the laws governing incorporation, I thought about them while studying in France." His French experiences naturally led Shibusawa to stress the importance of management.

> In organizing a company, the most important factor one ought to consider is to obtain the services of the right person to oversee its operation. In the early years of Meiji, the government also encouraged incorporation of companies and organized commercial firms and development companies. The government actively participated in these companies'

affairs and saw to it that their various needs were met fully. However, most of these companies failed because their management was poor. To state it simply, the government failed to have the right men as their managers.

He also endeavored to raise the prestige of businesspeople, and, rather than trying to convince the public of the national importance of business activities (the public, it appears, was already convinced that they were important, but this failed to change the contemptuous attitude toward those who engaged in them), he advised that a businessman rise to the moral level of and behave like a gentleman—that is, like a samurai brought up on Confucian values—and set the first example of such behavior by "studying and practicing the teachings of the *Analects of Confucius*." He felt that these teachings, "first enunciated more than twenty-four hundred years ago," were wonderfully consistent with the spirit of modern economy and provided "the ultimate in practical ethics for all of us to follow in our daily living." For instance, they contained such sage words as: "Wealth and respect are what men desire, but unless a right way is followed, they cannot be obtained; poverty and lowly position are what men despise, but unless a right way is found, one cannot leave that status once reaching it." This "shows very clearly," commented Shibusawa, "how a businessman must act in this world."

It is safe to assume that not all of the Meiji entrepreneurs went as far in their desire to impart nobility to business as Shibusawa and studied the *Analects*. All of them, however, subscribed to the properly modernized samurai ethic of *bushido*—the way of the warrior. The essence of this ethic was selfless, in fact self-sacrificial, devotion to duty which was now interpreted as service to the nation. The "men of affairs" scorned material wealth for their own sake, and personal profit, they claimed, rarely if ever entered their thoughts. It was not self-interest, however enlightened, much less greed that moved them. Some of them still found money repulsive. The son of Matsukata Masayoshi, the finance minister responsible for the privatization of Japan's industries in the 1880s, Matsukata Kojiro, who in 1896 became the president of the Kawasaki Shipbuilding Company, recalled that when he first went to Osaka to enter business, "the continual bowing and scraping" made him uncomfortable. "I felt as if I was bowing to [money]," he wrote. "Although I could endure it, I felt it was inhuman to bow down to money." Instead, they were moved by nationalism, and while money did not attract them, the necessity to endure things which they found unpleasant apparently did, for the ability to endure proved how ardent and sincere their love of country was. A friend of Matsukata Kojiro, also a "man of affairs" of samurai stock with whom he shared his sense of unease about business life, found such delicate sensibility unworthy of a patriot. "His face flushed and he cried angrily, 'What! Is it not for the sake of the State that we undertake these enterprises? What is painful about bowing for the State?'"[18]

From the point of view of economic rationality, the men responsible for Japan's economic takeoff were raving lunatics. But they were men of exceptional civic courage and determination. By and large, they went against the prevailing attitudes which remained suspicious of business well into the twentieth century, changing only slowly, and they did so by choice.[19] Time and again they were attacked by their peers for making this choice and had to defend it. Their paramount consideration, they would respond invariably, was the interest of the nation. In the late 1870s such a disagreement arose between two friends, Hara Rokuro and Kaneko Kentaro, who studied together in the United States, where they made a pledge to "devote themselves to the good of the State." Upon his return Hara decided to become a banker. Kaneko, who stayed behind a while longer, found his friend in flagrante delicto and could hardly believe his eyes: "There was Hara the samurai wholly engrossed in making money at the bank." Later he wrote, indignantly, "If all he had intended was to become a mere shopkeeper or take up a trade, there was no need for him to have gone abroad to study." Hara, however, insisted that he was doing his duty as pledged. "After all," he reasoned, "from the point of view of rendering service to the country, is there really any difference . . . between taking part in the government as an official and enriching the nation by devoting one's efforts to business?" Kaneko was to reach a high rank as a government expert on financial matters; one hopes he was persuaded.

In the business press, entrepreneurs were commended for "putting themselves last and the public first" and having service to the nation "as their single guiding thought." For their own part, they constantly referred to their selfless concern for the general good. "It has never been my hope to spend my life in idleness and pleasure," an Osaka businessman, Godai Tomoatsu, replied in the early 1880s when asked whether the fortune he had already accumulated ever made him consider retirement. "The wealth of the Empire must never be considered a private thing . . . My hopes will be fulfilled when the happiness of the nation is secured, even if I have failed, and this wealth has disappeared." The CEO of the copper works of Sumitomo (whose clearheaded selfishness in the seventeenth century made it such an exception among its self-abnegating contemporaries) insisted that "this great wealth does not belong to the House [of Sumitomo] alone; in larger terms, this wealth belongs to the country." Such "professions of altruism and patriotic devotion" appeared with what, to an American, seems "tedious regularity," leading Byron Marshall, the author of the very informative *Nationalism and Capitalism in Prewar Japan*, to conclude—against evident disbelief and the assumption that businessmen, as rational actors, should "utilize" ideas to "justify" and "further" the development of their business—that it is "quite probable that Japanese business leaders were sincere in their claims about their patriotic motives."

Though rarely, there lurked behind these claims another motive which indeed was rendered legitimate by them. This was the love of business as an art form, for its own sake, which, in the seventeenth century, animated the founder of Mitsui. In 1908 an industrialist, Suzuki Tosaburo, implicitly confessed to a similar passion, saying in regard to a recent setback:

> I am a businessman. I have no interest in dabbling in books or paintings, or in taking my ease in luxurious mansions. My calling [*honbun*] is to run businesses. Even if I lose the capital I have invested in a business, I do not regret it in the slightest, since business [as a whole] has gained. Even if my work should prove unsuccessful, the research will be inherited by those who come after . . . Once an enterprise has been launched, society ultimately benefits.

This indifference to personal gain was reflected in the singular Meiji notions of business success and failure. The bottom line had surprisingly little significance in their assessment. "To go bankrupt because of moral principle," ruled Shibusawa, "is not to fail, even though it is to go bankrupt. To become rich without moral principle is not to succeed, even though it is to become rich." Success was measured in prestige and respect of one's peers rather than money, and prestige in business was bestowed upon those who did their utmost to advance the national economy. Matsukata Kojiro could write admiringly of a fellow entrepreneur: "Even if his enterprise had proven unprofitable, it would still have benefited the nation," for profitability was a secondary consideration at most. Nevertheless, since Meiji businessmen were generally remarkably successful in the sense we attribute to the word, they made profits, and profits had a place, however minor, in this moral scheme. As in early modern Europe (for instance, Savary) and in *Shingaku,* they were believed to be a function of righteous conduct, in this case selfless dedication to the nation's economic interest. Patriotism and devotion to duty, similarly to Savary's godliness or Ishida Baigan's *honshin,* was a necessary condition for profits, and, like Ishida, though in marked contrast to his Western counterpart (who considered godliness thoroughly insufficient as a method of moneymaking), Meiji "men of affairs" appeared to regard profits as an unintended but necessary consequence of the right attitude. In 1874 the newspaper *Yubin Hochi* published the following report regarding the House of Mitsui:

The House of Mitsui has rendered distinguished service to the Emperor since the time of the Restoration, as is well known among the Japanese people. From the first year of Meiji (1868) until the present, it has made financial assistance available to the government ministries and prefectural governments, and has recently accrued profits on its investments. Today it shared these profits among its employees from the first to thirteenth ranks . . . Reports are that the Mitsui profits are the result of its great efforts in works in the public interest with little concern for private gain.

(The reporter was not entirely certain that these profits reflected nothing else, however, for he added—as an afterthought, but nevertheless—"and the family is managed so well that people are quick to cooperate with it.")

Morimura Ichizaemon, who made a name for himself in foreign trade and was made a baron for his success in cultivating trade relations with the United States, in particular, was convinced that a business he started as a young man failed because he had the wrong motivation. Rather than being moved by the "spirit of [patriotic] dedication", he "had merely a shallow desire to make a profit." As a result, he said, "I was negligent in a number of matters." This early experience made him realize that success was reserved only for such a man "who has in his breast the great concept of 'nation,' and has resolved never to quit until he drops." Since, for a samurai especially, dedication to the nation implied such resolve, Morimura never had the chance to test the two theoretically distinct variables separately. Shibusawa used the example of the sustained growth of his own assets to explain the mechanism which connected patriotism to profits:

Business could not be carried on without adequate funds. Hence I bought shares or stocks and received salaries. In this way my fortune increased; but that was not my real purpose . . . I buy shares with one hundred thousand yen. Times being favorable, they may increase to two hundred thousand or three hundred thousand yen. My object does not lie in the increase of wealth, but from the nature of the business it so happens. That is all. Never for a moment did I aim at my own profit.

Later, his son, Shibusawa Hideo, summarized his father's simple philosophy in this regard: "Money is the by-product of work. Just as grime collects on a machine long in operation, so work produces an accumulation of money."

Apparently the principle "ask not what your economy can do for you but what you can do for your economy" by which Meiji entrepreneurs, who belonged to the first generations of Japanese nationalists, lived, survived far past the Meiji period. Günther Stein, worried about Japan's relentless economic advancement in 1935, described a typical small businessman of that day, "a short, modest little workman," but a technical genius, who began as a hired hand and then opened his own workshop.

He still remains the modest little workman. He works from dawn to dusk in his gear-cutting plant which is the largest in Japan and probably one of the finest in the world. He wears a worker's blue overall; his hands are oily. His three brothers are now working with him. Together they own their factory worth 3,000,000 yen, and employing 260 workers.

The chief and his three brothers do not take more pay from the factory than the highest-paid employee's 5.30 yen per day (6s. 6d. at present rates). The engineers just reach the average wage of the staff at 3.50 yen (4s. 3d.) per day. The profits, which are considerable, are invariably reinvested in the factory. The owner has never taken a day off, does not drink, smoke, or gamble, but is happy and enthusiastic. From a special fund he allows himself an expense account not exceeding 200 yen (£12) per month, but he hardly ever touches it except for the education of his children. He says that he considers the factory not as his property but as a trust which he is called upon to administer. Money, he says, does not interest him, it does not even give him an incentive. What he really wants is to cut beautiful gears, and as far as he has any other interests, he is proud of being an example for many Japanese industrialists who, in his view, spend far too much, live far too well and work far too little!"[20]

One Heart Band

In the late 1970s, Yamamoto Shichihei had very similar stories to tell about the generation of businessmen who were responsible for the reconstruction of the Japanese economy and "stood behind Japan's phenomenal economic growth" after World War II. They were still driven by the spirit of service to the community and devotion to duty, thought little of profit, trusting, as before, that the right attitude would not leave them penniless, and preferred "spiritual rewards" (including status, which remained largely independent of wealth) to money. Of course, the national patriotic rhetoric of yore was attenuated, and one's loyalty appeared to be transferred from the nation to the company in which one worked. But national sentiment remained very much alive; if it was voiced less strenuously and less often than before, this was (apart from the U.S.-imposed restraint), probably, mostly because it matured and became unproblematic. The company did not replace the nation as the ultimate object of civic loyalty; it was the intermediary link between the individual and the nation, the central channel through which the participant in the economy did his duty by it and expressed his national loyalty. In Japan's socio-cognitive structure, it played a part similar to the one in Germany Hegel assigned to class, and it assumed that role long before the defeat in World War II made patriotic effusions politically incorrect. "The spirit of loyalty and love of country," maintained the president of the semigovernmental Kogyo Bank, Soeda Juichi, in 1908, "is by no means limited to the relationship between the sovereign and subject." It is expressed, he said, in an equal measure in the relations of employers and employees of business enterprise.[21]

Like the national army of Yamagata Aritomo, which elevated peasant conscripts to the dignity of samurai, allowing them to share in the duty of the military nobility, the business firm welcomed workers, also for the most part recruited from the peasantry, to become soldiers in the "war of enterprise" and share in the honor of the "men of affairs." Alongside schools and the army, and, during the Meiji years, probably to a greater extent than either, companies contributed to the moral education of the populace, making people patriots and imparting to them the ethic of selfless dedication and contempt for personal gain. The nationalized and modernized warrior ethic— *bushido*—was transmitted to the employees via the company rules, which even today are often recited at the beginning of each working day. Sometimes these rules were supplemented with a company song, sung in unison, whose hymnal cadences and vague but pervasive didacticism helped each worker to feel a part of a larger moral entity. The song of a factory that in the 1930s produced bicycles, mainly for the domestic market, was called the "Song of the One Heart Band" ("Isshindan"), which undoubtedly drove the point still closer. Literally translated, its words had no connection whatsoever to its humble product and no identifiable reference in the real world, but were calculated to foster the sense of unity and self-confidence among the singers, as well as lift their spirits generally. They went as follows:

> However overwhelmingly the waves of the world's seas
> May come on like flooding tides,
> The One Heart Band'll rouse itself, sturdy as a rock,
> With its iron arms of co-operation.
> With the power of righteousness and the heart of chivalry,
> Helping the weak and holding the strong,
> Our brotherhood goes even through fire and water,
> Of which the One Heart Band is proud before the world.
> Looking forward to a Utopia of co-existence
> Where our noble ideal is attainable,

Lo! the One Heart Band'll shine forever
Gloriously with its glaring zeal.

The company rules were displayed, alongside the text of the song, in the factory office. The preamble read:

We, with a view to assisting national industrialization, shall try to develop social enterprises by the brotherhood organization of the working masses.

We, with a view to promoting the interests of the consumers at large, shall primarily aim at establishing a most rationalized system of producing and distributing bicycles.

We shall try fully to protect the interests of each member of our concern and secure him or her an appropriate means of living.

We, with a view of promoting the common interest of our factory, distributing stations and agents, shall try to realize the unification of the whole enterprise as one and the same heart and body.

Each member shall try intently to promote the interest of all members and shall never forget the demands of the whole body. No member shall do anything against the interest of the whole.

Then followed more specific work rules, stipulating, among other things, that apprentices would be supplied with free housing, health insurance, soap and twenty-five bath tickets a month, and that during work hours there was to be no playing with fire, smoking, loud singing, or gossiping. The fact that all workers under age twenty-one and unmarried workers above that age for the first four years on the job lived in the factory dormitories (providing company housing—and dormitories for young employees and those living away from their families—remains a common practice in Japan), that all of them took their meals there, that the working day was from 7 o'clock in the morning till 5 in the afternoon and, when business was good, from 6 to 9:30 P.M., probably facilitated the enforcement of these rules and greatly contributed to their internalization. The worker's wages to a certain extent, but more important his status, depended on it; each employee's "responsibility," "devotion," "kindness," and "common sense," as well as productivity, were evaluated monthly, with the score kept in the office index card file, and the best were awarded bronze and silver medals.[22]

From very early on the "men of affairs," who selflessly exerted themselves for the sake of the nation's economy, felt that they could count on their employees to selflessly exert themselves for the sake of their companies. This was what the "equality of obligations" (as the Japanese interpreted the major tenet of nationalism) implied. Sometimes it involved working longer hours, taking cuts in pay, and, under certain circumstances, losing one's job. In 1878 Mitsubishi's Iwasaki Yataro issued a set of bylaws which stipulated that, since Mitsubishi was a family business, the profits of the company rightfully belonged to, and the losses were rightfully sustained by, the president. But it was additionally ruled that "if the company prospers and receives a large amount of profit, there may be times when the monthly salary may be increased across the board. On the other hand, if the company's enterprise suffers and there is a certain loss, then the monthly salary may be reduced across the board and employment may be terminated." In 1876, when Mitsubishi was fighting the British Peninsula & Oriental Steam Navigation Company for the control of Japan's coastal trade, exactly such an exigency arose. To attract customers, the Japanese company cut its fares in half, with an obvious implication for earnings. Iwasaki asked his employees for cooperation. He argued, as Sir Walter Raleigh did some three centuries earlier, though perhaps without the latter's directness:

> Many people have expressed differing opinions concerning the principles to be followed and advantages to be obtained in engaging foreigners or Japanese in the task of coastal trade. Granted, we may permit a dissenting voice, which suggests that in principle both foreigners and Japanese must be permitted to engage in coastal trade, but once we look into the question of advantages, we know that coastal trade is too important a matter to be given over to the control of foreigners. If we allow the right of coastal navigation to fall into the hands of foreigners in peacetime, it means a loss of business and employment opportunities for our own people, and in wartime it means yielding the vital right of gathering information to foreigners. In fact, this is not too different from abandoning the rights of our country as an independent nation.

He then pledged "to do my utmost, and along with my 35 million compatriots, perform my duty as a citizen of this country. That is to recover the right of coastal trade in our hands and not to delegate that task to foreigners." He knew, he said, "that our responsibilities are even greater than the full weight of Mt. Fuji thrust upon our shoulders." Crafty foreigners made them heavier still:

> There have been many who wish to hinder our progress in fulfilling our obligations. However, we have been able to eliminate one of our worst enemies, the Pacific Mail Company of the United States, from contention by applying appropriate means available to us. Now another rival

has emerged. It is the Peninsula & Oriental Steam Navigation Company of Great Britain, which is setting up a new line between Yokohama and Shanghai and is attempting to claim its rights over the ports of Nagasaki, Kobe, and Yokohama. The P&O Company is backed by its massive capital, its large fleet of ships, and by its experiences of operating in Oriental countries. In competing against this giant, what methods can we employ?

Clearly, this was the time to forget about self-interest and make the requisite sacrifices for the sake of the nation. "There is no other alternative but to eliminate unnecessary positions and unnecessary expenditures," Iwasaki urged:

> By eliminating unnecessary personnel from the payroll, eliminating unnecessary expenditures, and engaging in hard and arduous tasks, we shall be able to solidify the foundation of our company. If there is a will, there is a way. Through our own efforts, we shall be able to repay the government for its protection and answer our nation for its confidence shown in us. Let us work together in discharging our obligations and let us not be ashamed of ourselves. Whether we succeed or fail, whether we can gain profit or sustain loss, we cannot anticipate at this time. Hopefully, all of you will join me in a singleness of heart to attain this cherished goal, forbearing and undaunted by setbacks, to restore to our own hands the right to our own coastal trade. If we succeed it will not only be an accomplishment for our company but also a glorious event for our Japanese Empire, which shall let its light shine to all four corners of the earth.

"We may succeed and we may fail," he concluded, "and it depends on your effort or lack of it. Do your utmost in this endeavor!"

Who could resist such an appeal, which called on one's noblest sentiments (taking for granted their existence) and flattered one's vanity? That in exchange it exacted material self-denial and perhaps the sacrifice of one's paycheck did not make its implicit offerings any less precious. Besides, such ultimate monetary sacrifice was demanded only in extreme need and in circumstances which surpassed in their gravity the presence of the P&O Company in Japan's coastal waters. In the end, Mitsubishi employees had to give up one third of their salaries, but few, it appears, if any, were discharged. In fact, Japanese companies preferred the policy of lifetime employment, reflecting, on the one hand, the considerable investment they had to make in the training and general education of their work force owing to the shortage of skilled labor in the early modern period, and, on the other, the tradition of familism (*kazoku shugi*) or affectionism (*onjo shugi*), which was to some extent carried over from the Tokugawa period and led employers to regard their employees as their own family or household. Tamura Masanori of the Shimano Spinning Mills, for instance, compared the business company to the household of a *daimyo*. "From ancient times," he said, "in our country there have been warm feelings [*onjo*] between employer and employee. It has been a relationship similar to that between the lord and his retainer. The lord treats the retainer just like one of his own children. The retainer, besides performing his duties in return for his sustenance, has every intention of giving up his life [for the lord] without regret if the occasion should arise."

This tradition of familism was behind the institution of extensive benefits programs, such as insurance and pension plans, and on-site services for employees, which became typical of Japan's companies within the first decades of its modernity and promoted the sense of community in them. The founder of the largest Japanese copper and silver mining company, Furukawa Ichibe, declared that building a mining business was "exactly like creating a colony. Since the mines are far back in the mountains, a new town or village must be built, with hospitals for public health, schools for education, relief measures for charity, and temples to encourage religious faith among the miners and employees . . . One must attend to all the things that human beings need in this world." Admittedly, this was a special case, but, as Marshall points out, it was quite characteristic, and the emergence of *zaibatsu*, or combinations of different businesses, each with its employee welfare programs, under the same holding company, necessarily contributed to the spread of this pattern, bringing the worker's entire world to revolve around the company.[23] Work was life for the entrepreneurs, and they made it life for their employees as well.

These arrangements, as well as the principle of promotion by seniority, which by the 1920s applied to manual workers as well as managers and promised everyone not only a secure but also a dignified future, made employees identify with their companies and see the professed interests of the entrepreneurs as their own. Since, for the entrepreneurs, the purpose of business was service to the nation, the work force was converted to nationalism. Undoubtedly, by and large, the workers did believe that by serving their companies they were serving the nation. They were assured of this incessantly. Company rules commanded them never to forget that the ultimate goal of work was "repaying the debt to the nation"; senior executives taught that to be successful one needed, above all, "determination to distinguish oneself through dedication to the future of the nation"; and so on and so forth. Moreover, the managers insisted that one's place in the business hierarchy was of no importance and attempted "to make those in the lower ranks conscious of how essential the connection is between their jobs and the progress of the enterprise as a whole." They also practiced what they preached, taking meals alongside production workers in factory cafeterias, like Asabuki Eiji or Dan Takuma of Mitsui, personally overseeing working conditions, making rounds of factory halls to check—and lift—the mood in them.

Did every executive show such concern for his employees? Was the concern shown always sincere? Were all the workers convinced, and did all of them dedicate themselves selflessly to the service of the nation via their respective companies? The answer to all these questions is: certainly not. Social systems are man-made and never perfect. But there is no question that the economic system constructed by Meiji nationalists made possible for most participants, entrepreneurs and wage laborers alike, a dignified and meaningful existence—a life centered on a common effort, where everyone belonged and was needed and appreciated. There were frictions between labor and management, but, on the whole, their relations in Japan, given the degree and the rapidity of its industrialization, were remarkably harmonious by comparison to other industrial powers. Judging by this record, which continues today, Japanese economic actors are indeed irrational, for they do value "spiritual rewards" disbursed by the system above material ones which it withholds.[24] They are indoctrinated, to be sure. But, secure in their sense of purpose and membership, they might also be sensible enough to recognize that what they have is just as good as working nine to five for higher wages and spending the rest of the day struggling with the meaninglessness of life (which, as we know, happens too).

The sense of participation in a collective enterprise was also reflected in the relations among entrepreneurs (specifically, their view of competition), and between the business community and the government. The latter from the beginning of the Meiji period was very interested in economic modernization and, during its early years, played the central role in the process, assuming the responsibilities of private entrepreneurs as well as management. Government officials were sent abroad to study Western industrial methods and import technology, and, upon their return, set up plants and ran them. Within a decade of the Restoration they established numerous modern factories, laid the foundations of the modern banking system, and began the construction of modern communications networks. From the start, however, the officials regarded the government's active involvement in the economy as temporary: they did what needed to be done, because, given the state of the economy they had inherited from the *bakufu*, "the very existence of the nation was in peril," yet "the people" possessed neither the right motivation nor the sufficient resources to do the job on its own and had, therefore, to be shown the way. The development of the economy, nevertheless, as numerous official speeches and decrees constantly stressed, was the people's, not the government's, responsibility. In a samurai nation, guided by *bushido,* everyone had his sacred duty and was expected to perform it. For this reason, nationalization was never considered, except by socialists, who were regarded (wrongly but inevitably) as unpatriotic: Japanese nationalism implied trust in individual initiative.

In the 1880s, owing, partly, to a financial crisis and the necessity to cut government spending, Finance Minister Matsukata Masayoshi decided on a policy of privatization and sold most of the government-owned enterprises, factories and mines, to private entrepreneurs. "The natural function of the government is chiefly to protect the public interest and guarantee peace to the community," he declared. "The government should never attempt to compete with the people in industry and commerce. It falls within the sphere of government to look after matters of education, armament, and the police, while matters concerning trade and industry fall outside its sphere." The state never withdrew from the economy completely and was always ready to put its mighty shoulder to the wheel; it continued to support industry and foreign trade, in particular, by means of protective taxation and sometimes direct subsidies, but its involvement never again reached the early Meiji level of actual management.[25]

For this there was neither justification nor need. Soon private entrepreneurs became full "partners and supporters of the State in the great patriotic drive for industrial expansion." For their own part, entrepreneurs considered active—though more or less limited (there were disagreements as to the optimal degree)—participation of government in the national economic effort both natural and necessary: it was, after all, a part of the nation and had powers other parts lacked. It was its authority to which business leaders appealed and its arbitration on which they relied in cases of conflicts in their midst. The prevailing opinion was that relations between Japanese businesses ought to be based on cooperation, the better to compete against the outside world; but sometimes the competitive spirit got the better of them and they tried to outdo one another.

A primary example of such internecine competition during the Meiji period was the "duel" between the two modern shipping companies, Mitsubishi Shipping Lines and the United Transportation Company (Kyodo Un'yu Kaisha), which drove both to the brink of bankruptcy. The business community, concerned about the damage to the national economy, decided to intervene and asked the government to restrain the opponents. The representative of Mitsubishi protested that it was not the government's business to regulate competition, but agreed that it was an evil, for "if it is left to the survival of the fittest, the inferior will certainly suffer a crushing defeat." On these grounds, and to eliminate the very possibility of competition between the two companies, he proposed a merger. Those arguing on behalf of the community countered that a little competition was not bad at all (and, therefore, there was no reason for a merger), but unrestrained competition which could harm the national economy should be regulated by the government; and, since protecting national interest was precisely the government's business, such regulation could by no means be considered "unwarranted interference." A little competition, it was believed, promoted "a spirit of independence in businessmen" and thus was "very essential to the development of business" and progress in general. It is unclear what "the spirit of independence" meant in this context, but if it had the meaning Fukuzawa attributed to it of national sentiment or spirit of competition against foreigners, this approval of competition at home might have had to do with the idea that it encouraged greater effort in everyone. The argument was not well articulated.

On the whole, Japanese entrepreneurs wished to keep domestic competition under control. Most accepted government regulation, and those who believed that the government had (or had to have) other concerns were prepared to control it themselves. This general attitude was behind the formation of characteristic cartels and trusts, or "combines" (*zaibatsu* and, after World War II, *keiretsu*), and numerous trade associations, whose function was to ensure smooth cooperation among member businesses. The government, when it did not initiate this process, encouraged it through legislation. The government and private companies which comprised the business community saw each other as allies, and more than that, as units in the same army; they were all "partners . . . in the great patriotic drive towards industrial expansion."[26]

Studying the Enemy's Language

One more subject must be considered before I conclude: the influence of Western economic ideas. Could the reorientation of economic action toward growth and the dramatically changed economic practice of the Meiji period be to any extent attributed to the importation of European and American economic science? The answer is no, it could not. And this is so despite the fact that Western economics profoundly affected business education and was wholly absorbed by academic economic thought in Japan.

The first school to teach economics in Japan, as was pointed out earlier, was Fukuzawa Yukichi's Keio Gijuku, which he had founded in 1858. At first and inevitably it was mainly a language school; but by 1867, it appears, Fukuzawa made economics a required subject (along with physics, chemistry, mathematics, philosophy, and history), introducing into the curriculum Francis Wayland's *Elements of Political Economy*. Economics also figured prominently in the curriculum of Japan's first—Tokyo Imperial—university, incorporated as such in 1877. It, too, developed on the foundations of a language school (Bansho Shirabesho, the Institute for the Study of Barbarian Writing), which operated from the mid-1850s, being formed specifically to prepare future government officials. Its first professor of economics was a Bostonian philosopher, Ernest Fenollosa, who eventually made a name for himself in the study of Japanese art and was instrumental in the creation of the exquisite collection of the Boston Museum of Fine Arts, as well as of the Freer Gallery in Washington, D.C. The economics course he taught introduced students to the heterogeneous ideas of American, British, and German economists, such as Roscher, List, J. S. Mill, Jevons, and Macleod, which, judging by the extant set of lecture notes taken by his listeners, made to them very little sense. The notes contain the following entry regarding Macleod, for instance: "Mr Macleod says Political Economy is the science of Exchange. He tries to find out some of universal which explain every thing. He speaks of exchangeable quantities . . . Law of Demand and Supply. Law of Cost of Production. Law of Utility. Law of Labor in things. There are many such assertions. But they are valueless and the real use of Pol. Econo. is to find out certain forces which are really acting actually."

The first business school was founded by Mori Arinori, the first Japanese ambassador to the United States and the first minister of education, in 1875. Mori, writes Sugiyama Chuhei, "is generally believed to have been a progressive liberal, one of the so-called champions of the Japanese Enlightenment who characterized the intellectual climate during the years following the end of the long-lived feudal regime. He became, as did many others, a reactionary nationalist later in life." Before that he was a nationalist of the progressive liberal, or what the Russians were the first to call "Westernist," variety, that is, one firmly convinced that it was necessary for Japan to adopt Western ways as soon as possible and fervently devoted to the cause of modernization. Indeed, becoming like the West appeared to him so important that he was willing to consider replacing Japanese with "a rationalized version of English" as the national language (on the grounds that Japanese could not support the modern economic and political discourse). During his stay in Washington, Mori approached several American academics, mostly college and university presidents, with a request to share with him their views on how Japan could best elevate its education, intellectual, moral, and physical. The particular subjects on which he wished to have their opinions were: "The effect of education 1. Upon the material prosperity of a country; 2. Upon its commerce; 3. Upon its agricultural and industrial interests; 4. Upon the social, moral, and physical condition of the people; and 5. The influence upon the laws and government."

The learned men were in their element and willing to oblige. Professor J. H. Steele of Amherst College informed the Japanese ambassador that

the production and accumulation of wealth follow great laws as exactly as do the movements of the tide and the planets. There is a science of public economy, that is, a science of wealth, as true and as beautiful as the science of astronomy. All the mistakes which governments have ever made in their financial legislation, or which individuals make in their business transactions, come from ignorance of the fundamental truths of this science. Knowledge of this, therefore, is all-important for any nation, but such knowledge is not easily gained. The science, though now in its main principles well established, is very intricate, and demands well-trained intellects to master it.

Education, obviously, helped to train intellects. Therefore, Steele advised, "for the sake of commerce I would say, make education thorough and universal." The president of Princeton University, James McCosh, admonished similarly, "Commerce can be extensively carried on only in nations in which there is a body of enlightened mercantile men, who know the wants of the country, and the products to be had in other countries," while a professor at Rutgers University, writing on behalf of the president, W. H. Campbell, stressed:

National prosperity is held to consist in the accumulation of wealth in the hands of the inhabitants, in the general activity of trade and exchange, in the increase of the productions of a country, and in its general growth in population. These circumstances, which constitute material growth, are sure evidence also of the existence of happiness and contentment among the people, and have no small share in producing them . . . [Education] stimulates in the mind of the individual a desire to improve his present condition, and aids him in devising ways and means to do so.

He also commended commerce for bringing nations into (presumably peaceful) relations with one another.

Armed with such advice and impressed with American prosperity, Mori, upon his return to Japan in 1873, applied to the Tokyo Council for a plot of land where he could establish a school to implement it, as well as for funds to employ "a suitable American" as a professor of the true and beautiful science of economics. His requests granted, the school, called Shoho Koshujo (Commercial Training School), which later became the Hitotsubashi University, was established. Fukuzawa Yukichi, who was one of its three trustees, wrote a prospectus on the school's behalf, reflecting the motives behind its foundation and giving some indication of its educational philosophy. As might be expected, it differed somewhat from that of the advice proffered by Americans. The prospectus announced:

> In the past when Japan closed itself to the outer world, its merchants had only to be acquainted with inland trade, and it was sufficient for them to be smart enough not to miss any business chance there . . . Now that foreign trade has begun, things have changed drastically. Until now the wealth or skill of a merchant has only been a private matter. Now he must recognize his public duty in knowing how to deal with Western merchants . . . In every Western country it has been recognized that where there are merchants, there are also commercial schools. Similarly in Japan in the feudal ages, where there were samurai, there were fencing schools. In fighting one another by means of the sword, one cannot go to the battlefield without learning the art of fencing beforehand. Likewise, in the age of battles by means of business, one cannot be confronted with foreigners without learning the art of business in advance.[27]

The "suitable American" to teach Japanese students economic swordsmanship, a certain Dr. Whitney of Newark, was recommended by the then acting Japanese consul in New York, Tomita Tetsunosuke, who was later to assume the posts, first, of vice president of the Bank of Japan and then governor of Tokyo prefecture. He happened to be a graduate of the Newark branch of the Bryant and Stratton chain of commercial colleges and knew Whitney personally. Tomita's own views on economics and business education would be congenial to the trustees of Shoho Koshujo: he had great respect for the American protectionist Henry Carey and wrote the preface to his 1859 *Principles of Social Science,* which he encouraged his friend Inukai Tsuyoshi (a graduate of the Keio school) to translate. He mentioned there that Carey had advised him to beware of Westerners and watch carefully their actions in Asia. He also contributed a preface to the translation of List's *National System,* warning Japan against the "cosmopolitical" principles of Adam Smith. Tomita's choice, Whitney, perhaps not fully aware of his new employers' agenda and preferences, however, proved unable to instruct aspiring Japanese fighters in business *bushido.* Probably for this reason he was almost immediately replaced by two other Americans who specialized in practical business subjects. At the same time, the trustees did not seem to be bothered by the noticeable inconsistency between their ethical program and the theoretical literature on which they based their courses. "The political economy that was taught in the Commercial Training School," says Sugiyama, "was nothing but the popularized version of classical political economy, despite the nationalist spirit that lay at the basis of the school."

Similar inconsistencies characterized economic discourse in general. Japanese intellectuals, who were interested in economics perhaps more than any other subject, read and translated everything they could lay their hands on. They did not always subscribe to the ideas they translated. Reading "as many Western books as possible" was a necessary means to the glorious end of making Japan "civilized," and one could not afford to be selective: the principle behind Japanese Enlightenment was "know thy enemy."[28]

The first economic theory to be imported was indeed the classical liberal theory, but this did not happen by design. The only Western language with which the Japanese intellectuals were familiar to any significant extent was Dutch, and at first they therefore used Dutch as their conduit to Western ideas. The Dutch economic discourse of the time was dominated by the laissez-faire tradition. In 1862 two students of "Barbarian Writings," Tsuda Mamichi and Nishi Amane, were sent to Leiden, where they became private students of Simon Vissering, an economics professor at the university. An expert on French and British economic theories, he was a devotee, particularly, of Bastiat and John Stuart Mill, and, apparently, a very good teacher. His two Japanese students became disciples and were to remain the most doctrinaire exponents of liberal economics during the Meiji period. The first general introduction to economics was translated into Japanese in 1867 by Kanda Takahira, who was a teacher of Dutch in Bansho Shirabesho. It was the *Outline of Social Economy* by William Ellis, a popular laissez-faire text, and Kanda translated it from Vissering's Dutch translation.

The Japanese translation, like most early Japanese translations, was liberal in a different sense; it was more of a free rendition than a translation properly so called, which made it possible to see that the translator found the theory convincing. For instance, Kanda not only accepted but also developed the argument for liberty of personal enrichment, adding to it an ethical dimension. Some people, he wrote, are clever while others are dull, some strive industriously but others remain lazy, some tend to be thrifty but others are wasteful. Thus "it is only natural that those who are at the same time clever, industrious and thrifty grow rich, whereas those who are at once dull, lazy and wasteful can only become poor. Therefore to try to eliminate the inequality of property is nothing other than to rob the rich in order to give to the poor, the result of which would only be to discourage virtue and encourage vice."

In contrast, Fukuzawa was evidently not convinced by a similar defense of material self-interest in *Chambers' Educational Course in Political Economy*, which he translated, also in 1867, as *Seiyo Jijo Gaihen* (Conditions in the West, volume 2), for he simply omitted the chapter in which the author articulated the metaphor of the invisible hand. In general, Fukuzawa's views on self-interest were uncertain. The intense collectivistic nationalism which permeated all his thinking made him inherently opposed to it (this was reflected, among other things, in his rejection of domestic competition, as well as his general idea of liberty). But, on occasion, he would endorse it, as in his 1877 article in *Minkan Zasshi,* where he declared that "private interest is the basis of public benefit, the latter of which can be attained only by those who pursue the former," or in a later essay, where he predicted that "the private profit of each merchant will eventually be gathered and accumulated to contribute to Japan's victory in the business world." It seems, however, that, similarly to his idea of "spirit of independence," which actually meant "spirit of competition against foreigners," Fukuzawa's notion of self- or "private" interest implied, rather, the sense of one's individual duty to the nation, being a sort of Marxian "class consciousness." (In the thought of Shibusawa Eiichi, it corresponded to the self-interest of the "objective" self, which perceived itself primarily as a part of a society and identified with its needs, rather than of the "subjective," self-centered self.)

The same pluralism prevailed in regard to freedom of (foreign) trade versus protectionism. Teachers, for the most part, advocated protectionism, but included theories of free traders in their curricula. Henry Carey, who was the main authority for protectionists before they discovered List, was quoted as early as 1871 and translated in 1874 and again ten years later. In 1878 Taguchi Ukichi, aged twenty-four, published a defense of free trade—*Jiyu Koeki Nihon Keizairon* (On the Free Trade Japanese Economy) and the next year founded a journal, *Tokyo Keizai Zasshi* (The Tokyo Economist), to advance the cause. He owed the idea to do so to a chance conversation with an "employee foreigner," A. A. Shand, who advised the Ministry of Finance on banks, and on whose desk Taguchi noticed an issue of *The Economist.* He said Japan should have a magazine of this kind also, to which Shand replied that the country was probably not yet rich enough for that. Taguchi was stung to the quick. "Although it was no more than a passing remark in a conversation," he later confessed, "it left a very great impression on me. I promised him that I would some day launch an economic periodical of this kind and would show it to him." In 1880 a rival periodical appeared, *Tokai Keizai Shinpo* (Tokai New Economic Review) attacking Taguchi's position in its first editorial. "The National economy," it announced,

is not the same as a cosmopolite economy, nor is it the same as a private economy . . . Each state has its own race, language, custom, law, and civilization. That is why their interests are nothing less than various, and so are their economies. If it is not possible to combine all countries of the world in one single community without different interests and without conflict and strife for evermore, it is equally impossible to establish an economy which is universally applicable.

For about a year the two journals hotly debated the issue, repeating their arguments over and over again, and then, exhausted, let it be. The opinion of other pundits, unaffected by the debate, tended toward protectionism. Fukuzawa, who in his early days briefly supported free trade, became a pragmatist. The choice depended on the condition of the country in question, he argued, using Britain and the United States as examples: "In a country such as Britain, where there is surplus of commodities manufactured by human art and exported with profit all over the world, free trade is defended by most scholars, whereas in a country such as America, where there are plenty of natural goods but not as yet many manufactured commodities, protection is defended. It is no wonder that the argument between both sides continues *ad infinitum*." Of course, he noted, what was allowed to the strong America would not be to "a mere country in Asia," but, should opportunity arise, for Japan in its current state he recommended old-fashioned mercantilism.

In the meantime, translation of Western economists proceeded apace, works by free traders and protectionists appearing simultaneously or in quick succession. The first translation of *The Wealth of Nations* began publication, in installments, in 1884, and only five years later Friedrich List's *National System of Political Economy* became available in Japanese. This, as Morris-Suzuki points out, was "a particularly important milestone in the development of Japanese protectionist thought." Oshima Sadamatsu, List's translator, boldly attacked the British classical "natural liberty" school: "People tend to be attracted by the word 'freedom,' but freedom in politics and freedom in foreign trade are entirely different from each other. The former liberates a nation, whereas the latter liberates other nations at the expense of one nation." He also wrote, following his role model:

If all apples fall towards the ground in England, we can presume that all apples will fall towards the ground in every country of the world. But in the case of politics, law or economics, what is suitable for England may not be applicable to France, for nations may be old or new, large or small, strong or weak, and their position, climate, customs and etiquette are also interconnected . . . Yet there are those who, having read two or three English economic texts, then want to take these and apply them to our country, whose circumstances, population, wealth and strength are entirely different.[29]

Among practicing businessmen there were now fewer and fewer of those. Thanks to the labors of people concerned with Japanese "civilization," Westernization by the 1880s had proceeded so far and so fast that they had Western authorities aplenty to support any position and could pick and choose among them and customize their model of modernity. More and more often they picked List rather than Smith. German influence increased across the board, and in politics as well as in economics, it was a matter of active choice rather than passive and inevitable submission to a theoretically superior or "more scientific" argument. The movers and shakers of the new Japan found German theories persuasive because they were already persuaded, because, in fact, they shared most of the assumptions on which these theories were based.

With the increasing differentiation of functions which accompanied modernization, "men of affairs" and academic economists drifted apart and soon lost touch with each other (a situation, of course, which is not unique to Japan). Classical economics, assured an honored place in the curricula of universities and business schools, assumed an ever more theoretical character and lost its practical importance.[30] (Later this also happened to Marxism.) Thus, despite the massive importation of Western economic ideas and the great respect the Japanese public had for them, none of these ideas had a noticeable impact on the development of the Japanese economy. They were either ignored or used in support of native tendencies.[31] The only Western offering that the Japanese adopted and that directly and significantly affected their thinking and behavior was nationalism, and they adopted it because it dovetailed so perfectly with the needs and interests of the most articulate and ultimately influential segment of the Japanese elite.

The economic system created during the Meiji period has lasted for over a century. With certain modifications of the vocabulary and changes of emphasis accounted for by internal as well as external developments, it remains essentially the same today as it was at the moment of Japan's takeoff. It is animated by the same spirit—a distillate of the national consciousness, cooperative within and combatively competitive vis-à-vis the outside world—which was responsible for it and has consistently oriented Japanese economy toward growth. This spirit, like any enthusiasm, is subject to routinization, which both ensures its durability as a collective orientation and weakens its grip on the individual psyche, and it waxes and wanes in intensity. So far it has been intense enough to propel little Japan to, and keep it at, the top of the economic world, where it vies for leadership with the United States. Occasionally it outdoes its rival; more often it does not. This should not surprise anyone, for it is not a competition between equals. This particular week or month—what with the yen's stature periodically diminished and Japanese officials humbly listening to the pontifications of American statesmen and Harvard professors, who teach them how to live—may not be the best time to sing the praises of the Japanese economy. Western economic commentators tend to interpret relative decline (i.e., decline relative to someone else's performance) as failure, and—amnesia being an occupational disease—when Japan scores low, hasten to find inherent flaws in precisely those ways of doing business and organizational structures which perhaps a year or two ago they hailed as the causes of its scoring enviably high.[32] But its relative woes are temporary. So long as its fighting spirit is alive, Japan will stay in the race, and, from time to time, it might score again. It would take a very long period of frustration or a cataclysmic event worse than Hiroshima and Nagasaki to eradicate this spirit completely, and there is no reason whatsoever at present to predict that this will happen anytime soon.

IV | The Economic Civilization: The Spirit of Capitalism in the New World

There is no puzzle in the prodigious economic growth of a society begun as an economic enterprise and from its infancy accustomed to the notion of profit seeking as a commendable orientation in life, made all the more attractive by the fact that, in the absence of a native nobility, wealth was the surest road to social eminence; a society whose population swelled at an unprecedented rate owing to immigration, and territorial expansion kept pace with this swelling population until it was in possession of a vast stretch of land, second, perhaps, in its natural abundance only to the "enormous bulk"[1] of the Russian Empire. It was to be expected that, after the West was won and the many millions of Europeans who kept pouring into the new country throughout the nineteenth century were inducted into the new economic consciousness—the "spirit of capitalism"—that was America's inheritance, the United States would emerge as the world's economic front-runner and dwarf its competition. Adam Smith had already predicted as much in 1776. If those who witnessed this emergence a century later did not expect it, only their own nearsightedness was to blame. They were oblivious to the connection between English nationalism and the drive behind modern economy and overlooked the fact that Americans were Englishmen first, and with their national consciousness which they brought with them from seventeenth-century England, they transported to the New World the potent idea that economies grew and that it was one's duty to help them grow.

The American "takeoff" thus, unlike those of England, France, Germany, and Japan, while a fascinating story, fully deserving to be told and retold, does not require an explanation. With the vigorous economic spirit and a stout body, the sustained and stupendous growth of the American economy—unlike economic growth in general—was indeed natural; it would be a riddle to wear out any intelligence if it had not occurred. The causes of natural developments are remote and are not to be sought in immediate contexts.[2] The economic history of the United States, like the history of the American nation in general, was a direct (though, of course, not inevitable)

363

continuation of the English one: its causes lie in sixteenth- and seventeenth-century England. American nationalism did not have the same direct motivating influence on the process of American economic development, specifically the takeoff of the American economy into sustained growth, which nationalism had on respective takeoffs in other cases; it was a condition for this development rather than its cause.

Transplanted from England to America in the course of the seventeenth century, the "spirit of capitalism" was already to a significant extent routinized, as it also was in England at the time.[3] One participated in capitalist activity, oriented to profit and growth, because this was what most people did in life, unreflectively, without giving oneself an account as to one's reasons for such participation, or feeling the need to justify it. Were one to feel such a need, however, justifications were readily available, found among the very first principles of the colonial society. In other words, modern economy, capitalism, was carried to the New English World already institutionalized, as a ready-made iron cage: an iron cage not because it was uncomfortable and restricted one's freedom (this happened to be a very large cage), but because it was sturdy, reliable, and firmly in place, as is true of all Weberian iron cages. It was left to its inhabitants only to gild it.

This was begun in earnest during the age that was called "Gilded" (although "gilding" might have been more appropriate), when Americans also took the new economic consciousness a giant step further and in the direction which could not be foreseen at its birth. Then in the United States, the modern civilization created in England and distinguished, among other things, by the honorable place which the economy occupied in it was transformed into an economic civilization over which the economy held sway and in which it came to be generally considered the fundamental sphere of social reality and the end-all of human existence. Human imagination, whose sovereign sphere expanded infinitely because of the vistas opened to it by nationalism and, specifically, the reorientation of economic action to growth, was changing the material world, but was imagined as a function of the animal struggle for survival, a "conscious awareness" (as Marx would say in Germany, where, of course, nobody believed him) of material necessity. Though it was only in the twentieth century that this economistic consciousness came to truly dominate the American society, in their economic determinism Americans were Marxists before Marx and did not need German logic to see his fantastic "reality" beyond appearances: it was apparent to them almost from the beginning of their collective existence.

Two developments were responsible for the ascendancy of this consciousness and its establishment in the position of a hegemonic idea by the end of the nineteenth century. One was a development in the organization of the economy—the rise of big business and giant corporations, which turned the United States (ostensibly) into a nation of corporate employees, dependent for their livelihood and security, for their work, health care, education, and leisure, neither on themselves nor on the government, but on private enterprises largely independent from the government, and yet as remote from and seemingly overpowering the average individual as was the latter. More than anywhere else in the world, the lives of Americans came to be shaped by the interests, decisions, and actions of a group whose constantly shifting membership always remained small, of successful entrepreneurs and managers of big business, driven by the desire to become bigger and bigger and competing for the status of the biggest ever. The continued accumulation of wealth—for its own sake—was their professed goal, and they controlled the economy and the destinies of millions of Americans.[4] It was reasonable to conclude that the economy ruled the world and that the desire for ever greater accumulation of wealth was the ruling principle of the economy, and thus the fundamental human drive.

The other factor that contributed to the establishment of this notion, bestowing on a vague sentiment the form and the magisterial authority of a scientific doctrine, was the institutionalization of the social sciences, foremost among them economics. A central element in the late nineteenth-century "revolution" in American education, this development, paradoxically, was an expression of the opposition to the growth of big business and its animating spirit, and was inspired by the desire to dislodge the ambitious entrepreneur from the position of social influence he was speedily acquiring. Economics as an academic discipline, to put this differently, emerged as a reaction (in the sense we attribute to the word "reactionary") to contemporary economic developments. And yet it served to reinforce the thinking which these developments suggested, particularly to the uneducated mind, contributing the essential element of a system of arguably clear and certainly authoritatively formulated principles—that is, an ideology—to the economic civilization which they were in the process of creating.

Both these phenomena—big business and the intellectual opposition to it, which prompted the establishment of economics—were products of a singular feature of American nationalism: its unreserved and unparalleled egalitarianism. Equality is a central value in all nationalisms. But while other nations constructed a civic Pantheon, worshipping equality together with, for instance, liberty and fraternity, which moderated their dedication to any single deity and made them relatively tolerant of inconsistencies between their ideals, or between these ideals and reality, America—despite its tolerance for pluralism in other respects—was a rigorously monotheistic nation, equality being its one true God. This was so, on the one hand, because American society was new, and ideals could be realized in it to a fuller extent than elsewhere, for they were by definition unopposed by vested interests and social inertia (which reduced tolerance to inconsistencies between ideals and reality). On the other hand, of all the ideals of nationalism, equality most directly connected to the universal human concern for status, which, because American society was new, was particularly intense. Equality became the standard for one's social position and aspirations. Theoretically, one was equal to all other members of society and measured oneself against them. In practice, this implied desire for parity only with those who were "more equal" than the others and, as a result, a constant race, justified and spurred on by the supreme national ideal, for social superiority.

In the economic sphere, where status was to be achieved for the great majority of Americans, this meant continuous competition for profits, continuous search for new ways to make them, and thus continuous stimulus for diversification, technological and organizational innovation, and growth. One was as good as anyone else, but there always was somebody who was doing better. This deprived the ambitious man of sleep. Moneymaking became an addiction, a sport in which one tested oneself and found *certitudo salutis,* the surest way to and method of secular salvation. It became an end in itself and—combined with a special talent, a unique organizational, commercial, or technical ability, on the one hand, and vast and for a long time untapped American resources, human and otherwise, on the other—it brought into being the American system of mass production, the multidivisional corporation, huge new markets for every conceivable product, and an economy whose growth, while from time to time checked, was, in this framework, in principle unstoppable.

Not everyone cared for status, of course, even in America, and not everyone who cared was willing to compete in the economic sphere. Most uncommon things were done in it, and most uncommon fortunes made, but it remained the sphere of the common man. People who considered themselves above the multitude did not appreciate, and in fact resented, the opportunities it offered the common man's ambition. In this land of the common man, one group—the intellectuals—became particular prey to such resentment. The relentless devotion of the American society to equality, namely, to the right of everyone to do better than everyone else, presented a problem for the intellectuals. Owing to their very nature, as I have argued elsewhere, egalitarianism was a foreign sentiment to them, and they were willing to tolerate equality only so long as they remained at the top.

Intellectuals are people characterized by an uncommon taste for the contemplation of, and finding order in, social life (that is people watching and its rationalization). This taste is often accompanied by a certain facility of verbal expression, and, as a result, talking and writing is the way professional intellectuals usually earn their living; but this linguistic ability is not the definitive characteristic of intellectuals, and can be associated with very different propensities. Natural scientists, who can be very able writers and orators, for instance, by and large are not intellectuals; neither, frequently, are lawyers or genuinely religious thinkers; and even modern secular writers and poets may at times be distinguished rather sharply from, and in certain cases (such as those of the greatest Russian writers, for example) themselves refuse to be identified as, intellectuals. Nevertheless, a professional intellectual, that is, one able to turn his (or her) natural inclination into a way of earning a living, must either cultivate or be endowed from birth with a superior ability of verbal expression, and most professional intellectuals, since the time they emerged as a group, have been writers or litterateurs of some sort.

It was the national reinterpretation of social reality that made possible the transformation of the contemplation and rationalization of social reality, which in earlier epochs could only be a leisure pastime, into a gainful occupation. Intellectuals everywhere played the central role in this reinterpretation, but after it was accomplished, their collective fate differed in different societies, depending on the character of the nationalism they helped to construct. In Russia, France, and Germany, as well as in Japan—all collectivistic nations—the intellectuals emerged as the new priesthood, qualified to understand the collective spirit and invested with undisputed authority to express the will of the nation, and as the new, alternative aristocracy; thus they were assured high social status. This, in turn, stimulated the professionalization of the intellectual pursuit, attracting to it relatively large numbers of people, as well as the formation of a characteristic ethos, style of life, and other attributes of a class. In distinction, in individualistic nations such as England and the United States, where the national will was identified with that of the electoral majority, no need was felt for special qualifications to interpret it, and, consequently, those who claimed to be specially qualified did not automatically command authority or enjoy superior status. By and large, people watching remained a leisure pastime for people who derived their income from some other occupation, and there was no particular impetus for the professionalization of intellectual activity and increase in the numbers of intellectuals. In the United States, in addition, the clergy for a long time retained a great deal of authority, which extended to the articulation of the national values, so that there was no place for a new secular priesthood.

Only a minority of American intellectuals, in these inauspicious circumstances, became professional intellectuals, but this minority, from its earliest collective infancy, was a deeply discontented group. Always in need of social recognition, owing to the nature of their occupations, they suffered from their nation's refusal to bestow it on them as a group and its general indifference to their interests. A comparison to the enviable lot of intellectuals in other nations (France, Germany, and even Britain) led them to believe that these interests were lofty and that social deference was their due, which made them feel still more miserable, leading them to complain bitterly about the lack of cultivation of their fellow citizens and to deceive themselves—and the world—with notions of the inherent anti-intellectualism of American society.[5]

It is hard to estimate how acute was their sense of status deprivation when most of them, while dissatisfied with society's treatment of them as intellectuals, came from old and established families and enjoyed considerable prestige as a result of their background and family wealth. Probably it was less acute than after the advent of big business dwarfed the significance of the former and made the latter appear laughable in comparison with the astronomical fortunes of a Carnegie or a Rockefeller. In any case, until the advent of big business they could do little to improve their status. The enormous rise in the prestige of science following the publication of Darwin's *Origin of Species* prompted them to redefine themselves as social scientists, which made such improvement possible. Paradoxically, big business, the emergence of which coincided with this unrelated development, in sponsoring the modern university, with its emphasis on research and the concomitant redefinition of the role of the college professor, provided them with an institutional framework and the means to do so.

The "economic civilization" was thus a result of a series of historical accidents, some of them tenuously related (through their relation to the national passion for "equality," so called), others (such as the publication of *Origin of Species*, which played an essential evolutionary role in this context) completely independent. The rise of this civilization was quite rapid and could not have been predicted from a much longer (though also relatively short) history of the modern economy in America and the evolution of its specific "spirit of capitalism." Since, in contrast to other cases in this book, no single potent force (such as self-assertive nascent nationalism) directed the development of this spirit, it was characterized by some rather striking reversals. The wider cultural significance of the rise of "economic civilization" demands that we focus on it rather than on this development, but the inherently fascinating adventures of the American "spirit of capitalism" on its meandering course make it worth our while to follow it at least part of the way.

7 | Searching for the American System

That the chief motive behind the original colony at Jamestown, Virginia, was profit is amply attested to by the wording of the First Charter that King James granted on April 10, 1606, to "certain knights, gentlemen, merchants, and other adventurers" of his fairest cities. In the language of the time "adventurers" meant "investors": people who speculated on the success of an enterprise, risking their capital in the hope of increasing it. The presence among them of knights and gentlemen reflected the general respectability of such speculative ventures: the company was, indeed, distinguished. The king considered the gamble "well-intended" and was quite willing to sponsor "so noble a work."[1] The flattering royal opinion of venture capitalism reflected its recognition in England of the 1600s as a central factor in the promotion of public welfare. It made the English economy grow, and adventurers, therefore, were presumed to be patriots and men of civic virtue. Many of them, in fact, were patriots; they sincerely identified their personal interests with the interest of the nation, or vice versa, and were evidently moved by considerations of general good as much as by the selfish desire to improve their social position (which reflected the new attitude to wealth and its importance for status) or to experience the now legitimate thrill of risk taking.

Moneymaking as Religion

One of the Virginia adventurers, Richard Hakluyt, the author of *Principal Navigations . . . of the English Nation,* which eloquently argued the superiority of the English as seamen and explorers, a man of undoubted patriotic credentials, contended that the profit he and his companions sought was, first and foremost, profit to England: the increase of the nation's dominions, dignity, and independence. In a document advocating public support of American colonization, Hakluyt advanced a classical mercantilist argument. America, he maintained, was a territory "most convenient for the supply of those

369

defects which this Realm of England most requires," for, trade being the main support of a state and England being an island, it could not be "otherwise fortified than by strong ships and mariners," yet lacked the raw materials necessary for building an adequate marine and "at this present time [enjoyed] them only by the favor of a foreign country." Private entrepreneurs lacked sufficient capital to support such a major undertaking on their own and were reluctant to invest what they had in a project the success of which was uncertain. A public enterprise was more likely to succeed, and it was "honorable for a state to back an exploit by a public [corporation] rather than a private monopoly." In Hakluyt's opinion, self-interest did not provide enough motivation for decent people and, while a sufficient motive for those of low character to attract them to the venture, could not be relied on to sustain their efforts in difficulties, in better times being certain to make all collective effort impossible. And then even the success of an enterprise designed for private gain alone was not good for the state.

The colonization of America, Hakluyt argued, was becoming urgent, for foreign powers were plotting to enrich themselves at England's expense and ready to rob it of its trade and labor alike. "It is publicly known that trade with our neighbor countries is beginning to be of small request," he told his audience.

> Foreign states either have already or at this present time are preparing to enrich themselves with wool and cloth of their own which they heretofore borrowed of us, which purpose of theirs is now being achieved in France, as it already has been done in Spain and Italy. Therefore, we must, of necessity, forgo our great showing if we do not wish to prepare a place fit for the vent of our wares and so set our mariners to work, who daily run to serve foreign nations for want of employment and cannot be restrained by any law when necessity forces them to serve in the hire of a stranger rather than to serve at home.

He reiterated the mercantilist ideal of self-sufficiency, apparently accepted as an axiom, and the related preference for exports over imports: "That realm is more complete and wealthy which either has the sufficiency to serve itself, or can find the means to export its natural commodities, than if it has occasion necessarily to import." Colonies were the way to self-sufficiency. Hakluyt explained: "A colony transported into a good and plentiful climate able to furnish our wants, our moneys, and wares, that now run into the hands of our adversaries or cold friends, shall pass unto our friends and natural kinsmen and from them likewise we shall receive such things as shall be most available to our necessities. This intercourse of trade may rather be called a homebread traffic than a foreign exchange."

The argument was popular among the colonists until the Revolution: the economic importance of the colonies for the mother country was a proof of the Americans' English identity and the very reason for their being American (rather than European) English; it was essentially a matter of patriotic exertion and thus—so the Americans thought—entitled them to a special consideration by their compatriots at home. But the importance of such mercantilist reasoning as a rationalization of the everyday economic activity of the colonists and their dealings with one another rapidly decreased. Founded as "a comfortable addition to our Great Britain," the "virgin or maiden Britain" in America naturally developed a unique identity of its own, complementing the English nationality of the colonists yet stressing characteristics which distinguished them from Englishmen in other parts of England. Central among these was godliness, the superior piety, reflected in such phrases as "American Jerusalem," "New-English Jerusalem," "God's American Israel," and "American Canaan," which over the course of time was inconspicuously translated into superior virtue in general. Since, to the contemporary mind, the Protestant and the English cause were one, religious devotion was in no way considered contradictory to the settlers' commitment to England's worldly interests, and piety, which was arguably the paramount motive only for the Puritan settlements in New England, was from the very beginning believed to characterize Americans everywhere. In 1609, for instance, the Reverend William Symonds referred to the Adventurers for the Plantation of Virginia as "advancers of the standard of Christ among gentiles."

From early on the proof of the Americans' election was seen in the material prosperity of the colonial society. By 1616 John Smith had forgotten the starving time in Virginia, when, in the first five months of the settlement, he saw 50 of his 104 comrades buried, "such extreme weakness and sickness oppressed" the small troop. Their diet was "half a pint of wheat, and as much barley boiled with water for a man a day . . . [D]rink was water . . . lodgings castles in the air." Nine years later he could hardly contain his excitement, describing the natural plenty of the yet unsettled New English coast. Everything necessary "for the nourishing of man's life" was to be had there "for the taking up"; all that was required, "without any other tax, [was] labor." America was a veritable paradise on earth, though Smith used the epithet only in regard to "the country of the Massachusetts." The Reverend Francis Higginson of Salem in 1629 boasted:

It is scarce to be believed how our kine [cows] and goats, horses and hogs do thrive and prosper here and like well of this country. In our plantation we have already a quart of milk for a penny; but the abundant increase of corn proves this country to be a wonderment. Thirty, forty, fifty, sixty are ordinary here. Yea, Joseph's increase in Egypt is outstripped here with us . . . It is almost incredible what great gain some of our English planters have had by our indian corn . . . where you may see how God blesses husbandry in this land. There is not such great and plentiful ears of corn, I suppose, anywhere else to be found but in this country.

The country excelled in every food group. "Our governor has a store of green peas growing in his garden," Higginson wrote proudly, "as good as ever I ate in England." "Our turnips, parsnips, and carrots," he insisted, "are here both bigger and sweeter than is ordinarily to be found in England." For wood there was "no better in the world." New England's water was plentiful, both salt and fresh. In fact, "the greatest sea in the world, the Atlantic Sea, [ran] along the coast thereof." "The abundance of sea fish [was] almost beyond believing." So was the abundance of lobsters: "The least boy in the plantation may both catch and eat what he will of them." Thus both land and sea abounded "with store of blessings for the comfortable sustenance of man's life in New England." Nine years after the landing at Plymouth (with mortality in the early days higher than in Virginia), Higginson believed "experience [to] manifest that there is hardly a more healthful place to be found in the world that agrees better with our English bodies." "A sup of New England's air," he proverbially opined, "is better than a whole draft of old England's ale." The quality of the air was reflected in the quality of the poultry; the reverend noted, in particular, that the turkeys of the American woods were "far greater than our English turkeys, and exceeding fat, sweet, and fleshy." And the list went on.

It was "through the mercy of Christ" that the "remote, rocky, barren, bushy, wild-woody wilderness . . . becom a second England for fertilness" and was transformed into "the wonder of the world." The hardly to be believed prosperity of the American colonies could only be explained as a sign of the "Wonder-Working Providence," of the *Magnalia Christi Americana*—the marvels wrought by God for his chosen people. There was no place in this American imagination for Saint Matthew's view of the rich man's predicament: virtue was tied to material wealth, and poverty had no redeeming qualities. Therefore, it was one's moral duty, a good in itself, to make and keep oneself rich.[2]

Given the prevailing notion of what being rich meant, it was not difficult to be so in seventeenth-century English America. All men, declared John Winthrop in "A Modell of Christian Charity," written aboard the *Arabella* in

1630, are "(by Divine Providence) ranked into two sorts, rich and poor; under the first are included all men such as are able to live comfortably by their own means duly improved; and all others are poor according to the former distribution." In the America of his time, after the hardships of settlement were overcome, poverty should have been virtually unknown. Nevertheless, "for the glory of his Creator and the common good of the creature, man," some men were made wealthier than others, and the relations between men who were more and less rich were to be governed by the principles of justice and mercy.

The rule of mercy, taught Winthrop, was exercised in giving, lending, and forgiving. Giving was helping one's neighbor in time of need, when the latter had no "present or probable or possible means of repaying." To do so was one's duty as a Christian. When, however, the neighbor in need had "present or probable or possible means of repaying," one was expected not to give but to lend and "to look at him not as the recepient of mercy, but by way of commerce." Lending on the assumption of only probable or possible means involved a risk, which one, as a Christian, was obliged to take, and if the assumption proved wrong, one was obliged to forgive the debt. Commercial transactions were to be conducted according to the rule of justice, on which Winthrop did not fully elaborate in the text, but justice clearly did not contradict self-interest. Self-interest was a natural and universal drive, Winthrop explained, inherited by humanity from Adam, who "rent himself from his Creator, rent all his posterity also from one another; whence it comes that every man is born with this principle in him, to love and seek himself only. And thus a man continues till Christ comes and takes possession of his soul." This tolerant attitude, while still anchored in religion, was very different from the one found in the European discussions of usury and implied the legitimacy and normality of the desire for personal gain.

By 1675 Benjamin Tompson lamented in "The New England's Crisis":

> These golden times (too fortunate to hold)
> Were quickly sinned away for love of gold.

Under the American skies the spirit of capitalism apparently became routinized with distressing speed, and the values with which it was originally associated and which formed its ethical foundation were soon forgotten. The new—American—English were unreflectively and unapologetically moved by self-interest and seemed unaware that prosperity was a sign of godliness. In 1651, to arrest the Tawnean move away from religion, a sumptuary law was introduced in the Massachusetts Bay Colony. The legislators complained in the preamble: "Intolerable excess and bravery have crept in upon us, and especially among people of meaner condition, to the dishonor of God, the scandal of our profession, the consumption of estates, and altogether unsuitable to our poverty." The said excess and "bravery" expressed themselves in the citizens' unabashed enjoyment of their prosperity (which proved that their estates were far from being consumed, while the poverty of the colony was a cherished memory rather than a contemporary reality), men walking in "great boots" and womenfolk wearing silk and tiffany hoods, or scarves, "which, though allowable to persons of greater estates or more liberal education, yet" the Court could not "but judge intolerable." Its scandalized representatives obviously concurred in defining status as a function of wealth and education (thus unconsciously encouraging the evil they attempted to combat).

Driving the point home, the Court declared "that no person within this jurisdiction, nor any of their relations depending upon them, whose visible estates, real and personal, shall not exceed the true and indifferent value of £200, shall wear any gold or silver lace, or gold and silver buttons, or any bone lace above 2s. per yard, or silk hoods, or scarves, upon the penalty of 10s. for every such offence." Foreseeing problems in enforcing this law, the legislators further ordered

> that the selectmen of every town, or the major part of them, [be] enabled and required, from time to time, to have regard and take notice of apparel of any of the inhabitants of their several towns respectively; and whosoever they shall judge to exceed their ranks and abilities in the costliness of fashion of their apparel in any respect . . . the selectmen aforesaid shall have power to assess such persons . . . in the country rates, at £200 estates, according to that proportion that such men use to pay to whom such apparel is suitable and allowed; provided this law shall not extend to the restrain of any magistrate or public officer of this jurisdiction, their wives and children, who are left to their discretion in wearing of apparel, or any settled military officer or soldier in the time of military service, or any other whose education and employment have been above the ordinary degree, or whose estate have been considerable, though now decayed.

The last stipulation made the enforcement of the law absolutely impossible. It was drowned in contradictions. If status depended on wealth (and the education that wealth could afford), conspicuous consumption of the wealth one had, the purpose of which was to express the status to which it gave one the claim, was legitimate—lawful—by definition and could not well be required to accord with feudal, or simply rigid, notions of propriety.

By 1700 it was clear that endless (thus irrational) accumulation of wealth had emerged in America as an end in itself, an ethical ideal in its own right.

Those who articulated this ideal, the intellectuals of the time, were Puritan divines, and in their writings, in contrast to those of their English counterparts, we indeed find the paradigmatic Weberian idea of business as *praxis pietatis*, a calling. In 1701 a man of no lesser eminence than Cotton Mather devoted to it a tract entitled *A Christian at His Calling*, which, among other things, highlighted how secular, despite the language in which it was couched, the idea of piety had become. A Christian, Mather argued, had two callings in life: the general one, which is to serve God and save his own soul, and a particular, "a certain particular employment, by which his usefulness in his neighbourhood is distinguished." The two callings were equal in value, and a Christian owed equal attention to both:

A Christian, at his two callings, is a man in a boat, rowing for heaven, the house which our Heavenly Father hath intended for us. If he mind but one of his callings, be it which it will, he pulls the oar, but on one side of the boat, and will make but a poor dispatch to the shore of eternal blessedness. It is not only necessary that a Christian should follow his general calling; it is of necessity that he follow his personal calling, too.

The salvation of a man's soul thus depended on having a gainful occupation, and on making this occupation the focus of one's earthly existence. "Every Christian ordinarily should have a calling," Mather elaborated. "That is to say, there should be some special business and some settled business wherein a Christian should for the most part spend the most of his time; and this, that so he may glorify God by doing of good for others and getting of good for himself." A calling was supposed to be allowable and agreeable, which implied that it was not such by definition (as one would expect a divine calling to be), and that it was a matter of choice, rather than an assignment. This raises the question in which sense, then, was this a "calling," and it appears that the distinguished clergyman used the word as a metaphor, in its modern secular sense of a choice of occupation in agreement with one's natural inclinations. "What can any man be the better for a calling that will bring him under the wrath of God?" Mather asked.

The man and his posterity will gain but little by a calling whereto God hath not called him. For our course of life, then, we must consult the Word of God if we would not fall into a course of sin when we go to choose our occupation . . . But this is not enough. A Christian should have it contrived that his calling be agreeable as well as allowable. It is a wonderful inconvenience to man to have a calling that won't agree with him. See to it, O parents, that when you choose callings for your children, you wisely consult their capacities and their inclinations, lest you ruin them.

He also added: "When a man is become unfit for his business, or his business becomes unfit for him, unquestionably he may leave; and a man may be otherwise invited, sometimes justly, to change his business." Though such steps were not to be taken lightly, a calling was not necessarily a lifetime commitment; occupational mobility, the freedom of labor, in which both Marx and Weber saw a necessary condition for capitalist economy, was taken for granted.

A Christian, of course, had to "mind his occupation, as it becomes a Christian." That is to say, he was to conduct his business industriously, rationally (in Mather's words, "with discretion"), and honestly. "A Christian should follow his occupation with industry," Mather stressed. "It seems a man slothful in business is not a man serving the Lord. By slothfulness men bring upon themselves, what, but poverty, but misery, but all sorts of confusion." He evidently drew no distinctions between the secular and transcendental consequences of this religious virtue and its complementary vice. But his emphasis was on the secular. "A man by diligence in his business, what may he not come to? A diligent man is very rarely an indigent man. Would a man rise by his business? I say, then, let him rise by his business . . . I tell you, with diligence a man may do marvelous things. Young man, work hard while you are young; you'll reap the effects of it when you are old." And he admonished the loafer: "Thou wicked and slothful person, reform thy ways or thou art not far from outer darkness. Is it nothing to thee that by much slothfulness thy money and credit and all is decaying, and by the idleness of thy hands thy house is coming to nothing?" The identification of the decay of credit with hell must have left a powerful impression on Mather's audience.

Regarding the Christian virtue of "discretion" or reason, Mather advised:

Let every man have the discretion to be well instructed in, and well acquainted with, all the mysteries of his occupation. Be a master of your trade; count it a disgrace to be no workman. And as discretion would bid you to have an insight in your business, thus it also bids you have a foresight in it . . . Let every man, therefore, in his business, observe the most proper time for everything; for there is a time to every purpose. The wise man says, "There is a time to buy, and a time to sell." And a wise man will do what he can to discern the time.

The same discretion must show a man how to proportion his business unto his ability. 'Tis an indiscreet thing for a man to overcharge himself in his business; for a man to distract his mind, to confound his health, to launch out beyond his estate in his business, is a culpable indiscretion.

Be therewithal well advised by the rules of discretion with another caveat: and that is to suit your expenses unto your revenues. Take this advice, O Christians: 'Tis a sin, I say, 'tis ordinarily a sin, and it will at length be a shame, for a man to spend more than he gets, or make his layings out more than his comings in. A frequent inspection into the state of your business is, therefore, not among the least rules of discretion. It was among the maxims of wisdom given of old, Be thou diligent for to know the state of thy flocks; that is to say, often examine the condition of thy business to see whether thou go forward or backward, and learn how to order thy concerns accordingly.

Mather's remarks on honesty demonstrated how deeply modern economic ideas penetrated the American consciousness by his time. "You aim at the getting of silver and gold by your occupation," he granted his audience at the outset of the discussion,

but you should always act by the Golden Rule . . . Shall I be more particular? I say then: Let a principle of honesty in your occupation cause you to speak the truth, and nothing but the truth, on all occasions . . . Let a principle of honesty cause you carefully to pay the debts which in your business must fall on you. Run into debt as little as you may . . . But being in debt, be as ready to get out of it as ever you were to get into it . . . Don't carelessly run into debt, and then as carelessly live in it. Indeed, business cannot ordinarily be carried on (especially as the world now goes) without something of debtor and creditor. Well, but let it be uneasy unto you, at any time to think, I have so much of another man's estate in my hands, and I to his damage detain it from him.

As in Winthrop, there is no trace here of the traditional Christian (whether Catholic or Protestant) attitude to usury. The concept of credit is accepted as unproblematic, almost self-evidently necessary for the smooth running of a Christian society—in which everyone is engaged in business. Similarly, no moral questions are raised about the desire for personal gain: Mather assumes that profit is what people are in business for and constructs his moral discourse around this axiom.

Any allowable (i.e., not criminal) business was good. "For my part," Mather confessed, "I can't see an honest man hard at work in the way of his occupation, be it never so mean (and though, perhaps, driving of a wheelbarrow) but I find my heart sensibly touched with respect for such a man." Nevertheless, for his "own part," he had "a special value for the neighbors who go down to the sea in ships, and do business on the great waters," that is, for foreign trade. "They are the sort of men," he said, "that lay the public under as great obligation as almost the men of any occupation whatsoever. And the genius of many young men leading them to the sea, it must not be discouraged." Still, his advice to the young men without such genius was to stick to their true calling, the occupation which agreed best with their personality, and not to think that "you might be, yourselves, greater and richer if you were in some other business," which would not be prudent.[3]

If these admonitions remind us more of a Savary or a Mitsui than Baxter or Bunyan, of a business manual than a religious sermon—which they were— this is because business in America was emerging as a religion. Not in the sense of the worship of Mammon, with which it is so commonly identified, of course, but in that of a methodical practice of piety, a moral discipline, a religion more akin to Buddhism or Judaism, perhaps, than Christianity. Most of all, however, they remind us of Benjamin Franklin. Indeed, the argument of *A Christian at His Calling* is virtually identical to Franklin's 1748 "Advice to a Young Tradesman"; the differences appear to be purely stylistic. Like Mather, Franklin insists on industry, rationality, and honesty; though addressing a businessman eager to succeed, he has no need to stress the importance of business. "Remember, that credit is money," he says, and that "he that is known to pay punctually and exactly to the time he promises may, at any time and on any occasion, raise all the money his friends can spare. This is sometimes of great use. After industry and frugality, nothing contributes more to the raising of a young man in the world than punctuality and justice in all his dealings; therefore never keep borrowed money an hour beyond the time you promised, lest a disappointment shut up your friend's purse forever." His aphoristic "Time is money" is no different from Mather's injunction that "a Christian should for the most part spend the most of his time" in his business. And if Franklin supports his formula with a rational-sounding "Money is of the prolific, generating nature. Money can beget money, and its offspring can beget more, and so on" (thus, nothing should be wasted "either in time or expense"), Mather says much the same thing, asking grandiloquently: "If the Lord Jesus Christ might find thee in thy storehouse, in thy shop, or in thy ship, or in thy field, or where thy business lies, who knows what blessings He might bestow upon thee?" What truly distinguishes Franklin's advice from that of his compatriot half a century earlier is that it no longer has any connection to the salvation of one's soul, any transcendental connotation (despite the deistic genuflection to the beneficent "Being who governs the world"); the only rationale for the endless accumulation of wealth, if there is any rationale at all, remains status: the "raising of a young man in the world."

By the time Franklin penned his "Advice to a Young Tradesman," the passion for moneymaking had liberated itself from the tutelage of ethical ideals which nursed the spirit of capitalism in England, and was gratified on a mass scale with no regard whatsoever to these ideals. The ideals thus overlooked were not religious—in the spirit of capitalism, religion has long since been replaced by a new, secular, ethic—but national. In the eighteenth century, American entrepreneurs, otherwise as patriotic Englishmen as any, were no longer moved by the economic interest of the British nation, and thought nothing of undermining it whenever an opportunity presented itself. Defoe's economic nationalism was most assuredly foreign to them. For instance, the advocate general of Massachusetts, William Bollan, complained in 1743 to the London Board of Trade:

> There has lately been carried on here a large illicit trade (destructive to the interest of Great Britain in her trade to her own plantations and contrary to the main intent of all her laws made to regulate that trade) by importing into this province large quantities of European goods of almost all sorts from diverse parts of Europe, some of which are by the laws wholly prohibited to be imported into the plantations, and the rest are prohibited to be imported there unless brought directly from Great Britain.

Apparently, Dutch and French products, brought aboard Dutch and French ships directly from Holland and France, were disposed of in Massachusetts ports, to the delight of the colonists. As a material proof, Mr. Bollan presented himself, informing their lordships that he was writing "clad in a superfine French cloth which I bought on purpose that I might wear about the evidence of these illegal traders having already begun to destroy the vital parts of the British commerce; and to use a memento to myself and to custom-house officers to do everything in our power toward cutting off this trade so very pernicious to the British nation."

The colonists' disregard for the national interest was so complete that they would buy goods produced in Spain (with which Great Britain was at war and whose merchandise it was prohibited to import into the British territories under great penalties). What made the deplorable situation difficult to control, however, was not the indiscriminate and unpatriotic demand of the colony, but its active involvement on the side of supply. A considerable part of the illicit trade, Bollan reported, was carried on "by factors here for the sake of their commission." Moreover, he wrote, "persons concerned in this trade [were] many, some of them of the greatest fortunes in this country," and they had

> made great gains by it . . . and having all felt the sweets of it, they begin to espouse and justify it, some openly, some covertly; and having per-

suaded themselves that their trade ought not to be bound by the laws of Great Britain, they labor, and not without success, to poison the minds of all the inhabitants of the province, and matters are brought to such a pass that it is sufficient to recommend any trade to their general approbation and favor that it is unlawful.[4]

It was not far from this to demands for independence.

Political Economy "Colonial Style": Benjamin Franklin

It is of no importance whether the national economic interest, as defined by the Board of Trade, corresponded to the objective interest of the nation and whether the trade laws that Parliament imposed on the colonies were objectively fair. Whatever the definition of the national interest, Americans did not identify their personal economic interests with it and would therefore tend to believe that the trade laws were bad. For a long time, however, people who wouldn't think twice about transgressing these laws also wouldn't think of questioning their British identity and allegiance to the mother country and, when called upon to articulate their economic principles, fell back on the old mercantilist rhetoric, stressing the value of the colonies for Britain and insisting on the identity of the colonial interests with those of the metropolis. In his "Observations Concerning the Increase of Mankind," written in 1751 but reprinted in 1760 and as late as 1769, Franklin in this manner celebrated the population of North America: "What an accession of power to the British empire by sea as well as by land! What increase of trade and navigation! What numbers of ships and seamen!" He argued it was in the British interest—and a duty of a responsible government toward its people, as of a wise and good mother—to promote the economic development of the colonies, for any possibility of a conflict of interest between Englishmen in the Old World and the New was ruled out by the dearness of labor in the latter:

> So vast is the territory of North America that it will require many ages to settle it fully; and, till it is fully settled, labor will never be cheap here, where no man continues long a laborer for others, but gets a plantation of his own; no man continues long a journeyman to a trade, but goes among those new settlers and sets up for himself; etc. Hence labor is no cheaper now in Pennsylvania than it was thirty years ago, though so many thousand laboring people have been imported.
>
> The danger, therefore, of these colonies interfering with their mother country in trades that depend on labor, manufactures, etc., is too remote to require the attention of Great Britain.
>
> But in proportion to the increase of the colonies, a vast demand is

growing for British manufactures, a glorious market wholly in the power of Britain in which foreigners cannot interfere, which will increase in a short time even beyond her power of supplying, though her whole trade should be to her colonies; therefore Britain should not too much restrain manufactures in her colonies. A wise and good mother will not do it. To distress is to weaken, and weakening the children weakens the whole family.

The logic of the last statement did not apply generally: with minor concessions to local circumstances, Franklin subscribed to a conventional mercantilist position which presupposed the subordination of the parts to the whole. For instance, he argued in regard to luxuries:

Foreign luxuries and needless manufactures, imported and used in a nation, do . . . increase the people of the nation that furnishes them and diminish the people of the nation that uses them. Laws, therefore, that prevent such importations, and on the contrary promote the exportation of manufactures to be consumed in foreign countries, may be called (with respect to the people that make them) generative laws as by increasing subsistence they encourage marriage. Such laws likewise strengthen a country doubly by increasing its own people and diminishing its neighbors.

Some European nations prudently refuse to consume the manufactures of East India. They should likewise forbid them to their colonies; for the gain to the merchant is not to be compared with the loss, by these means, of people to the nation.

Or so it was so long as the merchant in question was not Franklin himself. Since by his time the spirit of capitalism in America was fully routinized, the dictates of this spirit, which made it one's interest endlessly (that is, for no end) to increase one's fortune, were unproblematic. Franklin's economic ideas, therefore, were not a product of a search for answers to troubling questions, for economic questions were not troubling, or of serious reflection, for there was no need to reflect. Rather, they were nuggets of the by then established wisdom on the subject, and Franklin, having at his disposal the mental bag in which they were contained, reached into it, whenever a reiteration was required, and produced one or another of these nuggets. This was a mixed bag: protectionist notions in it were found alongside those of free trade (as we saw in the case of England, both could serve the purposes of economic nationalism), and mercantilist emphasis on trade coexisted with the Physiocratic preference for agriculture. That is why Franklin's economic philosophy, if his various pronouncements can be presented as a system, was so contradictory and unoriginal at the same time.

His choice of arguments on any given occasion appeared to depend on the support they lent to the advancement of his personal interest (the endless increase of his fortune). Convinced that this interest, specifically the land promotions in the Ohio Valley, was best advanced within the British Empire, he resorted to mercantilist reasoning, stressing the essential importance of westward colonization for British manufacture and trade in the 1760 tract *The Interest of Great Britain Considered,* or, quite disinterestedly and moved by patriotic considerations alone, arguing in an anonymous pamphlet in 1768 for the freedom of the corn trade, despite the hardship this would imply for the poor in Britain, on the grounds that English grain exports would enrich the nation as a whole at the expense of foreigners. Between 1764 and 1766, Franklin also advocated the establishment of a London-controlled bank which would provide the colonies with currency, while channeling all the specie from America to the metropolis and also, through interests on loans, providing a considerable annual revenue to the Crown and so rendering Crown officials independent from colonial assemblies—a scheme that could be interpreted as a device for "taxation without representation." But by 1769—not a moment too soon—Franklin concluded that Britain was putting unreasonable obstacles in the Americans' way to wealth. His attitude to the mother country changed dramatically. Whereas in 1768 he still thought England blessed with "the best constitution [and] the best king" and an ideal place to live, in 1772 he declared that had he not been an American but judged the advantages of civilization solely on the basis of his acquaintance with England, he would not advise savages to become civilized, so inequitable was that "handicraft, shop-keeping State," and so miserable the life of people there. Anticipating George Fitzhugh, he wrote that the working poor in England were worse off in every respect than African slaves on southern plantations, that indeed they, and not slaves in America, were the real slaves, forced to work from morning to night for a pittance and denied the possibility to improve their condition, while England—that is, a tiny class of the rich in England—went on being the workshop of the world. With this change of heart, the emphasis in his inventory of economic ideas shifted to Physiocracy. In *Positions to be Examined, concerning National Wealth* of 1769, for instance, he opined that there were three ways to increase it—war, commerce, and agriculture—but the only honest way was the last, for war was robbery and commerce cheating, while in agriculture a man received a "real increase of the seed thrown into the ground, in a kind of continual miracle, wrought by the hand of God in his favor, as a reward for his innocent life and his virtuous industry." It was, apparently, agriculture that made "the general happy

Mediocrity," so starkly different from the starving and ragged masses and the few indecently rich of England, prevail in America. At the same time, though now as "a friend to the poor" rather than a British patriot, Franklin argued in 1774 for abolishing all English restrictions on trade. (Cheating or not, commerce was, after all, a remarkably efficient way to make a fortune.)

With such an eclectic collection of arguments it would be surprising if Franklin consistently practiced what he preached, and in fact his economic activity was wholly independent of the ideas with the help of which, on different occasions and under different circumstances, he sought to promote it. Did this make him a hypocrite? No. The economic activity of colonial Americans, fueled by the modern desire for the increase of wealth, was generally consistent with both mercantilism and Physiocracy, the two economic systems of which an educated person at the end of the eighteenth century was expected to be aware. Mercantilism—the view that commerce, especially foreign trade, was the chief means for increasing national wealth, a view which could be, depending on the definition of the national interest, protectionist, as well as associated with free trade—was much older, and it was dominant. The "agricultural system" of the French Économistes, though conceived as a challenge to Britain, posed no challenge to this view and was not considered by its proponents as such, since mercantilism obviously served the British interest quite well. The two systems were in a sense parallel: they addressed the same general subject but did not come into direct contact. Applying, as did Franklin, mercantilist and Physiocratic ideas in different contexts, an informed (but not intellectually engaged) person could certainly find it possible to hold both systems valid.

Charles F. Dunbar, the first incumbent of the chair of Political Economy at Harvard, believed that Franklin's economic writings exemplified "the condition in which the breaking out of our Revolution found the study of economic science in this country." Franklin, Dunbar wrote, was marked by his activity and personality alike "as the American who must deal with political economy if any one did, and the one who could rise to the level of the national thought in economic speculation, if he did not soar much beyond it." Unfortunately, the collection of writings on economic issues he left us

rests on no well-defined systematic body of opinions; indeed, [it] raises questions as to his clearness of perception in morals as well as in political economy. He is quoted with admiration by writers of the protectionist school, and he might equally well be quoted by their opponents. He was in fact a man of expedients rather than principles, often sagacious in dealing with immediate practical questions, but satisfied with the crudest speculation as to the operation of causes in any degree remote.

His theoretical legacy was "a mass of ill-digested reasoning." With regret, Dunbar was moved to conclude that "it must be said of Franklin that he not only did not advance the growth of economic science, but that he seems not even to have mastered it as it was already developed."[5] One implication of this harsh but fair judgment (which Dunbar would not wish to consider) was that the colonial economy had done very well without economics. The so-cial—and economic—value of "economic science" the underdevelopment of which the professor lamented was questionable; economic success was possible without familiarity with its principles, whatever they were.

Economic Nationalism Embattled: The Many Duels of Alexander Hamilton

The struggle for independence only briefly interrupted Americans' efforts to make themselves rich; by 1786 the economy was booming and the country awash in wealth. In Boston—that hub of revolutionary discontent—people could not complain, it was said, because their mouths were "stopped with white bread and roast beef." Philadelphia, which in the last decade of the century was the nation's capital, astonished European visitors—including aristocrats from Paris and London, who might be trusted to have seen luxury at its most ostentatious and were familiar with the prodigious lengths to which one could carry conspicuous consumption—by the splendor of its beau monde: at Mrs. Washington's New Year's Day levee, one reported, it was "as much crowded as a Birth Night at St. James and with company as brilliantly drest." (Frugality, apparently, was less conspicuous than consumption in the City of Brotherly Love.) True, Boston and Philadelphia were among the most affluent cities, but, according to Washington, wherever one looked in the newly independent nation there was "no City, Town, Village, or even farm, but what exhibit[ed] evidences of increasing wealth and prosperity." The price of land, said the first president, had increased "beyond all calculation"; wheat fetched a dollar a bushel; American exports doubled in value in five years. Between 1790 and 1794, so did the number of American ships in the merchant marine. The infant United States indeed presented "a spectacle of national happiness never surpassed, if ever before equaled, in the annals of human affairs."[6]

The ways to wealth in this earthly paradise were many, and though no one questioned the legitimacy of the pursuit itself, there were profound disagreements as to which of them were truly consistent with religion, enlightened morality, and patriotism. The most common business was that of farming the land. It was a commercial enterprise, oriented to profit and the increase of wealth, rather than mere satisfaction of natural wants, and its name, "farming" reflected this. "Farming" (from medieval Latin *firma:* "fixed payment") in the seventeenth and eighteenth centuries referred to a rent paid for an economic privilege: in this sense, the most notorious farmers of the period, and ones likely to be familiar to the reader, were French tax farmers, who had a monopoly on the collection of taxes for the Crown, worth every centime in the substantial sum they paid for it, for they grew magnificently rich on the spoils of their office. In agriculture farmers at the time were known only in Britain: both gentlemen farmers, landowners engaged in capitalist enterprise on their extensive domains, and entrepreneurs of peasant origin, who tried to rise in the world with the help of modest, often rented plots of land. In other countries the soil was tilled mostly by peasants whose ambitions did not extend far beyond filling their stomachs, while gentlemen, who lived on their labor, by and large considered active pursuit of wealth beneath their dignity. In America there were neither peasants nor gentlemen who doubted the respectable character of moneymaking (especially in agriculture), and "farmer [was] the only apellation of the rural inhabitants." By the time of independence, most Americans were in the farming business.

Some of them farmed on such a large scale that it was not clear where the business of a farmer ended and that of a merchant began. Southern planters certainly needed to—and did—combine the two sets of skills. Many, in addition, were land speculators ("by the time of the Revolution it was difficult to find a large landowner or merchant who was not," says J. O. Robertson); they bought and rented farming land, or acquired, perhaps as a land grant, surveyed, divided, and resold land in the yet unsettled areas. This apparently was the preferred method of moneymaking among the Founding Fathers below the Mason-Dixon line, though—as the example of Franklin demonstrates—it had its votaries farther north as well.

This example more generally demonstrates that northern businessmen from very early on were diversifying their interests. Franklin was made rich by industry (if not frugality) in such disparate areas of endeavor as literature (*Poor Richard's Almanack* was a best-seller), the exploitation of a Crown office, land schemes, and other investments. "Like others of the day, his Philadelphia print shop dealt in slaves, indentured servants, imports from the West Indies and elsewhere, and a variety of other items as well as printed matter. Before long Franklin had a successful newspaper, had acquired that most lucrative field of the printing business—the public printing—not only in Pennsylvania but also in neighboring colonies, and through partnerships was operating a chain of print shops and newspapers in various provinces." Northern states were the home of the nascent "manufacturing interest," an infant whose robust constitution unpleasantly surprised the British consul, forcing him to complain as early as 1791 about the excessive American production of nails, iron tools, farming equipment, and certain items of apparel. Around Boston, 2,500 people were engaged in manufactures, as were over 2,000 men in Philadelphia—a quarter of the city's adult male population. Early in 1789 Washington remarked that more factories (cotton, wool, and iron) had been founded in the new nation in the previous year and a half than in the course of its entire colonial history. But the method of moneymaking which distinguished the northern states, even if it was only a hobby rather than a regular business to which most of its practitioners devoted most of their waking hours, appears to have been speculation in securities and stocks. Indeed, within twenty years of the Declaration of Independence, New Englanders and Yankees, in particular, several times abandoned themselves to such a feverish "delirium of speculation" that even Alexander Hamilton, who thought of the "moneyed interest" as an inestimable aid to the national interest and sought to stimulate it in every "allowable" way, was taken aback.[7]

Twice only between 1789 and 1792, what Madison regarded as the "impatient avidity for immediate and immoderate gain" among his countrymen was provoked by the efforts of the first Secretary of the Treasury to fan the spirit and build the institutional infrastructure for the development of capitalism in the new nation. The first time this national appetite was excited by Hamilton's "Report on Public Credit," which included his plan for the funding of the public debt; the second time the *agiotage* flared up because of the Bank of the United States. The secretary was activated by civic concern, but the majority of his supporters clearly were moved by naked self-interest (however unreasonably defined) and did not care a hoot for the general good. The conduct of Hamilton's friend William Duer, a relative by marriage, and the Assistant Secretary of the Treasury under him, was not typical, for Duer operated on a scale that few others could afford, but it nevertheless offers a good example of the gambling passion that fueled investment in the nascent American securities market.

An Englishman by birth, Duer was a member of the Continental Congress, entrusted with the post of Secretary of the Board of Treasury, and the most glittering (if not brilliant) personage in the high society of New York, where "he lived in almost ducal magnificence," serving fifteen different kinds of wine at dinner and otherwise entertaining his friends to the most "ostentatious display of wealth." While not frugal, he was, without question, very industrious in his attempts to raise himself in the world, and tirelessly accumulated wealth by all the means at his disposal, never pausing (for he remembered that time was money) to examine their legitimacy. A valued member of the "international set of bankers and speculators," he formed with several of them (including the French revolutionary Brissot) a syndicate to buy the American debt from France and tried to use his position on the

Board of Treasury to have the American government ratify this transaction. Though this characteristic attempt was not successful, Duer's "career was an almost unbroken record of financial coups"; his friends claimed he had a "golden touch," and his ability as a businessman was undeniable. Hamilton had a great respect for business ability and, apparently convinced of the universal applicability of Franklin's dictum "Honesty is the best policy," wished to see it represented among the Treasury appointees. But Duer, who followed Poor Richard's advice only when it agreed with his own inclinations, used his office to further increase his fortune, trading in government securities and liberally leaking inside information to his familiars. Among those who profited handsomely from his counsel was William Bingham (he reportedly borrowed £60,000 from Dutch sources to invest in American bonds, as well as, possibly, Secretary of War Knox—the richest man in Washington's administration after Washington himself, and General Schuyler. (Since Schuyler was Hamilton's father-in-law, it was rumored among Hamilton's many detractors that in this case the privileged information was passed on by the Secretary of the Treasury himself, but it is hard to imagine—and would be hard to explain—why a person so meticulous in all his financial dealings, who never put his interest, or that of his wife, above the public good, would make an exception and endanger his unspotted reputation for the sake of his wife's father.)

Duer, who was a clever man, did not abuse his office for too long: the law prohibited officers of the Treasury to buy and sell government securities; aware that he might overstep and find himself in legal trouble, he exercised the "discretion" recommended by Cotton Mather and in April 1790 resigned from the department. A year later, however, he was available to participate in an even greater "orgy of speculation," invited to the festivities, again, by the personally incorruptible Hamilton. The scrip (stock) of the Bank of the United States, which the Secretary of the Treasury conceived and brought into being against most determined opposition, was about to go on sale on July 4, 1791, and in May the *Gazette of the United States* proudly informed its readers that "no equal object of speculation is perhaps presented in any quarter of the globe." Here was the opportunity for William Duer to satisfy his "ambition of making himself the richest man in the country." Feeling the imminent realization of this (status-aggrandizing) dream, the man with the golden touch forgot the sage advice of the "get-rich" experts, threw caution to the wind, and, borrowing left and right (including from the Secretary of War), attempted to corner the market. The price of the bank scrip plummeted, affecting that of government securities as well. The market crashed.

According to J. C. Miller, an excellent biographer, Hamilton thought

Duer was "a bit too sanguine." But, unwilling to let such foolhardy optimism undermine the financial health of the nation, which he had worked so hard to ensure, the Secretary of the Treasury in August led his department, acting through the Bank of New York, into the securities market, sinking over $200,000 in it from the sinking fund to support the price of the government bonds.[8]

An expression of original individualistic nationalism, American society was pluralistic from its earliest inception, and, however widespread was the passion for moneymaking in it, it was never universal. Some people were entirely devoid of pecuniary interests, claiming, as did Franklin's contemporary John Woolman, that "wealth desired for its own sake obstructs the increase of virtue."[9] Alexander Hamilton—the founding father of American economic greatness—offered a more typical example of indifference to personal monetary gain. This extraordinary man contributed more than any other single individual to the institutionalization of the spirit of capitalism in this country, but his own actions were animated by this spirit (at least in its routinized American version) very little. A different sentiment moved him. If ever he desired to raise himself in the world, he wished to do so on the battlefield, yearning for military glory rather than money—a strange and old-worldly disposition that clearly distinguished him among his materialistic compatriots. But his governing passion was nationalism, the concern for the honor and standing of the United States of America. It was this passion that prompted him to accept, and then guided his actions in, that most ungrateful of offices, the post of the Secretary of the Treasury. He was appointed on the suggestion of James Madison (then still Hamilton's friend) and Robert Morris, because he was "damned sharp" (though his ready acceptance of the offer, which came with a measly salary of $3,000 a year, raised doubts on this count), and the state of the nation's finances—"a deep, dark, and dreary chaos"—called for an acute intelligence. Hamilton knew that "his going into public life would materially affect his pecuniary prospects, but he thought it would be in his power, in the financial department, to do the country great good; and this consideration outweighed, with him, every consideration of a private nature." He admitted that he "hazarded much" in undertaking the task, but, he said, "I thought it an occasion that called upon me to hazard."

During his time in office Hamilton did everything in his power to place the nation economically on its feet—to make it self-sufficient, independent of the goodwill, and caprice, of other nations—and "to promote," as he put it in the "Report on the Public Credit," "the increasing respectability of the American name." In other words, while there was not a mercantile bone in his body, as a statesman he was decidedly a mercantilist. A man of exceptional moral integrity (the sad entanglement with the Reynolds couple notwithstanding), he held no theoretical principles sacred. His political audacity, the willingness to risk his popularity, which to most politicians appeared as reckless then as it would now, in order to do what in his view was in the nation's interest, was matched by his ingenuity and pragmatic clear-sightedness: his politics were "politics of responsibility." Thus he was able to promulgate several revolutionary measures and, as his biographer wrote, offer "Americans wealth and greatness, not by war and conquest, but by the utilization of the human and material resources at their command."

The first order of business upon Hamilton's assumption of his office in the summer of 1789 was to provide the federal government with the means to discharge the national debt. The future credit of the infant United States, essential for economic development, among other things, depended on the government's meeting its extant obligations, but these could not be met without the further extension of the credit. The domestic debt, accrued by all the "means of going into debt known to governments," at the time stood at over $27 million, plus $13 million of accumulated interest. The foreign debt of close to $12 million in principal and interest combined added to this burden. This was the optimistic estimate, and the figure was growing as the possibilities of diminishing it were considered, for the revenue was not sufficient even to cover the interest payments. To many, repudiation appeared the only realistic strategy, and, under the circumstances, it was quite justified, but Hamilton insisted that the debt could, and therefore should, be paid, saying that "states, like individuals, who observe their engagements are respected and trusted; while the reverse is the fate of those who pursue an opposite conduct." Moreover, he thought it essential that the federal government assume the debts of the states and reimburse their creditors too. "If all the public creditors receive their dues from one source, distributed with an equal hand," he reasoned, "their interests will be the same; and, having the same interests, they will unite in the support of the fiscal arrangements of the government." Such assumption, however, would raise the national debt to $80 million. To top it all, Hamilton was adamant that the debt be paid to its current, rather than original, holders, namely, to the speculators, who acquired government securities on the cheap, on a sporting chance that their little investment would pay off big later—not out of *amor patriae* and desire to extricate it from financial difficulties, by which some of the original purchasers might have been moved, but out of love of money and moneymaking.

These propositions made some of Hamilton's erstwhile friends realize that they had grievously misplaced their affections and led to a prolonged and acrimonious debate in the Congress which, in Hamilton's words, "laid the foundation of the great schism which has since prevailed" between Republicans and Federalists. Opinion broke down the sectional line then as surely as today it breaks down the party line. Though the "moneyed interest," concentrated in the North, was not entirely absent in the South either, the South took a grim and unforgiving view of it. James Madison, emerging as a leader of the Republican faction, attacked Hamilton's plan as a tool of iniquity, and though he refrained from attacking Hamilton himself (whose patriotism and disinterestedness were, apparently, unassailable), the selfless Secretary of the Treasury was nevertheless identified as the friend of the "stockjobbing herd" of northern capitalists and the enemy of the "honest part of the community," consisting of soldiers, widows, and orphans, whom they dispossessed.[10]

This was an unfair inference. Like most committed mercantilists, Hamilton was not an admirer of material self-interest as such and despised those who pursued it to the exclusion of more altruistic motives. As Washington's aide-de-camp, he had been known to castigate "pecuniary motives" and "dishonest artifices of a mercantile projector" as symptoms of a disease of the state, which could turn fatal if avarice were allowed to take the lead over other considerations. He thought a person motivated solely by the desire of personal material gain worthy of contempt if one was forced by necessity to spend all one's energies on scraping a living; of indignation if one was not so forced and was a person of standing; and of abhorrence and "vengeance of the people" if one happened to be entrusted with the affairs of the state.

At the same time, he believed that, insofar as the multitude of humanity was concerned, considerations of material self-interest exercised the strongest influence on men's imaginations. Hamilton's goal was to have it defined in terms of the public good. He wanted to exploit avarice and ambition; his plan was to attach the holders of the public debt—people with means and the mentality of modern businessmen, who had money, wanted to make more of it, and were willing to take risks in order to do so—to the nation by the ties of their selfishness, make them identify the interest of the nation with their self-interest. In the minds of these people, he determined, the creditability of the American government must become, as that of the British had in the minds of its creditors, "an article of faith, and . . . no longer an article of reason." Not a believer in the invisible hand, he would not rely on self-interest exclusively. He was certain it was not always "rightly understood" as implying constant and careful reinvestment of accumulated capital; one could sink the money in plantations and slaves, which was not the wisest use of it, or get carried away and in the heat of speculative excitement forget the need for "discretion," a possibility "ruinous to the fortunes of many individuals and . . . hurtful to the public credit," as he was to caution at the time of the bank scrip *agiotage*. Of course, he did not think that self-interest was identical with public interest. Therefore, though it was to be allowed every possibility of expression and even stimulated, it also had to be regulated, channeled (as one would channel natural forces, such as water or steam) into venues beneficial for the society as a whole. There always was a place for the directing influence of the government, and in all his far-reaching proposals Hamilton made sure to indicate where exactly that place was. His position was that of a realist. He never deceived himself regarding the moral virtues of speculators, convinced that, like any other description of men, given the chance they would always put themselves first and general good second. But he also believed that speculation—investment in risky ventures, in other words—was an essential ingredient of the fuel which made the economic machine run, and that the continuous increase of national wealth, which he thought necessary to sustain the power and prestige of the United States, was impossible without it. He wanted, in short, to put self-interest—the spirit of adventure, avarice, and ambition—to good public use.

The calculated gamble of the Secretary of the Treasury paid off promptly and handsomely. The avidity of some Americans for quick and easy gain, activated (apparently it needed very little stimulation) by Madison's attack on Hamilton's plan and the opposition he led in the Congress to the passage of the funding and assumption bill, ensured that capital was concentrated in the hands of those who were ready to invest it in the expansion of the national economy. Frightened into thinking that Hamilton's plans would never be realized, the "honest part of the community" in possession of government securities unloaded, and the speculators in Boston, New York, and Philadelphia, "vulture-like" creatures always on the lookout for "where they shall perch to the greatest advantage," descended on the national debt "like crows [upon] a carcass" and gobbled it up. When the bill did pass, at the price of the agreement Hamilton concluded over a bottle of wine with Madison and Jefferson to construct the nation's capital on the banks of the Potomac—a site inhospitable to human life in the summer months, and to Hamilton's ideas all year round—these scavengers, whose appetite for easy gain increased *en mangeant*, were able to invest on a vast scale, mightily energizing the economy, which could hardly be characterized as sluggish to begin with.

The federal government's creditworthiness did become an article of faith with domestic as well as foreign creditors. As experienced a player on the financial market as Talleyrand placed in it his trust. Only in the United States, he said, were the bonds "safe and free from reverses. They have [been] funded in such a sound manner and the prosperity of this country is growing so rapidly that there can be no doubt of their solvency." The outbreak of war in Europe added to the attraction of investment in American securities, with the result that the United States government had at its disposal $20 million of European capital in 1795, and $33 million in 1801. The 6 percent interest on this money that had to be shouldered by the taxpayers, in Hamilton's view, was small change in comparison with the 20 percent profit to be derived from its proper employment at home. The financial position of the new nation was now solid as a rock.

None of this convinced Hamilton's southern opponents that his ideas made any sense. Having established the procedure for coping with the national debt, the indefatigable Secretary of the Treasury turned his attention to the actual means with which the taxpayers were supposed to pay and thus keep it growing for the benefit of the economy, namely, money, which in the young United States was in short supply, and submitted to the Congress his plan for the Bank of the United States. The bank bill passed the House because representatives from the North, who were sympathetic to the "moneyed interest," held a substantial majority, but the South almost as a body voted against it. The likes of Thomas Jefferson and James Madison were not the type to take defeat lying down, and indeed the two future presidents (together with another Virginian, Attorney General Edmund Randolph) lost no time in presenting President Washington with arguments suggesting in the strongest possible terms that he should veto the proposed law. They claimed that the establishment of the bank, a public institution under mostly private control, was unconstitutional, because the powers of the government enumerated in the Constitution did not include one named "the power to establish a bank," and the bank, obviously, could not be considered as "indispensably necessary" for the implementation of any of the powers that were specifically mentioned. The objection that the bank, whose purpose was to provide the economy with circulating medium which it lacked, did seem to be related to the power of the government to regulate commerce, Jefferson countered, as behooved an authority on the matter, with a declarative statement which admitted no further discussion: "To erect a bank and to regulate commerce are very different acts." Madison met with astonishment the very idea: "What has this bill to do with trade? Would any plain man suppose [a bank] had anything to do with trade?"[11] Clearly, to his mind, no plain man was so unreasonable.

But Hamilton was not a plain man, and his explanation of the connection persuaded President Washington to sign the bank bill. The "Little Lion" scored another victory for the predominantly northern "vultures," who celebrated in a virtual bacchanalia of moneymaking, causing the price of scrip to skyrocket from $25 in July to $325 in August and upward and onward, while "the men who had resigned their lives in the war, or who had parted with their patrimonies or hard earned estates, to save the public liberty stood at a distance, and with astonishment beheld the singular and unexpected phenomenon." Tacitly, these men—mostly southern planters—and the bank agreed on a policy of mutual disregard: the bank showed no interest in the business of the land, and representatives of the "agrarian interest" ignored the bank. The enthusiasm of the bank's supporters, as was mentioned earlier, eventually led to the fall of the stock and securities market; Hamilton's prompt action, however, helped it to land on its feet: by October 1791, two months after the fall, both the bank stock and government securities had gained back all that they had lost and more.

Summing up the epopee of the bank's foundation, John Miller wrote:

> Hamilton seemed to have won a complete triumph. His objectives were seldom as fully realized as they were in the case of the Bank of the United States. By increasing and stabilizing the circulating medium, making credit available where credit had not existed before, and discounting bills of exchange, the Bank made itself to a great degree "the mainspring and regulator of the whole American business world." It was of inestimable value to the government in paying the foreign and domestic debt, transmitting funds from one part of the country to another and to Europe, collecting revenue, loaning money and serving as a depository for government funds. It facilitated the payment of taxes by increasing the amount of money in circulation, and the directors co-operated with the Treasury in controlling the money market and maintaining the value of its notes. As a means of raising up a moneyed class, the Bank was second only to the funding system: the high dividends it yielded to stockholders and the opportunities it afforded businessmen to embark upon new ventures made it a potent instrument of capitalism.[12]

In fact, however, it was not until the establishment of the Federal Reserve Board in 1913 that what "seemed" a complete triumph turned into one.

Defense of Industrialization

Finally, there was the "Report on Manufactures," which "contained the embryo of modern America: here, if a date can be assigned to a development so amorphous and far-reaching in its consequences, was conceived the grand design by which the United States became the greatest industrial power in the world." A quintessential expression of economic nationalism—thus of modern economic consciousness—the document was pragmatic in its temper and mercantilist in its ideals. With the British experience as its model, it reflected—and reflected on—the lessons of a two-centuries-old tradition of economic policy and thought, but only its headiness could suggest that this was wine from an old bottle. The report represented a most momentous departure from the American economic orthodoxy. It must have appeared disturbingly innovative, even visionary (in either the positive or negative sense, depending on where one's sympathies lay), to Hamilton's contemporaries, for the audacious Secretary of the Treasury was far ahead of his time. He proved to be prescient, and today may appear to have been clairvoyant, but this was so not because he saw into the future but because he made it happen.

In January 1790 the House of Representatives, whose members shared Hamilton's fundamental mercantilist presuppositions, asked the Secretary of the Treasury to prepare a plan "for the encouragement and promotion of such manufactures as will tend to render the United States independent of other nations for essentials." In response he presented the body with a program and justification of the nation's industrialization. The idea that industrialization—namely, the development of manufacturing industry—beyond essentials was something to be desired was novel (it was, Hamilton noted in the introduction to his report, "not long since deemed very questionable," though he pretended that at the time of his writing it already appeared "to be pretty generally admitted"). The opinion that prevailed was Physiocratic, of a homegrown variety, quite independent of the views of the French Économistes, however much admired for their agreement with the native disposition. It held that manufacturing, of all industries, was the least productive of wealth, in fact, unproductive, and that a country with abundant agricultural resources had no need of it (beyond essentials such as military ammunition, which pertained primarily to concerns other than production of wealth). As in France, this native American Physiocracy reflected the evident economic strengths of the new nation, as well as most readily available opportunities that the latter presented to its enterprising citizens and, therefore, their interests; and, as in France, it seemed to offer the most efficient way to realize mercantilist, that is, nationalist, objectives.

But Hamilton, as was widely recognized, was "damned sharp," his intelligence penetrated beyond what was readily accessible and clearly evident to others, and as he had no personal economic interests but was moved solely by considerations of the national good, there was nothing to obstruct the clarity of his vision. While unable to see into the future, he perceived the possibilities concealed in the present, and also saw the inconsistencies in the reasoning of his opponents, with which they rationalized their blindness. His task was made easier by the fact that this reasoning was lazy and haphazard, for before the brave Secretary of the Treasury challenged it, no one was called upon to examine and bolster it. Hamilton thus began by dismantling the "agricultural system," proving, step by step, that agriculture could not be justifiably considered (as it was) the only truly productive sphere of activity, that all the arguments adduced in defense of its productivity could with equal success be applied to manufactures (from which it followed that the latter were at least as productive), and that, in fact, they were significantly more productive and added infinitely more wealth to the community.

The factors that he believed accounted for the superior productivity of manufacturing industry were the division of labor and technology, specifically the use of machinery. It is likely that in stressing the importance of the division of labor, Hamilton appealed to the authority of Adam Smith, which seems to have been established earlier on this side of the Atlantic; perhaps he even borrowed the idea from the father of modern economics. But the emphasis on machinery was entirely original. It is in fact quite astonishing how early Hamilton recognized technology as a major economic force, how little empirical evidence there was to support this recognition. The "industrial revolution" in Britain had barely begun; the steam engine had been in use for only fifteen years; few perceived what was happening. Hamilton's confidence must have appeared unfounded to the members of the House of Representatives, who had their feet firmly on the ground they knew; empirically it *was* unfounded. Skepticism was the natural reaction to his assertions, which sound almost banal today. Hamilton wrote:

> The employment of machinery forms an item of great importance in the general mass of national industry [i.e., economy]. It is an artificial force brought in aid of the natural force of man; and, to all the purposes of labor, is an increase of hands—an accession of strength, unencumbered, too, by the expense of maintaining the laborer. May it not, therefore, be fairly inferred that those occupations which give greatest scope to the use of this auxiliary contribute most to the general stock of industrious effort and, in consequence, to the general product of industry [economy]?
>
> It shall be taken for granted, and the truth of the position referred to observation, that manufacturing pursuits are susceptible in a greater degree of the application of machinery than those of agriculture. If so, all the difference is lost to a community which, instead of manufacturing for itself, procures the fabrics requisite to its supply from other countries. The substitution of foreign for domestic manufactures is a transfer to foreign nations of the advantages accruing from the employment of machinery in the modes in which it is capable of being employed with most utility and to the greatest extent.
>
> The cotton mill, invented in England within the last twenty years, is a signal illustration of the general proposition which had just been advanced. In consequence of it, all the different processes for spinning cotton are performed by means of machines which are put in motion by water, and attended chiefly by women and children; and by a smaller number of persons, in the whole, than are requisite in the ordinary mode of spinning. And it is an advantage of great moment that the operations of this mill continue, with convenience, during the night as well as

through the day. The prodigious effect of such a machine is easily conceived. To this invention is to be attributed, essentially, the immense progress which has been so suddenly made in Great Britain in the various fabrics of cotton.

How reasonable, how self-evident this argument sounds at the turn of the twenty-first century—so few of us would question today the fundamental role of technology in economic expansion, so many equate technological proficiency with competitive advantage as such. And yet how remarkably narrow are the parameters of Hamilton's economy, growing and mechanized though it is, in comparison with our infinite vision, how close still to the economy of subsistence: its function is limited to the provision of man with food, clothing, and shelter; the only manufacturing industry of importance, even to Hamilton's daring imagination, appears to be textiles. What, then, is the purpose of economic growth? Why constantly increase the wealth of the nation? One can digest only so much food and wear so many clothes. The natural human needs the economy satisfies impose natural limits on its growth. Only as an end in itself (which, to a significant degree, economic growth has become for us) or geared as a means to the political ends of power and prestige—the desire for which is by definition insatiable—can it transcend these limits.

The power and prestige of the United States were uppermost in Hamilton's mind. It was the thought of national greatness—defined in terms of power and prestige—which inspired all of his initiatives as Secretary of the Treasury, all of his public life. Whether or not he believed, as John Miller claims, that "wealth and power were passing rapidly into the hands of those countries that devoted their energies to commerce and manufacturing" (there was at the time only one such country, and it had enjoyed its superior wealth and power for a century) or that industrial development "was the wave of the future upon which nations would rise to greatness," he certainly considered manufacturing essential for safeguarding the nation's honor in the sense of securing its independence from, and favorable comparison with, other nations. Agriculture alone, however flourishing, and with commerce based on agricultural surplus, could not do it. An emphasis on agriculture at the expense of manufacturing industry in domestic economy not only made the country dependent on foreigners for military supplies, therefore weak, but also necessarily placed it at a disadvantage in commercial relations with its manufacturing partners, and thus perpetuated this dependence and increased its relative weakness. In this context Hamilton argued as one would expect a mercantilist: "There is always a higher probability of a favorable balance of trade in regard to countries in which manufactures founded on the basis of a thriving agriculture flourish than in regard to those which are confined wholly, or almost wholly, to agriculture; [from which it followed] that countries of the former description are likely to possess more pecuniary wealth, or money, than those of the latter." Manufactures, it was clear, had the capacity, which agriculture lacked, to increase both the pecuniary wealth and the productivity of labor, which created wealth in general. Only with their help could one take the economy beyond the limits of subsistence and achieve economic growth. Therefore, the encouragement of manufactures in a nation such as the United States, where they were not sufficiently developed, Hamilton claimed, was "recommended by the most cogent and persuasive motives of national policy."

Growth was in the interest of the nation rather than that of individuals (or, to put it differently, it was in the interest of individuals only as members of the nation rather than in their private capacity). Since Hamilton did not believe these to be naturally congruent, he dismissed the likely objection that it was not "wise in a government to attempt to give a direction to the industry of its citizens," as that was best left "under the quick-sighted guidance of private interest," sure to show it the way to the most profitable employment and, consequently, most effectually promote public prosperity. Private interest, in the opinion of the Secretary of the Treasury, was prone rather to near- and not quick-sightedness, its vision obscured by the strong influence of habit, the fear of failure in untried enterprises, and the like, not to speak of "the bounties, premiums, and other artificial encouragements with which foreign nations second the exertions of their own citizens in the branches in which they are to be rivaled." The probable argument to the effect that similar artificial encouragements of American manufactures would serve only the interests of particular classes, at the expense of the rest of the community, forced to support expensive domestic production and to give up the right to enjoy the better prices, and perhaps quality, of foreign goods, Hamilton also countered with the familiar mercantilist riposte. Though it be true that the immediate effect "of regulations controlling the competition of foreign with domestic" production would be a discomfort to the consumer, in the long run protection will pay off in terms of price and quality alike, and in the process encourage domestic competition. Thus, he concluded, it was "the interest of a community, with a view to eventual and permanent economy, to encourage the growth of manufactures. In a national view, a temporary enhancement of price must always be well compensated by a permanent reduction of it." Again, the interests (private and therefore temporary by definition) of a part were sacrificed to the long-term, fundamentally unchanging interest of the whole.[13]

In many ways, Hamilton's economic philosophy resembled that of the leaders of Japanese modernization a century later, unaware as they must have been of this affinity with such a central personage in the history of the Land of Free Trade. Like them, he thought nothing of putting frail women and children of tender age (who otherwise would be "useless" for the community) to work for the nation; like them, he valued private enterprise, entrusting it with the task of promoting economic growth, but would not leave it alone, as it was the duty of the government to encourage, protect, and (however gently) push it in the right direction; like them, he favored domestic competition, but only insofar as it fostered the national interest. He was a proponent of a judiciously measured economic liberalism, never forgetting that economic liberty—the right to follow one's material self-interest—was only a means to the end that was the power and prestige of the United States. Liberty never became a fetish for him. He was an idealist, not a doctrinaire, and, never losing sight of his ideal, was able to distinguish clearly what was, in its light, instrumental, and therefore rational, from what was not—both in his thinking and in the conduct of affairs of the state.

Resistance to Industrialization

However ambitious were Hamilton's financial and monetary policies, the immense project of the industrialization of the American economy, outlined in the "Report on Manufactures," was far more ambitious and in the most auspicious of circumstances could be expected to take many years. The circumstances were not auspicious. In 1804, by the time of Hamilton's tragic death ("Oh, Aaron Burr, what hast thou done? / Thou hast shooted dead great Hamilton" went the popular lament) the transformation had barely begun. The call to patriotic exertion sounded by the first Secretary of the Treasury found little response among his countrymen: they had long been in business for themselves and knew that this was a perfectly moral position; guided by self-interest (irrationally defined and contrary to the logic of *Homo economicus* though it was), they were deaf to the appeal to their better selves. Self-interest pointed to agriculture. "Had Alexander Hamilton been content to be the spokesman of the majority of the people of the United States and to reflect faithfully their ideals and aspirations," wrote a perceptive historian, "he would never have written his reports or, had they been written, they would have been dedicated to furthering the immediate interests of agriculture. The prevailing ideas of the day were hostile to the kind of financial and economic planning that emanated from the office of the Secretary of the Treasury . . . With characteristic audacity, he undertook to run a farmers' republic for the immediate profit of businessmen."

But, though uninterested, the American farmers were too busy making a good living off the land to pay much attention to Hamilton's plans for the industrial development of the country and left active and vocal opposition to the more leisured class of southern planters. Rich, but, in the words of Jefferson, who knew and liked them well, "careless of their interests . . . thoughtless in their expenses and in all their transactions of business," the southern magnates resented the all too quick rise in the world of enterprising young men from the North, whose newly acquired wealth allowed them to pretend to equality with gentlemen of old standing as they "embraced the pride of distinction without its refinements." It appears that this offended them in particular and "was most repulsive of all": the insolent upstarts did not live nobly, they did not take time to wash off the traces of their mediocre origins, the vulgar odors of menial occupations still followed them. They paraded in coaches but belonged in "buttermilk-carts, or at the arms of bakers' wheelbarrows." Not long ago the gentlemen declared that all men were created equal; it was clear that far from regarding the realization of this lofty principle as self-evident, they were unpleasantly surprised by it. Unfortunately for them, they lived in the United States of America, and no other language but that of equality was available to express their discomfiture at the vulgar onslaught on privilege mounted from the North, where they took them at their word. So they used that language shamelessly, carelessly oblivious of the multiple inconsistencies such usage implied. Their desire was to prevent the upward mobility, made possible by the new methods of moneymaking, from the lower orders of society into the American aristocracy, such as it was; incongruously, they argued for "the banishment of [all] privileged orders from the world."[14]

Thomas Jefferson felt their pain. A far more capable politician than Hamilton, sensitive to public opinion and adept at courting it (though, it must be said, he did this only when it corresponded to his principles), Jefferson led the opposition to the ideas of the farsighted and fearless but lonely "Little Lion." The promotion of industry was only one of these ideas and, at the time, not of central concern to the planters; their grievances probably focused on the "fiscal" or "moneyed interest," which was, it was widely feared, ready to transform the United States into the "United States of the Bank." But industrialization was an integral part of Hamilton's policies and, as such, was identified with the other evil economic forces—finance and, to a certain extent, even commerce—aligned by the crafty Secretary of the Treasury against the only honest method of moneymaking, the business of agriculture.

Jefferson's preference for agriculture predated his conflict with Hamilton. "Those who labor in the earth are the chosen people of God," he wrote in the 1784 *Notes on Virginia*, "if ever he had a chosen people, whose breasts He has made His peculiar deposit for substantial and genuine virtue. It is the focus in which He keeps alive that sacred fire, which otherwise might escape from the face of the earth." Farmers were "the most vigorous, the most inde-

pendent, the most virtuous" of men, and were certain to be the most patriotic, too, "tied [as they were] to their country, and wedded to its liberty and
interests by the most lasting bonds." Thus agriculture was the "wisest pursuit" and contributed "most to the real wealth, good morals and happiness of
the people." The affinity of his views with Physiocracy was profound (possibly explaining his sympathy for Adam Smith, or at least for his chief early interpreter in France, J.-B. Say), but he was "no doctrinaire Physiocrat" and, as
a landowner and planter, was sufficiently involved in commerce not to judge
it as harshly as did the French Économistes. Indeed, he recognized it as the
"modern source of wealth and power" and, maintaining his country's "natural right" to a fair share of the latter, sought by every means at his disposal in
his many important public offices to expand American foreign trade. A part
of him clearly remained mercantilist, even bullionist: he was convinced that
specie constituted a crucial element in the wealth of a nation and, during the
Revolutionary War, even advocated the sale of tobacco and provisions to
Britain as a means of changing the balance of power in favor of the newborn
American Confederation.

Later, as Secretary of State in Washington's administration, Jefferson advised American diplomats to insist on the right of the United States to free
trade with the European powers (i.e., unencumbered sale to the latter of
American agricultural produce), suggesting that they threaten those that
would not cooperate with the possibility of America's turning to manufactures. But, while a cunning diplomatic ruse, this possibility must have appeared at least as frightening to himself: unlike English mercantilists and
unlike Hamilton, he had not yet perceived any connection between national wealth and industrial capability and rather believed the effects of industrial development to be deleterious for the manufacturing nation first of all.
Large-scale manufactories were instruments of degeneracy: they produced
"starved and rickety paupers and dwarfs" whose infirm bodies could not be
expected to support the independent republican spirit. It was best that "for
the general operations of manufacture [American] workshops remain in Europe." Jefferson's opinion of finance, or "tricks with paper," was even worse.
It was the province of "gamblers" and "jugglers," of people who were merce-
nary and corrupt to the core, and had no sense of honor or loyalty that could
restrain their brazen ambition. Above all, they were "monarchists." Financial
and industrial capitalism of the kind conceived by Hamilton, in Jefferson's
mind, stood to "monarchism" in the same relationship today assumed to exist between that very capitalism and democracy. "Stockjobbers" were the natural kin of "King makers"—the natural enemies, that is, of the republican
form of government and the sovereign people it represented.

Presenting Hamilton's economic policies as a strategy in the plot to undermine the republic was a brilliant political move. At the time, "monarchist" in the United States was the equivalent of today's "right-wing reactionary" or "fascist," "a substitute for argument, and its overmatch," in the words of Fisher Ames. It was a word whose very utterance terrified and repelled, a charge that damaged irreparably simply by being leveled. Were Jefferson engaged in calculated character assassination (which would be more in character for his future assassin of a vice president), he could not have done better than hurling it at his rival. But he seems to have truly believed that Hamilton was a monarchist. How such a preposterous idea could have occurred to one of the most intelligent and high-minded personalities of the age belongs to those questions whose examination proves that the human mind works far more mysteriously than rational action theory would have one suppose and that, specifically, rather than being always dictated by reason, interests often dictate to it. Perhaps this condemnatory opinion of the intention and economic policies of a great patriot whose life was so evidently devoted to the service of the republic was related to Jefferson's belief in the inherent goodness of human nature in general and his trust in self-interest, through which operated the invisible hand of the beneficent providence. If man was naturally good and self-interest led to common welfare, individuals could err, but the majority was never wrong. The majority engaged in agriculture; it was justly uninterested in manufactures and finance. Hamilton claimed he knew better, he placed himself above the majority; he wished to force it on a path of inefficiency and sin, seducing the weak. He had no respect for the will of the people. What else could one think but that he wanted to become a progenitor of kings or plotted to make some available royal (the fourth son of George III, the duke of Kent, was rumored to be his candidate) king of the United States?

Things look different in opposition than they do when one is called upon to decide the fate of the nation—at least, fortunately for the nation, so they did to Jefferson. "Anti-Hamiltonian out of supreme office, [he] became in good part Hamiltonian as President." He learned to appreciate the importance of banking and its "tricks with paper," of protection, when it was needed, and of manufactures. As he grew older, he became what Hamilton had always been, a pragmatist in regard to the means of achieving the ideal, which the two men shared, of the power and prestige of the United States, and exchanged the politics of ultimate ends for the politics of responsibility. In 1816, an elder statesman, he wrote to a Republican leader in Massachusetts, Benjamin Austin, in awkward defense of his earlier views which were now quoted by enemies of American manufactures and "friends of England." These views had long since changed, and their change made Jefferson forget the ideological sharpness of his opposition to Hamilton's policies.

You tell me I am quoted by those who wish to continue our dependence on England for manufactures. There was a time when I might have been so quoted with more candor, but within the thirty years which have since elapsed, how are circumstances changed! Our independent place among nations was acknowledged. A commerce which offered the raw material in exchange for the same material after receiving the last touch of industry was worthy of welcome to all nations. It was expected that those especially to whom manufacturing industry was important would cherish the friendship of such customers by every favor, by every inducement, and particularly cultivate their peace by every act of justice and friendship.

Under this prospect the question seemed legitimate whether, with such an immensity of unimproved land courting the hand of husbandry, the industry of agriculture, or that of manufactures would add most to the national wealth. And the doubt on the utilities of the American manufactures was entertained on this consideration chiefly, that to the labor of the husbandman a vast addition is made by the spontaneous energies of the earth on which it is employed . . .

This was the state of things in 1785, when the Notes on Virginia were first published; when the ocean being open to all nations, and their common right in it acknowledged and exercised under regulations sanctioned by the assent and usage of all, it was thought that the doubt might claim some consideration. But who in 1785 could foresee the rapid depravity which was to render the close of that century a disgrace of the history of men?

Austin could have answered "Hamilton," but that would have been cruel to an old man so eager to correct past mistakes.

Referring to the restrictions placed before the War of 1812 on American commerce, which forced many Americans to reconsider their self-interest and look on manufactures with favor bordering on enthusiasm, Jefferson continued:

Compare this state of things with that of '85, and say whether an opinion founded in the circumstances of that day can be fairly applied to those of the present. We have experienced what we did not then believe, that there exists both profligacy and power enough to exclude us from the field of interchange with other nations; that to be independent for the comforts of life we must fabricate them ourselves. We must now place the manufacturer by the side of the agriculturist . . .

The grand inquiry now is, shall we make our own comforts or go without them at the will of a foreign nation? He, therefore, who is now against domestic manufacture must be for reducing us either to dependence on that foreign nation, or to be clothed in skins and to live like wild beasts in dens and caverns. I am not one of these; experience has taught me that manufactures are now as necessary to our independence as to our comfort; and if those who quote me as of a different opinion will keep pace with me in purchasing nothing foreign where an equivalent of domestic fabric can be obtained, without regard to difference in price, it will not be our fault if we do not soon have a supply at home equal to our demand, and wrest the weapon of distress from the hand which had wielded it.

Jefferson ended his letter with an admonition never to treat elements of economic policy as matters of principle (for the economic interest of the nation changed with circumstances) and rejected those who relied on his earlier authority as unpatriotic:

In so complicated a science as political economy, no one axiom can be laid down as wise and expedient for all times and circumstances, and for their contraries. Inattention to this is what has called for this explanation, which reflection would have rendered unnecessary with the candid, while nothing will do with those who use the former opinion only as a stalking-horse to cover their disloyal propensities to keep us in eternal vassalage to a foreign and unfriendly people.

In this duel—for the outcome of which he cared far more than for that in which his life was at stake—Hamilton had triumphed.[15]

Economic Nationalism Triumphant: The "American System"

He triumphed, even though Jefferson changed his opinions again,[16] for the views of the first Secretary of the Treasury had been embraced as the "American system." Several political developments contributed to this emphatic nationalization of an economic program which only years before had appeared so obviously foreign. Among these developments were the Franco-British hostilities, which repeatedly induced both parties to interfere with the profitable commerce in which the United States engaged as a neutral power; the embargo Jefferson imposed to avoid conflict; and finally the war for "free trade and seamen's rights," declared by his peace-loving successor, President Madison, against the opposition of Federalist New England (where the ostensibly offended commercial interest was concentrated) and under the irresistible pressure of bellicose Republican leaders from the South (John Calhoun) and West (Henry Clay), who put the national interest—as they understood it at the time—above that of a section. Northern merchants believed the free trade rhetoric ridiculous, and were far more upset by the measures designed to protect them than by the occasional altercations with the warring Europeans, which only marginally added to the risk involved in their business or subtracted from its profits. New Englanders did not want to support the war effort and thought of secession, Reverend Elijah Parish of Massachusetts calling on them from the pulpit in July 1812 to "proclaim an honorable neutrality [and] let the southern Heroes fight their own battles and guard . . . against the just vengeance of their lacerated slaves." "Break those chains, under which you have sullenly murmured, during the long, long reign of democracy," he advised, "and once more breathe that free, commercial air of New England which your fathers always enjoyed."

What, if not commercial interests, animated the "hawks" of 1812? Nationalism—of the loud, chauvinistic variety—was surely one of the sentiments. It reflected the exuberant sense of strength, which could not but be inspired by the tremendous increase in the nation's territory (and resources) as a result of the Louisiana Purchase. The young United States, not yet thirty years of age, was larger than any European state with the exception of Russia. Bursting with confidence, Americans welcomed the opportunity to put this strength to a test: they knew they were no longer to be dictated to; they wished to know whether they could dictate.

The Louisiana Purchase added a new section, the West, to the Union, which had previously consisted of only two sections. It was a country of young males with raging hormones, unfamiliar with the concept of delayed gratification, who wanted to—and believed they could—have it all now. They were even more confident than their compatriots elsewhere, and less patient. They also tended to think "continentally"; unburdened by the memories of colonial rivalries, unfettered by inveterate vested interests, national consciousness in the West was starker than in the older regions; there were no atavistic identities which interfered with the national identity. The West had no past, just the future, and its special interests—seen as national—were defined by the latter. Britain and France stood (and placed Indians) in the way of the western, American, expansion. They had to be taught a lesson, that much was clear. The disagreements in the war faction concerned which of the two, Britain or France, was to be taken on first, and Britain was chosen, among other reasons, because it represented a greater challenge.

The voice that spoke most convincingly in favor of the war belonged to the young senator from Kentucky, Henry Clay—the (adopted) "child of the West," the "statesman for the Union." On February 22, 1810, he delivered in the Senate an "essential Clay" speech. "It breathed western passion to smite the foreign forces that unceasingly humiliated and shamed the American people." "I am for resistance by the sword," he declared. "No man in the nation desires peace more than I. But I prefer the troubled ocean of war . . . to the tranquil, putrescent pool of ignominious peace." He was for war with Britain, rather than France, for Britain was "prior in aggression," and victory over it, involving a greater risk, perhaps, offered a greater payoff. Some claimed that no object was attainable by such a war. Clay replied: "The conquest of Canada is in your power. I trust I shall not be deemed presumptuous when I state, what I verily believe, that the militia of Kentucky are alone competent to place Montreal and Upper Canada at your feet." And he demanded rhetorically: "Is it nothing to us to extinguish the torch that lights up savage warfare? Is it nothing to acquire the entire fur trade connected with that country, and to destroy the temptation and the opportunity of violating your revenue and other laws?"[17]

As it happened, the Kentucky militia disgraced themselves, but Jackson's spectacular performance in the Battle of New Orleans and the honorable Treaty of Ghent further boosted Americans' self-confidence and fired civic sentiments. Nationalism roused spirits which had been indifferent to its suggestions earlier and appeared in the new form of economic nationalism, among others. National economic interest, traditionally defined by the Republicans in terms of self-interest, came to be seen by many as separate from, and superior to, if still dependent on the latter. And self-interest itself was gradually redirected into new channels—such as the manufacturing industry—which not long before had seemed to be contrary to its logic.

Disturbances in the nation's trade with Europe alerted American entrepreneurs to the opportunities for moneymaking offered by manufactures, and nationalism made them morally attractive. Such entrepreneurs remained relatively few throughout the first half of the nineteenth century, but their absolute numbers grew rapidly. The first mechanized industry, as in Britain, was cotton spinning; it suggested itself as a natural investment for an American businessman, given that the country, with the help of the native genius in the person of Eli Whitney and his "'gin," was becoming the largest producer of raw cotton in the world. Again, New England, with the fertility of imagination compensating for the barrenness of the soil, led the way. About 100 spinning mills were operating there in 1812. Three years later, within thirty miles of Providence alone there were at least 140 of them. The first mill was set up in 1787, by George Cabot, in Beverly, Massachusetts. It was not particularly successful. But the interest in mechanized production was passed down the family line, and in 1813 Francis Cabot Lowell founded the Boston Manufacturing Company, which funded "the first modern industrial factory." Located in Waltham, it worked raw cotton into cloth, spinning, weaving, dyeing, and all. The work was done by machines designed, manufactured, and repaired on the premises, and later a print shop was added to make possible an elegant finished fabric. This "invention of the industrial factory by Lowell and his associates," wrote J. O. Robertson, "was the first major American contribution to industrialization. (British industrialists did not adopt the idea until much later in the century.) The factory was itself a complex machine which required the integration of energy, capital, numbers of human beings, and many complicated engines into a self-contained process which produced a volume product."

Pooling of capital for undertakings of this kind was made easier by the changes in the corporation law. Originally monopolies, created to promote public goals (however defined) with the help of private enterprise, corporations were imported to colonial America from England. Some of the colonies were corporations, so were cities and colleges, but businesses seldom incorporated before the Revolution. The first business corporation in the new nation was created in 1781; it was the Bank of North America. Ten years later the Congress chartered another—the Bank of the United States—and in the meantime individual states created thirty or so corporations of their own. In the next decade business corporations mushroomed, with 295 of them in existence by the beginning of the new century. As their numbers grew, so did the sentiment against them. Whatever contribution they made to the public welfare, it was claimed, was negated by the fact that they implied "a privilege given to one order of citizens which others [did] not enjoy, and [thus were] destructive of that principle of equal liberty" which was the supreme American ideal. The tug-of-war between American ideals of individualism and egalitarianism which was based on and reinforced it was developing a pattern: American individuals, jealous of their equality, attempted to avail themselves of all the "allowable" means to raise themselves in the world, if possible above the multitude, while the multitude of these same individuals, jealous of their equality, tried to keep them down.

The agitation reached its peak with Jackson's attack on the "monster" Bank of the United States, but by Jackson's time corporations were already being stripped of their most offensive privileges: in particular (since 1799, when the legislature of Massachusetts enacted a law for the creation of library corporations), they were no longer monopolies. By the 1830s, anyone who filled out the necessary forms and paid the requisite fees could incorporate. From a tool of the political community which harnessed self-interest to the promotion of public good, the corporation was transformed into a tool of self-interest which facilitated the funding of large-scale private enterprise. Its most important privilege now was freedom from outside interference.[18]

At the same time, industrialization was actively promoted by the government on all levels. On March 26, 1810, Henry Clay delivered yet another momentous speech in the Senate, one rather discordant with the valiant defense, to the point of war, of free trade he had mounted from the same seat a month earlier. The March speech was related to the war effort, however. It was provoked by the opposition to John Pope's amendment to the bill regarding the purchase of war supplies, which provided for the preference of home-produced naval stores, such as hemp, cordage, sailcloth, and the like. Ironically, the protectionist amendment was opposed by a Federalist, James Lloyd of Boston, whom Clay, as he rallied to the cause of American manufactures, accused of representing the commercial interest. At that early moment in the development of what was to become "the American system," Clay was still an old-fashioned mercantilist of the Continental European type, rather than a modern economic nationalist. His goal was national self-sufficiency, not competition. Therefore, he argued, "it is important to diminish our imports. The nation that imports its cloathing from abroad is but little less dependent than if it imported its bread." Clay briefly touched upon the issue of national security (asserting that United States Navy operations ought not "to depend upon casualties of foreign supply"), but the emphasis was on clothing. It was in the interest of everyone in America, insisted the spirited Kentuckian, to dress in American-made garments, the selfish protestations of "dame commerce" to the contrary. "She is a flirting, flippant, noisy jade," Clay maintained, "and if we are governed by her fantasies we shall never put off the muslins of India and the cloths of Europe. But I trust that the yeomanry of the country, the true and genuine landlord of this tenement, called the United States, disregarding her freaks, will persevere in reform until the whole national family is furnished by itself with the cloathing necessary for its own use." He was certain that, "fostered by the government," American manufactures would before long be "fully competent to supply us with at least every necessary article of cloathing." Therefore, he "for one" was in favor of encouraging them "to such an extent as will redeem us entirely from all dependence on foreign countries." There was "a pleasure," Clay argued, "a pride" in being arrayed in raiment of domestic make, and he demanded bravely, "Others may prefer the cloths [of] Leeds and of London, but give me those of Humphreysville." (He was true to his word, it seems, his manner of dress being "slovenly," which accorded little with his otherwise graceful person.)

Humphreysville was a pioneering enterprise, a woolen factory, established in 1806 by Colonel David Humphreys (who imported Merino sheep from Spain, to which he was a consul) along the lines a century later thought to be uniquely characteristic of Japanese capitalism. It was "staffed mostly by unpaid apprentice boys, some of them orphans . . . and by women at wages of fifty cents to a dollar a week." The colonel was a patriot and an enthusiast, from time to time given to poetic outbursts, such as, for instance, the grandiloquent "Poem on the Industry of the United States of America," calling on Washington to foster domestic manufactures:

> While thou presid'st, in useful arts direct,
> Create new fabrics and the old protect,

and exhorting the nation in the following words:

> First let the loom each lib'ral thought engage,
> Its labours growing with the growing age;
> Then true utility with taste allied,
> Shall make our homespun garbs our nation's pride.
> See wool, the boast of Britain's proudest hour,
> Is still the basis of her wealth and pow'r!
> From her the nations wait their wintry robe,
> Round half this idle, poor, dependant globe.
> Shall we, who foil'd her sons in fields of fame,
> In peace add noblest triumphs to her name?
> Shall we, who dar'd assert the rights of man,
> Become the vassals of her wiser plan?
> Then, rous'd from lethargies—up! men! increase,
> In every vale, on every hill, the fleece!

Humphreys envisaged his role as the patriarch of a family, rather than simply an employer: he not only thought that his duty was to "teach tiny hands with engin'ry to toil," but also believed that he was responsible for the morals and general education of those whom he provided with work. If every manufacturer in the United States assumed such responsibility, industrial development in the country could proceed free from the deleterious side effects which blackened its name in Britain. Americans could reap the benefits of the new economic thinking, invented across the Atlantic, without paying its social costs; this was not a package deal.

The wisdom of this position was quickly appreciated, and in 1808 the elected representatives of the state of Connecticut lauded Humphreys's establishment in terms that appeared to be taken verbatim from Hamilton's disregarded report. It was most praiseworthy of Humphreys to use machines and child labor, they declared: this not only allowed him to avoid the "embarrassments resulting from the dearness of labor," but also made it possible to transform into "active capital the exertions of persons who otherwise would be idle, and in many instances a burthen to the community," and this "in a mode very honourable to himself and useful to the State." The legislature thus regarded with "much satisfaction the exertions of Colonel

Humphreys to render the exertions of women and children more useful, and those of the latter more nearly useful." His was a magic formula: "Nothing [was] drained from tillage and yet the funds of national industry [were] increased." It was only just to reward his ingenious contribution to these funds with an exemption of all his superintendents, foremen, and apprentices from poll tax and assessments, military duty, and working on highways, and to leave the factory tax-free for ten years.

Such legislative largesse must have encouraged others to follow Humphreys's example, undoubtedly also recommended by its high-mindedness. "Patriarchal" industrial establishments were founded in the other northeastern states. In Massachusetts, Francis Cabot Lowell of the Boston Manufacturing Company in 1820 expanded the first modern industrial factory into "the first planned industrial city in America"—Lowell. Its worker-residents—mostly young women—recruited from rural New England, lived in dormitories under the supervision of house "mothers," where they had to observe strict etiquette, designed to keep them out of mischief, and could profit from various educational programs and activities. Apparently the girls valued the experience. It gave them a sense of independence, expanded their mental horizons, and allowed them to amass a dowry that improved their marriage possibilities. Other planned manufacturing towns, such as Manchester, New Hampshire, or Holyoke, Massachusetts, bore a closer resemblance to natural urban growth. Their labor force was more heterogeneous, including men and married people of both sexes, and, in addition to dormitories for the young and single, they provided family housing and numerous services, such as shops, medical and legal offices, and churches. Work hours were long and the discipline rigorous. In 1850, in Holyoke, the morning bells rang at 4:40 and 5:00 A.M. The mill gates opened at the first bell and were closed ten minutes past the second one, when the work began. Those who did not make it through this window of opportunity could not work until after dinner (and lost their morning wages). Breakfast was taken at the mill during the half hour after 6:30 or 7:00, depending on the time of year. Then work went on for another five to five and a half hours until the half-hour dinner recess at 12:30. The day ended at 6:30 (earlier on Saturdays if sunset was before 6:30).

In 1845, when "the first planned industrial city" had come to resemble others more, John Greenleaf Whittier, who for six months edited a Lowell reform newspaper, wrote about it:

This, then, is Lowell—a city, springing up, like the enchanted palaces of the Arabian tales, as it were in a single night—stretching far and wide its chaos of brick masonry and painted shingles, filling the angle of the confluence of the Concord and the Merrimack with the sights and sounds of trade and industry! Marvelously here has Art wrought its modern miracles. I can scarcely realize the fact, that a few years ago these rivers, now tamed and subdued to the purposes of man, and charmed into slavish subjection to the Wizard of Mechanism, rolled unchecked . . . in the wild freedom of Nature. A stranger, in view of all this wonderful change, feels himself as it were thrust forward into a new century; he seems treading on the outer circle of the millennium of steam engines and cotton mills. Work is here the Patron Saint. Every thing bears his image and superscription. Here is no place for that respectable class of citizens called gentlemen, and their much vilified brethren, familiarly known as loafers . . . The Gospel of Industry preached daily and hourly from some thirty temples; each huger than the Milan Cathedral or the temple of Jeddo . . . its thousand priests, and its thousands priestesses, ministering around their spinning-jenny and power-loom altars.

This was wonderful indeed, but Whittier had doubts whether such miracles were, in the final analysis, good for man. In a later edition of his *Stranger in Lowell,* a passage was added which stated: "After all, it may well be questioned whether this gospel according to Poor Richard's Almanac, is precisely calculated for the redemption of humanity. Labor, graduated to man's simple wants, necessities, and unperverted tastes, is doubtless well; but all beyond this is weariness of flesh and spirit."[19]

Turnpikes, Canals, Railroads

More important for run-of-the-mill entrepreneurs than the attraction of the role of the nation's teachers were new opportunities for moneymaking which presented themselves with the emerging industrial infrastructure. The latter, by definition, was the foundation of American industrialization, but it was intended to serve the "commercial" and the "money interest," which promoted it with little if any thought for industrial development. Its laying down began with the construction of roads and bridges by individual states with the help of the chartered transportation corporations. Massachusetts, as in so many other endeavors, blazed the trail with the Proprietors of Charles River Bridge in 1785. The bridge, considered "a most pleasing proof" and "the greatest effect" of the powers of "private enterprise in the United States," was opened in 1786—with great fanfare, including a parade of the builders, the stockholders, and state and city officials, cheered by twenty thousand spectators. It was a very successful venture and made many people rich, increasing land values in its neighborhood and paying stockholders the minimum of 10 percent annually. In 1837, during the attack on monopolies, the Charles River Bridge Corporation was declared unconstitutional.

The honor of building "the first of the great American turnpikes" belonged to Pennsylvania, which in 1792 incorporated the President, Managers, and Company of the Philadelphia and Lancaster Turnpike Road. An English observer in 1797 characterized the road as "a masterpiece of its kind." It was sixty-two miles long and cost half a million dollars, a very large sum at the time. Though not as successful as the Charles River Bridge, it also proved a wise investment, which could not be said of most other turnpikes. The boom in their construction began after the War of 1812 and lasted for the next several decades. Tens of thousands of miles of roads were built all over the growing American territory, with Pennsylvania and Kentucky investing most lavishly. The returns were disappointing: shipping goods via turnpikes—the reason for their construction—proved too expensive, especially when compared with transportation by plentiful waterways. But they failed to subdue the enthusiasm of capitalists who, despite the clear evidence to the contrary, believed in their inherent profitability (thereby demonstrating that they were complex creatures of flesh, blood, and passions, capable of strong convictions and misconceptions, and not programmed "rational" mannequins which economic theorists would imagine them to be).

In 1808 Secretary of the Treasury Albert Gallatin argued in his "Report on Public Roads and Canals" that the federal government was under an obligation to contribute actively to the construction of the transportation network, since private capital was insufficient for, and private interest precluded committing it to, ventures which promised only "remote and moderate profits." He underestimated the resourcefulness of his compatriots. In New York, Gouverneur Morris and others were at the time promoting a state canal that would connect Lake Erie to the Hudson, making New York City an even greater commercial center than it already was and the entrepôt for western commodities. The promoters did not conceal their personal interest in raising the value of the land, which they owned, along the projected waterway, but, as the canal was in the common interest as well, counted on the state's support and expected to be rewarded by it for their efforts and expenses. The state obliged by appointing an advisory committee with Morris as a member and in 1811 received a report which, as could be expected, recommended the construction. Downplaying the rivalry between the states, the commissioners argued that the canal would strengthen the ties between them, contribute to the national prosperity (boosting agriculture, manufactures, and commerce alike), and prevent the commercial ascendancy of foreign harbors, such as Montreal. A great national interest was at stake, they insisted. This implied the need for a chartered corporation, for matters of such importance were not to be entrusted to self-interest alone.

Since decisions of this magnitude could not be taken lightly, it was not until 1817 that the New York State legislature acted upon this recommendation. The reasons behind its hesitancy were as good as they come: Americans had little experience in canal construction. The longest one in existence at the time, the Middlesex Canal, which connected the Merrimack River to Boston, extended for only 27 miles, while the projected length of the Erie Canal was 350 miles, three and a half times the length of all American canals combined. The young surveyor who became the project's chief engineer was sent to England to learn the secrets of the art, and got his education from walking the two thousand miles along English canals. The estimated cost of the construction—$6 million—appeared prohibitive as well, but the audacious New Yorkers, nudged by Governor De Witt Clinton (no stranger to risky speculations), took the risk, and the payoff was staggering. The canal opened for traffic in 1825; the net profit, calculated in 1882, was $42.6 million. The profit to the nation was far greater. The "mighty ditch," dug, according to a popular 1830s ballad, by the rich of New York, became the mother of all ditches and started a boom in canal construction across the country. Canals provided cheap and convenient transportation for agricultural products, raised their prices, and boosted commerce. They were vessels that carried vital juices and literally infused life into the great land mass that the United States now possessed. The population along the canal routes swelled and business flourished.

But the canals were dainty capillaries compared to the iron arteries of railroads, which between 1830 and 1850 were to spurt throughout the body of the young nation. American railroads, the first of which began operating in 1833, extended to 3,000 miles by 1840 (1,200 miles more than the combined length of railroads in Europe) and to 9,000 miles (more than twice the combined length of the canals) by 1850. The payoffs were enormous, the risks contributed to the thrill. "The most adventurous and resilient among Americans, men who in still earlier days would have engaged in whaling or the desperate fur trade, turned their energies into the construction of railways." Very expensive to build, they were subsidized by the local and state governments through chartered corporations and direct investment. Their promoters, however, were merchants, who were turning from competitive foreign commerce to the expanding (in no small degree owing to their efforts) domestic market. It was this "commercial interest" that supplied private capital. By 1850 the biggest American businesses, railroads were the first "big" businesses. They were, by their very nature, industrial and stimulated industrialization in multiple ways.

The creation—from scratch and within the span of one generation—of a formidable communications network effected a tremendous change in people's lives, which was deeply appreciated by those who were older. In 1847, speaking at the opening of the Northern Railroad to Grafton, New Hampshire, Daniel Webster remembered:

We are on Smith's River, which, while in college, I had occasion to swim. Even that could not always be done; and I have occasionally made a circuit of many rough and tedious miles to get over it. At that day, steam, as a motive power, acting on water and land, was thought of by nobody; nor were there good, practicable roads in this part of the State . . . So late as when I left college, there was no road from river to river for a carriage fit for the conveyance of persons. I well recollect the commencement of the system of turnpike roads. The granting of a charter of the fourth turnpike, which led from Lebanon to Boscawen, was regarded as a wonderful era . . . I remember to have attended the first meeting of the proprietors of this turnpike at Andover. It was difficult to persuade men that it was possible to have a passable carriage road over these mountains . . . Perhaps the most valuable result of making these and other turnpike roads was the diffusion of knowledge upon road-making among the people; for in a few years afterward, great numbers of the people went to church, to electoral and other meetings, in chaises and wagons, over very tolerable roads. The next step after turnpikes was canals. Governor Sullivan, Dr. Dexter, Colonel Baldwin, and other eminent citizens of Massachusetts, had planned the Middlesex Canal, connecting the Merrimack River at Pawtucket Falls, near where Lowell now is, with Boston . . . This was thought to be a great and most useful achievement, and so indeed it was. But a vastly greater was now approaching, the era of steam. That is the invention which distinguishes this age. The application of steam to the moving of heavy bodies, on the water and on the land, towers above all other inventions of this or the preceding age.

For Webster, at least, the development was a wonderment, and he called upon his audience to recognize the manifold benefits it implied:

Fellow-citizens, this railroad may be said to bring the sea to your doors. You cannot, indeed, snuff its salt water, but you will taste its best products, as fresh as those who live on its shores. I cannot conceive of any policy more useful to the great mass of the community than the policy which established these public improvements. Let me say, fellow-citizens, that in the history of human inventions there is hardly one so well calculated as that of railroads to equalize the condition of men. The richest must travel in the cars, for there they travel fastest; the poorest can travel in the cars, while they could not travel otherwise, because this mode of conveyance costs but little time or money . . . Men are thus brought together as neighbors and acquaintances, who live two hundred miles apart.[20]

Protection as a National Principle

The federal government converted to the "industrial system" several decades earlier than the American people: victorious, Republicans came to appreciate the merit of the literal interpretation of "leadership" by the Federalists. This conversion (paradoxically, if one associates the "industrial system" with Adam Smith) was accompanied by the wide and enthusiastic acceptance of the central element of the Federalist economic doctrine: Hamiltonian protectionism. Protection of the economy by the government, argued John Calhoun, the leader of the Republicans in the postwar (of 1812) House and the champion of "the policies of high Federalism," was necessary, in the first place because of the natural economic competitiveness of the nation's chief rival, Britain, and its nationalist jealousy of the United States' rapid development. For this reason, among other things, he sponsored the resurrection of the Bank of the United States, dead since 1811, strenuously advocating for the second bank the very same powers he opposed before, and urged that the increased revenue to the government be spent on internal improvements, such as roads tying Maine to Louisiana, eastern commercial centers to the West, and the West to New Orleans. He also argued against the "abstract principle that, industry [economy] left to pursue its own course, will find [the reasons for development] in its own interest." Self-interest was not the wisest adviser where national good was concerned, and it was the duty of the government to make sure that the former was channeled into directions that were conducive to the latter.

Manufactures were no longer seen as a poor and unworthy relation of agriculture and commerce. It was decided that of all branches of the national industry, they were the most "eminently calculated to build up a National character, and insure the real independence of our beloved country." The eminent instrument of their encouragement, the protective tariff, was therefore elevated from the humble rank of a stopgap measure, to be used when expedient and abandoned without regret, to that of a national—American—principle. The best economic minds and ablest politicians (if not the businessmen) lined up behind the new position. As before, Britain was in part responsible for the metamorphosis in American attitudes (though, clearly, its policies only strengthened rather than provoked them). In 1815 it introduced, and in 1817 started to enforce, the Corn Laws, which prohibited the importation of grain when it fell below a certain price at home. This directly affected American "agrarian interest," unrivaled in its loyalty to the ideals of free trade throughout the period, and brought many a farmer to the side of protection.

In 1819 Mathew Carey, a Pennsylvania banker, and nine like-minded individuals formed the Philadelphia Society for the Promotion of National Industry, and Carey used it as a platform from which to spread the anti-British protectionist gospel. Carey's Anglophobia was of long standing: as a young man in Ireland he had called for an armed insurrection against England and was forced to emigrate as a result. His *Pennsylvania Herald* preached resistance to everything British and, on one occasion, proclaimed a commercial treaty with this enemy nation a negation of the Declaration of Independence, which made the United States as good as a colony of "the most corrupt and degenerate government in Europe." He had as much energy and was as devoted to the cause as his German contemporary Friedrich List, who that very year, at the head of the newborn Society of German Merchants and Manufacturers, was embarking on a lifelong career as propagandist of "national economy" and industrialization in his Fatherland. Like List, Carey went straight for the theoretical foundations of the enemy position, wasting no time in acquainting himself with the defenses he was determined to demolish. Though an experienced businessman and a veteran of the interminable bank wars, Carey confessed that he had not given to the theory of political economy three days of study. But in less than three days he became sufficiently familiar with both the new and the old school in approaching the subject to compare and render a judgement on their relative merits—an achievement that should qualify him as a genius. The new, laissez-faire school was represented by Adam Smith and his followers, such as Ricardo; it had its root in the fantastic imagination of philosophers, was abstract and removed from the real world. The old, mercantilist school, had the authority of practice behind it; it was a lesson taught by history and had the great merit of making England a superpower. Carey preferred the old school. It was not a "theory" in the sense that the new one was, of neatly organized arguments, however groundless, but then "theories" were created by "theorists" who had nothing better to do, and not by men of affairs. Perhaps it would be useful for the old school to acquire a theorist of its own, to wrest the palm of intellectual prestige, which, Carey conceded, belonged to the disciples of Smith, from the hands of the supporters of laissez-faire. But before such a theorist could be found (which was to happen, as we know, with the arrival of Friedrich List from Germany), Carey believed his plain talk would do.

For some even less was sufficient. Henry Clay, who was later to rely on Carey and praise him for "the disinterested diligence with which he has collected a large mass of highly useful facts and . . . the clear and convincing reasoning with which he generally illustrates them," insisted in Congress in 1816 that it was high time to "effectually protect our manufacturers" from foreign competition. Moreover, he claimed that protection was in "the general interest" more than in the interest of manufacturers themselves. Clay's position at times appeared pragmatic: he argued for selective protection in accordance with the concrete and changing circumstances, being particularly eager to encourage Kentucky "hempen and sail cloths" manufactures. But pragmatic considerations clearly were subsumed in a general ideology, and it was this ideology that determined his vote. "Clay, Calhoun, and some other southern representatives supported [the tariff of 1816] largely for nationalistic reasons," says Robert Remini. In this they were different both from the majority of northeasterners and westerners, who favored it "because it advanced their economic interests," and the minority, such as Daniel Webster from New Hampshire, who sided with the majority of the southerners in their opposition to it, "because he believed it would injure the shipping interests of New England."[21]

The tariff bill passed, establishing 25 percent duties on cottons and woolens (with East Indian cottons particularly hard hit) and 30 percent on iron goods. But this did not satisfy the nationalists. The Panic of 1819 gave rise to demands for more protection, especially in Pennsylvania (which was the leader in manufacturing), where Mathew Carey and Hezekiah Niles of the *Weekly Register* pushed for a tariff reform. In 1820 Henry Baldwin, the chairman of the newly established House Committee on Manufactures, introduced a higher and more comprehensive tariff bill. Some of the supporters of the 1816 tariff opposed it on the familiar grounds that freedom of trade was most conducive to the public welfare, but Clay inveighed against "the maxim of let alone," arguing that though closet theorists subscribed to it, no sensible statesman ever would.[22]

Baldwin's tariff was defeated, yet the victory of free trade forces proved to be short-lived, for while the battle was lost, the war, it turned out, was about to be won by protectionists. In 1824, as he was gearing up for an attempt to get himself elected president, Clay used his position as the Speaker of the House to present his vision for the nation. The debate on the tariff provided him with a sterling opportunity to formulate it. He was to run as the Father of the American System—a distinctively American program, a reflection of the nation's ideals and character, uniquely suited to assure its unity and prosperity. "The idea of the system," wrote Remini,

> had been in [Clay's] mind for years. In numerous speeches he had discussed several of its parts. Now he grasped the unity of his program as a unique expression of what needed to be done by the government to benefit Americans in all sections and among all classes and economic endeavors. It was a vision of progress, a bold reformulation of the relationship between government and society. But most important of all, in view of the near breakup of the Union occasioned by the dispute over the admission of Missouri, Clay's American System was intended to strengthen

the bonds that tied the nation together into a single whole. It was intended to ensure the perpetuity of a united country.

The American System was based on two principles: industrialization and protection. Clay spelled them out in a historic speech, which lasted six and a half hours on March 30 and was completed on March 31, 1824. He wished the United States to declare its independence from foreigners:

> The policy of all Europe refuses to receive from us anything but those raw materials of smaller value, essential to their manufactures, to which they can give a higher value, with the exception of tobacco and rice, which they cannot produce . . . We must give a new direction to some portion of our industry. We must speedily adopt a genuine American policy. Still cherishing the foreign market, let us create also a home market to give further scope to the consumption of the produce of American industry. Let us counteract the policy of foreigners and withdraw the support which we now give to their industry and stimulate that of our own country.

The wealth of the nation was inseparable from its independence and willingness to defend it, he argued:

> It is in vain to tantalize us with the greater cheapness of foreign fabrics . . . The superiority of the home market results, first, from its steadiness and comparative certainty at all times; second, from its greater security; and, last, from an ultimate and not distant augmentation of consumption (and consequently of comfort) from increased quantity and reduced prices. But this home market . . . can only be created and cherished by the protection of our own legislation against the inevitable prostration of our industry, which must ensue from the action of foreign policy and legislation . . . The measure of the wealth of a nation is indicated by the measure of its protection of its industry; and . . . the measure of the poverty of a nation is marked by that of the degree in which it neglects and abandons the care of its own industry, leaving it exposed to the action of foreign powers.

Failure to protect the domestic economy inevitably resulted in its depression, even if it appeared blooming and the only sign of its ill health was the superior prosperity of others. It was the duty of the government to make sure that the United States was no laggard. The Speaker insisted:

> The committee will agree with me in thinking that it is the solemn duty of government to apply a remedy to the evils which afflict our country, if it can apply one. Is there a remedy within the reach of the government? . . . [T]here is a remedy, and that remedy consists in modifying our for-

eign policy, and in adopting a genuine American system. We must naturalize the arts in our country; and we must naturalize them by the only means which the wisdom of nations has yet discovered to be effectual—by adequate protection against the otherwise overwhelming influence of foreigners.

Clay ridiculed the fears of the opposition and its feigned solicitude for the interests of the people. The nation would be the beneficiary of the protective measures, and if there were any costs to particular interests, they were incurred voluntarily, he claimed:

[The tariff] seems to have been regarded as a sort of a monster, huge and deformed—a wild beast, endowed with tremendous powers of destruction, about to be let loose among our people, if not to devour them, at least to consume their substance. But let us calm our passions and deliberately survey this alarming, this terrific being. The sole object of the tariff is to tax the produce of foreign industry with the view of promoting American industry. The tax is exclusively leveled at foreign industry. That is the avowed and the direct purpose of the tariff. If it subjects any part of American industry to burdens, that is an effect not intended, but is altogether incidental and perfectly voluntary . . . No man pays the duty assessed on the foreign article by compulsion, but voluntarily; and this voluntary duty, if paid, goes into the common exchequer for the common benefit of all.

He had no patience for the complaints of the South, thundering:

But it is said that the South, owing to the character of a certain portion of its population, cannot engage in the business of manufacturing . . . [Those who make this claim] would have us abstain from adopting a policy called for by the interest of the greater and freer part of our population. But is that reasonable? Can it be expected that the interests of the greater part should be made to bend to the conditions of the servile part of our population? That, in effect, would be to make us the slaves of slaves.

The objection that "Europe will not buy of us if we do not buy of her," thus diminishing the amount of American exports, was countered with a suggestion "to take care of the European ability in legislating for American interests."

Clay found no merit in the old argument that "the proposed system will force capital and labor into new and reluctant employments; [that the United States were] not prepared, in consequence of the high price of wages, for the successful establishment of manufactures, and [therefore] must fail in the experiment." "We have seen," he protested,

> that the existing occupations of our society, those of agriculture, commerce, navigation, and the learned professions, are overflowing with competitors, and that the want of employment is severely felt. Now what does this bill propose? To open a new and extensive field of business in which all that choose may enter. There is no compulsion upon anyone to engage in it. An option only is given to industry to continue in the present unprofitable pursuits, or to embark in a new and promising one. The effect will be to lessen the competition in the old branches of business and to multiply our resources for increasing our comforts and augmenting the national wealth.

The mantra of laissez-faire was dismissed as unfounded.

> It is said that wherever there is a concurrence of favorable circumstances manufactures will arise of themselves, without protection; and that we should not disturb the natural progress of industry, but leave things to themselves . . . I contend that this proposition is refuted by all experience, ancient and modern, and in every country. If I am asked why unprotected industry should not succeed in a struggle with protected industry, I answer, the fact has ever been so, and that is sufficient; I reply that uniform experience evinces that it cannot succeed in such an unequal contest, and that is sufficient.

As to the adverse social effects of industrialization (the claim "that the manufacturing system is adverse to the genius of our government in its tendency to the accumulation of large capitals in a few hands; in the corruption of the public morals, which is alleged to be incident to it; and in the consequent danger to the public liberty"), Clay denied them, though admitting that agriculture was the most proper occupation for the citizens of a republic. He was not worried about manufactures developing to excess and at the expense of agriculture, believing, like Franklin and many others, that the abundance of land guaranteed the preeminence of agricultural pursuits in America. "The greatest danger to public liberty is from idleness and vice," and not manufactures, he argued:

> If manufactures form cities, so does commerce. And the disorders and violence which proceed from the contagion of the passions are as frequent in one description of those communities as in the other.
>   There is no doubt but that the yeomanry of a country is the safest depository of public liberty. In all time to come, and under any probable direction of the labor of our population, the agricultural class must be

much the most numerous and powerful, and will ever retain, as it ought to retain, a preponderating influence in our councils. The extent and the fertility of our lands constitute an adequate security against an excess in manufactures, and also against oppression, on the part of capitalists, toward the laboring portion of the community.

Clay concluded his speech with an impassioned plea, for the sake of the Union, to protect and encourage every "interest"—or segment of the economy—which contributed to the nation's prosperity:

Our Confederacy comprehends, within its vast limits, great diversity of interests: agricultural, planting, farming, commercial, navigating, fishing, manufacturing. No one of these interests is felt in the same degree and cherished with the same solicitude throughout all parts of the Union. Some of them are peculiar to particular sections of our common country. But all these great interests are confided to the protection of one government—to the fate of one ship—and a most gallant ship it is, with a noble crew. If we prosper and are happy, protection must be extended to all; it is due to all . . . This is the only mode by which we can preserve, in full vigor, the harmony of the whole Union.

Clay's nationalism, says his biographer,

never rang out more strongly, never more fervently . . . It was a stunning performance, a bold and mighty speech, a stupendous effort to win over his colleagues to his vision of what the United States could become: a great and powerful nation, materially prosperous, with a prosperity that would be shared by every citizen of every class and section. It involved sacrifices; it involved compromises. But the net result would lift the nation to world power and dominance. Henry Clay was one of the few early statesmen to have this vision of America's future greatness and provide the ideas to transform it into reality.

The bill passed, by a small margin, against the opposition of the South, which closed ranks against it, and the divided New England. The new tariff raised duties to about 35 percent on most imports. "The measure of protection which it extends to Domestic industry is short of what it should have been," commented Clay. "But we have succeeded in establishing the principle, and hereafter I apprehend less difficulty will be encountered in giving to it a more comprehensive and vigorous application."

By 1828 the American System had achieved the status of a dominant creed in the country. New England converted to it en masse, led by such erstwhile champions of free trade as Edward Everett and Daniel Webster. Webster, who was Clay's most formidable opponent in 1824, now praised the tariff which had stimulated manufactures in the northeastern states. He no longer trusted philosophers, such as Smith, who presented the doctrine of laissez-faire as the "science of political economy." "There is no such science," he declared. "There are no rules on these subjects so fixed and invariable as that their aggregate constitutes a science." He based this judgment on a thorough study of *The Wealth of Nations* and more than twenty other treatises by representatives of the school, finding little in them besides "mere truisms" and "doubtful propositions." The South thus remained alone in its loyalty to the classics. Indeed, as the country at large was turning decidedly against them, the loyalty of this tragically isolated section was becoming more passionate. Calhoun, who earlier had supported the tariff for nationalist reasons, was now resentful of the great strides made under its protection by every other region but his, kept down by the millstone of slavery hung about its neck, and embraced the claim, raised and abandoned by Massachusetts, that protection of industry was unconstitutional. But the South was a minority, and there were dissenting voices even there. An editorial in the *Georgia Courier* in 1827 concluded that the section had no one to blame for its woes but itself, and hailed the tariff as a possible remedy. "That we have cultivated cotton, cotton, cotton, and bought everything else, has long been our opprobium," wrote the anonymous author:

> It is time we should be roused by some means or other to see that such a course of conduct will inevitably terminate in our ultimate poverty and ruin. Let us manufacture, because it is our best policy . . . This we can do without manifesting any ill nature to any of the members of the same great family, all whose earnings go to swell the general prosperity and happiness. Much of our chagrin and ill nature on this subject may be justly, because truly, ascribed to a sense of shame which we of the Southern states feel, that we have been so long behind our Northern neighbors in the production of everything that substantially administers to the elegance or the comforts of life. It has been our own fault—not theirs . . . Let us change our policy, but without that spirit and those expressions which leave a festering sore in the hearts of those who should be brothers . . . [L]et those who have capital and enterprise manufacture on a more extensive scale. There is nothing to prevent us from doing it. We have good land, unlimited waterpower, capital in plenty, and a patriotism which is running over in some places. If the tariff drives us to this, we say, let the name be sacred in all future generations.

There was never any doubt about the filiation of the American system which half a century after independence at last firmly placed the nation on the path to industrialization. "We contend not for a new principle," claimed Samuel Woodson, representative from Kentucky, during the debates over the tariff in 1823, "but for the extension of that system most ably vindicated in Hamilton's Report which has received the sanction of every other distinguished patriot." The latter part of the sentence was patently untrue, but it had already become a habit to invoke the collective authority of the Founding Fathers, whatever the position one wished to defend.[23]

Finally, Industrialization

As Clay predicted, the American System opened a new and extensive field for the native businessman. It gave him an option, which he was free to reject, but was likely to accept if he wished to avoid competition in the crowded branches of industry or had an adventurous spirit, to embark on a new and exciting pursuit with every chance also to be profitable. The old prejudices against manufacture were being erased, and it acquired a hue of nobility and civic virtue heretofore associated with agriculture. The business itself became more attractive to the entrepreneur owing to the simultaneous development of legal and organizational mechanisms for funding large-scale new ventures, and of a far-flung communication system which created and opened to view extensive, accessible, hungry markets. The government pushed the businessman and new opportunities pulled him in the same direction. The manufacturing industry was beginning to appear the rational choice: a most natural application for the energies of the individual and an evident course for the development of the economy. But, as Edward Shils says of traditions, there was no continuous line of change. The accretion of new elements in what from our perspective appears a mighty trend was neither explicit nor intentional. No connection existed between the developments that combined to change men's minds and produce American industrialization. Very often people who supported one opposed others or repeatedly changed positions on the same issue. Technology came from across the Atlantic. Insofar as the organizational structure and the system of communications are concerned, industrialization was a wholly unintended consequence of uncoordinated actions of diverse individuals, mostly merchants and financiers, motivated by the desire to promote their various (but uniformly nonindustrial) interests. Industrialization, therefore, was a contingent development; it could not be predicted and did not have to happen. It was also remarkably slow (by comparison, let's say, with that in Britain which preceded it, or in Germany and Japan which followed): for it was not before 1850 that the attention of a critical mass of entrepreneurs was finally attracted to the new opportunities, created by the machines invented in England, the redefinition of the corporation, and vastly expanded transportation possibilities, and assiduously fostered by the government.

In the 1850s "the spirit of manufacturing," which at the time of Hamilton's report was most noticeable in America for its absence, finally became "the general spirit of the nation, and [was] incorporated, as it were, into their very essence." A new era was dawning, the industrial age. Its most striking characteristic was technology, and it obscured other features, no less important, that went into its making. In November 1847, on the occasion of the opening of the Northern Railroad to Lebanon, New Hampshire, Daniel Webster commented:

It is an extraordinary era in which we live. It is altogether new. The world has seen nothing like it before. I will not pretend, no one can pretend, to discern the end; but every body knows that the age is remarkable for scientific research into the heavens, the earth, and what is beneath the earth; and perhaps more remarkable still for the application of this scientific research to the pursuits of life. The ancients saw nothing like it. The moderns have seen nothing like it till the present generation . . . We see the ocean navigated and the solid land traversed by steam power, and intelligence communicated by electricity. Truly this is almost a miraculous era. What is before us no one can say, what is upon us one can hardly realize. The progress of the age has almost outstripped human belief.

Webster's great contemporary Ralph Waldo Emerson, who also believed that it was "that wonderful machinery which differences this age from any other age," considered the (new) interest of American entrepreneurs in industry self-evident. They were predisposed to manufacturing—which by the time he wrote had become *the* industry and monopolized the name—by the very climate of the country. In 1847 Emerson noted in his diary (with that knowledge of the business mind that has characterized intellectuals ever since):

An American in this ardent climate gets up early some morning and buys a river; and advertises for twelve or fifteen hundred Irishmen; digs a new channel for it, brings it to his mills, and has a head of twenty-four feet of water; then to give him an appetite for his breakfast, he raises a house; then carves out within doors, a quarter township into streets and building lots, tavern, school and the Methodist meeting-house—sends up an engineer into New Hampshire, to see where his water comes from, and after advising with him, sends a trusty man of business to buy of all the farmers such mill privileges as will serve him among their waste hill and pasture lots, and comes home with great glee announcing that he is now owner of the great Lake Winipeseogee, as reservoir for his Lowell mills at midsummer. They are an ardent race, and are fully possessed with that hatred of labor, which is the principle of progress in the human race, as any other people. They must and will have the enjoyment without the sweat. So they buy slaves, where the women will permit it; where they will not, they make the wind, the tide, the waterfall, the stream, the cloud, the lightning, do the work, by every art and device their cunningest brain can achieve.

Emerson appreciated these industrial entrepreneurs; in his view it was to them—though perhaps despite themselves—that the nation owed its exceptional prosperity. The chapter "Wealth" in his 1860 *The Conduct of Life* was a panegyric to them—"the men of the mine, telegraph, mill, map, and survey—the monomaniacs, who talk up their project in marts, and offices, and entreat men to subscribe." "How did our factories get built?" asked Emerson. "How did North America get netted with iron rails, except by the importunity of these orators, who dragged all the prudent men in?" Fanatics, driven by the desire for "power to execute their design, power to give legs and feet, form and actuality to their thought" (rather than love of money, significantly), they took the risks for all of us. "This speculative genius is the madness of few for the gain of the world. The projectors are sacrificed, but the public is the gainer. Each of these idealists, working after his thought, would make it tyrannical, if he could. He is met and antagonized by other speculators, as hot as he. The equilibrium is preserved by these counteractions, as one tree keeps down another in the forest, that it may not absorb all the sap in the ground." There were, of course, social costs to this. Technology and capital, the forces of "industrial power," were "the new agents [by which] our social system [was] moulded." They created a new, industrial society. And here Emerson—in 1856—proposed what we today would associate with the coming of the postindustrial society, the stage of late capitalism, produced by the "information" rather than the "industrial revolution." "By dint of steam and of money," he said, "war and commerce are changed. Nations have lost their old omnipotence; the patriotic tie does not hold. Nations are getting obsolete, we go and live where we will. Steam has enabled men to choose what law they will live under. Money makes place for them. The telegraph is a limp-band that will hold the Fenris-wolf of war."[24]

The Other "American System"

Soon after American businessmen began to realize that manufacturing offered better profits than the more conventional employments of industry and capital, the term "American system" acquired a new meaning.[25] It came to refer to the mass machine production of industrial goods with interchangeable parts. The idea apparently belonged to the inventor of the cotton gin, Eli Whitney, who thought of "assembling" guns in this fashion early in the nineteenth century. Though Whitney himself was not able to make all the machines that the process required, other gun makers decided to give the method a try, and the federal government, anxious to become independent of foreign suppliers in "essentials," adopted it in the arsenals of Springfield, Massachusetts, and Harpers Ferry, Virginia. But it was left to another Connecticut son, like Whitney, fascinated with technology, to impress the world with the possibilities of mass production of instruments of slaughter, and it was he who was credited with the creation of "the American system of manufacturing." This American Hephaestus was Samuel Colt, who had none of the sedate virtues of a businessman, but had the stamina, the daring, and the sharpness of mind which more than compensated for this deficiency. It is unlikely that his lifelong preoccupation with means of mechanical destruction was a response to a social demand (which, no doubt, was as widespread in the United States as in any other country keen on its independence). He seems to have been born with it, offering a spectacular demonstration of the nature of his interests at the age of fifteen (in 1829), when he blew up a raft with gunpowder in Ware Pond, igniting it "with an electric spark from a battery on shore transmitted under the water through wires he had coated with rubber." To prevent further expressions of such explosive creativity, his parents shipped him off, first to school at the Amherst Academy, a year later to Calcutta, aboard the brig *Cordo,* to whose Captain Spaulding he was apprenticed. When Colt returned in 1831, he had with him a wooden model of a revolving pistol that would make him famous, the idea of the mechanism being suggested to him by the clutch on a ship's capstan.

The boy went to work on his father's mill in Ware, and the father paid a gunsmith for the two pistols necessary for a patent, but they did not work. So Colt awarded himself a doctoral degree and, as "Dr. Coult of New York, London, and Calcutta," embarked on a three-year tour of North America, lecturing on and demonstrating the effects of "laughing gas" to pay for more pistols. When his lectures took him to the Mississippi and Ohio rivers, his brother, a riverboat gambler, kept him company. In 1835 a Baltimore gunsmith, convinced by Colt's solvency (but, as it happened, never paid), made for him two working pistols he needed for the patent. Before requesting an American patent, which was promptly granted, Colt traveled to London and secured himself several European ones, including the British, after which he founded the Patent Arms Manufacturing Company in New Jersey. Between 1836 and 1840 it manufactured 2,700 revolvers and 2,500 other guns, some of which, in an attempt to attract government contracts, Colt gave away to soldiers in the Seminole Wars and in Texas. He also pawned them to support an extravagant lifestyle: clearly, moneymaking for moneymaking's sake was not his goal. In a few years he succeeded in making the "Colt" very popular (President Jackson was among its admirers) and in antagonizing his stockholders. As government contracts were not forthcoming, they dissolved the company in 1845. For a time Colt devoted himself to other pursuits—all expressions of his long-standing interest in long-distance murder machinery—which had occupied his attention on and off, while the Patent Arms Company was in operation. He developed a waterproof cartridge and an underwater stationary mine, on the principle of his early experiments with coated wire and electricity, and in 1841 founded the Submarine Battery Company with $20,000 in federal contract money. In 1842 he blew up a ship in New York Harbor, but failed to sell his mines, and, instead, sold cable for Morse's telegraph, forming a cable company in 1844 and, under license from Morse, a telegraph company in 1845.

The Mexican War, which began in 1846, created a lively demand—and contracts—for Colt revolvers. He subcontracted to Whitney's heir and other gunmakers in Connecticut and in 1847 produced a thousand pistols. The next year he went into production himself, first with machines acquired from Whitney, then with new ones he designed with Elisha Root, a friend from his days in Ware, and soon was doing a brisk business, arming California gold diggers. He traveled to Europe again, where the demand for his product was strong owing to the revolutions of 1848, and armed Kossuth in Hungary and the sultan in Turkey. It was then that "his advertising, entertaining, and lobbying began to spread the word in Europe that there was an American system of manufacture, which could make more of anything, faster, and more uniformly than humanity had ever dreamed possible."

The impression created by Colt and his revolver at the 1851 Crystal Palace Industrial Exhibition in London, reinforced by other American machines, gave credence to this word and compelled industrialists in Britain, heretofore undisturbed in the consciousness of their comparative strength, to take a closer look at that "American system." Colt offered them a chance by opening a plant in England. At the outbreak of the Crimean War (which was fought with Colt revolvers), the workshop of the world dispatched to the United States a team of two artillery officers and an engineer to study the American system at its source. The Committee of the Ordnance Board visited all the principal manufacturing sites in the former colonies and submitted a lengthy report to Parliament. "The Americans display an amount of ingenuity," it stated, "combined with undaunted energy, which as a nation we would do well to imitate, if we mean to hold our present position in the great market of the world." This ingenuity and energy, however, expressed themselves best not in American-made machines (which were "upon the whole behind those of England"), but in the organization of work in the factories "got up by Corporations," which, "with machinery applied to almost every single process," used an "extreme subdivision of labor" and "cheaply and quickly" made the entire product "on the premises from the raw material." The productivity of American labor suffered from "the extreme heat of the weather during summer" (when operatives drank "immense quantities of [iced] water") and from poor discipline, workers being "absent from their employment to an extent which could not be tolerated with us." At the same time, the report emphasized, "every workman seems continually devising some new thing to assist him in his work," which led to the creation of ever newer machines "in order to obtain the article at the smallest possible cost." All in all, the committee was duly impressed. The Americans were not yet up to a competition with Britain, but their system of manufacture was clearly worthy of respect and in some aspects even of imitation. The members were "quite astonished" by the magnitude of Colt's "new establishment, [at the time of their visit] in the course of erection"—the Hartford Armory began full operation in the spring of 1856—and concluded, with admiration, that "when completed, this will be the largest and finest armory in the world."[26]

8 | The Thrust

It was in 1867, according to Henry Adams, that "for the first time in history, the American felt himself almost as strong as an Englishman." In thirty years, he predicted, "he should feel himself stronger." Some Englishmen thought that the prediction came true sooner. William Gladstone believed it realized already in 1878, writing:

> While we have been advancing with portentous rapidity, America is passing us as if in a canter. There can hardly be a doubt, as between America and England, of the belief that the daughter at no very distant time will, whether fairer or less fair, be unquestionably yet stronger than the mother . . . It is America who at a given time, and probably will wrest from us [our] commercial primacy. We have no title: I have no inclination to murmur at the prospect. If she acquires it, she will make the acquisition by the right of the strongest; but in this instance the strongest means the best. She will probably become what we are now—head servant in the great household of the world, the employer of all employed, because her service will be the most and ablest.

The United States had not yet arrived, but it was fast arriving at the position of the greatest industrial power in the world, and in the United States the day had dawned on the age of the grand arrivistes.[1]

The Employers of All Employed

Countless books have been written on the stupendous growth of the American economy, and its speedy and irreversible industrialization, in the period between the Civil War and the beginning of the new century. This not being a history of that growth, there is no need to dwell on its endlessly scrutinized indices; a few illustrations will suffice:

Between 1867 and 1873, more than 30,000 miles of new [railroad] track were opened to traffic in the United States; and by 1893, though more than eight years of depression intervened, 150,000 miles had been laid since the war. Capital invested in American railroads jumped in this period from two to nearly ten billion dollars . . . By 1893, New England alone was producing manufactured goods more valuable per capita than those of any country in the world. In the manufacture of timber and steel, the refinement of crude oil, the packing of meat, the extraction of gold, silver, coal, and iron, the United States surpassed all competitors. America had more telephones, more incandescent lighting and electric traction, more miles of telegraph wires than any other nation. In specialties like hardware, machine tools, arms, and ammunition, she retained the leadership assumed before the Civil War, while her pianos as well as her locomotives had become the best in the world.[2]

Gone were the days when the largest factory complex in America (Pepperell Mills) employed eight hundred people and operated at the cost of just over $300,000 per annum; the 1850s, with its focus on textiles, must have appeared to the children who grew up forty years later a distant age, as remote from their reality as the time of the American Revolution.

To Henry Adams, the change appeared striking already in 1868, when he returned to his native land, at the age of thirty, from a ten-year sojourn in Europe. His famous autobiography offers us a glimpse of what this meant in terms of personal experience. "One could divine pretty nearly where the [new] force lay," he wrote,

> since the last ten years had given to the great mechanical energies—coal, iron, steam—a distinct superiority in power over the old industrial elements—agriculture, handwork, and learning; but the result of this revolution on a survivor from the fifties resembled the action of the earthworm; he twisted about, in vain, to recover his starting-point; he could no longer see his own trail; he had become an estray; a flotsam or jetsam of wreckage; a belated reveler, or a scholar-gypsy like Mathew Arnold's. His world was dead. Not a Polish Jew from Warsaw or Cracow—not a furtive Yacoob or Ysaac still reeking of the Ghetto, snarling a weird Yiddish to the officers of the customs—but had a keener instinct, an intenser energy, and a freer hand than he—American of Americans, with Heaven knew how many Puritans and Patriots behind him, and an education that had cost a civil war. He made no complaint and found no fault with his time . . . The defeat was not due to him, nor yet to any superiority of his rivals. He had been unfairly forced out of the track, and must get back into it as best he could.

One comfort he could enjoy in the full. Little as he might be fitted for the work that was before him, he had only to look at his father and [people of that generation] to see figures less fitted for it than he. All were equally survivors from the forties—bric-a-brac from the time of Louis Philippe; stylists; doctrinaires; ornaments that had been more or less suited to the colonial architecture . . . They could scarcely have earned five dollars a day in any modern industry.

E. C. Kirkland's hypothetical and (unlike Henry Adams) unexceptional contemporary, looking at this experience half a century later, makes it easy to identify with it:

A youth entering business at the age of fifteen in 1860 would have faced a world of industry which manufactured hardly a ton of steel and where kerosene from petroleum obtained from driven wells was a novelty of a year or so. If he survived to retire forty years later, he would have seen the United States the leading nation in the manufacture of steel by all methods—steel has displaced iron—and he would have realized beyond peradventure that oil industry was one of the great economic mainstays of the country. Change of this magnitude and rapidity penetrated every cranny of the industrial structure. In 1886 the *Commercial and Financial Chronicle,* giving tonnage statistics for the dressed beef trade, commented incidentally that this beef industry "is a growth of recent years," and in the middle of the next decade it marveled at the fact that in 1860 probably nine-tenths of all underclothes were made at home rather than in the factory. In terms of communications, the same youngster of 1860 would have seen a nation with 30,626 miles of railroad; no transcontinental line yet connected the Mississippi with the Pacific. Forty years later the railroad mileage of the nation was 258,784. More significant than mere statistics was the fact that the railroad had shattered the protections which distance had once given the local producers and merchants [yes, the creation of a global village was depicted in terms of shattering the protections of yesteryear] and had made the market a national one.[3]

In 1960 I was younger than Henry Adams when he left for Europe, or than Kirkland's imaginary young businessman of 1860, but I can attest that no changes of similar magnitude in material reality have shaken my generation in the forty years that have passed since.

While changes in material reality were the most dramatic, a profound transformation was occurring in the nature of economic activity and in the understanding of economic and social reality. This transformation, in the first place, had to do with the development in the organization of industrial enterprises and the emergence of "big business."[4] In 1900, at the Chicago Conference on Trusts (which reportedly attracted "scores of gaily dressed women," and was described as "as brilliant and intellectual a gathering as ever assembled in Chicago" which "bore testimony to the interest of all classes in the question under debate"), the reformer William Dudley Foulke declared this organizational development to be the most momentous of all:

> The question we are called to consider dwarfs in importance all other issues now before the country or the world . . . When Dreyfus shall have been forgotten, when the war in the Philippines shall be regarded only as one of the episodes of history, when men shall speak no longer of the tariff or the currency, the present era may well be remembered by coming generations as the epoch of that great organic change when the system of competition began to give way to the system of co-operation—a change leading inevitably . . . to the radical reconstruction of the world's industrial and social life.

Despite the widespread belief, contemporary with "big business," that it was "simply a product of natural laws," an evolutionary stage which every society had to reach at one or another point and which was in the participants' objective economic interest, this development, like industrialization in general, in the United States and elsewhere was contingent, essentially voluntary (i.e., dependent on the unpredictable creativity of exceptional individuals), and proceeded from causes that were not economic. Many of the conditions of "big business"—above all the corporation, which allowed people capable of conceiving fantastic schemes to finance them with "other people's money," and the speculative temper, which induced the latter to risk their savings at the flimsiest promise of gain—had been present in the United States for some time. Others were added with the development of communications infrastructure and the realization of the labor-saving and profit-generating capacity of machines. The railroads (which were the first "big businesses" in the nation, but not businesses of industrial production) already in the 1840s and 1850s revealed, and utilized, the extraordinary opportunities for growth which the corporate structure contained, as they excited the characteristic avidity of the American public, noticed by Madison. "The seminal development of the period," noted Thomas Cochran and William Miller of these years,

> was the spread of corporate stocks and bonds among a larger and larger investing public. Related to this development was the growth of private banking houses. Investment capital began to flow confidently to the

eastern money markets, and through these banking houses such capital was finding its way to the new securities of railroad construction companies, textile and iron factories, shipbuilding corporations, commercial banks, and insurance companies. Increased speculation in stocks and bonds symbolized the change that was coming over American business, and the development of stock exchanges in key cities speeded this change.

In 1838 the Western Railroad in Massachusetts had 2,331 stockholders; the Lebanon line of the Northern Railroad in New Hampshire in 1847 had 1,500 (according to Daniel Webster, farmers referred lovingly to the line of shingles stretching across fields three or four years before it was constructed: "It is the line of our railroad"). Disinterested observers, such as Channing or Emerson, whose social position demanded that they distance themselves from the preoccupations of the vulgar multitude, making plain their unease and embarrassment before foreigners whom they suspected of greater gentility, commented: "The opening of vast prospects of wealth to the multitude of men has stirred up a fierce competition, a wild spirit of speculation, a feverish, insatiable cupidity, under which fraud, bankruptcy, distrust, distress are fearfully multiplied, so that the name American has become a byword beyond the ocean." (Thus Channing.) "The rapid wealth which hundreds in the community acquire in trade enchants the eyes of the rest, the luck of one is the hope of thousands, and the whole generation is discontented with the tardy rate of growth which contents every European community" (Emerson).[5]

"Rails" ruled the stock market from the early 1830s (significantly, channeling capital away from other—smaller—industrial ventures). "Between 1850 and 1857," write Cochran and Miller,

> 2,300 miles of track were constructed annually in the United States at an average cost of $60,000,000. Funds from every walk of life, from every section of the land, were pouring into eastern money markets and out again to western railroads to push construction of the Illinois Central, the Rock Island, the Hannibal & St. Joseph, the Pacific Railroad of Missouri; to extend the Pennsylvania, the Erie, the Michigan Central and scores of other lines in the North, East, South, and West. By 1860, $1,500,000,000 was invested in American railroads, more than 25 per cent of the total active capital in the country. No wonder the financial structure collapsed when railroad profits proved smaller or slower than expected.

In 1855 the Pennsylvania Railroad employed four thousand workers; the Erie's annual operation costs amounted to $3 million; the railroads implied management of "shops, terminals, stations, warehouses, office buildings, bridges, telegraph lines"; the number of business transactions in which they daily participated was of an order different from anything encountered at the time anywhere in the economy.

The unprecedented size and complexity of these businesses required a commensurately large and complex organization. Thus they became, in the words of Alfred Chandler, "the pioneers in modern corporate management." The "first functionally departmentalized, administrative structures for an American business" were created by Louis McLane and Benjamin Latrobe of the Baltimore and Ohio Railroad, refined by Daniel McCallum of the Erie, and adopted by the "Pennsy's" J. E. Thomson. Robertson writes:

> The system divided the railroad into operational divisions, headed by superintendents and charged with the complicated day-to-day running of the trains and traffic. There were also functional divisions, headed by agents and engineers, responsible for planning, policies, and general supervision of the various kinds of work the company did: divisions for passengers, freight, wood (later coal), telegraph, road repair and maintenance, locomotive repair and maintenance. All the operational divisions reported to a general superintendent. He, in turn, along with the heads of the functional divisions, reported to the president, who was ultimately responsible for the entire company. There was also a Financial Department responsible for collecting, assessing, and presenting to the president and the Board of Directors financial information on all operations, and responsible for supervising the company's finances. Reports, both immediate and accumulated, a carefully arranged hierarchy of authority and responsibility, and a system of rapid communication were the essentials of big railroad management. McCallum on the Erie insisted on hourly telegraphic reports (on train movement and delays), as well as daily, weekly, and monthly reports from those responsible for departments and divisions. Modern accounting was developed to determine costs and profitability, and to arrive at standardized management decisions. Thus, modern corporate bureaucracies were invented.

But the line from railroads to big business in the production of industrial goods was indirect. Apart from having a ravenous appetite for capital, which deprived of nurture less robust organisms, railroads were, on occasion, directly opposed to other industrial interests and had the power to subvert them. For instance, they were naturally in favor of the free trade in British iron goods, while underdeveloped domestic ironmasters demanded protection. Under the pressure of the transportation giants (who early became experts in greasing politicians' palms) and in the name of the "general welfare of the United States," the American system temporarily gave way and "until after 1860, most of the rails used in American railroads were imported from England at prices American producers could not match. So discouraged were they that as late as 1857, 'Pittsburgh did not have a single mill engaged in the manufacture' of rails."

Even when all the conditions that could allow American industrialization were in place (as they possibly were by 1860), it was not a foregone conclusion. We are reminded that "industrial culture" in the United States was extremely young, that before the Civil War it was represented by a small minority of entrepreneurs, who "had always to contend with a political state dominantly agrarian in attitude," that in 1860, "for the first time in American history, the output of factory, mill, shop, and mine exceeded in value that of the farm," that as late as 1863, American industry lacked the capacity to provide the industrial North with necessities: soldiers' uniforms, as well as munitions, had to be imported (the South, obviously, fared worse), and only by 1865 was its supremacy at last proved. Still, in 1867, Henry Adams later recalled, "no one could yet guess which of his contemporaries was most likely to play a part in the great world. A shrewd prophet in Wall Street might perhaps set a mark on Pierpont Morgan, but hardly on the Rockefellers."[6]

It was the war that finally changed that, propelling industry to "the envied position of a pampered only child" of both the federal government and, more important, the nation's ambitious entrepreneurs. The war at last opened the eyes of the latter to the immense opportunities implied in the use of machinery and corporations. It trained the businessman to organize the work force to produce and distribute manufactured goods—ready-to-wear boots and clothes, munitions and arms—for millions. "The great operations of war, the handling of large masses of men, the influence of discipline, the lavish expenditure of unprecedented sums of money, the immense financial operations, the possibilities of effective cooperation, were lessons not likely to be lost on men quick to receive and apply all new ideas."[7] Furthermore, the war deprived the South of its national political leadership, and with it went the agrarian attitude of the government and its atavistic free trade sympathies. During the war the Union government courted manufacturers with generous gifts of land and ever-increasing protective tariffs, some of them interpreted as compensation for new taxes. After the war the taxes were eliminated, but the tariffs remained. The party of Lincoln "wrote into law most of Hamilton's theories," enacting "the greatest program of nationalism" since Federalists. The war inevitably favored large enterprises; so did the mechanization of production, for machines required capital, to which small producers had little access. The spectacular growth of the Gilded Age—which amounted to the industrialization of the American economy—was entirely the doing of big businesses organized in corporations, with which a lone manufacturer was unable to compete.[8]

The rewards of success grew enormous, but its price increased proportionally: the competition among corporations, confronting one another in a still very limited number of industries on the same market, vast but rendered manageable by railroads and telegraph, which each of them could potentially control, was savage—"cutthroat" must have been a word invented especially for it, for the country had never known anything like it.[9] It was wasteful and ruinous. "In the three decades after the Civil War," wrote Cochran and Miller,

> as confident entrepreneurs raced to take advantage of every ephemeral rise in prices, of every advance in tariff schedules, of every new market opened by the railroads and puffed up by immigration, they recklessly expanded and mechanized their plants, each seeking the greatest share of the new melon. The more successful they were in capturing such shares and the more efficient they were in promptly satisfying the market, however, the greater was the number of buildings and machines left idle when the new market approached the saturation point and the rate of expansion declined. The result was that all the competitors were left with the problem of amortizing their new buildings and machines precisely at the time when the operation of those new buildings and machines was unable any longer to produce a profit.

This was true from bread and whiskey to the iron industry and a nascent branch such as petroleum. To protect themselves, corporations began to combine, at first on the basis of gentlemanly agreements in pools, which did not work, later in trusts. A little competition (perhaps on the level that existed before the Civil War) was fine, but too much was bad for business. "I like a little competition," confessed J. P. Morgan, "but I like combination better."

Rational economic defense, however, was not the only motive behind consolidation. Some wanted glory rather than reasonable profits. They desired personal greatness, equality—on an epic scale—with the best, and the post–Civil War economy offered them a field in which to make their mark. Only incidentally was business a way of making a living for them (and moneymaking, too, was only incidental to it): the great capitalists of the Gilded Age would agree with FDR's statement—which he thought expressed a radical disagreement with their view—that "happiness lies not in the mere possession of money; it lies in the joy of achievement, in the thrill of creative effort." It was the way they chose to challenge their destiny, a most serious, vital game, in which they took the measure of themselves. They were guided by the principle of "winner takes all," and they played to win. American society always encouraged such players; it was a competitive society by definition, not in the economic sense, but in the sense of its essential, profound egalitarianism, which made for an incessant scramble for status. After the Civil War, business was the arena which promised the most rigorous trial and the highest prizes. The sport was "the race for wealth," yet the prize—"the crown that all were striving for"—as ever, was recognition, respect (and self-respect), social honor.[10]

That behind many of the titanic accomplishments of American business in that vilified age was not base cupidity but grand ambition is best demonstrated by the actions of the so-called (by Matthew Josephson, a Marxist, who could not be expected to know much about the feudal times with which he was drawing a parallel) "robber barons"—such as, among other things, the unprecedented and unequaled scale of their philanthropy. "Truly, the new men of wealth organized their philanthropies as grandiosely as they organized their businesses." On occasion, however, they revealed their motives in words. The context of such revelations was rarely an attempt at self-analysis, and they were often made quite unconsciously. Moreover, businessmen felt no pride in these motives, which were irrelevant to and at times contradicted the rational calculation of interests, which they believed should guide them. For instance, a personage as mundane as the president of the National Millers Association (not one of the giants of the age and therefore nameless) in 1888 addressed the bread-making community, which, like many other business communities, suffered from unregulated competition, in the following strong terms. "Our ambition," he said,

> overreached our discretion and judgment. We have all participated in the general steeplechase for pre-eminence; the thousand-barrel mill of our competitor had to be put in the shade by a two-thousand-barrel mill of our own construction; the commercial triumph of former seasons had to be surpassed by still more dazzling figures. As our glory increased our profits became smaller, until now the question is not how to surpass the record, but how to maintain our position and how to secure what we have in our possession . . . In the general scramble we have gradually lost sight of the inexorable laws of supply and demand.

John D. Rockefeller, in his *Reminiscences,* claimed that the wastefulness of competition was the reason for the formation of the Standard Oil Trust: when "the butcher, the baker, and the candlestick maker began to refine oil," because at first it was easy and profitable, saturating the market and bringing the profits down in no time, "it seemed absolutely necessary to extend the market for oil . . . and also greatly improve the processes of refining so that oil could be made and sold cheaply, yet with profit"; thus "we proceeded to buy the largest and best refining concerns and centralize the administration of them with a view to securing greater economy and efficiency." He believed (like so many economic historians since) that in creating Standard Oil he had no choice, that his actions were dictated by recognized necessity, a law of economic progress. Consolidation "was the origin of the whole system of modern economic administration," he said. "It has revolutionized the way of doing business all over the world. The time was ripe for it. It had to come, though all we saw at the moment was the need to save ourselves from wasteful conditions." His company succeeded where others failed simply because "we have taken steps of progress that our rivals could not take."

But why was he not satisfied with smaller profits and bothered by wasteful conditions? What made him perceive a trend of history which no one noticed before? Rockefeller did not love money more than the next man; he was apparently indifferent to the comforts it bought; indeed, Ida Tarbell, the censorious historian of the Standard Oil Company, accused him of being "poor in his pleasures": instead of building himself a mansion of the kind for which other critics attacked other millionaires, this mogul was satisfied to live in "cheap ugliness." It was not an opportunity to earn more that sharpened his sensitivity and spurred on his business genius, but a chance to do something big, "to carry on a business of some magnitude and importance," as he himself said, explaining the incorporation of several refineries into the "Rockefeller Associates" (Standard Oil Company) only years after "Colonel" Drake had struck oil in Pennsylvania in 1859, "in place of the small business that each separately had theretofore carried on." At the end of his career, Rockefeller insisted: "I had no ambition to make a fortune. Mere money-getting has never been my goal. I saw a marvelous future for our country, and I wanted to participate in the work of making our country great. I had an ambition to build."[11]

Nor did pecuniary considerations move Andrew Carnegie. His attitude to money was at most ambivalent, and he considered an annual income of $50,000 at thirty-three far more than adequate, writing despondently: "Whatever I engage in I must push inordinately . . . To continue much longer overwhelmed by business cares and with most of my thoughts wholly upon the way to make more money in the shortest time, must degrade me beyond hope of permanent recovery. I will resign business at thirty-five." If he did not, this was not because "rational economic interest" drove him to go on. He came from poverty, of which he was proud, and thought it was the responsibility of a rich man to give away all his wealth in his lifetime—a principle, we are told, in the adherence to which Carnegie was relentless. "Whether the millionaire wishes it or not," he wrote in *Empire of Business,* "he cannot evade the law which under present conditions, compels him to use his millions for the good of the people. All that he gets during a few years of his life is that he may live in a finer house, surround himself with finer furniture . . . He can eat richer food and drink richer wines." Even this, however, the businessman was allowed only in moderation, for, Carnegie thought, it was the duty of the millionaire "to set an example of modest, unostentatious living, shunning display or extravagance." He had a castle in Scotland, where display was de rigueur, but in his adopted home, the United States, lived in a—relatively—plain house on upper Fifth Avenue, without a yacht, without an opera box, without Old Masters or first editions. Perhaps because things of this nature gave him no particular pleasure, he could say that

> truly the modern millionaire is generally a man of very simple tastes and even miserly habits. He spends little upon himself, and is the toiling bee laying up honey in the industrial hive, which all the inmates of that hive, the community in general, will certainly enjoy . . . Under our present conditions the millionaire who toils on is the cheapest article which the community secures at the price it pays for him, namely, his shelter, clothing, and food . . . It will be a great mistake for the community to shoot the millionaires.

Carnegie's desire was "to make something tangible," not to make himself rich. If profits, in his view, were essential for business, this was because they tested the businessman. A businessman, he said, "must be at least part owner of the enterprise which he manages and to which he gives his attention, and chiefly dependent for his revenues not upon salary but upon its profits"; he had to plunge and toss upon the waves of human affairs "without a life-preserver in the shape of salary," risking it all. Self-interest was involved, of course, but it was interest in dignity, not greed. The "star-spangled Scotchman" dedicated his *Triumphant Democracy* ("with an intensity of gratitude and admiration which the native-born citizen can neither feel nor understand") "to the BELOVED REPUBLIC under whose equal laws I am made the peer of any man, although denied political equality by my native land." The book, he said, was

> a labor of love—the tribute of a very dutiful and grateful adopted son to the country which has removed the stigma of inferiority which his native land saw proper to impress upon him at birth, and has made him, in the estimation of its great laws as well as in his own estimation (much the more important consideration), the peer of any human being who draws the breath of life, be he pope, kaiser, priest or king—henceforth the subject of no man."[12]

It is significant that he was not grateful for the opportunity to become one of the richest men in the world.

Most "robber barons" admittedly spent more on themselves than these lords of oil and steel, though of most it could be said, as Charles Elliott Perkins said of Huntington and Gould, that their wealth "does them personally very little good—a small part of their incomes may be wasted on show or champagne, but most of it is invested in some form of industry which directly benefits the masses by making something cheaper." And while Henry Adams might have wished to emphasize the millionaires' lack of ability, rather than desire, for display, he too remarked, "The men who commanded high pay were as a rule not ornamental." They erected luxurious homes to house their families—structures that were baroque rather than baronial in their extravagance. There was the house of Charles Crocker in San Francisco, which sported a seventy-six-foot observation tower (offering a view of the harbor and an athletic challenge to the overweight owner), and which was called "a delirium of the wood carver"; Potter Palmer's "mansion to end all mansions" in Chicago, "an American architect's best thought of what a baronial castle should be"; the "cottages" in Newport, which Henry James characterized as "white elephants." Why did they do it, wondered a historian. "Why did the business leaders from San Francisco to Bar Harbor have to live in houses with libraries, billiard rooms, art galleries, several rooms in which to eat, at least one of which had to be two stories high and paneled to the ceiling, buildings sometimes equipped with small theatres and perhaps even a chapel capable of holding a considerable congregation?" They were compelled to do so by "the vanity of wealth," which some contemporaries still recognized as the ruling motive for its acquisition, hoping that their copious investments in conspicuous consumption would generate returns in status.

Old Masters and first editions were other forms of cultural sophistication, used to the same status-aggrandizing purpose, though some of the vulgar rich, such as J. P. Morgan, clearly developed a genuine taste for the finer things in life. James Caldwell, a smaller "baron" from Tennessee, recorded how, coming to New York to see the banker "on a matter of business," he was a witness to the latter's lengthy conference with "the superintendent of the Art Museum," as the two admired "a treasure which had just arrived from Europe." "It proved," remembered Caldwell, "to be a plain-looking picture, executed upon a board, and called the 'Fra Angelica.' It clearly was antique, and no doubt a very rare piece, but not pretty, and to me, who am no art critic, it seemed quite ordinary; but he and the art superintendent took on over it mightily and it was quite some time before we could get him back to 'business.'" The attitude to "culture" of Commodore Vanderbilt, who probably shared Caldwell's taste in art, was more astute: one couldn't cut a figure without it. "I've been to England, and seen them lords, and other fellows," he once confessed, "and knew that I had twice as much brains as they had maybe, and yet I had to keep still, and couldn't say anything through fear of exposing myself." He was no doubt sincere when he exclaimed in a conversation with a clergyman invited to his home, "I'd give a million dollars today, Doctor, if I had your education!"

The desire to cut a figure certainly was behind some of the endowments and gifts to colleges and universities, which were as typical of "robber barons" as they were incongruous with this collective label which denied them generosity. The theme in Carnegie's *Gospel of Wealth,* "that the province and office of wealth was the diffusion and advancement of culture," we are told, "proved strangely attractive to men whose one goal had been accumulation and who were themselves extravagantly uncultivated." A steel producer, Abram Hewitt (the singular business mogul, counted as a friend by the likes of Henry Adams), declared in 1896, on the occasion of the dedication of the new Morningside Heights campus to his alma mater, Columbia: "In this country patents of nobility are wisely prohibited, but a title to immortality is surely within the reach of those to whom the trustees may finally award the privilege and the glory of erecting any one of these buildings."[13] Most of the princely contributions to higher education in America, made by the "robber barons" of the Gilded Age, however, were inspired by a grander ambition—also an aspiration to a superior status of a kind—to be benefactors to humanity.

The national sentiment was relatively unimportant among the motivations of American entrepreneurs of that age. To be sure, they were patriots; but it was not the desire to make the United States great among nations that spurred them on in their ventures. Even the "star-spangled" Carnegie, whose devotion to his adopted country admitted no doubt and was probably more ardent, and certainly more effusive, than that of others, was largely insensible to economic nationalism. Like their German or Japanese counterparts, and in harmony with the Darwinian-Spencerian fashion of the time, captains of American industry might have seen business activity as a form of struggle and even at times as a form of international struggle (J. H. Francis, in 1899, lobbying for business education in the United States, suggested that "the struggle of the future will not be on the battlefields, but in the arena of trades, markets, and exchanges"). But on the whole, the struggle they envisioned was between individuals rather than collective entities, and if they claimed that their activity promoted general interests, those were the interests not of the American nation but of humanity as a whole. E. L. Godkin, whose opinion of big business was more favorable than that of most contemporary intellectuals, maintained that the great capitalists were appointed by natural selection to be the "explorers for the race." Carnegie defended large corporations because they improved the condition "of the race," and advised patience regarding bitter competition, for "while the law may be sometimes hard for the individual, it is best for the race, because it insures the survival of the fittest in every department." Clearly, it was the human race these people spoke about. The actions of the great business leaders backed their ideology and reflected its universalist orientation. They saw the world as their oyster, and as soon as the American market was sufficiently impressed with their powers, needed larger and larger audiences to demonstrate them anew. They competed indiscriminately with the entrepreneurs of any nation, but they did so not in order to submit other economies to American control, but in order to prove to themselves that they could do it, or simply because they could no longer stop.

One of the early twentieth-century critics of the Gilded Age, Walter Weyl, wrote of the railroads which made possible America's industrialization: "Peculation, speculation, force, fraud, genius, and courage,—all went into the new lines." The railroad promoter, like the pioneer, though on a greater scale, "wasted, ravaged, and laid fire; like the pioneer, though on a much greater scale, he built for himself and for the nation. Ruthless, greedy, imaginative, he erected, by fair means or foul, by his own brains and the tributary science of the world, an edifice overpowering in its immensity." The same, though on a still greater scale, could be said of all new industries and industrialists of that pregnant time. "Robber barons" were men of exceptional ability, imagination, and willpower, but not saints. Some of them were in fact cheats and crooks, who could be called robbers with good reason. Their actions were described often enough. They might have been indeed chiefly, if not exclusively, interested in material gain and used indiscriminately the means available to them to achieve their goals, enriching themselves at the expense of the public so long as they could get away with it. These true "malefactors of great wealth" were neither the most prominent nor the most vilified members of their group. The "unbroken chorus of protests," which, according to Henry Lloyd, accompanied the rise of the great corporations, was provoked not by the dishonesty of their directors and founders, but—despite the alleged chivalry and generosity of the American people, "always rejoicing in the victories of those runners of the race for wealth who have won the right to wear the crown that all were striving for"—by their success.[14]

The secret of this success lay in resolute ambition, coupled with superior ability to use the available resources creatively. The ambition could blind one to the illegality or immorality of the means employed; in the case of the two greatest fortunes of the period—the main object of public outrage—it did not. It is absolutely clear that both Rockefeller and Carnegie did what others did (or, at any rate, were expected to do), only better than others. There were no legal restrictions on their actions (though some were introduced later), in fact, sanctioned by the American tradition of free competition. Henry Lloyd did not know how to restrain his annoyance with the Standard Oil Company; the disapproval gushed out of him like the mineral substance on which the obnoxious business was based from a newly tapped field. What was the problem? He could not explain how it could "lubricate poverty into its almost unaccountable millions." For the men who formed it "were neither capitalists, nor oil discoverers, nor oil experts in any branch." Of Rockefeller he wrote with unconcealed spite:

> The first of them came tardily into the field about 1862. He started a little refinery in Cleveland, hundreds of miles from the oil wells. The sixty and more manufacturers who had been able to plant themselves before 1860, when they had to distil coal into petroleum before they could refine petroleum into kerosene, had been multiplied into hundreds by the arrival of petroleum ready made from below. Some of the richest and most successful business men of the country had preceded him and were flourishing. He had been a book-keeper, and then a partner, in a very small country-produce store in Cleveland. As described by his councel some years later, he was a "man of brains and energy without money."

It never occurred to Lloyd that brains and energy—business acumen and ambition—were factors of economic importance comparable to money, luck, or technical expertise. Therefore, he suspected black magic. Its sinister working was clearly evident, he thought, in Rockefeller's ability to hypnotize the railroads into aiding and abetting him. On examination, however, it appears that the only sentiment behind the infamous rebates (according to Lloyd and other critics, responsible for the Standard Oil's fortune) was self-interest, which, in America, has been traditionally considered a purely natural phenomenon.

In his *Random Reminiscences,* John D. Rockefeller referred to the "question of rebates," which was the uppermost "of all the subjects which seem to have attracted the attention of the public to his affairs." "The Standard Oil Company of Ohio, of which I was president," he wrote,

> did receive rebates from the railroads prior to 1880, but received no advantages for which it did not give full compensation. The reason for rebates was that such was the railroads' method of business. A public rate was made and collected by the railroad companies, but, so far as my knowledge extends, was seldom retained in full; a portion of it was repaid to the shippers as a rebate. By this method the real rate of freight which any shipper paid was not known by his competitors nor by other railroad companies, the amount being a matter of bargain with the carrying company. Each shipper made the best bargain that he could, but

whether he was doing better than his competitor was only a matter of conjecture. Much depended upon whether the shipper had the advantage of competition of carriers.

The Standard Oil Company of Ohio, being situated in Cleveland, had the advantage of different carrying lines, as well as of water transportation in the summer; taking advantage of those facilities, it made the best bargains possible for its freights. Other companies sought to do the same. The Standard gave advantages to the railroads for the purpose of reducing the cost of transportation of freight. It offered freights in large quantities, car-loads and train-loads. It furnished loading facilities and discharging facilities at great cost. It provided regular traffic, so that a railroad could conduct its transportation to the best advantage and use its equipment to the full extent of its hauling capacity without waiting for the refiner's convenience. It exempted railroads from liability for fire and carried its own insurance. It provided at its own expense terminal facilities which permitted economies in handling. For these services it obtained contracts for special allowances on freights.

But notwithstanding these special allowances, this traffic from the Standard Oil Company was far more profitable to the railroad companies than the smaller and irregular traffic, which might have paid a higher fare.

Whatever advantage the company received from reduced rates of freight, Rockefeller explained, "was only one of the many elements of lessening cost to the consumer which enabled us to increase our volume of business the world over because we could reduce the selling price." He added a little later:

I well remember a bright man from Boston who had much to say about rebates and drawbacks. He was an old and experienced merchant, and looked after his affairs with a cautious and watchful eye. He feared that some of his competitors were doing better than he in bargaining for rates, and he delivered himself of this conviction: "I am opposed on principle to the whole system of rebates and drawbacks—unless I am in it."

Equally innocent of black magic were the methods of competition employed by Andrew Carnegie, who early recognized the superior contribution which could be made to his business by disciplined accounting and chemistry. He recalled in his *Autobiography:*

As I became acquainted with the manufacture of iron, I was greatly surprised to find that the cost of each of the various processes was unknown . . . I felt as if we were moles burrowing in the dark, and this to me was intolerable. I insisted upon such a system of accounting being introduced throughout our works as would enable us to know what our cost was for each process and especially what each man was doing, who saved material, who wasted it, and who produced the best results.

The system allowed Carnegie to calculate that an expensive furnace of a new type, the cost of which was considered exorbitant by manufacturers, in heating great masses of iron saved almost half the waste that would have resulted from the use of a less expensive facility and would have justified double the expense. He bought it, and "it was many years before we were followed in this new departure." An additional benefit was the discovery of a valuable worker, who surprised Carnegie "one day by presenting a detailed statement showing results for a period, which seemed incredible. All the needed labor in preparing this statement he had performed at night unasked and unknown to us. The form adopted was uniquely original. Needless to say, William soon became superintendent of the works and later a partner, and the poor German lad died a millionaire." He "well deserved his fortune," thought the steel king.

Chemistry added to the advantages of accounting. Here, too, Carnegie was ahead of the competition. He wrote:

Looking back to-day it seems incredible that only forty years ago (1870) chemistry in the United States was an almost unknown agent in connection with the manufacture of pig iron. It was the agency, above all others, most needful in the manufacture of iron and steel. The blast-furnace manager of that day was usually a rude bully, generally a foreigner, who in addition to his other acquirements was able to knock down a man now and then as a lesson to the other unruly spirits under him. He was supposed to diagnose the condition of the furnace by instinct, to possess some almost supernatural power of divination, like his congener in the country districts who was reputed to be able to locate an oil well or water supply by means of a hazel rod. He was a veritable quack doctor who applied whatever remedies occurred to him for the troubles of his patient.

The Lucy Furnace was out of one trouble and into another, owing to the great variety of ores, limestone, and coke which were then supplied with little or no regard to their component parts. This state of affairs became intolerable to us. We finally decided to dispense with the rule-of-thumb-and-intuition manager.

Instead, the company hired "a learned German, Dr. Fricke," a chemist, and "nine tenths of all the uncertainties of pig-iron making were dispelled under the burning sun of chemical knowledge." "What fools we had been!" marveled the retired magnate.

> But then there was this consolation: we were not as great fools as our competitors. It was years after we had taken chemistry to guide us that it was said by the proprietors of some other furnaces that they could not afford to employ a chemist. Had they known the truth then, they would have known that they could not afford to be without one. Looking back it seems pardonable to record that we were the first to employ a chemist at blast furnaces—something our competitors pronounced extravagant. The Lucy Furnace became the most profitable branch of our business, because we had almost the entire monopoly of scientific management.[15]

"We do what we must and call it by the best name possible," wrote Emerson.[16] The protesting choristers called their chant "an opposition to monopoly." In general, "monopoly" was a term of opprobrium for any large and successful corporation, but its sting was reserved for corporations that controlled a significant share of the market for a particular product. The method of achieving such control was of no importance: a business which emerged victorious in free competition, owing to the natural ability of its founders who inherited no wealth, contacts, or social position, was as much, and as vicious, a monopoly as the one that owed it to special privileges and legal restrictions on competition; the word was used in its etymological sense, abstracted from the historical context and purified from the sediment of tradition which gave meaning to the concept. The inevitable result of supreme business success was the end, or at least a severe limitation, of further competition, in the same way that a result of the victory in a race was the end of a race (with that difference, of course, that successful businessmen continued to compete against themselves, spurred on by the desire to beat their own record). This similarity of result justified condemning as a "monopoly" a corporation which realized the spirit of competition best, and while in the past the surest method to fight this evil (and to foster liberty of trade) was thought to be the lifting of all restrictions on competition at the starting point, now it seemed to be the establishment of a ceiling on the possible achievement. Nobody should aspire to be so much more than others, was the implied message; this did not agree with the American notion of equality. Moreover, though large corporations, in the first place corporations called "monopolies," reduced consumer prices, created jobs, and in general contributed to the material prosperity and comfort of the community, it was assumed that in the future, in the absence of such a ceiling, their effect must necessarily turn adverse, for, in accordance with the immutable laws of the human nature, success was certain to go to the heads of the corporations' directors, however good their intentions, and turn them into tyrants. In this instance, Americans believed that wealth corrupts and corporate wealth corrupts absolutely.[17]

William Jennings Bryan, "the darling of the rural masses," learned this, appropriately, from observations on hogs. He was a man with an open mind, ready for all sorts of suggestions. "We get our ideas from every source," he said. "We get them from our fellow men. We get them from inanimate nature. We get them from the animals about us." Hogs, he told an audience at the Chicago Conference on Trusts in 1900, taught him to oppose "monopolies." "I was riding through Iowa once," he recounted,

> and saw some hogs rooting in the field. The first thought that came to me was that those hogs were destroying a great deal in value, and then my mind ran back to the time when I lived upon a farm and when we had hogs.
>
> Then I thought of the way in which we used to protect property from the hogs by putting rings in the noses of the hogs; and then the question came to me, why did we do it? Not to keep the hogs from getting fat, for we were more interested in their getting fat than they were; the sooner they got fat the sooner we killed them; the longer they were in getting fat the longer they lived. But why did we put rings in their noses? So that while they were getting fat they would not destroy more than they were worth. And then the thought came to me that one of the great purposes of government was to put rings in the noses of hogs.

In Mr. Bryan's elegant metaphor, founders and directors of giant corporations were hogs, while corporations themselves were man-made hogs, and it was a supreme duty of the government to put rings in their noses. "I do not believe," he declared, "it is safe for a society to permit any man or group of men to monopolize any article of merchandise or any branch of industry." Curiously, the great Democrat thought that the "destruction of property" argument, which led him to advocate nose rings in the case of hogs in the field, was irrelevant insofar as monopoly hogs were concerned. "What is the defense made of the monopoly?" he demanded.

> The defense of the monopoly is always placed on the ground that if you will allow a few people to control the market and fix the price they will be good to the people who purchase of them. The entire defense of the trusts rests upon a money argument. If the trust will sell to a man an article for a dollar less than the article will cost under other conditions, then in the opinion of some that proves a trust to be a good thing. In the first place I deny that under a monopoly the price will be reduced. In the sec-

ond place, if under a monopoly the price is reduced the objections to a monopoly from other standpoints far outweigh any financial advantage that the trust could bring. But I protest in the beginning against settling every question upon the dollar argument. I protest against the attempt to drag every question down to the low level of dollars and cents.

The hoggishness of the monopolies, Bryan feared, transcended monetary calculation. Monopolies were hogs on a much higher, indeed monstrous, level, and the damage their existence portended to the community made one's hair stand on end. Bryan admitted that "we have not had in this country a taste of a complete trust, a complete monopoly, and we cannot tell what will be the results of a complete monopoly by looking at the results that have followed from an attempt to secure a monopoly." He was nevertheless certain that they would undermine the republic. "I may be in error," he declared in a manner sure to convince his audience that the suggestion was absurd,

> but, in my judgment, a government of the people, by the people, and for the people, will be impossible when a few men control all the sources of production and dole out daily bread to all the rest on such terms as the few may prescribe. I believe that this nation is the hope of the world. I believe that the Declaration of Independence was the grandest document ever penned by human hands. The truths of that declaration are condensed into four great propositions: That all men are created equal; that they are endowed with inalienable rights; that governments are instituted among men to preserve those rights, and that governments derive their just powers from the consent of the governed. Such a government is impossible under an industrial aristocracy.

It was not for nothing that Bryan was the great Populist leader and, perhaps, the greatest demagogue of nineteenth-century America: he read the mind of the crowd; he knew precisely what nerve to touch to produce the desired reaction. The ideal he appealed to was equality, the emotion—envy. Under the conditions of a national market and mechanized production, grand business success was offensive to American sensibilities ("un-American," one of the first American economists and the founder of the American Economic Association was to say): it made some men conspicuously unequal to the rest.

But America was a pluralist society. Its underlying ideology, its civic spirit, the consciousness that characterized it as a nation, was individualism, and, contrary to what many, including business leaders, were saying at the time, this spirit was not destroyed, nor even weakened, by the organizational transformation in the economy. There remained plenty of people—as many as there ever were—willing to take a chance, perhaps more willing when the chance was slim; intolerant of limitations placed on their ambition; and determined to think for themselves. In such a society populist leaders would do better in some years than in others, but on the whole they had a hard time. Thus it was not entirely in vain to attempt to bring the discussion, as did W. Bourke Cockran, from the lofty sphere of Populist fancy down to earth, experience, and logic. "Dangerous intoxication of phrases," argued Cockran, was not the way to address the problem of monopolies. Rather, one needed to establish what precisely a monopoly is and whether it was found in the United States. If an oppressive monopoly existed in his country, he would be the first, he said, to join Bryan in the efforts to suppress it; but "to call an industrial organization—a combine—a hydra-headed monster—or even an octopus [he left out the hog metaphor]—does not cast any light upon what it is, or illumine my pathway in attempting to deal with it." If the conference was to reach a conclusion of any significance on trusts, it had to focus on its actual effects on the community. The participants had to ask: "Are we prosperous, or are we suffering? Is anybody injured, and by whom? Has this octopus of which we hear so much taken possession of anybody or anything? On whom or on what is it preying? Where is its lair?" Cockran continued, spelling out the inconsistency of the Populist position on big business:

> What is the evil of which gentlemen here complain? The chief cause of alarm seems to be fear that competition will be stifled, yet the natural, nay, the inevitable result of competition, is the object of their most vehement denunciations. I confess I am at a loss to understand the mental processes which lead men to laud competition and yet to condemn the fruit which competition must always bear. Do you want competition, or do you not? . . . Can you have competition without competitors? If there be competition must not somebody succeed in it? If one competitor far excels all others, will not that excellence constitute a monopoly? Will you suppress competition when it develops unapproachable merit? Will you place limits upon excellency? . . . There is no way to suppress a monopoly arising from conspicuous merit except by the suppression of merit. If the producer of the best commodity may not dominate the market for that particular article, neither should the possessor of particular ability in any other department of human endeavor. Must we place restrictions on capacity in law and medicine, so as to place the capable and the incapable on a common level? . . . Mr. Bryan's position, as he states it, is that monopoly in private hands is always oppressive. Instead of distinguishing between corporations which dominate the market by excellence and those dominating it by favor, he appears to distinguish between those which are successful and those which are not.

He next addressed fears regarding the future effects of large corporations, assessing them against actual experience:

If corporate organization be an evil thing, if you can show me an evil flowing out of it and inseparable from it, I would not hesitate a moment to adopt Mr. Bryan's remedy [regulation]. But when it is admitted, as Mr. Bryan admitted this morning, that these evils of monopoly have not yet become apparent,—that they are evils anticipated, not suffered,— why, then, I say to him or to anybody who agrees with him, you are simply exciting yourself over a fanciful picture of your own creation.

Experience did not warrant opposition to big business. In Cockran's opinion, it justified praise and gratitude on the part of the community:

The change which has come over this world within the last ten years is the great phenomenon of civilization. A dozen years ago none but the largest cities contained public parks. The pleasure grounds laid out at the public expense, and the drives which led to them, were fully available only to those who owned their own carriages. To-day every town of considerable size possesses its place of recreation, while every mechanic and laborer can use the driveway on a bicycle of his own. The journey to and from the place of labor which formerly the laborer made every day at a snail's pace in wretched street cars, with splattering oil lamps, drawn by miserable horses or mules, is made to-day in rapid comfortable vehicles, lighted and moved by electricity. Every workman is better housed, earns higher wages, eats more abundant and more wholesome food, reads more books and better books than ever before in the history of the race.

He may have been carried away a little. He may have exaggerated insofar as better books were concerned or the incontestable superiority of the electric vehicles to horse-drawn streetcars. But he was correct in insisting on the better quality of food overall, and housing, and wages, and the general level of prosperity, and was right to conclude, as he did, "When we realize that this is an age of marvelous improvement, that the conditions of men are growing better and better every day, we ought to hesitate a while before we change the industrial system evolved from experience, for fanciful experiments suggested by exuberant rhetoric."[18]

The truth of the matter was that as the "robber barons" attempted to raise themselves in the world, they did an awful lot of good for their country. Propelled by their ambition, the United States emerged as the greatest industrial power on earth, the economic colossus it now is. This ambition was an objective economic force at least as potent as railroads, corporations, the enormous natural resources of the American land, or capital; in fact, it was the greatest capital and the most creative natural resource itself, for it was this ambition that made the other forces multiply and fill the earth (or that part of it which was the United States) with immense wealth, hardly imaginable before. This ambition was a species of self-interest, though not of the material economic kind recognized by economic theory. The great entrepreneurs pursued their own ends, only marginally concerned with the society as a whole; but the effect of this pursuit, unintentional or only partly intended, was nevertheless to improve tremendously the material condition of this society, and, if the general interest be defined in terms of material strength and prosperity, spectacularly advance its general interest. The hard fact about the Gilded Age, as H. Wayne Morgan put it, was that "the nation *did* grow stronger in all spheres."

The gap between the super-rich and those on the lower rungs of the economic scale necessarily widened, but the situation of the latter was incomparably better at the end of the period than at its beginning: real wages were higher and working days shorter; living standards rose. The "industrial class"—the new lower class created by big business, whose "division of labor [substituted] for the versatile frontiersman the specialized factory-hand"— was better off than other lower classes insofar as the material conditions of labor were concerned, and the perspectives of the laborer were infinitely brighter. The scope of social mobility widened with the possibilities created by the growing economy; few families remained below for generations. Ambition drove them—or their children—up the ladder of success, and the examples of "robber barons" gave them encouragement and reasonable hope. "Among American working classes," wrote Charles A. Beard, "all save the most wretched had aspirations; there was a baton in every tool kit."

For those who wished to rise in the world of business, but were incapable or unwilling to risk all upon the waves of human affairs without a life preserver in the form of a salary, the giant corporations provided a new venue for mobility: a career in management. The idea of economic success (and competition) was redefined to include advancement in the corporate hierarchy. The urban middle class—the class of those who could without undue strain afford all the amenities of life, and of which the ever-growing number of business managers formed a subclass—expanded tremendously; its influence grew in proportion to this expansion, the elites of the American society being recruited from it. Urban America, a novel phenomenon, was fed, clothed, and supplied with increasingly diverse goods by big business. The majority of urban Americans, it seemed, were also employed by it. "A new economic society" came into being. The economic landscape of the country, like the physical, was transformed beyond recognition, the occupational structure changed dramatically, and though the social dynamic remained very much what it was before industrialization began—because the nation was still animated by the same spirit and guided by the same consciousness—the economic framework for the operation of the characteristic motive forces was new. The outlines of today's economy were becoming distinct. One could welcome or—as was more often the case—be alarmed by the vision, but it was clear. "If, in a century we have increased from seven to ninety millions," wrote Walter Weyl in 1912,

> we may well increase, in the coming century, to two or three hundreds of millions. In the lifetime of babes already born, the United States may be a Titanic commonwealth bestriding the world; a nation as superior in power to England or Germany as those countries are to Holland or Denmark . . . It may be the greatest single factor, for good or evil, in the destinies of the world . . . If to-day we have individual fortunes of four or five hundreds of millions, whereas in Washington's day we had not a single millionaire, how overwhelming may not be our fortunes in the year 2000.[19]

He was not far off the mark, for the structure of the economy we know today was already in place. The only element of the economic civilization that was still to be added was the articulate consciousness of its fundamental, unchanging, and universal character.

The Rise of Economics

The creation of this economic consciousness was directly related to the rise of big business, though not because it "reflected" the new mode of production in a Marxian fashion, or "corresponded" in some mystical manner to the systemic needs of industrializing economy, but because it provoked the creators of this consciousness. These creators—the first American economists—came from the traditional social elite of American society, "almost entirely native-born Protestants" and college graduates, many of whom "had considerably more than moderate means" and "had inherited their money." They had no direct experience of the new economic reality, and the ideas they formed of it were rationalizations of the revulsion it inspired in them rather than a result of a dispassionate analysis of facts. The reasons for their revulsion, remarkably, had little if anything to do with the economic changes effected by industrialization and big business; the problem to which the profound, peculiarly American economism (and the American discipline of economics, which was its original form) was a response was not economic at all. "Curiously," wrote

Richard Hofstadter regarding the Progressive movement, of which the early economics may be considered a part,

> the Progressive revolt—even when we have made allowance for the brief panic of 1907 and the downward turn in business in 1913—took place almost entirely during a period of sustained and general prosperity . . . [M]en [became] Progressives not because of economic deprivations but primarily because they were victims of an upheaval in status that took place in the United States during the closing decades of the nineteenth and the early years of the twentieth century. Progressivism, in short, was to a very considerable extent led by men who suffered from the events of their time not through a shrinkage in their means but through the changed pattern in the distribution of deference and power.

The "status revolution" to which Hofstadter drew attention was a consequence of the emergence of the new class of super-rich, produced by big business, which of necessity upset the system of existing class relations and undermined the position of the traditional elite. Wealth has always been the basis of status in American society, but with the passing of generations it acquired the patina of gentility and gracious living, covering its nakedness under layers of cultural sophistication or at least form. It was civilized and ennobled. Closely associated with social eminence, it came to be regarded as the latter's extension: being a lawyer or a merchant placed one somewhat above the rest of the community in terms of one's pecuniary rewards, which made these "the fairest titles" this land, characterized as it was by "happy mediocrity," could afford, and money which made lawyers and merchants stand out appeared as a natural appurtenance of their position rather than the other way around. Until very late in American history, merchants were the richest men in the nation. Only a few of them became millionaires: in 1831 Stephen Girard died, leaving $6 million, while the estate of John Jacob Astor at the time of his death in 1848 was three times that amount. These fortunes were considered "immense." The professions, especially law, offered the surest avenue of upward mobility, "along which a man who started with only moderate social advantages might, without capital, rise upward through the ranks to a position of wealth or power." In his old age Henry Adams recalled that "down to 1850, and even later, New England society was still directed by the professions[:] lawyers, physicians, professors, merchants." It was not much different elsewhere, at least in the North. The liberal professions (money which was tied to education), it appears, had a higher status—in the eyes of the professionals themselves, at any rate—than trade, despite merchants' superior wealth. An eminent architect remembered wistfully at the end of his career in 1902 how in his youth "an architect was somebody . . . He ranked with the judge, the leading lawyer, the eminent physician—several pegs higher in the social rack than the merely successful merchant or broker."

When Henry Adams returned from Europe at the end of the 1860s, as we saw, the situation had already changed. Hofstadter writes:

> The newly rich, the grandiosely or corruptly rich, the masters of great corporations, were bypassing . . . the old gentry, the merchants of long standing, the small manufacturers, the established professional men, the civic leaders of an earlier era. In a score of cities and hundreds of towns, particularly in the East but also in the nation at large, the old-family, col-lege-educated class that had deep ancestral roots in local communities and often owned family businesses, that had traditions of political lead-ership, belonged to the patriotic societies and the best clubs, staffed the governing boards of philanthropic and cultural institutions, and led the movements for civic betterment, were being overshadowed and edged aside in the making of basic political and economic decisions. In their personal careers, as in their community activities, they found themselves checked, hampered, and overridden by the agents of the new corpora-tions, the corrupters of legislatures, the buyers of franchises, the allies of the political bosses. In this uneven struggle they found themselves lim-ited by their own scruples, their regard for reputation, their social stand-ing itself. To be sure, the America they knew did not lack opportuni-ties, but it did seem to lack opportunities of the highest sort for men of the highest standards. In a strictly economic sense these men were not growing poorer as a class, but their wealth and power were being dwarfed by comparison with the new eminences of wealth and power. They were less important, and they knew it.[20]

The deprivation felt by the traditional elite was a relative deprivation (which is to say that they suffered not from a want of something, but from the knowledge that someone else had more of what they had), yet it was rela-tive deprivation of heroic proportions that corresponded to the vast distance separating the old rich from the new. Whereas, in the 1850s and early 1860s, according to the 1885 Senate Education and Labor Committee report on the relations between labor and capital, "a man that had a farm worth $1,500 or $2,000 was considered 'A, No. 1'," and the "richest man in town was worth some $4,000 or $5,000," a reporter who visited Andrew Carnegie in 1901, after Carnegie sold his company to J. P. Morgan's United States Steel Corpo-ration for a quarter of a billion dollars, calculated that the daily income of the retired magnate amounted to $40,000. No wonder the old rich were coming to perceive poverty in an entirely different light, believed themselves destitute, and bitterly resented the so-called plutocracy. Walter Weyl left us a pointed description of the sentiment that was at the root of their reaction:

> The most curious factor in this antagonism [to big business] is that an increasing bitterness is felt by a majority which is not worse but better off than before. This majority suffers not an absolute decline but a relatively slower growth. It objects that a plutocracy grows too fast; that in growing so rapidly it squeezes its growing neighbors. Growth is right and proper, but there is, it is alleged, a rate of growth which is positively immoral. It is urged against the plutocracy that, because of its growth, it subjects an increasing number of people to a pressure to which they are becoming increasingly sensitive. This pressure is not for the most part the pang of hunger. Our society is too well padded for that. It is a subtler pressure on a higher economic plane . . . [I]t is the mere existence of a plutocracy, the mere "being" of our wealthy contemporaries, that is the main offense. Our over-moneyed neighbors cause a relative deflation of our personalities . . . Our jogging horses are passed by their high-power automobiles. We are obliged to take their dust.
>
> By setting the pace for a frantic competitive consumption, our infinite gradations in wealth (with which gradations the plutocracy is inevitably associated) increase the general social friction and produce an acute social irritation. There was ostentatious spending before the plutocratic period, as there will be after, for display is an inveterate form of individuation, older than humanity. Our plutocracy, however, intent upon socially isolating itself and possessing no title to precedence other than the visible possession of money, makes of this competitive consumption a perennial handicap-race of spenders. We are developing new types of destitutes—the automobileless, the yachtless, the Newport-cottageless. The subtlest of luxuries become necessities, and their loss is bitterly resented. The discontent of to-day reaches very high in the social scale.[21]

Other people's money has traditionally aroused lively indignation in America. The traditional elite, perched—yachtless and Newport-cottageless—on the highest rung of the social ladder, suffered from an uncommonly acute variety of common envy. Its condition was similar to that of a European nobility (most clearly, the *noblesse de race* and *d'épée* in France) threatened by the advance of the enterprising middle classes, and its reaction closely resembled that of the duc de Saint-Simon to "vile bourgeoisie." Like the French nobility, American notables sought solace in those aspects of their status that were inaccessible to the parvenus from below, however wealthy: the numbers of exclusive patriotic and genealogical societies, which played up the relative antiquity of the elite's American descent and the participation of their families in the formative episodes of the national history, apparently grew in direct proportion to big business and the fortunes of "robber barons."[22] But solace was not to be found there. Like the French nobility, American notables therefore also sought to diminish in their own eyes the great industrial capitalists. In the process they constructed a sinister mythical image, at once revolting and terrifying. In utter disregard of the American ideal of equality, the old elite denied the merit of the big businessmen and was unsparing in the ridicule of their self-made character, their humble origins, and their lack of cultivation. In every essential, this was a replay of the reaction of the "honest part of the community" to the "stock-jobbing herd" of the 1790s, though the enormous wealth of the "robber barons" naturally necessitated a stronger language. Henry Demarest Lloyd, one of the just and humiliated, obviously felt that, when it came to portraying our captains of industry, no hyperbole was too extravagant and no calumny too malicious. The end justified the means. "If our civilization is destroyed," Lloyd suggested, giving every impression, that this was both likely and imminent,

it will not be by barbarians from below. Our barbarians come from above. Our great money-makers have sprung in one generation into seats of power kings do not know . . . Without restraints of culture, experience, the pride, or even the inherited caution of class or rank, these men, intoxicated, think . . . that they have created the business which has created them . . . They claim a power without control, exercised through forms which make it a secret, anonymous, and perpetual . . . They are gluttons of luxury and power, rough, unsocialized, believing that mankind must be kept terrorized . . . Of gods, friends, learnings, of the uncomprehended civilization they overrun, they ask but one question: How much? What is a good time to sell? What is a good time to buy? The Church and the Capitol, incarnating the sacrifices and triumphs of a procession of martyrs and patriots since the dawn of freedom, are good enough for a money-changer's shop for them, and a market and shambles. Their heathen eyes see in the law and its consecrated officers nothing but an intelligence-office and hired men to help them burglarize the treasures accumulated for thousands of years at the altars of liberty and justice, that they may burn their marbles for the lime of commerce.

What respectable men in America wrote about American businessmen sounded much like what German Romantic nationalists would write about the Jews or Russian Slavophils about the West. But the "crass materialism" of the "robber barons," their alleged lack of respect for and understanding of high culture and religion, their presumed incapacity for friendship—all this was not enough to justify the elite's revulsion and savored too distinctly of sour grapes. The notables needed to give "a higher note to their complaint," to elevate their envy to the level of a nobler sentiment. The claim that big businessmen were insufficiently patriotic was a step in the right direction. Still, the focus on the personal deficiencies of the super-rich was counterproductive; as Walter Weyl noted, "Everywhere . . . we meet the millionaire's good and evil works, and we seem to resent the one as much as the other." The American people were of necessity "looking beyond the titular offender in the search for a greater anonymous culprit." They found it in the giant corporation, the organizational structure of big business, and the crime of which the latter, paradoxically but inevitably, was accused was "having ended our old-time equality."[23] A grievance of the social elite was reinterpreted as a national affliction, a threat to the core American ideal, and a privileged group of people, intolerant of equality at work, appointed themselves its guardians on behalf of the community of those whom they considered their natural inferiors.

In the meantime, a revolution was under way in American higher education, which dramatically affected the situation of one particular group within the elite—the intellectuals. Up to the Gilded Age which they so mercilessly derided, intellectuals occupied no clear place in American society. Their emergence as a social category sometime in the 1830s was a result of a natural self-selection, made possible by the affluence of their families, which afforded them a life of leisurely observation and ratiocination. But while they lived that good life, they answered no expressed need in the community, fulfilled no manifest function, and formed no recognizable profession. From the very outset they had characteristic grievances, interests, and therefore an incipient ethos. But they did not constitute a community, and their sense of collective identity was "inchoate." As intellectuals, they stood outside existing organizational structures and had no structure of their own which could perpetuate their traditions and give form to their style of life. In other words, they did not represent a status-honor group, or what in common parlance is called a class.

Denominational colleges which proliferated throughout the period offered them no congenial home. The office of the college president was virtually monopolized by clergymen, and the office of the professor, who, in the words of Walter Metzger, had "something of the status of the nursemaid" to unruly adolescent boys, with few exceptions had little appeal to the scions of the best American families. The college was an essentially religious institution. According to reliable estimates, as many as one in three students at midcentury was preparing for the ministry, which, in combination with the equally or more clerical composition of the faculty (90 percent of college presidents and about 35 percent of the teaching staff were ministers between

1800 and 1860), lent the institution the look, if not the atmosphere, of a theological seminary.

The atmosphere of the college was rather more like that of an exclusive boarding school for boys, for the other two thirds of the student body attended simply because respectable people did so, biding their time and expecting from this extended moratorium no advantages for the adult life that lay ahead. If they wished to enter such learned professions as law or medicine, the way to them lay outside the college, through a system of apprenticeship, and their college education was largely irrelevant to their aspirations. If they desired intellectual excitement and wished to acquire a general education, as did Henry Adams, the college certainly was not the place to find it, for, as we know from Adams, it was an enemy of intellectual excitement and defined its function as disciplinary rather than educational: "Students took prescribed courses and recited their lessons by rote; professors acted like schoolmasters, drillmasters, and prisonkeepers." The assumptions of American pedagogy were "dreary." Adams wrote of Harvard in 1854: "No one took Harvard College seriously. All went there because their friends went there, and the College was their ideal of social self-respect . . . Four years of Harvard College, if successful, resulted in an autobiographical blank." Yet, he added, "Harvard College was probably less hurtful than any other university then in existence. It taught little, and that little ill, but it left the mind open." The students had to entertain themselves as best they could. According to Adams, this involved "substantial whiskey"; according to other sources, they made creative use of firecrackers.

Their wards' irrepressible joie de vivre and determined efforts to avoid dying of boredom were a source of intolerable nuisance for the college authorities, but in the end contributed greatly to the well-being of professors. The latter, as was already mentioned, were a humble, downtrodden lot. At the time, political correctness was not a major consideration, yet, rather like today, college teachers were often hired not on the basis of subject competence (which was not "of prime importance when professors had to 'double on the brass' in tiny tutorial orchestras"), but on the grounds of sectarian affiliation. In colleges which presented themselves as nonsectarian, neutrality was "presumed to lie in an equal division of the spoils" between sects, "in proportion to their respective strength in the community." In accordance with this early commitment to diversity, the University of Michigan, for instance, "for years pursued a policy of even-handed injustice, and named a minister of a different sect to each of its professorships." Teachers whose chief qualification consisted in subscribing to an orthodoxy could not be expected to shine with the light of genius or even of acquired learning, and did not. As a result, they did not carry much authority. The trustees, who were even more orthodox and at least as competent in most subjects of instruction as the professors, had little respect for them and treated them as low-level employees. At Princeton, we are told, they criticized the grammatical construction of sentences in the faculty "minutes." "It is doubtful," wrote Metzger, "that the most intrusive board of trustees today would ever display toward its faculty so marked an attitude of contempt."

The lowliness of the professorial office was felt all the more sharply because of the status differential between the faculty and the trustees: the latter were pillars of the community, who enjoyed above-average wealth and prestige; the former, as a rule, lacked social luster altogether, for little but necessity would attract one to a career of college teaching until late in the nineteenth century. They were "hopelessly outclassed." Thanks to the student indomitability, however, the professors had to be, little by little, granted more respect, for it was not to be expected that, abject as they were, they would be obeyed by the rambunctious progeny of the social elite. Thus "the college teacher was elevated from the position of a powerless subaltern to the status of an executive officer in the realm of discipline and instruction," the crucial factor being "the prosaic and commonplace, but disquieting and relentless, problem of the lack of student discipline."[24]

Another persistent problem that plagued antebellum colleges—the constant budget deficit—also profited the professors. To ease their distress, the colleges had to appeal to the generosity of the alumni, who were equal, if not superior, to the trustees in status. The presence of a powerful secular group disturbed the college hierarchy, weakened the position of the clerical boards, and by default added to the authority of the professoriate. With the change in their position came a change in the methods, and eventually subjects, of teaching.

While student discipline and financial difficulties pushed the colleges toward reform which beneficially affected the status of the professors, other factors pulled them in the same direction. The most important of these factors was the emergence of German universities as the model for American academics. The pilgrimage of American intellectuals (not college professors) to Germany began in earnest after 1850, though some pioneers made the journey earlier. Unlike in the United States, the universities in Germany did represent the center of intellectual life, and professors, especially in the humanities, who were intellectuals by definition, enjoyed great prestige.[25] Altogether, some nine thousand Americans were educated in Germany in the nineteenth century (two hundred before, the rest after 1850), most of them in Göttingen and Berlin, the two greatest universities, where the social superiority of the German professor was most pronounced. Duly impressed, they, in the words of a historian, "reacted enviously." Longfellow, who attended

Göttingen in 1829, compared the shining example of the Teutonic world of letters to the sectarian parochialism of the college at home. The German university gathered together "professors in whom the spirit moved—who were well enough known to attract students to themselves." And "what has heretofore been the idea of an University with us?" The answer was simple and depressing: "Two or three large brick buildings,—with a chapel, and a President to pray in it!" The German professor was a scholar, a priest at the altar of knowledge, an expert, more than that, a creator, a perfect man with an authority to advise rulers; he "appeared to be the very embodiment of learning in its most exalted form." His American counterpart was "a nondescript, a jack of all trades, equally ready to teach surveying and Latin eloquence, and thankful if his quarter's salary is not docked to whitewash the college fence." The pilgrims returned with their aspirations inflated, bitterly resentful of the orphan existence to which American society condemned its best and brightest, and convinced that the university was the rightful home of the intellectual and "professor" his proper title. Having seen their "ideal of a university not only realized, but extended and glorified" in Germany, they determined to transplant it to the native shores—to "do something" for the nation, as they put it.[26]

Fortunately, this was the age of big business and "robber barons" who were philanthropically inclined, and they provided the money for the realization of the intellectuals' ambition. Magnificent new institutions, conceived as research universities came into being: Johns Hopkins, the Göttingen of Baltimore, blessed at birth with $3.5 million by a local capitalist who played fairy godmother; Stanford, launched with $24 million its founder made in his railroad business; the University of Chicago, revived and swept into greatness with Rockefeller's gift of $34 million. Modeled specifically on the German faculty of philosophy—the leading and most prestigious faculty in German universities, exclusively devoted to the disinterested pursuit of knowledge and cultivation of intellectual superiority (and the intellectually superior)—the American research university developed differently. The graduate school, the preserve of the professor (accomplished and in the making) rather than the student, was only one of its many divisions, the rest of which catered primarily to the needs of other groups. There was the undergraduate college, the chief function of which was still to educate adolescents and mold them into men, and professional schools, which trained doctors, lawyers, engineers, and—yes—business managers. Nevertheless, the university provided a definite social position for intellectuals, which they previously lacked, a structural foundation which would support their collective ethos, a self-perpetuating organizational framework within which they could realize their social interests and maintain their status, and from within which they boldly faced the rest of society. It allowed them to perceive themselves as a community, "an order of learning" (defined as the "academic order"), of which it became the center, making possible formal careers and granting degrees—the closest this society came to titles of nobility. It gave them a "sense of strength," a "new dignity," "a new conception of the self, of its powers, privileges and obligations." In short, it made American intellectuals into a class.

An unrelated revolution in thought endowed this class with prestige which was at least equal in value to the millions supplied by the "robber barons." This revolution was launched by the publication of Darwin's *Origin of Species* in 1859, and accompanied by a shift in attitudes which propelled science to the apex of the social value scale. "The acceptance of Darwinism by American scientists [or, rather, the order of learning] was remarkably rapid," wrote Metzger. "The American Philosophical Society awarded Darwin honorary membership as early as 1869, and the gesture was soon repeated by other American societies."

The colleges resisted. In 1880 nine eastern college presidents, including those of Yale and Princeton (but not including President Eliot of Harvard, who was among the first to defect to the revolutionary evolutionary camp), were asked whether they encouraged the teaching of Darwinian evolution on their campuses. Unanimously they rejected the idea as preposterous. The president of Amherst, the Reverend Julius H. Seelye, spoke for all of them when he responded: "So long as the notion that man is evolved from the monkey has not a single fact to rest upon, and is in flat contradiction to all the facts of history, I think we may leave it with the socialists . . . This college does not yet teach groundless guesses for ascertained truths of science." Noah Porter, Yale's president, in 1879 ordered William Graham Sumner to stop using Spencer's Darwinian *(avant le nom) Study of Sociology* in his classes. But these were no longer the dark ages, and German-educated professors, many of them in new rich universities founded and funded by "robber barons," and some in reforming ones such as Harvard, were no longer lowly nursemaids to unruly upper-class adolescents, but upper-class adults, more than any other group in society conscious and jealous of their superior status.

They countered with an "imperious claim to gnostic superiority." Scientists, they said—using the term in the German manner, as a synonym for "intellectuals," "scholars," and "professors"—knew best; they represented human intellect in all its power, and human intellect—as even Frances G. Abbot, who was not a professor, insisted—was "the sole discoverer of truth"; they were the only ones who had the mastery of scientific method, and this method was "the sole organon of its discovery." "No other method of inquiry now commands respect," asserted President Eliot. This was true: the

Darwinian revolution dealt a lethal blow to the image of empirical, especially human, reality sponsored by the Christian religion, elevating science to the position of unquestionable authority previously reserved for religious and civic leaders of the nation. "The two decades between 1880 and 1900 were decades of praise for science . . . Great businessmen and leading state politicians as well as a few major national politicians and important publicists and, in a vague way, much of the electorate, joined in the appreciation of this kind of knowledge and the university as its proper organ."[27]

The science so elevated was natural science, but humanistic scholarship—and, in particular, the favorite pastime of secular intellectuals, social philosophy (and criticism)—upheld its cause against clerical detractors, professed devotion to its truth, and, by virtue of such interested services, pretended to its proud status. The identification of science and university in public opinion encouraged such pretensions. Besides, in a time of frightening economic growth and social upheaval which it implied, the thought that change was implicit in the natural process and occurred for the better brought comfort, and people were ready to see society as an extension of Darwinian evolution. They were not about to quibble over such minor matters as the record and credentials of those who told them what they wanted to hear. Herbert Spencer was wildly popular. Edward L. Youmans, the editor of *Popular Science Monthly*, who propagandized his Darwinian sociology in America, did not distinguish between (actual) natural and (projected) social sciences. The authority of the former, which reflected their world-shaking accomplishment, was complacently and eagerly generalized to include the latter, though they had nothing to show for it. In the America of "robber barons," there was a palpable desire—a social demand—for social sciences. American intellectuals capitalized on it. The first area of social philosophy and criticism to declare itself a science in America was that of political economy.

Before the Gilded Age which inaugurated the age of the universities, the American social elite, and in particular the intellectuals, showed little interest in economic questions. Political economy preoccupied lesser mortals: college presidents and an occasional professor; recent immigrants (who had an axe to grind with the mother country), and practicing businessmen, whose hands (and minds) were anyhow already dirty. This led Charles Dunbar, a professor at the reformed Harvard of President Eliot, to declare in 1876 that there was no political economy in the United States, which, he said, "have, thus far, done nothing towards developing [its] theory."

Dunbar's conclusion, however, was not warranted by the evidence. It is true, college presidents who taught Smithian economics as a unit of the required course on moral philosophy, which it was their privilege and responsibility to deliver, added nothing to the English classics, before whose majesty, to paraphrase Henry Adams, they knelt in self-abasement. Protestant clergy-men, they were attempting to bring errant Britons back into the fold of Christian religion, and thus equated the invisible hand with the hand of the rational, benevolent Christian God. They saw no difference between the principles of political economy and those of morality, for "almost every question in the one [could] be argued on grounds belonging to the other," and believed that free trade, which they revered "as something holy," was, literally, "the will of God." It was such worthies, utterly disregarded in their own country, who lectured the leaders of Japan's modernization. Textbooks were their only production, and where other textbooks were available, their exegetic wares had no market.

But this was not so with exponents—mostly men of affairs—of the protectionist "American System," also called the "national school," "which dominated the practical policy of the country" well into the twentieth century. Preached vigorously by Henry Carey, it enjoyed wide acclaim around the economically alert world, was regarded with interest in Britain and France, and taken very seriously in Germany and Japan, where it was taught in business schools. Dunbar dismissed Carey's importance. "It cannot be said," he admitted, "that Mr. Carey has not engaged attention outside of his own country, for his works have been translated and circulated in nearly every important language of Europe," and Mr. Mill himself on several occasions paid "him the distinguished tribute of singling him out in an especial manner from a throng of opponents." Nevertheless, he was unwilling to forget that "to lead a school is not necessarily making a contribution to the science," and was confident that "not much of Mr. Carey's work will be found wrought into the political economy of the future." As it happened, he was in a position to see that the prophecy was fulfilled.

While people of Carey's ilk tried to uncover the springs of American economic life, upper-class intellectuals reacted to it with uncomprehending amusement and sometimes a sourer sentiment. They kept aloof from the national sport and lifework of getting rich. Already in the 1830s, one could hear them complain. "In the former age," Emerson lamented in 1834, "men of might were men of will; now they are men of wealth." With the coming of big business, such coquetry came to reflect reality, and they began paying attention to the sphere of social activity which suddenly loomed so uncomfortably large in their heretofore comfortable world, desperately attempting to explain it away. Intellectual curiosity was not the motive behind their interest, and, obviously, they did not like what they saw. Their economic thought therefore took the form of mournful philosophizing and ethical preaching. They regarded the prodigious economic growth of their time, as Walter Weyl so well put it, as "positively immoral." Their delicate stomachs turned by the

"Great Barbecue," they oozed contempt, but before "robber barons" built for them great universities within which they were allowed to believe that social criticism was science (thanks to Darwin, endowed with the authority of religion), they had no audience and could do little to assuage their chagrin. When all these conditions were in place, however, these intellectuals, in the words of Richard Hofstadter, "had become disposed . . . to agitate themselves [visibly] about things that had previously left them unconcerned" or, rather, reserved, and took their place at the head of the so-called "main stream of liberal dissent."[28]

It was clearly not "the avidity of intellectual desire," the "irrepressible desire to understand" an aspect of empirical reality—which Edward Shils, projecting his own ideals onto the members of the world of learning in general, believed to have inspired American social sciences—that motivated the founders of the native discipline of economics. To the empirical reality in question they were still quite indifferent. The 1876 volume of *North American Review*—the most influential intellectual magazine of the period—which took account of the achievements of American society in the century since the Declaration of Independence, included in this order surveys of religion, politics, abstract (i.e., natural) science, economic (i.e., social) science, law, and education, but did not contain an essay on business. It appears that future economists did not notice, insofar as it did not touch upon their sensitive status spot, the wondrous economic development that was taking place before their eyes. The motive behind the emergence of economics was revealed by one of its first professors, Simon N. Patten, who taught at the University of Pennsylvania. In an 1893 essay in the *Yale Review* titled "The Scope of Political Economy," he wrote:

The boundary lines between the various social sciences have not been fixed by any systematic study of their relations nor by any logical order or sequence. They have their place in history because of the practical interest which social reformers have had in them as means of securing progress, or at least as a means of maintaining the existing social order against retrogression or decay. Each succeeding social science has had the same aim—to give new sanctions to the progressive forces of society. Each science, however, has succeeded in conquering but a section of the general field of social science, and this section it holds against its newer rivals. Religion, morality, natural law, politics, and economics have arisen to answer the one supreme question: What is the binding authority to which appeal can be made and for which men will have respect? For a time, the potent force that held men and nations in peaceful relations was religion. When its authority began to decline, an appeal was made to moral principles, in the hope that they would increase the respect for law, and thus advance the interests of social progress. When this hope failed, resort was had to natural law, to politics, and finally to economics; and from each of these sciences laws and practical rules were secured that have helped to resist the forces that tended to dissolve society, and in many cases have been real causes of social progress.

The interest behind economics was practical; it was an interest in the binding authority and respect which would allow social reformers (presumably, people who discerned the optimal direction of societal development, an elite of intelligence and virtue) to orient society in that optimal direction and resist the forces of evil that tended to dissolve it. Economics thus was a functional equivalent of religion, morality, a certain kind of political philosophy, and politics, all of which were, by fiat of poetic license, created "sciences," thereby justifying identifying economics as a science as well. What distinguished this younger sister from its venerable siblings was its rationality. "Economics," defined Patten, "is the science of positive utilities—the realm where no other motives are recognized except those resulting from changes in the amount of our measurable pleasures and pains. If all our actions depended upon judgments reached by reasoning from premise to conclusion, there would be no social science but economics . . . [A]ll social science would be purely utilitarian—a mere calculus of pleasure and pain,—and at the same time economic." Such rationality made economics the most scientific of the "social sciences." It was also the broadest, for, while not all judgments were reached by reasoning from premise to conclusion, they were all ultimately reducible to such reasoning. Patten lamented "confining" or "reducing" economics to a theory of the production of goods, the increase of material wealth. Combined with "the popular belief that the pursuit of wealth was the source of moral and political degeneration," this could only deprive the discipline of its legitimate subject: "the general welfare of the community."[29] This American conception, formulated just years before the beginning of the twentieth century in one of the leading modern universities, was quite similar to the one found in the German *Hausväterliteratur* of the late 1600s and the Japanese notion of *keizai* entertained by eighteenth-century samurai scholars.

But American intellectuals of the Gilded Age were not advisers to territorial princes or shoguns, and their project was a good deal more self-centered than that of their unlikely predecessors. They wanted to have political influence, of course, but the main reason for their hankering for the authority of science was the desire to protect, maintain, and improve their status, always unsatisfactory and now threatened by the Juggernaut of big business. So-

cial reform was the most ambitious but, as it happened, not the best strategy to achieve this goal, though it was adopted by several very influential
early economists besides Patten, among them Richard Ely, the founder and
longtime first secretary of the American Economic Association. In view of
the intellectuals' objectives, it was essential that their "science" be accepted
as an academic discipline. Yet there were weighty objections to defining a
new academic discipline in this manner. On the one hand, the German ideal
of "pure" scholarship spurned partisanship (even though it approved of nationalism)—and would-be economists were almost without exception "Ger-
many-returned." On the other hand, pronounced policy orientation undermined and offended the already established professors of political economy
or its variously titled equivalents in old elite schools (such as Dunbar, Taussig,
and Laughlin at Harvard, Sumner at Yale, and so on), who believed—with
the fervor and certainty one associates with religious belief—in the truths of
the classical, laissez-faire school. According to Francis A. Walker, the second
president of MIT and the first president of the American Economic Association, with these illustrious personages, whose allegiance had to be secured at
all costs, laissez-faire "was not made the test of economic orthodoxy, merely.
It was used to decide whether a man were an economist at all."

For a while the disparate contingents of the little troop followed separate
paths. In April 1882 J. L. Laughlin, at the time an instructor at Harvard,
wrote to Edward Atkinson:

> The matter of the "American Society of Political Economy" (?) has been
> simmering in my mind, and I have now thought it worth proposing
> some plan. As you say, "bores" must be excluded. So, it seems best to
> approach a few of the leading economists first . . . It ought to be made a
> dignified body, for it can be authoritative and useful in many ways. It
> could encourage economic studies by offering prizes, as in France, for
> work which deserves it well, and propose many subjects affecting our
> own country for which it offers honorable rewards.

The motley group of ten "leading economists" he proposed consisted of two
businessmen, Edward Atkinson—the addressee—and David A. Wells; two
university presidents, Francis Walker of MIT and Andrew D. White of Cor-
nell; Carl Schurz, a statesman and publicist; and five professors, of whom four
actually taught political economy—Simon Newcomb, professor of mathematics in the U.S. Navy; Charles Dunbar, professor of political economy at
Harvard; William Graham Sumner, professor of political and social science at
Yale; Arthur Latham Perry, professor of political economy and history at Williams College—and Laughlin himself.

The Political Economy Club (as the organization was named), modeled on its British namesake, was formed at the end of 1883, with an inaugural meeting at the home of Horace White of the *New York Evening Post*. Newcomb was elected president. "Your reign is undisputed," commented Laughlin. "We are only too glad to have a double star at the head of our constellation." Disputed were the topics of discussion at the club's meetings. Horace White and David Wells (two men of affairs) proposed the question "What ought to be the policy of the Democratic Party with regard to the tariff?" This was "far better," they thought, "than an academic discussion" on something else. Laughlin retorted in a letter to Newcomb: "The one who regards a discussion of principles as 'academic' will not further the progress of our science. And as economists we ought to meet this tendency at once, gently but firmly ... I think it would be very undignified for a Club of professed economists to talk at their dinner of the policy of the Democratic party." White countered Laughlin's objection with the claim that "the English and the French societies of economists take up questions relating to party politics, and I don't see why we may not." He was seconded by Atkinson, who did not like "the 'Socialists of the Chair' [i.e., *Kathedersozialisten*, the German "academic socialists"] or the 'Economists of the Closet,'" and wished "to make the Political Economy Club a little more of a force" than a faculty club, which it promised to become. Evidently, businessmen and professors among the "professed economists" did not see eye to eye.

There was dissension among the professors as well. Younger members, such as Ely, were impatient with the timidity of the "conservative" academic position. In 1884 Ely proposed an alternative organization for "economists who repudiate *laissez-faire* as a scientific doctrine," and in September 1885 the American Economic Association was "officially inaugurated . . . following discussions among a miscellaneous group of scholars, ministers and social reformers who were attending the second meeting of the American Historical Association." The Historical Association, in the person of its founder and secretary Henry Baxter Adams, Ely's senior colleague in the history department at Johns Hopkins University, gave its blessing, and a faction of recently baptized historians enthusiastically converted and professed themselves economists. "The idea of an economic association," write A. W. Bob Coats, "was undoubtedly German in origin," being inspired by the Verein für Sozialpolitik. But

Ely's call met with a warm response not only from the young scholars who had been impressed by the reigning German school of historical economics but also from leading historians, prominent past, present, and future university presidents like Gilman, Andrew White, C. K. Adams, W. W. Folwell and Francis A. Walker (who was also a distinguished representative of the older generation of economists), such outstanding liberal ministers as Lyman Abbott and Washington Gladden, and officers of the American Social Science Association.

Ely's economic ideas were derived largely from German sources: he considered economics, or, rather, political economy, to be an essentially ethical teaching, whose purpose was the promotion of the highest welfare of all citizens; defined economic freedom as "merely relative"; favored restrictions, insofar as they were "in the interest of the whole people, not of a few privileged individuals or classes" (restrictions kept "the strong and cunning from injuring others," thus increasing liberty); and believed that it was the duty of the state (which he consistently capitalized) to regulate economic institutions and manage "natural monopolies, such as gas, electric light, water supply, street-car lines, steam railways, etc." In a modern democracy, where the state was "not something apart from us and outside us, but we ourselves," it was rightfully the chief economic actor, the beneficence of whose intervention was revealed with particular clarity by the example of Germany (presumably a model democratic society). "Governmental action is one of the most powerful factors promoting civilization," Ely wrote in the 1889 *Introduction to Political Economy,* "and in a country like Germany we observe a high civilization, every part of which is largely the result of governmental activity." Remarkably, while true to the theoretical principles of *Nazionaloekonomie,* his rendition of it entirely lacked its sentiment: he wished to change his society rather than make it great among others.[30]

According to Newcomb, Ely's association was "intended to be a sort of church, requiring for admission to its full communion a renunciation of ancient errors, and an adhesion to the supposed new creed." As the main tenet of this creed appeared to be the faith in direct state action as the means of righting all wrongs, the "conservative" classicists, ensconced in the best universities, considered the association a travesty and scornfully ignored repeated invitations to join it. They were convinced, writes Coats, "that prestige and influence could be earned only by exercising sound scholarship and wise statesmanship," one of them declaring that "the economists as a body . . . strongly disapprove the attempt to 'popularize' economics by giving too much weight to the conclusions of uninstructed public sentiment." Within years this had indeed become the position of the economists as a body. After all, what they wanted was "scientific status and prestige," and "they sought to attain [it] by dissociating themselves from the past, and by establishing economics as an independent scholarly discipline, free from theological, ethical, historical and sociological connotations and, above all, free from the taint of missionary zeal and political partisanship." In 1892 the American Economic Association, following a heated discussion in which Ely's program was "effectively repudiated," elected Dunbar president. Ely left Johns Hopkins and moved to the University of Wisconsin, where he became a professor of economics and director of the School of Economics, Political Science, and History. (This was a sign of the persistent uncertainty as to what economics, political science, or even history was, not of a precocious interest in the interdisciplinary approach.) In 1894–95 Ely supported his friend John R. Commons, also an "economist," in founding ("on ideas similar to those prevailing when the AEA was started") the American Political Science Association. Other onetime economists in the meantime were redefining their commitment to social reform as "sociology."

The ideological stringency of the American Economic Association was briefly replaced by broad tolerance of competing agendas, and, as there was a need for a new common ground to replace the one ceded to softer social sciences, for a while a belief prevailed that "political economy [was] swinging back to a renewed attention to practical or business affairs." This tolerance went so far indeed that certain members entertained the idea of electing a businessman president in 1899. Of course, this misguided attempt at fraternization with the enemy was instantly brought to a stop, there being a wide agreement that "we should remain a scientific body." J. B. Clark explained: "At bottom even the philistines will have more respect for such a body than they would for one that should put a man of affairs at its head. I may be wrong, but I dread any yielding to the view that economic wisdom resides outside of the schools and inside of the counting house."[31]

Unclear as to what their discipline was, early American economists never doubted that business education it was not. They must have taken pride in the uselessness of their "economic wisdom" for practical men, whether in countinghouses or industrial plants; that it was indeed useless is attested by the constant and, until the twentieth century, largely unsuccessful attempts of the business community to establish business schools alongside the proliferating departments of economics. The latter did not prepare their students for life in the real world. Governor Leland Stanford thus explained to Francis Walker the purpose of the great university he founded and named after his son:

> I have been impressed with the fact that of all the young men who come to me with letters of introduction from friends in the East, the most helpless class are college men . . . They are generally prepossessing in appearance and of good stock, but when they seek employment, and I ask them what can they do, all they can say is "anything." They have no definite technical knowledge of anything. They have no specific aim,

no definite purpose. It is to overcome that condition, to give an education which shall not have that result, which I hope will be the aim of this university.

Joseph Wharton, a Philadelphia merchant whose Wharton School of Finance and Economy, opened in 1881 at the University of Pennsylvania, was conceived with the special needs of the children of wealthy self-made men in mind, at a reception in 1890 declared, "The education given today in our colleges is a positive disadvantage." As the young men in question lacked the clear sense of direction which characterized their parents, they were to be supplied with it at a university. The aspiration of the Wharton School was to educate "young men with a taste for business, vigorous, active workers, of sturdy character and independent opinion, having a lofty faith in all things good, and able to give a reason for a faith that is in them." The way to such character lay through the understanding of accounting, mercantile law, money, banking, industry, commerce, and transportation. Among other things, the aspiring (even though hereditary) businessmen had to learn

how a great nation should be as far as possible self-sufficient, maintaining a proper balance between agriculture, mining, and manufactures, and supplying its own wants; how mutual advantage results from reciprocal exchange of commodities natural to one land for the diverse commodities natural to another, but how by craft in commerce one nation may take the substance of a rival and maintain for itself a virtual monopoly of the most profitable and civilizing industries; how by suitable tariff legislation a nation may thwart such designs, may keep its productive industry active, cheapen the cost of commodities, and oblige foreigners to sell to it at low prices while contributing largely toward defraying the expenses of the government.

For the practical Mr. Wharton, in the booming economy of his day, economic wisdom apparently still meant old-fashioned seventeenth-century mercantilism.

Other businessmen "most earnestly" recommended "the founding of schools of finance and economy for the business training of our children . . . upon . . . the Wharton plan." The University of Chicago (no doubt encouraged by its benefactor) established one earlier than most. But, President Harper reported in 1903, its progress was intentionally kept slow, "the desire of the authorities being not to lay too great emphasis upon work of this character, in contrast with the longer-established college work, in the early years of the University." Columbia, for its part, successfully resisted formation of a business school until much later and managed to block even the establishment of a course in commercial history, geography, law, and accounting which the New York State Chamber of Commerce offered to finance. When the business school was finally established in 1916, Professor Seligman of the Department of Economics revealed the reason behind the university's dawdling: "[The] Department of Economics and others realized the real obligation was graduate work and research rather than professional teaching." Economists were preoccupied with bringing up more economists to carry on their values and represent their interests; they had no wish to abet the sinister forces which it was the responsibility of all social sciences to resist. Indeed this was the position of academics in general. "We must educate away from the controlling forces of society," declared members of the National Educational Association in 1898; "those forces are not ideal, and it is the business of education to strive for the ideal."[32]

In the Gilded Age, the "professed economists" who were professors of economics were among the most idealistic of the nation's teachers. Material reality interested them very little and they knew very little about it. Their concerns were strictly spiritual, or in the Durkheimean sense "moral"; they were preoccupied with their position on the scale of social honor. Their academic subjects, the agenda that drew them to economics in the first place, reflected their fear of losing status to the successful entrepreneurs and irritation at the enormous gains in prestige the latter seemed to owe to their fabulous wealth but in fact owed to their business ability. Their first and natural impulse was therefore to diminish these upstarts—and it was a long time before this impulse died away. But social criticism as such could not accomplish their objective, which was to assert their superiority and improve their status in American society, with which they were never happy. Their best chance lay in becoming scientists. Scientists were indeed elevated in this nation to the position of high priests and diviners of ultimate meanings which in European societies, such as Germany and France, belonged to secular intellectuals in general. But this eminently attractive identity came with a hefty price tag.

The idea of science among American intellectuals who professed themselves economists could not reflect the nature of their social subject matter, of which they were ignorant; nor could it reflect a deep understanding of the activity of natural scientists, of which they were ignorant as well. They were left, therefore, with the model natural scientists constructed for the benefit of the lay audience, and this was a very demanding model. Knowledge becomes science, said the astronomer and mathematician Chauncey Wright, "when it ceases to be associated with our fears, our respects, our aspirations—our emotional nature; when it ceases to prompt questions as to what relates to our personal destiny, our ambition, our moral worth; when it ceases to have man, his personal and social nature, as its central and controlling objects."[33]

The poor professors, who were desperately interested in questions relating to their personal destiny and ambition, thus were pushed into the cold embrace of the classical—laissez-faire—theory, for it was the only approach that could be fitted into this Procrustean bed. It was impersonal, ahistorical, and long since separated from the social context in which it had its roots. It was so abstract that the man of whom it ostensibly treated became as remote as a distant star and assumed the respectable qualities of a mathematical equation. It reduced the immense complexity of social reality to a few relatively simple rules, and it presented these rules, which it called "economic laws," as unchanging and universal.

The dynamics of intellectual development normally responsible for the emergence of new scientific disciplines were absent, and nothing but status considerations stood behind the choice of a paradigm in this case. Once made, however, it implied its own dynamics. Possessors of a body of a highly formalized, esoteric knowledge, which made them "experts," economists were irresistibly impelled along the path of its increasing formalization, creating a tradition that was ever more "theoretical, mathematical, and quantitative." This development, more akin to scholasticism, or to Mannerism in art, than to science, encouraged and increasingly necessitated cultivation of very special skills. This both attracted to economics, and created a niche for, people with special abilities and inclinations, whose social interests were significantly different from those of the founders of this academic profession, for instance, those who were good at math, though perhaps not passionate enough about it to devote their lives to pure mathematics, or those who enjoyed formal, abstract reasoning for the sake of it. The stringent standards of excellence, common to esoteric traditions, contributed to making the group ever more exclusive.

Secluded in their ivory towers, high above—or, at the very least, far away from—the wheeling-and-dealing world of business, before long the economists were talking mostly to themselves, for what they said had meaning only to the initiated. A distinguished member of the group, George Stigler, wrote in 1984 that the profession was producing "a literature that no person could possibly read—the limits imposed by sanity are stricter than those imposed by time. Indeed, it is a literature that perhaps is read by a number of economists only moderately larger than the number of writers. The best memories can recall only a tiny fraction of this literature, and if the literature were irrevocably destroyed, most of it would utterly perish from human knowledge."[34]

This development resulted in a paradox. The more exclusive economists became as a group, the more special grew their skills and the more formalized and abstract their theories, the surer became their hold on their chosen identity, for the society at large concurred with them in the idea of science as formal, quantitative, and inherently incomprehensible to laymen. The surer became their identity, the greater was their authority as a science. And the greater their authority as a science, the more often highly credentialed economists exchanged mathematical modeling for social preaching and parlayed their technical proficiency into positions of generalized opinion leaders.

Their influence grew in proportion to their remoteness; they were believed to be in possession of magical formulas and were expected to work magic, as other sciences so often did, when economic trends created in the Gilded Age disappointed expectations or got out of control. Faith is infinitely stronger than experience. Economists never fulfilled these expectations, but faith in their power never waivered. And because of this faith, their theoretical assumptions—as often as not belied by their practical recommendations—were raised to the level of first principles in the national consciousness. The rarefied ideas of the English classics, the ideas of the bogeyman *Smithianismus* of German Cameralists, permeated the thinking of the average American, becoming as natural for him as basic categories of time and space, and reinforced the sense, suggested since the Gilded Age by big business, that the human world was the world of *Homo economicus*. Inhabitants of "economic civilization," we do not question or examine them. They spur us on in our unending "handicap-race" of wealth, in which we compete for status. And we forget—as men always forget—that this world is of our own making, and if we wish, we can stop at any moment.

Epilogue: Looking Backward from Year 2000

The preceding pages focused on the periods of the emergence of the modern economy in England/Britain, France, Germany, and Japan, culminating with the respective "takeoffs," and on the developments leading to the formation of the "economic civilization" in the United States. The nature of the questions has made the examination of subsequent events theoretically inconsequential: they would have no bearing on the nature of the argument. Thus we could stop at the beginning of the twentieth century (earlier in some cases), the length of the book encouraging one to forgo inessential excursuses. The conclusions, however, remain relevant to the realities at the dawn of the new millennium.

These conclusions may be summarized as follows.

1. The sustained orientation of economic activity to growth, the characteristic "spirit of capitalism" which makes modern economy modern, owes its existence to nationalism. In general, this "spirit of capitalism" is the economic expression of the collective competitiveness inherent in nationalism—itself a product of the members' investment in the dignity or prestige of the nation. In the American case in particular, it is, in addition and primarily, the result of the refraction of the core nationalist principle of the equality of membership in the unique conditions of a structurally unformed society without an aristocratic tradition.

2. Though at the turn of the twenty-first century nationalism appears inevitable, its emergence and even spread, at least as far as the eighteenth century in Europe (and, as the case of Japan clearly demonstrates, the late nineteenth century elsewhere), were a matter of an unconnected series of historical accidents. Being in a very important sense a product of nationalism, economic growth, too, therefore, must be regarded as a historical, contingent phenomenon, and cannot be seen as natural and expected as a matter of course. It is not endemic to the historical process, nor does it represent an efflux of any number of economic forces (be they technology, business organization, financial flows, or whatnot) at a certain stage of development. These forces,

473

the significance of which as *conditions* of growth I would not dream of under-estimating, are inert unless put to use by the human will, and it is this will, in the form of the historically shaped competitive motivation, which powers modern economy. Because it is not natural but essentially historical, the search for the universally applicable formula of economic growth is a wild goose chase; it can never be found.

3. The economic thought of nations reflects their particular nationalisms, producing national economic traditions as different as are traditions in phi-losophy or literature. Classical, or liberal, economics represents one such na-tional tradition. It is informed by the peculiar characteristics of English (and then British and American) nationalism, specifically the composite definition of the nation, reflecting the image of society as an association of naturally free and equal individuals. The internationalization of this national tradition, its lasting dominance, and its elevation to the status of a universally valid and ap-plicable scientific theory must be attributed to the fact that it was the only na-tional tradition of economic thought that lent itself to mathematical formal-ization (and thus could be interpreted as science).

4. While a product of nationalism, the orientation to economic growth is not a necessary product of nationalism. The "spirit of capitalism" is to be found only where the economy is included among the areas of international competition in which the nation in question wishes to participate. In individ-ualistic nations, such as England/Britain or the United States, it is likely to be so included at the birth of national consciousness itself. But in nations that are collectivistic, such inclusion is, again, contingent on circumstances whose presence cannot be predicted, and (as in Germany, where the crucial circum-stance was the activity of Friedrich List) may occur years and even genera-tions after the original formulation of the national consciousness. Growth-producing nationalisms further differ in their impact on the style of economic development: the nature of the particular business ethic, forms of conduct and organization, preference for certain sectors of economic activity, and so on.

5. Where nationalism embraces economic competitiveness, the "take-off into sustained growth" can be expected to take place within a generation: at least, such is the record of the cases analyzed here. Having begun, economic growth should logically continue so long as the motivation which sustains it lasts, despite temporary setbacks, unavoidable because no single economy can fully control the complex *conditions* within which growth occurs. The *conditions* of economic growth may slow it down or speed it up, making a certain rate more difficult or easier to achieve; they may favor certain sectors and allow them to lunge ahead while holding back others; but they are not responsible for the trend itself. The only certain threat to economic growth is

a change in motivation—a reorientation of the economy to other goals, or simply away from growth, as a result of the waning nationalist enthusiasm. So long as the economically active strata in Britain, Germany, Japan, and other societies which have built a component of economic nationalism into their national consciousness are animated by the national sentiment, they will remain oriented to growth and stay—within the limits allowed by their natural resources and external conditions—economically competitive. The trend of economic growth in the United States is not likely to be significantly affected even by the cooling of the national sentiment and the loss of interest in international competition (themselves quite unlikely possibilities at present) so long as Americans feel compelled to "keep up with the Joneses"—so long, that is, as the nationalist ideal of equality spurs them on in their constant competition for individual status.

Not every nationalism has a built-in component of economic nationalism. In some nationalisms the attitude to economic activity and its role in upholding national dignity is inconsistent, as it clearly is in France—a case of inconsistent, ambivalent nationalism. Others may be consistently opposed to linking national dignity (and, by implication, personal status) to moneymaking, denying it dignity, and may lack the element of economic nationalism altogether. Such is, emphatically, the case in Russia. The puzzling inability of this giant to achieve levels of economic performance commensurate with its enormous natural wealth, size, cultural development, and power, breaking through the barriers of the inertia allegedly induced by seventy years of communism exasperates Western experts. Economic theory provides no explanation for such sluggishness, leaving them to their own devices, and so they hope against hope that perhaps this time—this decade, this year, or this week—Russia will wake up to its potential, ever predicting this, however cautiously, and ever proposing new (or forgotten) ad hoc arguments as to why it has not as yet when it disappoints them again. They see the world through glasses tinted by and almost opaque with the thick economism of our collective imagination, blinded to the deep truth in the scriptural "not by bread alone," and incredulous of the possibility that some human beings may be driven by other desires than that for material prosperity. We are deceived in regard to ourselves and our own society.[1] How can we comprehend that Russia, of which we know so very little, does not—as a nation—want to participate in the economic competition, that material prosperity belongs at the very bottom of its value scale, that moneymaking is despised, that, proud of its *soul*, which it believes the West lacks, it has developed its own ideal of *Homo anti-economicus*?

This possibility, which escapes the mind of the "economic civilization" and must escape it, is implied in the logic of the argument proposed in this volume. Russia was among the first societies to develop national consciousness, but there was nothing in the lives of the architects of its nationalism, the educated nobility, and little in its later history as a nation to suggest that economic prowess had anything to contribute to its prestige. From the time they first acquired national identity late in the eighteenth century, patriotic Russians could take pride in the military might of their country, feared by every European power and admired in not a few of them, including France. When the Crimean War, several generations later, demonstrated that the Russian army could be beaten, Russian nationalists had already reinvested their trust in the superiority of Russian culture. The dignity and independence of the nation has never been linked to its ability to withstand the commercial pressures of the outside world, as in Japan; and the Russian intelligentsia of noble and common origins, which furnished all of Russia's ideologues and spokesmen of its national consciousness, never spawned an equivalent of Friedrich List who would translate this consciousness for the specific use of the economically active strata, elevating them to the dignity of the nationalist elite, and create Russian economic nationalism. Thus business in Russia remained ignoble, and all of the Marxist rhetoric was not able to raise the status of the Russian working classes.

True, on the cusp of the twentieth century Russia had the enterprising Sergei Witte, who, as minister of finance and then prime minister of the last Romanov, inaugurated and was close to accomplishing Russia's rapid industrialization. But Witte, apart from being a powerful minister of an autocrat (which in large measure explains his success in this enterprise), was a man of foreign ancestry and name, whose alien temperament was reflected in the disturbing (to a patriot) predilection for appointing to posts of authority other aliens, such as Jews and Poles, and that based solely on merit rather than on the politically correct ethnic quotas. His labors therefore contributed to the definition of the very interest in economic growth as un-Russian and, stiffening the Russian elite in its traditional aversion to moneymaking, ruled out the establishment of the "spirit of capitalism" in Russia at that time.

Of course, in the Russian case as in others, the dislike for moneymaking in no sense implied a dislike of money and what it could afford. The anthropological ideal of *Homo anti-economicus,* like its Western counterpart, was only an ideal, a theoretical aspiration which reality never approximated. Greed was as common among Russians as in any other segment of the human race, and conspicuous consumption, if not more widespread, was practiced perhaps more magnificently among certain sectors of Russian society. When I shared my thoughts on the subject with one very important economist—arguably the most prominent adviser of governments in ostensible transition to market economy, he retorted that he would never believe that a nation can consistently put anything above economic advantage and be uninterested in economic growth, for he knew many Russians and they wanted to have money as much as anybody else. His observation was obviously correct, although its juxtaposition with Russia's protracted economic record should have led him to doubt, as Weber suggested some hundred years ago, the relevance of such universal covetousness to modern capitalism. Yes, Russians want to have money, among other things (as their great writers remind us) so that they could light cigarettes from rolls of banknotes or purchase the best crystal goblets to smash them against walls when emptied. Nor are they impervious to the occasional suggestion of that elementary rationality which constitutes the conceptual core of the ideal of *Homo economicus:* after all, it was one of them who concluded that "it is better to be rich and healthy than poor and sick."[2] But, as we know from the Dutch experience, the rationality of *Homo economicus* is no more related to the "peculiar rationalism" which makes for economic growth than irrational greed, and may, rather, be antithetical to the modern economy. In any case, the fact remains that Russia's economic reformers and doers to this very day tend to bear outlandish names such as Gaidar or Chubais, have suspicious if not downright unacceptable genealogies, and more often than not (or than is good for either themselves or the Russian economy) be Jewish. Russian national consciousness—the very prism through which Russians view, and construct, their reality—being both collectivistic and ethnic, such an economic elite is more likely to cause the radicalization of national sentiment, with Russia moving farther away from the alien values, including market capitalism, than to promote the spirit of this capitalism in the Russian people and foster economic growth.[3]

Were Russian nationalism to radicalize, however, the native aliens in the economic elite would not be the only ones to blame. The interference of the United States would unquestionably be an important contributing factor: it has already led to notable exacerbation of anti-American (and consequently anti-Western, antidemocratic, anticapitalist) feeling. Whatever it was on the whole, the twentieth century certainly ended as the American century. The Soviet Union collapsed, and the one remaining nuclear superpower was left to rule the roost. As a result, the United States, never retiring, has been unusually active in peddling—pushing—the principles of its singular civilization around the globe, or, if one prefers, spreading the gospel of its theoretical economics, for these principles came to be identified with the premises and dictates of classical economics more closely than ever. This activism is in part a reflection of the sense of freedom which comes with America's post–Cold War status. But it is also a semiconscious attempt to prevent further loss of confidence in American ideals among Americans—another consequence of the demise of the Soviet Union, whose menacing presence kept American morale high—which can be regained only if others come to believe in these ideals. Given this predicament (and a predicament it is), it is no wonder that the reluctance of the potential converts adds zeal to the missionaries instead of deterring them. It also explains the academic nature of the crusade (as well as quite a few of the crusaders): with every social value in dispute, one naturally seeks shelter behind values that are scientifically prescribed.

By the late 1990s the economy had been made "a centerpiece of foreign policy," reflecting "the growing enthusiasm" of the Clinton administration "for markets." The establishment of the National Economic Council raised economic interests (of the nation?) to the significance of security concerns— that is, concerns with national defense and independence itself—a symbolically striking gesture. The task put before the National Economic Council was, among other things, to increase opportunities for the American banking industry, but the spirit that apparently breathed life into it was "the American passion for free trade," which it saw as its mission to communicate to the benighted world. In the first few years of its existence its battle cry was "financial liberalization."

The actions of the council bore a greater resemblance to a religious than to an economic campaign: they had little to do with the sober calculus of costs and benefits. The men in command clearly believed free capital flow to be a good in its own right, by definition in the best interest of everyone concerned. Only this belief would justify forcing countries to liberalize against their will (reflected in penalties imposed on resisters, or at least threatened, and praise and rewards showered on those who comply). To paraphrase Rousseau, they believed that mankind must be forced to prosper. Without question, the trouble that is now brewing in Russia is to some extent attributable to this presumptuous solicitude for the soul of humanity dressed in the garb of crass materialism: Russians like to think that their soul is good enough as it is. But Russia would be in trouble with or without American missionaries. With Asia the case may be different. Some observers maintain that Washington's pursuit of speedy and essentially unconditional economic liberalization significantly contributed to the "Asian crisis" which began with the devaluation of the Thai baht in July 1997. The argument had a definite appeal in Tokyo or Jakarta, where it was naturally preferred to harping on the deficiencies of "Asian values" (overnight transformed from the secret of the region's enviable success into the obvious cause of its predictable failure), but it was also advanced by eminent Western economists.[4]

At the same time, the practices of the federal government at home remained as inconsistent with the principles of economic freedom as they were in the days of the first "American system," though not for reasons of economic nationalism. The government systematically interfered in business in the name of the ideal of equality. It legislated personnel policies, imposing rules and quotas blatantly hostile to the logic of business enterprise and more in tune with the anticapitalist spirit of the French ancien régime, lamented by Abbé Coyer, than with that of Adam Smith: indeed, if the dead were given to such calisthenics, these rules would make that venerable man turn in his grave. As in the time of Rockefeller and before, it also punished exceptional success.[5] That such anti-business government policy failed to sap the American economy of its vitality is attributable to the fact that no amount of imposed equality can satisfy the thirst for status in an open society, and the economy must remain the field where most people seek status. People who want to get ahead won't be kept down. The leveling laws provide them with ever new stimuli for innovation as they try to find ways around them. Thus, despite itself, the government contributed to economic growth.

The stakes in this game we play are getting higher. Rockefeller's billion no longer looks so impressive; Carnegie's $250 million, which once made him the richest man in the world, seem picayune. The safety net is far wider now; our definition of poverty, changed again and again to keep up with the times, in 1994 presupposed a higher standard of living than in 1971 was implied in the definition of an "average household."[6] The race is, therefore, not harder than it was. Still, the country has grown mightily, and so there are many more people who find it hard and opt out. A small segment of this population are not satisfied with simply leaving the fast lane (possibly because they are uncertain of their personal decision) and devote their thus released energies to spreading the word and persuading others to do likewise. Somewhat like the Quaker John Wolman, Benjamin Franklin's contemporary, or the parents of Clyde Griffiths of Dreiser's *American Tragedy,* they preach a return to a simpler life off "the work-and-spend treadmill," poor in money but, for this very reason, rich in community and meaning. (Whether they are better able to protect their children from the pressures of our perfectly modern world remains an important question.) In fact, they do not give up their ambitions, but simply transform them and make the simple living propaganda their business—often quite successful. Their message is carried on scores of Web sites, a few periodicals, numerous books (with at least a couple of best-sellers among them), and is promoted by various foundations and on public television.[7]

The intellectual elite, whose members by and large prefer printed to electronic media, but whose opinions profoundly influence their lesser brethren whose pulpit is the former, add their authoritative voice to the discordant chorus of politicians and pundits, which sings praises to American capitalism and condemns it at the same time. On the whole, the intellectuals like it no more than they did in the Gilded Age, when both business and the intellectual stratum as we know them came into being in America. They still consider capitalism immoral and crass. Their views percolate down to the deepest recesses of the American mind: indeed, they seem to affect business students. It is fortunate for the American economy that the majority of entrepreneurs still dispense with professional education, for those who go through it are likely to graduate with a conscience as guilty as was that of usurers in medieval Europe and with ideas that are in sharp contrast to the American credo, now broadcast with such ardor around the world. With accreditation standards that insist on diversity rather than merit among business school professors, and curricula that emphasize "ethical and global issues; the influence of political, social, legal and regulatory, environmental and technological issues, and the impact of demographic diversity on organizations," these students feel they must agree that capitalism is the source of all poverty and (for the wrong reasons) find it quite improbable that market economics are in any way related to democracy.[8] The intellectuals' traditional dislike of capitalism is bolstered by new outrages. It really does offend one's sense of propriety that a Harvard dropout should be able to succeed so much more spectacularly than, say, an economics professor.

Still, economists—professors for the most part—rule the world. At least, such is the claim of *Fortune* magazine, a reputable business publication, not given, as a rule, to using names of academics in vain. And, as a matter of fact, their influence has never been greater, their social position more exalted. The ascendancy of economists as the *scientific* advisers to presidents par excellence began with Woodrow Wilson, continued with the New Deal (their explicit commitment to laissez-faire economics notwithstanding), and then continued further. But never before were American academic economists given the authority to instruct governments the world over. The collapse of the Soviet Union, which brought the Cold War to an end, prompted an American administration to define economic policy as a central element of foreign policy; this transformed presidential economists from advisers to mostly otherwise engaged statesmen into tutors who have a claim to their undivided attention. And America's emergence as the only superpower made them schoolmasters to the world. Economists today have more name recognition among the general public than any other intellectual denomination taken as a group. The homage they receive from the media far exceeds that received, for example, by physicists or biologists. Indeed, it is hardly conceivable that *Scientific American* or any other counterpart of *Fortune* in science would claim that either of these eminent professional groups rules the world. It would be absurd to claim that. And yet physicists and biologists have a relatively clear grasp of their subject matters and, as a result, have been able to manipulate them for the benefit of humanity—an achievement that has, so far, escaped economists. The original aspiration, responsible for the rise of economics as an academic discipline a century ago, has been realized with a vengeance.

There is a problem: economists rule the world, *Fortune* tells us, but "they aren't quite sure what to do with it." "They still can't answer the big questions." This irks some economists whose position makes them notice this lamentable inconsistency and whose responsibilities allow them the leisure to reflect on it. Peter Drucker, who insists that he is not an economist, is annoyed enough to suggest that the world would be better off without economists. There is no doubt, he says, "that we are at the end of economic theory as we know it," because the reality for which it was created has changed beyond recognition. One striking aspect of this change is, Drucker claims, the disappearance of the national economy—the one economy for which we have economic theory. Though not everyone agrees with this, it is a popular argument, a variant of the "demise of the nation-state" thesis, which alleges that, in consequence of economic globalization, we are nearing—or witnessing— the end of the age of nationalism. Of course, social change—insofar as it is not a change in human nature—can undermine a set of economic laws, which are as immutable as the laws of nature and represent a subset of the latter, only if they are in fact not laws. If this is what Drucker has in mind, he is raising questions not simply in regard to economic theory as we know it—*an* economic theory—but about the very scientific premises, and therefore status, of the discipline of economics.[9]

Nevertheless, economists have no reason to worry. Nationalism shows no signs of weakening its grip on the souls of men, though this grip is not equally tight everywhere—it never was. What more proof of its vitality does one need at a time when it takes all of NATO, with its super–high tech, billion-dollar-apiece aircraft, almost three months to bomb into submission the tiny Yugoslavia, sustained solely by the fervor of its nationalist xenophobia and wounded pride, and make it withdraw its forty thousand troops from Kosovo? Or when desperately poor India and Pakistan test nuclear devices, in the face of the general consternation of the rich Western powers and despite the threats of economic sanctions with which they resolve to punish the two upstarts, and the destitute citizenry of both meet the news with jubilation on the streets for they know that the costly and dangerous action of their governments gained them the respect of the world that feeding the millions of the famished among them would not? They have stood their ground. They have shown the world their mettle. "It takes guts to say 'no' to the repeated calls of the head of the sole superpower," they say, and they were able to do this. Is there any question that national dignity beats prosperity any day? And, who knows, it may bring prosperity on better terms, compatible with one's sense of honor, in the long run. As an Indian commentator put it, "A soft state that yields on vital national security issues cannot project an image of a tough negotiator on trade and commerce."[10]

Besides, economic globalization is unlikely to undermine the nation either as a polity or as an economy. It is, as we have seen, not a new trend: it has been quite pronounced in the last 500 years; there is no basis for claiming that it was significantly modified in the recent half century, and it would be most unreasonable to expect that it would suddenly have an effect opposite to the one it is known to have had for the first 450 years of its recorded history. During those years globalization promoted the spread of nationalism, rather than retarding it, in the first place, because a diffusion of cultural norms (of which the spread of nationalism represents a particular case) is possible only in conditions of considerable integration. If we assume that the essential nature of the process of globalization itself has not changed, it could not contribute now to the dismantling of the social system based on nationalism unless a new cultural canon, or paradigm, replaced nationalism, as nationalism once replaced, for instance, the principles of the society of orders. But so far there is no such new cultural canon.

In the meantime, much of what is regarded as economic "globalization," ostensibly an "objective" secular trend, required by the state of development of world economic forces and independent of particular interests and cultural values, is in fact a function of the normal working of particular national economies, guided by their particular—often national—interests and reflecting their particular cultural traditions (i.e., nationalisms). Most of the so-called global companies are both founded and run by Americans. As a rule, their objective is to succeed, to grow, rather than to advance the interests of the American economy or contribute to the nation's prestige. If continued success requires the internationalization of a company's management, or moving the headquarters out of the United States, its American leadership will, in all probability, go forward with such changes, and do so with an easy conscience. Yet such conduct on its part is neither an expression of the iron laws of economic rationality nor a sign of indifference to the national interest. It is a reflection of the specific American tradition—its peculiar business ethic, which condones and encourages competition on an individual basis, and which is a product of the nature and development of American national consciousness. American businessmen compete in their private capacity, not as representatives of their nation. There is nothing new in this: as we saw with Rockefeller and even Colt, Americans, however attached to their country, never regarded the sphere of their activity as forever confined to it: the moment they were capable of expanding beyond its borders, they expanded.

But the situation is different in the case of multinational corporations founded and headed by nationals of other countries. While their work force and middle management may be "global," it cannot be doubted that their character remains emphatically national, with each of the companies associated with a particular nation and their success and failure—in the eyes of the respective nationals—reflecting on the nation's standing. The merger of Daimler and Chrysler, in which the German company assumed the control of the American one, was a great event in Germany. The German CEO-elect of DaimlerChrysler was celebrated as a national hero. Citizens in no way connected to the enterprise exulted, "Finally, Germany has a global company!" There is no doubt that the reaction would have been more subdued were the very same global company—which, we were assured, would remain faithful to the "key elements" at least of German business tradition and corporate culture—a result of Chrysler's acquisition of Daimler. But the celebratory mood in this case should be attributed to the fact that the takeover involved a great American company, for, as we have seen, Germany has successfully pursued "globalization" at a closer range since before the First World War.

It is doubtful that the development of the European Monetary Union, hailed as the surest sign of the demise of the state and nationalism, represents an exception to the foregoing interpretation. Society being an open system, everything is possible, of course, and we must wait and see. But, so far, it has been a union in a very limited sense, with the euro signifying neither a waning national sentiment nor a significant diminution in the authority of the participating states. In France, Germany (and, on the whole, standoffish Britain), the popular mood, if not the attitudes of politicians, has been swaying in accordance with the perceived possibilities for the union leadership, namely, the possibilities of using the European Union for the advancement of the respective national interests in power and prestige. And even weaker nations, with the leadership out of reach, have not been uniformly supportive of denationalizing initiatives of any kind—including those cases in which these initiatives were unambivalently suggested by growth-oriented economic rationality. Olivetti's successful 1999 bid for the control of the newly privatized Telecom Italia, over the better-equipped Deutsche Telekom, attracted attention. The *International Herald Tribune* reported that "Olivetti won largely because it is Italian. The government was thought to have blessed its offer, and many of the institutions that tendered their shares to Olivetti are Italian."[11]

We can foresee the future only insofar as it remains part of the present. The foreseeable future of nationalism looks bright. We still live in the social world created by national consciousness—it cannot be otherwise. For the same reason, the future of economic growth looks bright, and so do the prospects of the discipline of economics. The fate of the economists is interwoven with the fate of their civilization more than that of representatives of any other academic profession. To this *economic* civilization the economists stand in the relation of Delphic oracles to the civilization of ancient Greece: what they say is law in a weightier sense than a mere description of empirical regularity, and they are not going to be judged by their misconstructions of the latter. Given the insatiable appetite for status in this as nearly egalitarian society as any society can be, America will go on racing and continue to uphold its economistic worldview, upholding this unique civilization. For at least part of the way, perhaps the length of it, Japan and the European powers, obedient to the dictates of their different nationalisms, will keep racing against it. The economies of these great nations will continue to grow and the aggregate wealth of the world will increase. As to whether this is good or bad in the larger scheme of things, such judgment is beyond the scope of social science.

Notes

Index

Notes

Introduction

1. The famous author is Marx, the text "The German Ideology." For the structuralist position, see Ernest Gellner, *Nations and Nationalism* (Oxford: Basil Blackwell, 1983), and Eric Hobsbawm, *Nations and Nationalism since 1780* (Cambridge: Cambridge University Press, 1990).
2. A brief discussion of premodern scorn for economic activities may be found in Albert Hirschman, *The Passions and the Interests: Political Arguments for Capitalism before Its Triumph* (Princeton: Princeton University Press, 1977). The subject of the book is precisely the shift in attitudes resulting in the positive reevaluation of the economy which is the focus of these pages. Hirschman traces this shift in the thought of moral and political philosophers from the Renaissance to the late eighteenth century, quoting generously from French and especially English seventeenth- and eighteenth-century sources. But he does not explain why this shift occurred or why the complex arguments of a few elite intellectuals appealed to and were able to exert such a profound influence on the life of the society at large.
3. "Take-off into self-sustained growth" is the phrase Rostow used when he first introduced his concept, quoted in M. W. Flinn, *The Origins of the Industrial Revolution* (New York: Barnes and Noble, 1967), p. 8. David S. Landes, "On Technology and Growth," introduction to Patrice Higonnet, D. S. Landes, and Henry Rosovsky, eds., *Favorites of Fortune: Technology, Growth, and Economic Development since the Industrial Revolution* (Cambridge, Mass.: Harvard University Press, 1991), pp. 4–5, 11.
4. Flinn, *Origins,* pp. 36, 54; Dwight Perkins, "Government as an Obstacle to Industrialization: The Case of Nineteenth-Century China," *Journal of Economic History,* 27:4 (1967), 485; W. W. Rostow, *How It All Began: Origins of the Modern Economy* (New York: McGraw Hill, 1975), p. 2; Flinn, *Origins,* p. 77; Peter Mathias, *The Transformation of England: Essays in the Economic and Social History of England in the Eighteenth Century* (New York: Columbia University Press, 1979), esp. chap. 1, "British Industrialization: Unique or Not?" and chap. 3, "Who Unbound Prometheus? Science and Technical Change, 1600–1800."
5. Rostow, *How It All Began.*
6. W. W. Rostow, *The Stages of Economic Growth: A Non-Communist Manifesto,* 3rd ed. (1960; Cambridge: Cambridge University Press, 1990), pp. 39, 29.

7. Flinn, *Origins,* p. 8.

8. Rostow, *Stages,* p. 26; Rostow, *How It All Began,* pp. 193, 94, 222.

9. Rostow, "Coda: Reflections on the Debate as of 1990," in *Stages,* p. 247.

10. Max Weber, *The Protestant Ethic and the Spirit of Capitalism,* trans. Talcott Parsons (New York: Scribner's, 1976), pp. 17–24, 26, 13. Reprinted by permission of Prentice-Hall, Inc., Upper Saddle River, N.J.

11. In light of the specific definition of Weber's *explanandum*—(the spirit of) capitalism—as both a form of rationalization potentially conducive to growth and a societal, rather than individual, phenomenon allowing for the realization of this potential, many of the criticisms leveled against his thesis lose their relevance. To claim that certain individuals among late medieval Catholics possessed the capitalist spirit as defined by Weber is in no way to undermine his thesis (as some would have it; see Werner Sombart, *The Quintessence of Capitalism* [New York: Dutton, 1915]; Amintore Fanfani, *Catholicism, Protestantism, and Capitalism* [New York: Sheed and Ward, 1955]), because what is in question is not the dispositions of individuals but a cultural—that is, societal—propensity. And to reject Weber's definition of the capitalist spirit, as did, for example, H. M. Robertson, on the grounds that it disregarded men's natural "appetite for riches" and would astonish "a realist like Marx, who originated the discussions on capitalism" (which, presumably, gives him a prior claim on how it should be defined), is, obviously, to engage in an altogether different discussion. H. M. Robertson, *Aspects of the Rise of Economic Individualism* (Cambridge: Cambridge University Press, 1933).

12. R. H. Tawney, *Religion and the Rise of Capitalism* (1926; New York: Mentor Books, 1953); Albert Hyma, *Renaissance to Reformation* (Grand Rapids, Mich.: Eerdmans, 1955).

13. Weber, *Protestant Ethic,* p. 17.

14. Tawney, *Religion,* pp. 76, 228, 192–193, 207, 182, 188–195, 98.

15. Weber, *Protestant Ethic,* p. 53.

16. Ibid., pp. 64–65.

1. The Capitalist Spirit and the British Economic Miracle

1. Adam Smith, *The Theory of Moral Sentiments* (Oxford: Oxford University Press, 1976), pp. 57, 62, 342.

2. Citation from J. S. Nicholson, introduction to Friedrich List, *The National System of Political Economy* (London: Longmans, Green, 1822), p. xiv. See Liah Greenfeld, *Nationalism: Five Roads to Modernity* (Cambridge, Mass.: Harvard University Press, 1992), hereafter cited as Greenfeld, *Nationalism,* in particular the chapter on English nationalism, "God's Firstborn," pp. 27–87; and Chapter 2 below. Nicolai quoted in *Nationalism,* p. 314.

3. Thomas Milles's 1604 "Customer's Reply [to John Wheeler]," quoted in G. B.

Hotchkiss, "Introduction," in John Wheeler, *A Treatise of Commerce* (1601; New York: New York University Press, 1931), p. 82.

4. This is a line from a poem (probably by William Glanvill) about Gresham College, which introduced Gresham thus:

> If to be rich and to be learn'd
> Be every nation's cheifest glory
> How much are English men concern'd,
> Gresham, to celebrate thy story
> Who built th'Exchange t'enrich the Citty
> And a College founded for the witty.

5. Gresham's letter to the queen, quoted in Hotchkiss, "Introduction," p. 41.

6. Ibid., pp. 46–47.

7. "Dutch" (plural: "Dutches") was used as a synonym for "German" at the time. "Hollander" was the proper term for "Dutch."

8. Hotchkiss, "Introduction," p. 11; Wheeler, *Treatise;* facsimile text, pp. 119–305; edited text, pp. 307–460; all quotations are from the edited text, pp. 340, 373, 371, 375, 374, 428, 366; 340, 438–439, 425, 360–361, 366, 368, 403, 368. For Hotchkiss's and early seventeenth-century characterizations, see Hotchkiss, "Introduction," p. 8; Wheeler, *Treatise,* pp. 316–317; Hotchkiss, "Introduction," p. 71.

9. Hotchkiss, "Introduction," p. 101. B. E. Supple's *Commercial Crisis and Change in England, 1600–1642* (Cambridge: Cambridge University Press, 1964) contains an extensive list of contemporary publications on business matters. The argument of Thomas Mun's "England's Treasure by Forraign Trade, or the Ballance of our Forraign Trade is The Rule of our Treasure," published in 1664 after Mun's death by his son, John Mun (who drew attention to his father's patriotism in the dedication), first appeared in print in 1621 as "A Discourse of Trade from England." Thomas Mun (1664), *Reprints of Economic Classics* (Fairfield, N.J.: Augustus Kelley, 1986), p. iv; Supple, *Crisis,* p. 188. Robert Brenner, who by and large focused on matters other than the national sentiment of seventeenth-century businessmen, in *Merchants and Revolution: Commercial Change, Political Conflict, and London's Overseas Traders, 1550–1653* (Princeton: Princeton University Press, 1993) characterized Mun, for instance, as "the great theorist and propagandist of English national power through English commercial power" (p. 272).

10. Walter Raleigh, "Observations touching Trade and Commerce with the Hollander, and other Nations" (1605), reprinted in J. R. McCulloch, ed., *Scarce and Valuable Tracts on Commerce* (London, 1859), pp. 9–27.

11. Samuel Fortrey, *Englands Interest and Improvement* (1663), Reprints of Economic Tracts (Baltimore: Johns Hopkins University Press, 1907), introduction by J. H. Hollander, p. 3; quotations are from pp. 11–36.

12. A fellow of the College of Physicians, Barbon founded the first insurance firm in London after the fire of 1666, as well as a land bank in 1690s, and was twice elected a member of Parliament. Nicholas Barbon, *A Discourse of Trade* (1690),

Reprints of Economic Tracts (Baltimore: Johns Hopkins University Press, 1905), p. 36; introduction by J. H. Hollander, p. 1. Gregory King, "Of the Naval Trade of England A[round] 1688," in *Two Tracts by Gregory King,* Reprints of Economic Tracts (Baltimore: Johns Hopkins University Press, 1936), p. 61; Barbon, *Discourse,* pp. 19, 5–6, 22–23, 32, 33, 11.

13. John Robert Moore, "Daniel Defoe and Modern Economic Theory," *Indiana University Studies,* 21 (June 1934), 4. Facsimile edition, *Defoe's Review,* vol. 1 (New York: Columbia University Press for the Facsimile Text Society, 1938), introduction by A. W. Secord, p. xv.

14. *Defoe's Review,* p. xvii. Defoe was assigned by Robert Harley to work for the Union, and wrote some forty poems and pamphlets, in addition to numerous articles in the *Review, History of the Union,* and *Memoirs of the Church of Scotland,* which may be considered propaganda for it, including a series of essays titled "Removing National Prejudices." See Paula R. Backscheider, *Daniel Defoe: Ambition and Innovation* (Lexington: University Press of Kentucky, 1986), pp. 55–58.

15. Daniel Defoe, *A Plan of the English Commerce* (1728; Oxford: Basil Blackwell, 1927), pp. 81–82, vii.

16. Daniel Defoe, *The Complete English Tradesman* (Manila: Historical Conservation Society, 1989) (reprint of 4th ed., 1738), pp. 143, 144–145, 146–147, 173; chap. 25, pp. 174–182.

17. The phrase is Linda Colley's in *Britons: Forging the Nation, 1707–1837* (New Haven: Yale University Press, 1992), p. 61. Colley's quotations suggest that, while in the period on which she focuses the arguments remained essentially what they had become toward the end of the seventeenth century, their prose had improved, acquiring the smoothness which comes from use.

2. "The Great Seventeenth-Century Exception"

1. Characterization of the Indian historian K. M. Panikkar, quoted in *The Times Atlas of World History,* 4th ed., ed. Geoffrey Parker (London: Hammond, 1993), p. 148. Discussion of the period prior to the emergence of the Dutch Republic is based largely on the maps and text of this edition. In this context, also see Fernand Braudel, *Civilisation matérielle, économie et capitalisme, XV–XVIII siècle: le temps du monde,* vol. 3 (Paris: Armand Colin, 1979), pp. 12–14; Jonathan Israel, *Dutch Primacy in World Trade: 1585–1740* (Oxford: Clarendon Press, 1989), pp. 1–3; Immanuel Wallerstein, *The Modern World System* (New York: Academic Press, 1974), pp. 15, 16.

2. Charles P. Kindleberger, *World Economic Primacy, 1500 to 1990* (New York: Oxford University Press, 1996), pp. 83–85. Israel, *Dutch Primacy,* pp. 1–3.

3. *Encyclopaedia Britannica,* 15th ed., s.v. "Charles V," "Fugger"; *Atlas,* p. 143.

4. Braudel, *Civilisation,* pp. 80–86. Pieter Geyl, *The Revolt of the Netherlands (1555–1609)* (New York: Barnes and Noble, 1958), p. 89. *Atlas,* p. 147; Geyl, *Revolt,* pp. 34, 63. Kindleberger, *Primacy,* p. 86. *Atlas,* p. 143; J. A. van Houtte, "Anvers," in Amintore Fanfani, ed., *Città mercanti dottrine nell'economia europea dal IV al XVIII secolo* (Milan: A. Giuffrè, 1964), pp. 297–319; Israel, *Primacy,* pp. 6, 4–5. Geyl, *Revolt,* p. 43. Israel, *Primacy,* p. 6. Jan de Vries and Ad

van der Woude, *The First Modern Economy: Success, Failure, and Perseverance of the Dutch Economy, 1500–1815* (Cambridge: Cambridge University Press, 1997), p. 92; reprinted with the permission of Cambridge University Press.

5. Jonathan Israel, *The Dutch Republic: Its Rise, Greatness, and Fall, 1477–1806* (Oxford: Clarendon Press, 1995), pp. 129–154, 132. On the institution of public debt in the Netherlands, see in addition, de Vries and van der Woude, *First Modern Economy*, and Marjolein C. 't Hart, *The Making of a Bourgeois State: War, Politics, and Finance during the Dutch Revolt* (Manchester: Manchester University Press, 1993). Israel, *Republic*, p. 130. Geyl, *Revolt*, pp. 40, 69.

6. Geyl, *Revolt*, p. 71. This was very similar to the reaction of the French nobility to the absolutist policies of their kings. See Greenfeld, *Nationalism*, esp. pp. 133–145.

7. Israel, *Republic*, pp. 135–137. Kindleberger, *Primacy*, p. 74; Israel, *Republic*, pp. 141–144, 140, 145.

8. *Encyclopaedia Britannica*, 11th ed., s.v. "Brothers of Common Life." R. B. Drummond, quoted in *Encyclopaedia Britannica*, 11th ed., s.v. "Erasmus." Geyl, *Revolt*, pp. 54–56; Anna Bijns quoted p. 57. John Foxe's book, popularly referred to as *The Book of Martyrs* (whose actual lengthy title began with the words "Actes and Monuments"), was first published in 1554. On its effect in England, see Haller, *The Book of Martyrs and the Elect Nation*, and Greenfeld, *Nationalism*, pp. 54–67. Geyl, *Revolt*, pp. 58, 72–78; Israel, *Republic*, pp. 143–145. William of Orange quoted in Geyl, *Revolt*, p. 78. Israel, *Republic*, p. 145; petition quoted p. 146.

9. Johan Huizinga, "Dutch Civilization in the Seventeenth Century," in *Dutch Civilization in the Seventeenth Century and Other Essays* (New York: Frederick Ungar Publishing, 1968), pp. 14–15. Israel, *Primacy*, p. 12. Wallerstein dates Dutch "hegemonic victory" between 1590 and 1620, and considers the period between 1620 and 1650 as that of the Republic's "hegemonic maturity." See Terence K. Hopkins, Immanuel Wallerstein et al., "Cyclical Rhythms and Trends of the Capitalist World Economy," in *World-Systems Analysis: Theory and Methodology* (Beverly Hills, Calif.: Sage Publications, 1982). Fernand Braudel, *Civilisation*, p. 91. Israel argues that Braudel's view of the Dutch Republic as the "city-state of Amsterdam" is misleading and unfounded: in fact, Amsterdam, though the largest of the Dutch cities and the center of the global economy, never exerted an influence similar to that of Italian city-states on the polity as a whole, which, throughout its existence, was characterized by relative lack of coordination between its constitutive parts, pulled in different directions by centrifugal, particularistic forces. Israel, *Primacy*, p. 25. Bernard H. Slicher van Bath, "The Economic Situation in the Dutch Republic during the Seventeenth Century," in Maurice Aymard, ed., *Dutch Capitalism and World Capitalism* (Cambridge: Cambridge University Press, 1982), pp. 23–35. Munn quoted in Simon Schama, *The Embarrassment of Riches: An Interpretation of Dutch Culture in the Golden Age* (New York: Knopf, 1987), p. 185; Sir Josiah Child, *Brief Observations Concerning Trade and Interest of Money* (1668), quoted in Kindleberger, *World Economic Primacy*, pp. 90–93. De Vries and van der Woude, *First Modern Economy*, p. 710.

10. *Atlas,* p. 174; de Vries and van der Woude, *First Modern Economy,* pp. 29–30; Paul Zumthor, *Daily Life in Rembrandt's Holland* (Stanford: Stanford University Press, 1994), pp. 314–315. Israel, *Dutch Primacy,* p. 25. De Vries and van der Woude, *First Modern Economy,* p. 624; Schama, *Embarrassment,* pp. 150–188. Zumthor, *Daily Life,* pp. 311–312. Schama, *Embarrassment,* p. 163. De Vries and van der Woude, *First Modern Economy,* pp. 645, 636, 614. Zumthor, *Daily Life,* p. 307; Schama, *Embarrassment,* p. 164, also regards herring as "the foundation of the national fortune." Munn (1664) quoted in Schama, *Embarrassment,* p. 190. Israel, *Dutch Primacy,* p. 23. Zumthor, *Daily Life,* pp. 306–307; according to other estimates, the annual value of the trade was "around one million pounds, or half the total exports of Britain at this time" (Schama, *Embarrassment,* p. 230). De Vries and van der Woude, *First Modern Economy,* p. 267, quote smaller figures: 3 million guilders a year between 1630 and 1640. Israel, *Dutch Primacy,* p. 24; de Vries and van der Woude, *First Modern Economy,* p. 266. Munn quoted in Schama, *Embarrassment,* p. 230. Zumthor, *Daily Life,* p. 307; de Vries and van der Woude, *First Modern Economy,* p. 268. Alfred Marshall, *Industry and Trade: A Study of Industrial Technique and Business Organization; and of Their Influences on the Conditions of Various Classes and Nations* (London: MacMillan, 1920), p. 677. Kindleberger, *World Economic Primacy,* pp. 93–94. The tsar's certificate quoted in Zumthor, *Daily Life,* p. 304. Israel, *Dutch Primacy,* p. 21; Kindleberger, *World Economic Primacy,* p. 94; and Zumthor, *Daily Life,* p. 286. Kindleberger, *World Economic Primacy,* p. 94. Israel, *Dutch Primacy,* p. 24; Zumthor, *Daily Life,* pp. 285–286; de Vries and van der Woude, *First Modern Economy,* pp. 457, 673. Israel, *Dutch Primacy,* pp. 6, 17, and throughout. De Vries and van der Woude, *First Modern Economy,* p. 669. Figures quoted in 't Hart, *Bourgeois State,* p. 17, from Johan de Vries, *De economische achteruitgang der Republiek in de achttiende eeuw* (Leiden, 1968), p. 27. Davenant quoted in Schama, *Embarrassment,* p. 224. Zumthor, *Daily Life,* pp. 291–293. De Vries and van der Woude, *First Modern Economy,* pp. 385, 388. Zumthor, *Daily Life,* p. 294. De Vries and van der Woude, *First Modern Economy,* pp. 458–464, 40, 180.

11. P. G. M. Dickson, *The Financial Revolution in England: A Study in the Development of Public Credit* (New York: St. Martin's Press, 1967). In regard to the Netherlands, see James D. Tracy, *A Financial Revolution in Habsburg Netherlands: Renten and Rentiers in the County of Holland, 1515–1565* (Berkeley: University of California Press, 1985); and, in particular, 't Hart, *Bourgeois State;* De Vries and van der Woude, *First Modern Economy,* pp. 88–89, 82, 88; Zumthor, *Daily Life,* p. 268. De Vries and van der Woude, *First Modern Economy,* pp. 131, 147, 136; Zumthor, *Daily Life,* pp. 273, 274. Dutch and French sources quoted in Schama, *Embarrassment,* pp. 198 and 188, respectively. De Vries and van der Woude, *First Modern Economy,* p. 669. 't Hart, *Bourgeois State,* pp. 62, 71, 122–123; de Vries and van der Woude, *First Modern Economy,* pp. 107, 535, 111, 100; 't Hart, *Bourgeois State,* p. 81. De Vries and van der Woude, *First Modern Economy,* pp. 116–118, 124, 129, 139–146, 150; Sir William Temple quoted p. 116. Kindleberger, *World Economic Primacy,* p. 96.

12. De Vries and van der Woude, *First Modern Economy,* pp. 162, 60–63, 159, 161, 529, 715, 654, 693–694.

13. Kindleberger, *World Economic Primacy,* pp. 4–22.

14. De Vries and van der Woude, *First Modern Economy,* pp. 684, 30, 540, 39, 35, 41, 49, 78, 60, 64, 171, 570–571, 118, 122, 119, 696, 125, 129, 187, 673, 678, 682, 685, 678, 673.

15. Ibid., pp. 718–722, 698, 687–688, 698–699, 712.

16. Schama, *Embarrassment,* pp. 3, 6. Huizinga, "Dutch Civilization," pp. 10–11. Geyl, *Revolt,* p. 24 and passim. De Vries and van der Woude, *First Modern Economy,* pp. 91, 10, 159, 96–98, 102, 172. 't Hart, *Bourgeois State,* pp. 6, 19, 20. De Vries and van der Woude, *First Modern Economy,* pp. 192, 178; de Witt quoted p. 177.

17. 't Hart, *Bourgeois State,* p. 5. Geyl, *Revolt,* p. 28. For Schama's view of Geyl, see Schama, *Embarrassment,* p. 63.

18. Clifford Geertz, "Religion as a Cultural System," in *The Interpretation of Cultures* (New York, Basic Books, 1973), p. 104.

19. Andries Vierlingh, a dike master to the princes of Orange, quoted in Schama, *Embarrassment,* p. 42. The context is the fight against water (thus the list of provinces, which were to be divided between several states), but, as Schama argues, Vierlingh's "terms could have been interchangeable for the war with Spain" (p. 42).

20. It must be stressed that most recent Dutch scholarship on Dutch national identity locates the emergence of such identity at the end of the eighteenth and the beginning of the nineteenth centuries, thus in agreement with the present argument. Some often cited works include N. C. F. van Sas, "Vaderlansliefde, nationalisme en vaterlands gevoel in Nederland, 1770–1813," *Tijdschrift voor Geschiedenis,* 102 (1989), 471–495, whose author declares: "I count myself among those who view the emergence of nationalism as a product of the last decades of the eighteenth century which arose in Koselleck's *Sattelsezeit* [Reinhart Koselleck, "Einleitung," in *Geschichtliche Grudbegriffe,* vol. 1 (Stuttgart, 1972), pp. xiii–xxvii]. Norms and notions that perhaps had themselves been in circulation already for centuries were at that time welded [*aaneengesmeed*] into an ideology whereby the past was critically evaluated and was developed into a program of action for the future" (p. 471). He further argues: "The pan-(northern) Netherlands idea was based on the veritable cult of the Fatherland which emerged in the 1760s and especially in the 1770s. These [ideas] were closely linked to the ideals, means of expression and metaphorical mechanisms of the Enlightened Dutch public" (p. 473). Another text is Wantje Fritschy and Joop Toebes, eds. "Modernisering, staats- en natie- vorming," in *Het Onstaan van het Moderne Nederland: staats- en natievorming tussen 1780 en 1830* (Nijmegen: Sun, 1996). Following Benedict Anderson and Ernest Gellner, Toebes places the emergence of Dutch national identity toward the end of the eighteenth century with the changed modes of communication and in the nineteenth century with increased industrialization. "This late blossoming of [Dutch] nationalism," he writes, "could, according to Gellner's theory, possibly have something to do with the late industrialization of

our country evident around 1890" (p. 31). Toebes relies on the work by Hans Knippenberg and Ben De Pater, often referenced as an authority on the formation of Dutch national identity, *De eenwording van Nederland: schaalvergroting en intergratie sinds 1800* (Nijmegen: Sun, 1988). The authors are concerned with the process of social, economic, and political unification since 1800 and employ Karl Deutsch's typology of social mobilization in their account of how this came about. The emergence of national identity is conceived of as a function of social integration. Toebes writes: "That the penetration [*doordringen*] of the national idea, that is, the idea of belonging to one people [*volk*], was a slow process in the Netherlands, it lasted two centuries, was made clear by Knippenberg and De Pater in their book *De eenwording van Nederland*. They establish that in the first half of the nineteenth century 'people with supra-regional orientation and those with the greatest feeling of common purpose with the Fatherlandish Protestants were those who belonged to the established citizenry of the cities of Holland. People with a strict local or regional orientation, for whom the concept of Fatherland was a symbol without meaning, were Catholics of lower station who lived in the countryside in outlying areas [*excentrisch gelegen*].' But [Knippenberg and De Pater] add that 'these were the extremes; most people would certainly have found themselves somewhere in the middle, strung between their place of residence, religious conviction, and socioeconomic position'" (pp. 31–32). And: "[Knippenberg and De Pater] place the beginning of the period of greatest change—that of modernization—'in any event no earlier than 1860' with the expansion of the railroad system. But they also believe that [modernization and national identity] could plausibly be the result of the beginning of urbanization and industrialization in the 1880s or 1890s" (p. 32). Knippenberg and De Pater write: "In the first half of the nineteenth century the Netherlands formed a state but its inhabitants not yet a nation. Many felt themselves to be primarily residents of a city or region and only remotely Netherlanders. This would remain so for a long while" (p. 38). I owe these references—and translations from the Dutch—to Michael Thurman.

21. Schama, *Embarrassment,* p. 52. E. H. Kossmann, "Freedom in Seventeenth-Century Dutch Thought and Practice," in Jonathan I. Israel, *The Anglo-Dutch Moment: Essays on the Glorious Revolution and Its World Impact* (Cambridge: Cambridge University Press, 1991), pp. 287, 288. Schama, *Embarrassment,* p. 283; Kossmann, "Freedom," p. 292. Schama, *Embarrassment,* pp. 8, 124; Lydius quoted p. 45. Petrus Cunaeus, drawing an explicit comparison between the Dutch Republic and ancient Israel in the preface to his *De Republica Hebraeorum* of 1617, an interpretation of a fire on De Rijp in 1655, quoted in Schama, *Embarrassment,* p. 47.

22. Hans-Juergen Wagener, "Free Seas, Free Trade, Free People: Early Dutch Institutionalism," *History of Political Economy,* 26 (1994), 396–422, disagrees that the Dutch contributed nothing to economic theory. He looks at the works of Hugo Grotius (1583–1645), Dirk Graswinckel (1600–1666), Peter de la Court (1618–1685), and to some degree Baruch Spinoza (1632–1677), noting that it "is rather astonishing that the political and economic literature of the Low Countries was completely ignored in England. The main work of de la Court, the *Interest van Holland* of 1662, was translated within three years in German. French

and English translations appear only later, and after the Dutch decline has commenced—1743." For all these authors, however, economics was of only marginal interest, and in dealing with it they departed little from the traditional Christian view. "If there is one central [economic] proposition to be extracted from their texts," writes Wagener, "it ought to be the free-trade proposition: free trade increases the wealth of nations and socializes the people" (p. 419). Apart from this, though somewhat inconsistent, Wagener seems to be in agreement with the general argument proposed here. He claims that "the Netherlands and England . . . succeeded in establishing a commercial and growth-oriented economic order," but then contradicts himself in asserting that in the Netherlands "about 1650, growth came to a halt, and the next one and a half centuries were characterized by a stationary state" (pp. 419, 420). I owe this reference to Michael Thurman.

23. De Vries and van der Woude, *First Modern Economy*, p. 664. Kossmann, "Freedom," p. 293; de Vries and van der Woude, *First Modern Economy*, pp. 164–167; Huizinga, "Dutch Civilization," pp. 48–60; Geyl, *Revolt*, pp. 45–51; and J. C. Riemersma, *Religious Factors in Early Dutch Capitalism, 1550–1650* (The Hague: Mouton, 1967), in regard to noninterference of the Calvinist clergy in particular in matters of economic policy and practice. Wagener, "Free Seas," p. 399; Grotius quoted p. 415.

24. David Ricardo, *The Principles of Political Economy and Taxation*, quoted in Doug Henwood, *Wall Street* (New York: Verso, 1997), p. 113. On Abraham Ricardo, see de Vries and van der Woude, *First Modern Economy*, pp. 155–156.

3. The First Convert: France

1. Eli F. Heckscher, *Mercantilism*, trans. Mendel Shapiro, rev. ed., ed. E. F. Soderlund (New York: Macmillan, 1955), 1:29. Frances Acomb, *Anglophobia in France* (Durham, N.C.: Duke University Press, 1950), pp. 42–43. Charles Gouraud, *Histoire de la politique commerciale de la France* (Paris, Auguste Durand, 1854), pp. 360–364.

2. Adam Smith, *An Inquiry into the Nature and Causes of the Wealth of Nations* (Indianapolis: Liberty Classics, 1981), pp. 610, 429. J. W. Horrocks, *A Short History of Mercantilism* (London: Methuen, 1925), pp. 2–3. Max Beer, in *An Inquiry into Physiocracy* (1939; New York: Russell & Russell, 1966), p. 13, defines "mercantilism" as follows: "The characteristics of mercantilism are: (i) Conception of money (coin and bullion or treasure) as the essence of wealth. (This conception prevailed from the end of the Middle Ages up to the end of the seventeenth century.) (ii) Regulating foreign trade with a view to bringing in money by the balance of trade. (iii) Making the balance of trade the criterion of national prosperity or decline. (iv) Promotion of manufacture by supplying it with cheap raw materials and cheap labor. (v) Protective customs duties on, or prohibition of, import of manufactured commodities. (vi) The view that the economic interests of nations are mutually antagonistic."

3. Smith, *Wealth*, pp. 428, 663, 666, 671, 428, 431, 430, 431–432, 434–435, 428.

4. Heckscher, *Mercantilism*, pp. 19, 20; Gustav Schmoller, *Merkantilsystem in seiner historischen Bedeutung* (1884), and William Cunningham, *Growth of English In-*

dustry and Commerce during the Early and Middle Ages, quoted p. 28. Lawrence Stone, "State Control in Sixteenth-Century England," *Economic History Review,* 17 (1947), 110. Horrocks, *History,* pp. 6, 4, 3, 26–27. J. M. Keynes, *The General Theory of Employment Interest and Money* (London: Macmillan, 1936), pp. 335, 339, 350.

5. Though, he adds parenthetically, Belgium and Switzerland shared this latter distinction. François Crouzet, *Britain Ascendant: Comparative Studies in Franco-British Economic History* (Cambridge: Cambridge University Press, 1990), p. 6.

6. Smith, *Wealth,* 2:663. Charles W. Cole, *French Mercantilist Doctrines before Colbert* (New York, R. R. Smith, 1931), p. xi; Joseph J. Spengler, "Mercantilist and Physiocratic Growth Theories," in Bert F. Hoselitz, ed., *Theories of Economic Growth* (Glencoe, Ill.: Free Press, 1961), app., pp. 302–307. Beer, *Physiocracy,* p. 39.

7. Cole gives the date of the document's appearance between 1453 and 1461; see discussion in Cole, *Doctrines,* pp. 1–5. According to Funck-Brentano, it was published in 1456; Th. Funck-Brentano, introduction to Antoyne de Montchrétien, *Traicté de l'oeconomie politique* (Paris: Plon, 1889); *Debate* quoted pp. lxxxv–lxxxvi. Unless otherwise indicated, translations are mine.

8. The contact with the more advanced Italian civilization was responsible for the emergence of what has become a distinguishing characteristic of the French economy, "cet amour et cette recherche du fini et du beau par-dessus tout, qui compose aujourd'hui ce que j'appellerais volontiers son tempérament industriel." This noble "maladie du goût" made it at times difficult for French manufacturers to compete against the methods of their rivals abroad, "qui, marchands plus encore que manufacturiers, se soucient peu de produire grossier, s'ils vendent bon marché." Gouraud, *Histoire,* pp. 114, 115; 100–101. Cole, *Doctrines,* pp. 7–8, 10; discussion of Bodin's economic views pp. 47–57 (quotation is from p. 57).

9. Indeed, Sully, with his emphasis on agriculture and perfect indifference to both commerce and industry, would become a model for the Physiocrats.

10. It is interesting to note that the word enters French discourse much earlier than English, and also that it is used in its original and etymologically correct meaning of "household management," with an emphasis on management. However large the household, or the estate, the science of economy is, in this framework, the knowledge not of objective laws operating in the economic sphere, but of the principles of efficient management of resources in the presumed interests of the household. It is, therefore, inherently subjective and particularistic. There is no assumption of the invisible hand, naturally arranging everything for the general good; the arranging hand, which, depending on the nature of the household, may be the hand of a manager (who may or may not also be an owner) of a farm, a business firm, or a king's minister, is necessarily visible, and it is up to this visible regulating hand to arrange everything for the general good. It is clear that the "mercantile system" is much closer to this original conception of economics than the one that replaced it, which, paradoxically, then reveals itself to be anti-management.

11. *Essai sur l'histoire du tiers état,* quoted in Gouraud, *Histoire,* p. 164. Barthélemy de Laffemas, preface to *La Commission édit et partie des memoires de l'ordre et establissement du Commerce général des manufactures en ce Royaume* (Paris,

1601). Laffemas, *Premier Traicté*, p. 7; trans. in Cole, *Doctrines*, p. 70. Gouraud, *Histoire*, p. 162; Cole, *Doctrines*, p. 76. Gouraud, *Histoire*, p. 156; Cole, *Doctrines*, pp. 96–97, 104–105. Gouraud, *Histoire*, p. 168, and, quoting from Voltaire's *Essai sur les moeurs*, pp. 168–169.

12. Xavier Treney, *Extraits des économistes des XVIII et XIX siècles* (Paris: Maison Quantin, 1889), p. vi.

13. Montchrétien, *Traicté*, pp. 4, 11, 17, 31, 6, 25–26, 23–24, 29.

14. Montchrétien, *Traicté*, pp. 161–162, 192–193, 240, 165, 92; trans. Cole, *Doctrines*, pp. 137–138, 139–140, 147, 137, 133.

15. Montchrétien, *Traicté*, pp. 5, 49, 194–195, 198, 132; trans. Cole, *Doctrines*, pp. 124, 140, 141, 146, 129. It is interesting to note that the Dutch—the greatest commercial power of the time, whom Colbert later in the century would consider the "mortal enemies" of France and its most dangerous competitor—were treated by Montchrétien rather benignly. See Cole, *Doctrines*, p. 142, fn. 1.

16. Montchrétien, *Traicté*, pp. 58, 66, 276; trans. Cole, *Doctrines*, pp. 127–128, 151, and pp. 160–161 of Cole's text. It should be noted that, "though a little skeptical," as Cole points out, Montchrétien did consider gold and silver the "two great and faithful friends, which supply the needs of all men and are honored among all peoples." Montchrétien, *Traicté*, pp. 141–142; trans. Cole, *Doctrines*, p. 135.

17. Montchrétien, *Traicté*, pp. 5, 12–13. "Ce tiers ordre est composé de trois sortes d'hommes, Laboureurs, Artisans et Marchands. . . . Imaginez-vous que ce sont . . . les trois canaux de l'utilité commune, qui portent et versent l'eau dans les grandes places de vos citéz, la où viennent abreuver tous les autres hommes" (pp. 12–13).

18. Sully quoted in Gouraud, *Histoire*, p. 171.

19. Exhibit 182 of the exhibition of the Ministère de la Culture, *Colbert*, October 4–November 30, 1983; catalogue, pp. 132–133.

> Money today makes the destiny of men;
> Money is a power before which all gives way;
> Money, without moving, moves all designs;
> Money is a sovereign remedy for misfortunes;
> Money is the pivot of bankers, of merchants;
> Money is the recourse of the good and of the wicked;
> Money is the chief thought of authors;
> Money is the object of desire for all arts;
> Money breaks walls and obstacles;
> And money is the agent that sets everything in motion.
> Money alone can change an unhappy fate;
> Money is a key to sweet power;
> Money opens for us the door in danger,
> For it bewitches everyone to whom it is advanced.
> In this vast universe everyone courts it;
> Money subjects to its laws both honor and love:
> For honor and love it breaks all the obstacles.
> Money conquers hearts in a chaste pursuit;
> Money makes the ugly beautiful and the sick healthy,

> And money, in a word, almost works miracles.
> Money has all the power on earth and on the seas;
> Money saves lives and frees from bondage;
> Money opens the heavens and closes the hells;
> Money does all the good and all the evil in the world.

20. This was very well understood by Romantics of the nineteenth century. Dumas, in *Le vicomte de Bragelonne,* paints a memorable portrait of Colbert as a symbol of a new breed of men—base, leveling, calculating, soulless, interested only in money—who were to crowd out everything noble and beautiful.

21. Henri Hauser, "Le 'Parfait Négociant' de Jacques Savary," *Revue d'histoire économique et sociale* (1925), 1–6, 3, 6, 7, 12, 11, 18, 9.

22. D'Argenson quoted in Jacques Godechot, "Nation, patrie, nationalisme et patriotisme en France au XVIII siècle," *Annales historiques de la révolution française,* 206 (October–December 1971), 489; the "lassez-faire" rule was recommended by d'Argenson with some urgency, its original formulation apparently being "Laissez faire, morbleu, Laissez faire!" (Laissez faire, damn it, Laissez faire!); quoted in André Alem, *Le Marquis d'Argenson et l'Économie politique au début du XVIII siècle* (Paris: Arthur Rousseau, 1900), p. 2.

23. L'Abbé Coyer, *La Noblesse commerçante* (London and Paris, 1756), p. 5. Edgard Depitre, "Le Système et la querelle de la *Noblesse commerçante* (1756–1759)," *Revue d'histoire économique et sociale,* 2 (1913), 137–176, quote 147.

24. De Lassay quoted in Jean Lebreton-Savigny, *Les Idées économiques de l'Abbé Coyer* (Poitiers: Nicolas, Renault & Cie., 1920), pp. 21, 35. Coyer, *Développement et défense du système de la Noblesse Commerçante* (Paris: Duchesne, 1757). The *Journal Économique* raised the issue anew in 1761 in an article whose title spelled out the connection between it and the national project in general, "Examen de la noblesse par rapport au commerce et à la gloire de la nation." Mably treated it in the 1763 *Entretiens de Phocion sur le rapport de la morale avec la politique,* which was republished in 1793; it was discussed in Tixedor's *Nouvelle France ou France commerçante* in 1765, and so on.

25. Coyer, *Développement,* 1:113. Declaration quoted in Depitre, "Système," p. 143. The list of edicts limiting the law of *dérogeance* may be found in the already mentioned *Dictionnaire universel de commerce* of Savary de Bruslons, in the entry on "Profession mercantile." Depitre, "Système," pp. 144–145. Montesquieu, *De l'Esprit des Lois* (Paris: Garnier, 1877), pp. 389–391. Coyer, *Noblesse,* pp. 214–215; *Développement,* 1:78; *Noblesse,* pp. 98, 107; *Développement,* 2:21; and Depitre, "Système," pp. 151–152, 162. Coyer, *Développement,* 1:72; 2:82, 44–46.

26. For a discussion of the dynamics of the development of national consciousness and the importance of the model—the source from which the idea of the nation is imported—see Greenfeld, *Nationalism;* France is the subject of chap. 2. On various aspects and phases of Anglomania, see Josephine Grieder, *Anglomania in France, 1740–1789: Fact, Fiction, and Political Discourse* (Geneva: Librairie Droz, 1985), who quotes Rigoley de Juvigny's assessment of the situation in a note on p. 11.

27. Louis-Philippe, Comte de Ségur, *Mémoires, souvenirs et anecdotes* (Paris: Librairie de Firmin Didot Frères, 1859), 1:14. Mlle. de l'Espinasse quoted in Hans Kohn,

"France between Britain and Germany," *Journal of the History of Ideas,* 17:3 (June 1956), 283. Henri Carre, *La noblesse de France et l'opinion publique au XVIII siècle* (Paris: Champion, 1920), p. 141. Depitre, "Système," pp. 148–149.

28. De Lassay quoted in Coyer, *Noblesse,* p. 8.

29. The similarity is all the more striking since d'Arcq, too, was captain of the king's Musketeers, and it is quite probable that his was not simply an assumed pose. In any event, his views deserve close attention: according to Lebreton-Savigny (*Idées,* p. 38), they represented the dominant opinion of the nobility.

30. Lebreton-Savigny, *Idées,* pp. 37–45; d'Arcq, *La Noblesse militaire,* quoted pp. 85, 86. D'Arcq's assumption that power and prosperity were mutually exclusive desiderata serves to underscore how novel the idea of the economy's very importance was. J. Le Rond d'Alembert, *Histoire des membres de l'Académie française morts depuis 1700 jusqu'en 1771,* Darnton's translation (Paris: Chez Panckoucke et Moutard, 1779), pp. xxxii–xxxiii. V. de Pennes *Noblesse ramenée à ses vrais principes,* p. 72, quoted in Depitre, "Système," p. 169, see also p. 170. The latter characterization of the English government appeared in Henri Misson de Valbourg's *Mémoires et observations faites par un voyageur en Angleterre,* published in La Haye in 1698.

31. On the changing sentiments toward England, see, in particular, the two complimentary studies Acomb, *Anglophobia,* and Grieder, *Anglomania.*

32. The fact that the French edition of the *Lettres* was condemned by the Parlement of Paris upon publication and burned for infamy by a common hangman would scarcely diminish their influence. In that time of disaffection, as Ségur, among others, related to us, "la condamnation d'un livre était un titre de considération pour l'auteur" (*Mémoires,* 1:11). Some contemporaries, in fact, believed Voltaire responsible for creating Anglomania: Montbron (who is quoted in Grieder, *Anglomania,* p. 8), in 1757 thought that his "plus grand miracle [was] la Métamorphose surprenante qu'il a faite des Anglois." Voltaire, *Philosophical Letters,* trans. Ernest Dilworth (New York: Macmillan, 1961), pp. 39–40, Letter 10, "On Commerce." F. A. Taylor, introduction to Voltaire's *Lettres* (Oxford: Basil Blackwell, 1979), p. xi. Voltaire to Mme. d'Epinay, July 6, 1766, in *Correspondence complète* (Banbury: Voltaire Foundation, 1968), 30:299.

33. Crouzet, *Britain,* pp. 17–25. Guy Palmade, *French Capitalism in the Nineteenth Century* trans. Graeme M. Holmes (New York: Barnes and Noble, 1972), pp. 43, 60, 65. Crouzet, *Britain,* pp. 29, 26–27. Shelby T. McCloy, *French Inventions of the Eighteenth Century* (Lexington: University of Kentucky Press, 1952), p. 189; societies for the encouragement of invention and industry, including Baudeau's, are discussed on p. 181. Crouzet, *Britain,* p. 43. W. W. Rostow, *How It All Began: Origins of the Modern Economy* (New York: McGraw Hill, 1975), p. 38. Palmade, *Capitalism,* p. 68, 56–59; Mercier quoted p. 56; the rest of the paragraph relies on pp. 46–56. *Prospectus de la fourniture et distribution des eaux de la Seine, à Paris, par les machines à fer* (Paris, 1781), pp. 1–2, 6, quoted in Grieder, *Anglomania,* p. 28. Palmade, *Capitalism,* pp. 59, 60, 63. French text: Guy P. Palmade, *Capitalisme et capitalistes français au XIX siècle,* (Paris: Armand Colin, 1961), pp. 51, 43.

34. Palmade, *Capitalisme,* p. 70. Rondo E. Cameron, "Economic Growth and Stagnation in France," *Journal of Modern History,* 30 (March 1958), 2. David S.

Landes, *The Unbound Prometheus: Technological Change and Industrial Development in Western Europe from 1750 to the Present* (New York: Cambridge University Press, 1969), pp. 10, 11, 126–147, 131–133, 147, 188–192, 209–210, 526–528; idem, *The Wealth and Poverty of Nations* (New York: W. W. Norton, 1998), pp. 516, 260–261, 454–459, 446–447. Crouzet, *Britain,* p. 30.

35. J.-J. Rousseau, *The Government of Poland,* trans. Willmore Kendall, (Indianapolis: Bobbs-Merill, 1972), pp. 68–70; idem, *Social Contract,* in *The Social Contract and Discourses,* trans. G. D. H. Cole (London: Everyman's Library, 1952), p. 77. *L'improvisateur français,* vols. 3–4 (Paris: Goujon Fils, year xii [1804]), pp. 45–46. Palmade quotes the same definition from the *National and Anecdotal Dictionary* of 1790 in *Capitalisme,* p. 35; Mirabeau quoted p. 34.

36. Rousseau's correspondent quoted in Palmade, *Capitalism,* p. 34. My discussion of the Physiocrats relies on pp. 35, 60, 105–130.

4. The Power of Concerted Action: Germany

1. Henri Hauser, *Economic Germany: German Industry Considered as a Factor Making for War,* trans. P. E. Matheson (London: Thomas Nelson and Sons, 1915), p. 6. John H. Clapham, *The Economic Development of France and Germany, 1815–1914* (Cambridge: Cambridge University Press, 1936), p. 43.

2. Greenfeld, *Nationalism,* pp. 322–352.

3. Johann Gottfried Herder, "Übers Erkennen und Empfinden in der Menschlichen Seele," in *Sämtliche Werke* (Hildesheim: Georg Olms Verlag, 1967), 8:261.

4. One should note that this was not a confusion peculiar to Romantics, though. The concept of the state was relatively new in Germany. When Botero's *Della ragio di stato* was translated in 1596, a liberal interpretation was substituted for the precise translation of the title, for there was no term that could render *stato* in German. The treatise therefore bore the name "Thorough Account of the Arrangement of Good Police [*Polizei*] and Rule, also the Stand of Ruler and Lord." More than half a century later, the author of *Biblische Policey,* Reinking, thought that the word *Staat,* which was invented for the purpose, was not "proper German." Apparently, when he was writing, the common German translation of the Latin *status,* which was the source of the English *state* and French *état,* was *Stand*—which corresponded to the English and French concepts of "estate" in the sense of legal stratum, from which the concept of "state" in both languages had long since separated. When the term *Staat* finally entered discourse in the later seventeenth century, it meant both "the government"—the ruler and his court—and (so Keith Tribe tells us) "*bürgerliche Gesellschaft,* a political association or political society *per se.*" "The German terminology," says Tribe, "derived directly from a Latinate tradition and remained uncontaminated by the very different French and English understandings of 'state' and 'civil society' until the later eighteenth century." Keith Tribe, *Governing Economy: The Reformation of German Economic Discourse, 1750–1840* (Cambridge: Cambridge University Press, 1988), p. 28; reprinted with the permission of Cambridge University Press.

5. Adam Müller, "Elements of Politics," lecture no. 2, in H. S. Reiss, ed., *The Political Thought of the German Romantics* (Oxford: Basil Blackwell, 1955), pp. 144, 154, 155, 146, 150. Müller quoted in Hans Kohn, "Romanticism and German

Nationalism," *Review of Politics,* 12 (1950), 466. Müller, "Elements," pp. 160, 159, 158. Hegel quoted in Leonard Krieger, *The German Idea of Freedom: History of a Political Tradition* (Boston: Beacon Press, 1957), pp. 133, 132, 133. Friedrich Schlegel, *Lucinde or the Fragments* (Minneapolis: University of Minnesota Press, 1971), "Ideas," no. 64, p. 247; no. 54, p. 246. Novalis, *Fragmente,* no. 1614, quoted in Kohn, "Romanticism," p. 449.

6. Much literature on German economic history, and an overwhelming majority of general studies, concentrate on Prussia. In the context of discussing agrarian development in the eighteenth century, Clapham writes: "As Prussia after 1815 was the sole state representative of almost all Germany, with lands stretching from the servile Slavonic east to the free Dutch west, the Prussian development deserves the closest study. It illustrates every point of importance" (*Development,* p. 42). Tribe, in turn, points out that "the history of the German economy in the eighteenth century is dominated by Prussia—whose territories and institutions extended across northern and eastern Germany . . . Cameralism first developed in Prussian universities" (*Governing,* p. 8). Schmoller, "Friedrich Wilhelm I und das politische Testament von 1722," and Friedrich II quoted in Tribe, *Governing,* pp. 9, 19. Also see discussion in Hajo Holborn, "Welfare and Power," in *A History of Modern Germany, 1648–1840* (New York: Knopf, 1964), pp. 240–242.

7. J. W. Horrocks, *A Short History of Mercantilism* (London: Methuen, 1925), p. 142. Also Joseph J. Spengler, "Mercantilist and Physiocratic Growth Theories," in Bert F. Hoselitz (ed.), *Theories of Economic Growth* (Glencoe, Ill.: Free Press, 1961), p. 320. Tribe, *Governing,* pp. 24, 51; Hochberg, Schröder, and Wolff quoted pp. 19, 31.

8. Tribe, *Governing,* pp. 35–36. Tribe's translation of the passages from Zincke's *Lexicon,* which appear in *Governing,* pp. 54, 51, are slightly modified to highlight the nature of the German terms in brackets. Tribe, *Governing,* pp. 42–44, 39.

9. Tribe, *Governing,* p. 60. J. H. G. von Justi, *Staatswirtschaft, oder systematische Abhandlung aller oekonomischen und Cameralwissenschaften, die zur Regierung eines Landes erfordert werden* (Leipzig, 1958), 1:32, 59–60, 45, 48; Hasek's translation: C. W. Hasek, *The Introduction of Adam Smith's Doctrines into Germany* (New York: Columbia University Press, 1925), pp. 36, 37, 38; Tribe's translation in *Governing,* p. 68; first edition quoted in Tribe, *Governing,* p. 73; Justi's Vienna lecture notes p. 62.

10. Hasek, *Smith,* p. 39; W. F. Bruck, *Social and Economic History of Germany from William II to Hitler, 1888–1938: A Comparative Study* (Oxford: Oxford University Press, 1938), pp. 35–39. Tribe, *Governing,* pp. 86, 66. Justi, *Staatswirtschaft,* p. 152 (Hasek's trans., *Smith,* p. 42), pp. 178, 198. *The Theory of Moral Sentiments,* in which Smith announced his plan for his latter work, it will be remembered, appeared in 1759.

11. Clapham, *Development,* pp. 36–43 (quotation from G. F. Knapp p. 41); Hasek, *Smith,* pp. 19–21; William O. Henderson, *Studies in the Economic Policy of Frederick the Great* (London: Frank Cass & Co., 1963), Macaulay quoted p. 162. Clapham, *Development,* pp. 41, 42. Hasek, *Smith,* p. 21; Clapham, *Development,* pp. 42–43 (the ditty is quoted p. 43). Henderson, *Policy,* pp. 128–136, 162–163 (Friedrich quoted p. 129); Hasek, *Smith,* pp. 24–25.

12. Hasek, *Smith,* p. 19. Regarding guilds Hasek also writes: "Each and every guild

was made a unit independent of any central [guild] organization. Legal decisions of the guilds were invalid beyond the bounds of the territory. Punishments within the power of the guild were reduced to trifling fines. Meetings could be held only in the presence of a member of [government] council. The punishment of exclusion from the guild could be pronounced only by a magistrate. The oath of secrecy and participation in secret organizations was forbidden. In certain trades customers could order goods from masters in other cities, a provision which broke down the exclusiveness of the local market. Merchants were permitted to deal in guild products" (*Smith,* pp. 29, 30).

13. Ibid., pp. 16, 31.

14. As was mentioned in a previous chapter, "patriotism" does not always refer to "national patriotism" and is often entirely unrelated to any national sentiment. In eighteenth-century Prussia, "patriotic" meant "devoted to the king" and "civic-minded" in the manner encouraged by the king.

15. The account of Gotzkowsky's life relies on the discussion in Henderson, *Policy,* chap. 2, "The Rise of the Berlin Silk and Porcelain Industries," pp. 17–36, including all the quotations from Gotzkowsky and other contemporary sources.

16. See Tribe, *Governing,* pp. 83, 79, 104, 110. "Approximately twice as many translations from the French language as from the English were published in the later 18th century," Tribe comments. "It was France rather than Britain that was regarded as the dominant foreign cultural influence" (p. 135).

17. J. G. H. Feder in *Göttingische gelehrte Anzeigen,* March 10, 1777, and April 5, 1777 (quoted in Hasek, *Smith,* pp. 63–64). *Allgemeine deutsche Bibliothek,* 38 (1777), 300 (quoted p. 65). According to W. Roscher, Smith's book was quoted now and then, mostly by Cameralists, but in a rather perfunctory manner, reflecting familiarity with his name more than his ideas (see p. 66).

18. F. K. Wittichen, *Briefe von und an Friedrich von Gentz* (Berlin, 1909), 1:181–182; Garve quoted in Hasek, *Smith,* p. 69. Smith's publisher quoted in Tribe, *Governing,* p. 144. *Göttingische gelehrte Anzeigen,* October 19, 1793, p. 1662; Kraus quoted in Hasek, *Smith,* pp. 66, 73; and see p. 79. The critic E. Kühn quoted in Tribe, *Governing,* p. 147. Hasek, *Smith,* pp. 116–117, 86–87.

19. This idea was backed by the additional authority of the Physiocrats, who also enjoyed a brief vogue in Germany in the 1770s and 1780s, though the final judgment on their contribution was quite similar to Smith's: it was irrelevant. A German professor in 1786 put it rather unkindly: Physiocracy, he said, was like "a girl as beauteous as an angel, but unfortunately a virgin" (quoted in Tribe, *Governing,* p. 130).

20. C. D. H. Bensen, *Versuch eines systematischen Grundrisses der reinen und angewandten Staatslehre für Kameralisten* (Erlangen, 1798), 1:9, 2:15; quoted in Tribe, *Governing,* p. 161.

21. Tribe, who does not at all focus on nationalism and the place of *Nationalökonomie* in its development, notes nevertheless that at first "the name for this 'new economics' had a strategic value and was itself the object of controversy" (*Governing,* p. 171).

22. "At no time before had so many books on economics appeared in so short a time," writes Hasek of this period (*Smith,* p. 94). Jakob, quoted in Tribe, *Governing,* p. 170; p. 167.

23. Clapham, *Development*, p. 43. Holborn, *1648–1840*, p. 395. "It is certain," wrote a nineteenth-century observer, "that in the years 1792–1797 many commercial houses increased their capital at a rate which had never before been heard of." J. G. Büsch, *Geschichtliche Beurtheilung der grossen Handelsverwirrung im Jahre 1799*, quoted in Hasek, *Smith*, p. 56.

24. In 1792 France declared war on Austria, on whose side Prussia was obliged to join in accordance with the provisions of the 1791 Declaration of Pillnitz. The separate Treaty of Basel between France and Prussia was concluded on April 5, 1795. Friedrich Wilhelm's favorite minister, Hardenberg—who earlier ministered in Hanover and Brunswick—negotiated the agreement, claiming that the aim of this isolationist action was actually to "rally Germany around the king of Prussia." Quoted in Walter M. Simon, "Variations in Nationalism during the Great Reform Period in Prussia," *American Historical Review*, 59 (1953–54), 308. On Friedrich Wilhelm, see J. A. R. Marriott and C. G. Robertson, *The Evolution of Prussia* (Oxford: Oxford University Press, 1915), p. 193.

25. Hasek, *Smith*, pp. 45–59; Holborn, *1648–1840*, pp. 386–423. Simon, "Variations," p. 305. Holborn, *1648–1840*, p. 393. Werner F. Bruck, *Social and Economic History of Germany from Wilhelm II to Hitler, 1888–1938* (Oxford: Oxford University Press, 1938), p. 42. T. A. H. Schmaltz, *Berichtigung einer Stelle* (Berlin, 1815), quoted in Simon, "Variations," p. 313; regarding the *Encyclopaedie der Cameralwissenschaften*, see Tribe, *Governing*, p. 160. Stein, letter of December 1, 1812, and Niebuhr, "Preussens Recht gegen den sächsischen Hof," quoted in Simon, "Variations," pp. 307, 311. Holborn, *1648–1840*, pp. 398, 393; in regard to other states, see pp. 386–392.

26. Stein, "Nassauer Denkschrift," June 1807, and letter to Münster, December 1, 1812, both quoted in Simon, "Variations," pp. 305, 307. Extracts from the Prussian Reform Edict of October 9, 1807, in Louis L. Snyder, ed., *Documents of German History* (New Brunswick, N.J.: Rutgers University Press, 1958), pp. 132–133. Hasek, *Smith*, p. 142. Theodor von Schön, *Aus den Papieren des Ministers und Burggrafen von Marienburg Theodor von Schön* (Halle, 1875), 1:43, quoted in Hasek, *Smith*, p. 142. Holborn, *1648–1840*, p. 407.

27. Introduction to selections from Müller, in Reiss, *Thought*, pp. 142–143; Müller on Smith is quoted in Goetz A. Briefs, "The Economic Philosophy of Romanticism," *Journal of the History of Ideas*, 2:3 (1941), 289, and in Kohn, "Romanticism," p. 466. The discussion of Müller's economic views relies on Briefs, "Philosophy," with quotations from a selection of Müller's works taken from pp. 287–295; the quotation from *Elements of Politics*, public lectures Müller delivered in 1808–9 before Prince Bernhard of Saxe-Weimar, whose tutor he was, and an audience of statemen, is from Reiss, *Thought*, pp. 149–150.

28. Roman Szporluk, *Communism and Nationalism: Karl Marx versus Friedrich List* (New York: Oxford University Press, 1988), pp. 104, 107. Friedrich List, *The National System of Political Economy*, trans. S. S. Lloyd, intro. J. S. Nicholson (London: Longmans, Green and Company, 1922), pp. xxx, xxxi, xxxvii. General James Hamilton, representative from South Carolina, quoted in Joseph Dorfman, *The Economic Mind in American Civilization, 1606–1865*. vol. 2 (New York: Viking, 1946), p. 582.

29. List, *System*, pp. 117, 156, 208, 111, 116, 132, 40, 97–98, 141, 278, 279, 106–

107; and quoted in Szporluk, *Communism,* p. 112, from List's "On the Use of the Railway." Regarding the attraction of Marxists to fascism, see Zeev Sternhell, *Fascist Ideology: From Cultural Rebellion to Political Revolution* (Princeton: Princeton University Press, 1994), and, particularly, Jacob L. Talmon, *The Myth of the Nation and Vision of Revolution: Ideological Polarization in the Twentieth Century* (New Brunswick, N.J.: Transaction Books, 1991). Also see my review of Talmon in *Theory and History,* 32:3 (October 1993), 339–349.

30. Kossuth quoted in W. O. Henderson, *Friedrich List: Economist and Visionary, 1789–1846* (London: Frank Cass, 1983), p. 109; List's characterization is Hajo Holborn's, in *A History of Modern Germany, 1840–1945* (New York: Knopf, 1973), p. 21. Louis L. Snyder, *German Nationalism: The Tragedy of a People* (Harrisburg, Pa.: Stackpole, 1952), chap. 4, "Economics: The Role of Friedrich List in the Establishment of the *Zollverein,*" pp. 76–77, 80; Friedrich Lenz, *Friedrich List und Grossdeutschland* (Leipzig–Berlin, ca. 1942), quoted in Snyder, p. 99. Keith Tribe, in *Strategies of Economic Order* (New York: Cambridge University Press, 1995), chap. 3, "Die Vernunft des List: National Economy and the Critique of Cosmopolitical Economy," p. 36, n. 12, quotes another German text of 1942, H. Voss's introduction to List's writings: "List's economic attempts from the middle, Bismarck's political consolidation from above, all this had to collapse before, on the basis of a new and solid foundation, Adolph Hitler completed *volkspolitisch* the construction of the Great German Reich from below."

31. Holborn, *1648–1840,* p. 461; Henderson, *List,* pp. 34–35; Clapham, *Development,* pp. 98–99. Lenz quoted in Snyder, *Nationalism,* p. 90. The three factors, besides List's activity, that led to the establishment of *Zollverein* were, according to Price, "the coordination of practical and theoretical elements in the Prussian Customs Law of 1818; Hofmann's synthesis of particularism, with the necessity of a customs system; and Motz's integration of Prussia's fiscal and foreign policy." Arnold H. Price, *The Evolution of the Zollverein, a Study of the Ideas and Institutions Leading to German Economic Unification between 1815 and 1833* (Ann Arbor: Michigan University Press, 1949), pp. 255–256. Snyder, *Nationalism,* pp. 88, 75–76.

32. There was serious disagreement as to what the common welfare was: List's involvement in the German Union of Merchants, for instance, was defined by the Württemberg minister of the interior as service "in a foreign country" and cost the unlucky patriot his Tübingen professorship (Henderson, *List,* p. 41). As to Prussia's diplomatic skills, Prussia "exploited her diplomatic successes with great ability. Little princes learnt that it was well to be in favour at Berlin. If they were, Berlin would find money for building valuable roads across their territory. Not for love of them, but because the roads were part of a systematic policy for diverting German trade from the territory of those who were not friends of hers" (Clapham, *Development,* p. 101).

33. Henderson, *List,* pp. 51, 107–109. Clapham, *Development,* p. 101; Banfield quoted p. 101. During this tour, at a banquet in Vienna, List proposed a toast to the future economic might of Germany: "Germany—in science, art, and literature a star of the first magnitude among the nations of the world! Germany—destined by its natural resources, by the genius of its inhabitants, and by a wise com-

mercial policy to be the richest country on the Continent!" (Henderson, *List*, p. 76).

34. Holborn, *1840–1945*, pp. 11, 12–13. Henderson, *List*, pp. 78–83. Treitschke cited in Clapham, *Development*, p. 280.

35. Tribe, "List," pp. 38–39. Also see J. J. Sheehan, *German Liberalism in the Nineteenth Century* (Chicago: University of Chicago Press, 1978). Snyder, *Nationalism*, p. 76. William Carr, *A History of Germany, 1815–1945* (London: Edward Arnold, 1969), p. 21. For data on List's journalistic activities, I rely on Henderson, *List*, pp. 78–89, 206; last quotation, from the Prussian ambassador in London, writing in 1846, is from p. 123; also on List's renown, pp. 100, 117; Tribe, "List," esp. pp. 36–37; Schmoller quoted p. 36.

36. On List's posthumous popularity, see Henderson, *List*, pp. 100–123, 204–215; Richelot quoted p. 100; Bismarck on p. 211; also Snyder, *Nationalism*, p. 76.

37. Clapham, *Development*, pp. 96, 97, 88–89, 82, 279, 281; Banfield quoted p. 88. See also Charles W. Cole, *French Mercantilist Doctrines before Colbert* (New York: R. R. Smith, 1931), p. 280. Holborn, *1840–1945*, pp. 4, 12, 122, 124; Sombart quoted p. 122.

38. Prussian officer quoted in Hauser, *Germany*, pp. 3–4. Hauser is right in pointing out that "it matters little whether the words are apocryphal: they express a profound and symbolic truth, and admirably render the thought of an entire nation." E. E. Williams, *"Made in Germany"* (1896; Brighton: Harvester Press, 1973), p. 91. On the development of the iron industry, see Clapham, *Development*, pp. 283–285; Keynes quoted p. 284.

39. Clapham, *Development*, pp. 284, 295, 308.

40. "Between 1815 and 1845 the population of Germany (excluding Austria) grew from 25 to 34.5 million. The German governments were alarmed, and Malthus' predictions about the dire consequences of a multiplying population prompted some of them, chiefly in southern and central Germany, to issue laws making marriages contingent on a means test. These rather ineffective laws, some of which were abolished only after 1867, were signs of prevailing doubts about the chances for an expansion of the economy, and optimism was certainly ill-founded [for] Germany lacked the capital required for any large-scale development." Holborn, *1840–1945*, p. 4.

41. Hauser, *Germany*, p. 3. Karl Lamprecht, *Zur jüngsten deutschen Vergangenheit*, quoted, possibly with some paraphrasing, p. 17, fn.

42. Hauser, *Germany*, pp. 23–26, 20–23, including quotations from Italian and Swiss sources. Paul Arndt, *Deutschlands Stellung in Weltwirthschaft*, and G. von Below, *Militarismus und Kultur in Deutschland* (1915), quoted pp. 30, 16, fn.

43. Gustav Stresemann, "La politique mondiale de l'Allemagne," *Revue économique internationale* (1913), quoted in Hauser, *Germany*, p. 28, fn. Williams, *"Made in Germany,"* pp. 19–20, 48, 95, 155, 156–157, 44; 1884 Report quoted p. 67; Sir Charles Oppenheimer on p. 6. *Saturday Review* quoted in Austen Albu, introduction to Williams, *"Made in Germany,"* pp. xxxii, xiv.

44. Albu, introduction, pp. xxx–xxxii, including quotations. Clapham, *Development*, p. 311. Lassalle, in particular, continued the work of List, being in a way the German—and far more sophisticated, it goes without saying—counterpart of

Gerard Winstanley. Nationalist inspiration behind Marxism has been discussed in Greenfeld, *Nationalism.*

5. Japanese Nationalism

1. G. B. Sansom, *The Western World and Japan: A Study in the Interaction of European and Asiatic Cultures* (New York: Alfred A. Knopf, 1950), p. 238. Edwin O. Reischauer, *Japan: The Story of a Nation,* 3rd ed. (New York: Alfred A. Knopf, 1981), pp. 131–132.
2. Reischauer, *Japan,* pp. 89, 95. See also S. N. Eisenstadt, *Japanese Civilization: A Comparative View* (Chicago: University of Chicago Press, 1996), p. 2. David J. Lu, introduction to chap. 9, "Intellectual Currents in Tokugawa Japan," in *Japan: A Documentary History* (New York: Sharpe, 1997), 1:243. Reprinted with permission from M.E. Sharpe, Inc., Publisher, Armonk, N.Y. 10504. Also see Yamamoto Shichihei, *The Spirit of Japanese Capitalism and Other Essays,* trans. Lynn E. Riggs (New York: Madison Books [Library of Japan], 1992), esp. chap. 4, "Roots of the Modern Ethos." Sansom, *Western World,* pp. 187, 197; Will Adams quoted p. 188.
3. Cosme de Torres on Japanese receptivity (ca. 1550); Saint Francis Xavier's view of Japanese (ca. 1550); Alessandro Valigniano on Japanese prudence and discretion, and on patience and resignation (ca. 1580); all in Lu, *Documentary History,* pp. 198; 199–200. Will Adams in Sansom, *Western World,* p. 188.
4. In 1594 Henri Bourbon adopted Catholicism and was crowned Henri IV of France, ending a forty-year period of civil wars, and in 1590 Hideyoshi finally united all of Japan under one government, having subdued the last important opponent, the Hojo. *Baku-han:* from *bakufu*—the central government of the shogun, and *han,* the domains of the feudal lords, *daimyo,* redistributed by the *bakufu* to ensure compliance with its prescriptions and replicating the *bakufu* administrative arrangements. For the 1595 Edict on *Daimyo* and 1587 Limitation on the Propagation of Christianity, see Lu, *Documentary History,* pp. 195, 196.
5. One *koku* was approximately equal to five bushels.
6. Amendment of Kanei to Buke Shohatto (1635), in Lu, *Documentary History,* p. 208. The original Ieyasu's law stipulated, among other things, "The *daimyo*'s visits *(sankin)* to Edo must follow the following regulations [which were justified by appeal to immemorial tradition]: The *Shoku Nihongi* (Chronicles of Japan) contains a regulation saying that 'Unless entrusted with some official duty, no one is permitted to assemble his clansmen at his own pleasure. Furthermore no one is to have more than twenty horsemen as his escort within the limits of the capital.' Hence it is not permissible to be accompanied by a large force of soldiers," and so on (p. 207). G. B. Sansom, *Japan: A Short Cultural History* (Stanford: Stanford University Press, 1978), p. 448, note.
7. Edicts on Collection of Swords (1588); Change of Status (1591); Limitation on the Propagation of Christianity (1587); all in Lu, *Documentary History,* pp. 191, 194, 196.
8. The tax rate was estimated as 40 to 50 percent of the peasant's yield, like ours today—"extraordinarily high," says Reischauer, *Japan,* p. 98.

9. Lord of Echizen (1632), "The Group of Five," and "Farmers and Annual Tax" (1603); both in Lu, *Documentary History,* pp. 209–210, 210–211.

10. Simon Schama, *The Embarrassment of Riches: An Interpretation of Dutch Culture in the Golden Age* (New York: Knopf, 1987), pp. 16–24. "The work was so grueling and the rewards so paltry . . . that the distinction between rehabilitation and punishment must have been lost on those who were bound to it." But this was punishment, and there was a sincere intention on the part of the authorities, and thus hope for the inmates, of rehabilitation. The inmates were paid (!) a "meager wage" of only eight and a half stuivers a day, and forced to save two stuivers a week so as to have something to take with them upon discharge, and while incarcerated they were on a plain but ample diet: "dark bread, grits, porridge, peas and beans; a little pork or stockfish once or twice a week. It was, at least, to be sufficiently varied that its deprivation for bread and water would seem like a punishment" (pp. 19–20, 17). A Japanese peasant, neither a social offender nor a prisoner, would have envied that.

11. Naoe Kanetsugu, a retainer of the *daimyo* of Aizu, Injunctions for Peasants (ca. 1619); Regulations for Villagers (1643); both in Lu, *Documentary History,* pp. 212–213, 213–215.

12. Reischauer, *Japan,* p. 85; Sansom, *Western World,* 234; regarding French nobility, see Greenfeld, *Nationalism,* p. 134 and references. Saint Francis Xavier's view of Japanese; Laws of Military Households (1615), in Lu, *Documentary History,* p. 206.

13. Delmer M. Brown, in *Nationalism in Japan: An Introductory Historical Analysis* (New York: Russell and Russell, 1971), p. 51, credits the teacher of Hayashi, Fujiwara Seika (1561–1619), with introducing Chu Hsi to the Tokugawa, but he agrees that Hayashi's contribution was far more important. Hayashi Razan, "Natural Order and Social Order," in Lu, *Documentary History,* pp. 245–247. The implication of Hayashi's vision for social stratification has been spelled out by a later author (Hori Isao, *Hayashi Razan* [Tokyo: Yoshikawa Kobunkan, 1964]). D. Howard Smith, *Confucius* (London: Paladin, 1974), p. 62. Reischauer, *Japan,* p. 96; Sansom, *Western World,* pp. 197–198, 184. Sansom, *Japan,* p. 499.

14. Reischauer characterizes *bushido* as "an idealized combination of Confucianism and feudal ethics" (*Japan,* p. 103). It stressed the virtues of loyalty and duty, but its distinguishing characteristic was, perhaps, the contempt for death. Hayashi Razan, "On the Unity of Shinto and Confucianism," in Lu, *Documentary History,* p. 247.

15. Reischauer, *Japan,* p. 84. Kada Azumamaro, "Petition for the Establishment of a School of National Learning," and Motoori Norinaga, "The True Tradition of the Sun Goddess," in Ryusaku Tsunoda, W. Theodore de Bary, and Donald Keene, eds., *Sources of Japanese Tradition* (hereafter *Sources*), vol. 2 (New York: Columbia University Press, 1964), pp. 6–7 and pp. 15, 18; reprinted by permission of the publisher. The belief in the superior quality of Japanese rice persists and is reflected, among other things, in the opposition of the country's consumers to the deregulation of agricultural imports (which would reduce the relatively high domestic food prices). Chikashi Moriguchi, "Rice and Melons—Japanese Agriculture in the Showa Era," in Carol Gluck and Stephen R. Graubard, eds.,

Showa: The Japan of Hirohito (New York: W. W. Norton, 1992), p. 139. See also Walter LaFeber, *The Clash: A History of U.S.–Japan Relations* (New York: W. W. Norton, 1997), pp. 399–400.

16. Hirata Atsutane, "The Land of the Gods" and "Ancient Japanese Ethics," pp. 39, 42–43; Kamo Mabuchi, pp. 11–12, 13, 14, 15; Motoori Norinaga, "The Error of Rationalism," pp. 24, 23; and "Wonder," pp. 20–21; all in *Sources*. German authors quoted in Greenfeld, *Nationalism*, pp. 333, 332.

17. Tokugawa Mitsukuni (1628–1700) was the "related" *daimyo* of Mito. *Dai ni honshi—History of Great Japan—*was a compilation of historical materials, on which the *daimyo* apparently spent more than half his fortune, collected and edited, under his leadership, by the disciples of the neo-Shintoist scholar Yamazaki Ansai, who are referred to as the "Mito school." See Brown, *Nationalism*, pp. 54–55. Reischauer, *Japan*, p. 103; Sansom, *Western World*, p. 210.

18. Kamo, in "The Land," pp. 12, 15, 18. Introduction to chap. 22, "The Shinto Revival," in *Sources*, p. 5. "National Learning" is this volume's translation for *kokugaku*, but it is incorrect. *Koku* is a word predating the appearance of the idea of the nation in Japan by several centuries; it is roughly equivalent to "country." When the idea of the nation was introduced, a new term was invented to denote it: *kokumin*, that is, "the people of the country."

19. From Japanese for Holland, "Oranda," as David Landes explains in *The Wealth and Poverty of Nations* (New York: W. W. Norton: 1998), p. 366.

20. Sansom, *Western World*, 202, 204, 255; Ogyu quoted pp. 200–201; Sugita Gempaku, "The Beginning of Dutch Studies in Japan," in Lu, *Documentary History*, pp. 264–266.

21. Tessa Morris-Suzuki, *A History of Japanese Economic Thought* (London: Routledge, 1989), p. 15; Ogyu quoted p. 10. Sansom, *Western World*, p. 197. By the early 1700s, a futures market for rice had been established in Osaka. See Jeffrey A. Bernstein, "Japanese Capitalism," in T. K. McCraw, ed., *Creating Modern Capitalism* (Cambridge, Mass.: Harvard University Press, 1997), p. 445.

22. Ogyu Sorai, "Spread of the Money Economy," in Lu, *Documentary History*, p. 229. Sansom, *Western World*, p. 235; Sugita quoted p. 234. Reischauer *Japan*, p. 83.

23. Ogyu Sorai, "Proposal for Employing Men of Talent," in Lu, *Documentary History*, pp. 251–254. Reischauer, *Japan*, p. 91.

24. Ihara Saikaku quoted in Morris-Suzuki, *History*, p. 11.

25. This is Reischauer's opinion (*Japan*, p. 101). I expect that the belief that "the first art for the masses" was the Dutch art of the Golden Age is more common (among those who give any thought to such matters), but it is worth noting that Simon Schama qualifies himself, stating that the Dutch was "the first mass consumers' art market in European history" (*Embarrassment*, p. 318). It would be interesting to know if he wrote this with Japan in mind. As it happens, the Dutch Golden Age and the *ukiyo* period were roughly contemporary.

26. Around 1800 the rate of literacy in Japan is estimated at 35 percent (Reischauer, *Japan*, p. 95). On *'t Amsterdamsch Hoerdom*, see Schama, *Embarrassment*, pp. 470–473. He characterizes its illustrations as "crude." Sansom, *Western World*, p. 217. Regarding the similarities between the art of the Dutch Golden

Age and Japanese *ukiyo-e,* compare the following statements. "'What other people,' wrote the nineteenth-century critic-politician Theophile Thore, 'has written its history in its art?' Unlike the art of Renaissance Italy, Dutch art, he thought, was so much the record of the here and now, of *la vie vivante,* anchored in a specific time and place. It was the record of 'the men and the matter, the sentiments and habits, the deeds and gestures of a whole nation.'" This is Schama (pp. 9–10), justifying using Dutch art as a source in cultural history. "The Ukiyo-e with all its limitations contains some of the true essence of Japanese art. It is, as has been observed by Professor Yashiro, an admirable record of the emotional life of the Japanese people, so eminently their *art intime* that it 'lays bare those charming weaknesses which one does not readily disclose to others.'" This is Sansom (*Western World,* p. 217) on "pictures of the fleeting, floating world." It would be wrong, Schama claims, to regard the Dutch Golden Age painting "as a sort of photography of their great seventeenth century," for underlying its seemingly descriptive realism was an image of reality, "a way of seeing," a philosophical conception which suggested "an acute sense of the mutable world," of "a state of organic flux, forever composing, decomposing and recomposing itself." This conception behind the canvas gave the Dutch art its "élasticité secrète," and made the artists focus on "the zenith before the fall; the moment of perfect ripeness before the decay" (*Embarrassment,* p. 11). Similarly, *ukiyo-e* was distinguished by "a profusion of genre paintings which portray faithfully and for the most part with only a faint idealistic tinge the common contemporary life in its many-colored aspects. This is the heyday of a realistic art which takes for its themes the streets, the theatres, the tea-houses, and the easy-going ladies or the fashionable actors who frequent them" (*Western World,* p. 192). And yet, behind this art was the idea of *ukiyo*—"a Buddhist expression which connoted first 'this world of pain,' with the derived sense of 'this transient, unreliable world.' Etymologically it thus meant 'this fleeting, floating world.'" The philosophy of *ukiyo-e* was captured in an eighteenth-century epigram: "Neither Kano nor Tosa / can paint it: / Main Street—Yoshiwara." Richard Lane, *Masters of Japanese Print* (London: Thames and Hudson, 1962), pp. 10, 7. And whereas Schama discerned "an embarrassed self-consciousness" behind the superabundance of Dutch art, Tessa Morris-Suzuki perceived "a certain sense of fragility and unease" in "the splendour of Tokugawa urban culture." Schama, *Embarrassment,* p. 8 and passim; Morris-Suzuki, *History,* p. 19.

27. Sansom, *Western World,* pp. 219, 222; Bakin's party is described, and the letter quoted, pp. 220–221.

28. The first of these recoinages took place in 1695, and, before 1868, there were eleven more of them. Morris-Suzuki, *History,* p. 19.

29. Kumazawa and Ogyu quoted in Morris-Suzuki, *History,* pp. 16–17, 20–21, 24. Sakuma Shozan, "The Eight-Point Program," in *Sources,* p. 98.

30. Morris-Suzuki, *History,* p. 14. Brown, *Nationalism,* p. 47. On the development of attitudes to Christianity in Japan, see, among others, Brown, *Nationalism,* pp. 42–46; Sansom, *Japan,* pp. 417–428; Sansom, *Western World,* pp. 115–133; and Lu, *Documentary History,* pp. 173, 187, 196–197.

31. Norma Field, *In the Realm of the Dying Emperor* (New York: Pantheon Books,

1991), p. 69, suggests "body politic" as the translation of the term, but this may not do justice to its modernity.

32. Aizawa Seishisai, *Shinron* [New Proposals] (1825), in *Sources,* pp. 88–95, 86–87.

33. The text of President Fillmore's letter to the emperor, which did not omit to mention the "powerful squadron" of Commodore Perry, may be found in, among other publications, Donald R. Bernard, *The Life and Times of John Manjiro* (New York: McGraw-Hill, 1992), pp. 160–162. Sakuma Shozan, *Reflections on My Errors (Seiken-roku),* in *Sources,* pp. 103–104.

34. Tsunoda Ryusaku et al., introduction to Fukuzawa Yukichi, in *Sources,* pp. 116–117. The incident with the peasant quoted in Sansom, *Western World,* p. 239. All the following appear in *Sources:* Fukuzawa Yukichi, excerpts from *Autobiography,* pp. 119, 127–128, 120–121, 124, 130, 118–119; Kido Koin, "The Voluntary Surrender of Feudal Domains" and "Observations on Returning from the West," pp. 141–142, 143–144, 145; Ito Hirobumi, "Speech on the Constitution," pp. 161–162 (the argument was fairly common; see Carol Gluck, *Japan's Modern Myths: Ideology in the Late Meiji Period* [Princeton, N.J.: Princeton University Press, 1985], p. 48); Tsunoda Ryusaku and Saigo Takamori, p. 150; Okubo Toshimichi, "Reasons for Opposing the Korean Expedition," pp. 153–155; Ito Hirobumi, "Speech on the Restoration" (1899), "Speech on the Constitution of 1889," and "Memorandum on Okubo's Views on Constitutional Government" (1873), pp. 171, 164, 159, 163.

35. The depiction of the Japanese *(Wa)* in the early—Han and Wei—Chinese records. See *Encyclopedia Britannica,* 11th ed., s.v. "Japan, Domestic History."

36. Okuma Shigenobu, "Conclusion to *Fifty Years of New Japan*" (1907–8), in *Sources,* pp. 191–192. Many of the Meiji nationalists were Westernizers. Carol Gluck writes, "It is a trivialization of their task to regard the ideologists [of the late Meiji period] as anti-Western, which the majority emphatically were not, or as apostles of a return to the past, which had little hold on most of them" (*Myths,* p. 20).

37. Ito Hirobumi, "Restoration," in *Sources,* pp. 164–165, 160–161, 162, 163–164. Itagaki Taisuke, "Address on Liberty," and Yamagata Aritomo, "Official Notice" on Military Conscription Ordinance, Imperial Precepts to Soldiers and Sailors (1882), in *Sources,* pp. 178, 180, 197–198, 198–199. Ito, "Restoration," pp. 171–172. Okuma Shigenobu, speech, "Citizenship in the New World," and speech of March 2, 1915, in *Sources,* pp. 191, 188–189.

6. Racing and Fighting

1. Guenther Stein, *Made in Japan* (London: Methuen, 1935), pp. 1–2 (emphasis added), 3–6, 167–170, 54, 62–63; 6. The title of this chapter is the Japanese term for competition, *kyoso,* which literally means "racing and fighting," invented during the early Meiji period specifically to apply to economic competition between nations. Productivity was spurred, no doubt, by the exhortations of Meiji leaders half a century earlier not to spend Sundays in "excess and dissipation": "Even if we now cause the people to run day and night, we shall not overtake the West in less than a few decades. If such is the case, how much longer will it take if

they waste a day each week?" From an 1875 speech by Kashiwabara Takaaki, quoted in Carol Gluck, *Japan's Modern Myths: Ideology in the Late Meiji Period* (Princeton, N.J.: Princeton University Press, 1985), p. 18.

2. Yamamoto Shichihei, "Whence the Economic Animal?" in *The Spirit of Japanese Capitalism and Other Essays,* trans. Lynn E. Riggs (New York: Madison Books [Library of Japan], 1992), pp. 200, 202–206; *Joei* Code, article 145, quoted p. 211.

3. Tessa Morris-Suzuki, *A History of Japanese Economic Thought* (London: Routledge, 1989), pp. 13–14; Dazai quoted p. 14; Baudeau, Kumazawa, Arai, and Kaiho quoted pp. 12, 17, 21–22, and 33–34. See also Tetsuo Najita, *Visions of Virtue in Tokugawa Japan: The Kaitokudo Merchant Academy of Osaka* (Chicago: University of Chicago Press, 1987).

4. The discussion of Suzuki Shosan relies on Yamamoto, *Spirit,* chap. 5, "Zen and the Economic Animal," pp. 75–90; dialogue p. 80.

5. Clifford Geertz, "Religion as a Cultural System," in *The Interpretation of Cultures* (New York: Basic Books, 1973), p. 104.

6. Yamamoto, *Spirit,* pp. 82 (original Japanese differs slightly from the translation), 84–85, 87, 75.

7. Ishida in Yamamoto, *Spirit,* pp. 69, 70. Bellah compares Ishida's concept of *shokubun* to Luther's *Beruf.* See Robert Bellah, *Tokugawa Religion: The Values of Pre-industrial Japan* (New York: Free Press, 1957), pp. 115, 123, 125, 164; Ishida Baigan, *Tohi Mondo,* quoted p. 158.

8. One could translate *Shingaku,* without changing the meaning, as "A Theory of Moral Sentiments." In his discussion of honesty Ishida uses the word *sokuin no jo,* which is literally translated as the emotion of "compassion"; but "compassion" does not seem to make sense in the context of the entire sentence. "Emotion" captures Ishida's meaning better, in my opinion. *Sekimon* refers to Ishida himself, consisting of the first character of his surname, which can be read *seki* and *mon,* which means "gate." See Yamamoto, *Spirit,* p. 92, fn., and p. 96. Herder, letter to Caroline Flachsland, January 9, 1773, in *Herders Briefwechsel mit Caroline Flachsland,* vol. 2 (Weimar: Verlag der Goethe-Gesellschaft, 1926–1928), p. 325. Ferdinand Tönnies, *Community and Society,* and Karl Marx "Economic and Philosophical Manuscripts of 1844." Ishida quoted in Yamamoto, *Spirit,* pp. 99, 107.

9. David J. Lu, *Japan: A Documentary History,* vol. 1 (New York: Sharpe, 1997), commentary to Sumitomo's "Precepts," p. 237; Sumitomo Masatomo, "Precepts" (ca. 1630), p. 239. Mitsui's *Observations* were composed sometime in the late 1720s and early 1730s, a couple of years before his death in 1737, and thus before Ishida Baigan articulated his views in *Tohi Mondo,* which appeared only in 1739 and had little resonance until the end of the eighteenth century. Mitsui Takahira Hachirouemon, "On Being a Good Merchant" (1726–1733), in Lu, *Documentary History,* pp. 229–231. Eamonn Fingleton, *Blindside: Why Japan Is Still on Track to Overtake the U.S. by the Year 2000* (Boston: Houghton Mifflin, 1995), pp. 27–29.

10. Sato quoted in Morris-Suzuki, *History,* pp. 31, 35, 37–38.

11. Sugiyama Chuhei, *Origins of Economic Thought in Modern Japan* (London:

Routledge, 1994), p. vi. David J. Lu, *Japan: A Documentary History,* vol. 2, *The Late Tokugawa Period to the Present* (New York: Sharp, 1997), p. 345; Fukuzawa Yukichi, *Encouragement of Learning,* chap. 5 (1874), 2:348. Dallas Finn, *Meiji Revisited: The Sites of Victorian Japan* (New York: Weatherhill, 1995), p. 118. G. B. Sansom, *The Western World and Japan* (New York: Alfred A. Knopf, 1950), p. 235. Wakayama in Sugiyama, *Origins,* p. 8. Inoue quoted in Byron K. Marshall, *Capitalism and Nationalism in Prewar Japan: The Ideology of the Business Elite, 1868–1941* (Stanford: Stanford University Press, 1967), pp. 15–16.

12. Okubo Toshimichi, "Opinion on Encouragement of Industries" (1874), in Lu, *Documentary History,* 2:321–322; Fukuzawa, *Encouragement of Learning,* pp. 347, 348, 347–350, and quoted in Sugiyama, *Origins,* pp. 51, 46, 45, 54 (emphasis added), 46. Sugiyama, *Origins,* p. 43.

13. All quotations from Fukuzawa in the preceding section are taken from Sugiyama, *Origins,* pp. 47–58.

14. Compare, for instance the 1885 *Datsu-a* (Good-bye Asia), in Lu, *Documentary History,* 2:351–353, to the already quoted *Jiji Shogen,* where he declares that "without [military] strength there cannot be wealth," and urges Japan to "help [the Chinese and Koreans] militarily." "We must strive," he says, "to protect them [from Western commercial encroachment] with force of arms and to lead them by cultural example, so that they too may enter the sphere of modern civilization. And, if there is no alternative, we may forcibly urge them to progress" (Sugiyama, *Origins,* pp. 51–52).

15. Marshall, *Prewar Japan,* pp. 47–48. Sugiyama, *Origins,* p. 12.

16. Marshall, *Prewar Japan,* p. 10; Shibusawa, Inoue, Fukuzawa, Nishimura, and editorial in *Oriental Economist,* quoted pp. 10–11, 48. Johannes Hirschmeier, *The Origins of Entrepreneurship in Meiji Japan* (Cambridge, Mass.: Harvard University Press, 1964), pp. 248–249; Thomas C. Smith, "Landlords' Sons in the Business Elite," *Economic Development and Cultural Change,* 9:1, pt. 2 (October 1960), 93–107. Joseph Ben-David, "Roles and Innovation in Medicine" and (with R. Collins) "Social Factors in the Origins of a New Science: The Case of Psychology," chaps. 1 and 2, in Gad Freudental, ed., *Scientific Growth* (Berkeley: University of California Press, 1991).

17. Finn, *Meiji,* p. 118. Yamamoto, *Spirit,* pp. 175–186; Shibusawa cited pp. 185, 186. Japan's success in following Shibusawa's vision and the West's continuing failure to comprehend it was demonstrated in another Paris exhibition more than a century later. When, in May 1986, the Japan Traditional Crafts Fair was held in Paris, a local newspaper ran its report on the exhibition under the headline "First Encounter with Japan." Relating this story and the long history of cultural exchanges between France and Japan, the organizer of the exhibition, Sakaiya Taichi, a longtime MITI official, asked: "With all this interchange with Japan, how could such a small exhibition be called a 'First Encounter with Japan'? This extraordinary billing was given the exhibition because it was perceived as shedding light not only on Japan's traditional crafts and performances but also on the effects of traditional ways on the modern industrially optimized society. For Europeans, it is almost impossible to connect the nation ruled by samurai with the incredible industrial might of today's Japan. For them Japan is a 'black

box' belching boatloads of high-quality industrial goods, a nation whose cultural forms are obscure and whose inhabitants have names they do not know. Why were the other countries of Asia and Africa unable to incorporate successfully European and American innovations into their societies while Japan was? The answer is that Japan has traditions that facilitate the embrace of foreign technology and systems and their digestion." For Sakaiya, Shibusawa's mandate has become a cultural trait. What was a conscious effort to guide an emerging modern economy is perceived today as a national idiosyncrasy, a historical predilection for flexibility and adaptability. Sakaiya Taichi, *What Is Japan? Contradictions and Transformations* (New York: Kodansha International, 1995), pp. 101–103.

18. Shibusawa Eiichi, "Reasons for Becoming a Businessman," in Lu, *Documentary History*, 2:354–356. Matsukata and his friend quoted in Marshall, *Prewar Japan*, pp. 41–42, 43.

19. Matsushita Konosuke, the founder of Matsushita Electric, tells of his visit to a temple community in 1932, a visit that inspired a new mission for his company and a way to justify profit making. Impressed with the fine buildings, the diligence of the workers, and the enthusiasm of the construction laborers who were donating their time, he asked himself why businesses go up and down while religion is steady and prosperous. The difference, he thought, was that religion, "bringing spiritual peace and enlightenment to people," is respected, while manufacturers, who do not serve the spirit, cannot depend and flourish on the support of the public. This attitude toward manufacturers, however, is valid only when they concentrate on making money. If manufacturers produce to satisfy not their own needs but the material needs of society, they perform a task of equal dignity to that of religion. He told his employees: "The mission of a manufacturer is to overcome poverty, to relieve society as a whole from the misery of poverty and bring it wealth. Business and production are not meant to enrich only the shops or the factories of the enterprise concerned, but all the rest of society as well. Possessing material comforts in no way guarantees happiness. Only spiritual wealth can bring true happiness. If that is correct, should business be concerned only with the material aspects of life and leave the care of the human spirit to religion or ethics? I do not think so. Businessmen too should be able to share in creating society that is spiritually rich and materially affluent." Matsushita Konosuke, *Not for Bread Alone: A Business Ethos, A Management Ethic* (Tokyo: PHP Institute, 1984), pp. 87–88.

20. Kaneko, Hara, Godai, Suzuki, Matsukata, and Morimura quoted in Marshall, *Prewar Japan*, pp. 42, 48, 36–37. In present-day Japan, moral principles are still more important than profits. In 1998, the time of the "Asian crisis," a thirty-seven-year old businessman described to a *New York Times* reporter his bankrupt business "as based not on contracts or prices but rather on traditional values." The business lost money for years because of the rise in the volume of competitive Chinese imports, but he did not take the cost-cutting steps that might have saved it: "What I kept thinking about was the employees. They depend on us. I just couldn't bring myself to dismiss the inefficient ones." Also still prevalent in Japan is the notion that the nation's interest supersedes all other interests. From the same *New York Times* report on reactions to Japan's economic turmoil in Omiya,

a small town two hundred miles southwest of Tokyo: "There is a broad agreement in Omiya that sweeping change is coming to create an economy based more on the concept of 'the strong gobble up the meat of the weak.' Indeed, many people favor it, saying that even if they themselves are consumed, economic Darwinism is in the interests of the nation. They say this even though Omiya could be a loser in a more open system." Nicholas D. Kristof, "Shops Closing, Japan Still Asks, 'What Crisis?'" *New York Times,* April 21, 1998. *Yubin Hochi* quoted in Yamamoto, *Spirit,* pp. 158–159. The discussion of Shibusawa relies on Marshall, *Prewar Japan,* pp. 30–50; his son quoted in Yamamoto, *Spirit,* p. 191. Stein, *Made in Japan,* pp. 32–33. For current data on the relatively narrow wage differentials in Japanese companies, see Koike Kazuo, *Understanding Industrial Relations in Modern Japan* (New York: St. Martin's Press, 1988), pp. 35–42.

21. Yamamoto, *Spirit,* p. 11 and passim. Soeda quoted in Marshall, *Prewar Japan,* p. 58.

22. Stein, *Made in Japan,* pp. 28–31; the song and rules quoted on pp. 66–69. Compare with Matsushita's business principles (articulated first in the 1930s): "1. National service through industry. 2. Fairness. 3. Harmony and cooperation. 4. Struggle for betterment. 5. Courtesy and humility. 6. Adjustment and assimilation. 7. Gratitude." And its business philosophy: "To recognize our responsibilities as industrialists, to foster progress, to promote the general welfare of society, and to devote ourselves to the further development of world culture. Progress and development can be realized only through the combined efforts and cooperation of each member of our Company. Each of us, therefore, shall keep this idea constantly in mind as we devote ourselves to the continuous improvement of our Company." Richard Pascale and Anthony Athos, who provide this translation in their 1981 business best-seller, *The Art of Japanese Management: Applications for American Executives* (New York: Simon and Schuster, 1981), also quote a Matsushita executive saying in 1980: "It seems silly to Westerners, but every morning at 8:00 A.M., all across Japan, there are 87,000 people reciting the code of values and singing together. It's like we are all a community" (pp. 50–51). By the 1990s, the reinforcement of this business philosophy in the face of growing doubts took many forms, including certain popular and widely read business *manga* (comics). One such *manga,* created by Hirokane Kenshi, centered on Shima Kosaku ("Japan's most famous salaryman," according to the *Mainichi Shimbun*), a section chief at Hatsushiba Electric Company, a thinly disguised Matsushita. In one episode he is transferred from the firm's Tokyo offices to a manufacturing plant in Kyoto. There we see a group of employees crying in unison: "One: Service to society!" and the caption explains that every morning starts with radio calisthenics and a recitation of the founder's principles. Shima makes the following observation: "The crew at the head office were generally critical of this recitation. The people here, however, are surprisingly cooperative, and take it very seriously." T. R. Reid, in his introduction to the English version of this *manga,* describes the current "clash" between the traditional and the new, more individualistic attitudes toward work: "In the spring of 1995, NHK's Sunday morning show *Keizai Scope* arranged a debate pitting two styles of salaryman against one another. In one corner was Hirokane, representing Section Chief

Shima and other earnest, hard-working *shigoto ningen*. In the other was Yamazaki Juzo, creator of the beloved "Hama-chan," the laid-back hero of the *manga* series *Diary of a Fishing Freak*. Hirokane presented the case for hard work, Yamazaki presented the case for going fishing. The moderator and the studio audience, comprising 50 male and female executives from major companies, were asked to choose the winner. The result was a landslide: these real-life salarymen and career women declared by more than a two to one margin that they would prefer to emulate Shima Kosaku, still the paradigm of the hard-working company man—and still Japan's most famous salaryman." T. R. Reid, "Section Chief Shima Kosaku," in Laura K. Silverman, ed., *Bringing Home the Sushi: An Inside Look at Japanese Business through Japanese Comics* (Atlanta: Mangajin, 1995), p. 114.

23. Iwasaki Yataro, "Articles of 1878" and letter of instructions to Mitsubishi employees (1876), in Lu, *Documentary History*, 2:357–358, 356–357. Tamura in Marshall, *Prewar Japan*, p. 58. The most important of the benefits, including lifelong employment, promotion by seniority, and family allowances, at first applied only to white-collar or supervisory personnel, but were extended to blue-collar workers by the 1920s; see Marshall, *Prewar Japan*, p. 70, fn.; Furukawa quoted p. 67.

24. Marshall, *Prewar Japan*, pp. 70–72, 66. See also Ronald P. Dore, *Flexible Rigidities: Industrial Policy and Structural Adjustment in the Japanese Economy, 1970–1980* (Stanford: Stanford University Press, 1986); Kamata Satoshi, *Japan in the Passing Lane: An Insider's Account of Life in a Japanese Auto Factory* (New York: Pantheon Books, 1982); James C. Abegglen, *The Strategy of Japanese Business* (Cambridge, Mass.: Ballinger, 1984), pp. 79–81; S. N. Eisenstadt, *Japanese Civilization: A Comparative View* (Chicago: University of Chicago Press, 1996), pp. 58–59.

25. Matsukata in Morris-Suzuki, *History*, p. 58. See also Haru Matsukata Reischauer, *Samurai and Silk: A Japanese and American Heritage* (Cambridge, Mass.: Harvard University Press, 1986). Eisenstadt, *Civilization*, pp. 54–57; Edward J. Lincoln, "The Showa Economic Experience," in Carol Gluck and Stephen R. Graubard, eds., *Showa: The Japan of Hirohito* (New York: W. W. Norton, 1992), pp. 199–202; Komine Takao, "The Role of Economic Planning in Japan," in Komiya Ryutaro et al., eds., *Industrial Policy of Japan* (Orlando, Fla: Academic Press, 1988), p. 328.

26. Stein, *Made in Japan*, p. 7. Marshall, *Prewar Japan*, pp. 27–28; Okuma Shigenobu (1897), p. 23. "The majority of the Meiji business class accepted not only the principle of restricted competition but also the view expressed by Shibusawa that it was the proper function of the government to enforce such restrictions. Again, as in the case of government management of economic enterprises, those in favor of government intervention used the argument that such intervention was justified by the backward condition of the Japanese economy and the need to meet the economic challenge of the West." Marshall, *Prewar Japan*, p. 27. According to Jeffrey Bernstein, the fear of *kato kyoso*, or "excessive competition," is often cited today as the basis for the "sanction and often the deliberate creation of cartels in Japan. By one count, in the mid-1960 there were over 1,000

cartels in operation, in roughly 20 percent of all manufacturing sectors, and 43 percent of all Japanese manufacturing output came from sectors involving some cartel activity." Jeffrey Bernstein, "Japanese Capitalism," in Thomas K. McCraw, ed., *Creating Modern Capitalism* (Cambridge, Mass.: Harvard University Press, 1997), pp. 478–479. On "excessive competition," see also Komiya Ryutaro, *The Japanese Economy: Trade, Industry, and Government* (Tokyo: Tokyo University Press, 1990), pp. 297–298; Bai Gao, *Economic Ideology and Japanese Industrial Policy: Developmentalism from 1931 to 1965* (Cambridge: Cambridge University Press, 1997), pp. 51–55.

27. Lawrence W. Chisolm, *Fenollosa: The Far East and American Culture* (New Haven: Yale University Press, 1963); Jan Fontein, "A Brief History of the Collections," in *Selected Masterpieces of Asian Art* (Tokyo: Museum of Fine Arts, Boston, 1992). Morris-Suzuki, *History*, pp. 46–48; student notes cited p. 47. Sugiyama, *Origins*, p. 64; Steele, McCosh, Campbell, and Fukuzawa quoted pp. 65–67, 69. Mori was assassinated in 1899.

28. Sugiyama, *Origins*, pp. 71, 74. The 1868 Charter Oath article stating, "Knowledge shall be sought for throughout the world so that the welfare of the empire may be promoted" is still a major tenet of the contemporary Japanese business ethos with its emphasis on the gathering of information and the management of information flows within the corporation. See Larry Kahaner, *Competitive Intelligence* (New York: Simon and Schuster, 1997), pp. 159–185; Eisenstadt, *Civilization*, p. 61; Ikujiro Nonaka and Hirotaka Takeuchi, *The Knowledge-Creating Company: How Japanese Companies Create the Dynamics of Innovation* (New York: Oxford University Press, 1995); W. Mark Fruin, *Knowledge Works: Managing Intellectual Capital at Toshiba* (New York: Oxford University Press, 1997).

29. Sugiyama, *Origins*, pp. 41–44, 62; Kanda, Taguchi, *Tokai Keizai Shinpo*, and Fukuzawa quoted pp. 3, 86–87, 87–88, 59; regarding Shibusawa, see Marshall, *Prewar Japan*, p. 34. Morris-Suzuki, *History*, p. 60. Oshima Sadamatsu, "On the Present Situation" (1891), quoted in Sugiyama, *Origins*, p. 12, and in Morris-Suzuki, *History*, p. 60. Compare to Sakakibara Eisuke, a top Ministry of Finance official, who reacted in a 1993 interview to American pressures for "reform": "If they [the Americans] start saying Japan should become the fifty-first of the United States we will resist. We can be partners without making our systems converge. We will retain our culture. We have integrity as a nation." Quoted in Christopher Wood, *The End of Japan Inc.* (New York: Simon and Schuster, 1994), p. 25. In his own book, Sakakibara wrote: "Calls for reform that lack a clear awareness of Japan's systemic realities have only led to a subservient Japanese pandering to frequent U.S. and European demands . . . It is about time we take stock of our situation, live our lives at our own pace, and form our policies accordingly." Sakakibara Eisuke, *Beyond Capitalism: The Japanese Model of Market Economics* (Lanham, Md.: University Press of America, 1993), p. 11.

30. This has not changed much in the intervening century. "The role of the economist in government or business is merely one of many examples of the differences between Japan's culture and human relations and their counterparts in countries with European traditions. In Japan, there is no profession of economist or statistician . . . [I]n order to affect economic policy even slightly . . . economists would

have needed to be able to speak the language used by bureaucrats and politicians and to cooperate closely with generalist administrators; few Japanese academic economists have been able to do this. Many academic economists are . . . too theoretical to be effective in government." Komiya, *Japanese Economy*, pp. 385–386.

31. "The Japanese, in spite of what their political leaders say at summit conferences about the glories of free enterprise in the Free World, and in spite of the fact that a British publisher with a new book about Adam Smith can expect to sell half the edition in Japan, have never really caught up with Adam Smith. They have never managed to bring themselves to believe in the invisible hand." Ronald Dore, *Taking Japan Seriously: A Confucian Perspective on Leading Economic Issues* (Stanford: Stanford University Press, 1987), p. 181.

32. Writing in 1986, Ronald Dore commented on observers at the time who were quick to interpret changes in the Japanese economy as a general trend toward individualism and a loss of the work ethic: "It is a debatable issue, about which we will know more when ten years have passed. But we already know more than we did ten years ago, when predictions about the eventual triumph of western individualism, the break-down of lifetime employment and all the other collective constraints on market mobility, were being made with even greater frequency and confidence than they are today." Dore, *Rigidities*, p. 249.

IV. The Economic Civilization

1. Characterization of Russia in Henry Adams, *The Education of Henry Adams: An Autobiography* (New York: Modern Library, 1996), p. 439.

2. Any attempt to *explain* such developments while focusing on the immediate context must necessarily result in the substitution of process for cause (to use Landes's phrase again), or in circular statements, and in the best of cases remain on the level of pure description, this time, in distinction to the "naturalistic" theories of economic growth, because of the very nature of the evidence considered. A preeminent (in many senses) example of such a predicament in the case of American economic history is the work of Alfred D. Chandler. A 1997 summary by Richard R. John of Chandler's main arguments, as well as his followers' additions and his critics' objections, while most appreciative, highlights the circularity of Chandler's reasoning. To choose but one of several examples, Chandler's book *The Visible Hand* (which John recognizes as a great work of history) "revolved around a deceptively simple question. How, Chandler asked, could the rise of the modern business enterprise in the United States [i.e., the characteristic American *organization* of big business] best be explained? To answer this question, Chandler surveyed the history of every industrial enterprise in the United States in 1917 that had assets of more than $20 million." Chandler's conclusion was that "new technologies and burgeoning markets were necessary but not sufficient preconditions for the rise of the modern business enterprise. Even more important was the establishment of an administrative hierarchy to coordinate the flow of resources through the firm. Lacking such a hierarchy, business leaders could never hope to realize the potential 'economies of speed' that modern technology made possible. Organization, in short—even more than technology and markets—was

the key." Richard R. John, "Elaborations, Revisions, Dissents: Alfred D. Chandler, Jr.'s, *The Visible Hand* after Twenty Years," *Business History Review*, 71 (Summer 1997), 151–200; quotations pp. 153, 155. In other words, it happened because it happened. The organization of the modern business enterprise was the key to its rise. The focus on "preconditions" (rather than "causes") reveals the assumption that the development to be "explained" is natural. The project is akin to looking for the origin of life in the anatomy of an organism.

3. "Capitalism came in the first ships," in the words of Carl N. Degler, *Out of Our Past: The Forces That Shaped Modern America* (New York: Harper, 1959), p. 1, quoted in Thomas K. McCraw, "American Capitalism," in Thomas K. McCraw, ed., *Creating Modern Capitalism* (Cambridge, Mass.: Harvard University Press, 1997), p. 303. McCraw states: "No nation has been more market-oriented in its origin and subsequent history than the United States of America."

4. "As modern business enterprise acquired functions hitherto carried out by the market, it became the most powerful institution in the American economy and its managers the most influential group of economic decision makers." Alfred D. Chandler, *The Visible Hand: The Managerial Revolution in American Business* (Cambridge, Mass.: Harvard University Press, 1977), p. 1. See also Olivier Zunz, *Making America Corporate: 1870–1920* (Chicago: University of Chicago Press, 1990). In 1990, corporations accounted for 19 percent of all non-farm businesses and for 90 percent of their sales and receipts. Some seven thousand corporations (with assets of more than $250 million or more) accounted for 51 percent of the total sales and receipts for all businesses. See Carl Kaysen, ed., *The American Corporation Today* (New York: Oxford University Press, 1996), pp. 5, 22. Alfred D. Chandler, *Strategy and Structure: Chapters in the History of the American Industrial Enterprise* (Cambridge, Mass.: MIT Press, 1962); Alfred D. Chandler, "The United States: Competitive Managerial Capitalism," in *Scale and Scope: The Dynamics of Industrial Capitalism* (Cambridge, Mass.: Harvard University Press, 1990); Alfred D. Chandler, "The United States: Engines of Economic Growth in the Capital-Intensive and Knowledge-Intensive Industries," in Alfred D. Chandler, Franco Amatori, and Takashi Hikino, eds., *Big Business and the Wealth of Nations* (New York: Cambridge University Press, 1997); Richard S. Tedlow, *New and Improved: The Story of Mass Marketing in America* (Boston: Harvard Business School Press, 1996); Glenn Porter, *The Rise of Big Business: 1860–1920* (Arlington Heights, Ill.: Harlan Davidson, 1992).

5. Greenfeld, *Nationalism,* pp. 460–472, 564–565, fn. 119.

7. Searching for the American System

1. First Charter of Virginia, April 10, 1606, in *Annals of America,* vol. 1, *1493–1754* (Chicago: Encyclopaedia Britannica, 1976), pp. 15–16.

2. Richard Hakluyt (alternatively attributed to Sir John Popham), "On the Value of Colonies to England" (1607), in *Annals,* 1:18–20: "Where colonies are founded for a public-weal," wrote Hakluyt, "they may continue in better obedience and become more industrious than when private men are absolute backers of the voyage. Men of better behavior and quality will engage themselves in a public service,

which carries more reputation with it, than a private, which is for the most part ignominous in the end, because it is presumed to aim at a [private] profit and is subject to rivalry, fraud, and envy, and when it is at the greatest height of fortune can hardly be tolerated because of the jealousy of the state." William Symonds, sermon preached at "White-Chappel," London, April 25, 1609, in *Annals*, 1:33, 32; John Smith, "A Description of New England" (1616), pp. 36–39; Francis Higginson, "On the Riches of New England" (1629), pp. 95–99. Edward Johnson, *History of New England, or Wonder-Working Providence of Sions Saviour, 1628–1652*, ed. J. Franklin Jameson (New York: Scribner, 1952), pp. 209–210.

3. John Winthrop, "A Modell of Christian Charity" (1630), Tompson, "Crisis," in *Annals*, 1:109–115, 245. *The Colonial Laws of Massachusetts* (Boston, 1887), p. 5. Cotton Mather, *A Christian at His Calling*, 2nd Discourse ("Directing a Christian in his Personal Calling," 1701), in *Annals*, 1:319–324.

4. Benjamin Franklin, "Advice to a Young Tradesman" (1748), *Annals*, 1:479–480. Mather, *Christian*, pp. 320–321. It is true that, as any reader of Weber will remember, Franklin also advocates frugality, but this surely cannot be regarded as honest advice, and is mentioned rather out of loyalty to the canons of the genre, or out of unwillingness to sacrifice, for the sole purpose of utility, good literary material. As we are told by, among others, Daniel Bell, in *Cultural Contradictions of Capitalism* (New York: Basic Books, 1978), where the homilies of Poor Richard are characterized as "partly cunning, and perhaps even deceit," "in personal life [he] was a *bon viveur*" (pp. xix, 58). He knew very well that frugality, unless understood as abstention from willful and needless prodigality, had little to do with economic success. William Bollan, *Publications of the Colonial Society of Massachusetts*, vol. 6, in *Annals*, 1:454–457.

5. Benjamin Franklin, "Observations Concerning the Increase of Mankind, Peopling of Countries, etc.," in *Annals*, 1:489–493. There can be no doubt that, while making this argument, Franklin wrote in good faith: he attached a somewhat exaggerated value to being English at this point, holding, for example, that, given the abundant (and, in England, expendable) supply of Englishmen to populate America, there was no justification for allowing lesser breeds of men, such as Germans, to settle there. As there was no justification, he confined his argument to a rhetorical question: "Why should the Palatine boors be suffered to swarm into our settlements and, by herding together, establish their language and manners to the exclusion of ours? Why should Pennsylvania, founded by the English, become a colony of *aliens*, who will shortly be so numerous as to germanize us instead of us anglifying them, and will never adopt our language or customs any more than they can acquire our complexion?" This led Franklin to a thought that was still more surprising, to say the least, in so enlightened a character. "The number of purely white people in the world is proportionally very small," he proposed. "All Africa is black or tawny; Asia chiefly tawny; America (exclusive of the newcomers), wholly so. And in Europe, the Spaniards, Italians, French, Russians, and Swedes are generally of what we call a swarthy complexion; as are the Germans also, the Saxons only excepted, who, with the English, make the principal body of white people on the face of the earth. I could wish their numbers were increased. And while we are, as I may call it, scouring our planet by clearing

America of woods, and so making this side of our globe reflect a brighter light to the eyes of inhabitants in Mars or Venus, why should we, in the sight of superior beings, darken its people? Why increase the sons of Africa by planting them in America, where we have so fair an opportunity, by excluding all blacks and tawnies, of increasing the lovely white and red? But perhaps I am partial to the complexion of my country, for such kind of partiality is natural to mankind." Joseph Dorfman, *The Economic Mind in American Civilization, 1606–1865* (New York: Viking, 1946), 1:186–187, 188–190; Franklin, letter to John Ross, May 14, 1768, quoted p. 186; letter to Joshua Babcock, January 13, 1772; letter to Samuel Cooper, April 27, 1769, "Positions to be Examined . . . ," quoted pp. 193, 192; "A Conversation . . . on . . . Slavery" (1770), discussed p. 194; "Information to those who would remove to America," quoted in James Oliver Robertson, *America's Business* (New York: Hill and Wang, 1985). Charles F. Dunbar, "Economic Science in America, 1776–1876," *North American Review*, 122 (January 1876), 129–130.

6. Washington and other contemporary sources quoted in John C. Miller, *Alexander Hamilton: Portrait in Paradox* (New York: Harper, 1959), pp. 279–281. The last quotation is from Hamilton. Surveying probate inventories in the thirteen colonies in 1774, Alice Jones concluded, "Americans of 1774 had attained substantial wealth which compared favorably with that of 'ordinary people' in England and Europe and, on average, may have not been far behind that of England even when the wealth of the lords and barons is included." Alice H. Jones, *Wealth of a Nation to Be: The American Colonies on the Eve of the Revolution* (New York: Columbia University Press, 1980), p. 341.

7. Robertson, *America's Business*, pp. 23–28, 30; J. Hector St. John de Crevecoeur, *Letters from an American Farmer* (1782; New York: Penguin American Library, 1981), p. 67. Regarding Franklin, see Dorfman, *Mind*, p. 179. Miller, *Portrait*, p. 283. Regarding diversification: "His own storehouse no more monopolized the merchant's attention than the plow did the farmer's or the last, the cobbler's. Everyone dabbled in a variety of ventures, trading, lending, going on shares with partners in mills, forges, glass-, candle-, and brickmaking, all on the chance of some greater gain. The speculative use of capital was the prevailing feature of colonial life." Oscar Handlin and Mary F. Handlin, *The Wealth of the American People: A History of American Affluence* (New York: McGraw-Hill, 1975), p. 24. Landes writes: "New England and the middle colonies of Pennsylvania and New Jersey became the 'industrial heartlands' of the new nation. Ironmaking got its start in the 1640s (bog iron on the Saugus [at Lynn] in Massachusetts), only two decades after the Pilgrims' landing at Plymouth. By the time of the Revolution (1770s), some two hundred iron forges were in operation in Britain's American colonies, and the annual make was some 30,000 tons. Only Britain, France, Sweden, and Russia made more. Along with smelting went refining, hammering, cutting, slitting, rolling, and the sundry other operations that turn iron into tools and objects. Inevitably, the demand for British metallurgical products fell sharply." David Landes, *The Wealth and Poverty of Nations* (New York: W. W. Norton, 1998), p. 298. The mood, seen by contemporaries as "delirium of speculation" and first inspired by the founding of the Bank of the United States (Miller,

Portrait, p. 270), was two hundred years later characterized by Federal Reserve chairman Alan Greenspan as "irrational exuberance."

8. Madison in Miller, *Portrait,* p. 240; all quotations and characterizations regarding Duer and Hamilton, pp. 244–246, 270–271. Essentially, Hamilton's bold action was not unlike the much-talked-about 207 years later $3.6 billion bailout of the Long-Term Capital Management (LTCM) hedge fund by the chairman of the Federal Reserve Board, acting through private investment firms. Of course, Chairman Greenspan's laissez-faire economic ideas could not have been more different from the openly dirigist notions of America's Colbert, but it is doubtful that, when push came to shove, these ideas had more effect on his actions than they did on those of the first secretary of the U.S. Treasury, who dismissed them as "reveries" of "incorrigible theorists."

9. John Woolman, "A Plea for the Poor" (1763), *Annals of America,* vol. 2, *1755–1783: Resistance and Revolution* (Chicago: Encyclopaedia Britannica, 1976), p. 78. Woolman was a very unusual case, for he was a born businessman who resisted his obvious "calling": his moral position, a result of independent reflection, did not, as is common, reinforce what he himself recognized as his "natural inclination for merchandizing," but caused him to suppress it forcibly. He was a Quaker "of a middle station between riches and poverty," and, as a member of the Council of Ministers and Elders of the Annual Meeting of Philadelphia, played an important role in the Quaker community, acting, at different times, as a schoolteacher, surveyor, notary, executor of estates, accountant, and scribe. He chose as his particular business the trade of a tailor "with a little shopkeeping on the side," hoping that this would not make him too rich, but it did, even though he did his best to dissuade his customers from buying what they did not absolutely need and could not afford with ready cash. He tried to downsize his operations and frequently closed shop to go on prolonged travels in New England, the South, the West Indies, and even England, but it was all to no avail. Finally, to prevent his wealth from accumulating, he gave up shopkeeping altogether. Dorfman, *Mind,* pp. 196–204. He was perhaps the earliest native precursor of the late twentieth-century anti-"Affluenza" advocates.

10. Miller, *Portrait,* pp. 225–226, 289, including quotations from Hamilton and contemporaries. Alexander Hamilton, "First Report on the Public Credit" and "Report on the Public Credit," in *Annals of America,* vol. 3, *Organizing the Nation: 1784–1796* (Chicago: Encyclopaedia Britannica, 1976), pp. 407–415, 409, 408, 413–414; the epithets at the end of the section are Jefferson's, *Annals,* 3:420.

11. Alexander Hamilton as "Publius," letter of October 19, 1778, to the *New-York Journal,* in *Annals,* 2:509. Miller, *Portrait,* pp. 237, 270, 243–244, 253, including contemporaries, Hamilton's views, and Talleyrand. Jefferson, "Against the Bank," in *Annals,* 3:450; Madison quoted in Miller, *Portrait,* p. 264. Jefferson's argument is very similar to one regarding the meaning of an impeachable offense in the case of a president, specifically the claim that perjury cannot constitute such an offense because the phrase "Treason, Bribery, or other high Crimes and Misdemeanors" makes no mention of it.

12. Miller, *Portrait,* pp. 276–277; contemporary source quoted p. 268.

13. Miller, *Portrait*, pp. 289, 284. On the popularity of Adam Smith, see Joseph Dorfman, *The Economic Mind in American Civilization*, vol. 2, *From Independence to Civil War* (New York: Viking, 1946), p. 512. Hamilton, "Report on Manufactures," in *Annals*, 3:459–472. Hamilton's contemporary Tench Coxe also stressed machinery.

14. Contemporary rhyme quoted in Robert V. Remini, *Henry Clay, Statesman for the Union* (New York: W. W. Norton, 1991), p. 41. Miller, *Portrait*, p. 311; Jefferson (1785), Representative from Virginia William Giles, one of Hamilton's most vocal opponents in Congress, and other contemporary sources quoted pp. 295, 312.

15. John Taylor "of Carolina," quoted in Miller, *Portrait*, p. 311. Jefferson, *Notes on the State of Virginia*, in *The Complete Jefferson*, ed. Saul K. Padover (New York: Duell, Sloan and Pierce, 1943), p. 678; letter to John Jay, August 23, 1785, in *The Papers of Thomas Jefferson*, ed. J. P. Boyd (Princeton: Princeton University Press, 1953), 8:426. Dorfman, *Mind* 2:514, 435. Jefferson, *Notes*, "Ideas on Finance," in *Complete*, pp. 679, 364. Fisher Ames quoted in Miller, *Portrait*, p. 316; see also pp. 311–321. Dorfman, *Mind* 2:440. Jefferson, letter to Benjamin Austin, January 9, 1816, in *Annals of America*, vol. 4, *1797–1820: Domestic Expansion and Foreign Entanglements* (Chicago: Encyclopaedia Britannica, 1976), pp. 412–413. See Alfred E. Eckes, *Opening America's Market: U.S. Foreign Trade Policy since 1776* (Chapel Hill: University of North Carolina Press, 1995), pp. 19–20, for opinions similar to Jefferson's regarding manufacturing and trade policies by Presidents Madison, Adams, Monroe, and Jackson. The triumph of manufacturing and technology, however, ensured that the vocal resistance to industrialization continued unabated. In 1833 Thomas Mann wrote in "Picture of a Factory Village":

> For liberty our fathers fought
> Which with their blood, they dearly bought,
> The factory System sets at naught.
> A slave at morn, a slave at eve,
> It doth my inmost feelings grieve;
> The blood runs chilly from my heart,
> To see fair Liberty depart;
> And leave the wretches in their chains,
> To feed a vampire from their veins.
> Great Britain's curse is now our own;
> Enough to damn a King and Throne.

Quoted in Brooke Hindle and Steven Lubar, *Engines of Change: The American Industrial Revolution, 1790—1860* (Washington, D.C.: Smithsonian Institution Press, 1986), p. 92. Also see John F. Kasson, *Civilizing the Machine: Technology and Republican Values in America, 1776–1900* (New York: Penguin Books, 1977), pp. 129, 130.

16. According to Dorfman, *Mind*, 2:582, denouncing protection "root and branch."

17. Parish in Dorfman, *Mind*, 1:345. "Statesman for the Union" is the subtitle of Remini, *Clay*; on Clay, see p. 59; quotation from Clay's speech p. 60; "Josiah

Quincy reportedly said that Henry Clay 'was the man whose influence and power more than that of any other produced the War of 1812 between the United States and Great Britain'" (p. 91).

18. Robertson, *Business*, pp. 93, 95. According to Landes: "In 1788, Philadelphia's Fourth of July parade featured a hand-powered cotton carding machine and an eighty-spindle jenny—symbols of a pre-industrial (pre-power) economic independence. Twenty years later, the young United States was powering almost 100,000 cotton spindles; between 1810 and 1820 the number tripled, and in the next decade more than tripled again. So, by 1831, the industry counted 1.2 million spindles and 33,500 looms, most of them power-driven by piedmont streams from New Hampshire in the North to Maryland in the south" (*Wealth*, p. 300). The first "working spinning machines" were, apparently, installed in 1790 by Samuel Slater in Providence, Rhode Island. Landes, *Wealth*, p. 299. Robertson, *Business*, pp. 70–76; contemporary opinion quoted p. 73. See also Oscar Handlin and Mary Handlin, "Origins of the American Business Corporation," *Journal of Economic History*, 5 (May 1945), pp. 1–23; Thomas K. McCraw, "The Evolution of the Corporation in the United States," in John R. Meyer and James M. Gustafson, eds., *The U.S. Business Corporation: An Institution in Transition* (Cambridge, Mass. Ballinger, 1988), pp. 1–20.

19. Henry Clay, speech of March 26, 1810, quoted in Remini, *Clay*, pp. 61–62. David Humphreys, "A Poem on the Industry of the United States of America," in Michael B. Folsom and S. D. Lubar, eds., *The Philosophy of Manufactures: Early Debates over Industrialization in the United States* (Cambridge, Mass.: MIT Press, 1982) pp. 129, 136–137; on Humphreys, see Dorfman, *Mind*, 1:327–328. Also see Robert F. Dalzell, Jr., *Enterprising Elite: The Boston Associates and the World They Made* (Cambridge, Mass.: Harvard University Press, 1987); Margaret Crawford, *Building the Workingman's Paradise: The Design of American Company Towns* (London: Verso, 1995); Philip Scranton, *Proprietary Capitalism: The Textile Manufacture at Philadelphia, 1800–1885* (Cambridge: Cambridge University Press, 1983). While "some features of a factory organization existed at Humphreysville," the Boston Manufacturing Company "erected the first modern factory in America. It differed from previous establishments of equal size, either here or abroad, in performing all operations of cloth-making by power at a central plant . . . [T]he commercial, technical, and operative elements of a factory were brought together in accordance with an intelligent plan and so coordinated as to make a more efficient producing unit than had hitherto existed in this country . . . The idea of the factory, as we know it, was conceived and demonstrated so that its application at other places and to other industries was a mere matter of adjustment." Victor S. Clark, *History of Manufactures in the United States*, vol. 1, *1607–1860* (New York: McGraw-Hill, 1929), pp. 453, 450. On the Lowell mills, see Hindle and Lubar, *Engines*, pp. 200–201. According to Charles Dickens, who in 1842 visited Lowell's factories ("each of which belongs to what we should term a Company of Proprietors, but what they call in America a Corporation"), "no fewer than nine-hundred and seventy-eight of these girls were depositors in the Lowell Savings Bank; the amount of whose joint savings was estimated at $100,000." Dickens did not include this fact among those he thought "will star-

tle a large class of readers on this side of the Atlantic"—the existence of a joint-stock piano in many of the boarding houses; that nearly all the girls subscribed to the circulating libraries; and that they established and wrote for a periodical, the *Lowell Offering*. Charles Dickens, *American Notes and Pictures from Italy* (Oxford: Oxford University Press, 1957), p. 68. On the organization of work in Lowell, see Robertson, *Business,* pp. 99–105. The comparison with Japan is natural; see Landes, *Wealth,* p. 300, note (Landes argues that "hours were long, but shorter for example than in Japanese mills at the same stage"). As in Japan later on (see Chapter 6), work regulations went far beyond establishing discipline and accountability. As Hindle and Lubar put it in their discussion of the 1816 Springfield Armory, "Managers at the armories, like those at other factories, believed that careful regulation of the work force would instill values conducive to the well-being of the country." Hindle and Lubar, *Engines,* p. 233. John Greenleaf Whittier, "The City of a Day" (1845), in Folsom and Lubar, *Philosophy,* pp. 422–426.

20. On bridges and turnpikes, including quotations, see Robertson, *Business,* pp. 77–78, 78–79, 80–82; Dorfman, *Mind,* 1:375–376. Quotations on railroads from Walter E. Weyl, *The New Democracy: An Essay on Certain Political and Economic Tendencies in the United States* (New York: Macmillan, 1913), p. 28. Alfred D. Chandler, "The Railroads: Pioneers in Modern Corporate Management," *Business History Review,* 39 (Spring 1965), 16–40; "Henry Varnum Poor: Business Analyst," *Explorations in Entrepreneurial History,* May 15, 1950, pp. 180–202. Daniel Webster, speech on the opening of the Northern Railroad to Grafton, New Hampshire, August 28, 1847, in Folsom and Lubar, *Philosophy,* pp. 438–440. "A critical fact in the world of 1801 was that nothing moved faster than the speed of a horse . . . But only sixty years later, Americans could move bulky items in great quantity farther in an hour than Americans of 1801 could do in a day, whether by land (twenty-five miles per hour on railroads) or water (ten miles an hour upstream on a steamboat)." Stephen E. Ambrose, *Undaunted Courage: Meriwether Lewis, Thomas Jefferson, and the Opening of the American West* (New York: Touchstone, 1997), pp. 52, 54.

21. On Calhoun and changes of sentiment on protection, see Dorfman, *Mind,* 1:362, 362–383. Hans Kohn, *American Nationalism: An Interpretive Essay* (New York: Collier, 1961), p. 37. Henry Clay, 1824 speech quoted in Dorfman, *Mind,* 1:390. Remini, *Clay,* pp. 138–139. Also see Eckes, *Opening,* pp. 17ff.

22. Again, as in the case of the first Bank of the United States, the opponents of the proposed economic measures used the Constitution as a shield, though this time it was a representative of the "commercial interest" in Massachusetts, rather than of the "agrarian interest" in Virginia, who pointed out the obvious (to him, at least) disapproval of the newfangled ways of moneymaking the text was intended to convey. Ezekiel Whitman "thought it strange that Congress should have a standing Committee on Manufactures, for the general government was not constituted with a view to manufactures. The Constitution grants no specific delegation of power for the object. Hitherto we have been content to do what the Constitution explicitly authorized Congress to do—namely, to regulate commerce." Dorfman, *Mind,* 1:388.

23. Remini, *Clay,* pp. 225, 229. Clay, speech in Congress, March 30–31, 1824, *An-*

nals of America, vol. 5, *1821–1832: Steps Toward Equalitarianism,* pp. 114–118. Remini, *Clay,* pp. 230–232; Clay quoted p. 232. Dorfman, *Mind,* 2:596; 1:92, 392, 393. Editorial in *Georgia Courier* (Augusta), June 21, 1827, in *Annals* 5:226–227. Woodson in Dorfman, *Mind,* 2:574.

24. Hindle and Lubar, *Engines,* pp. 59–73. An English observer, quoted in Robertson, *Business,* p. 97, wrote late in the eighteenth century: "It is not enough that a few, or even a greater number of people, understand manufactures; the spirit of manufacturing must become the general spirit of the nation, and be incorporated, as it were, into their very essence. Knowledge may be soon acquired; but it requires a long time before the personal, and still longer time before national habits are formed." Daniel Webster, speech on the opening of the Northern Railroad to Lebanon, N.H., November 17, 1847, and Ralph Waldo Emerson, "Several Opinions on 'Wealth'" (1847, 1856, 1860), in Folsom and Lubar, *Philosophy,* pp. 445–446, 447–462.

25. By the 1940s the term had acquired a third meaning, "the American System of free enterprise and limited government" going full circle to denote a national economic policy and a system of values, albeit one dedicated to "free markets" and "free trade." Francis X. Sutton et al., *The American Business Creed* (Cambridge, Mass.: Harvard University Press, 1956); Eckes, *Opening,* pp. 278–289.

26. Robertson, *Business,* pp. 111–119 ("Samuel Colt and the American System"); the report of the Committee of the Ordnance Board quoted pp. 115–118. See also Hindle and Lubar, *Engines,* pp. 218–235, 259–260. For the full text of the Ordnance Board report and other similar reports, see Nathan Rosenberg, ed., *The American System of Manufactures: The Report of the Committee on the Machinery of the United States, 1855, and the Special Reports of George Wallis and Joseph Witworth, 1854* (Edinburgh: Edinburgh University Press, 1969).

8. The Thrust

1. Henry Adams, *The Education of Henry Adams: An Autobiography* (New York: Modern Library, 1996), p. 235; Gladstone (1878), quoted in Hans Kohn, *American Nationalism: An Interpretive Essay* (New York: Collier, 1961), p. 49.

2. Thomas C. Cochran and William Miller, *The Age of Enterprise: A Social History of Industrial America* (1942; New York: Harper, 1961), pp. 131, 136. Also see J. F. Normano, *The Spirit of American Economics* (London: Deanis Dobson, 1943), pp. 117, 118; Peter Temin, *Causal Factors in American Economic Growth in the Nineteenth Century* (London: Macmillan, 1975); Nathan Rosenberg, *Technology and American Economic Growth* (New York: Harper & Row, 1972); Thomas Weiss and Donald Schaefer, eds., *American Economic Development in Historical Perspective* (Stanford: Stanford University Press, 1994).

3. James Oliver Robertson, *America's Business* (New York: Hill and Wang, 1985), p. 124. Adams, *Education,* p. 238. Edward Chase Kirkland, *Dream and Thought in the Business Community, 1860–1900* (1956; Chicago: Elephant Paperbacks, 1990), pp. 3–5.

4. "The element of 'bigness' was just entering American economy—the mass movement," writes Normano, *Spirit,* p. 118.

5. Chicago Conference and Foulke in Ari Hoogenboom and Olive Hoogenboom,

eds., *The Gilded Age* (Englewood Cliffs, N.J.: Prentice-Hall, 1967), pp. 40–41 (a collection of eyewitness accounts). Cochran and Miller, *Enterprise,* pp. 52–53. Daniel Webster in Michael B. Folsom and S. D. Lubar, eds., *The Philosophy of Manufactures* (Cambridge, Mass.: MIT Press, 1982), pp. 444–445. Channing and Emerson quoted in Cochran and Miller, *Enterprise,* p. 68.

6. Cochran and Miller, *Enterprise,* pp. 82–83 (railroads), 79 (effect on other industries), 58, 77, 113 (youth of American industry). Robertson, *Business,* p. 126, including quotations from Alfred D. Chandler, "The Railroads." See also Chandler, *Strategy and Structure* (Cambridge, Mass.: MIT Press, 1962), pp. 20–24; and *The Visible Hand* (Cambridge, Mass.: Harvard University Press, 1977), pp. 81–121. Normano, *Spirit,* p. 117. Adams, *Education,* pp. 234–235.

7. John Tipple, "The Robber Baron in the Gilded Age: Entrepreneur or Iconoclast?" in H. Wayne Morgan, ed., *The Gilded Age: A Reappraisal* (Syracuse, N.Y.: Syracuse University Press, 1963), p. 16. Charles F. Adams, Jr., and Henry Adams, *Chapters of the Erie and Other Essays* (Boston, 1871), p. 135. Perhaps equally important was the training of the work force that the war offered. Robertson (*Business,* p. 135) thinks it was more important: "The experience of large-scale national organization was the Civil War's contribution to the big-business revolution. The experiences businessmen had in financing the war, in producing goods for it, in collecting, transporting, and distributing goods were used, applied, and transformed in creating big businesses after the war was over. But more important was the experience of millions—more than ten percent of the population—in the mass armies of the Civil War. In those armies, for the first time young Americans had the experience of being regimented to work, move, fight, eat, and sleep in company with and in coordination with thousands of others. Six hundred thousand young men died . . . And millions carried their experiences home with them—the experiences of regimentation, mass life, and mass work."

8. H. Wayne Morgan, "An Age in Need of Reassessment: A View Beforehand," in Morgan, *Reappraisal,* p. 7. Also see Cochran and Miller, *Enterprise,* pp. 92–106; Thomas K. McCraw, "American Capitalism," in Thomas K. McCraw, ed., *Creating Modern Capitalism* (Cambridge, Mass.: Harvard University Press, 1997), pp. 318–320.

9. "What in earlier and more halcyon days had been attributed to the benign operation of the law of competition had been, in most instances, an absence of competition," writes Tipple ("Robber," p. 27). "Before the Civil War, competition was virtually dormant in many parts of the United States largely because of intervening geographical factors, and where it did exist, it usually operated on a local rather than a national scale, cushioning a large portion of the economy from the hardships of rigorous competition . . . These imperfections of competition in the ante-bellum period, however, tended to be eliminated by tremendous postwar advances in transportation and communication. Business rivalry also was intensified by the application of new technology to industry and nationalized by the substitution of the big interstate corporation for smaller local individual and partnership enterprises. The immediate outcome was competition with a vengeance and the inauguration of a species of commercial warfare of a magnitude and violence unheralded in economic history."

10. Cochran and Miller, *Enterprise,* p. 139. J. P. Morgan quoted in Tipple, "Robber," p. 26. FDR quoted in Normano, *Spirit,* p. 193. Henry D. Lloyd, *The Independent,* March 4, 1897, in Hoogenboom and Hoogenboom, *Gilded Age,* p. 33. "An early muckraker," Lloyd believed that the race for wealth was a natural national sport and that all Americans, indeed, strove to win in it. This, for him, was the essence of the national competitive spirit. "The Americans are a competitive people," he wrote in another attack on the "Oil Combination," which was the main object of his critical attention. "They are devoted to business, making money, developing the resources of the country; and they are a chivalrous and generous people, always rejoicing in the victories of those runners of the race for wealth who have won the right to wear the crown that all were striving for. Why is it that the success of the group of men who have . . . in the oil business achieved the greatest fortunes that have ever, in the history of commerce, been got in one generation has excited from the beginning till now without cessation an unbroken chorus of protests?" (pp. 33–34).

11. Josephson himself borrowed the nomenclature from an 1880 Kansas anti-monopoly pamphlet; Matthew Josephson, *The Robber Barons* (San Diego: Harcourt Brace & Company, 1962), p. vi. On the scale of new philanthropy, see Walter P. Metzger, *Academic Freedom in the Age of the University* (New York: Columbia University Press, 1961), p. 140. Millers' president and Rockefeller in Cochran and Miller, *Enterprise,* pp. 140, 143, 144. Tarbell in Kirkland, *Dream,* p. 38. Cochran and Miller, *Enterprise,* p. 116; Robertson, *Business,* pp. 136–137. J. T. Flynn, *God's Gold: The Story of Rockefeller and His Times* (New York: Harcourt Brace & Co., 1940), p. 201.

12. Carnegie from B. J. Hendrick, *The Life of Andrew Carnegie,* quoted in Kirkland, *Dream,* pp. 9–10. Carnegie, *Autobiography* and *Empire of Business,* quoted in Edward C. Kirkland, *Business in the Gilded Age* (Madison: University of Wisconsin Press, 1952), pp. 57–58, 49, 58, 51. Andrew Carnegie, *Triumphant Democracy or Fifty Years' March of the Republic* (1885; Garden City, N.Y.: Doubleday, Doran & Co, 1933), dedication, pp. vii–viii.

13. Kirkland, *Dream,* pp. 29–32, 33 (businessmen's taste in architecture); Perkins, John Bascom (president of the University of Wisconsin), J. E. Caldwell (*Recollections of a Life Time* [Nashville: Baird-Ward Press, 1923]), A. S. Hewitt ("Liberty, Learning, and Property") and Vanderbilt quoted pp. 48, 46, 102, 85. Adams, *Education,* p. 238. Metzger, *Freedom,* p. 144.

14. Francis, "The Claims of Business Education to a Place in Our Public Schools," quoted in Kirkland, *Dream,* p. 59. Godkin, Carnegie in Kirkland, *Business,* p. 35. Cochran and Miller, *Enterprise,* p. 143; Robertson, *Business,* p. 164. Walter E. Weyl, *The New Democracy* (New York: Macmillan, 1913), pp. 28, 33; Henry Demarest Lloyd, *Wealth against Commonwealth* (New York: Harper, 1902), p. 33.

15. Lloyd in Hoogenboom and Hoogenboom, *Gilded Age,* p. 34; Lloyd, *Wealth,* p. 44; John D. Rockefeller, *Random Reminiscences of Men and Events* (New York: Doubleday, Page & Co, 1909), pp. 107–109, 111–112. Carnegie, *Autobiography* (Boston: Houghton Mifflin, 1920), pp. 135–136, 181–184.

16. Emerson, in Lloyd, *Wealth,* p. 57.

17. In the words of Louis D. Brandeis, the "most incisive critic of the trusts during his generation," the chief economic adviser to President Wilson, and one whose thought is "still remarkably influential three generations later": "I have considered and do consider that the proposition that mere bigness can not be an offense against society is false, because I believe that our society, which rests upon democracy, can not endure under such conditions," and "Our society could not endure half free and half slave. The essence of the trust is a combination of the capitalist, by the capitalist, for the capitalist." Quoted in Thomas K. McCraw, "Rethinking the Trust Question," in Thomas K. McCraw, ed., *Regulation in Perspective: Historical Essays* (Cambridge, Mass.: Harvard University Press, 1981), pp. 37, 52. McCraw states in the conclusion to his survey of antitrust regulation: "Economic regulation typically has not been the ally but the enemy of competition. Because of the preference for small enterprise shared by so many Americans, this has been a fact sometimes difficult to grasp . . . [N]umerous American intellectuals still have difficulty disentangling their personal predispositions from their otherwise democratic economics" (p. 55).

18. Normano, *Spirit*, p. 157. William Jennings Bryan, speech at the Chicago Conference on Trusts (1900); Richard T. Ely, "Pullman: A Social Study"; and W. Bourke Cockran, speech at the Chicago Conference on Trusts, all in Hoogenboom and Hoogenboom, *Gilded Age*, pp. 41–44, 80, 45–49.

19. Morgan, *Reappraisal*, p. 12. Normano, *Spirit*, p. 119 (quoting Parrington). Beard, *The Rise of American Civilization*, quoted in Morgan, *Reappraisal*, p. 4; on the same point, see Cochran and Miller, *Enterprise*, p. 153. Normano, *Spirit*, p. 121. Weyl, *Democracy*, p. 3.

20. Richard Hofstadter, *The Age of Reform: From Bryan to F.D.R.* (New York: Vintage Books, 1955), pp. 144, 134–135, 157; reprinted by permission of Alfred A. Knopf, a Division of Random House, Inc. J. Hector St. John de Crevecoeur, *Letters from an American Farmer* (1782; New York: Penguin American Library, 1981), p. 67. Robertson, *Business*, pp. 87–89. Adams, *Education*, p. 32. F. W. Fitzpatrick, *Inland Architect*, 39 (June 1902), quoted in Hofstadter, *Reform*, p. 153, n. 8; last quotation p. 137.

21. Kirkland, *Dream*, p. 6 (quoting 1885 report and 1901 repartee). Weyl, *Democracy*, pp. 244–246.

22. On Saint-Simon, see Greenfeld, *Nationalism*, p. 139–140. "Of 105 patriotic orders founded between 1783 and 1900, 34 originated before 1870 and 71 between 1870 and 1900." Hofstadter, *Reform*, p. 138, n. 8. Hofstadter continues: "The increase of patriotic and genealogical societies during the status revolution suggests that many old-family Americans, who were losing status in the present, may have found satisfying compensation in turning to family glories of the past. Of course, a large proportion of these orders were founded during the nationalistic outbursts of the nineties; but these too may have had their subtle psychological relation to status changes. Note the disdain of men like Theodore Roosevelt for the lack of patriotism and aggressive nationalism among men of great wealth."

23. Lloyd, *Wealth*, pp. 510–511. Weyl, *Democracy*, pp. 245–246, 247. Weyl continued: "In actual fact we always had less equality than we now like to believe . . . Americans have never worshiped a rigid equality of wealth. They have always been

willing to condone inequality which was measurable, which could be overcome in a lifetime, which represented, or might represent, superior attainments of the wealthier. But present inequalities differ so widely in degree from our old inequalities as to differ in kind. The rich are so rich that they can hardly help growing richer. A multimillionaire may be dissipated, lazy, imbecile, spendthrift, and yet automatically he gains more in a month than the average man earns in a lifetime" (pp. 247–248). This was a theoretical possibility, however. As far as we know, neither Rockefeller nor Carnegie nor any number of other eminent capitalists was an imbecile or an idler. They were resented all the same, and since it was awkward to resent them for their virtues, they were assigned imaginary vices.

24. Edward Shils, "The Order of Learning in the United States from 1865 to 1920: The Ascendancy of the Universities," *Minerva*, 16:2 (1978), writes: "Until the formation of the Johns Hopkins University, the learned world in the United States was rather inchoate. It had no center, it had no hierarchy" (p. 187). On college professors, see Metzger, *Freedom*, pp. 31, 5, 24, 26–27, 30, 32. Henry Adams, *Education*, pp. 54–55.

25. This was chiefly the result of their role as architects of German nationalism, which allowed them to position themselves advantageously within the German culture and national consciousness. See Greenfeld, *Nationalism*, chap. 4 on Germany.

26. Metzger, *Freedom*, p. 100; Longfellow, "Higher Education in America" (1871), and Andrew Dickson White quoted pp. 100–101. Only Shils's own idealism and dedication to learning could lead him to believe that this determination reflected in the first place "the avidity of intellectual desire," "the all-decisive fact of the love of learning," and an "irrepressible desire to understand," to which noble sentiments the wish "to confer legitimacy on and elevate the status of the new academic professions and to increase their public influence" (which he admits) was but secondary ("The Order of Learning," pp. 162, 167, 168, 174. As in any social movement which inevitably unites people on the basis of the lowest common denominator, behind it was an avidity of a very different kind.

27. Metzger, *Freedom*, pp. 46–48, 75–77 (including quotations from Abbot and Eliot); Seelye quoted p. 60. Shils, "Order," pp. 174, 176, 168, 194.

28. Dunbar, "Economic Science," pp. 140, 137–138. Regarding the godliness of economics, see Normano, *Spirit*, pp. 60–63. Francis Wayland, preface to *The Elements of Political Economy*, and John McVickar, *First Lesson in Political Economy*, quoted p. 62. (Wayland was the president of Brown University; his book, published in 1837, was the most popular textbook on the subject before the Civil War. The Reverend McVickar was the first professor of political economy at Columbia College and, apparently, the first to teach it in the country. His textbook dates from 1825.) Regarding dominance of American System, see Normano, *Spirit*, p. 81. Paul K. Conkin, *Prophets of Prosperity: America's First Political Economists* (Bloomington: Indiana University Press, 1980), pp. 171–280. Emerson in Cochran and Miller, *Enterprise*, p. 70. Weyl, *Democracy*, p. 244. Hofstadter, *Reform*, p. 149.

29. Simon N. Patten, "The Scope of Political Economy," *Yale Review* (November 1893), pp. 264–265, 274–275, 267, 268, 269.

30. A. W. Bob Coats, *The Sociology and Professionalization of Economics: British and*

American Economic Essays (London: Routledge, 1993), pp. 207, 225–238, 205–206 (including quotations from Walker, Laughlin, Atkinson, Ely). Richard T. Ely, *An Introduction to Political Economy* (New York: Hunt & Eaton, 1894), pp. 85–86, 72, 87–90.

31. Coats, *Sociology,* pp. 205–214, 216; Newcomb quoted p. 207, Clark, p. 216. Also see, among numerous other early testimonials, Albion W. Small, "Relations of Sociology to Economics," *Journal of Political Economy* (March 1895), 169–184.

32. Stanford, Wharton, and other sources quoted in Kirkland, *Dream,* pp. 93–94, 86, 96–101, 66.

33. Wright quoted in Metzger, *Freedom,* p. 80.

34. George Stigler, *The Economist as Preacher* (1984), quoted in Coats, *Sociology,* p. 197.

Epilogue

1. While President Coolidge's remark that "the business of America is business" is often quoted as an eloquent summation of the paramount place moneymaking has in American life, few bother to get acquainted with the rest of his address: "The chief ideal of the American people is idealism. I cannot repeat too often that America is a nation of idealists." William Allen White, *Calvin Coolidge* (New York: Macmillan 1925), p. 218.

2. The conversation, with Jeffrey Sachs, took place at a session of Glenn Loury's "Theory and Description" seminar on economic nationalism at Boston University in late 1997. The last delicious phrase, representative of characteristic Russian wit and enjoying the status of folk wisdom, appears to be a free and rather recent rendition of Schopenhauer's pronouncement to the effect that "a healthy pauper is happier than a sick prince."

3. This diagnosis is in line with Peter Drucker's suggestion in an interview in *Context* (Spring 1999): "One looks at a country's history and traditions and culture and not just the economic statistics because countries do not change their fundamental behavior, or at least not fast. And there is nothing in Russia's history that should encourage anybody to truck with Russia. If you're the International Monetary Fund, and it's other people's money you're throwing away, go ahead. If it's your shareholders' money, stay out. I'm sorry I'm so brutal, but one has to be brutal because it is a brutal country" (p. 39). See also Peter Reddaway, "Anatoly Chubais, No Friend of the People," *Washington Post National Weekly Edition,* September 1, 1997; Steve Liesman and Andrew Higgins, "Some Astonishing Missteps Helped Grease the Slope," *Wall Street Journal,* September 23, 1998.

4. See, among others, Nicholas D. Kristof and D. E. Sanger, "How U.S. Wooed Asia to Let Cash Flow In," *New York Times,* February 16, 1999; David Wessel and Bob Davis, "Missteps of the U.S.'s Best Experts May Have Fostered Economic Crisis," *Wall Street Journal,* September 24, 1998.

5. See, for example, "Justice Charges Gates Was Key in Planning Attack on Netscape," *Wall Street Journal,* October 19, 1998; John R. Wilke, "Greenspan Questions Antitrust Enforcement Campaign," *Wall Street Journal,* June 17, 1998; John Steele Gordon, "Read Your History, Janet," *Forbes,* February 23,

1998; Steve Lubove, "Damned If You Do, Damned If You Don't," *Forbes*, December 15, 1997.

6. W. Michael Cox and Richard Alm, *Myths of Rich and Poor: Why We're Better Off Than We Think* (New York: Basic Books, 1999).

7. There has aired on the subject a series of programs, *Affluenza* and *Escape from Affluenza*. The first program diagnosed a "modern-day plague of materialism and overconsumption," a social disease of epidemic proportions, the symptoms of which included "stress, overwork, waste, and indebtedness," and which was caused by "dogged pursuit of the American dream." In 1998, "Americans, who make up only five percent of the world's population, used nearly a third of its resources and produced almost half of its hazardous waste." And in addition to thus despoiling Earth, our mother, and causing overwork and stress, the wicked virus was responsible for the erosion of family and community, skyrocketing debt, and the growing gap between rich and poor.

   Escape from Affluenza proposed various cures for the illness, all of which had to do with "*working* and shopping less" (emphasis added), in consequence of which the patients/viewers were assured they would enjoy their lives more. The program came supplemented—on PBS's Web site—with suggestions for further reading, discussion questions, self-administered tests, and a "teacher's guide" for the benefit of fifth-grade through high school teachers, who were advised that the two programs would be a useful resource in classes on language, social studies, communications, business, economics, mathematics, and art. The Web site introduced *Escape from Affluenza* as "a prime example of PBS' commitment to enlightening programming on today's important issues." PBS Online, www.pbs.org.

8. Marianne M. Jennings, "Business Students Who Hate Business," *Wall Street Journal*, May 3, 1999. Jennings is a professor of legal and ethical studies in the College of Business at Arizona State University.

9. Justin Fox, "What in the World Happened to Economics?" *Fortune*, March 15, 1999, pp. 91–102. One Nobel laureate opines, "I don't care who writes a nation's laws . . . if I can write its economics textbooks," quoted in "The Puzzling Failure of Economics," *The Economist*, August 23, 1997, p. 11. See also an interview with then–Treasury Secretary Robert Rubin in which he "dismisses the notion that he's Atlas holding up the world," in "The Circumstances Are Unprecedented," *Fortune*, September 28, 1998; Milton Friedman, "Markets to the Rescue," *Wall Street Journal*, October 13, 1998; Nigel Holloway, "Doctor Knows Best," *Forbes*, April 6, 1998; Michael M. Phillips and Dagmar Aalund, "U.S. Differs with Europe and Japan on Cause of Global Economy's Woes," *Wall Street Journal*, February 22, 1999; Eduardo Lachica, "Oh Brother: The World Bank, IMF Jockey for Position," *Wall Street Journal*, October 5, 1998. Drucker, *Context*. An editorial in *Business Week* explains: "There are moments in history when a confluence of events brings sudden, piercing clarity to changes that, while deep, are outside the focus of eyes trained on the familiar . . . The shock of recent events brings these new realities into view: Capital trumps nationalism . . . Globalism trumps regionalism . . . Free-market trumps mercantilism." "Lessons from our Fast-changing World," *Business Week*, May 18, 1998, p. 210.

10. According to reports, NATO dropped more than 23,000 bombs achieving its goal, more than one bomb per every two Serbian soldiers—or policemen. On India and Pakistan, see Inayatullah, *The Nation* (Lahore), June 3, 1998; K. Subrahmanyam, *Economic Times* (New Delhi), May 14, 1998.

11. Surveying the historical data on the movement of goods, services, capital, and labor, *The Economist* observed that "trade and cross-border investment . . . boomed in 1870–1913 . . . a period . . . during which the world economy approached integration at an even faster pace than has been seen in the past 40 years . . . One measure, the growth of world trade, is slowing rather than accelerating." The only evidence of greater economic integration *The Economist* found was increased movement of capital (since 1980), but even this only between developing countries, where "a number of governments allowed it to." *The Economist* concluded: "Proper global economic integration is a distant prospect, and even continued progress toward it cannot be taken for granted." Bill Emmott, "Multinationals: Back in Fashion," *The Economist,* March 27, 1993. See also Timothy J. Hatton and Jeffrey G. Williamson, *The Age of Mass Migration: Causes and Economic Impact* (New York: Oxford University Press, 1998), and John Micklethwait and Adrian Wooldridge, *A Future Perfect: The Challenge and Hidden Promise of Globalization* (New York: Crown Business, 2000). After surveying 11,678 managers (who "were not selected at random") in twenty-five countries, the *Harvard Business Review* concluded that the "idea of a corporate global village where a common culture of management unifies the practice of business around the world is more dream than reality . . . Look at the third of the survey respondents who say that businesses should be willing to pay a premium to support domestic suppliers, or the quarter who want business owners to care more about their country's success than their company's." Rosabeth Moss Kanter, "Transcending Business Boundaries: 12,000 World Managers View Change," *Harvard Business Review* 69:3 (May–June 1991), 151, 155. Karen Lowry Miller, "A Secret Weapon for German Reform," *Business Week,* October 12, 1998, p. 138; Peter Passell, "Capitalism Victorious (Thanks, Everyone)," *New York Times,* May 10, 1998; Hollman W. Jenkins Jr., "DaimlerChrysler: Just Another German Car Company," *Wall Street Journal,* May 26, 1999; Bill Vlasic and Bradley A. Stertz, *Taken for a Ride: How Daimler-Benz Drove Off with Chrysler* (New York: William Morrow & Co., 2000). The official guide distributed to the citizens of France on the eve of the introduction of the euro included a chart titled "L'euro fait la force," comparing the economies of France, Japan, the United States, and the "euro zone," with the last taking first place in population count and falling just slightly behind the first-place United States in the size of the economy (as opposed to distant France on its own). "Guide Pratique de l'euro," Ministère de l'économie des finances et de l'industrie, November 1998, p. 2. See also Charles Wolf, Jr., "All for the Currency," *Wall Street Journal,* April 1, 1998; Robert Frank, "Europe's 'on Freud's Couch' as Countries Vie for Identity," *Wall Street Journal,* October 19, 1998; Enter the Euro," *The Economist,* May 9, 1998. Conrad de Aenlle, "Second Thoughts on Telecom Italia," *International Herald Tribune,* June 5–6, 1999, p. 19.

Index

Abbot, Frances G., 460
Abbott, Lyman, 467
Acts of Navigation, 47, 77, 101, 110, 132, 136, 329
Adams, C. K., 466
Adams, Henry, 428, 429, 430, 434, 439, 440, 452, 453, 457, 462
Adams, Henry Baxter, 466
Adams, Will, 229, 231
Adventurer, definition of, 369
Agiotage, 147, 386, 390
Agriculture: 75, 108, 384–385, 399, 400, 401; vs. industry, 151, 394–397, 401, 414, 419
Aizawa, Seishisai, 270–273
Alembert, Jean le Rond d', 138, 170
American Economic Association, 447, 465, 466, 467
American Historical Association, 466
American Political Science Association, 468
American Social Science Association, 467
American system (of mass production), 425–426
American system (of protectionism), 201, 403, 407, 416–418, 420, 421, 422, 433, 462, 478
Ames, Fisher, 401
Anglo-Dutch Wars, 98–99, 101
Anglomania, 137, 139–140
Anglophobia, 108, 140, 149, 153, 415
Arai, Hakuseki, 251, 306; a Japanese "mercantilist," 308
Arcq, Ph.-A., Chevalier d', 134, 137–139, 149, 170
Argenson, R. L. de Voyer de Paulmy, Marquis d', 132, 151
Armada, 36
Arndt, Ernst Moritz, 206
Artagnan, d', 137
Asabuki, Eiji, 351
"Asian Crisis," 478

Association (Society, Union) of German Merchants and Manufacturers, 200, 207, 209, 415
Astor, John Jacob, 452
Atkinson, Edward, 465, 466
Aufklärung, 156, 157, 165, 179, 229, 249, 251
Austin, Benjamin, 401, 402

Bakin, Takizawa, 264
Bakufu. See Tokugawa
Baku-han, 231
Balance of trade, 48, 109, 112, 124, 136
Baldwin, Henry, 416
Bank of Amsterdam, 78–79
Bank of New York, 388
Bank of North America, 406
Bank of the United States, 386, 387, 392–393, 406, 414
Barbon, Nicholas, 48–50, 55–56
Barrême, B.-F., 126–127
Bastiat, Frédérick, 357
Bauernschutz, 187, 193, 194
Baxter, Richard, 313, 378
Beard, Charles A., 450
Beaudeau, Abbé, 144, 181, 307
Bellah, Robert, 313
Ben-David, Joseph, 338
Bensen, C. D. H., 185
"Big business" (large corporations), 365, 368, 412, 431, 433, 434, 435, 445, 448, 449, 450, 451, 454, 456, 459, 464, 482
Bismarck, Otto von, 214, 217, 290
Bodin, Jean, 116, 121, 128
Bollan, William, 379
Boston Manufacturing Company, 405–406, 409
Bourgeoisie: France, 142, 145; vs. business class, 147–148; Prussia, 194; inclusion in the German nation, 207; Tokugawa merchants, 263–267, 337–338

Braudel, Fernand, 73
Brederode, Hendrik van, 72
Brown, Delmer, 268
Brunschwig, Henri, 156
Bryan, William Jennings, 446, 447, 448, 449
Buddhism, 242, 243, 246, 251, 320; as economic ethic, 309–311; attitude to profits, 312–313; compared to Protestant ethic and Pietism, 313
Bullionism, 112, 116
Bunyan, John, 313, 378
Bureaucracy, Prussian, 155, 191
Burr, Aaron, 398
Bushido, 242, 273, 288, 352, 356; as business ethic, 338, 341, 346
Business as art, 343
Business education: Japan, 354–356; U.S.A., 468–470, 480

Cabot, George, 405
Caldwell, James, 439
Calhoun, John, 403, 414, 416, 421
Calling, 15; in Shingaku, 314; Mitsui's, 320; in Mather, 375–376, 378
Cameralism, 162–171, 179, 185–187, 472; parallels to in Japan, 307, 325
Campbell, W. H., 355
"Capitalist," concept of, 80, 149–150
Carey, Henry, 328, 356, 358, 414, 415, 462
Carey, Mathew, 416
Carnegie, Andrew, 368, 437, 438, 440, 441, 443, 444, 453, 479
Catherine the Great, 262
Chandler, Alfred, 433
Channing, W. E., 432
Charles II (King of England), 46, 54
Charles V (Emperor, King Charles I of Spain), 62–70, 163
Charter Oath, 281
Chicago Conference on Trusts, 431, 446
Child, Josiah, 44, 74, 137
Chu Hsi, 240–242, 249, 250, 251, 256, 269
"Civilization": as a national goal in Japan, 285, 327; as "modernization" in Japan, 331
Civil War: English (Puritan Rebellion), 18, 43, 45; American, 428, 429, 434, 435, 436
Clapham, John, 155, 173, 208, 215, 217
Clark, Colin, 301
Clark, J. B., 468
Classical school (*laissez-faire* economics), 111, 113, 180, 190, 203, 222, 357, 360, 415, 461, 465, 466, 467, 471, 472, 474, 480; Webster's attitude toward, 421

Clay, Henry, 403, 404, 405, 406, 407, 415, 416, 417–420, 421, 422
Clinton, De Witt, 412
Coal production, 115, 143, 215, 216, 217
Coats, A. W. Bob, 466, 467
Cochran, Thomas, 431, 432, 435
Cockran, Bourke, 448, 449
Colbert, J.-B., 108, 111, 114, 125–127, 128, 129, 134, 137, 172, 174
Cold War, 480
Cole, C. W., 124
Colleges, American, 456–457; influence of German universities on, 458–459
Colt, Samuel, 425, 426, 427, 482
"Commercial classes," 18, 19, 55, 142
Confucianism, 240–242, 243, 246, 248, 249, 250, 251, 252, 256, 259, 263, 269, 314, 320; as a guide for business, 341
Constitution of 1889, 282, 290, 292
Corporations, 406, 410, 411, 427, 431
Court, Pieter de la, 102
Coyer, G. P. Abbé, 132–139, 309, 479
Crimean War, 426, 476
Crocker, Charles, 439
Crouzet, François, 114, 142, 143, 145, 148
"Cultural capital," 199
Cunningham, William, 111

DaimlerChrysler, 483
Dan, Takuma, 351
Darwin, Charles, 368, 460, 463
Davenant, Charles, 77
Dazai, Shundai, 306, 329
Defoe, Daniel, 50–56, 103, 128, 166, 379
Depitre, Edgar, 136
Dithmar, J. C., 166, 167
Dreiser, Theodore, 479
Drucker, Peter, 481
Duer, William, 386–388
Dunbar, Charles F., 383–384, 461, 462, 465, 468
Durkheim, Emile, 25, 91–92, 470
Dutch carrying trade, 47, 65, 76–77
Dutch studies *(rangaku),* 251–255

East India Company, 36, 40–41
East India Company (VOC), 77–78, 87
Economic civilization, 1, 24, 364, 368, 451, 472, 473, 475, 484
Economic competition: Anglo-German, 33, 180, 203, 217, 220, 300; England, 44–45; Anglo-Dutch, 101; Franco-Dutch, 101; Anglo-French, 136, 145, 153; as war by

other means, 218–220, 334–337, 356;
concept of, in Japan (*kyoso*), 328, 358;
attitude toward, in Japan, 351–353; U.S.A,
366, 435, 441, 448, 482
Economic decline, concept of, 84–86, 87–89
Economic growth: concept of, 6–10, 51–52,
170; emergence as desideratum, 22; as an
equivalent of military expansion, 218; in
Hamilton's thinking, 396–398; as immoral,
454, 462
Economic liberalism, 26, 101, 136, 153, 478;
Prussian, 194, 208, 217; attack on in
Germany, 196, 197, 215; in Tokugawa
Japan, 265; Hamilton's, 398; Clay's attack
on, 419
Economic miracle: British, 29; Dutch, 73
Economic nationalism, 475; English, 33,
112, 114; German, 154, 195, 196, 199,
200; as the original form of Japanese
nationalism, 326–328; U.S.A., 384, 393,
403, 407, 440; absence of, in Russia, 476
Economic rationality, 90, 103, 319, 342,
437, 477
Economics as academic discipline:
Germany, Cameralism: 162, 164, 165, 168,
179, 187; definition and scope, 166, 167,
169; as a species of mercantilism, 170,
171; "new economics," 185, 186, 187
Japan: 353–360; alienation from business,
360
U.S.A: 365, 384, 447, 451, 463, 466, 467,
471, 480, 481; as science, 461, 464, 465
Economics as the craft of management, 119–
120, 163–165, 169, 175, 187
Economy, concept of:
England, 40, 49–52, 56
France, 112–113, 117, 119
Germany: as a dimension of political reality,
163; *Hauswirtschaft, Wirtschaft,* 164; as
an area of discourse, 166, 179; as ener-
gies of a nation, 185
Japan. See *Keizai*
U.S.A., 365, 396
Economy, management of, in Japan, 340,
352, 353
Edict of Emancipation, 192–194
Edict on the Change of Status, 235–236
Edict on the Collection of Swords, 234–235
Edward VI (King of England), 35
Egmont, counts of, 64, 66, 68, 72
Eliot, Charles William, 460, 461
Elizabeth I, 35–36, 39, 98
Ellis, William, 357

Ely, Richard, 465, 466, 467, 468
Emerson, Ralph Waldo, 423–424, 432, 445,
462
Engels, Friedrich, 208, 214
English/American national consciousness,
363, 371, 474
English (British) national consciousness, 31,
51, 474
Éon, Jean, Chevalier d', 134
Equality, idea of, in nationalism, 2, 32; in
Germany, 160; importation to Japan, 277,
278; interpretation under Meiji, 293–296,
340, 348; as a central American value,
365–366, 399, 438, 445, 447, 455, 456,
475; in America, as opposed to
individualism, 406
Erasmus, 70, 163
European Monetary Union, 483
Everett, Edward, 420

Fairs, 61–62, 79
Familism, 350
Fascism, 204
Feder, J. G. H., 180
Fenellosa, Ernest, 354
Ferdinand of Aragon, 62, 64
"Financial Revolution," 78–79
Fingleton, Eamonn, 323
Florinus, F. P., 164
Fluyt, 76
Fonvisin, Denis, 262, 275
Forbonnais, 137, 150, 179
Foreign trade: free, 26, 358, 359; England,
34, 40, 42, 46; Netherlands, 34, 42, 74,
77, 79, 131; France, 126, 131, 135, 142;
Prussia, 175; Japan, 299–301, 344; U.S.A.,
400
Fortrey, Samuel, 43–48
Foulke, William Dudley, 431
Fouquet, Nicolas, 128
Francis, J. H., 440
Franco-Prussian War, 216
Franklin, Benjamin, 313, 317, 378, 380–384,
385, 387, 388, 419, 479
Frederick the Great (Frederick II), 156, 161,
163, 171, 172, 173, 174, 176, 177, 178,
181, 191; as the supreme manager, 175
Free trade, 26, 37–38, 48, 101, 109–110,
121, 132, 136, 152, 180, 197–198, 203,
214, 222, 383, 398, 404, 416, 478; as a
tool of English nationalism, 205–206
French Revolution, 139, 140, 142, 147, 148,
149, 184, 191, 194

Friedrich Wilhelm I (King of Prussia), 163, 173, 174, 195
Friedrich Wilhelm III (King of Prussia), 188, 189, 192, 195
Frois, Louis, 229
Fuggers, 63
Fukoku kyohei, 284
Fukuyama, Francis, 169
Fukuzawa, Yukichi, 277, 279, 284, 286, 327, 328, 330–334, 335–336, 337, 338, 353, 356, 357, 358, 359, 353, 356, 357, 358, 359; idea of independence, 331; idea of equality and national interest, 332; understanding of modern economy, 333; idea of economic liberty, 334
Furukawa, Ichibe, 350

Gallatin, Albert, 411
Garve, Christian, 181, 182
Gasser, S. P., 167
Gentz, Friedrich von, 181
German Confederation, 195, 200, 209
German unification, 214
Gerschenkron, Alexander, 89
Geyl, Pieter, 64–65, 71–72, 90, 93, 96
Girard, Stephen, 452
Gladden, Washington, 467
Gladstone, William, 428
Globalization, 59, 61–63, 69, 481, 482, 483
Godai, Tomoatsu, 342
Godkin, E. L., 440
Goningumi, 236
Göttingen, University of, 180, 181, 196, 458, 459
Gotzkowsky, J. E., 175–179
Gould, Jay, 439
Gournay, Vincent de, 137
Granvelle, Antoine Perrenot de, 68–69, 71–72
Gresham, Thomas, 35
Grimm, Jakob and Wilhelm, 206
Grotius, Hugo, 102
Guilds, 174, 265

Habsburgs, 62–64, 66–67
Hakluyt, Richard, 369–370
Hamilton, Alexander, 384, 386–403, 408, 414, 422, 423, 434; "Report on Public Credit," 386; "Report on Manufactures," 393–398
Hanseatic League, 34–37, 39–40, 42, 60–61, 206
Happiness: German idea of, 165, 170; Japanese idea of, 235, 325

Hara, Rokuro, 342
Hardenberg, K. von, 189, 191, 192, 194, 195, 209
Haughton, William, 37
Hauser, Henri, 155, 219
Hausväterliteratur, 164, 165, 181, 235, 281; parallels to in Japan, 307
Hauswirtschaft, 164
Hayashi, Razan, 240, 241, 242
Heckscher, Eli, 111
Hegel, G. W. F., 160, 317
Henderson, W. O., 211
Henry, Patrick, 292, 293
Henry IV (King of France), 116–119
Henry VII (King of England), 34–35
Henry VIII (King of England), 34–35
Henslowe, Philip, 37
Herder, J. G., 247, 248, 316, 317
Herring fishing, 75–76
Hewitt, Abram, 440
Hideyoshi, 231, 234, 235, 268
Higginson, Francis, 371–372
Hirata, Atsutane, 245, 246
Hitotsubashi, 339
Hofstadter, Richard, 452, 453, 463
Hohenzollerns, 173
Holborn, Hajo, 191
Homo economicus, 90, 103, 398, 472, 477
Honshin, 315, 343; compared to *Wesenwille* and "species-being," 316; compared to class consciousness, 317
Horrocks, J. W., 112
Hotchkiss, G. B., 36, 41
Houtte, J. A. van, 65
Huizinga, Johan, 90, 93
Humboldt, Wilhelm von, 185, 191, 195
Hume, David, 48, 179
Humphreys, David, 407, 408

Ienobu, 251
Ietsugu, 251
Ieyasu, 231, 232, 233, 240, 243, 256, 279, 310
Ihara, Saikaku, 263, 264
Individualism: as a moral position, 25; English/British, 196, 205, 222–223; American, 388, 406, 447, 475
"Industrial Class," 450
Industrialization:
    Germany, 215, 218
    Japan, 302
    U.S.A.: Hamilton's defense of, 393–398; resistance to, 398–403; first signs, 405, 406, 409–410; "industrial infrastruc-

ture," 410–413, 417, 419; ascendance, 422–426, 428, 434, 441
Industrial Revolution, 7, 9, 22, 50, 58, 78, 145, 395, 424
Inoue, Kaoru, 337
Inoue, Shozo, 328
Inquisition, 70–72
Instrumental rationality, 323
Intellectuals:
  France, 133, 149
  Germany: as architects of German national-ism, 155, 207, 214; *Aufklärung* and Ro-manticism among, 156; status-inconsis-tency of, 156; view of modernity, 158; attitude to equality, 160; lack of interest in economics, 162
  Japan: Samurai intelligentsia, 262, 276; as the new business class, 337–345; notions of success, 343–344
  Russian intelligentsia, 476
  U.S.A., 366–368, 456, 458, 459, 460, 461, 462, 463, 470, 479; professors, 368, 457, 458–463, 466, 470, 480; economists, 451, 464, 465, 466, 467, 470, 471–472, 480, 481, 484
Interest, public vs. private, 47–49, 102, 203–204, 397–398, 405, 406, 411, 414, 418
Inukai, Tsuyoshi, 356
Invisible hand, 17, 19, 54, 199, 203, 307, 358, 401
Iron production, 45, 216, 217
Isabella of Castille, 62, 64
Ishida, Baigan, 313–319, 343
Israel, Jonathan, 65, 67–68, 91
Itagaki, Taisuke, 292–293
Italian wars, 116
Ito, Hirobumi, 282, 285, 288, 290–292, 293, 296–297
Ivan the Terrible, 231
Iwasaki, Yataro, 348

J. H. G., 166
Jackson, Andrew, 405, 406, 426
Jakob, L. H., 186
James, Henry, 439
James I (King of England), 43, 119, 369
Japan compared: with Germany, 228, 235, 244, 259; with Spain, 229; with France, 231, 234, 256, 258; with Russia, 231, 232, 236, 262; with the West, 231, 274, 277, 289; with the Netherlands, 244, 264, 264n26; with England, 257, 280
"Japanese Industrial Revolution," 336
Jefferson, Thomas, 391, 392, 399, 401, 403

Jevons, W. S., 354
Jitsugyoka, 338, 343
Josephson, Matthew, 436
Justi, J. H. G., 168, 169, 170, 171, 179, 307

Kada, Azumamaro, 243, 244
Kamo, Mabuchi, 246, 247, 248, 249, 250
Kanda, Takahira, 357
Kant, Immanuel, 183, 184
Keiretsu, 319, 353
Keizai, 305–306, 324–325, 327, 328, 464
Kentaro, Kaneko, 341
Keynes, J. M., 113, 216
Kido, Koin, 280, 281, 282, 286
Kindleberger, Charles, 81, 84–85
King, Gregory, 48, 137
Kirkland, E. C., 430
Kokugaku, 243–251, 255, 277; anti-rationalism, 245–246, parallels with Romanticism, 246–249; view of the emperor, 250, 269
Kokumin, 278
Kokutai, 272, 280, 291
Kossmann, E. H., 98
Kossuth, Louis, 206
Kraus, Ch. J., 183, 191
Kumazawa, Banzan, 251, 256, 265, 307–309
Kuznetz, Simon, 6

Lafayette, M. J. P. Y. R. G. du Motier, Marquis de, 200, 201
Laffemas, Barthélemy de, 116–121, 123, 308
Laissez-faire: origin of phrase, 132, 498n22; use by Physiocrats, 150, 151
Laissez-faire economics. *See* Classical school
Lamprecht, Karl, 218
Landes, David, 6–7, 22
Large corporations. *See* "Big business"
Lassay, Marquis de, 133, 137
Latrobe, Benjamin, 433
Laughlin, J. J., 465, 466
Laws of the Military Households, 233–234, 240
Lincoln, Abraham, 434
List, Friedrich, 6, 31–32, 112, 196, 199–214, 218, 354, 356, 358, 359, 360, 415, 474, 476
Lloyd, Henry Demarest, 441, 442, 455
Lloyd, James, 407
Locke, John, 48, 109
Longfellow, H. W., 458
Louis XIII, 119
Louis XIV, 125, 127, 131, 132, 134
Louis XV, 151

Lowell, Francis Cabot, 405, 406, 409
Lydius, Jacobus, 99

McCloy, Shelby, 144
McCosh, James, 355
MacFarlane, Alan, 82
McLane, Louis, 433
Macleod, H. D., 354
Madison, James, 386, 388, 390, 391, 392, 403, 431
Malthusian model, 7, 88–89
Margaret of Parma, 68, 72
Marshall, Alfred, 76
Marshall, Byron, 337, 342, 350
Marx, Karl, 5, 6, 11, 29, 144, 197, 199, 201, 202, 204, 214, 293, 316, 317, 326, 364, 376
Marxism, 6, 18, 92, 147, 148, 204, 451, 476
Mary of Burgundy, 62, 64
Mary Tudor, 35
Mather, Cotton, 375–378
Matsukata, Kojiro, 341, 343
Matsukata, Masayoshi, 341, 352
Matthew, Saint, 5, 372
Maximilian of Austria, 62
Mazarin, Cardinal, 125
Meiji Restoration, 227, 228, 251, 277, 280, 281, 284, 285, 293, 320, 328, 333, 340, 344, 351
Meinecke, Friedrich, 195
Mercantilism, 48, 101, 107–114, 116, 119–120, 124, 132, 136, 152, 163, 170, 171, 180, 181, 182, 185, 210, 359, 369, 370, 381, 383, 388, 394, 396, 397, 400, 407, 415, 469; parallels to, in Japan, 307
Merchants Adventurers, 34–40, 42
Mercier, Louis-Sébastien, 146, 149
Metternich, C. W. L., 195, 207, 208, 214
Metzger, Walter, 456, 458, 460
Mill, J. S., 354, 357, 462
Miller, J. C., 387, 393, 396
Miller, William, 431, 432, 435
Mirabeau, Marquis de, 150
Mitchell, James, 87
Mitsubishi, 336, 338, 348, 349, 352
Mitsui, 319, 324, 337, 338, 343, 344, 351, 378
Mitsui, Takahira, 320–323; on profit, 322
"Modern devotion," 69, 244
Money economy, in Japan, 258, 303–305
Monopoly, 34, 406, 410, 445, 447, 448
Montchrétien, Antoine de, 116, 121–125, 132, 164

Montesquieu, Charles de Secondat, 134, 291
"Moral capital," 198
Morgan, H. Wayne, 450
Morgan, J. P., 434, 435, 439, 453
Mori, Arinori, 354, 355
Morimura, Ishizaemon, 344
Morris, Robert, 388
Morris-Suzuki, Tessa, 268, 306, 359
Motoori, Norinaga, 244, 246, 248, 249, 250, 251
Movement for National Efficiency, 221
Müller, Adam, 159, 196–199, 247, 293
Mun (Munn), Thomas, 41, 50, 73, 75, 109–110

Napoleon, 127, 189, 191, 195
Napoleon III, 339
National Economic Council, 478
National identity, definition, 93–97
Nationalism: definition, 1–4, 24–25; types, 2, 3, 23–25, 474; "reactive," 9, 24
Nationaloekonomie, 184, 186, 197, 467; parallels to in Japan, 329
National Socialism, 158
"Nations," commercial, 60–61, 65
Newcomb, Simon, 465, 466, 467
Nicolai (Nikolai), Ch., 181
Niles, Hezekiah, 416
Nishi, Amane, 357
Nishimura, Shigeki, 337
Nobility:
  England, 54, 136, 141
  France, 117, 129–131, 143, 144, 149, 454, 455; noblesse commerçante, 132–139
  Germany: reaction to French invasion, 161; Junkers, 172, 173
  Japan: daimyo, 232–234; surrender of domains, 280; samurai, 239, redefinition as a cultural elite, 240–242; lack of opportunities, 244, 255–262; ronin, 256, 257, 258, 263; detestation of merchants, 265, 266; receptivity to nationalism, 270; disaffection from the bakufu, 277
  Netherlands, 66–67, 71–72, 102
Nobunaga, Oda, 229, 231
Novalis (Hardenberg, Freidrich von), 161, 272

Oguri, Ryoun, 314
Ogyu, Sorai, 251, 257, 258, 259–262, 266–267, 268, 269, 319
Okubo, Toshimichi, 280, 282, 285, 328–330

Okuma, Shigenobu, 287, 293, 297–298
"One Heart Band," 345–347
Oshima, Sadamatsu, 359
Oymei (Wang Yang-ming), 251, 256

Palmade, Guy, 142, 143, 146, 147
Palmer, Potter, 439
Parish, Elijah, 403
Patriotism, definition of, 97; and profit, 343–345
Patten, Simon N., 463, 464, 465
Perkins, Charles Elliot, 439
Perry, Arthur Latham, 465
Perry, M. C., Commodore, 274
Peter the Great, 76, 286
Philadelphia Society for the Promotion of National Industry, 415
Philanthropy, 436, 440, 459
Philip II (King of Spain), 39, 64, 66–68, 72, 98
Physiocracy (économistes), 107–108, 139, 147, 150–153, 171, 179, 181, 382, 383, 394, 400; parallels to, in Japan, 307
Political economy: England, 37, 41; France, 116, 119; Germany, 186, 201–206; Confucian, 305–309; Japan, 324; U.S.A., 380–384, 461, 462, 463, 465, 468
Political Economy Club, 465, 466, 467
Pope, John, 407
Porter, Noah, 460
"Productive power" (of intellectuals), 203
Progressive movement, 452
Property, German idea of, 196–197
Protectionism, 109, 123, 359, 414, 417
Protective tariff: England/Britain, 45, 132, 222; Germany, 202–203, 209, 210; U.S.A., 414, 416, 418, 420, 421, 466
Protestantism (Calvinism, Pietism), 17, 18–19, 21, 23, 25, 44–45, 49, 70–71, 99, 157, 371
Protestant Reformation, 16, 69–70
Prussian tariff, 208, 209
Public debt: Dutch, 78, 80, 87; U.S.A., 386–388, 389, 390

Quesnay, Francois, 150–152, 171, 307

Railroads: Germany, 210–211, 213, 215; U.S.A., 412, 413, 429, 430, 431, 432, 433, 434, 435
Raleigh, Walter, 42–43, 348
Randolph, Edmund, 392
Rationalization, 12–14, 20

Reischauer, Edwin, 228, 242, 259, 263
Remini, Robert, 416
Renten, 66, 80
"Republican Diet," 75
Revolt of the Netherlands, 36, 65–66, 68–69, 72–73, 76–77, 79, 102, 104
Ricardo, Abraham, 103
Ricardo, David, 103, 415
Richelieu, A. J. du Plessis, Cardinal, 125, 129, 134
"Robber barons," 436, 438, 439, 440, 441, 449, 455, 459, 460, 461, 463
Robertson, J. O., 385, 406, 433
Rockefeller, John D., 368, 434, 436, 437, 441, 442, 443, 459, 479, 482
Romanticism, 156, 161, 189, 316; notions of "totality and individuality," 157, 158, 159, 160; Romantic nationalism, 199, 202, 455
Root, Elisha, 426
Rostow, W. W., 8–10, 104, 142
Rousseau, J.-J., 149, 150, 153, 293, 478
Russia, 22, 131, 158, 174, 475, 476, 478; pressure to adopt market reforms, 5; occupation of Berlin, 177, 178; compared to Prussia in 1790s, 188; unwillingness to participate in economic competition, 475–477
Russo-Japanese War, 222, 287, 288

Saigo, Takamori, 280, 282, 284–285
Sakuma, Shozan, 267, 268, 273–276
Sankin-kotai, 233–234, 257, 263
Sansom, George, 227, 258
Sartorius, George, 182, 183, 196
Sato, Nobuhiro, 324–326, 329
Savary, Jacques, 127–132, 164, 166, 307, 320, 343, 378
Savary de Bruslons, Jacques, 127
Schama, Simon, 81, 90–93, 96–99, 103
Schiller, J. F., 180
Schlegel, Friedrich, 160, 162
Schmaltz, Theodor, 190
Schmoller, Gustav, 111, 163
Schön, H. Th. von, 191, 192, 193
Schrötter, von, 183, 192, 193
Schutz, Carl, 465
Seelye, Julius H., 460
Se-i tai shogun, 269
Sekigahara, battle of, 231, 310
Sekimon Shingaku: 313–319, 320, 322, 323, 343; idea of honesty in, 316; attitude to profit in, 317–318; attitude toward economic growth, 318

Self-interest, 43, 48, 103, 334, 349, 357, 370, 373, 398, 401, 402, 438, 442; as "class consciousness," 358, 390, 391
Serfdom: in Prussia, 172, 173, 194–195; in Japan, 236–237
Seven Years' War, 177
Shand, A. A., 358
Shibusawa, Eiichi, 337, 338–341, 343, 344, 358
Shibusawa, Hideo, 344
Shils, Edward, 422, 463
Shinto, 242, 243, 244, 247, 269, 320, 326
Sino-Japanese War, 286, 336
Sinophobia, 243, 250
Smith, Adam, 6, 17, 19, 29, 40, 48, 50, 56, 107, 111, 114, 159, 164, 170, 171, 179, 221, 230, 295, 307, 329, 356, 360, 363, 395, 400, 414, 415, 421, 479; idea of the nation, 31–32; attack on, in Germany, 196–199
Smith, Adam, works of:
 The Theory of Moral Sentiments, 29–32
 The Wealth of Nations, 30–33, 108–110, 421; German translation, 180, 181, 182, 183; and *Nationaloekonomie,* 184, 185, 186, 187, 190; and Prussian reform, 191; Japanese translation, 359
Smith, J. P., 214
Smithianismus, 31, 184, 187, 196, 215, 472
Snyder, Louis, 206, 208
Social sciences, 365, 461, 463, 464
Society of orders, 32, 156, 227
Soden, F. J. H., von, 186
Soeda, Juichi, 346
Solow, Robert, 10
Sombart, Werner, 11, 215
Sonnenfels, Joseph von, 168, 169, 170–171, 179
Sonno-joi, 269, 270, 273, 289, 336, 338
Speculation, 81, 385, 386–387, 390, 391, 432
Spencer, Herbert, 460, 461
Staatswirtschaft, 168, 169, 184, 187, 210, 218, 222–223; redefinition as *Nationaloekonomie,* 186; parallels to, in Japan, 306, 324–326
Standard Oil, 437, 442, 443
Stanford, Leland, 468
Steel, J. H., 355
Steelyard, 34–35, 60
Stein, Günther, 299–302, 304, 344
Stein, Karl vom, 189, 191–195, 196
Steuart, James, 180
Stigler, George, 471

Stone, Lawrence, 112
Sugita, Gempaku, 252–255, 258
Sugiyama, Chuhei, 327, 354, 356
Sully, M. de Béthune, duc de, 116, 119, 125, 307
Sumitomo, 319, 337, 342
Sumitomo, Masatomo, 319–320
Sumner, William Graham, 460, 465
Sun Goddess, 244
Supple, B. E., 42
Suzuki, Shosan, 310–312, 314, 315
Suzuki, Tosaburu, 343
Symonds, William, 371

Taguchi, Ukichi, 358
Takeoff: Britain, 9, 22, 52, 59; Netherlands, 59; France, 145; Germany, 215, 218; Japan, 227, 337, 360; U.S.A., 363, 364
Talleyrand, Ch.-M. de, 143, 147, 391
Tamura, Masanori, 350
Tarbell, Ida, 437
Tawney, R. H., 15, 17–19, 40, 48, 104, 215, 373
Taxation, Dutch, 66–67, 78–80
Technology: role in economic modernization, 7, 84; France, 143–144; U.S.A.: 395–396, 423, 424
Temple, William, 80
't Hart, Marjolein, 79, 91–94
Thierry, Augustin, 117
Thomson, J. E., 433
Tokugawa, 228, 229, 231, 232, 233, 259, 269, 279, 282, 305; treatment of the emperor, 244; expressions of discontent with, 262–263; growth of opposition to, 266–267; internal inconsistencies, 268; humiliation by the West, 274
Tomita, Tetsunosuke, 356
Tompson, Benjamin, 373
Torres, Cosme de, 229
Treitschke, Heinrich von, 206, 211, 212
Trevelyan, G. M., 51
Triangular trade, 62
Tribe, Keith, 168, 170, 179, 213
Tsuda, Mamichi, 357
Tsunoda, Ryusaku, 284

Ukiyo-e, 264, 265, 508n26
Unequal treaties, 285, 326
Union of Utrecht, 80, 90–91

Valigniano, Alessandro, 230
Vanderbilt, Cornelius (Commodore), 439

Vissering, Simon, 357
Voltaire, 137, 140–142
Vries, Jan de, and Ad van der Woude, 74, 77, 79, 81–84, 86–88, 90–94, 101, 104

Wagner, Richard, 207
Wakayma, Norikazu, 328
Walker, Francis A., 465, 466, 468
Wallerstein, Immanuel, 91
War of Liberation, 155
Washington, George, 278, 384, 386, 387, 390, 392, 400, 451
Wayland, Francis, 354
Wealth: status as a function of, 30, 374, 452; and poverty, 453, 454; idea of: England, 42; Netherlands, 100; Germany, 171, 198–199; Japan, 309; U.S.A., 372–373
Webb, Sidney, 221, 222
Weber, Max, 5, 10, 13–14, 16–17, 19–23, 25, 50, 99, 103, 220, 313, 318, 364, 375, 376, 477; *Protestant Ethic,* 11–16, 18, 21–22; notion of capitalism, 11–13; concepts of calling and predestination, 15
Webster, Daniel, 412, 413, 416, 420, 423, 432
Wells, David A., 465, 466
Weyl, Walter, 440, 451, 454, 456, 462
Wharton, Joseph, 469
Wheeler, John, 37–42, 103, 128, 131
White, Andrew D., 465, 466

White, Horace, 466
Whitney, Dr., 356
Whitney, Eli, 405, 425
Whittier, John Greenleaf, 409, 410
William of Orange, 68–69, 71–72
Williams, Ernest Edwin, 220–221, 299
Wilson, Woodrow, 480
Winthrop, John, 372–373, 377
Wirtschaft, 164
Witte, Sergei, 476
Wolff, Christian, 165
Woodson, Samuel, 422
Woolman, John, 388, 479, 521n9
World War I, 155, 300, 483
World War II, 221, 345, 346, 353
Wright, Chauncey, 470

Xavier, Saint Francis, 229, 230, 239

Yamagata, Aritomo, 293–295, 346
Yamamoto, Shichihei, 303, 304, 312, 313, 315, 316, 338, 345
Yoshimune, 243, 244, 252
Youmans, Edward L., 461
Young, Arthur, 180, 183

Zaibatsu, 350, 353
Zincke, G. H., 167, 168
Zollverein, 154, 208–210, 214, 215
Zumthor, Paul, 75